Real World Haskell

Real World Haskell

Bryan O'Sullivan, John Goerzen, and Don Stewart

O'REILLY®

Beijing · Cambridge · Farnham · Köln · Sebastopol · Tokyo

Real World Haskell

by Bryan O'Sullivan, John Goerzen, and Don Stewart

Published by O'Reilly Media, Inc., 1005 Gravenstein Highway North, Sebastopol, CA 95472.

O'Reilly books may be purchased for educational, business, or sales promotional use. Online editions are also available for most titles (*http://safari.oreilly.com*). For more information, contact our corporate/ institutional sales department: (800) 998-9938 or *corporate@oreilly.com*.

Editor: Mike Loukides	**Indexer:** Joe Wizda
Production Editor: Loranah Dimant	**Cover Designer:** Karen Montgomery
Copyeditor: Mary Brady	**Interior Designer:** David Futato
Proofreader: Loranah Dimant	**Illustrator:** Robert Romano

Printing History:

November 2008:   First Edition.

ISBN: 978-0-596-51498-3

[LSI]   [2010-12-17]

1292541328

To Cian, Ruairi, and Shannon, for the love and joy they bring.

—Bryan

For my wife, Terah, with thanks for all her love, encouragement, and support.

—John

To Suzie, for her love and support.

—Don

Table of Contents

Preface

Have We Got a Deal for You!

Haskell is a deep language; we think learning it is a hugely rewarding experience. We will focus on three elements as we explain why. The first is *novelty*: we invite you to think about programming from a different and valuable perspective. The second is *power*: we'll show you how to create software that is short, fast, and safe. Lastly, we offer you a lot of *enjoyment*: the pleasure of applying beautiful programming techniques to solve real problems.

Novelty

Haskell is most likely quite different from any language you've ever used before. Compared to the usual set of concepts in a programmer's mental toolbox, functional programming offers us a profoundly different way to think about software.

In Haskell, we deemphasize code that modifies data. Instead, we focus on functions that take immutable values as input and produce new values as output. Given the same inputs, these functions always return the same results. This is a core idea behind functional programming.

Along with not modifying data, our Haskell functions usually don't talk to the external world; we call these functions *pure*. We make a strong distinction between pure code and the parts of our programs that read or write files, communicate over network connections, or make robot arms move. This makes it easier to organize, reason about, and test our programs.

We abandon some ideas that might seem fundamental, such as having a `for` loop built into the language. We have other, more flexible, ways to perform repetitive tasks.

Even the way in which we evaluate expressions is different in Haskell. We defer every computation until its result is actually needed—Haskell is a *lazy* language. Laziness is not merely a matter of moving work around, it profoundly affects how we write programs.

Power

Throughout this book, we will show you how Haskell's alternatives to the features of traditional languages are powerful and flexible and lead to reliable code. Haskell is positively crammed full of cutting-edge ideas about how to create great software.

Since pure code has no dealings with the outside world, and the data it works with is never modified, the kind of nasty surprise in which one piece of code invisibly corrupts data used by another is very rare. Whatever context we use a pure function in, the function will behave consistently.

Pure code is easier to test than code that deals with the outside world. When a function responds only to its visible inputs, we can easily state properties of its behavior that should always be true. We can automatically test that those properties hold for a huge body of random inputs, and when our tests pass, we move on. We still use traditional techniques to test code that must interact with files, networks, or exotic hardware. Since there is much less of this impure code than we would find in a traditional language, we gain much more assurance that our software is solid.

Lazy evaluation has some spooky effects. Let's say we want to find the k least-valued elements of an unsorted list. In a traditional language, the obvious approach would be to sort the list and take the first k elements, but this is expensive. For efficiency, we would instead write a special function that takes these values in one pass, and that would have to perform some moderately complex bookkeeping. In Haskell, the sort-then-take approach actually performs well: laziness ensures that the list will only be sorted enough to find the k minimal elements.

Better yet, our Haskell code that operates so efficiently is tiny and uses standard library functions:

```
-- file: ch00/KMinima.hs
-- lines beginning with "--" are comments.

minima k xs = take k (sort xs)
```

It can take a while to develop an intuitive feel for when lazy evaluation is important, but when we exploit it, the resulting code is often clean, brief, and efficient.

As the preceding example shows, an important aspect of Haskell's power lies in the compactness of the code we write. Compared to working in popular traditional languages, when we develop in Haskell we often write much less code, in substantially less time and with fewer bugs.

Enjoyment

We believe that it is easy to pick up the basics of Haskell programming and that you will be able to successfully write small programs within a matter of hours or days.

Since effective programming in Haskell differs greatly from other languages, you should expect that mastering both the language itself and functional programming techniques will require plenty of thought and practice.

Harking back to our own days of getting started with Haskell, the good news is that the fun begins early: it's simply an entertaining challenge to dig into a new language—in which so many commonplace ideas are different or missing—and to figure out how to write simple programs.

For us, the initial pleasure lasted as our experience grew and our understanding deepened. In other languages, it's difficult to see any connection between science and the nuts-and-bolts of programming. In Haskell, we have imported some ideas from abstract mathematics and put them to work. Even better, we find that not only are these ideas easy to pick up, but they also have a practical payoff in helping us to write more compact, reusable code.

Furthermore, we won't be putting any "brick walls" in your way. There are no especially difficult or gruesome techniques in this book that you must master in order to be able to program effectively.

That being said, Haskell is a rigorous language: it will make you perform more of your thinking up front. It can take a little while to adjust to debugging much of your code before you ever run it, in response to the compiler telling you that something about your program does not make sense. Even with years of experience, we remain astonished and pleased by how often our Haskell programs simply work on the first try, once we fix those compilation errors.

What to Expect from This Book

We started this project because a growing number of people are using Haskell to solve everyday problems. Because Haskell has its roots in academia, few of the Haskell books that currently exist focus on the problems and techniques of the typical programming that we're interested in.

With this book, we want to show you how to use functional programming and Haskell to solve realistic problems. We take a hands-on approach: every chapter contains dozens of code samples, and many contain complete applications. Here are a few examples of the libraries, techniques, and tools that we'll show you how to develop:

- Create an application that downloads podcast episodes from the Internet and stores its history in an SQL database.
- Test your code in an intuitive and powerful way. Describe properties that ought to be true, and then let the QuickCheck library generate test cases automatically.
- Take a grainy phone camera snapshot of a barcode and turn it into an identifier that you can use to query a library or bookseller's website.
- Write code that thrives on the Web. Exchange data with servers and clients written in other languages using JSON notation. Develop a concurrent link checker.

A Little Bit About You

What will you need to know before reading this book? We expect that you already know how to program, but if you've never used a functional language, that's fine.

No matter what your level of experience is, we tried to anticipate your needs; we go out of our way to explain new and potentially tricky ideas in depth, usually with examples and images to drive our points home.

As a new Haskell programmer, you'll inevitably start out writing quite a bit of code by hand for which you could have used a library function or programming technique, had you just known of its existence. We packed this book with information to help you get up to speed as quickly as possible.

Of course, there will always be a few bumps along the road. If you start out anticipating an occasional surprise or difficulty along with the fun stuff, you will have the best experience. Any rough patches you might hit won't last long.

As you become a more seasoned Haskell programmer, the way that you write code will change. Indeed, over the course of this book, the way that we present code will evolve, as we move from the basics of the language to increasingly powerful and productive features and techniques.

What to Expect from Haskell

Haskell is a general-purpose programming language. It was designed without any application niche in mind. Although it takes a strong stand on how programs should be written, it does not favor one problem domain over others.

While at its core, the language encourages a pure, lazy style of functional programming, this is the *default*, not the only option. Haskell also supports the more traditional models of procedural code and strict evaluation. Additionally, although the focus of the language is squarely on writing statically typed programs, it is possible (though rarely seen) to write Haskell code in a dynamically typed manner.

Compared to Traditional Static Languages

Languages that use simple static type systems have been the mainstay of the programming world for decades. Haskell is statically typed, but its notion of what types are for and what we can do with them is much more flexible and powerful than traditional languages. Types make a major contribution to the brevity, clarity, and efficiency of Haskell programs.

Although powerful, Haskell's type system is often also unobtrusive. If we omit explicit type information, a Haskell compiler will automatically infer the type of an expression or function. Compared to traditional static languages, to which we must spoon-feed large amounts of type information, the combination of power and inference in Haskell's type system significantly reduces the clutter and redundancy of our code.

Several of Haskell's other features combine to further increase the amount of work we can fit into a screenful of text. This brings improvements in development time and agility; we can create reliable code quickly and easily refactor it in response to changing requirements.

Sometimes, Haskell programs may run more slowly than similar programs written in C or C++. For most of the code we write, Haskell's large advantages in productivity and reliability outweigh any small performance disadvantage.

Multicore processors are now ubiquitous, but they remain notoriously difficult to program using traditional techniques. Haskell provides unique technologies to make multicore programming more tractable. It supports parallel programming, software transactional memory for reliable concurrency, and it scales to hundreds of thousands of concurrent threads.

Compared to Modern Dynamic Languages

Over the past decade, dynamically typed, interpreted languages have become increasingly popular. They offer substantial benefits in developer productivity. Although this often comes at the cost of a huge performance hit, for many programming tasks productivity trumps performance, or performance isn't a significant factor in any case.

Brevity is one area in which Haskell and dynamically typed languages perform similarly: in each case, we write much less code to solve a problem than in a traditional language. Programs are often around the same size in dynamically typed languages and Haskell.

When we consider runtime performance, Haskell almost always has a huge advantage. Code compiled by the Glasgow Haskell Compiler (GHC) is typically between 20 to 60 times faster than code run through a dynamic language's interpreter. GHC also provides an interpreter, so you can run scripts without compiling them.

Another big difference between dynamically typed languages and Haskell lies in their philosophies around types. A major reason for the popularity of dynamically typed languages is that only rarely do we need to explicitly mention types. Through automatic type inference, Haskell offers the same advantage.

Beyond this surface similarity, the differences run deep. In a dynamically typed language, we can create constructs that are difficult to express in a statically typed language. However, the same is true in reverse: with a type system as powerful as Haskell's, we can structure a program in a way that would be unmanageable or infeasible in a dynamically typed language.

It's important to recognize that each of these approaches involves trade-offs. Very briefly put, the Haskell perspective emphasizes safety, while the dynamically typed outlook favors flexibility. If someone had already discovered one way of thinking about types that was always best, we imagine that everyone would know about it by now.

Of course, we, the authors, have our own opinions about which trade-offs are more beneficial. Two of us have years of experience programming in dynamically typed languages. We love working with them; we still use them every day; but usually, we prefer Haskell.

Haskell in Industry and Open Source

Here are just a few examples of large software systems that have been created in Haskell. Some of these are open source, while others are proprietary products:

- ASIC and FPGA design software (Lava, products from Bluespec, Inc.)
- Music composition software (Haskore)
- Compilers and compiler-related tools (most notably GHC)
- Distributed revision control (Darcs)
- Web middleware (HAppS, products from Galois, Inc.)

The following is a sample of some of the companies using Haskell in late 2008, taken from the Haskell wiki (*http://www.haskell.org/haskellwiki/Haskell_in_industry*):

ABN AMRO
　　An international bank. It uses Haskell in investment banking, in order to measure the counterparty risk on portfolios of financial derivatives.

Anygma
　　A startup company. It develops multimedia content creation tools using Haskell.

Amgen
　　A biotech company. It creates mathematical models and other complex applications in Haskell.

Bluespec
　　An ASIC and FPGA design software vendor. Its products are developed in Haskell, and the chip design languages that its products provide are influenced by Haskell.

Eaton
> Uses Haskell for the design and verification of hydraulic hybrid vehicle systems.

Compilation, Debugging, and Performance Analysis

For practical work, almost as important as a language itself is the ecosystem of libraries and tools around it. Haskell has a strong showing in this area.

The most widely used compiler, GHC, has been actively developed for over 15 years and provides a mature and stable set of features:

- Compiles to efficient native code on all major modern operating systems and CPU architectures
- Easy deployment of compiled binaries, unencumbered by licensing restrictions
- Code coverage analysis
- Detailed profiling of performance and memory usage
- Thorough documentation
- Massively scalable support for concurrent and multicore programming
- Interactive interpreter and debugger

Bundled and Third-Party Libraries

The GHC compiler ships with a collection of useful libraries. Here are a few of the common programming needs that these libraries address:

- File I/O and filesystem traversal and manipulation
- Network client and server programming
- Regular expressions and parsing
- Concurrent programming
- Automated testing
- Sound and graphics

The Hackage package database is the Haskell community's collection of open source libraries and applications. Most libraries published on Hackage are licensed under liberal terms that permit both commercial and open source use. Some of the areas covered by these open source libraries include the following:

- Interfaces to all major open source and commercial databases
- XML, HTML, and XQuery processing
- Network and web client and server development
- Desktop GUIs, including cross-platform toolkits
- Support for Unicode and other text encodings

A Brief Sketch of Haskell's History

The development of Haskell is rooted in mathematics and computer science research.

Prehistory

A few decades before modern computers were invented, the mathematician Alonzo Church developed a language called *lambda calculus*. He intended it as a tool for investigating the foundations of mathematics. The first person to realize the practical connection between programming and lambda calculus was John McCarthy, who created Lisp in 1958.

During the 1960s, computer scientists began to recognize and study the importance of lambda calculus. Peter Landin and Christopher Strachey developed ideas about the foundations of programming languages: how to reason about what they do (operational semantics) and how to understand what they mean (denotational semantics).

In the early 1970s, Robin Milner created a more rigorous functional programming language named *ML*. While ML was developed to help with automated proofs of mathematical theorems, it gained a following for more general computing tasks.

The 1970s also saw the emergence of lazy evaluation as a novel strategy. David Turner developed SASL and KRC, while Rod Burstall and John Darlington developed NPL and Hope. NPL, KRC, and ML influenced the development of several more languages in the 1980s, including Lazy ML, Clean, and Miranda.

Early Antiquity

By the late 1980s, the efforts of researchers working on lazy functional languages were scattered across more than a dozen languages. Concerned by this diffusion of effort, a number of researchers decided to form a committee to design a common language. After three years of work, the committee published the Haskell 1.0 specification in 1990. It named the language after Haskell Curry, an influential logician.

Many people are rightfully suspicious of "design by committee," but the output of the Haskell committee is a beautiful example of the best work a committee can do. They produced an elegant, considered language design and succeeded in unifying the fractured efforts of their research community. Of the thicket of lazy functional languages that existed in 1990, only Haskell is still actively used.

Since its publication in 1990, the Haskell language standard has seen five revisions, most recently in 1998. A number of Haskell implementations have been written, and several are still actively developed.

During the 1990s, Haskell served two main purposes. On one side, it gave language researchers a stable language in which to experiment with making lazy functional programs run efficiently and on the other side researchers explored how to construct programs using lazy functional techniques, and still others used it as a teaching language.

The Modern Era

While these basic explorations of the 1990s proceeded, Haskell remained firmly an academic affair. The informal slogan of those inside the community was to "avoid success at all costs." Few outsiders had heard of the language at all. Indeed, functional programming as a field was quite obscure.

During this time, the mainstream programming world experimented with relatively small tweaks, from programming in C, to C++, to Java. Meanwhile, on the fringes, programmers were beginning to tinker with new, more dynamic languages. Guido van Rossum designed Python; Larry Wall created Perl; and Yukihiro Matsumoto developed Ruby.

As these newer languages began to seep into wider use, they spread some crucial ideas. The first was that programmers are not merely capable of working in expressive languages; in fact, they flourish. The second was in part a byproduct of the rapid growth in raw computing power of that era: it's often smart to sacrifice some execution performance in exchange for a big increase in programmer productivity. Finally, several of these languages borrowed from functional programming.

Over the past half decade, Haskell has successfully escaped from academia, buoyed in part by the visibility of Python, Ruby, and even JavaScript. The language now has a vibrant and fast-growing culture of open source and commercial users, and researchers continue to use it to push the boundaries of performance and expressiveness.

Helpful Resources

As you work with Haskell, you're sure to have questions and want more information about things. The following paragraphs describe some Internet resources where you can look up information and interact with other Haskell programmers.

Reference Material

The Haskell Hierarchical Libraries reference
    Provides the documentation for the standard library that comes with your compiler. This is one of the most valuable online assets for Haskell programmers.
Haskell 98 Report
    Describes the Haskell 98 language standard.

GHC Users's Guide
> Contains detailed documentation on the extensions supported by GHC, as well as some GHC-specific features.

Hoogle and Hayoo
> Haskell API search engines. They can search for functions by name or type.

Applications and Libraries

If you're looking for a Haskell library to use for a particular task or an application written in Haskell, check out the following resources:

The Haskell community
> Maintains a central repository of open source Haskell libraries called Hackage (*http://hackage.haskell.org/*). It lets you search for software to download, or browse its collection by category.

The Haskell wiki (http://haskell.org/haskellwiki/Applications_and_libraries)
> Contains a section dedicated to information about particular Haskell libraries.

The Haskell Community

There are a number of ways you can get in touch with other Haskell programmers, in order to ask questions, learn what other people are talking about, and simply do some social networking with your peers:

- The first stop on your search for community resources should be the Haskell website (*http://www.haskell.org/*). This page contains the most current links to various communities and information, as well as a huge and actively maintained wiki.

- Haskellers use a number of mailing lists (*http://haskell.org/haskellwiki/Mailing _lists*) for topical discussions. Of these, the most generally interesting is named haskell-cafe. It has a relaxed, friendly atmosphere, where professionals and academics rub shoulders with casual hackers and beginners.

- For real-time chat, the Haskell IRC channel (*http://haskell.org/haskellwiki/IRC _channel*), named #haskell, is large and lively. Like haskell-cafe, the atmosphere stays friendly and helpful in spite of the huge number of concurrent users.

- There are many local user groups, meetups, academic workshops, and the like; there is a list of the known user groups and workshops (*http://haskell.org/haskell wiki/User_groups*).

- The Haskell Weekly News (*http://sequence.complete.org/*) is a very-nearly-weekly summary of activities in the Haskell community. You can find pointers to interesting mailing list discussions, new software releases, and similar things.

- The Haskell Communities and Activities Report (*http://haskell.org/communities/*) collects information about people that use Haskell and what they're doing with it. It's been running for years, so it provides a good way to peer into Haskell's past.

Conventions Used in This Book

The following typographical conventions are used in this book:

Italic
> Indicates new terms, URLs, email addresses, filenames, and file extensions.

`Constant width`
> Used for program listings, as well as within paragraphs to refer to program elements such as variable or function names, databases, data types, environment variables, statements, and keywords.

`Constant width bold`
> Shows commands or other text that should be typed literally by the user.

`Constant width italic`
> Shows text that should be replaced with user-supplied values or by values determined by context.

 This icon signifies a tip, suggestion, or general note.

 This icon indicates a warning or caution.

Using Code Examples

This book is here to help you get your job done. In general, you may use the code in this book in your programs and documentation. You do not need to contact us for permission unless you're reproducing a significant portion of the code. For example, writing a program that uses several chunks of code from this book does not require permission. Selling or distributing a CD-ROM of examples from O'Reilly books does require permission. Answering a question by citing this book and quoting example code does not require permission. Incorporating a significant amount of example code from this book into your product's documentation does require permission.

We appreciate, but do not require, attribution. An attribution usually includes the title, author, publisher, and ISBN. For example: "*Real World Haskell*, by Bryan O'Sullivan, John Goerzen, and Don Stewart. Copyright 2009 Bryan O'Sullivan, John Goerzen, and Donald Stewart, 978-0-596-51498-3."

If you feel your use of code examples falls outside fair use or the permission given above, feel free to contact us at *permissions@oreilly.com*.

Safari® Books Online

Safari When you see a Safari® Books Online icon on the cover of your favorite technology book, that means the book is available online through the O'Reilly Network Safari Bookshelf.

Safari offers a solution that's better than e-books. It's a virtual library that lets you easily search thousands of top tech books, cut and paste code samples, download chapters, and find quick answers when you need the most accurate, current information. Try it for free at *http://safari.oreilly.com*.

How to Contact Us

Please address comments and questions concerning this book to the publisher:

O'Reilly Media, Inc.
1005 Gravenstein Highway North
Sebastopol, CA 95472
800-998-9938 (in the United States or Canada)
707-829-0515 (international or local)
707-829-0104 (fax)

We have a web page for this book, where we list errata, examples, and any additional information. You can access this page at:

http://www.oreilly.com/catalog/9780596514983

To comment or ask technical questions about this book, send email to:

bookquestions@oreilly.com

For more information about our books, conferences, Resource Centers, and the O'Reilly Network, see our website at:

http://www.oreilly.com

Acknowledgments

This book would not exist without the Haskell community: an anarchic, hopeful cabal of artists, theoreticians and engineers, who for 20 years have worked to create a better, bug-free programming world. The people of the Haskell community are unique in their combination of friendliness and intellectual depth.

We wish to thank our editor, Mike Loukides, and the production team at O'Reilly for all of their advice and assistance.

Bryan

I had a great deal of fun working with John and Don. Their independence, good nature, and formidable talent made the writing process remarkably smooth.

Simon Peyton Jones took a chance on a college student who emailed him out of the blue in early 1994. Interning for him over that summer remains a highlight of my professional life. With his generosity, boundless energy, and drive to collaborate, he inspires the whole Haskell community.

My children, Cian and Ruairi, always stood ready to help me to unwind with wonderful, madcap, little-boy games.

Finally, of course, I owe a great debt to my wife, Shannon, for her love, wisdom, and support during the long gestation of this book.

John

I am so glad to be able to work with Bryan and Don on this project. The depth of their Haskell knowledge and experience is amazing. I enjoyed finally being able to have the three of us sit down in the same room—over a year after we started writing.

My 2-year-old Jacob, who decided that it would be fun to use a keyboard too and was always eager to have me take a break from the computer and help him make some fun typing noises on a 50-year-old Underwood typewriter.

Most importantly, I wouldn't have ever been involved in this project without the love, support, and encouragement from my wife, Terah.

Don

Before all else, I'd like to thank my amazing coconspirators, John and Bryan, for encouragment, advice, and motivation.

My colleagues at Galois, Inc., who daily wield Haskell in the real world, provided regular feedback and war stories and helped ensure a steady supply of espresso.

My Ph.D. supervisor, Manuel Chakravarty, and the PLS research group, who provided encouragement, vision, and energy and showed me that a rigorous, foundational approach to programming can make the impossible happen.

And, finally, thanks to Suzie, for her insight, patience, and love.

Thank You to Our Reviewers

We developed this book in the open, posting drafts of chapters to our website as we completed them. Readers then submitted feedback using a web application that we developed. By the time we finished writing the book, about 800 people had submitted over 7,500 comments—an astounding figure.

We deeply appreciate the time that so many people volunteered to help us to improve our book. Their encouragement and enthusiasm over the 15 months we spent writing made the process a pleasure.

The breadth and depth of the comments we received have profoundly improved the quality of this book. Nevertheless, all errors and omissions are, of course, ours.

The following people each contributed over 1% of the total number of review comments that we received. We would like to thank them for their care in providing us with so much detailed feedback:

Alex Stangl, Andrew Bromage, Brent Yorgey, Bruce Turner, Calvin Smith, David Teller, Henry Lenzi, Jay Scott, John Dorsey, Justin Dressel, Lauri Pesonen, Lennart Augustsson, Luc Duponcheel, Matt Hellige, Michael T. Richter, Peter McLain, Rob deFriesse, Rüdiger Hanke, Tim Chevalier, Tim Stewart, William N. Halchin.

We are also grateful to the people below, each of whom contributed at least 0.2% of all comments:

Achim Schneider, Adam Jones, Alexander Semenov, Andrew Wagner, Arnar Birgisson, Arthur van Leeuwen, Bartek Cwikłowski, Bas Kok, Ben Franksen, Björn Buckwalter, Brian Brunswick, Bryn Keller, Chris Holliday, Chris Smith, Dan Scott, Dan Weston, Daniel Larsson, Davide Marchignoli, Derek Elkins, Dirk Ullrich, Doug Kirk, Douglas Silas, Emmanuel Delaborde, Eric Lavigne, Erik Haugen, Erik Jones, Fred Ross, Geoff King, George Moschovitis, Hans van Thiel, Ionut Artarisi, Isaac Dupree, Isaac Freeman, Jared Updike, Joe Thornber, Joeri van Eekelen, Joey Hess, Johan Tibell, John Lenz, Josef Svenningsson, Joseph Garvin, Josh Szepietowski, Justin Bailey, Kai Gellien, Kevin Watters, Konrad Hinsen, Lally Singh, Lee Duhem, Luke Palmer, Magnus Therning, Marc DeRosa, Marcus Eskilsson, Mark Lee Smith, Matthew Danish, Matthew Manela, Michael Vanier, Mike Brauwerman, Neil Mitchell, Nick Seow, Pat Rondon, Raynor Vliegendhart, Richard Smith, Runar Bjarnason, Ryan W. Porter, Salvatore Insalaco, Sean Brewer, Sebastian Sylvan, Sebastien Bocq, Sengan Baring-Gould, Serge Le Huitouze, Shahbaz Chaudhary, Shawn M Moore, Tom Tschetter, Valery V. Vorotyntsev, Will Newton, Wolfgang Meyer, Wouter Swierstra.

We would like to acknowledge the following people, many of whom submitted a number of comments:

Aaron Hall, Abhishek Dasgupta, Adam Copp, Adam Langley, Adam Warrington, Adam Winiecki, Aditya Mahajan, Adolfo Builes, Al Hoang, Alan Hawkins, Albert Brown, Alec Berryman, Alejandro Dubrovsky, Alex Hirzel, Alex Rudnick, Alex Young, Alexander Battisti, Alexander Macdonald, Alexander Strange, Alf Richter, Alistair Bayley, Allan Clark, Allan Erskine, Allen Gooch, Andre Nathan, Andreas Bernstein, Andreas Schropp, Andrei Formiga, Andrew Butterfield, Andrew Calleja, Andrew Rimes, Andrew The, Andy Carson, Andy Payne, Angelos Sphyris, Ankur Sethi, António

Pedro Cunha, Anthony Moralez, Antoine Hersen, Antoine Latter, Antoine S., Antonio Cangiano, Antonio Piccolboni, Antonios Antoniadis, Antonis Antoniadis, Aristotle Pagaltzis, Arjen van Schie, Artyom Shalkhakov, Ash Logan, Austin Seipp, Avik Das, Avinash Meetoo, BVK Chaitanya, Babu Srinivasan, Barry Gaunt, Bas van Dijk, Ben Burdette, Ben Ellis, Ben Moseley, Ben Sinclair, Benedikt Huber, Benjamin Terry, Benoit Jauvin-Girard, Bernie Pope, Björn Edström, Bob Holness, Bobby Moretti, Boyd Adamson, Brad Ediger, Bradley Unterrheiner, Brendan J. Overdiep, Brendan Macmillan, Brett Morgan, Brian Bloniarz, Brian Lewis, Brian Palmer, Brice Lin, C Russell, Cale Gibbard, Carlos Aya, Chad Scherrer, Chaddaï Fouché, Chance Coble, Charles Krohn, Charlie Paucard, Chen Yufei, Cheng Wei, Chip Grandits, Chris Ball, Chris Brew, Chris Czub, Chris Gallagher, Chris Jenkins, Chris Kuklewicz, Chris Wright, Christian Lasarczyk, Christian Vest Hansen, Christophe Poucet, Chung-chieh Shan, Conal Elliott, Conor McBride, Conrad Parker, Cosmo Kastemaa, Creighton Hogg, Crutcher Dunnavant, Curtis Warren, D Hardman, Dafydd Harries, Dale Jordan, Dan Doel, Dan Dyer, Dan Grover, Dan Orias, Dan Schmidt, Dan Zwell, Daniel Chicayban Bastos, Daniel Karch, Daniel Lyons, Daniel Patterson, Daniel Wagner, Daniil Elovkov, Danny Yoo, Darren Mutz, Darrin Thompson, Dave Bayer, Dave Hinton, Dave Leimbach, Dave Peterson, Dave Ward, David Altenburg, David B. Wildgoose, David Carter, David Einstein, David Ellis, David Fox, David Frey, David Goodlad, David Mathers, David McBride, David Sabel, Dean Pucsek, Denis Bueno, Denis Volk, Devin Mullins, Diego Moya, Dino Morelli, Dirk Markert, Dmitry Astapov, Dougal Stanton, Dr Bean, Drew Smathers, Duane Johnson, Durward McDonell, E. Jones, Edwin DeNicholas, Emre Sevinc, Eric Aguiar, Eric Frey, Eric Kidd, Eric Kow, Eric Schwartz, Erik Hesselink, Erling Alf, Eruc Frey, Eugene Grigoriev, Eugene Kirpichov, Evan Farrer, Evan Klitzke, Evan Martin, Fawzi Mohamed, Filippo Tampieri, Florent Becker, Frank Berthold, Fred Rotbart, Frederick Ross, Friedrich Dominicus, Gal Amram, Ganesh Sittampalam, Gen Zhang, Geoffrey King, George Bunyan, George Rogers, German Vidal, Gilson Silveira, Gleb Alexeyev, Glenn Ehrlich, Graham Fawcett, Graham Lowe, Greg Bacon, Greg Chrystall, Greg Steuck, Grzegorz Chrupała, Guillaume Marceau, Haggai Eran, Harald Armin Massa, Henning Hasemann, Henry Laxen, Hitesh Jasani, Howard B. Golden, Ilmari Vacklin, Imam Tashdid ul Alam, Ivan Lazar Miljenovic, Ivan Miljenovic, J. Pablo Fernández, J.A. Zaratiegui, Jaap Weel, Jacques Richer, Jake McArthur, Jake Poznanski, Jakub Kotowski, Jakub Labath, James Cunningham, James Smith, Jamie Brandon, Jan Sabbe, Jared Roberts, Jason Dusek, Jason F, Jason Kikel, Jason Mobarak, Jason Morton, Jason Rogers, Jeff Balogh, Jeff Caldwell, Jeff Petkau, Jeffrey Bolden, Jeremy Crosbie, Jeremy Fitzhardinge, Jeremy O'Donoghue, Jeroen Pulles, Jim Apple, Jim Crayne, Jim Snow, Joan Jiménez, Joe Fredette, Joe Healy, Joel Lathrop, Joeri Samson, Johannes Laire, John Cowan, John Doe, John Hamilton, John Hornbeck, John Lien, John Stracke, Jonathan Guitton, Joseph Bruce, Joseph H. Buehler, Josh Goldfoot, Josh Lee, Josh Stone, Judah Jacobson, Justin George, Justin Goguen, Kamal Al-Marhubi, Kamil Dworakowski, Keegan Carruthers-Smith, Keith Fahlgren, Keith Willoughby, Ken Allen, Ken Shirriff, Kent Hunter, Kevin Hely, Kevin Scaldeferri, Kingdon Barrett, Kristjan Kannike, Kurt Jung, Lanny Ripple, Laurentiu Nicola, Laurie Cheers, Lennart

Kolmodin, Liam Groener, Lin Sun, Lionel Barret de Nazaris, Loup Vaillant, Luke Plant, Lutz Donnerhacke, Maarten Hazewinkel, Malcolm Reynolds, Marco Piccioni, Mark Hahnenberg, Mark Woodward, Marko Tosic, Markus Schnell, Martijn van Egdom, Martin Bayer, Martin DeMello, Martin Dybdal, Martin Geisler, Martin Grabmueller, Matúš Tejiščák, Mathew Manela, Matt Brandt, Matt Russell, Matt Trinneer, Matti Niemenmaa, Matti Nykänen, Max Cantor, Maxime Henrion, Michael Albert, Michael Brauwerman, Michael Campbell, Michael Chermside, Michael Cook, Michael Dougherty, Michael Feathers, Michael Grinder, Michael Kagalenko, Michael Kaplan, Michael Orlitzky, Michael Smith, Michael Stone, Michael Walter, Michel Salim, Mikael Vejdemo Johansson, Mike Coleman, Mike Depot, Mike Tremoulet, Mike Vanier, Mirko Rahn, Miron Brezuleanu, Morten Andersen, Nathan Bronson, Nathan Stien, Naveen Nathan, Neil Bartlett, Neil Whitaker, Nick Gibson, Nick Messenger, Nick Okasinski, Nicola Paolucci, Nicolas Frisby, Niels Aan de Brugh, Niels Holmgaard Andersen, Nima Negahban, Olaf Leidinger, Oleg Anashkin, Oleg Dopertchouk, Oleg Taykalo, Oliver Charles, Olivier Boudry, Omar Antolín Camarena, Parnell Flynn, Patrick Carlisle, Paul Brown, Paul Delhanty, Paul Johnson, Paul Lotti, Paul Moore, Paul Stanley, Paulo Tanimoto, Per Vognsen, Pete Kazmier, Peter Aarestad, Peter Ipacs, Peter Kovaliov, Peter Merel, Peter Seibel, Peter Sumskas, Phil Armstrong, Philip Armstrong, Philip Craig, Philip Neustrom, Philip Turnbull, Piers Harding, Piet Delport, Pragya Agarwal, Raúl Gutiérrez, Rafael Alemida, Rajesh Krishnan, Ralph Glass, Rauli Ruohonen, Ravi Nanavati, Raymond Pasco, Reid Barton, Reto Kramer, Reza Ziaei, Rhys Ulerich, Ricardo Herrmann, Richard Harris, Richard Warburton, Rick van Hattem, Rob Grainger, Robbie Kop, Rogan Creswick, Roman Gonzalez, Rory Winston, Ruediger Hanke, Rusty Mellinger, Ryan Grant, Ryan Ingram, Ryan Janzen, Ryan Kaulakis, Ryan Stutsman, Ryan T. Mulligan, S Pai, Sam Lee, Sandy Nicholson, Scott Brickner, Scott Rankin, Scott Ribe, Sean Cross, Sean Leather, Sergei Trofimovich, Sergio Urinovsky, Seth Gordon, Seth Tisue, Shawn Boyette, Simon Brenner, Simon Farnsworth, Simon Marlow, Simon Meier, Simon Morgan, Sriram Srinivasan, Stefan Aeschbacher, Stefan Muenzel, Stephan Friedrichs, Stephan Nies, Stephan-A. Posselt, Stephyn Butcher, Steven Ashley, Stuart Dootson, Terry Michaels, Thomas Cellerier, Thomas Fuhrmann, Thomas Hunger, Thomas M. DuBuisson, Thomas Moertel, Thomas Schilling, Thorsten Seitz, Tibor Simic, Tilo Wiklund, Tim Clark, Tim Eves, Tim Massingham, Tim Rakowski, Tim Wiess, Timo B. Hübel, Timothy Fitz, Tom Moertel, Tomáš Janoušek, Tony Colston, Travis B. Hartwell, Tristan Allwood, Tristan Seligmann, Tristram Brelstaff, Vesa Kaihlavirta, Victor Nazarov, Ville Aine, Vincent Foley, Vipul Ved Prakash, Vlad Skvortsov, Vojtech Fried, Wei Cheng, Wei Hu, Will Barrett, Will Farr, Will Leinweber, Will Robertson, Will Thompson, Wirt Wolff, Wolfgang Jeltsch, Yuval Kogman, Zach Kozatek, Zachary Smestad, Zohar Kelrich.

Finally, we wish to thank those readers who submitted over 800 comments anonymously.

CHAPTER 1

Getting Started

As you read the early chapters of this book, keep in mind that we will sometimes introduce ideas in restricted, simplified form. Haskell is a deep language, and presenting every aspect of a given subject all at once is likely to prove overwhelming. As we build a solid foundation in Haskell, we will expand upon these initial explanations.

Your Haskell Environment

Haskell is a language with many implementations, two of which are widely used. Hugs is an interpreter that is primarily used for teaching. For real applications, the Glasgow Haskell Compiler (GHC) is much more popular. Compared to Hugs, GHC is more suited to "real work": it compiles to native code, supports parallel execution, and provides useful performance analysis and debugging tools. For these reasons, GHC is the Haskell implementation that we will be using throughout this book.

GHC has three main components:

ghc
> An optimizing compiler that generates fast native code

ghci
> An interactive interpreter and debugger

runghc
> A program for running Haskell programs as scripts, without needing to compile them first

How we refer to the components of GHC

When we discuss the GHC system as a whole, we will refer to it as GHC. If we are talking about a specific command, we will mention ghc, ghci, or runghc by name.

We assume that you're using at least version 6.8.2 of GHC, which was released in 2007. Many of our examples will work unmodified with older versions. However, we *recommend* using the newest version available for your platform. If you're using Windows or Mac OS X, you can get started easily and quickly using a prebuilt installer. To obtain a copy of GHC for these platforms, visit the GHC download page (*http://www.haskell .org/ghc/download.html*) and look for the list of binary packages and installers.

Many Linux distributors and providers of BSD and other Unix variants make custom binary packages of GHC available. Because these are built specifically for each environment, they are much easier to install and use than the generic binary packages that are available from the GHC download page. You can find a list of distributions that custom build GHC at the GHC page distribution packages (*http://www.haskell.org/ghc/ distribution_packages.html*).

For more detailed information about how to install GHC on a variety of popular platforms, we've provided some instructions in Appendix A.

Getting Started with ghci, the Interpreter

The interactive interpreter for GHC is a program named ghci. It lets us enter and evaluate Haskell expressions, explore modules, and debug our code. If you are familiar with Python or Ruby, ghci is somewhat similar to python and irb, the interactive Python and Ruby interpreters.

 The ghci command has a narrow focus

We typically cannot copy some code out of a Haskell source file and paste it into ghci. This does not have a significant effect on debugging pieces of code, but it can initially be surprising if you are used to, say, the interactive Python interpreter.

On Unix-like systems, we run ghci as a command in a shell window. On Windows, it's available via the Start menu. For example, if you install the program using the GHC installer on Windows XP, you should go to All Programs, then GHC; you will see ghci in the list. (See "Windows" on page 641 for a screenshot.)

When we run ghci, it displays a startup banner, followed by a Prelude> prompt. Here, we're showing version 6.8.3 on a Linux box:

```
$ ghci
GHCi, version 6.8.3: http://www.haskell.org/ghc/  :? for help
Loading package base ... linking ... done.
Prelude>
```

The word Prelude in the prompt indicates that Prelude, a standard library of useful functions, is loaded and ready to use. When we load other modules or source files, they will show up in the prompt, too.

Getting help

If you enter `:?` at the ghci prompt, it will print a long help message.

The `Prelude` module is sometimes referred to as "the standard prelude" because its contents are defined by the Haskell 98 standard. Usually, it's simply shortened to "the prelude."

About the ghci prompt

The prompt displayed by ghci changes frequently depending on what modules we have loaded. It can often grow long enough to leave little visual room on a single line for our input.

For brevity and consistency, we replaced ghci's default prompts throughout this book with the prompt string ghci>.

If you want to do this yourself, use ghci's `:set prompt` directive, as follows:

```
Prelude> :set prompt "ghci> "
ghci>
```

The `Prelude` is always implicitly available; we don't need to take any actions to use the types, values, or functions it defines. To use definitions from other modules, we must load them into ghci, using the `:module` command:

```
ghci> :module + Data.Ratio
```

We can now use the functionality of the `Data.Ratio` module, which lets us work with rational numbers (fractions).

Basic Interaction: Using ghci as a Calculator

In addition to providing a convenient interface for testing code fragments, ghci can function as a readily accessible desktop calculator. We can easily express any calculator operation in ghci and, as an added bonus, we can add more complex operations as we become more familiar with Haskell. Even using the interpreter in this simple way can help us to become more comfortable with how Haskell works.

Simple Arithmetic

We can immediately start entering expressions, in order to see what ghci will do with them. Basic arithmetic works similarly to languages such as C and Python—we write expressions in *infix* form, where an operator appears between its operands:

```
ghci> 2 + 2
4
ghci> 31337 * 101
3165037
ghci> 7.0 / 2.0
3.5
```

The infix style of writing an expression is just a convenience; we can also write an expression in *prefix* form, where the operator precedes its arguments. To do this, we must enclose the operator in parentheses:

```
ghci> 2 + 2
4
ghci> (+) 2 2
4
```

As these expressions imply, Haskell has a notion of integers and floating-point numbers. Integers can be arbitrarily large. Here, (^) provides integer exponentiation:

```
ghci> 313 ^ 15
27112218957718876716220410905036741257
```

An Arithmetic Quirk: Writing Negative Numbers

Haskell presents us with one peculiarity in how we must write numbers: it's often necessary to enclose a negative number in parentheses. This affects us as soon as we move beyond the simplest expressions.

We'll start by writing a negative number:

```
ghci> -3
-3
```

The - used in the preceding code is a unary operator. In other words, we didn't write the single number "-3"; we wrote the number "3" and applied the operator - to it. The - operator is Haskell's only unary operator, and we cannot mix it with infix operators:

```
ghci> 2 + -3

<interactive>:1:0:
    precedence parsing error
        cannot mix `(+)' [infixl 6] and prefix `-' [infixl 6] in the same infix
                                                                     expression
```

If we want to use the unary minus near an infix operator, we must wrap the expression that it applies to in parentheses:

```
ghci> 2 + (-3)
-1
ghci> 3 + (-(13 * 37))
-478
```

This avoids a parsing ambiguity. When we apply a function in Haskell, we write the name of the function, followed by its argument—for example, f 3. If we did not need to wrap a negative number in parentheses, we would have two profoundly different ways to read f-3: it could be either "apply the function f to the number -3," or "subtract the number 3 from the variable f."

Most of the time, we can omit whitespace ("blank" characters such as space and tab) from expressions, and Haskell will parse them as we intended. But not always. Here is an expression that works:

```
ghci> 2*3
6
```

And here is one that seems similar to the previous problematic negative number example, but that results in a different error message:

```
ghci> 2*-3

<interactive>:1:1: Not in scope: `*-'
```

Here, the Haskell implementation is reading *- as a single operator. Haskell lets us define new operators (a subject that we will return to later), but we haven't defined *-. Once again, a few parentheses get us and ghci looking at the expression in the same way:

```
ghci> 2*(-3)
-6
```

Compared to other languages, this unusual treatment of negative numbers might seem annoying, but it represents a reasoned trade-off. Haskell lets us define new operators at any time. This is not some kind of esoteric language feature; we will see quite a few user-defined operators in the chapters ahead. The language designers chose to accept a slightly cumbersome syntax for negative numbers in exchange for this expressive power.

Boolean Logic, Operators, and Value Comparisons

The values of Boolean logic in Haskell are True and False. The capitalization of these names is important. The language uses C-influenced operators for working with Boolean values: (&&) is logical "and", and (||) is logical "or":

```
ghci> True && False
False
ghci> False || True
True
```

While some programming languages treat the number zero as synonymous with False, Haskell does not, nor does it consider a nonzero value to be True:

```
ghci> True && 1

<interactive>:1:8:
    No instance for (Num Bool)
      arising from the literal `1' at <interactive>:1:8
    Possible fix: add an instance declaration for (Num Bool)
    In the second argument of `(&&)', namely `1'
```

```
In the expression: True && 1
In the definition of `it': it = True && 1
```

Once again, we are faced with a substantial-looking error message. In brief, it tells us that the Boolean type, Bool, is not a member of the family of numeric types, Num. The error message is rather long because ghci is pointing out the location of the problem and hinting at a possible change we could make that might fix it.

Here is a more detailed breakdown of the error message:

```
No instance for (Num Bool)
```
Tells us that ghci is trying to treat the numeric value 1 as having a Bool type, but it cannot

```
arising from the literal '1'
```
Indicates that it was our use of the number 1 that caused the problem

```
In the definition of 'it'
```
Refers to a ghci shortcut that we will revisit in a few pages

Remain fearless in the face of error messages

We have an important point to make here, which we will repeat throughout the early sections of this book. If you run into problems or error messages that you do not yet understand, *don't panic*. Early on, all you have to do is figure out enough to make progress on a problem. As you acquire experience, you will find it easier to understand parts of error messages that initially seem obscure.

The numerous error messages have a purpose: they actually help us write correct code by making us perform some amount of debugging "up front," before we ever run a program. If you come from a background of working with more permissive languages, this may come as something of a shock. Bear with us.

Most of Haskell's comparison operators are similar to those used in C and the many languages it has influenced:

```
ghci> 1 == 1
True
ghci> 2 < 3
True
ghci> 4 >= 3.99
True
```

One operator that differs from its C counterpart is "is not equal to". In C, this is written as !=. In Haskell, we write (/=), which resembles the ≠ notation used in mathematics:

```
ghci> 2 /= 3
True
```

Also, where C-like languages often use ! for logical negation, Haskell uses the not function:

```
ghci> not True
False
```

Operator Precedence and Associativity

Like written algebra and other programming languages that use infix operators, Haskell has a notion of operator precedence. We can use parentheses to explicitly group parts of an expression, and precedence allows us to omit a few parentheses. For example, the multiplication operator has a higher precedence than the addition operator, so Haskell treats the following two expressions as equivalent:

```
ghci> 1 + (4 * 4)
17
ghci> 1 + 4 * 4
17
```

Haskell assigns numeric precedence values to operators, with 1 being the lowest precedence and 9 the highest. A higher-precedence operator is applied before a lower-precedence operator. We can use ghci to inspect the precedence levels of individual operators, using ghci's :info command:

```
ghci> :info (+)
class (Eq a, Show a) => Num a where
  (+) :: a -> a -> a
  ...
        -- Defined in GHC.Num
infixl 6 +
ghci> :info (*)
class (Eq a, Show a) => Num a where
  ...
  (*) :: a -> a -> a
  ...
        -- Defined in GHC.Num
infixl 7 *
```

The information we seek is in the line infixl 6 +, which indicates that the (+) operator has a precedence of 6. (We will explain the other output in a later chapter.) infixl 7 * tells us that the (*) operator has a precedence of 7. Since (*) has a higher precedence than (+), we can now see why 1 + 4 * 4 is evaluated as 1 + (4 * 4), and not (1 + 4) * 4.

Haskell also defines *associativity* of operators. This determines whether an expression containing multiple uses of an operator is evaluated from left to right or right to left. The (+) and (*) operators are left associative, which is represented as infixl in the preceding ghci output. A right associative operator is displayed with infixr:

```
ghci> :info (^)
(^) :: (Num a, Integral b) => a -> b -> a      -- Defined in GHC.Real
infixr 8 ^
```

The combination of precedence and associativity rules are usually referred to as *fixity* rules.

Undefined Values, and Introducing Variables

Haskell's `Prelude`, the standard library we mentioned earlier, defines at least one well-known mathematical constant for us:

```
ghci> pi
3.141592653589793
```

But its coverage of mathematical constants is not comprehensive, as we can quickly see. Let us look for Euler's number, e:

```
ghci> e

<interactive>:1:0: Not in scope: `e'
```

Oh well. We have to define it ourselves.

Don't worry about the error message

If the `not in scope` error message seems a little daunting, do not worry. All it means is that there is no variable defined with the name e.

Using ghci's `let` construct, we can make a temporary definition of e ourselves:

```
ghci> let e = exp 1
```

This is an application of the exponential function, `exp`, and our first example of applying a function in Haskell. While languages such as Python require parentheses around the arguments to a function, Haskell does not.

With e defined, we can now use it in arithmetic expressions. The (^) exponentiation operator that we introduced earlier can only raise a number to an integer power. To use a floating-point number as the exponent, we use the (**) exponentiation operator:

```
ghci> (e ** pi) - pi
19.99909997918947
```

This syntax is ghci-specific

The syntax for `let` that `ghci` accepts is not the same as we would use at the "top level" of a normal Haskell program. We will see the normal syntax in "Introducing Local Variables" on page 61.

Dealing with Precedence and Associativity Rules

It is sometimes better to leave at least some parentheses in place, even when Haskell allows us to omit them. Their presence can help future readers (including ourselves) to understand what we intended.

Even more importantly, complex expressions that rely completely on operator precedence are notorious sources of bugs. A compiler and a human can easily end up with different notions of what even a short, parenthesis-free expression is supposed to do.

There is no need to remember all of the precedence and associativity rules numbers: it is simpler to add parentheses if you are unsure.

Command-Line Editing in ghci

On most systems, ghci has some amount of command-line editing ability. In case you are not familiar with command-line editing, it's a huge time saver. The basics are common to both Unix-like and Windows systems. Pressing the up arrow key on your keyboard recalls the last line of input you entered; pressing up repeatedly cycles through earlier lines of input. You can use the left and right arrow keys to move around inside a line of input. On Unix (but not Windows, unfortunately), the Tab key completes partially entered identifiers.

Where to look for more information

We've barely scratched the surface of command-line editing here. Since you can work more effectively if you're familiar with the capabilities of your command-line editing system, you might find it useful to do some further reading.

On Unix-like systems, ghci uses the GNU readline library (*http://tiswww .case.edu/php/chet/readline/rltop.html#Documentation*), which is powerful and customizable. On Windows, ghci's command-line editing capabilities are provided by the **doskey** command (*http://www.microsoft .com/resources/documentation/windows/xp/all/proddocs/en-us/doskey .mspx*).

Lists

A list is surrounded by square brackets; the elements are separated by commas:

```
ghci> [1, 2, 3]
[1,2,3]
```

Commas are separators, not terminators

Some languages permit the last element in a list to be followed by an optional trailing comma before a closing bracket, but Haskell doesn't allow this. If you leave in a trailing comma (e.g., [1,2,]), you'll get a parse error.

A list can be of any length. An empty list is written []:

```
ghci> []
[]
ghci> ["foo", "bar", "baz", "quux", "fnord", "xyzzy"]
["foo","bar","baz","quux","fnord","xyzzy"]
```

All elements of a list must be of the same type. Here, we violate this rule. Our list starts with two `Bool` values, but ends with a string:

```
ghci> [True, False, "testing"]
```

```
<interactive>:1:14:
    Couldn't match expected type `Bool' against inferred type `[Char]'
    In the expression: "testing"
    In the expression: [True, False, "testing"]
    In the definition of `it': it = [True, False, "testing"]
```

Once again, ghci's error message is verbose, but it's simply telling us that there is no way to turn the string into a Boolean value, so the list expression isn't properly typed.

If we write a series of elements using *enumeration notation*, Haskell will fill in the contents of the list for us:

```
ghci> [1..10]
[1,2,3,4,5,6,7,8,9,10]
```

Here, the `..` characters denote an *enumeration*. We can only use this notation for types whose elements we can enumerate. It makes no sense for text strings, for instance—there is not any sensible, general way to enumerate `["foo".."quux"]`.

By the way, notice that the preceding use of range notation gives us a *closed interval*; the list contains both endpoints.

When we write an enumeration, we can optionally specify the size of the step to use by providing the first two elements, followed by the value at which to stop generating the enumeration:

```
ghci> [1.0,1.25..2.0]
[1.0,1.25,1.5,1.75,2.0]
ghci> [1,4..15]
[1,4,7,10,13]
ghci> [10,9..1]
[10,9,8,7,6,5,4,3,2,1]
```

In the second case, the list is quite sensibly missing the endpoint of the enumeration, because it isn't an element of the series we defined.

We can omit the endpoint of an enumeration. If a type doesn't have a natural "upper bound," this will produce values indefinitely. For example, if you type `[1..]` at the ghci prompt, you'll have to interrupt or kill ghci to stop it from printing an infinite succession of ever-larger numbers. If you are tempted to do this, hit Ctrl-C to halt the enumeration. We will find later on that infinite lists are often useful in Haskell.

Beware of enumerating floating-point numbers

Here's a nonintuitive bit of behavior:

```
ghci> [1.0..1.8]
[1.0,2.0]
```

Behind the scenes, to avoid floating-point roundoff problems, the Haskell implementation enumerates from 1.0 to 1.8+0.5.

Using enumeration notation over floating-point numbers can pack more than a few surprises, so if you use it at all, be careful. Floating-point behavior is quirky in all programming languages; there is nothing unique to Haskell here.

Operators on Lists

There are two ubiquitous operators for working with lists. We concatenate two lists using the (++) operator:

```
ghci> [3,1,3] ++ [3,7]
[3,1,3,3,7]
ghci> [] ++ [False,True] ++ [True]
[False,True,True]
```

More basic is the (:) operator, which adds an element to the front of a list (this is pronounced "cons" [short for "construct"]):

```
ghci> 1 : [2,3]
[1,2,3]
ghci> 1 : []
[1]
```

You might be tempted to try writing [1,2]:3 to add an element to the end of a list, but ghci will reject this with an error message, because the first argument of (:) must be an element, and the second must be a list.

Strings and Characters

If you know a language such as Perl or C, you'll find Haskell's notations for strings familiar.

A text string is surrounded by double quotes:

```
ghci> "This is a string."
"This is a string."
```

As in many languages, we can represent hard-to-see characters by "escaping" them. Haskell's escape characters and escaping rules follow the widely used conventions established by the C language. For example, '\n' denotes a newline character, and '\t' is a tab character. For complete details, see Appendix B.

```
ghci> putStrLn "Here's a newline -->\n<-- See?"
Here's a newline -->
<-- See?
```

The putStrLn function prints a string.

Haskell makes a distinction between single characters and text strings. A single character is enclosed in single quotes:

```
ghci> 'a'
'a'
```

In fact, a text string is simply a list of individual characters. Here's a painful way to write a short string, which ghci gives back to us in a more familiar form:

```
ghci> let a = ['l', 'o', 't', 's', ' ', 'o', 'f', ' ', 'w', 'o', 'r', 'k']
ghci> a
"lots of work"
ghci> a == "lots of work"
True
```

The empty string is written "", and is a synonym for []:

```
ghci> "" == []
True
```

Since a string is a list of characters, we can use the regular list operators to construct new strings:

```
ghci> 'a':"bc"
"abc"
ghci> "foo" ++ "bar"
"foobar"
```

First Steps with Types

While we've talked a little about types already, our interactions with ghci have so far been free of much type-related thinking. We haven't told ghci what types we've been using, and it's mostly been willing to accept our input.

Haskell requires type names to start with an uppercase letter, and variable names must start with a lowercase letter. Bear this in mind as you read on; it makes it much easier to follow the names.

The first thing we can do to start exploring the world of types is to get ghci to tell us more about what it's doing. ghci has a command, :set, that lets us change a few of its default behaviors. We can tell it to print more type information as follows:

```
ghci> :set +t
ghci> 'c'
'c'
it :: Char
ghci> "foo"
"foo"
it :: [Char]
```

What the +t does is tell ghci to print the type of an expression after the expression. That cryptic it in the output can be very useful: it's actually the name of a special variable, in which ghci stores the result of the last expression we evaluated. (This isn't a Haskell language feature; it's specific to ghci alone.) Let's break down the meaning of the last line of ghci output:

- It tells us about the special variable it.
- We can read text of the form x :: y as meaning "the expression x has the type y."
- Here, the expression "it" has the type [Char]. (The name String is often used instead of [Char]. It is simply a synonym for [Char].)

The Joy of it

That it variable is a handy ghci shortcut. It lets us use the result of the expression we just evaluated in a new expression:

```
ghci> "foo"
"foo"
it :: [Char]
ghci> it ++ "bar"
"foobar"
it :: [Char]
```

When evaluating an expression, ghci won't change the value of it if the evaluation fails. This lets you write potentially bogus expressions with something of a safety net:

```
ghci> it
"foobar"
it :: [Char]
ghci> it ++ 3

<interactive>:1:6:
    No instance for (Num [Char])
      arising from the literal `3' at <interactive>:1:6
    Possible fix: add an instance declaration for (Num [Char])
    In the second argument of `(++)', namely `3'
    In the expression: it ++ 3
    In the definition of `it': it = it ++ 3
ghci> it
"foobar"
it :: [Char]
ghci> it ++ "baz"
"foobarbaz"
it :: [Char]
```

When we couple it with liberal use of the arrow keys to recall and edit the last expression we typed, we gain a decent way to experiment interactively: the cost of mistakes is very low. Take advantage of the opportunity to make cheap, plentiful mistakes when you're exploring the language!

Here are a few more of Haskell's names for types, from expressions of the sort that we've already seen:

```
ghci> 7 ^ 80
40536215597144386832065866109016673800875222251012083746192454448001
it :: Integer
```

Haskell's integer type is named `Integer`. The size of an `Integer` value is bounded only by your system's memory capacity.

Rational numbers don't look quite the same as integers. To construct a rational number, we use the (%) operator. The numerator is on the left, the denominator on the right:

```
ghci> :m +Data.Ratio
ghci> 11 % 29
11%29
it :: Ratio Integer
```

For convenience, ghci lets us abbreviate many commands, so we can write :m instead of :module to load a module.

Notice there are *two* words on the righthand side of the :: in the preceding code. We can read this as a "Ratio of Integer." We might guess that a `Ratio` must have values of type `Integer` as both numerator and denominator. Sure enough, if we try to construct a `Ratio` where the numerator and denominator are of different types or of the same nonintegral type, ghci complains:

```
ghci> 3.14 % 8

<interactive>:1:0:
    Ambiguous type variable `t' in the constraints:
      `Integral t' arising from a use of `%' at <interactive>:1:0-7
      `Fractional t'
        arising from the literal `3.14' at <interactive>:1:0-3
    Probable fix: add a type signature that fixes these type variable(s)
ghci> 1.2 % 3.4

<interactive>:1:0:
    Ambiguous type variable `t' in the constraints:
      `Integral t' arising from a use of `%' at <interactive>:1:0-8
      `Fractional t'
        arising from the literal `3.4' at <interactive>:1:6-8
    Probable fix: add a type signature that fixes these type variable(s)
```

Although it is initially useful to have **:set +t** giving us type information for every expression we enter, this is a facility we will quickly outgrow. After a while, we will often know what type we expect an expression to have. We can turn off the extra type information at any time, using the :unset command:

```
ghci> :unset +t
ghci> 2
2
```

Even with this facility turned off, we can still get that type information easily when we need it, using another ghci command:

```
ghci> :type 'a'
'a' :: Char
ghci> "foo"
"foo"
ghci> :type it
it :: [Char]
```

The :type command will print type information for any expression we give it (including it, as we see here). It won't actually evaluate the expression; it checks only its type and prints that.

Why are the types reported for these two expressions different?

```
ghci> 3 + 2
5
ghci> :type it
it :: Integer
ghci> :type 3 + 2
3 + 2 :: (Num t) => t
```

Haskell has several numeric types. For example, a literal number such as 1 could, depending on the context in which it appears, be an integer or a floating-point value. When we force ghci to evaluate the expression 3 + 2, it has to choose a type so that it can print the value, and it defaults to Integer. In the second case, we ask ghci to print the type of the expression without actually evaluating it, so it does not have to be so specific. It answers, in effect, "its type is numeric." We will see more of this style of type annotation in Chapter 6.

A Simple Program

Let's take a small leap ahead and write a small program that counts the number of lines in its input. Don't expect to understand this yet—it's just fun to get our hands dirty. In a text editor, enter the following code into a file, and save it as *WC.hs*:

```
-- file: ch01/WC.hs
-- lines beginning with "--" are comments.

main = interact wordCount
    where wordCount input = show (length (lines input)) ++ "\n"
```

Find or create a text file; let's call it *quux.txt*:[*]

```
$ cat quux.txt
Teignmouth, England
Paris, France
Ulm, Germany
Auxerre, France
```

---

[*] Incidentally, what do these cities have in common?

```
Brunswick, Germany
Beaumont-en-Auge, France
Ryazan, Russia
```

From a shell or command prompt, run the following command:

```
$ runghc WC < quux.txt
7
```

We have successfully written a simple program that interacts with the real world! In the chapters that follow, we will continue to fill the gaps in our understanding until we can write programs of our own.

EXERCISES

1. Enter the following expressions into `ghci`. What are their types?

   - `5 + 8`
   - `3 * 5 + 8`
   - `2 + 4`
   - `(+) 2 4`
   - `sqrt 16`
   - `succ 6`
   - `succ 7`
   - `pred 9`
   - `pred 8`
   - `sin (pi / 2)`
   - `truncate pi`
   - `round 3.5`
   - `round 3.4`
   - `floor 3.7`
   - `ceiling 3.3`

2. From `ghci`, type `:?` to print some help. Define a variable, such as `let x = 1`, and then type `:show bindings`. What do you see?

3. The `words` function breaks a string up into a list of words. Modify the *WC.hs* example in order to count the number of words in a file.

4. Modify the *WC.hs* example again, in order to print the number of characters in a file.

CHAPTER 2

Types and Functions

Why Care About Types?

Every expression and function in Haskell has a *type*. For example, the value True has the type Bool, while the value "foo" has the type String. The type of a value indicates that it shares certain properties with other values of the same type. For example, we can add numbers and concatenate lists; these are properties of those types. We say an expression has type X, or is of type X.

Before we launch into a deeper discussion of Haskell's type system, let's talk about why we should care about types at all—what are they even *for*? At the lowest level, a computer is concerned with bytes, with barely any additional structure. What a type system gives us is *abstraction*. A type adds meaning to plain bytes: it lets us say "these bytes are text," "those bytes are an airline reservation," and so on. Usually, a type system goes beyond this to prevent us from accidentally mixing up types. For example, a type system usually won't let us treat a hotel reservation as a car rental receipt.

The benefit of introducing abstraction is that it lets us forget or ignore low-level details. If I know that a value in my program is a string, I don't have to know the intimate details of how strings are implemented. I can just assume that my string is going to behave like all the other strings I've worked with.

What makes type systems interesting is that they're not all equal. In fact, different type systems are often not even concerned with the same kinds of problems. A programming language's type system deeply colors the way we think and write code in that language.

Haskell's type system allows us to think at a very abstract level, and it permits us to write concise, powerful programs.

Haskell's Type System

There are three interesting aspects to types in Haskell: they are *strong*, they are *static*, and they can be automatically *inferred*. Let's talk in more detail about each of these ideas. When possible, we'll present similarities between concepts from Haskell's type system and related ideas in other languages. We'll also touch on the respective strengths and weaknesses of each of these properties.

Strong Types

When we say that Haskell has a *strong* type system, we mean that the type system guarantees that a program cannot contain certain kinds of errors. These errors come from trying to write expressions that don't make sense, such as using an integer as a function. For instance, if a function expects to work with integers and we pass it a string, a Haskell compiler will reject this.

We call an expression that obeys a language's type rules *well typed*. An expression that disobeys the type rules is *ill typed*, and it will cause a *type error*.

Another aspect of Haskell's view of strong typing is that it will not automatically coerce values from one type to another. (Coercion is also known as casting or conversion.) For example, a C compiler will automatically and silently coerce a value of type int into a float on our behalf if a function expects a parameter of type float, but a Haskell compiler will raise a compilation error in a similar situation. We must explicitly coerce types by applying coercion functions.

Strong typing does occasionally make it more difficult to write certain kinds of code. For example, a classic way to write low-level code in the C language is to be given a byte array and cast it to treat the bytes as if they're really a complicated data structure. This is very efficient, since it doesn't require us to copy the bytes around. Haskell's type system does not allow this sort of coercion. In order to get the same structured view of the data, we would need to do some copying, which would cost a little in performance.

The huge benefit of strong typing is that it catches real bugs in our code before they can cause problems. For example, in a strongly typed language, we can't accidentally use a string where an integer is expected.

Weaker and Stronger Types

It is useful to be aware that many language communities have their own definitions of a strong type. Nevertheless, we will speak briefly and in broad terms about the notion of strength in type systems.

In academic computer science, the meanings of *strong* and *weak* have a narrowly technical meaning. Strength refers to *how permissive* a type system is, whereas a weaker type system treats more expressions as valid than a stronger type system does.

For example, in Perl, the expression `"foo" + 2` evaluates to the number 2, but the expression `"13foo" + 2` evaluates to the number 15. Haskell rejects both expressions as invalid, because the (+) operator requires both of its operands to be numeric. Because Perl's type system is more permissive than Haskell's, we say that it is weaker under this narrow technical interpretation.

The fireworks around type systems have their roots in ordinary English, where people attach notions of *value* to the words "weak" and "strong"—we usually think of strength as better than weakness. Many more programmers speak plain English than academic jargon, and quite often academics *really are* throwing brickbats at whatever type system doesn't suit their fancy. The result is often that popular Internet pastime, a flame war.

Static Types

Having a *static* type system means that the compiler knows the type of every value and expression at compile time, before any code is executed. A Haskell compiler or interpreter will detect when we try to use expressions whose types don't match, and reject our code with an error message before we run it:

```
ghci> True && "false"
```

```
<interactive>:1:8:
    Couldn't match expected type `Bool' against inferred type `[Char]'
    In the second argument of `(&&)', namely `"false"'
    In the expression: True && "false"
    In the definition of `it': it = True && "false"
```

We've seen this kind of error message before. The compiler has inferred that the type of the expression `"false"` is `[Char]`. The (&&) operator requires each of its operands to be of type `Bool`, and its left operand indeed has this type. Since the actual type of `"false"` does not match the required type, the compiler rejects this expression as ill typed.

Static typing can occasionally make it difficult to write some useful kinds of code. In languages such as Python, *duck typing* is common, where an object acts enough like another to be used as a substitute for it.[*] Fortunately, Haskell's system of *typeclasses*, which we will cover in Chapter 6, provides almost all of the benefits of dynamic typing, in a safe and convenient form. Haskell has some support for programming with truly dynamic types, though it is not quite as easy as it is in a language that wholeheartedly embraces the notion.

Haskell's combination of strong and static typing makes it impossible for type errors to occur at runtime. While this means that we need to do a little more thinking up front, it also eliminates many simple errors that can otherwise be devilishly hard to find. It's a truism within the Haskell community that once code compiles, it's more likely to

---

[*] "If it walks like a duck, and quacks like a duck, then let's call it a duck."

work correctly than in other languages. (Perhaps a more realistic way of putting this is that Haskell code often has fewer trivial bugs.)

Programs written in dynamically typed languages require large suites of tests to give some assurance that simple type errors cannot occur. Test suites cannot offer complete coverage: some common tasks, such as refactoring a program to make it more modular, can introduce new type errors that a test suite may not expose.

In Haskell, the compiler proves the absence of type errors for us: a Haskell program that compiles will not suffer from type errors when it runs. Refactoring is usually a matter of moving code around, and then recompiling and tidying up a few times until the compiler gives us the "all clear."

A helpful analogy to understand the value of static typing is to look at it as putting pieces into a jigsaw puzzle. In Haskell, if a piece has the wrong shape, it simply won't fit. In a dynamically typed language, all the pieces are 1×1 squares and always fit, so you have to constantly examine the resulting picture and check (through testing) whether it's correct.

Type Inference

Finally, a Haskell compiler can automatically deduce the types of almost[†] all expressions in a program. This process is known as *type inference*. Haskell allows us to explicitly declare the type of any value, but the presence of type inference means that this is almost always optional, not something we are required to do.

What to Expect from the Type System

Our exploration of the major capabilities and benefits of Haskell's type system will span a number of chapters. Early on, you may find Haskell's types to be a chore to deal with.

For example, instead of simply writing some code and running it to see if it works as you might expect in Python or Ruby, you'll first need to make sure that your program passes the scrutiny of the type checker. Why stick with the learning curve?

While strong, static typing makes Haskell safe, type inference makes it concise. The result is potent: we end up with a language that's safer than popular statically typed languages and often more expressive than dynamically typed languages. This is a strong claim to make, and we will back it up with evidence throughout the book.

Fixing type errors may initially feel like more work than using a dynamic language. It might help to look at this as moving much of your debugging *up front*. The compiler

---

[†] Occasionally, we need to give the compiler a little information to help it make a choice in understanding our code.

shows you many of the logical flaws in your code, instead of leaving you to stumble across problems at runtime.

Furthermore, because Haskell can infer the types of your expressions and functions, you gain the benefits of static typing *without* the added burden of "finger typing" imposed by less powerful statically typed languages. In other languages, the type system serves the needs of the compiler. In Haskell, it serves *you*. The trade-off is that you have to learn to work within the framework it provides.

We will introduce new uses of Haskell's types throughout this book to help us write and test practical code. As a result, the complete picture of why the type system is worthwhile will emerge gradually. While each step should justify itself, the whole will end up greater than the sum of its parts.

Some Common Basic Types

In "First Steps with Types" on page 12, we introduced a few types. Here are several more of the most common base types:

A Char *value*

Represents a Unicode character.

A Bool *value*

Represents a value in Boolean logic. The possible values of type Bool are True and False.

The Int *type*

Used for signed, fixed-width integer values. The exact range of values represented as Int depends on the system's longest "native" integer: on a 32-bit machine, an Int is usually 32 bits wide, while on a 64-bit machine, it is usually 64 bits wide. The Haskell standard guarantees only that an Int is wider than 28 bits. (Numeric types exist that are exactly 8, 16, and so on bits wide, in signed and unsigned flavors; we'll get to those later.)

An Integer *value*

A signed integer of unbounded size. Integers are not used as often as Ints, because they are more expensive both in performance and space consumption. On the other hand, Integer computations do not silently overflow, so they give more reliably correct answers.

Values of type Double

Used for floating-point numbers. A Double value is typically 64 bits wide and uses the system's native floating-point representation. (A narrower type, Float, also exists, but its use is discouraged; Haskell compiler writers concentrate more on making Double efficient, so Float is much slower.)

We have already briefly seen Haskell's notation for types earlier in "First Steps with Types" on page 12. When we write a type explicitly, we use the notation `expression ::` `MyType` to say that `expression` has the type `MyType`. If we omit the `::` and the type that follows, a Haskell compiler will infer the type of the expression:

```
ghci> :type 'a'
'a' :: Char
ghci> 'a' :: Char
'a'
ghci> [1,2,3] :: Int

<interactive>:1:0:
    Couldn't match expected type `Int' against inferred type `[a]'
    In the expression: [1, 2, 3] :: Int
    In the definition of `it': it = [1, 2, 3] :: Int
```

The combination of `::` and the type after it is called a *type signature*.

Function Application

Now that we've had our fill of data types for a while, let's turn our attention to working with some of the types we've seen, using functions.

To apply a function in Haskell, we write the name of the function followed by its arguments:

```
ghci> odd 3
True
ghci> odd 6
False
```

We don't use parentheses or commas to group or separate the arguments to a function; merely writing the name of the function, followed by each argument in turn, is enough. As an example, let's apply the `compare` function, which takes two arguments:

```
ghci> compare 2 3
LT
ghci> compare 3 3
EQ
ghci> compare 3 2
GT
```

If you're used to function call syntax in other languages, this notation can take a little getting used to, but it's simple and uniform.

Function application has higher precedence than using operators, so the following two expressions have the same meaning:

```
ghci> (compare 2 3) == LT
True
ghci> compare 2 3 == LT
True
```

The parentheses in the preceding code don't do any harm, but they add some visual noise. Sometimes, however, we *must* use parentheses to indicate how we want a complicated expression to be parsed:

```
ghci> compare (sqrt 3) (sqrt 6)
LT
```

This applies compare to the results of applying sqrt 3 and sqrt 6, respectively. If we omit the parentheses, it looks like we are trying to pass four arguments to compare, instead of the two it accepts.

Useful Composite Data Types: Lists and Tuples

A composite data type is constructed from other types. The most common composite data types in Haskell are lists and tuples.

We've already seen the list type mentioned earlier in the "Strings and Characters" on page 11, where we found that Haskell represents a text string as a list of Char values, and that the type "list of Char" is written [Char].

The head function returns the first element of a list:

```
ghci> head [1,2,3,4]
1
ghci> head ['a','b','c']
'a'
```

Its counterpart, tail, returns all *but* the head of a list:

```
ghci> tail [1,2,3,4]
[2,3,4]
ghci> tail [2,3,4]
[3,4]
ghci> tail [True,False]
[False]
ghci> tail "list"
"ist"
ghci> tail []
*** Exception: Prelude.tail: empty list
```

As you can see, we can apply head and tail to lists of different types. Applying head to a [Char] value returns a Char value, while applying it to a [Bool] value returns a Bool value. The head function doesn't care what type of list it deals with.

Because the values in a list can have any type, we call the list type *polymorphic*.[‡] When we want to write a polymorphic type, we use a *type variable*, which must begin with a lowercase letter. A type variable is a placeholder, where we'll eventually substitute a real type.

[‡] We'll talk more about polymorphism in "Polymorphism in Haskell" on page 36.

We can write the type "list of a" by enclosing the type variable in square brackets: [a]. This amounts to saying, "I don't care what type I have; I can make a list with it."

Distinguishing type names and type variables

We can now see why a type name must start with an uppercase letter: it makes it distinct from a type variable, which must start with a lowercase letter.

When we talk about a list with values of a specific type, we substitute that type for our type variable. So, for example, the type [Int] is a list of values of type Int, because we substituted Int for a. Similarly, the type [MyPersonalType] is a list of values of type MyPersonalType. We can perform this substitution recursively, too: [[Int]] is a list of values of type [Int], i.e., a list of lists of Int.

```
ghci> :type [[True],[False,False]]
[[True],[False,False]] :: [[Bool]]
```

The type of this expression is a list of lists of Bool.

Lists are special

Lists are the bread and butter of Haskell collections. In an imperative language, we might perform a task many times by iterating through a loop. This is something that we often do in Haskell by traversing a list, either by recursing or using a function that recurses for us. Lists are the easiest stepping stone into the idea that we can use data to structure our program and its control flow. We'll be spending a lot more time discussing lists in Chapter 4.

A tuple is a fixed-size collection of values, where each value can have a different type. This distinguishes them from a list, which can have any length, but whose elements must all have the same type.

To help understand the difference, let's say we want to track two pieces of information about a book: its year of publication—a number—and its a title—a string. We can't keep both of these pieces of information in a list, because they have different types. Instead, we use a tuple:

```
ghci> (1964, "Labyrinths")
(1964,"Labyrinths")
```

We write a tuple by enclosing its elements in parentheses and separating them with commas. We use the same notation for writing its type:

```
ghci> :type (True, "hello")
(True, "hello") :: (Bool, [Char])
ghci> (4, ['a', 'm'], (16, True))
(4,"am",(16,True))
```

There's a special type, (), that acts as a tuple of zero elements. This type has only one value, which is also written (). Both the type and the value are usually pronounced "unit." If you are familiar with C, () is somewhat similar to void.

Haskell doesn't have a notion of a one-element tuple. Tuples are often referred to using the number of elements as a prefix. A 2-tuple has two elements and is usually called a *pair*. A 3-tuple (sometimes called a *triple*) has three elements; a 5-tuple has five; and so on. In practice, working with tuples that contain more than a handful of elements makes code unwieldy, so tuples of more than a few elements are rarely used.

A tuple's type represents the number, positions, and types of its elements. This means that tuples containing different numbers or types of elements have distinct types, as do tuples whose types appear in different orders:

```
ghci> :type (False, 'a')
(False, 'a') :: (Bool, Char)
ghci> :type ('a', False)
('a', False) :: (Char, Bool)
```

In this example, the expression (False, 'a') has the type (Bool, Char), which is distinct from the type of ('a', False). Even though the number of elements and their types is the same, these two types are distinct because the positions of the element types are different:

```
ghci> :type (False, 'a', 'b')
(False, 'a', 'b') :: (Bool, Char, Char)
```

This type, (Bool, Char, Char), is distinct from (Bool, Char) because it contains three elements, not two.

We often use tuples to return multiple values from a function. We can also use them any time we need a fixed-size collection of values, if the circumstances don't require a custom container type.

EXERCISE

1. What are the types of the following expressions?
   - False
   - (["foo", "bar"], 'a')
   - [(True, []), (False, [['a']])]

Functions over Lists and Tuples

Our discussion of lists and tuples mentioned how we can construct them but little about how we do anything with them afterwards. So far we have only been introduced to two list functions, head and tail.

Two related list functions, take and drop, take two arguments. Given a number n and a list, take returns the first n elements of the list, while drop returns all *but* the first n elements of the list. (As these functions take two arguments, notice that we separate each function and its arguments using whitespace.)

```
ghci> take 2 [1,2,3,4,5]
[1,2]
ghci> drop 3 [1,2,3,4,5]
[4,5]
```

For tuples, the fst and snd functions return the first and second element of a pair, respectively:

```
ghci> fst (1,'a')
1
ghci> snd (1,'a')
'a'
```

If your background is in any of a number of other languages, each of these may look like an application of a function to two arguments. Under Haskell's convention for function application, each one is an application of a function to a single pair.

Haskell tuples aren't immutable lists

If you are coming from the Python world, you'll probably be used to lists and tuples being almost interchangeable. Although the elements of a Python tuple are immutable, it can be indexed and iterated over using the same methods as a list. This isn't the case in Haskell, so don't try to carry that idea with you into unfamiliar linguistic territory.

As an illustration, take a look at the type signatures of fst and snd: they're defined *only* for pairs and can't be used with tuples of other sizes. Haskell's type system makes it tricky to write a generalized "get the second element from any tuple, no matter how wide" function.

Passing an Expression to a Function

In Haskell, function application is left-associative. This is best illustrated by example: the expression a b c d is equivalent to (((a b) c) d). If we want to use one expression as an argument to another, we have to use explicit parentheses to tell the parser what we really mean. Here's an example:

```
ghci> head (drop 4 "azerty")
't'
```

We can read this as "pass the expression drop 4 "azerty" as the argument to head." If we were to leave out the parentheses, the offending expression would be similar to passing three arguments to head. Compilation would fail with a type error, as head requires a single argument, a list.

Function Types and Purity

Let's take a look at a function's type:

```
ghci> :type lines
lines :: String -> [String]
```

We can read the -> as "to," which loosely translates to "returns." The signature as a whole thus reads as "lines has the type String to list-of-String". Let's try applying the function:

```
ghci> lines "the quick\nbrown fox\njumps"
["the quick","brown fox","jumps"]
```

The lines function splits a string on line boundaries. Notice that its type signature gives us a hint as to what the function might actually do: it takes one String, and returns many. This is an incredibly valuable property of types in a functional language.

A *side effect* introduces a dependency between the global state of the system and the behavior of a function. For example, let's step away from Haskell for a moment and think about an imperative programming language. Consider a function that reads and returns the value of a global variable. If some other code can modify that global variable, then the result of a particular application of our function depends on the current value of the global variable. The function has a side effect, even though it never modifies the variable itself.

Side effects are essentially invisible inputs to, or outputs from, functions. In Haskell, the default is for functions to *not* have side effects: the result of a function depends only on the inputs that we explicitly provide. We call these functions *pure*; functions with side effects are *impure*.

If a function has side effects, we can tell by reading its type signature—the type of the function's result will begin with IO:

```
ghci> :type readFile
readFile :: FilePath -> IO String
```

Haskell's type system prevents us from accidentally mixing pure and impure code.

Haskell Source Files, and Writing Simple Functions

Now that we know how to apply functions, it's time we turned our attention to writing them. While we can write functions in ghci, it's not a good environment for this. It accepts only a highly restricted subset of Haskell—most importantly, the syntax it uses for defining functions is not the same as we use in a Haskell source file.§ Instead, we'll finally break down and create a source file.

---

§ The environment in which ghci operates is called the IO monad. In Chapter 7, we will cover the IO monad in depth, and the seemingly arbitrary restrictions that ghci places on us will make more sense.

Haskell source files are usually identified with a suffix of *.hs*. A simple function definition is to open up a file named *add.hs* and add these contents to it:

```
-- file: ch03/add.hs
add a b = a + b
```

On the lefthand side of the = is the name of the function, followed by the arguments to the function. On the righthand side is the body of the function. With our source file saved, we can load it into ghci, and use our new add function straightaway (the prompt that ghci displays will change after you load your file):

```
ghci> :load add.hs
[1 of 1] Compiling Main             ( add.hs, interpreted )
Ok, modules loaded: Main.
ghci> add 1 2
3
```

What if ghci cannot find your source file?

When you run ghci, it may not be able to find your source file. It will search for source files in whatever directory it was run. If this is not the directory that your source file is actually in, you can use ghci's :cd command to change its working directory:

```
ghci> :cd /tmp
```

Alternatively, you can provide the path to your Haskell source file as the argument to :load. This path can be either absolute or relative to ghci's current directory.

When we apply add to the values 1 and 2, the variables a and b on the lefthand side of our definition are given (or "bound to") the values 1 and 2, so the result is the expression 1 + 2.

Haskell doesn't have a return keyword, because a function is a single expression, not a sequence of statements. The value of the expression is the result of the function. (Haskell does have a function called return, but we won't discuss it for a while; it has a different meaning than in imperative languages.)

When you see an = symbol in Haskell code, it represents "meaning"—the name on the left is defined to be the expression on the right.

Just What Is a Variable, Anyway?

In Haskell, a variable provides a way to give a name to an expression. Once a variable is *bound to* (i.e., associated with) a particular expression, its value does not change: we can always use the name of the variable instead of writing out the expression, and we will get the same result either way.

If you're used to imperative programming languages, you're likely to think of a variable as a way of identifying a *memory location* (or some equivalent) that can hold different values at different times. In an imperative language, we can change a variable's value at any time, so that examining the memory location repeatedly can potentially give different results each time.

The critical difference between these two notions of a variable is that in Haskell, once we've bound a variable to an expression, we know that we can always substitute it for that expression, because it will not change. In an imperative language, this notion of substitutability does not hold.

For example, if we run the following tiny Python script, it will print the number 11:

```
x = 10
x = 11
# value of x is now 11
print x
```

In contrast, trying the equivalent in Haskell results in an error:

```
-- file: ch02/Assign.hs
x = 10
x = 11
```

We cannot assign a value to x twice:

```
ghci> :load Assign
[1 of 1] Compiling Main             ( Assign.hs, interpreted )

Assign.hs:4:0:
    Multiple declarations of `Main.x'
    Declared at: Assign.hs:3:0
                 Assign.hs:4:0
Failed, modules loaded: none.
```

Conditional Evaluation

Like many other languages, Haskell has an `if` expression. Let's see it in action; then we'll explain what's going on. As an example, we'll write our own version of the standard `drop` function. Before we begin, let's probe a little into how `drop` behaves, so we can replicate its behavior:

```
ghci> drop 2 "foobar"
"obar"
ghci> drop 4 "foobar"
"ar"
ghci> drop 4 [1,2]
[]
ghci> drop 0 [1,2]
[1,2]
ghci> drop 7 []
[]
ghci> drop (-2) "foo"
"foo"
```

From this code, it seems that drop returns the original list if the number to remove is less than or equal to zero. Otherwise, it removes elements until it either runs out or reaches the given number. Here's a myDrop function that has the same behavior, and that uses Haskell's if expression to decide what to do. The following null function below checks whether a list is empty:

```
-- file: ch02/myDrop.hs
myDrop n xs = if n <= 0 || null xs
              then xs
              else myDrop (n - 1) (tail xs)
```

In Haskell, indentation is important: it *continues* an existing definition, instead of starting a new one. Don't omit the indentation!

You might wonder where the variable name xs comes from in the Haskell function. This is a common naming pattern for lists. You can read the s as a suffix, so the name is essentially "plural of x."

Let's save our Haskell function in a file named *myDrop.hs*, then load it into ghci:

```
ghci> :load myDrop.hs
[1 of 1] Compiling Main             ( myDrop.hs, interpreted )
Ok, modules loaded: Main.
ghci> myDrop 2 "foobar"
"obar"
ghci> myDrop 4 "foobar"
"ar"
ghci> myDrop 4 [1,2]
[]
ghci> myDrop 0 [1,2]
[1,2]
ghci> myDrop 7 []
[]
ghci> myDrop (-2) "foo"
"foo"
```

Now that we've seen myDrop in action, let's return to the source code and look at all the novelties we've introduced.

First of all, we have introduced --, the beginning of a single-line comment. This comment extends to the end of the line.

Next is the if keyword itself. It introduces an expression that has three components:

- An expression of type Bool, immediately following the if. We refer to this as a *predicate*.
- A then keyword, followed by another expression. This expression will be used as the value of the if expression if the predicate evaluates to True.
- An else keyword, followed by another expression. This expression will be used as the value of the if expression if the predicate evaluates to False.

We'll refer to the expressions that follow the then and else keywords as "branches." The branches must have the same types; the if expression will also have this type. An expression such as if True then 1 else "foo" has different types for its branches, so it is ill typed and a compiler or interpreter will reject it.

Recall that Haskell is an expression-oriented language. In an imperative language, it can make sense to omit the else branch from an if, because we're working with *statements*, not expressions. However, when we're working with expressions, an if that was missing an else wouldn't have a result or type if the predicate evaluated to False, so it would be nonsensical.

Our predicate contains a few more novelties. The null function indicates whether a list is empty, while the (||) operator performs a logical "or" of its Bool-typed arguments:

```
ghci> :type null
null :: [a] -> Bool
ghci> :type (||)
(||) :: Bool -> Bool -> Bool
```

Operators are not special

Notice that we were able to find the type of (||) by wrapping it in parentheses. The (||) operator isn't built into the language; it's an ordinary function.

The (||) operator "short circuits": if its left operand evaluates to True, it doesn't evaluate its right operand. In most languages, short-circuit evaluation requires special support, but not in Haskell. We'll see why shortly.

Next, our function applies itself recursively. This is our first example of recursion, which we'll talk about in some detail soon.

Finally, our if expression spans several lines. We align the then and else branches under the if for neatness. So long as we use some indentation, the exact amount is not important. If we wish, we can write the entire expression on a single line:

```
-- file: ch02/myDrop.hs
myDropX n xs = if n <= 0 || null xs then xs else myDropX (n - 1) (tail xs)
```

The length of this version makes it more difficult to read. We will usually break an if expression across several lines to keep the predicate and each of the branches easier to follow.

For comparison, here is a Python equivalent of the Haskell myDrop. The two are structured similarly—each decrements a counter while removing an element from the head of the list:

```
def myDrop(n, elts):
    while n > 0 and elts:
        n = n - 1
```

```
        elts = elts[1:]
    return elts
```

Understanding Evaluation by Example

In our description of myDrop, we have so far focused on surface features. We need to go deeper and develop a useful mental model of how function application works. To do this, we'll first work through a few simple examples, until we can walk through the evaluation of the expression myDrop 2 "abcd".

We've talked a lot about substituting an expression for a variable, and we'll make use of this capability here. Our procedure will involve rewriting expressions over and over, substituting expressions for variables until we reach a final result. This would be a good time to fetch a pencil and paper, so you can follow our descriptions by trying them yourself.

Lazy Evaluation

We will begin by looking at the definition of a simple, nonrecursive function:

```
-- file: ch02/RoundToEven.hs
isOdd n = mod n 2 == 1
```

Here, mod is the standard modulo function. The first big step to understanding how evaluation works in Haskell is figuring out the result of evaluating the expression isOdd (1 + 2).

Before we explain how evaluation proceeds in Haskell, let us recap the sort of evaluation strategy more familiar languages use. First, evaluate the subexpression 1 + 2, to give 3. Then apply the isOdd function with n bound to 3. Finally, evaluate mod 3 2 to give 1, and 1 == 1 to give True.

In a language that uses *strict* evaluation, the arguments to a function are evaluated before the function is applied. Haskell chooses another path: *nonstrict* evaluation.

In Haskell, the subexpression 1 + 2 is *not* reduced to the value 3. Instead, we create a "promise" that when the value of the expression isOdd (1 + 2) is needed, we'll be able to compute it. The record that we use to track an unevaluated expression is referred to as a *thunk*. This is *all* that happens: we create a thunk and defer the actual evaluation until it's really needed. If the result of this expression is never subsequently used, we will not compute its value at all.

Nonstrict evaluation is often referred to as *lazy evaluation*.[||]

[||] The terms "nonstrict" and "lazy" have slightly different technical meanings, but we won't go into the details of the distinction here.

A More Involved Example

Let us now look at the evaluation of the expression myDrop 2 "abcd", where we use print to ensure that it will be evaluated:

```
ghci> print (myDrop 2 "abcd")
"cd"
```

Our first step is to attempt to apply print, which needs its argument to be evaluated. To do that, we apply the function myDrop to the values 2 and "abcd". We bind the variable n to the value 2, and xs to "abcd". If we substitute these values into myDrop's predicate, we get the following expression:

```
ghci> :type  2 <= 0 || null "abcd"
2 <= 0 || null "abcd" :: Bool
```

We then evaluate enough of the predicate to find out what its value is. This requires that we evaluate the (||) expression. To determine its value, the (||) operator needs to examine the value of its left operand first:

```
ghci> 2 <= 0
False
```

Substituting that value into the (||) expression leads to the following expression:

```
ghci> :type  False || null "abcd"
False || null "abcd" :: Bool
```

If the left operand had evaluated to True, (||) would not need to evaluate its right operand, since it could not affect the result of the expression. Since it evaluates to False, (||) must evaluate the right operand:

```
ghci> null "abcd"
False
```

We now substitute this value back into the (||) expression. Since both operands evaluate to False, the (||) expression does too, and thus the predicate evaluates to False:

```
ghci> False || False
False
```

This causes the if expression's else branch to be evaluated. This branch contains a recursive application of myDrop.

Short-circuiting for free

Many languages need to treat the logical-or operator specially so that it short-circuits if its left operand evaluates to True. In Haskell, (||) is an ordinary function: nonstrict evaluation builds this capability into the language.

In Haskell, we can easily define a new function that short-circuits:

```
-- file: ch02/shortCircuit.hs
newOr a b = if a then a else b
```

If we write an expression such as newOr True (length [1..] > 0), it will not evaluate its second argument. (This is just as well: that expression tries to compute the length of an infinite list. If it were evaluated, it would hang ghci, looping infinitely until we killed it.)

Were we to write a comparable function in, say, Python, strict evaluation would bite us: both arguments would be evaluated before being passed to newOr, and we would not be able to avoid the infinite loop on the second argument.

Recursion

When we apply myDrop recursively, n is bound to the thunk 2 - 1, and xs is bound to tail "abcd".

We're now evaluating myDrop from the beginning again. We substitute the new values of n and xs into the predicate:

```
ghci> :type (2 - 1) <= 0 || null (tail "abcd")
(2 - 1) <= 0 || null (tail "abcd") :: Bool
```

Here's a condensed version of the evaluation of the left operand:

```
ghci> :type (2 - 1) <= 0
(2 - 1) <= 0 :: Bool
ghci> 2 - 1
1
ghci> 1 <= 0
False
```

As we should now expect, we didn't evaluate the expression 2 - 1 until we needed its value. We also evaluate the right operand lazily, deferring tail "abcd" until we need its value:

```
ghci> :type null (tail "abcd")
null (tail "abcd") :: Bool
ghci> tail "abcd"
"bcd"
ghci> null "bcd"
False
```

The predicate again evaluates to False, causing the else branch to be evaluated once more.

Because we've had to evaluate the expressions for n and xs to evaluate the predicate, we now know that in this application of myDrop, n has the value 1 and xs has the value "bcd".

Ending the Recursion

In the next recursive application of myDrop, we bind n to 1 - 1 and xs to tail "bcd":

```
ghci> :type (1 - 1) <= 0 || null (tail "bcd")
(1 - 1) <= 0 || null (tail "bcd") :: Bool
```

Once again, (||) needs to evaluate its left operand first:

```
ghci> :type (1 - 1) <= 0
(1 - 1) <= 0 :: Bool
ghci> 1 - 1
0
ghci> 0 <= 0
True
```

Finally, this expression evaluates to True!

```
ghci> True || null (tail "bcd")
True
```

Because the right operand cannot affect the result of (||), it is not evaluated, and the result of the predicate is True. This causes us to evaluate the then branch:

```
ghci> :type tail "bcd"
tail "bcd" :: [Char]
```

Returning from the Recursion

Remember, we're now inside our second recursive application of myDrop. This application evaluates to tail "bcd". We return from the application of the function, substituting this expression for myDrop (1 - 1) (tail "bcd") to become the result of this application:

```
ghci> myDrop (1 - 1) (tail "bcd") == tail "bcd"
True
```

We then return from the first recursive application, substituting the result of the second recursive application for myDrop (2 - 1) (tail "abcd") to become the result of this application:

```
ghci> myDrop (2 - 1) (tail "abcd") == tail "bcd"
True
```

Finally, we return from our original application, substituting the result of the first recursive application:

```
ghci> myDrop 2 "abcd" == tail "bcd"
True
```

Notice that as we return from each successive recursive application, none of them needs to evaluate the expression `tail "bcd"`: the final result of evaluating the original expression is a thunk. The thunk is only evaluated when `ghci` needs to print it.

```
ghci> myDrop 2 "abcd"
"cd"
ghci> tail "bcd"
"cd"
```

What Have We Learned?

We have established several important points:

- It makes sense to use substitution and rewriting to understand the evaluation of a Haskell expression.
- Laziness leads us to defer evaluation until we need a value and to evaluate just enough of an expression to establish its value.
- The result of applying a function may be a thunk (a deferred expression).

Polymorphism in Haskell

When we introduced lists, we mentioned that the list type is polymorphic. We'll talk about Haskell's polymorphism in more detail here.

If we want to fetch the last element of a list, we use the `last` function. The value that it returns must have the same type as the elements of the list, but `last` operates in the same way no matter what type those elements actually are:

```
ghci> last [1,2,3,4,5]
5
ghci> last "baz"
'z'
```

To capture this idea, its type signature contains a *type variable*:

```
ghci> :type last
last :: [a] -> a
```

Here, a is the type variable. We can read the signature as "takes a list, all of whose elements have some type a, and returns a value of the same type a."

Identifying a type variable

Type variables always start with a lowercase letter. You can always tell a type variable from a normal variable by context, because the languages of types and functions are separate: type variables live in type signatures, and regular variables live in normal expressions.

It's common Haskell practice to keep the names of type variables very short. One letter is overwhelmingly common; longer names show up infrequently. Type signatures are usually brief; we gain more in readability by keeping names short than we would by making them descriptive.

When a function has type variables in its signature, indicating that some of its arguments can be of any type, we call the function polymorphic.

When we want to apply `last` to, say, a list of `Char`, the compiler substitutes `Char` for each a throughout the type signature. This gives us the type of `last` with an input of `[Char]` as `[Char] -> Char`.

This kind of polymorphism is called *parametric* polymorphism. The choice of naming is easy to understand by analogy: just as a function can have parameters that we can later bind to real values, a Haskell type can have parameters that we can later bind to other types.

A little nomenclature

If a type contains type parameters, we say that it is a *parameterized* type, or a *polymorphic* type. If a function or value's type contains type parameters, we call it polymorphic.

When we see a parameterized type, we've already noted that the code doesn't care what the actual type is. However, we can make a stronger statement: *it has no way to find out what the real type is*, or to manipulate a value of that type. It can't create a value; neither can it inspect one. All it can do is treat it as a fully abstract "black box." We'll cover one reason that this is important soon.

Parametric polymorphism is the most visible kind of polymorphism that Haskell supports. Haskell's parametric polymorphism directly influenced the design of the generic facilities of the Java and C# languages. A parameterized type in Haskell is similar to a type variable in Java generics. C++ templates also bear a resemblance to parametric polymorphism.

To make it clearer how Haskell's polymorphism differs from other languages, here are a few forms of polymorphism that are common in other languages, but not present in Haskell.

In mainstream object-oriented languages, *subtype* polymorphism is more widespread than parametric polymorphism. The subclassing mechanisms of C++ and Java give them subtype polymorphism. A base class defines a set of behaviors that its subclasses can modify and extend. Since Haskell isn't an object-oriented language, it doesn't provide subtype polymorphism.

Also common is *coercion* polymorphism, which allows a value of one type to be implicitly converted into a value of another type. Many languages provide some form of coercion polymorphism; one example is automatic conversion between integers and floating-point numbers. Haskell deliberately avoids even this kind of simple automatic coercion.

This is not the whole story of polymorphism in Haskell. We'll return to the subject in Chapter 6.

Reasoning About Polymorphic Functions

In "Function Types and Purity" on page 27 we talked about figuring out the behavior of a function based on its type signature. We can apply the same kind of reasoning to polymorphic functions. Let's look again at `fst`:

```
ghci> :type fst
fst :: (a, b) -> a
```

First of all, notice that its argument contains two type variables, a and b, signifying that the elements of the tuple can be of different types.

The result type of `fst` is a. We've already mentioned that parametric polymorphism makes the real type inaccessible. `fst` doesn't have enough information to construct a value of type a, nor can it turn an a into a b. So the *only* possible valid behavior (omitting infinite loops or crashes) it can have is to return the first element of the pair.

Further Reading

There is a deep mathematical sense in which any nonpathological function of type (a,b) -> a must do exactly what `fst` does. Moreover, this line of reasoning extends to more complicated polymorphic functions. The paper "Theorems for free" by Philip Wadler (*http://citeseerx.ist.psu.edu/viewdoc/summary?doi=10.1.1.38.9875*) covers this procedure in depth.

The Type of a Function of More Than One Argument

So far, we haven't looked much at signatures for functions that take more than one argument. We've already used a few such functions; let's look at the signature of one, `take`:

```
ghci> :type take
take :: Int -> [a] -> [a]
```

It's pretty clear that there's something going on with an Int and some lists, but why are there two -> symbols in the signature? Haskell groups this chain of arrows from right to left; that is, -> is *right-associative*. If we introduce parentheses, we can make it clearer how this type signature is interpreted:

```
-- file: ch02/Take.hs
take :: Int -> ([a] -> [a])
```

From this, it looks like we ought to read the type signature as a function that takes one argument, an Int, and returns another function. That other function also takes one argument, a list, and returns a list of the same type as its result.

This is correct, but it's not easy to see what its consequences might be. We'll return to this topic in "Partial Function Application and Currying" on page 100, once we've spent a bit of time writing functions. For now, we can treat the type following the last -> as being the function's return type, and the preceding types to be those of the function's arguments.

We can now write a type signature for the myDrop function that we defined earlier:

```
-- file: ch02/myDrop.hs
myDrop :: Int -> [a] -> [a]
```

EXERCISES

1. Haskell provides a standard function, last :: [a] -> a, that returns the last element of a list. From reading the type alone, what are the possible valid behaviors (omitting crashes and infinite loops) that this function could have? What are a few things that this function clearly cannot do?

2. Write a function, lastButOne, that returns the element *before* the last.

3. Load your lastButOne function into ghci and try it out on lists of different lengths. What happens when you pass it a list that's too short?

Why the Fuss over Purity?

Few programming languages go as far as Haskell in insisting that purity should be the default. This choice has profound and valuable consequences.

Because the result of applying a pure function can only depend on its arguments, we can often get a strong hint of what a pure function does by simply reading its name and understanding its type signature. As an example, let's look at not:

```
ghci> :type not
not :: Bool -> Bool
```

Even if we don't know the name of this function, its signature alone limits the possible valid behaviors it could have:

- Ignore its argument and always return either `True` or `False`.
- Return its argument unmodified.
- Negate its argument.

We also know that this function *cannot* do some things: access files, talk to the network, and tell what time it is.

Purity makes the job of understanding code easier. The behavior of a pure function does not depend on the value of a global variable, or the contents of a database, or the state of a network connection. Pure code is inherently modular: every function is self-contained and has a well-defined interface.

A nonobvious consequence of purity being the default is that working with *impure* code becomes easier. Haskell encourages a style of programming in which we separate code that *must* have side effects from code that doesn't need side effects. In this style, impure code tends to be simple, with the "heavy lifting" performed in pure code.

Much of the risk in software lies in talking to the outside world, be it coping with bad or missing data or handling malicious attacks. Because Haskell's type system tells us exactly which parts of our code have side effects, we can be appropriately on guard. Because our favored coding style keeps impure code isolated and simple, our "attack surface" is small.

Conclusion

In this chapter, we've had a whirlwind overview of Haskell's type system and much of its syntax. We've read about the most common types and discovered how to write simple functions. We've been introduced to polymorphism, conditional expressions, purity, and lazy evaluation.

This all amounts to a lot of information to absorb. In Chapter 3, we'll build on this basic knowledge to further enhance our understanding of Haskell.

Defining Types, Streamlining Functions

Defining a New Data Type

Although lists and tuples are useful, we'll often want to construct new data types of our own. This allows us to add structure to the values in our programs. Instead of using an anonymous tuple, we can give a collection of related values a name and a distinct type. Defining our own types also improves the type safety of our code: Haskell will not allow us to accidentally mix values of two types that are structurally similar but have different names.

For motivation, we'll consider a few kinds of data that a small online bookstore might need to manage. We won't make any attempt at complete or realistic data definitions, but at least we're tying them to the real world.

We define a new data type using the `data` keyword:

```
-- file: ch03/BookStore.hs
data BookInfo = Book Int String [String]
                deriving (Show)
```

`BookInfo` after the `data` keyword is the name of our new type. We call `BookInfo` a *type constructor*. Once we define a type, we will use its type constructor to refer to it. As we've already mentioned, a type name, and hence a type constructor, must start with a capital letter.

The `Book` that follows is the name of the *value constructor* (sometimes called a data constructor). We use this to create a value of the `BookInfo` type. A value constructor's name must also start with a capital letter.

After `Book`, the `Int`, `String`, and `[String]` that follow are the *components* of the type. A component serves the same purpose in Haskell as a field in a structure or class would in another language: it's a "slot" where we keep a value. (We'll often refer to components as fields.)

In this example, the Int represents a book's identifier (e.g., in a stock database), String represents its title, and [String] represents the names of its authors.

To make the link to a concept we've already seen, the BookInfo type contains the same components as a 3-tuple of type (Int, String, [String]), but it has a distinct type. We can't accidentally (or deliberately) use one in a context where the other is expected. For instance, a bookstore is also likely to carry magazines:

```
-- file: ch03/BookStore.hs
data MagazineInfo = Magazine Int String [String]
                    deriving (Show)
```

Even though this MagazineInfo type has the same structure as our BookInfo type, Haskell treats the types as distinct because their type and value constructors have different names.

Deriving what?

We'll explain the full meaning of deriving (Show) later, in "Show" on page 139. For now, it's enough to know that we need to tack this onto a type declaration so that ghci will automatically know how to print a value of this type.

We can create a new value of type BookInfo by treating Book as a function and applying it with arguments of types Int, String, and [String]:

```
-- file: ch03/BookStore.hs
myInfo = Book 9780135072455 "Algebra of Programming"
         ["Richard Bird", "Oege de Moor"]
```

Once we define a type, we can experiment with it in ghci. We begin by using the :load command to load our source file:

```
ghci> :load BookStore
[1 of 1] Compiling Main             ( BookStore.hs, interpreted )
Ok, modules loaded: Main.
```

Remember the myInfo variable that we defined in our source file? Here it is:

```
ghci> myInfo
Book 9780135072455 "Algebra of Programming" ["Richard Bird","Oege de Moor"]
ghci> :type myInfo
myInfo :: BookInfo
```

We can construct new values interactively in ghci, too:

```
ghci> Book 0 "The Book of Imaginary Beings" ["Jorge Luis Borges"]
Book 0 "The Book of Imaginary Beings" ["Jorge Luis Borges"]
```

The ghci command :type lets us see what the type of an expression is:

```
ghci> :type Book 1 "Cosmicomics" ["Italo Calvino"]
Book 1 "Cosmicomics" ["Italo Calvino"] :: BookInfo
```

Remember that if we want to define a new variable inside ghci, the syntax is slightly different from that of a Haskell source file—we need to put a let in front:

```
ghci> let cities = Book 173 "Use of Weapons" ["Iain M. Banks"]
```

To find out more about a type, we can use some of ghci's browsing capabilities. The :info command gets ghci to tell us everything it knows about a name:

```
ghci> :info BookInfo
data BookInfo = Book Int String [String]
        -- Defined at BookStore.hs:4:5-12
instance Show BookInfo -- Defined at BookStore.hs:4:5-12
```

We can also find out why we use Book to construct a new value of type BookInfo:

```
ghci> :type Book
Book :: Int -> String -> [String] -> BookInfo
```

We can treat a value constructor as just another function—one that happens to create and return a new value of the type we desire.

Naming Types and Values

When we introduced the type BookInfo, we deliberately chose to give the type constructor BookInfo a different name from the value constructor Book, purely to make it obvious which was which.

However, in Haskell, the names of types and values are independent of each other. We use a type constructor (i.e., the type's name) only in a type declaration or a type signature. We use a value constructor only in actual code. Because these uses are distinct, there is no ambiguity if we give a type constructor and a value constructor the same name. If we are writing a type signature, we must be referring to a type constructor. If we are writing an expression, we must be using the value constructor:

```
-- file: ch03/BookStore.hs
-- We will introduce the CustomerID type shortly.

data BookReview = BookReview BookInfo CustomerID String
```

This definition says that the type named BookReview has a value constructor that is also named BookReview.

Not only is it *legal* for a value constructor to have the same name as its type constructor, it's *normal*. You'll see this all the time in regular Haskell code.

Type Synonyms

We can introduce a *synonym* for an existing type at any time, in order to give a type a more descriptive name. For example, the String in our BookReview type doesn't tell us what the string is for, but we can clarify this:

```
-- file: ch03/BookStore.hs
type CustomerID = Int
type ReviewBody = String

data BetterReview = BetterReview BookInfo CustomerID ReviewBody
```

The `type` keyword introduces a type synonym. The new name is on the left of the =, with the existing name on the right. The two names identify the same type, so type synonyms are *purely* for making code more readable.

We can also use a type synonym to create a shorter name for a verbose type:

```
-- file: ch03/BookStore.hs
type BookRecord = (BookInfo, BookReview)
```

This states that we can use `BookRecord` as a synonym for the tuple (`BookInfo`, `BookReview`). A type synonym creates only a new name that refers to an existing type.[*] We still use the same value constructors to create a value of the type.

Algebraic Data Types

The familiar `Bool` is the simplest common example of a category of type called an *algebraic data type*. An algebraic data type can have more than one value constructor:

```
-- file: ch03/Bool.hs
data Bool = False | True
```

The `Bool` type has two value constructors, `True` and `False`. Each value constructor is separated in the definition by a | character, which we can read as "or"—we can construct a `Bool` that has the value `True`, or the value `False`. When a type has more than one value constructor, they are usually referred to as *alternatives* or *cases*. We can use any one of the alternatives to create a value of that type.

 A note about naming

Although the phrase "algebraic data type" is long, we're being careful to avoid using the acronym "ADT," which is already widely understood to stand for "*abstract* data type." Since Haskell supports both algebraic and abstract data types, we'll be explicit and avoid the acronym entirely.

Each of an algebraic data type's value constructors can take zero or more arguments. As an example, here's one way we might represent billing information:

```
-- file: ch03/BookStore.hs
type CardHolder = String
type CardNumber = String
type Address = [String]
```

---

[*] If you are familiar with C or C++, it is analogous to a `typedef`.

```
data BillingInfo = CreditCard CardNumber CardHolder Address
                 | CashOnDelivery
                 | Invoice CustomerID
                   deriving (Show)
```

Here, we're saying that we support three ways to bill our customers. If they want to pay by credit card, they must supply a card number, the holder's name, and the holder's billing address as arguments to the CreditCard value constructor. Alternatively, they can pay the person who delivers their shipment. Since we don't need to store any extra information about this, we specify no arguments for the CashOnDelivery constructor. Finally, we can send an invoice to the specified customer, in which case, we need her CustomerID as an argument to the Invoice constructor.

When we use a value constructor to create a value of type BillingInfo, we must supply the arguments that it requires:

```
ghci> :type CreditCard
CreditCard :: CardNumber -> CardHolder -> Address -> BillingInfo
ghci> CreditCard "2901650221064486" "Thomas Gradgrind" ["Dickens", "England"]
CreditCard "2901650221064486" "Thomas Gradgrind" ["Dickens","England"]
ghci> :type it
it :: BillingInfo
ghci> Invoice

<interactive>:1:0:
    No instance for (Show (CustomerID -> BillingInfo))
      arising from a use of `print' at <interactive>:1:0-6
    Possible fix:
      add an instance declaration for (Show (CustomerID -> BillingInfo))
    In the expression: print it
    In a stmt of a 'do' expression: print it
```

The No instance error message arose because we did not supply an argument to the Invoice constructor. As a result, we were trying to print the Invoice constructor itself. That constructor requires an argument and returns a value, so it is a function. We cannot print functions in Haskell, which is ultimately why the interpreter complained.

Tuples, Algebraic Data Types, and When to Use Each

There is some overlap between tuples and user-defined algebraic data types. If we want, we can represent our BookInfo type from earlier as an (Int, String, [String]) tuple:

```
ghci> Book 2 "The Wealth of Networks" ["Yochai Benkler"]
Book 2 "The Wealth of Networks" ["Yochai Benkler"]
ghci> (2, "The Wealth of Networks", ["Yochai Benkler"])
(2,"The Wealth of Networks",["Yochai Benkler"])
```

Algebraic data types allow us to distinguish between otherwise identical pieces of information. Two tuples with elements of the same type are structurally identical, so they have the same type:

```
-- file: ch03/Distinction.hs
a = ("Porpoise", "Grey")
b = ("Table", "Oak")
```

Since they have different names, two algebraic data types have distinct types even if
they are otherwise structurally equivalent:

```
-- file: ch03/Distinction.hs
data Cetacean = Cetacean String String
data Furniture = Furniture String String

c = Cetacean "Porpoise" "Grey"
d = Furniture "Table" "Oak"
```

This lets us bring the type system to bear in writing programs with fewer bugs. With
the tuples we just defined, we could conceivably pass a description of a whale to a
function expecting a chair, and the type system could not help us. With the algebraic
data types, there is no such possibility of confusion.

Here is a more subtle example. Consider the following representations of a two-
dimensional vector:

```
-- file: ch03/AlgebraicVector.hs
-- x and y coordinates or lengths.
data Cartesian2D = Cartesian2D Double Double
                   deriving (Eq, Show)

-- Angle and distance (magnitude).
data Polar2D = Polar2D Double Double
               deriving (Eq, Show)
```

The Cartesian and polar forms use the same types for their two elements. However, the
meanings of the elements are different. Because Cartesian2D and Polar2D are distinct
types, the type system will not let us accidentally use a Cartesian2D value where a
Polar2D is expected, or vice versa.

```
ghci> Cartesian2D (sqrt 2) (sqrt 2) == Polar2D (pi / 4) 2

<interactive>:1:33:
    Couldn't match expected type `Cartesian2D'
           against inferred type `Polar2D'
    In the second argument of `(==)', namely `Polar2D (pi / 4) 2'
    In the expression:
        Cartesian2D (sqrt 2) (sqrt 2) == Polar2D (pi / 4) 2
    In the definition of `it':
        it = Cartesian2D (sqrt 2) (sqrt 2) == Polar2D (pi / 4) 2
```

The (==) operator requires its arguments to have the same type.

Comparing for equality

Notice that in the deriving clause for our vector types, we added another
word, Eq. This causes the Haskell implementation to generate code that
lets us compare the values for equality.

If we use tuples to represent these values, we could quickly land ourselves in hot water by mixing the two representations inappropriately:

```
ghci> (1, 2) == (1, 2)
True
```

The type system can't rescue us here: as far as it's concerned, we're comparing two (Double, Double) pairs, which is a perfectly valid thing to do. Indeed, we cannot tell by inspection which of these values is supposed to be polar or Cartesian, but (1,2) has a different meaning in each representation.

There is no hard and fast rule for deciding when it's better to use a tuple or a distinct data type, but here's a rule of thumb. If you're using compound values widely in your code (as almost all nontrivial programs do), adding data declarations will benefit you in both type safety and readability. For smaller, localized uses, a tuple is usually fine.

Analogues to Algebraic Data Types in Other Languages

Algebraic data types provide a single powerful way to describe data types. Other languages often need several different features to achieve the same degree of expressiveness. Here are some analogues from C and C++, which might make what we can do with algebraic data types and how they relate to concepts that might be more familiar or easier to understand.

The structure

With just one constructor, an algebraic data type is similar to a tuple: it groups related values together into a compound value. It corresponds to a struct in C or C++, and its components correspond to the fields of a struct. Here's a C equivalent of the BookInfo type that we defined earlier:

```
struct book_info {
    int id;
    char *name;
    char **authors;
};
```

The main difference between the two is that the fields in the Haskell type are anonymous and positional:

```
-- file: ch03/BookStore.hs
data BookInfo = Book Int String [String]
                deriving (Show)
```

By *positional*, we mean that the section number is in the first field of the Haskell type and the title is in the second. We refer to them by location, not by name.

Later in this chapter in "Pattern Matching" on page 50, we'll see how to access the fields of a BookInfo value. In "Record Syntax" on page 55, also in this chapter, we'll introduce an alternate syntax for defining data types that looks a little more C-like.

The enumeration

Algebraic data types also serve where we'd use an enum in C or C++ to represent a range of symbolic values. Such algebraic data types are sometimes referred to as *enumeration types*. Here's an example from C:

```
enum roygbiv {
    red,
    orange,
    yellow,
    green,
    blue,
    indigo,
    violet,
};
```

And here's a Haskell equivalent:

```
-- file: ch03/Roygbiv.hs

data Roygbiv = Red
             | Orange
             | Yellow
             | Green
             | Blue
             | Indigo
             | Violet
               deriving (Eq, Show)
```

We can try these out in ghci:

```
ghci> :type Yellow
Yellow :: Roygbiv
ghci> :type Red
Red :: Roygbiv
ghci> Red == Yellow
False
ghci> Green == Green
True
```

In C, the elements of an enum are integers. We can use an integer in a context where an enum is expected and vice versa—a C compiler will automatically convert values between the two types. This can be a source of nasty bugs. In Haskell, this kind of problem does not occur. For example, we cannot use a Roygbiv value where an Int is expected:

```
ghci> take 3 "foobar"
"foo"
ghci> take Red "foobar"

<interactive>:1:5:
    Couldn't match expected type `Int' against inferred type `Roygbiv'
    In the first argument of `take', namely `Red'
    In the expression: take Red "foobar"
    In the definition of `it': it = take Red "foobar"
```

The discriminated union

If an algebraic data type has multiple alternatives, we can think of it as similar to a union in C or C++. A big difference between the two is that a union doesn't tell us which alternative is actually present; we have to explicitly and manually track which alternative we're using, usually in another field of an enclosing struct. This means that unions can be sources of nasty bugs, where our notion of which alternative we should be using is incorrect:

```
enum shape_type {
    shape_circle,
    shape_poly,
};

struct circle {
    struct vector centre;
    float radius;
};

struct poly {
    size_t num_vertices;
    struct vector *vertices;
};

struct shape
{
    enum shape_type type;
    union {
    struct circle circle;
    struct poly poly;
    } shape;
};
```

In this example, the union can contain valid data for either a struct circle or a struct poly. We have to use the enum shape_type by hand to indicate which kind of value is currently stored in the union.

The Haskell version of this code is both dramatically shorter and safer than the C equivalent:

```
-- file: ch03/ShapeUnion.hs
type Vector = (Double, Double)

data Shape = Circle Vector Double
           | Poly [Vector]
```

If we create a Shape value using the Circle constructor, the fact that we created a Circle is stored. When we later use a Circle, we can't accidentally treat it as a Square. We will see why in the next section "Pattern Matching" on page 50.

A few notes

After reading the preceding sections, it should now be clear that *all* of the data types that we define with the `data` keyword are algebraic data types. Some may have just one alternative, while others have several, but they're all using the same machinery.

Pattern Matching

Now that we've seen how to construct values with algebraic data types, let's discuss how we work with these values. If we have a value of some type, there are two things we would like to be able to do:

- If the type has more than one value constructor, we need to be able to tell which value constructor was used to create the value.
- If the value constructor has data components, we need to be able to extract those values.

Haskell has a simple, but tremendously useful, *pattern matching* facility that lets us do both of these things.

A pattern lets us look inside a value and bind variables to the data it contains. Here's an example of pattern matching in action on a `Bool` value; we're going to reproduce the `not` function:

```
-- file: ch03/add.hs
myNot True  = False
myNot False = True
```

It might seem that we have two functions named `myNot` here, but Haskell lets us define a function as a *series of equations*: these two clauses are defining the behavior of the same function for different patterns of input. On each line, the patterns are the items following the function name, up until the = sign.

To understand how pattern matching works, let's step through an example—say, `myNot False`.

When we apply `myNot`, the Haskell runtime checks the value we supply against the value constructor in the first pattern. This does not match, so it tries against the second pattern. That match succeeds, so it uses the righthand side of that equation as the result of the function application.

Here is a slightly more extended example. This function adds together the elements of a list:

```
-- file: ch03/add.hs
sumList (x:xs) = x + sumList xs
sumList []     = 0
```

Let us step through the evaluation of sumList [1,2]. The list notation [1,2] is shorthand for the expression (1:(2:[])). We begin by trying to match the pattern in the first equation of the definition of sumList. In the (x:xs) pattern, the : is the familiar list constructor, (:). We are now using it to match against a value, not to construct one. The value (1:(2:[])) was constructed with (:), so the constructor in the value matches the constructor in the pattern. We say that the pattern *matches* or that the match *succeeds*.

The variables x and xs are now "bound to" the constructor's arguments, so x is given the value 1, and xs the value 2:[].

The expression we are now evaluating is 1 + sumList (2:[]). We must recursively apply sumList to the value 2:[]. Once again, this was constructed using (:), so the match succeeds. In our recursive application of sumList, x is now bound to 2, and xs to [].

We are now evaluating 1 + (2 + sumList []). In this recursive application of sumList, the value we are matching against is []. The value's constructor does not match the constructor in the first pattern, so we skip this equation. Instead, we "fall through" to the next pattern, which matches. The righthand side of this equation is thus chosen as the result of this application.

The result of sumList [1,2] is thus 1 + (2 + (0)), or 3.

Ordering is important

As we already mentioned, a Haskell implementation checks patterns for matches in the order in which we specify them in our equations. Matching proceeds from top to bottom and stops at the first success. Equations that are below a successful match have no effect.

As a final note, there is a standard function, sum, that performs this sum-of-a-list for us. Our sumList is purely for illustration.

Construction and Deconstruction

Let's step back and take a look at the relationship between constructing a value and pattern matching on it.

We apply a value constructor to build a value. The expression Book 9 "Close Calls" ["John Long"] applies the Book constructor to the values 9, "Close Calls", and ["John Long"] in order to produce a new value of type BookInfo.

When we pattern match against the Book constructor, we *reverse* the construction process. First of all, we check to see if the value was created using that constructor. If it was, we inspect it to obtain the individual values that we originally supplied to the constructor when we created the value.

Let's consider what happens if we match the pattern (Book id name authors) against our example expression:

- The match will succeed, because the constructor in the value matches the one in our pattern.
- The variable id will be bound to 9.
- The variable name will be bound to "Close Calls".
- The variable authors will be bound to ["John Long"].

Because pattern matching acts as the inverse of construction, it's sometimes referred to as *de*construction.

Deconstruction doesn't destroy anything

If you're steeped in object-oriented programming jargon, don't confuse deconstruction with destruction! Matching a pattern has no effect on the value we're examining: it just lets us "look inside" it.

Further Adventures

The syntax for pattern matching on a tuple is similar to the syntax for constructing a tuple. Here's a function that returns the last element of a 3-tuple:

```
-- file: ch03/Tuple.hs
third (a, b, c) = c
```

There's no limit on how "deep" within a value a pattern can look. This definition looks both inside a tuple and inside a list within that tuple:

```
-- file: ch03/Tuple.hs
complicated (True, a, x:xs, 5) = (a, xs)
```

We can try this out interactively:

```
ghci> :load Tuple.hs
[1 of 1] Compiling Main             ( Tuple.hs, interpreted )
Ok, modules loaded: Main.
ghci> complicated (True, 1, [1,2,3], 5)
(1,[2,3])
```

Wherever a literal value is present in a pattern (True and 5 in the preceding pattern), that value must match exactly for the pattern match to succeed. If every pattern within a series of equations fails to match, we get a runtime error:

```
ghci> complicated (False, 1, [1,2,3], 5)
*** Exception: Tuple.hs:10:0-39: Non-exhaustive patterns in function complicated
```

For an explanation of this error message, skip forward to the section "Exhaustive Patterns and Wild Cards" on page 54.

We can pattern match on an algebraic data type using its value constructors. Recall the BookInfo type we defined earlier; we can extract the values from a BookInfo as follows:

```
-- file: ch03/BookStore.hs
bookID      (Book id title authors) = id
bookTitle   (Book id title authors) = title
bookAuthors (Book id title authors) = authors
```

Let's see it in action:

```
ghci> bookID (Book 3 "Probability Theory" ["E.T.H. Jaynes"])
3
ghci> bookTitle (Book 3 "Probability Theory" ["E.T.H. Jaynes"])
"Probability Theory"
ghci> bookAuthors (Book 3 "Probability Theory" ["E.T.H. Jaynes"])
["E.T.H. Jaynes"]
```

The compiler can infer the types of the accessor functions based on the constructor that we're using in our pattern:

```
ghci> :type bookID
bookID :: BookInfo -> Int
ghci> :type bookTitle
bookTitle :: BookInfo -> String
ghci> :type bookAuthors
bookAuthors :: BookInfo -> [String]
```

If we use a literal value in a pattern, the corresponding part of the value that we're matching against must contain an identical value. For instance, the pattern (3:xs) first checks that a value is a nonempty list, by matching against the (:) constructor. It also ensures that the head of the list has the exact value 3. If both of these conditions hold, the tail of the list will be bound to the variable xs.

Variable Naming in Patterns

As you read functions that match on lists, you'll frequently find that the names of the variables inside a pattern resemble (x:xs) or (d:ds). This is a popular naming convention. The idea is that the name xs has an s on the end of its name as if it's the "plural" of x, because x contains the head of the list, and xs contains the remaining elements.

The Wild Card Pattern

We can indicate that we don't care what is present in part of a pattern. The notation for this is the underscore character (_), which we call a *wild card*. We use it as follows:

```
-- file: ch03/BookStore.hs
nicerID      (Book id _      _      ) = id
nicerTitle   (Book _  title  _      ) = title
nicerAuthors (Book _  _      authors) = authors
```

Here, we have tidier versions of the accessor functions that we introduced earlier. Now, there's no question about which element we're using in each function.

In a pattern, a wild card acts similarly to a variable, but it doesn't bind a new variable. As the previous examples indicate, we can use more than one wild card in a single pattern.

Another advantage of wild cards is that a Haskell compiler can warn us if we introduce a variable name in a pattern, but then not use it in a function's body. Defining a variable but forgetting to use it can often indicate the presence of a bug, so this is a helpful feature. If we use a wild card instead of a variable that we do not intend to use, the compiler won't complain.

Exhaustive Patterns and Wild Cards

When writing a series of patterns, it's important to cover all of a type's constructors. For example, if we're inspecting a list, we should have one equation that matches the non-empty constructor (:) and one that matches the empty-list constructor [].

Let's see what happens if we fail to cover all the cases. Here, we deliberately omit a check for the [] constructor:

```
-- file: ch03/BadPattern.hs
badExample (x:xs) = x + badExample xs
```

If we apply this to a value that it cannot match, we'll get an error at runtime—our software has a bug!

```
ghci> badExample []
*** Exception: BadPattern.hs:4:0-36: Non-exhaustive patterns in function badExample
```

In this example, no equation in the function's definition matches the value [].

Warning about incomplete patterns

GHC provides a helpful compilation option, -fwarn-incomplete-patterns, that will cause it to print a warning during compilation if a sequence of patterns doesn't match all of a type's value constructors.

If we need to provide a default behavior in cases where we don't care about specific constructors, we can use a wild card pattern:

```
-- file: ch03/BadPattern.hs
goodExample (x:xs) = x + goodExample xs
goodExample _      = 0
```

The wild card shown in the preceding code will match the [] constructor, so applying this function does not lead to a crash:

```
ghci> goodExample []
0
ghci> goodExample [1,2]
3
```

Record Syntax

Writing accessor functions for each of a data type's components can be repetitive and tedious:

```
-- file: ch03/BookStore.hs
nicerID      (Book id _      _      ) = id
nicerTitle   (Book _  title _       ) = title
nicerAuthors (Book _  _      authors) = authors
```

We call this kind of code *boilerplate*—necessary,but bulky and irksome. Haskell programmers don't like boilerplate. Fortunately, the language addresses this particular boilerplate problem: we can define a data type, and accessors for each of its components, simultaneously. (The positions of the commas here is a matter of preference. If you like, put them at the end of a line instead of the beginning.)

```
-- file: ch03/BookStore.hs
data Customer = Customer {
      customerID      :: CustomerID
    , customerName    :: String
    , customerAddress :: Address
    } deriving (Show)
```

This is almost exactly identical in meaning to the following, more familiar form:

```
-- file: ch03/AltCustomer.hs
data Customer = Customer Int String [String]
                deriving (Show)

customerID :: Customer -> Int
customerID (Customer id _ _) = id

customerName :: Customer -> String
customerName (Customer _ name _) = name

customerAddress :: Customer -> [String]
customerAddress (Customer _ _ address) = address
```

For each of the fields that we name in our type definition, Haskell creates an accessor function of that name:

```
ghci> :type customerID
customerID :: Customer -> CustomerID
```

We can still use the usual application syntax to create a value of this type:

```
-- file: ch03/BookStore.hs
customer1 = Customer 271828 "J.R. Hacker"
            ["255 Syntax Ct",
             "Milpitas, CA 95134",
             "USA"]
```

Record syntax adds a more verbose notation for creating a value. This can sometimes make code more readable:

```
-- file: ch03/BookStore.hs
customer2 = Customer {
            customerID = 271828
          , customerAddress = ["1048576 Disk Drive",
                               "Milpitas, CA 95134",
                               "USA"]
          , customerName = "Jane Q. Citizen"
          }
```

If we use this form, we can vary the order in which we list fields. Here, we moved the name and address fields from their positions in the declaration of the type.

When we define a type using record syntax, it also changes the way the type's values are printed:

```
ghci> customer1
Customer {customerID = 271828, customerName = "J.R. Hacker", customerAddress =
["255 Syntax Ct","Milpitas, CA 95134","USA"]}
```

For comparison, let's look at a BookInfo value; we defined this type without record syntax:

```
ghci> cities
Book 173 "Use of Weapons" ["Iain M. Banks"]
```

The accessor functions that we get "for free" when we use record syntax really are normal Haskell functions:

```
ghci> :type customerName
customerName :: Customer -> String
ghci> customerName customer1
"J.R. Hacker"
```

The standard System.Time module makes good use of record syntax. Here's a type defined in that module:

```
data CalendarTime = CalendarTime {
  ctYear                      :: Int,
  ctMonth                     :: Month,
  ctDay, ctHour, ctMin, ctSec :: Int,
  ctPicosec                   :: Integer,
  ctWDay                      :: Day,
  ctYDay                      :: Int,
  ctTZName                    :: String,
  ctTZ                        :: Int,
  ctIsDST                     :: Bool
}
```

In the absence of record syntax, it would be painful to extract specific fields from a type such as this. The notation makes it easier to work with large structures.

Parameterized Types

We've repeatedly mentioned that the list type is polymorphic: the elements of a list can be of any type. We can also add polymorphism to our own types. To do this, we introduce type variables into a type declaration. The Prelude defines a type named Maybe, which we can use to represent a value that could be either present or missing, for example, a field in a database row that could be null:

```
-- file: ch03/Nullable.hs
data Maybe a = Just a
             | Nothing
```

Here, the variable a is not a regular variable—it's a type variable. It indicates that the Maybe type takes another type as its parameter. This lets us use Maybe on values of any type:

```
-- file: ch03/Nullable.hs
someBool = Just True

someString = Just "something"
```

As usual, we can experiment with this type in ghci:

```
ghci> Just 1.5
Just 1.5
ghci> Nothing
Nothing
ghci> :type Just "invisible bike"
Just "invisible bike" :: Maybe [Char]
```

Maybe is a polymorphic, or generic, type. We give the Maybe type constructor a parameter to create a specific type, such as Maybe Int or Maybe [Bool]. As we might expect, these types are distinct.

We can nest uses of parameterized types inside each other, but when we do, we may need to use parentheses to tell the Haskell compiler how to parse our expression:

```
-- file: ch03/Nullable.hs
wrapped = Just (Just "wrapped")
```

To once again extend an analogy to more familiar languages, parameterized types bear some resemblance to templates in C++ and to generics in Java. Just be aware that this is a shallow analogy. Templates and generics were added to their respective languages long after the languages were initially defined, and they have an awkward feel. Haskell's parameterized types are simpler and easier to use, as the language was designed with them from the beginning.

Recursive Types

The familiar list type is *recursive*: it's defined in terms of itself. To understand this, let's create our own list-like type. We'll use Cons in place of the (:) constructor, and Nil in place of []:

```
-- file: ch03/ListADT.hs
data List a = Cons a (List a)
            | Nil
              deriving (Show)
```

Because List a appears on both the left and the right of the = sign, the type's definition refers to itself. If we want to use the Cons constructor to create a new value, we must supply one value of type a and another of type List a. Let's see where this leads us in practice.

The simplest value of type List a that we can create is Nil. Save the type definition in a file, and then load it into ghci:

```
ghci> Nil
Nil
```

Because Nil has a List type, we can use it as a parameter to Cons:

```
ghci> Cons 0 Nil
Cons 0 Nil
```

And because Cons 0 Nil has the type List a, we can use this as a parameter to Cons:

```
ghci> Cons 1 it
Cons 1 (Cons 0 Nil)
ghci> Cons 2 it
Cons 2 (Cons 1 (Cons 0 Nil))
ghci> Cons 3 it
Cons 3 (Cons 2 (Cons 1 (Cons 0 Nil)))
```

We could continue in this fashion indefinitely, creating ever-longer Cons chains, each with a single Nil at the end.

For a third example of what a recursive type is, here is a definition of a binary tree type:

```
-- file: ch03/Tree.hs
data Tree a = Node a (Tree a) (Tree a)
            | Empty
              deriving (Show)
```

A binary tree is either a node with two children—which are themselves binary trees—or an empty value.

Is List an acceptable list?

We can easily prove to ourselves that our List a type has the same shape as the built-in list type [a]. To do this, we write a function that takes any value of type [a] and produces a value of type List a:

```
-- file: ch03/ListADT.hs
fromList (x:xs) = Cons x (fromList xs)
fromList []     = Nil
```

By inspection, this clearly substitutes a Cons for every (:) and a Nil for each []. This covers both of the built-in list type's constructors. The two types are *isomorphic*—they have the same shape:

```
ghci> fromList "durian"
Cons 'd' (Cons 'u' (Cons 'r' (Cons 'i' (Cons 'a' (Cons 'n' Nil)))))
ghci> fromList [Just True, Nothing, Just False]
Cons (Just True) (Cons Nothing (Cons (Just False) Nil))
```

This time, let's search for insight by comparing our definition with one from a more familiar language. Here's a similar class definition in Java:

```
class Tree<A>
{
    A value;
    Tree<A> left;
    Tree<A> right;

    public Tree(A v, Tree<A> l, Tree<A> r)
    {
    value = v;
    left = l;
    right = r;
    }
}
```

The one significant difference is that Java lets us use the special value null anywhere to indicate "nothing," so we can use null to indicate that a node is missing a left or right child. Here's a small function that constructs a tree with two leaves (a leaf, by convention, has no children):

```
class Example
{
    static Tree<String> simpleTree()
    {
    return new Tree<String>(
            "parent",
        new Tree<String>("left leaf", null, null),
        new Tree<String>("right leaf", null, null));
    }
}
```

In Haskell, we don't have an equivalent of null. We could use the Maybe type to provide a similar effect, but that would bloat the pattern matching. Instead, we've decided to use a no-argument `Empty` constructor. Where the Java example provides `null` to the `Tree` constructor, we supply `Empty` in Haskell:

```
-- file: ch03/Tree.hs
simpleTree = Node "parent" (Node "left child" Empty Empty)
                           (Node "right child" Empty Empty)
```

EXERCISES

1. Write the converse of `fromList` for the `List` type: a function that takes a `List` a and generates a `[a]`.
2. Define a tree type that has only one constructor, like our Java example. Instead of the `Empty` constructor, use the `Maybe` type to refer to a node's children.

Reporting Errors

Haskell provides a standard function, `error :: String -> a`, that we can call when something has gone terribly wrong in our code. We give it a string parameter, which is the error message to display. Its type signature looks peculiar: how can it produce a value of any type `a` given only a string?

It has a result type of `a` so that we can call it anywhere and it will always have the right type. However, it does not return a value like a normal function. Instead, it *immediately aborts evaluation* and prints the error message we give it.

The `mySecond` function returns the second element of its input list but fails if its input list isn't long enough:

```
-- file: ch03/MySecond.hs
mySecond :: [a] -> a

mySecond xs = if null (tail xs)
              then error "list too short"
              else head (tail xs)
```

As usual, we can see how this works in practice in `ghci`:

```
ghci> mySecond "xi"
'i'
ghci> mySecond [2]
*** Exception: list too short
ghci> head (mySecond [[9]])
*** Exception: list too short
```

Notice the third case, where we try to use the result of the call to `mySecond` as the argument to another function. Evaluation still terminates and drops us back to the `ghci` prompt. This is the major weakness of using `error`: it doesn't let our caller distinguish between a recoverable error and a problem so severe that it really should terminate our program.

As we have already seen, a pattern matching failure causes a similar unrecoverable error:

```
ghci> mySecond []
*** Exception: Prelude.tail: empty list
```

A More Controlled Approach

We can use the Maybe type to represent the possibility of an error.

If we want to indicate that an operation has failed, we can use the Nothing constructor. Otherwise, we wrap our value with the Just constructor.

Let's see how our mySecond function changes if we return a Maybe value instead of calling error:

```
-- file: ch03/MySecond.hs
safeSecond :: [a] -> Maybe a

safeSecond [] = Nothing
safeSecond xs = if null (tail xs)
                then Nothing
                else Just (head (tail xs))
```

If the list we're passed is too short, we return Nothing to our caller. This lets them decide what to do, while a call to error would force a crash:

```
ghci> safeSecond []
Nothing
ghci> safeSecond [1]
Nothing
ghci> safeSecond [1,2]
Just 2
ghci> safeSecond [1,2,3]
Just 2
```

To return to an earlier topic, we can further improve the readability of this function with pattern matching:

```
-- file: ch03/MySecond.hs
tidySecond :: [a] -> Maybe a

tidySecond (_:x:_) = Just x
tidySecond _       = Nothing
```

The first pattern matches only if the list is at least two elements long (it contains two list constructors), and it binds the variable x to the list's second element. The second pattern is matched if the first fails.

Introducing Local Variables

Within the body of a function, we can introduce new local variables whenever we need them, using a let expression. Here is a simple function that determines whether we should lend some money to a customer. We meet a money reserve of at least 100, and we return our new balance after subtracting the amount we have loaned:

```
-- file: ch03/Lending.hs
lend amount balance = let reserve    = 100
                          newBalance = balance - amount
                      in if balance < reserve
                         then Nothing
                         else Just newBalance
```

The keywords to look out for here are let, which starts a block of variable declarations, and in, which ends it. Each line introduces a new variable. The name is on the left of the =, and the expression to which it is bound is on the right.

Special notes

Let us reemphasize our wording: a name in a let block is bound to an *expression*, not to a *value*. Because Haskell is a lazy language, the expression associated with a name won't actually be evaluated until it's needed. In the previous example, we could not compute the value of newBalance if we did not meet our reserve.

When we define a variable in a let block, we refer to it as a let-*bound* variable. This simply means what it says: we have bound the variable in a let block.

Also, our use of whitespace here is important. We'll talk in more detail about the layout rules later in this chapter in "The Offside Rule and Whitespace in an Expression" on page 64.

We can use the names of a variable in a let block both within the block of declarations and in the expression that follows the in keyword.

In general, we'll refer to the places within our code where we can use a name as the name's *scope*. If we can use a name, it's *in scope*; otherwise, it's *out of scope*. If a name is visible throughout a source file, we say it's at the *top level*.

Shadowing

We can "nest" multiple let blocks inside each other in an expression:

```
-- file: ch03/NestedLets.hs
foo = let a = 1
      in let b = 2
         in a + b
```

It's perfectly legal, but not exactly wise, to repeat a variable name in a nested let expression:

```
-- file: ch03/NestedLets.hs
bar = let x = 1
      in ((let x = "foo" in x), x)
```

Here, the inner x is hiding, or *shadowing*, the outer x. It has the same name, but a different type and value:

```
ghci> bar
("foo",1)
```

We can also shadow a function's parameters, leading to even stranger results. What is the type of this function?

```
-- file: ch03/NestedLets.hs
quux a = let a = "foo"
         in a ++ "eek!"
```

Because the function's argument a is never used in the body of the function, due to being shadowed by the let-bound a, the argument can have any type at all:

```
ghci> :type quux
quux :: t -> [Char]
```

Compiler warnings are your friends

Shadowing can obviously lead to confusion and nasty bugs, so GHC has a helpful -fwarn-name-shadowing option. When enabled, GHC will print a warning message any time we shadow a name.

The where Clause

We can use another mechanism to introduce local variables: the where clause. The definitions in a where clause apply to the code that *precedes* it. Here's a similar function to lend, using where instead of let:

```
-- file: ch03/Lending.hs
lend2 amount balance = if amount < reserve * 0.5
                       then Just newBalance
                       else Nothing
    where reserve    = 100
          newBalance = balance - amount
```

While a where clause may seem weird initially, it offers a wonderful aid to readability. It lets us direct our reader's focus to the important details of an expression, with the supporting definitions following afterwards. After a while, you may find yourself missing where clauses when using languages that lack them.

As with let expressions, whitespace is significant in where clauses. We will talk more about the layout rules shortly in "The Offside Rule and Whitespace in an Expression" on page 64.

Local Functions, Global Variables

You'll have noticed that Haskell's syntax for defining a variable looks very similar to its syntax for defining a function. This symmetry is preserved in let and where blocks; we can define local *functions* just as easily as local *variables*:

```
-- file: ch03/LocalFunction.hs
pluralise :: String -> [Int] -> [String]
pluralise word counts = map plural counts
    where plural 0 = "no " ++ word ++ "s"
          plural 1 = "one " ++ word
          plural n = show n ++ " " ++ word ++ "s"
```

We have defined a local function, plural, that consists of several equations. Local functions can freely use variables from the scopes that enclose them; here, we use word from the definition of the outer function pluralise. In the definition of pluralise, the map function (which we'll be revisiting in the next chapter) applies the local function plural to every element of the counts list.

We can also define variables, as well as functions, at the top level of a source file:

```
-- file: ch03/GlobalVariable.hs
itemName = "Weighted Companion Cube"
```

The Offside Rule and Whitespace in an Expression

In our definitions of lend and lend2, the left margin of our text wandered around quite a bit. This was not an accident; in Haskell, whitespace has meaning.

Haskell uses indentation as a cue to parse sections of code. This use of layout to convey structure is sometimes called the *offside rule*. At the beginning of a source file, the first top-level declaration or definition can start in any column, and the Haskell compiler or interpreter remembers that indentation level. Every subsequent top-level declaration must have the same indentation.

Here's an illustration of the top-level indentation rule; our first file, *GoodIndent.hs*, is well-behaved:

```
-- file: ch03/GoodIndent.hs
-- This is the leftmost column.

    -- It's fine for top-level declarations to start in any column...
    firstGoodIndentation = 1

    -- ...provided all subsequent declarations do, too!
    secondGoodIndentation = 2
```

Our second, *BadIndent.hs*, doesn't play by the rules:

```
-- file: ch03/BadIndent.hs
-- This is the leftmost column.

      -- Our first declaration is in column 4.
    firstBadIndentation = 1

    -- Our second is left of the first, which is illegal!
    secondBadIndentation = 2
```

Here's what happens when we try to load the two files into ghci:

```
ghci> :load GoodIndent.hs
[1 of 1] Compiling Main                ( GoodIndent.hs, interpreted )
Ok, modules loaded: Main.
ghci> :load BadIndent.hs
[1 of 1] Compiling Main                ( BadIndent.hs, interpreted )

BadIndent.hs:8:2: parse error on input `secondBadIndentation'
Failed, modules loaded: none.
```

An empty following line is treated as a continuation of the current item, as is a following line indented further to the right.

The rules for let expressions and where clauses are similar. After a let or where keyword, the Haskell compiler or interpreter remembers the indentation of the next token it sees. If the line that follows is empty, or its indentation is further to the right, it is considered as a continuation of the previous line. If the indentation is the same as the start of the preceding item, it is treated as beginning a new item in the same block:

```
-- file: ch03/Indentation.hs
foo = let firstDefinition = blah blah
          -- a comment-only line is treated as empty
                          continuation blah

          -- we reduce the indentation, so this is a new definition
          secondDefinition = yada yada

                          continuation yada
      in whatever
```

Here are nested uses of let and where:

```
-- file: ch03/letwhere.hs
bar = let b = 2
          c = True
      in let a = b
         in (a, c)
```

The name a is only visible within the inner let expression—it's not visible in the outer let. If we try to use the name a there, we'll get a compilation error. The indentation gives both us and the compiler a visual cue as to what is currently in scope:

```
-- file: ch03/letwhere.hs
foo = x
    where x = y
              where y = 2
```

Similarly, the scope of the first where clause is the definition of foo, but the scope of the second is just the first where clause.

The indentation we use for the let and where clauses makes our intentions easy to figure out.

A Note About Tabs Versus Spaces

If you use a Haskell-aware text editor (e.g., Emacs), it is probably already configured to use space characters for all whitespace when you edit Haskell source files. If your editor is *not* Haskell-aware, you should configure it to use only space characters.

The reason for this is portability. In an editor that uses a fixed-width font, tab stops are by convention placed at different intervals on Unix-like systems (every eight characters) than on Windows (every four characters). This means that no matter what your personal beliefs are about where tabs belong, you can't rely on someone else's editor honoring your preferences. Any indentation that uses tabs is going to look broken under *someone's* configuration. In fact, this could lead to compilation problems, as the Haskell language standard requires implementations to use the Unix tab width convention. Using space characters avoids this problem entirely.

The Offside Rule Is Not Mandatory

We can use explicit structuring instead of layout to indicate what we mean. To do so, we start a block of equations with an opening curly brace, separate each item with a semicolon, and finish the block with a closing curly brace. The following two uses of let have the same meanings:

```
-- file: ch03/Braces.hs
bar = let a = 1
          b = 2
          c = 3
      in a + b + c

foo = let { a = 1;  b = 2;
        c = 3 }
      in a + b + c
```

When we use explicit structuring, the normal layout rules don't apply, which is why we can get away with unusual indentation in the second let expression.

We can use explicit structuring anywhere that we'd normally use layout. It's valid for where clauses and even for top-level declarations. Just remember that although the facility exists, explicit structuring is hardly ever actually *used* in Haskell programs.

The case Expression

Function definitions are not the only place where we can use pattern matching. The case construct lets us match patterns within an expression. Here's what it looks like. This function (defined for us in Data.Maybe) unwraps a Maybe value, using a default if the value is Nothing:

```
-- file: ch03/Guard.hs
fromMaybe defval wrapped =
    case wrapped of
```

```
         Nothing    -> defval
         Just value -> value
```

The `case` keyword is followed by an arbitrary expression; the pattern match is performed against the result of this expression. The `of` keyword signifies the end of the expression and the beginning of the block of patterns and expressions.

Each item in the block consists of a pattern, followed by an arrow (`->`), followed by an expression to evaluate if that pattern matches. These expressions must all have the same type. The result of the `case` expression is the result of the expression associated with the first pattern to match. Matches are attempted from top to bottom.

To express "here's the expression to evaluate if none of the other patterns matches," we just use the wild card pattern _ as the last in our list of patterns. If a pattern match fails, we will get the same kind of runtime error that we saw earlier.

Common Beginner Mistakes with Patterns

There are a few ways in which new Haskell programmers can misunderstand or misuse patterns. The following are some attempts at pattern matching gone awry. Depending on what you expect one of these examples to do, there may be some surprises.

Incorrectly Matching Against a Variable

Take a look at the following code:

```
-- file: ch03/BogusPattern.hs
data Fruit = Apple | Orange

apple = "apple"

orange = "orange"

whichFruit :: String -> Fruit

whichFruit f = case f of
                 apple  -> Apple
                 orange -> Orange
```

A naive glance suggests that this code is trying to check the value f to see whether it matches the value `apple` or `orange`.

It is easier to spot the mistake if we rewrite the code in an equational style:

```
-- file: ch03/BogusPattern.hs
equational apple = Apple
equational orange = Orange
```

Now can you see the problem? Here, it is more obvious `apple` does not refer to the top-level value named `apple`—it is a local pattern variable.

Irrefutable patterns

We refer to a pattern that always succeeds as irrefutable. Plain variable names and the wild card _ (underscore) are examples of irrefutable patterns.

Here's a corrected version of this function:

```
-- file: ch03/BogusPattern.hs
betterFruit f = case f of
                  "apple"  -> Apple
                  "orange" -> Orange
```

We fixed the problem by matching against the literal values "apple" and "orange".

Incorrectly Trying to Compare for Equality

What if we want to compare the values stored in two nodes of type `Tree`, and then return one of them if they're equal? Here's an attempt:

```
-- file: ch03/BadTree.hs
bad_nodesAreSame (Node a _ _) (Node a _ _) = Just a
bad_nodesAreSame _               _         = Nothing
```

A name can appear only once in a set of pattern bindings. We cannot place a variable in multiple positions to express the notion "this value and that should be identical." Instead, we'll solve this problem using *guards*, another invaluable Haskell feature.

Conditional Evaluation with Guards

Pattern matching limits us to performing fixed tests of a value's shape. Although this is useful, we will often want to make a more expressive check before evaluating a function's body. Haskell provides a feature called *guards* that give us this ability. We'll introduce the idea with a modification of the function we wrote to compare two nodes of a tree:

```
-- file: ch03/BadTree.hs
nodesAreSame (Node a _ _) (Node b _ _)
    | a == b    = Just a
nodesAreSame _ _ = Nothing
```

In this example, we use pattern matching to ensure that we are looking at values of the right shape, and a guard to compare pieces of them.

A pattern can be followed by zero or more guards, each an expression of type `Bool`. A guard is introduced by a | symbol. This is followed by the guard expression, then an = symbol (or -> if we're in a `case` expression), then the body to use if the guard expression evaluates to `True`. If a pattern matches, each guard associated with that pattern is evaluated in the order in which they are written. If a guard succeeds, the body affiliated with it is used as the result of the function. If no guard succeeds, pattern matching moves on to the next pattern.

When a guard expression is evaluated, all of the variables mentioned in the pattern with which it is associated are bound and can be used.

Here is a reworked version of our lend function that uses guard:

```
-- file: ch03/Lending.hs
lend3 amount balance
     | amount <= 0            = Nothing
     | amount > reserve * 0.5 = Nothing
     | otherwise              = Just newBalance
   where reserve    = 100
         newBalance = balance - amount
```

The special-looking guard expression otherwise is simply a variable bound to the value True that aids readability.

We can use guards anywhere that we can use patterns. Writing a function as a series of equations using pattern matching and guards can make it much clearer. Remember the myDrop function we defined in "Conditional Evaluation" on page 29?

```
-- file: ch02/myDrop.hs
myDrop n xs = if n <= 0 || null xs
              then xs
              else myDrop (n - 1) (tail xs)
```

Here is a reformulation that uses patterns and guards:

```
-- file: ch02/myDrop.hs
niceDrop n xs | n <= 0 = xs
niceDrop _ []          = []
niceDrop n (_:xs)      = niceDrop (n - 1) xs
```

This change in style lets us enumerate up front the cases in which we expect a function to behave differently. If we bury the decisions inside a function as if expressions, the code becomes harder to read.

EXERCISES

1. Write a function that computes the number of elements in a list. To test it, ensure that it gives the same answers as the standard length function.

2. Add a type signature for your function to your source file. To test it, load the source file into ghci again.

3. Write a function that computes the mean of a list, i.e., the sum of all elements in the list divided by its length. (You may need to use the fromIntegral function to convert the length of the list from an integer into a floating-point number.)

4. Turn a list into a palindrome; i.e., it should read the same both backward and forward. For example, given the list [1,2,3], your function should return [1,2,3,3,2,1].

5. Write a function that determines whether its input list is a palindrome.

6. Create a function that sorts a list of lists based on the length of each sublist. (You may want to look at the **sortBy** function from the **Data.List** module.)

7. Define a function that joins a list of lists together using a separator value:

```
-- file: ch03/Intersperse.hs
intersperse :: a -> [[a]] -> [a]
```

The separator should appear between elements of the list, but it should not follow the last element. Your function should behave as follows:

```
ghci> :load Intersperse
[1 of 1] Compiling Main             ( Intersperse.hs, interpreted )
Ok, modules loaded: Main.
ghci> intersperse ',' []
""
ghci> intersperse ',' ["foo"]
"foo"
ghci> intersperse ',' ["foo","bar","baz","quux"]
"foo,bar,baz,quux"
```

8. Using the binary tree type that we defined earlier in this chapter, write a function that will determine the height of the tree. The height is the largest number of hops from the root to an **Empty**. For example, the tree **Empty** has height zero; **Node "x" Empty Empty** has height one; **Node "x" Empty (Node "y" Empty Empty)** has height two; and so on.

9. Consider three two-dimensional points, *a*, *b*, and *c*. If we look at the angle formed by the line segment from *a* to *b* and the line segment from *b* to *c*, it turns left, turns right, or forms a straight line. Define a **Direction** data type that lets you represent these possibilities.

10. Write a function that calculates the turn made by three two-dimensional points and returns a **Direction**.

11. Define a function that takes a list of two-dimensional points and computes the direction of each successive triple. Given a list of points [a,b,c,d,e], it should begin by computing the turn made by [a,b,c], then the turn made by [b,c,d], then [c,d,e]. Your function should return a list of **Direction**.

12. Using the code from the preceding three exercises, implement Graham's scan algorithm for the convex hull of a set of 2D points. You can find good description of what a convex hull (*http://en.wikipedia.org/wiki/Convex_hull*) is, and how the Graham scan algorithm (*http://en.wikipedia.org/wiki/Graham_scan*) should work, on Wikipedia (*http://en.wikipedia.org/*).

CHAPTER 4

Functional Programming

Thinking in Haskell

Our early learning of Haskell has two distinct obstacles. The first is coming to terms with the shift in mindset from imperative programming to functional: we have to replace our programming habits from other languages. We do this not because imperative techniques are bad, but because in a functional language other techniques work better.

Our second challenge is learning our way around the standard Haskell libraries. As in any language, the libraries act as a lever, enabling us to multiply our problem-solving ability. Haskell libraries tend to operate at a higher level of abstraction than those in many other languages. We'll need to work a little harder to learn to use the libraries, but in exchange they offer a lot of power.

In this chapter, we'll introduce a number of common functional programming techniques. We'll draw upon examples from imperative languages in order to highlight the shift in thinking that we'll need to make. As we do so, we'll walk through some of the fundamentals of Haskell's standard libraries. We'll also intermittently cover a few more language features along the way.

A Simple Command-Line Framework

In most of this chapter, we will concern ourselves with code that has no interaction with the outside world. To maintain our focus on practical code, we will begin by developing a gateway between our "pure" code and the outside world. Our framework simply reads the contents of one file, applies a function to the file, and writes the result to another file:

```
-- file: ch04/InteractWith.hs
-- Save this in a source file, e.g., Interact.hs

import System.Environment (getArgs)

interactWith function inputFile outputFile = do
  input <- readFile inputFile
```

```
    writeFile outputFile (function input)

main = mainWith myFunction
  where mainWith function = do
          args <- getArgs
          case args of
            [input,output] -> interactWith function input output
            _ -> putStrLn "error: exactly two arguments needed"

        -- replace "id" with the name of our function below
        myFunction = id
```

This is all we need to write simple, but complete, file-processing programs. This is a complete program, and we can compile it to an executable named *InteractWith* as follows:

```
$ ghc --make InteractWith
[1 of 1] Compiling Main          ( InteractWith.hs, InteractWith.o )
Linking InteractWith ...
```

If we run this program from the shell or command prompt, it will accept two filenames, the name of a file to read, and the name of a file to write:

```
$ ./Interact
error: exactly two arguments needed
$ ./Interact hello-in.txt hello-out.txt
$ cat hello-in.txt
hello world
$ cat hello-out.txt
hello world
```

Some of the notation in our source file is new. The do keyword introduces a block of *actions* that can cause effects in the real world, such as reading or writing a file. The <- operator is the equivalent of assignment inside a do block. This is enough explanation to get us started. We will talk in much more depth about these details of notation, and I/O in general, in Chapter 7.

When we want to test a function that cannot talk to the outside world, we simply replace the name id in the preceding code with the name of the function we want to test. Whatever our function does, it will need to have the type String -> String; in other words, it must accept a string and return a string.

Warming Up: Portably Splitting Lines of Text

Haskell provides a built-in function, lines, that lets us split a text string on line boundaries. It returns a list of strings with line termination characters omitted:

```
ghci> :type lines
lines :: String -> [String]
ghci> lines "line 1\nline 2"
["line 1","line 2"]
ghci> lines "foo\n\nbar\n"
["foo","","bar"]
```

While `lines` looks useful, it relies on us reading a file in "text mode" in order to work. Text mode is a feature common to many programming languages; it provides a special behavior when we read and write files on Windows. When we read a file in text mode, the file I/O library translates the line-ending sequence `"\r\n"` (carriage return followed by newline) to `"\n"` (newline alone), and it does the reverse when we write a file. On Unix-like systems, text mode does not perform any translation. As a result of this difference, if we read a file on one platform that was written on the other, the line endings are likely to become a mess. (Both `readFile` and `writeFile` operate in text mode.)

```
ghci> lines "a\r\nb"
["a\r","b"]
```

The `lines` function splits only on newline characters, leaving carriage returns dangling at the ends of lines. If we read a Windows-generated text file on a Linux or Unix box, we'll get trailing carriage returns at the end of each line.

We have comfortably used Python's "universal newline" support for years; this transparently handles Unix and Windows line-ending conventions for us. We would like to provide something similar in Haskell.

Since we are still early in our career of reading Haskell code, we will discuss our Haskell implementation in some detail:

```
-- file: ch04/SplitLines.hs
splitLines :: String -> [String]
```

Our function's type signature indicates that it accepts a single string, the contents of a file with some unknown line-ending convention. It returns a list of strings, representing each line from the file:

```
-- file: ch04/SplitLines.hs
splitLines [] = []
splitLines cs =
    let (pre, suf) = break isLineTerminator cs
    in  pre : case suf of
                 ('\r':'\n':rest) -> splitLines rest
                 ('\r':rest)      -> splitLines rest
                 ('\n':rest)      -> splitLines rest
                 _                -> []

isLineTerminator c = c == '\r' || c == '\n'
```

Before we dive into detail, notice first how we organized our code. We presented the important pieces of code first, keeping the definition of `isLineTerminator` until later. Because we have given the helper function a readable name, we can guess what it does even before we've read it, which eases the smooth "flow" of reading the code.

The `Prelude` defines a function named `break` that we can use to partition a list into two parts. It takes a function as its first parameter. That function must examine an element of the list and return a `Bool` to indicate whether to break the list at that point. The `break` function returns a pair, which consists of the sublist consumed before the predicate returned `True` (the *prefix*) and the rest of the list (the *suffix*):

```
ghci> break odd [2,4,5,6,8]
([2,4],[5,6,8])
ghci> :module +Data.Char
ghci> break isUpper "isUpper"
("is","Upper")
```

Since we need only to match a single carriage return or newline at a time, examining each element of the list one by one is good enough for our needs.

The first equation of splitLines indicates that if we match an empty string, we have no further work to do.

In the second equation, we first apply break to our input string. The prefix is the substring before a line terminator, and the suffix is the remainder of the string. The suffix will include the line terminator, if any is present.

The pre : expression tells us that we should add the pre value to the front of the list of lines. We then use a case expression to inspect the suffix, so we can decide what to do next. The result of the case expression will be used as the second argument to the (:) list constructor.

The first pattern matches a string that begins with a carriage return, followed by a newline. The variable rest is bound to the remainder of the string. The other patterns are similar, so they ought to be easy to follow.

A prose description of a Haskell function isn't necessarily easy to follow. We can gain a better understanding by stepping into ghci and observing the behavior of the function in different circumstances.

Let's start by partitioning a string that doesn't contain any line terminators:

```
ghci> splitLines "foo"
["foo"]
```

Here, our application of break never finds a line terminator, so the suffix it returns is empty:

```
ghci> break isLineTerminator "foo"
("foo","")
```

The case expression in splitLines must thus be matching on the fourth branch, and we're finished. What about a slightly more interesting case?

```
ghci> splitLines "foo\r\nbar"
["foo","bar"]
```

Our first application of break gives us a nonempty suffix:

```
ghci> break isLineTerminator "foo\r\nbar"
("foo","\r\nbar")
```

Because the suffix begins with a carriage return followed by a newline, we match on the first branch of the case expression. This gives us pre bound to "foo", and suf bound to "bar". We apply splitLines recursively, this time on "bar" alone:

```
ghci> splitLines "bar"
["bar"]
```

The result is that we construct a list whose head is `"foo"` and whose tail is `["bar"]`:

```
ghci> "foo" : ["bar"]
["foo","bar"]
```

This sort of experimenting with `ghci` is a helpful way to understand and debug the behavior of a piece of code. It has an even more important benefit that is almost accidental in nature. It can be tricky to test complicated code from `ghci`, so we will tend to write smaller functions, which can further help the readability of our code.

This style of creating and reusing small, powerful pieces of code is a fundamental part of functional programming.

A Line-Ending Conversion Program

Let's hook our `splitLines` function into the little framework that we wrote earlier. Make a copy of the *InteractWith.hs* source file; let's call the new file *FixLines.hs*. Add the `splitLines` function to the new source file. Since our function must produce a single `String`, we must stitch the list of lines back together. The `Prelude` provides an `unlines` function that concatenates a list of strings, adding a newline to the end of each:

```
-- file: cho4/SplitLines.hs
fixLines :: String -> String
fixLines input = unlines (splitLines input)
```

If we replace the `id` function with `fixLines`, we can compile an executable that will convert a text file to our system's native line ending:

```
$ ghc --make FixLines
[1 of 1] Compiling Main             ( FixLines.hs, FixLines.o )
Linking FixLines ...
```

If you are on a Windows system, find and download a text file that was created on a Unix system (for example, *gpl-3.0.txt* [*http://www.gnu.org/licenses/gpl-3.0.txt*]). Open it in the standard Notepad text editor. The lines should all run together, making the file almost unreadable. Process the file using the `FixLines` command you just created, and open the output file in Notepad. The line endings should now be fixed up.

On Unix-like systems, the standard pagers and editors hide Windows line endings, making it more difficult to verify that `FixLines` is actually eliminating them. Here are a few commands that should help:

```
$ file gpl-3.0.txt
gpl-3.0.txt: ASCII English text
$ unix2dos gpl-3.0.txt
unix2dos: converting file gpl-3.0.txt to DOS format ...
$ file gpl-3.0.txt
gpl-3.0.txt: ASCII English text, with CRLF line terminators
```

Infix Functions

Usually, when we define or apply a function in Haskell, we write the name of the function, followed by its arguments. This notation is referred to as *prefix*, because the name of the function comes before its arguments.

If a function or constructor takes two or more arguments, we have the option of using it in *infix* form, where we place it *between* its first and second arguments. This allows us to use functions as infix operators.

To define or apply a function or value constructor using infix notation, we enclose its name in backtick characters (sometimes known as backquotes). Here are simple infix definitions of a function and a type:

```
-- file: ch04/Plus.hs
a `plus` b = a + b

data a `Pair` b = a `Pair` b
                  deriving (Show)

-- we can use the constructor either prefix or infix
foo = Pair 1 2
bar = True `Pair` "quux"
```

Since infix notation is purely a syntactic convenience, it does not change a function's behavior:

```
ghci> 1 `plus` 2
3
ghci> plus 1 2
3
ghci> True `Pair` "something"
True `Pair` "something"
ghci> Pair True "something"
True `Pair` "something"
```

Infix notation can often help readability. For instance, the Prelude defines a function, elem, that indicates whether a value is present in a list. If we employ elem using prefix notation, it is fairly easy to read:

```
ghci> elem 'a' "camogie"
True
```

If we switch to infix notation, the code becomes even easier to understand. It is now clear that we're checking to see if the value on the left is present in the list on the right:

```
ghci> 3 `elem` [1,2,4,8]
False
```

We see a more pronounced improvement with some useful functions from the Data.List module. The isPrefixOf function tells us if one list matches the beginning of another:

```
ghci> :module +Data.List
ghci> "foo" `isPrefixOf` "foobar"
True
```

The `isInfixOf` and `isSuffixOf` functions match anywhere in a list and at its end, respectively:

```
ghci> "needle" `isInfixOf` "haystack full of needle thingies"
True
ghci> "end" `isSuffixOf` "the end"
True
```

There is no hard-and-fast rule that dictates when you ought to use infix versus prefix notation, although prefix notation is far more common. It's best to choose whichever makes your code more readable in a specific situation.

Beware familiar notation in an unfamiliar language

A few other programming languages use backticks, but in spite of the visual similarities, the purpose of backticks in Haskell does not remotely resemble their meaning in, for example, Perl, Python, or Unix shell scripts.

The only legal thing we can do with backticks in Haskell is wrap them around the name of a function. We can't, for example, use them to enclose a complex expression whose value is a function. It might be convenient if we could, but that's not how the language is today.

Working with Lists

As the bread and butter of functional programming, lists deserve some serious attention. The standard `Prelude` defines dozens of functions for dealing with lists. Many of these will be indispensable tools, so it's important that we learn them early on.

For better or worse, this section is going to read a bit like a laundry list of functions. Why present so many functions at once? Because they are both easy to learn and absolutely ubiquitous. If we don't have this toolbox at our fingertips, we'll end up wasting time by reinventing simple functions that are already present in the standard libraries. So bear with us as we go through the list; the effort you'll save will be huge.

The `Data.List` module is the "real" logical home of all standard list functions. The `Prelude` merely re-exports a large subset of the functions exported by `Data.List`. Several useful functions in `Data.List` are *not* re-exported by the standard `Prelude`. As we walk through list functions in the sections that follow, we will explicitly mention those that are only in `Data.List`:

```
ghci> :module +Data.List
```

Because none of these functions is complex or takes more than about three lines of Haskell to write, we'll be brief in our descriptions of each. In fact, a quick and useful learning exercise is to write a definition of each function after you've read about it.

Basic List Manipulation

The length function tells us how many elements are in a list:

```
ghci> :type length
length :: [a] -> Int
ghci> length []
0
ghci> length [1,2,3]
3
ghci> length "strings are lists, too"
22
```

If you need to determine whether a list is empty, use the null function:

```
ghci> :type null
null :: [a] -> Bool
ghci> null []
True
ghci> null "plugh"
False
```

To access the first element of a list, use the head function:

```
ghci> :type head
head :: [a] -> a
ghci> head [1,2,3]
1
```

The converse, tail, returns all *but* the head of a list:

```
ghci> :type tail
tail :: [a] -> [a]
ghci> tail "foo"
"oo"
```

Another function, last, returns the very last element of a list:

```
ghci> :type last
last :: [a] -> a
ghci> last "bar"
'r'
```

The converse of last is init, which returns a list of all but the last element of its input:

```
ghci> :type init
init :: [a] -> [a]
ghci> init "bar"
"ba"
```

Several of the preceding functions behave poorly on empty lists, so be careful if you don't know whether or not a list is empty. What form does their misbehavior take?

```
ghci> head []
*** Exception: Prelude.head: empty list
```

Try each of the previous functions in ghci. Which ones crash when given an empty list?

Safely and Sanely Working with Crashy Functions

When we want to use a function such as head, where we know that it might blow up on us if we pass in an empty list, there initially might be a strong temptation to check the length of the list before we call head. Let's construct an artificial example to illustrate our point:

```
-- file: ch04/EfficientList.hs
myDumbExample xs = if length xs > 0
                   then head xs
                   else 'Z'
```

If we're coming from a language such as Perl or Python, this might seem like a perfectly natural way to write this test. Behind the scenes, Python lists are arrays, and Perl arrays are, well, arrays. So we necessarily know how long they are, and calling len(foo) or scalar(@foo) is a perfectly natural thing to do. But as with many other things, it's not a good idea to blindly transplant such an assumption into Haskell.

We've already seen the definition of the list algebraic data type many times, and we know that a list doesn't store its own length explicitly. Thus, the only way that length can operate is to walk the entire list.

Therefore, when we care only whether or not a list is empty, calling length isn't a good strategy. It can potentially do a lot more work than we want, if the list we're working with is finite. Since Haskell lets us easily create infinite lists, a careless use of length may even result in an infinite loop.

A more appropriate function to call here instead is null, which runs in constant time. Better yet, using null makes our code indicate what property of the list we really care about. Here are two improved ways of expressing myDumbExample:

```
-- file: ch04/EfficientList.hs
mySmartExample xs = if not (null xs)
                    then head xs
                    else 'Z'

myOtherExample (x:_) = x
myOtherExample [] = 'Z'
```

Partial and Total Functions

Functions that have only return values defined for a subset of valid inputs are called partial functions (calling error doesn't qualify as returning a value!). We call functions that return valid results over their entire input domains total functions.

It's always a good idea to know whether a function you're using is partial or total. Calling a partial function with an input that it can't handle is probably the single biggest source of straightforward, avoidable bugs in Haskell programs.

Some Haskell programmers go so far as to give partial functions names that begin with a prefix such as unsafe so that they can't shoot themselves in the foot accidentally.

It's arguably a deficiency of the standard Prelude that it defines quite a few "unsafe" partial functions, such as head, without also providing "safe" total equivalents.

More Simple List Manipulations

Haskell's name for the append function is (++):

```
ghci> :type (++)
(++) :: [a] -> [a] -> [a]
ghci> "foo" ++ "bar"
"foobar"
ghci> [] ++ [1,2,3]
[1,2,3]
ghci> [True] ++ []
[True]
```

The concat function takes a list of lists, all of the same type, and concatenates them into a single list:

```
ghci> :type concat
concat :: [[a]] -> [a]
ghci> concat [[1,2,3], [4,5,6]]
[1,2,3,4,5,6]
```

It removes one level of nesting:

```
ghci> concat [[[1,2],[3]], [[4],[5],[6]]]
[[1,2],[3],[4],[5],[6]]
ghci> concat (concat [[[1,2],[3]], [[4],[5],[6]]])
[1,2,3,4,5,6]
```

The reverse function returns the elements of a list in reverse order:

```
ghci> :type reverse
reverse :: [a] -> [a]
ghci> reverse "foo"
"oof"
```

For lists of Bool, the and and or functions generalize their two-argument cousins, (&&) and (||), over lists:

```
ghci> :type and
and :: [Bool] -> Bool
ghci> and [True,False,True]
False
ghci> and []
True
ghci> :type or
or :: [Bool] -> Bool
```

```
ghci> or [False,False,False,True,False]
True
ghci> or []
False
```

They have more useful cousins, all and any, which operate on lists of any type. Each one takes a predicate as its first argument; all returns True if that predicate succeeds on every element of the list, while any returns True if the predicate succeeds on at least one element of the list:

```
ghci> :type all
all :: (a -> Bool) -> [a] -> Bool
ghci> all odd [1,3,5]
True
ghci> all odd [3,1,4,1,5,9,2,6,5]
False
ghci> all odd []
True
ghci> :type any
any :: (a -> Bool) -> [a] -> Bool
ghci> any even [3,1,4,1,5,9,2,6,5]
True
ghci> any even []
False
```

Working with Sublists

The take function, which we already discussed in "Function Application" on page 22, returns a sublist consisting of the first *k* elements from a list. Its converse, drop, drops *k* elements from the start of the list:

```
ghci> :type take
take :: Int -> [a] -> [a]
ghci> take 3 "foobar"
"foo"
ghci> take 2 [1]
[1]
ghci> :type drop
drop :: Int -> [a] -> [a]
ghci> drop 3 "xyzzy"
"zy"
ghci> drop 1 []
[]
```

The splitAt function combines the functions take and drop, returning a pair of the input lists, split at the given index:

```
ghci> :type splitAt
splitAt :: Int -> [a] -> ([a], [a])
ghci> splitAt 3 "foobar"
("foo","bar")
```

The takeWhile and dropWhile functions take predicates. takeWhile takes elements from the beginning of a list as long as the predicate returns True, while dropWhile drops elements from the list as long as the predicate returns True:

```
ghci> :type takeWhile
takeWhile :: (a -> Bool) -> [a] -> [a]
ghci> takeWhile odd [1,3,5,6,8,9,11]
[1,3,5]
ghci> :type dropWhile
dropWhile :: (a -> Bool) -> [a] -> [a]
ghci> dropWhile even [2,4,6,7,9,10,12]
[7,9,10,12]
```

Just as splitAt "tuples up" the results of take and drop, the functions break (which we already saw in "Warming Up: Portably Splitting Lines of Text" on page 72) and span tuple up the results of takeWhile and dropWhile.

Each function takes a predicate; break consumes its input while its predicate fails, and span consumes while its predicate succeeds:

```
ghci> :type span
span :: (a -> Bool) -> [a] -> ([a], [a])
ghci> span even [2,4,6,7,9,10,11]
([2,4,6],[7,9,10,11])
ghci> :type break
break :: (a -> Bool) -> [a] -> ([a], [a])
ghci> break even [1,3,5,6,8,9,10]
([1,3,5],[6,8,9,10])
```

Searching Lists

As we've already seen, the elem function indicates whether a value is present in a list. It has a companion function, notElem:

```
ghci> :type elem
elem :: (Eq a) => a -> [a] -> Bool
ghci> 2 `elem` [5,3,2,1,1]
True
ghci> 2 `notElem` [5,3,2,1,1]
False
```

For a more general search, filter takes a predicate and returns every element of the list on which the predicate succeeds:

```
ghci> :type filter
filter :: (a -> Bool) -> [a] -> [a]
ghci> filter odd [2,4,1,3,6,8,5,7]
[1,3,5,7]
```

In Data.List, three predicates—isPrefixOf, isInfixOf, and isSuffixOf—let us test for the presence of sublists within a bigger list. The easiest way to use them is with infix notation.

The isPrefixOf function tells us whether its left argument matches the beginning of its right argument:

```
ghci> :module +Data.List
ghci> :type isPrefixOf
isPrefixOf :: (Eq a) => [a] -> [a] -> Bool
ghci> "foo" `isPrefixOf` "foobar"
True
ghci> [1,2] `isPrefixOf` []
False
```

The isInfixOf function indicates whether its left argument is a sublist of its right:

```
ghci> :module +Data.List
ghci> [2,6] `isInfixOf` [3,1,4,1,5,9,2,6,5,3,5,8,9,7,9]
True
ghci> "funk" `isInfixOf` "sonic youth"
False
```

The operation of isSuffixOf shouldn't need any explanation:

```
ghci> :module +Data.List
ghci> ".c" `isSuffixOf` "crashme.c"
True
```

Working with Several Lists at Once

The zip function takes two lists and "zips" them into a single list of pairs. The resulting list is the same length as the shorter of the two inputs:

```
ghci> :type zip
zip :: [a] -> [b] -> [(a, b)]
ghci> zip [12,72,93] "zippity"
[(12,'z'),(72,'i'),(93,'p')]
```

More useful is zipWith, which takes two lists and applies a function to each pair of elements, generating a list that is the same length as the shorter of the two:

```
ghci> :type zipWith
zipWith :: (a -> b -> c) -> [a] -> [b] -> [c]
ghci> zipWith (+) [1,2,3] [4,5,6]
[5,7,9]
```

Haskell's type system makes it an interesting challenge to write functions that take variable numbers of arguments.[*] So if we want to zip three lists together, we call zip3 or zipWith3, and so on, up to zip7 and zipWith7.

---

[*] Unfortunately, we do not have room to address that challenge in this book.

Special String-Handling Functions

We've already encountered the standard `lines` function and its standard counterpart `unlines` in the section "Warming Up: Portably Splitting Lines of Text" on page 72. Notice that `unlines` always places a newline on the end of its result:

```
ghci> lines "foo\nbar"
["foo","bar"]
ghci> unlines ["foo", "bar"]
"foo\nbar\n"
```

The `words` function splits an input string on any whitespace. Its counterpart, `unwords`, uses a single space to join a list of words:

```
ghci> words "the  \r  quick \t  brown\n\n\nfox"
["the","quick","brown","fox"]
ghci> unwords ["jumps", "over", "the", "lazy", "dog"]
"jumps over the lazy dog"
```

EXERCISES

1. Write your own "safe" definitions of the standard partial list functions, but make sure they never fail. As a hint, you might want to consider using the following types:

    ```
    -- file: ch04/ch04.exercises.hs
    safeHead :: [a] -> Maybe a
    safeTail :: [a] -> Maybe [a]
    safeLast :: [a] -> Maybe a
    safeInit :: [a] -> Maybe [a]
    ```

2. Write a function `splitWith` that acts similarly to `words` but takes a predicate and a list of any type, and then splits its input list on every element for which the predicate returns `False`:

    ```
    -- file: ch04/ch04.exercises.hs
    splitWith :: (a -> Bool) -> [a] -> [[a]]
    ```

3. Using the command framework from the earlier section "A Simple Command-Line Framework" on page 71, write a program that prints the first word of each line of its input.

4. Write a program that transposes the text in a file. For instance, it should convert `"hello\nworld\n"` to `"hw\neo\nlr\nll\nod\n"`.

How to Think About Loops

Unlike traditional languages, Haskell has neither a `for` loop nor a `while` loop. If we've got a lot of data to process, what do we use instead? There are several possible answers to this question.

Explicit Recursion

A straightforward way to make the jump from a language that has loops to one that doesn't is to run through a few examples, looking at the differences. Here's a C function that takes a string of decimal digits and turns them into an integer:

```
int as_int(char *str)
{
    int acc; /* accumulate the partial result */

    for (acc = 0; isdigit(*str); str++) {
    acc = acc * 10 + (*str - '0');
    }

    return acc;
}
```

Given that Haskell doesn't have any looping constructs, how should we think about representing a fairly straightforward piece of code such as this?

We don't have to start off by writing a type signature, but it helps to remind us of what we're working with:

```
-- file: ch04/IntParse.hs
import Data.Char (digitToInt) -- we'll need digitToInt shortly

asInt :: String -> Int
```

The C code computes the result incrementally as it traverses the string; the Haskell code can do the same. However, in Haskell, we can express the equivalent of a loop as a function. We'll call ours `loop` just to keep things nice and explicit:

```
-- file: ch04/IntParse.hs
loop :: Int -> String -> Int

asInt xs = loop 0 xs
```

That first parameter to `loop` is the accumulator variable we'll be using. Passing zero into it is equivalent to initializing the `acc` variable in C at the beginning of the loop.

Rather than leap into blazing code, let's think about the data we have to work with. Our familiar `String` is just a synonym for `[Char]`, a list of characters. The easiest way for us to get the traversal right is to think about the structure of a list: it's either empty or a single element followed by the rest of the list.

We can express this structural thinking directly by pattern matching on the list type's constructors. It's often handy to think about the easy cases first; here, that means we will consider the empty list case:

```
-- file: ch04/IntParse.hs
loop acc [] = acc
```

An empty list doesn't just mean "the input string is empty"; it's also the case that we'll encounter when we traverse all the way to the end of a nonempty list. So we don't want to "error out" if we see an empty list. Instead, we should do something sensible. Here, the sensible thing is to terminate the loop and return our accumulated value.

The other case we have to consider arises when the input list is not empty. We need to do something with the current element of the list, and something with the rest of the list:

```
-- file: ch04/IntParse.hs
loop acc (x:xs) = let acc' = acc * 10 + digitToInt x
                  in loop acc' xs
```

We compute a new value for the accumulator and give it the name `acc'`. We then call the `loop` function again, passing it the updated value `acc'` and the rest of the input list. This is equivalent to the loop starting another round in C.

Single quotes in variable names

Remember, a single quote is a legal character to use in a Haskell variable name, and it is pronounced "prime." There's a common idiom in Haskell programs involving a variable—say, `foo`—and another variable—say, `foo'`. We can usually assume that `foo'` is somehow related to `foo`. It's often a new value for `foo`, as just shown in our code.

Sometimes we'll see this idiom extended, such as `foo''`. Since keeping track of the number of single quotes tacked onto the end of a name rapidly becomes tedious, use of more than two in a row is thankfully rare. Indeed, even one single quote can be easy to miss, which can lead to confusion on the part of readers. It might be better to think of the use of single quotes as a coding convention that you should be able to recognize, and less as one that you should actually follow.

Each time the `loop` function calls itself, it has a new value for the accumulator, and it consumes one element of the input list. Eventually, it's going to hit the end of the list, at which time the [] pattern will match and the recursive calls will cease.

How well does this function work? For positive integers, it's perfectly cromulent:

```
ghci> asInt "33"
33
```

But because we were focusing on how to traverse lists, not error handling, our poor function misbehaves if we try to feed it nonsense:

```
ghci> asInt ""
0
ghci> asInt "potato"
*** Exception: Char.digitToInt: not a digit 'p'
```

We'll defer fixing our function's shortcomings to "Exercises" on page 97.

Because the last thing that `loop` does is simply call itself, it's an example of a tail recursive function. There's another common idiom in this code, too. Thinking about the structure of the list, and handling the empty and nonempty cases separately, is a kind of approach called *structural recursion.*

We call the nonrecursive case (when the list is empty) the *base case* (or sometimes the *terminating case*). We'll see people refer to the case where the function calls itself as the recursive case (surprise!), or they might give a nod to mathematical induction and call it the *inductive case.*

As a useful technique, structural recursion is not confined to lists; we can use it on other algebraic data types, too. We'll have more to say about it later.

What's the big deal about tail recursion?

In an imperative language, a loop executes in constant space. Lacking loops, we use tail recursive functions in Haskell instead. Normally, a recursive function allocates some space each time it applies itself, so it knows where to return to.

Clearly, a recursive function would be at a huge disadvantage relative to a loop if it allocated memory for every recursive application—this would require linear space instead of constant space. However, functional language implementations detect uses of tail recursion and transform tail recursive calls to run in constant space; this is called *tail call optimization* (TCO).

Few imperative language implementations perform TCO; this is why using any kind of ambitiously functional style in an imperative language often leads to memory leaks and poor performance.

Transforming Every Piece of Input

Consider another C function, `square`, which squares every element in an array:

```
void square(double *out, const double *in, size_t length)
{
    for (size_t i = 0; i < length; i++) {
    out[i] = in[i] * in[i];
    }
}
```

This contains a straightforward and common kind of loop, one that does exactly the same thing to every element of its input array. How might we write this loop in Haskell?

```
-- file: ch04/Map.hs
square :: [Double] -> [Double]

square (x:xs) = x*x : square xs
square []     = []
```

Our `square` function consists of two pattern-matching equations. The first "deconstructs" the beginning of a nonempty list, in order to get its head and tail. It squares the first element, then puts that on the front of a new list, which is constructed by calling square on the remainder of the empty list. The second equation ensures that square halts when it reaches the end of the input list.

The effect of square is to construct a new list that's the same length as its input list, with every element in the input list substituted with its square in the output list.

Here's another such C loop, one that ensures that every letter in a string is converted to uppercase:

```
#include <ctype.h>

char *uppercase(const char *in)
{
    char *out = strdup(in);

    if (out != NULL) {
    for (size_t i = 0; out[i] != '\0'; i++) {
        out[i] = toupper(out[i]);
    }
    }

    return out;
}
```

Let's look at a Haskell equivalent:

```
-- file: ch04/Map.hs
import Data.Char (toUpper)

upperCase :: String -> String

upperCase (x:xs) = toUpper x : upperCase xs
upperCase []     = []
```

Here, we're importing the toUpper function from the standard Data.Char module, which contains lots of useful functions for working with Char data.

Our upperCase function follows a similar pattern to our earlier square function. It terminates with an empty list when the input list is empty; when the input isn't empty, it calls toUpper on the first element, then constructs a new list cell from that and the result of calling itself on the rest of the input list.

These examples follow a common pattern for writing recursive functions over lists in Haskell. The base case handles the situation where our input list is empty. The *recursive case* deals with a nonempty list; it does something with the head of the list and calls itself recursively on the tail.

Mapping over a List

The square and upperCase functions that we just defined produce new lists that are the same lengths as their input lists, and they do only one piece of work per element. This is such a common pattern that Haskell's Prelude defines a function, map, in order to make it easier. map takes a function and applies it to every element of a list, returning a new list constructed from the results of these applications.

Here are our `square` and `upperCase` functions rewritten to use `map`:

```
-- file: ch04/Map.hs
square2 xs = map squareOne xs
    where squareOne x = x * x

upperCase2 xs = map toUpper xs
```

This is our first close look at a function that takes another function as its argument. We can learn a lot about what map does by simply inspecting its type:

```
ghci> :type map
map :: (a -> b) -> [a] -> [b]
```

The signature tells us that map takes two arguments. The first is a function that takes a value of one type, a, and returns a value of another type, b.

Because map takes a function as an argument, we refer to it as a *higher-order* function. (In spite of the name, there's nothing mysterious about higher-order functions; it's just a term for functions that take other functions as arguments, or return functions.)

Since map abstracts out the pattern common to our `square` and `upperCase` functions so that we can reuse it with less boilerplate, we can look at what those functions have in common and figure out how to implement it ourselves:

```
-- file: ch04/Map.hs
myMap :: (a -> b) -> [a] -> [b]

myMap f (x:xs) = f x : myMap f xs
myMap _ _      = []
```

 What are those wild cards doing there?

If you're new to functional programming, the reasons for matching patterns in certain ways won't always be obvious. For example, in the definition of myMap in the preceding code, the first equation binds the function we're mapping to the variable f, but the second uses wild cards for both parameters. What's going on?

We use a wild card in place of f to indicate that we aren't calling the function f on the righthand side of the equation. What about the list parameter? The list type has two constructors. We've already matched on the nonempty constructor in the first equation that defines myMap. By elimination, the constructor in the second equation is necessarily the empty list constructor, so there's no need to perform a match to see what its value really is.

As a matter of style, it is fine to use wild cards for well-known simple types such as lists and Maybe. For more complicated or less familiar types, it can be safer and more readable to name constructors explicitly.

We try out our myMap function to give ourselves some assurance that it behaves similarly to the standard map:

```
ghci> :module +Data.Char
ghci> map toLower "SHOUTING"
"shouting"
ghci> myMap toUpper "whispering"
"WHISPERING"
ghci> map negate [1,2,3]
[-1,-2,-3]
```

This pattern of spotting a repeated idiom, and then abstracting it so we can reuse (and write less!) code, is a common aspect of Haskell programming. While abstraction isn't unique to Haskell, higher-order functions make it remarkably easy.

Selecting Pieces of Input

Another common operation on a sequence of data is to comb through it for elements that satisfy some criterion. Here's a function that walks a list of numbers and returns those that are odd. Our code has a recursive case that's a bit more complex than our earlier functions—it puts a number in the list it returns only if the number is odd. Using a guard expresses this nicely:

```
-- file: ch04/Filter.hs
oddList :: [Int] -> [Int]

oddList (x:xs) | odd x      = x : oddList xs
               | otherwise = oddList xs
oddList _                   = []
```

Let's see that in action:

```
ghci> oddList [1,1,2,3,5,8,13,21,34]
[1,1,3,5,13,21]
```

Once again, this idiom is so common that the Prelude defines a function, filter, which we already introduced. It removes the need for boilerplate code to recurse over the list:

```
ghci> :type filter
filter :: (a -> Bool) -> [a] -> [a]
ghci> filter odd [3,1,4,1,5,9,2,6,5]
[3,1,1,5,9,5]
```

The filter function takes a predicate and applies it to every element in its input list, returning a list of only those for which the predicate evaluates to True. We'll revisit filter again later in this chapter in "Folding from the Right" on page 94.

Computing One Answer over a Collection

It is also common to reduce a collection to a single value. A simple example of this is summing the values of a list:

```
-- file: ch04/Sum.hs
mySum xs = helper 0 xs
    where helper acc (x:xs) = helper (acc + x) xs
          helper acc _      = acc
```

Our `helper` function is tail-recursive and uses an accumulator parameter, `acc`, to hold the current partial sum of the list. As we already saw with `asInt`, this is a "natural" way to represent a loop in a pure functional language.

For something a little more complicated, let's take a look at the Adler-32 checksum. It is a popular checksum algorithm; it concatenates two 16-bit checksums into a single 32-bit checksum. The first checksum is the sum of all input bytes, plus one. The second is the sum of all intermediate values of the first checksum. In each case, the sums are computed modulo 65521. Here's a straightforward, unoptimized Java implementation (it's safe to skip it if you don't read Java):

```java
public class Adler32
{
    private static final int base = 65521;

    public static int compute(byte[] data, int offset, int length)
    {
    int a = 1, b = 0;

    for (int i = offset; i < offset + length; i++) {
        a = (a + (data[i] & 0xff)) % base;
        b = (a + b) % base;
    }

    return (b << 16) | a;
    }
}
```

Although Adler-32 is a simple checksum, this code isn't particularly easy to read on account of the bit-twiddling involved. Can we do any better with a Haskell implementation?

```haskell
-- file: ch04/Adler32.hs
import Data.Char (ord)
import Data.Bits (shiftL, (.&.), (.|.))

base = 65521

adler32 xs = helper 1 0 xs
    where helper a b (x:xs) = let a' = (a + (ord x .&. 0xff)) `mod` base
                                  b' = (a' + b) `mod` base
                              in helper a' b' xs
          helper a b _      = (b `shiftL` 16) .|. a
```

This code isn't exactly easier to follow than the Java code, but let's look at what's going on. First of all, we've introduced some new functions. The `shiftL` function implements a logical shift left; `(.&.)` provides a bitwise "and"; and `(.|.)` provides a bitwise "or".

Once again, our `helper` function is tail-recursive. We've turned the two variables that we updated on every loop iteration in Java into accumulator parameters. When our recursion terminates on the end of the input list, we compute our checksum and return it.

If we take a step back, we can restructure our Haskell `adler32` to more closely resemble our earlier `mySum` function. Instead of two accumulator parameters, we can use a pair as the accumulator:

```
-- file: ch04/Adler32.hs
adler32_try2 xs = helper (1,0) xs
    where helper (a,b) (x:xs) =
              let a' = (a + (ord x .&. 0xff)) `mod` base
                  b' = (a' + b) `mod` base
              in helper (a',b') xs
          helper (a,b) _      = (b `shiftL` 16) .|. a
```

Why would we want to make this seemingly meaningless structural change? Because as we've already seen with `map` and `filter`, we can extract the common behavior shared by `mySum` and `adler32_try2` into a higher-order function. We can describe this behavior as "do something to every element of a list, updating an accumulator as we go, and returning the accumulator when we're done."

This kind of function is called a *fold*, because it "folds up" a list. There are two kinds of fold-over lists: `foldl` for folding from the left (the start), and `foldr` for folding from the right (the end).

The Left Fold

Here is the definition of `foldl`:

```
-- file: ch04/Fold.hs
foldl :: (a -> b -> a) -> a -> [b] -> a

foldl step zero (x:xs) = foldl step (step zero x) xs
foldl _    zero []     = zero
```

The `foldl` function takes a "step" function, an initial value for its accumulator, and a list. The "step" takes an accumulator and an element from the list and returns a new accumulator value. All `foldl` does is call the "stepper" on the current accumulator and an element of the list, and then passes the new accumulator value to itself recursively to consume the rest of the list.

We refer to `foldl` as a *left fold* because it consumes the list from left (the head) to right.

Here's a rewrite of `mySum` using `foldl`:

```
-- file: ch04/Sum.hs
foldlSum xs = foldl step 0 xs
    where step acc x = acc + x
```

That local function step just adds two numbers, so let's simply use the addition operator instead, and eliminate the unnecessary where clause:

```
-- file: ch04/Sum.hs
niceSum :: [Integer] -> Integer
niceSum xs = foldl (+) 0 xs
```

Notice how much simpler this code is than our original mySum. We're no longer using explicit recursion, because foldl takes care of that for us. We've simplified our problem down to two things: what the initial value of the accumulator should be (the second parameter to foldl) and how to update the accumulator (the (+) function). As an added bonus, our code is now shorter, too, which makes it easier to understand.

Let's take a deeper look at what foldl is doing here, by manually writing out each step in its evaluation when we call niceSum [1,2,3]:

```
-- file: ch04/Fold.hs
foldl (+) 0 (1:2:3:[])
          == foldl (+) (0 + 1)            (2:3:[])
          == foldl (+) ((0 + 1) + 2)      (3:[])
          == foldl (+) (((0 + 1) + 2) + 3) []
          ==           (((0 + 1) + 2) + 3)
```

We can rewrite adler32_try2 using foldl to let us focus on the details that are important:

```
-- file: ch04/Adler32.hs
adler32_foldl xs = let (a, b) = foldl step (1, 0) xs
                   in (b `shiftL` 16) .|. a
    where step (a, b) x = let a' = a + (ord x .&. 0xff)
                          in (a' `mod` base, (a' + b) `mod` base)
```

Here, our accumulator is a pair, so the result of foldl will be, too. We pull the final accumulator apart when foldl returns, and then bit-twiddle it into a "proper" checksum.

Why Use Folds, Maps, and Filters?

A quick glance reveals that adler32_foldl isn't really any shorter than adler32_try2. Why should we use a fold in this case? The advantage here lies in the fact that folds are extremely common in Haskell, and they have regular, predictable behavior.

This means that a reader with a little experience will have an easier time understanding a use of a fold than code that uses explicit recursion. A fold isn't going to produce any surprises, but the behavior of a function that recurses explicitly isn't immediately obvious. Explicit recursion requires us to read closely to understand exactly what's going on.

This line of reasoning applies to other higher-order library functions, including those we've already seen, map and filter. Because they're library functions with well-defined behavior, we need to learn what they do only once, and we'll have an advantage when we need to understand any code that uses them. These improvements in readability also carry over to writing code. Once we start to think with higher-order functions in mind, we'll produce concise code more quickly.

Folding from the Right

The counterpart to foldl is foldr, which folds from the right of a list:

```
-- file: ch04/Fold.hs
foldr :: (a -> b -> b) -> b -> [a] -> b

foldr step zero (x:xs) = step x (foldr step zero xs)
foldr _     zero []    = zero
```

Let's follow the same manual evaluation process with foldr (+) 0 [1,2,3] as we did with niceSum earlier in the section "The Left Fold" on page 92:

```
-- file: ch04/Fold.hs
foldr (+) 0 (1:2:3:[])
         == 1 +           foldr (+) 0 (2:3:[])
         == 1 + (2 +      foldr (+) 0 (3:[])
         == 1 + (2 + (3 + foldr (+) 0 []))
         == 1 + (2 + (3 + 0))
```

The difference between foldl and foldr should be clear from looking at where the parentheses and the empty list elements show up. With foldl, the empty list element is on the left, and all the parentheses group to the left. With foldr, the zero value is on the right, and the parentheses group to the right.

There is a lovely intuitive explanation of how foldr works: it replaces the empty list with the zero value, and replaces every constructor in the list with an application of the step function:

```
-- file: ch04/Fold.hs
1 : (2 : (3 : []))
1 + (2 + (3 + 0 ))
```

At first glance, foldr might seem less useful than foldl: what use is a function that folds from the right? But consider the Prelude's filter function, which we last encountered earlier in this chapter in "Selecting Pieces of Input" on page 90. If we write filter using explicit recursion, it will look something like this:

```
-- file: ch04/Fold.hs
filter :: (a -> Bool) -> [a] -> [a]
filter p []     = []
filter p (x:xs)
    | p x       = x : filter p xs
    | otherwise = filter p xs
```

Perhaps surprisingly, though, we can write filter as a fold, using foldr:

```
-- file: ch04/Fold.hs
myFilter p xs = foldr step [] xs
```

```
    where step x ys | p x       = x : ys
                    | otherwise = ys
```

This is the sort of definition that could cause us a headache, so let's examine it in a little depth. Like `foldl`, `foldr` takes a function and a base case (what to do when the input list is empty) as arguments. From reading the type of `filter`, we know that our `myFilter` function must return a list of the same type as it consumes, so the base case should be a list of this type, and the `step` helper function must return a list.

Since we know that `foldr` calls `step` on one element of the input list at a time, then with the accumulator as its second argument, `step`'s actions must be quite simple. If the predicate returns `True`, it pushes that element onto the accumulated list; otherwise, it leaves the list untouched.

The class of functions that we can express using `foldr` is called *primitive recursive*. A surprisingly large number of list manipulation functions are primitive recursive. For example, here's `map` written in terms of `foldr`:

```
-- file: ch04/Fold.hs
myMap :: (a -> b) -> [a] -> [b]

myMap f xs = foldr step [] xs
    where step x ys = f x : ys
```

In fact, we can even write `foldl` using `foldr`!

```
-- file: ch04/Fold.hs
myFoldl :: (a -> b -> a) -> a -> [b] -> a

myFoldl f z xs = foldr step id xs z
    where step x g a = g (f a x)
```

Understanding foldl in terms of foldr

If you want to set yourself a solid challenge, try to follow our definition of `foldl` using `foldr`. Be warned: this is not trivial! You might want to have the following tools at hand: some headache pills and a glass of water, ghci (so that you can find out what the `id` function does), and a pencil and paper.

You will want to follow the same manual evaluation process as we just outlined to see what `foldl` and `foldr` were really doing. If you get stuck, you may find the task easier after reading "Partial Function Application and Currying" on page 100.

Returning to our earlier intuitive explanation of what `foldr` does, another useful way to think about it is that it *transforms* its input list. Its first two arguments are "what to do with each head/tail element of the list," and "what to substitute for the end of the list."

The "identity" transformation with `foldr` thus replaces the empty list with itself and applies the list constructor to each head/tail pair:

```
-- file: ch04/Fold.hs
identity :: [a] -> [a]
identity xs = foldr (:) [] xs
```

It transforms a list into a copy of itself:

```
ghci> identity [1,2,3]
[1,2,3]
```

If `foldr` replaces the end of a list with some other value, this gives us another way to look at Haskell's list append function, (++):

```
ghci> [1,2,3] ++ [4,5,6]
[1,2,3,4,5,6]
```

All we have to do to append a list onto another is substitute that second list for the end of our first list:

```
-- file: ch04/Fold.hs
append :: [a] -> [a] -> [a]
append xs ys = foldr (:) ys xs
```

Let's try this out:

```
ghci> append [1,2,3] [4,5,6]
[1,2,3,4,5,6]
```

Here, we replace each list constructor with another list constructor, but we replace the empty list with the list we want to append onto the end of our first list.

As our extended treatment of folds should indicate, the `foldr` function is nearly as important a member of our list-programming toolbox as the more basic list functions we saw in "Working with Lists" on page 77. It can consume and produce a list incrementally, which makes it useful for writing lazy data-processing code.

Left Folds, Laziness, and Space Leaks

To keep our initial discussion simple, we use `foldl` throughout most of this section. This is convenient for testing, but we will never use `foldl` in practice. The reason has to do with Haskell's nonstrict evaluation. If we apply `foldl (+) [1,2,3]`, it evaluates to the expression $(((0 + 1) + 2) + 3)$. We can see this occur if we revisit the way in which the function gets expanded:

```
-- file: ch04/Fold.hs
foldl (+) 0 (1:2:3:[])
         == foldl (+) (0 + 1)              (2:3:[])
         == foldl (+) ((0 + 1) + 2)        (3:[])
         == foldl (+) (((0 + 1) + 2) + 3)  []
         ==           (((0 + 1) + 2) + 3)
```

The final expression will not be evaluated to 6 until its value is demanded. Before it is evaluated, it must be stored as a thunk. Not surprisingly, a thunk is more expensive to store than a single number, and the more complex the thunked expression, the more space it needs. For something cheap such as arithmetic, thunking an expression is more computationally expensive than evaluating it immediately. We thus end up paying both in space and in time.

When GHC is evaluating a thunked expression, it uses an internal stack to do so. Because a thunked expression could potentially be infinitely large, GHC places a fixed limit on the maximum size of this stack. Thanks to this limit, we can try a large thunked expression in ghci without needing to worry that it might consume all the memory:

```
ghci> foldl (+) 0 [1..1000]
500500
```

From looking at this expansion, we can surmise that this creates a thunk that consists of 1,000 integers and 999 applications of (+). That's a lot of memory and effort to represent a single number! With a larger expression, although the size is still modest, the results are more dramatic:

```
ghci> foldl (+) 0 [1..1000000]
*** Exception: stack overflow
```

On small expressions, foldl will work correctly but slowly, due to the thunking overhead that it incurs. We refer to this invisible thunking as a *space leak*, because our code is operating normally, but it is using far more memory than it should.

On larger expressions, code with a space leak will simply fail, as above. A space leak with foldl is a classic roadblock for new Haskell programmers. Fortunately, this is easy to avoid.

The Data.List module defines a function named foldl' that is similar to foldl, but does not build up thunks. The difference in behavior between the two is immediately obvious:

```
ghci> foldl  (+) 0 [1..1000000]
*** Exception: stack overflow
ghci> :module +Data.List
ghci> foldl' (+) 0 [1..1000000]
500000500000
```

Due to foldl's thunking behavior, it is wise to avoid this function in real programs, even if it doesn't fail outright, it will be unnecessarily inefficient. Instead, import Data.List and use foldl'.

EXERCISES

1. Use a fold (choosing the appropriate fold will make your code much simpler) to rewrite and improve upon the asInt function from the earlier section "Explicit Recursion" on page 85.

```
-- file: ch04/ch04.exercises.hs
asInt_fold :: String -> Int
```

2. Your function should behave as follows:

```
ghci> asInt_fold "101"
101
ghci> asInt_fold "-31337"
-31337
ghci> asInt_fold "1798"
1798
```

3. Extend your function to handle the following kinds of exceptional conditions by calling error:

```
ghci> asInt_fold ""
0
ghci> asInt_fold "-"
0
ghci> asInt_fold "-3"
-3
ghci> asInt_fold "2.7"
*** Exception: Char.digitToInt: not a digit '.'
ghci> asInt_fold "314159265358979323846"
564616105916946374
```

4. The asInt_fold function uses error, so its callers cannot handle errors. Rewrite the function to fix this problem:

```
-- file: ch04/ch04.exercises.hs
type ErrorMessage = String
asInt_either :: String -> Ei

ghci> asInt_either "33"
Right 33
ghci> asInt_either "foo"
Left "non-digit 'o'"
```

5. The Prelude function concat concatenates a list of lists into a single list and has the following type:

```
-- file: ch04/ch04.exercises.hs
concat :: [[a]] -> [a]
```

6. Write your own definition of concat using foldr.

7. Write your own definition of the standard takeWhile function, first using explicit recursion, and then foldr.

8. The Data.List module defines a function, groupBy, which has the following type:

```
-- file: ch04/ch04.exercises.hs
groupBy :: (a -> a -> Bool) -> [a] -> [[a]]
```

9. Use ghci to load the Data.List module and figure out what groupBy does, then write your own implementation using a fold.

10. How many of the following Prelude functions can you rewrite using list folds?

- any
- cycle
- words

- unlines

For those functions where you can use either `foldl'` or `foldr`, which is more appropriate in each case?

Further Reading

The article "A tutorial on the universality and expressiveness of fold" by Graham Hutton (*http://www.cs.nott.ac.uk/~gmh/fold.pdf*) is an excellent and in-depth tutorial that covers folds. It includes many examples of how to use simple, systematic calculation techniques to turn functions that use explicit recursion into folds.

Anonymous (lambda) Functions

In many of the function definitions we've seen so far, we've written short helper functions:

```
-- file: ch04/Partial.hs
isInAny needle haystack = any inSequence haystack
    where inSequence s = needle `isInfixOf` s
```

Haskell lets us write completely anonymous functions, which we can use to avoid the need to give names to our helper functions. Anonymous functions are often called "lambda" functions, in a nod to their heritage in lambda calculus. We introduce an anonymous function with a backslash character (\) pronounced *lambda*.[†] This is followed by the function's arguments (which can include patterns), and then an arrow (->) to introduce the function's body.

Lambdas are most easily illustrated by example. Here's a rewrite of `isInAny` using an anonymous function:

```
-- file: ch04/Partial.hs
isInAny2 needle haystack = any (\s -> needle `isInfixOf` s) haystack
```

We've wrapped the lambda in parentheses here so that Haskell can tell where the function body ends.

In every respect, anonymous functions behave identically to functions that have names, but Haskell places a few important restrictions on how we can define them. Most importantly, while we can write a normal function using multiple clauses containing different patterns and guards, a lambda can have only a single clause in its definition.

The limitation to a single clause restricts how we can use patterns in the definition of a lambda. We'll usually write a normal function with several clauses to cover different pattern matching possibilities:

[†] The backslash was chosen for its visual resemblance to the Greek letter lambda (λ). Although GHC can accept Unicode input, it correctly treats λ as a letter, not as a synonym for \.

```
-- file: ch04/Lambda.hs
safeHead (x:_) = Just x
safeHead _ = Nothing
```

But as we can't write multiple clauses to define a lambda, we must be certain that any patterns we use will match:

```
-- file: ch04/Lambda.hs
unsafeHead = \(x:_) -> x
```

This definition of unsafeHead will explode in our faces if we call it with a value on which pattern matching fails:

```
ghci> :type unsafeHead
unsafeHead :: [t] -> t
ghci> unsafeHead [1]
1
ghci> unsafeHead []
*** Exception: Lambda.hs:7:13-23: Non-exhaustive patterns in lambda
```

The definition typechecks, so it will compile, and the error will occur at runtime. The moral of this story is to be careful in how you use patterns when defining an anonymous function: make sure your patterns can't fail!

Another thing to notice about the isInAny and isInAny2 functions shown previously is that the first version, using a helper function that has a name, is a little easier to read than the version that plops an anonymous function into the middle. The named helper function doesn't disrupt the "flow" of the function in which it's used, and the judiciously chosen name gives us a little bit of information about what the function is expected to do.

In contrast, when we run across a lambda in the middle of a function body, we have to switch gears and read its definition fairly carefully to understand what it does. To help with readability and maintainability, then, we tend to avoid lambdas in many situations where we could use them to trim a few characters from a function definition. Very often, we'll use a partially applied function instead, resulting in clearer and more readable code than either a lambda or an explicit function. Don't know what a partially applied function is yet? Read on!

We don't intend these caveats to suggest that lambdas are useless, merely that we ought to be mindful of the potential pitfalls when we're thinking of using them. In later chapters, we will see that they are often invaluable as "glue."

Partial Function Application and Currying

You may wonder why the -> arrow is used for what seems to be two purposes in the type signature of a function:

```
ghci> :type dropWhile
dropWhile :: (a -> Bool) -> [a] -> [a]
```

It looks like the -> is separating the arguments to dropWhile from each other, but that it also separates the arguments from the return type. Iin fact -> has only one meaning: it denotes a function that takes an argument of the type on the left and returns a value of the type on the right.

The implication here is very important. In Haskell, *all functions take only one argument*. While dropWhile *looks* like a function that takes two arguments, it is actually a function of one argument, which returns a function that takes one argument. Here's a perfectly valid Haskell expression:

```
ghci> :module +Data.Char
ghci> :type dropWhile isSpace
dropWhile isSpace :: [Char] -> [Char]
```

Well, *that* looks useful. The value dropWhile isSpace is a function that strips leading whitespace from a string. How is this useful? As one example, we can use it as an argument to a higher order function:

```
ghci> map (dropWhile isSpace) [" a","f","    e"]
["a","f","e"]
```

Every time we supply an argument to a function, we can "chop" an element off the front of its type signature. Let's take zip3 as an example to see what we mean; this is a function that zips three lists into a list of three-tuples:

```
ghci> :type zip3
zip3 :: [a] -> [b] -> [c] -> [(a, b, c)]
ghci> zip3 "foo" "bar" "quux"
[('f','b','q'),('o','a','u'),('o','r','u')]
```

If we apply zip3 with just one argument, we get a function that accepts two arguments. No matter what arguments we supply to this compound function, its first argument will always be the fixed value we specified:

```
ghci> :type zip3 "foo"
zip3 "foo" :: [b] -> [c] -> [(Char, b, c)]
ghci> let zip3foo = zip3 "foo"
ghci> :type zip3foo
zip3foo :: [b] -> [c] -> [(Char, b, c)]
ghci> (zip3 "foo") "aaa" "bbb"
[('f','a','b'),('o','a','b'),('o','a','b')]
ghci> zip3foo "aaa" "bbb"
[('f','a','b'),('o','a','b'),('o','a','b')]
ghci> zip3foo [1,2,3] [True,False,True]
[('f',1,True),('o',2,False),('o',3,True)]
```

When we pass fewer arguments to a function than the function can accept, we call it *partial application* of the function—we're applying the function to only some of its arguments.

In the previous example, we have a partially applied function, zip3 "foo", and a new function, zip3foo. We can see that the type signatures of the two and their behavior are identical.

This applies just as well if we fix two arguments, giving us a function of just one argument:

```
ghci> let zip3foobar = zip3 "foo" "bar"
ghci> :type zip3foobar
zip3foobar :: [c] -> [(Char, Char, c)]
ghci> zip3foobar "quux"
[('f','b','q'),('o','a','u'),('o','r','u')]
ghci> zip3foobar [1,2]
[('f','b',1),('o','a',2)]
```

Partial function application lets us avoid writing tiresome throwaway functions. It's often more useful for this purpose than the anonymous functions we introduced earlier in this chapter in "Anonymous (lambda) Functions" on page 99. Looking back at the isInAny function we defined there, here's how we'd use a partially applied function instead of a named helper function or a lambda:

```
-- file: ch04/Partial.hs
isInAny3 needle haystack = any (isInfixOf needle) haystack
```

Here, the expression isInfixOf needle is the partially applied function. We're taking the function isInfixOf and "fixing" its first argument to be the needle variable from our parameter list. This gives us a partially applied function that has exactly the same type and behavior as the helper and lambda in our earlier definitions.

Partial function application is named *currying*, after the logician Haskell Curry (for whom the Haskell language is named).

As another example of currying in use, let's return to the list-summing function we wrote in "The Left Fold" on page 92:

```
-- file: ch04/Sum.hs
niceSum :: [Integer] -> Integer
niceSum xs = foldl (+) 0 xs
```

We don't need to fully apply foldl; we can omit the list xs from both the parameter list and the parameters to foldl, and we'll end up with a more compact function that has the same type:

```
-- file: ch04/Sum.hs
nicerSum :: [Integer] -> Integer
nicerSum = foldl (+) 0
```

Sections

Haskell provides a handy notational shortcut to let us write a partially applied function in infix style. If we enclose an operator in parentheses, we can supply its left or right argument inside the parentheses to get a partially applied function. This kind of partial application is called a *section*:

```
ghci> (1+) 2
3
ghci> map (*3) [24,36]
```

```
[72,108]
ghci> map (2^) [3,5,7,9]
[8,32,128,512]
```

If we provide the left argument inside the section, then calling the resulting function with one argument supplies the operator's right argument, and vice versa.

Recall that we can wrap a function name in backquotes to use it as an infix operator. This lets us use sections with functions:

```
ghci> :type (`elem` ['a'..'z'])
(`elem` ['a'..'z']) :: Char -> Bool
```

The preceding definition fixes elem's second argument, giving us a function that checks to see whether its argument is a lowercase letter:

```
ghci> (`elem` ['a'..'z']) 'f'
True
```

Using this as an argument to all, we get a function that checks an entire string to see if it's all lowercase:

```
ghci> all (`elem` ['a'..'z']) "Frobozz"
False
```

If we use this style, we can further improve the readability of our earlier isInAny3 function:

```
-- file: ch04/Partial.hs
isInAny4 needle haystack = any (needle `isInfixOf`) haystack
```

As-patterns

Haskell's tails function, in the Data.List module, generalizes the tail function we introduced earlier. Instead of returning one "tail" of a list, it returns *all* of them:

```
ghci> :m +Data.List
ghci> tail "foobar"
"oobar"
ghci> tail (tail "foobar")
"obar"
ghci> tails "foobar"
["foobar","oobar","obar","bar","ar","r",""]
```

Each of these strings is a *suffix* of the initial string, so tails produces a list of all suffixes, plus an extra empty list at the end. It always produces that extra empty list, even when its input list is empty:

```
ghci> tails []
[[]]
```

What if we want a function that behaves like tails but *only* returns the nonempty suffixes? One possibility would be for us to write our own version by hand. We'll use a new piece of notation, the @ symbol:

```
-- file: ch04/SuffixTree.hs
suffixes :: [a] -> [[a]]
suffixes xs@(_:xs') = xs : suffixes xs'
suffixes _ = []
```

The pattern xs@(_:xs') is called an *as-pattern*, and it means "bind the variable xs to the value that matches the right side of the @ symbol."

In our example, if the pattern after the @ matches, xs will be bound to the entire list that matched, and xs' will be bound to all but the head of the list (we used the wild card (_) pattern to indicate that we're not interested in the value of the head of the list):

```
ghci> tails "foo"
["foo","oo","o",""]
ghci> suffixes "foo"
["foo","oo","o"]
```

The as-pattern makes our code more readable. To see how it helps, let us compare a definition that lacks an as-pattern:

```
-- file: ch04/SuffixTree.hs
noAsPattern :: [a] -> [[a]]
noAsPattern (x:xs) = (x:xs) : noAsPattern xs
noAsPattern _ = []
```

Here, the list that we've deconstructed in the pattern match just gets put right back together in the body of the function.

As-patterns have a more practical use than simple readability: they can help us to share data instead of copying it. In our definition of noAsPattern, when we match (x:xs), we construct a new copy of it in the body of our function. This causes us to allocate a new list node at runtime. That may be cheap, but it isn't free. In contrast, when we defined suffixes, we reused the value xs that we matched with our as-pattern. Since we reuse an existing value, we avoid a little allocation.

Code Reuse Through Composition

It seems a shame to introduce a new function, suffixes, that does almost the same thing as the existing tails function. Surely we can do better?

Recall the init function we introduced in "Working with Lists" on page 77—it returns all but the last element of a list:

```
-- file: ch04/SuffixTree.hs
suffixes2 xs = init (tails xs)
```

This suffixes2 function behaves identically to suffixes, but it's a single line of code:

```
ghci> suffixes2 "foo"
["foo","oo","o"]
```

If we take a step back, we see the glimmer of a pattern. We're applying a function, then applying another function to its result. Let's turn that pattern into a function definition:

```
-- file: ch04/SuffixTree.hs
compose :: (b -> c) -> (a -> b) -> a -> c
compose f g x = f (g x)
```

We now have a function, compose, that we can use to "glue" two other functions together:

```
-- file: ch04/SuffixTree.hs
suffixes3 xs = compose init tails xs
```

Haskell's automatic currying lets us drop the xs variable, so we can make our definition even shorter:

```
-- file: ch04/SuffixTree.hs
suffixes4 = compose init tails
```

Fortunately, we don't need to write our own compose function. Plugging functions into each other like this is so common that the Prelude provides function composition via the (.) operator:

```
-- file: ch04/SuffixTree.hs
suffixes5 = init . tails
```

The (.) operator isn't a special piece of language syntax—it's just a normal operator:

```
ghci> :type (.)
(.) :: (b -> c) -> (a -> b) -> a -> c
ghci> :type suffixes
suffixes :: [a] -> [[a]]
ghci> :type suffixes5
suffixes5 :: [a] -> [[a]]
ghci> suffixes5 "foo"
["foo","oo","o"]
```

We can create new functions at any time by writing chains of composed functions, stitched together with (.), so long (of course) as the result type of the function on the right of each (.) matches the type of parameter that the function on the left can accept.

As an example, let's solve a simple puzzle. Count the number of words in a string that begins with a capital letter:

```
ghci> :module +Data.Char
ghci> let capCount = length . filter (isUpper . head) . words
ghci> capCount "Hello there, Mom!"
2
```

We can understand what this composed function does by examining its pieces. The (.) function is right-associative, so we will proceed from right to left:

```
ghci> :type words
words :: String -> [String]
```

The words function has a result type of [String], so whatever is on the left side of (.) must accept a compatible argument:

```
ghci> :type isUpper . head
isUpper . head :: [Char] -> Bool
```

This function returns True if a word begins with a capital letter (try it in ghci), so filter (isUpper . head) returns a list of Strings containing only words that begin with capital letters:

```
ghci> :type filter (isUpper . head)
filter (isUpper . head) :: [[Char]] -> [[Char]]
```

Since this expression returns a list, all that remains is to calculate the length of the list, which we do with another composition.

Here's another example, drawn from a real application. We want to extract a list of macro names from a C header file shipped with libpcap, a popular network packet-filtering library. The header file contains a large number definitions of the following form:

```
#define DLT_EN10MB     1      /* Ethernet (10Mb) */
#define DLT_EN3MB      2      /* Experimental Ethernet (3Mb) */
#define DLT_AX25       3      /* Amateur Radio AX.25 */
```

Our goal is to extract names such as DLT_EN10MB and DLT_AX25:

```
-- file: ch04/dlts.hs
import Data.List (isPrefixOf)

dlts :: String -> [String]

dlts = foldr step [] . lines
```

We treat an entire file as a string, split it up with lines, and then apply foldr step [] to the resulting list of lines. The step helper function operates on a single line:

```
-- file: ch04/dlts.hs
  where step l ds
          | "#define DLT_" `isPrefixOf` l = secondWord l : ds
          | otherwise                     = ds
        secondWord = head . tail . words
```

If we match a macro definition with our guard expression, we cons the name of the macro onto the head of the list we're returning; otherwise, we leave the list untouched.

While the individual functions in the body of secondWord are familiar to us by now, it can take a little practice to piece together a chain of compositions such as this. Let's walk through the procedure.

Once again, we proceed from right to left. The first function is words:

```
ghci> :type words
words :: String -> [String]
ghci> words "#define DLT_CHAOS     5"
["#define","DLT_CHAOS","5"]
```

We then apply tail to the result of words:

```
ghci> :type tail
tail :: [a] -> [a]
ghci> tail ["#define","DLT_CHAOS","5"]
```

```
["DLT_CHAOS","5"]
ghci> :type tail . words
tail . words :: String -> [String]
ghci> (tail . words) "#define DLT_CHAOS     5"
["DLT_CHAOS","5"]
```

Finally, applying head to the result of drop 1 . words will give us the name of our macro:

```
ghci> :type head . tail . words
head . tail . words :: String -> String
ghci> (head . tail . words) "#define DLT_CHAOS     5"
"DLT_CHAOS"
```

Use Your Head Wisely

After warning against unsafe list functions earlier in this chapter in "Safely and Sanely Working with Crashy Functions" on page 79, here we are calling both head and tail, two of those unsafe list functions. What gives?

In this case, we can assure ourselves by inspection that we're safe from a runtime failure. The pattern guard in the definition of step contains two words, so when we apply words to any string that makes it past the guard, we'll have a list of at least two elements: "#define" and some macro beginning with "DLT_".

This is the kind of reasoning we ought to do to convince ourselves that our code won't explode when we call partial functions. Don't forget our earlier admonition: calling unsafe functions such as this requires care and can often make our code more fragile in subtle ways. If for some reason we modified the pattern guard to only contain one word, we could expose ourselves to the possibility of a crash, as the body of the function assumes that it will receive two words.

Tips for Writing Readable Code

So far in this chapter, we've come across two tempting features of Haskell: tail recursion and anonymous functions. As nice as these are, we don't often want to use them.

Many list manipulation operations can be most easily expressed using combinations of library functions such as map, take, and filter. Without a doubt, it takes some practice to get used to using these. In return for our initial investment, we can write and read code more quickly, and with fewer bugs.

The reason for this is simple. A tail recursive function definition has the same problem as a loop in an imperative language: it's completely general. It might perform some filtering, some mapping, or who knows what else. We are forced to look in detail at the entire definition of the function to see what it's really doing. In contrast, map and most other list manipulation functions do only *one* thing. We can take for granted what these simple building blocks do and can focus on the idea the code is trying to express, not the minute details of how it's manipulating its inputs.

Two folds lie in the middle ground between tail recursive functions (with complete generality) and our toolbox of list manipulation functions (each of which does one thing). A fold takes more effort to understand than, say, a composition of map and filter that does the same thing, but it behaves more regularly and predictably than a tail recursive function. As a general rule, don't use a fold if you can compose some library functions, but otherwise try to use a fold in preference to a hand-rolled tail recursive loop.

As for anonymous functions, they tend to interrupt the "flow" of reading a piece of code. It is very often as easy to write a local function definition in a let or where clause and use that as it is to put an anonymous function into place. The relative advantages of a named function are twofold: we don't need to understand the function's definition when we're reading the code that uses it, and a well-chosen function name acts as a tiny piece of local documentation.

Space Leaks and Strict Evaluation

The foldl function that we discussed earlier is not the only place where space leaks can happen in Haskell code. We will use it to illustrate how nonstrict evaluation can sometimes be problematic and how to solve the difficulties that can arise.

Do you need to know all of this right now?

It is perfectly reasonable to skip this section until you encounter a space leak "in the wild." Provided you use foldr if you are generating a list, and foldl' instead of foldl otherwise, space leaks are unlikely to bother you in practice for a while.

Avoiding Space Leaks with seq

We refer to an expression that is not evaluated lazily as *strict*, so foldl' is a strict left fold. It bypasses Haskell's usual nonstrict evaluation through the use of a special function named seq:

```
-- file: ch04/Fold.hs
foldl' _    zero []     = zero
foldl' step zero (x:xs) =
    let new = step zero x
    in  new `seq` foldl' step new xs
```

This seq function has a peculiar type, hinting that it is not playing by the usual rules:

```
ghci> :type seq
seq :: a -> t -> t
```

It operates as follows: when a seq expression is evaluated, it forces its first argument to be evaluated, and then returns its second argument. It doesn't actually do anything with the first argument. seq exists solely as a way to force that value to be evaluated. Let's walk through a brief application to see what happens:

```
-- file: ch04/Fold.hs
foldl' (+) 1 (2:[])
```

This expands as follows:

```
-- file: ch04/Fold.hs
let new = 1 + 2
in new `seq` foldl' (+) new []
```

The use of seq forcibly evaluates new to 3 and returns its second argument:

```
-- file: ch04/Fold.hs
foldl' (+) 3 []
```

We end up with the following result:

```
-- file: ch04/Fold.hs
3
```

Thanks to seq, there are no thunks in sight.

Learning to Use seq

Without some direction, there is an element of mystery to using seq effectively. Here are some useful rules for using it well.

To have any effect, a seq expression must be the first thing evaluated in an expression:

```
-- file: ch04/Fold.hs
-- incorrect: seq is hidden by the application of someFunc
-- since someFunc will be evaluated first, seq may occur too late
hiddenInside x y = someFunc (x `seq` y)

-- incorrect: a variation of the above mistake
hiddenByLet x y z = let a = x `seq` someFunc y
                    in anotherFunc a z

-- correct: seq will be evaluated first, forcing evaluation of x
onTheOutside x y = x `seq` someFunc y
```

To strictly evaluate several values, chain applications of seq together:

```
-- file: ch04/Fold.hs
chained x y z = x `seq` y `seq` someFunc z
```

A common mistake is to try to use seq with two unrelated expressions:

```
-- file: ch04/Fold.hs
badExpression step zero (x:xs) =
    seq (step zero x)
        (badExpression step (step zero x) xs)
```

Here, the apparent intention is to evaluate `step zero x` strictly. Since the expression is duplicated in the body of the function, strictly evaluating the first instance of it will have no effect on the second. The use of `let` from the definition of `foldl'` just shows illustrates how to achieve this effect correctly.

When evaluating an expression, `seq` stops as soon as it reaches a constructor. For simple types such as numbers, this means that it will evaluate them completely. Algebraic data types are a different story. Consider the value `(1+2):(3+4):[]`. If we apply `seq` to this, it will evaluate the `(1+2)` thunk. Since it will stop when it reaches the first `(:)` constructor, it will have no effect on the second thunk. The same is true for tuples: `seq ((1+2),(3+4))` `True` will do nothing to the thunks inside the pair, since it immediately hits the pair's constructor.

If necessary, we can use normal functional programming techniques to work around these limitations:

```
-- file: ch04/Fold.hs
strictPair (a,b) = a `seq` b `seq` (a,b)

strictList (x:xs) = x `seq` x : strictList xs
strictList []     = []
```

It is important to understand that `seq` isn't free: it has to perform a check at runtime to see if an expression has been evaluated. Use it sparingly. For instance, while our `strictPair` function evaluates the contents of a pair up to the first constructor, it adds the overheads of pattern matching, two applications of `seq`, and the construction of a new tuple. If we were to measure its performance in the inner loop of a benchmark, we might find that it slows down the program.

Aside from its performance cost if overused, `seq` is not a miracle cure-all for memory consumption problems. Just because you *can* evaluate something strictly doesn't mean you *should*. Careless use of `seq` may do nothing at all, move existing space leaks around, or introduce new leaks.

The best guides to whether `seq` is necessary, and how well it is working, are performance measurement and profiling, which we will cover in Chapter 25. From a base of empirical measurement, you will develop a reliable sense of when `seq` is most useful.

CHAPTER 5

Writing a Library: Working with JSON Data

A Whirlwind Tour of JSON

In this chapter, we'll develop a small, but complete, Haskell library. Our library will manipulate and serialize data in a popular form known as JSON (JavaScript Object Notation).

The JSON language is a small, simple representation for storing and transmitting structured data—for example—over a network connection. It is most commonly used to transfer data from a web service to a browser-based JavaScript application. The JSON format is described at *http://www.json.org/*, and in greater detail by RFC 4627 (*http://www.ietf.org/rfc/rfc4627.txt*).

JSON supports four basic types of value—strings, numbers, Booleans, and a special value named null:

```
"a string" 12345 true
      null
```

The language provides two compound types: an *array* is an ordered sequence of values, and an *object* is an unordered collection of name/value pairs. The names in an object are always strings; the values in an object or array can be of any type:

```
[-3.14, true, null, "a string"]
      {"numbers": [1,2,3,4,5], "useful": false}
```

Representing JSON Data in Haskell

To work with JSON data in Haskell, we use an algebraic data type to represent the range of possible JSON types:

```
-- file: ch05/SimpleJSON.hs
data JValue = JString String
            | JNumber Double
            | JBool Bool
            | JNull
            | JObject [(String, JValue)]
            | JArray [JValue]
              deriving (Eq, Ord, Show)
```

For each JSON type, we supply a distinct value constructor. Some of these constructors
have parameters: if we want to construct a JSON string, we must provide a String value
as an argument to the JString constructor.

To start experimenting with this code, save the file *SimpleJSON.hs* in your editor, switch
to a ghci window, and load the file into ghci:

```
ghci> :load SimpleJSON
[1 of 1] Compiling SimpleJSON        ( SimpleJSON.hs, interpreted )
Ok, modules loaded: SimpleJSON.
ghci> JString "foo"
JString "foo"
ghci> JNumber 2.7
JNumber 2.7
ghci> :type JBool True
JBool True :: JValue
```

We can see how to use a constructor to take a normal Haskell value and turn it into a
JValue. To do the reverse, we use pattern matching. Here's a function that we can add
to *SimpleJSON.hs* that will extract a string from a JSON value for us. If the JSON value
actually contains a string, our function will wrap the string with the Just constructor;
otherwise, it will return Nothing:

```
-- file: ch05/SimpleJSON.hs
getString :: JValue -> Maybe String
getString (JString s) = Just s
getString _           = Nothing
```

When we save the modified source file, we can reload it in ghci and try the new definition. (The :reload command remembers the last source file we loaded, so we do not
need to name it explicitly.)

```
ghci> :reload
Ok, modules loaded: SimpleJSON.
ghci> getString (JString "hello")
Just "hello"
ghci> getString (JNumber 3)
Nothing
```

A few more accessor functions and we've got a small body of code to work with:

```
-- file: ch05/SimpleJSON.hs
getInt (JNumber n) = Just (truncate n)
getInt _           = Nothing

getDouble (JNumber n) = Just n
```

```
getDouble _              = Nothing

getBool (JBool b) = Just b
getBool _          = Nothing

getObject (JObject o) = Just o
getObject _            = Nothing

getArray (JArray a) = Just a
getArray _          = Nothing

isNull v               = v == JNull
```

The `truncate` function turns a floating-point or rational number into an integer by dropping the digits after the decimal point:

```
ghci> truncate 5.8
5
ghci> :module +Data.Ratio
ghci> truncate (22 % 7)
3
```

The Anatomy of a Haskell Module

A Haskell source file contains a definition of a single *module*. A module lets us determine which names inside the module are accessible from other modules.

A source file begins with a *module declaration*. This must precede all other definitions in the source file:

```
-- file: ch05/SimpleJSON.hs
module SimpleJSON
    (
      JValue(..)
    , getString
    , getInt
    , getDouble
    , getBool
    , getObject
    , getArray
    , isNull
    ) where
```

The word `module` is reserved. It is followed by the name of the module, which must begin with a capital letter. A source file must have the same *base name* (the component before the suffix) as the name of the module it contains. This is why our file *SimpleJSON.hs* contains a module named `SimpleJSON`.

Following the module name is a list of *exports*, enclosed in parentheses. The `where` keyword indicates that the body of the module follows.

The list of exports indicates which names in this module are visible to other modules. This lets us keep private code hidden from the outside world. The special notation

(..) that follows the name JValue indicates that we are exporting both the type and all of its constructors.

It might seem strange that we can export a type's name (i.e., its type constructor), but not its value constructors. The ability to do this is important: it lets us hide the details of a type from its users, making the type *abstract*. If we cannot see a type's value constructors, we cannot pattern match against a value of that type, nor can we construct a new value of that type. Later in this chapter, we'll discuss some situations in which we might want to make a type abstract.

If we omit the exports (and the parentheses that enclose them) from a module declaration, every name in the module will be exported:

```
-- file: ch05/Exporting.hs
module ExportEverything where
```

To export no names at all (which is rarely useful), we write an empty export list using a pair of parentheses:

```
-- file: ch05/Exporting.hs
module ExportNothing () where
```

Compiling Haskell Source

In addition to the ghci interpreter, the GHC distribution includes a compiler, ghc, that generates native code. If you are already familiar with a command-line compiler such as gcc or cl (the C++ compiler component of Microsoft's Visual Studio), you'll immediately be at home with ghc.

To compile a source file, we first open a terminal or command prompt window, and then invoke ghc with the name of the source file to compile:

```
ghc -c SimpleJSON.hs
```

The -c option tells ghc to generate only object code. If we were to omit the -c option, the compiler would attempt to generate a complete executable. That would fail, because we haven't written a main function, which GHC calls to start the execution of a standalone program.

After ghc completes, if we list the contents of the directory, it should contain two new files: *SimpleJSON.hi* and *SimpleJSON.o*. The former is an *interface file*, in which ghc stores information about the names exported from our module in machine-readable form. The latter is an *object file*, which contains the generated machine code.

Generating a Haskell Program and Importing Modules

Now that we've successfully compiled our minimal library, we'll write a tiny program to exercise it. Create the following file in your text editor and save it as *Main.hs*:

```
-- file: ch05/Main.hs
module Main () where

import SimpleJSON

main = print (JObject [("foo", JNumber 1), ("bar", JBool False)])
```

Notice the `import` directive that follows the module declaration. This indicates that we want to take all of the names that are exported from the `SimpleJSON` module and make them available in our module. Any `import` directives must appear in a group at the beginning of a module, after the module declaration, but before all other code. We cannot, for example, scatter them throughout a source file.

Our choice of naming for the source file and function is deliberate. To create an executable, ghc expects a module named `Main` that contains a function named `main` (the `main` function is the one that will be called when we run the program once we've built it).

```
ghc -o simple Main.hs SimpleJSON.o
```

This time around, we omit the `-c` option when we invoke ghc, so it will attempt to generate an executable. The process of generating an executable is called *linking*. As our command line suggests, ghc is perfectly able to both compile source files and link an executable in a single invocation.

We pass ghc a new option, `-o`, which takes one argument: the name of the executable that ghc should create.[*] Here, we've decided to name the program *simple*. On Windows, the program will have the suffix *.exe*, but on Unix variants, there will not be a suffix.

Finally, we supply the name of our new source file, *Main.hs*, and the object file we already compiled, *SimpleJSON.o*. We must explicitly list every one of our files that contains code that should end up in the executable. If we forget a source or object file, ghc will complain about *undefined symbols*, which indicates that some of the definitions that it needs are not provided in the files we supplied.

When compiling, we can pass ghc any mixture of source and object files. If ghc notices that it has already compiled a source file into an object file, it will only recompile the source file if we've modified it.

Once ghc has finished compiling and linking our *simple* program, we can run it from the command line.

Printing JSON Data

Now that we have a Haskell representation for JSON's types, we'd like to be able to take Haskell values and render them as JSON data.

---

[*] Memory aid: -o stands for *output* or *object* file.

There are a few ways we could go about this. Perhaps the most direct would be to write a rendering function that prints a value in JSON form. Once we're done, we'll explore some more interesting approaches.

```
-- file: ch05/PutJSON.hs
module PutJSON where

import Data.List (intercalate)
import SimpleJSON

renderJValue :: JValue -> String

renderJValue (JString s)   = show s
renderJValue (JNumber n)   = show n
renderJValue (JBool True)  = "true"
renderJValue (JBool False) = "false"
renderJValue JNull         = "null"

renderJValue (JObject o) = "{" ++ pairs o ++ "}"
  where pairs [] = ""
        pairs ps = intercalate ", " (map renderPair ps)
        renderPair (k,v)   = show k ++ ": " ++ renderJValue v

renderJValue (JArray a) = "[" ++ values a ++ "]"
  where values [] = ""
        values vs = intercalate ", " (map renderJValue vs)
```

Good Haskell style involves separating pure code from code that performs I/O. Our renderJValue function has no interaction with the outside world, but we still need to be able to print a JValue:

```
-- file: ch05/PutJSON.hs
putJValue :: JValue -> IO ()
putJValue v = putStrLn (renderJValue v)
```

Printing a JSON value is now easy.

Why should we separate the rendering code from the code that actually prints a value? This gives us flexibility. For instance, if we want to compress the data before writing it out and intermix rendering with printing, it would be much more difficult to adapt our code to that change in circumstances.

This idea of separating pure from impure code is powerful, and it is pervasive in Haskell code. Several Haskell compression libraries exist, all of which have simple interfaces: a compression function accepts an uncompressed string and returns a compressed string. We can use function composition to render JSON data to a string, and then compress to another string, postponing any decision on how to actually display or transmit the data.

Type Inference Is a Double-Edged Sword

A Haskell compiler's ability to infer types is powerful and valuable. Early on, you'll probably face a strong temptation to take advantage of type inference by omitting as many type declarations as possible. Let's simply make the compiler figure the whole lot out!

Skimping on explicit type information has a downside, one that disproportionately affects new Haskell programmers. As such a programmer, we're extremely likely to write code that will fail to compile due to straightforward type errors.

When we omit explicit type information, we force the compiler to figure out our intentions. It will infer types that are logical and consistent, but perhaps not at all what we meant. If we and the compiler unknowingly disagree about what is going on, it will naturally take us longer to find the source of our problem.

Suppose, for instance, that we write a function that we believe returns a String, but we don't write a type signature for it:

```
-- file: ch05/Trouble.hs
upcaseFirst (c:cs) = toUpper c -- forgot ":cs" here
```

Here, we want to uppercase the first character of a word, but we've forgotten to append the rest of the word onto the result. We think our function's type is String -> String, but the compiler will correctly infer its type as String -> Char. Let's say we then try to use this function somewhere else:

```
-- file: ch05/Trouble.hs
camelCase :: String -> String
camelCase xs = concat (map upcaseFirst (words xs))
```

When we try to compile this code or load it into ghci, we won't necessarily get an obvious error message:

```
ghci> :load Trouble
[1 of 1] Compiling Main             ( Trouble.hs, interpreted )

Trouble.hs:9:27:
    Couldn't match expected type `[Char]' against inferred type `Char'
      Expected type: [Char] -> [Char]
      Inferred type: [Char] -> Char
    In the first argument of `map', namely `upcaseFirst'
    In the first argument of `concat', namely
        `(map upcaseFirst (words xs))'
Failed, modules loaded: none.
```

Notice that the error is reported where we *use* the upcaseFirst function. If we're erroneously convinced that our definition and type for upcaseFirst are correct, we may end up staring at the wrong piece of code for quite a while, until enlightenment strikes.

Every time we write a type signature, we remove a degree of freedom from the type inference engine. This reduces the likelihood of divergence between our understanding of our code and the compiler's. Type declarations also act as shorthand for us as readers of our own code, making it easier for us to develop a sense of what must be going on.

This is not to say that we need to pepper every tiny fragment of code with a type declaration. It is, however, usually good form to add a signature to every top-level definition in our code. It's best to start out fairly aggressive with explicit type signatures, and slowly ease back as your mental model of how type checking works becomes more accurate.

Explicit types, undefined values, and error

The special value `undefined` will happily typecheck no matter where we use it, as will an expression like `error "argh!"`. It is especially important that we write type signatures when we use these. Suppose we use `undefined` or `error "write me"` as a placeholder in the body of a top-level definition. If we omit a type signature, we may be able to use the value we defined in places where a correctly typed version would be rejected by the compiler. This can easily lead us astray.

A More General Look at Rendering

Our JSON rendering code is narrowly tailored to the exact needs of our data types and the JSON formatting conventions. The output it produces can be unfriendly to human eyes. We will now look at rendering as a more generic task: how can we build a library that is useful for rendering data in a variety of situations?

We would like to produce output that is suitable either for human consumption (e.g., for debugging) or for machine processing. Libraries that perform this job are referred to as *pretty printers*. Several Haskell pretty-printing libraries already exist. We are creating one of our own not to replace them, but for the many useful insights we will gain into both library design and functional programming techniques.

We will call our generic pretty-printing module `Prettify`, so our code will go into a source file named *Prettify.hs*.

Naming

In our `Prettify` module, we will base our names on those used by several established Haskell pretty-printing libraries., which will give us a degree of compatibility with existing mature libraries.

To make sure that `Prettify` meets practical needs, we write a new JSON renderer that uses the `Prettify` API. After we're done, we'll go back and fill in the details of the `Prettify` module.

Instead of rendering straight to a string, our `Prettify` module will use an abstract type that we'll call `Doc`. By basing our generic rendering library on an abstract type, we can choose an implementation that is flexible and efficient. If we decide to change the underlying code, our users will not be able to tell.

We will name our new JSON rendering module *PrettyJSON.hs* and retain the name renderJValue for the rendering function. Rendering one of the basic JSON values is straightforward:

```
-- file: ch05/PrettyJSON.hs
renderJValue :: JValue -> Doc
renderJValue (JBool True)  = text "true"
renderJValue (JBool False) = text "false"
renderJValue JNull         = text "null"
renderJValue (JNumber num) = double num
renderJValue (JString str) = string str
```

Our Prettify module provides the text, double, and string functions.

Developing Haskell Code Without Going Nuts

Early on, as we come to grips with Haskell development, we have so many new, unfamiliar concepts to keep track of at one time that it can be a challenge to write code that compiles at all.

As we write our first substantial body of code, it's a *huge* help to pause every few minutes and try to compile what we've produced so far. Because Haskell is so strongly typed, if our code compiles cleanly, we're assured that we're not wandering too far off into the programming weeds.

One useful technique for quickly developing the skeleton of a program is to write placeholder, or *stub*, versions of types and functions. For instance, we just mentioned that our string, text and double functions would be provided by our Prettify module. If we don't provide definitions for those functions or the Doc type, our attempts to "compile early, compile often" with our JSON renderer will fail, as the compiler won't know anything about those functions. To avoid this problem, we write stub code that doesn't do anything:

```
-- file: ch05/PrettyStub.hs
import SimpleJSON

data Doc = ToBeDefined
           deriving (Show)

string :: String -> Doc
string str = undefined

text :: String -> Doc
text str = undefined

double :: Double -> Doc
double num = undefined
```

The special value undefined has the type a, so it always typechecks, no matter where we use it. If we attempt to evaluate it, it will cause our program to crash:

```
ghci> :type undefined
undefined :: a
ghci> undefined
*** Exception: Prelude.undefined
ghci> :type double
double :: Double -> Doc
ghci> double 3.14
*** Exception: Prelude.undefined
```

Even though we can't yet run our stubbed code, the compiler's type checker will ensure that our program is sensibly typed.

Pretty Printing a String

When we must pretty print a string value, JSON has moderately involved escaping rules that we must follow. At the highest level, a string is just a series of characters wrapped in quotes:

```
-- file: ch05/PrettyJSON.hs
string :: String -> Doc
string = enclose '"' '"' . hcat . map oneChar
```

Point-free style

This style of writing a definition exclusively as a composition of other functions is called *point-free style*. The use of the word *point* is not related to the "." character used for function composition. The term *point* is roughly synonymous (in Haskell) with *value*, so a *point-free* expression makes no mention of the values that it operates on.

Contrast this point-free definition of string with this "pointy" version, which uses a variable, s, to refer to the value on which it operates:

```
-- file: ch05/PrettyJSON.hs
pointyString :: String -> Doc
pointyString s = enclose '"' '"' (hcat (map oneChar s))
```

The enclose function simply wraps a Doc value with an opening and closing character:

```
-- file: ch05/PrettyJSON.hs
enclose :: Char -> Char -> Doc -> Doc
enclose left right x = char left <> x <> char right
```

We provide a (<>) function in our pretty-printing library. It appends two Doc values, so it's the Doc equivalent of (++):

```
-- file: ch05/PrettyStub.hs
(<>) :: Doc -> Doc -> Doc
a <> b = undefined
```

```
char :: Char -> Doc
char c = undefined
```

Our pretty-printing library also provides hcat, which concatenates multiple Doc values into one—it's the analogue of concat for lists:

```
-- file: ch05/PrettyStub.hs
hcat :: [Doc] -> Doc
hcat xs = undefined
```

Our string function applies the oneChar function to every character in a string, concatenates the lot, and encloses the result in quotes. The oneChar function escapes or renders an individual character:

```
-- file: ch05/PrettyJSON.hs
oneChar :: Char -> Doc
oneChar c = case lookup c simpleEscapes of
              Just r -> text r
              Nothing | mustEscape c -> hexEscape c
                      | otherwise    -> char c
    where mustEscape c = c < ' ' || c == '\x7f' || c > '\xff'

simpleEscapes :: [(Char, String)]
simpleEscapes = zipWith ch "\b\n\f\r\t\\\"/" "bnfrt\\\"/"
    where ch a b = (a, ['\\',b])
```

The simpleEscapes value is a list of pairs. We call a list of pairs an *association list*, or *alist* for short. Each element of our alist associates a character with its escaped representation:

```
ghci> take 4 simpleEscapes
[('\b',"\\b"),('\n',"\\n"),('\f',"\\f"),('\r',"\\r")]
```

Our case expression attempts to see whether our character has a match in this alist. If we find the match, we emit it; otherwise, we might need to escape the character in a more complicated way. If so, we perform this escaping. Only if neither kind of escaping is required do we emit the plain character. To be conservative, printable ASCII characters are the only unescaped characters we emit.

The more complicated escaping involves turning a character into the string "\u" followed by a four-character sequence of hexadecimal digits representing the numeric value of the Unicode character:

```
-- file: ch05/PrettyJSON.hs
smallHex :: Int -> Doc
smallHex x = text "\\u"
          <> text (replicate (4 - length h) '0')
          <> text h
    where h = showHex x ""
```

The showHex function comes from the Numeric library (you will need to import this at the beginning of *Prettify.hs*) and returns a hexadecimal representation of a number:

```
ghci> showHex 114111 ""
"1bdbf"
```

The replicate function is provided by the Prelude and builds a fixed-length repeating list of its argument:

```
ghci> replicate 5 "foo"
["foo","foo","foo","foo","foo"]
```

There's a wrinkle: the four-digit encoding that smallHex provides can only represent Unicode characters up to 0xffff. Valid Unicode characters can range up to 0x10ffff. To properly represent a character above 0xffff in a JSON string, we follow some complicated rules to split it into two, which gives us an opportunity to perform some bit-level manipulation of Haskell numbers:

```
-- file: ch05/PrettyJSON.hs
astral :: Int -> Doc
astral n = smallHex (a + 0xd800) <> smallHex (b + 0xdc00)
    where a = (n `shiftR` 10) .&. 0x3ff
          b = n .&. 0x3ff
```

The shiftR function comes from the Data.Bits module and shifts a number to the right. The (.&.) function, also from Data.Bits, performs a bit-level *and* of two values:

```
ghci> 0x10000 `shiftR` 4    :: Int
4096
ghci> 7 .&. 2    :: Int
2
```

Now that we've written smallHex and astral, we can provide a definition for hexEscape:

```
-- file: ch05/PrettyJSON.hs
hexEscape :: Char -> Doc
hexEscape c | d < 0x10000 = smallHex d
            | otherwise   = astral (d - 0x10000)
  where d = ord c
```

Arrays and Objects, and the Module Header

Compared to strings, pretty printing arrays and objects is a snap. We already know that the two are visually similar: each starts with an opening character, followed by a series of values separated with commas, followed by a closing character. Let's write a function that captures the common structure of arrays and objects:

```
-- file: ch05/PrettyJSON.hs
series :: Char -> Char -> (a -> Doc) -> [a] -> Doc
series open close item = enclose open close
                        . fsep . punctuate (char ',') . map item
```

We'll start by interpreting this function's type. It takes an opening and closing character, then a function that knows how to pretty print a value of some unknown type a, followed by a list of values of type a. It then returns a value of type Doc.

Notice that although our type signature mentions four parameters, we listed only three in the definition of the function. We are just following the same rule that lets us simplify a definiton such as myLength xs = length xs to myLength = length.

We have already written enclose, which wraps a Doc value in opening and closing characters. The fsep function will live in our Prettify module. It combines a list of Doc values into one, possibly wrapping lines if the output will not fit on a single line:

```
-- file: ch05/PrettyStub.hs
fsep :: [Doc] -> Doc
fsep xs = undefined
```

By now, you should be able to define your own stubs in *Prettify.hs*, following the examples we have supplied. We will not explicitly define any more stubs.

The punctuate function will also live in our Prettify module, and we can define it in terms of functions for which we've already written stubs:

```
-- file: ch05/Prettify.hs
punctuate :: Doc -> [Doc] -> [Doc]
punctuate p []     = []
punctuate p [d]    = [d]
punctuate p (d:ds) = (d <> p) : punctuate p ds
```

With this definition of series, pretty printing an array is entirely straightforward. We add this equation to the end of the block we've already written for our renderJValue function:

```
-- file: ch05/PrettyJSON.hs
renderJValue (JArray ary) = series '[' ']' renderJValue ary
```

To pretty print an object, we need to do only a little more work. For each element, we have both a name and a value to deal with:

```
-- file: ch05/PrettyJSON.hs
renderJValue (JObject obj) = series '{' '}' field obj
    where field (name,val) = string name
                          <> text ": "
                          <> renderJValue val
```

Writing a Module Header

Now that we have written the bulk of our *PrettyJSON.hs* file, we must go back to the top and add a module declaration:

```
-- file: ch05/PrettyJSON.hs
module PrettyJSON
    (
      renderJValue
    ) where

import Numeric (showHex)
import Data.Char (ord)
import Data.Bits (shiftR, (.&.))
```

```
import SimpleJSON (JValue(..))
import Prettify (Doc, (<>), char, double, fsep, hcat, punctuate, text,
                 compact, pretty)
```

We export just one name from this module: renderJValue, our JSON rendering function. The other definitions in the module exist purely to support renderJValue, so there's no reason to make them visible to other modules.

Regarding imports, the Numeric and Data.Bits modules are distributed with GHC. We've already written the SimpleJSON module and filled our Prettify module with skeletal definitions. Notice that there's no difference in the way we import standard modules from those we've written ourselves.

With each import directive, we explicitly list each of the names we want to bring into our module's namespace. This is not required. If we omit the list of names, all of the names exported from a module will be available to us. However, it's generally a good idea to write an explicit import list for the following reasons:

- An explicit list makes it clear which names we're importing from where. This will make it easier for a reader to look up documentation if he encounters an unfamiliar function.

- Occasionally, a library maintainer will remove or rename a function. If a function disappears from a third-party module that we use, any resulting compilation error is likely to happen long after we've written the module. The explicit list of imported names can act as a reminder to ourselves of where we had been importing the missing name from, which will help us to pinpoint the problem more quickly.

- It is possible that someone will add a name to a module that is identical to a name already in our own code. If we don't use an explicit import list, we'll end up with the same name in our module twice. If we use that name, GHC will report an error due to the ambiguity. An explicit list lets us avoid the possibility of accidentally importing an unexpected new name.

This idea of using explicit imports is a guideline that usually makes sense, not a hard-and-fast rule. Occasionally, we'll need so many names from a module that listing each one becomes messy. In other cases, a module might be so widely used that a moderately experienced Haskell programmer will probably know which names come from that module.

Fleshing Out the Pretty-Printing Library

In our Prettify module, we represent our Doc type as an algebraic data type:

```
-- file: ch05/Prettify.hs
data Doc = Empty
         | Char Char
         | Text String
         | Line
```

```
      | Concat Doc Doc
      | Union Doc Doc
        deriving (Show,Eq)
```

Observe that the Doc type is actually a tree. The Concat and Union constructors create an internal node from two other Doc values, while the Empty and other simple constructors build leaves.

In the header of our module, we will export the name of the type, but none of its constructors. This will prevent modules that use the Doc type from creating and pattern matching against Doc values.

Instead, to create a Doc, a user of the Prettify module will call a function that we provide. Here are the simple construction functions. As we add real definitions, we must replace any stubbed versions already in the *Prettify.hs* source file:

```
-- file: ch05/Prettify.hs
empty :: Doc
empty = Empty

char :: Char -> Doc
char c = Char c

text :: String -> Doc
text "" = Empty
text s  = Text s

double :: Double -> Doc
double d = text (show d)
```

The Line constructor represents a line break. The line function creates *hard* line breaks, which always appear in the pretty printer's output. Sometimes we'll want a *soft* line break, which is only used if a line is too wide to fit in a window or page (we'll introduce a softline function shortly):

```
-- file: ch05/Prettify.hs
line :: Doc
line = Line
```

Almost as simple as the basic constructors is the (<>) function, which concatenates two Doc values:

```
-- file: ch05/Prettify.hs
(<>) :: Doc -> Doc -> Doc
Empty <> y = y
x <> Empty = x
x <> y = x `Concat` y
```

We pattern-match against Empty so that concatenating a Doc value with Empty on the left or right will have no effect, which keeps us from bloating the tree with useless values:

```
ghci> text "foo" <> text "bar"
Concat (Text "foo") (Text "bar")
ghci> text "foo" <> empty
Text "foo"
```

```
ghci> empty <> text "bar"
Text "bar"
```

A mathematical moment

If we briefly put on our mathematical hats, we can say that Empty is the identity under concatenation, since nothing happens if we concatenate a Doc value with Empty. In a similar vein, 0 is the identity for adding numbers, and 1 is the identity for multiplying them. Taking the mathematical perspective has useful practical consequences, as we will see in a number of places throughout this book.

Our hcat and fsep functions concatenate a list of Doc values into one. In "Exercises" on page 130 and in "How to Think About Loops" on page 84, we mentioned that we could define concatenation for lists using foldr:

```
-- file: ch05/Concat.hs
concat :: [[a]] -> [a]
concat = foldr (++) []
```

Since (<>) is analogous to (++), and empty to [], we can see how we might write hcat and fsep as folds, too:

```
-- file: ch05/Prettify.hs
hcat :: [Doc] -> Doc
hcat = fold (<>)

fold :: (Doc -> Doc -> Doc) -> [Doc] -> Doc
fold f = foldr f empty
```

The definition of fsep depends on several other functions:

```
-- file: ch05/Prettify.hs
fsep :: [Doc] -> Doc
fsep = fold (</>)

(</>) :: Doc -> Doc -> Doc
x </> y = x <> softline <> y

softline :: Doc
softline = group line
```

These take a little explaining. The softline function should insert a newline if the current line has become too wide, or a space otherwise. How can we do this if our Doc type doesn't contain any information about rendering? Our answer is that every time we encounter a soft newline, we maintain *two* alternative representations of the document, using the Union constructor:

```
-- file: ch05/Prettify.hs
group :: Doc -> Doc
group x = flatten x `Union` x
```

Our flatten function replaces a Line with a space, turning two lines into one longer line:

```
-- file: ch05/Prettify.hs
flatten :: Doc -> Doc
flatten (x `Concat` y) = flatten x `Concat` flatten y
flatten Line           = Char ' '
flatten (x `Union` _)  = flatten x
flatten other          = other
```

Notice that we always call flatten on the left element of a Union: the left of each Union is always the same width (in characters) as, or wider than, the right. We'll make use of this property in our rendering functions that follow.

Compact Rendering

We frequently need to use a representation for a piece of data that contains as few characters as possible. For example, if we're sending JSON data over a network connection, there's no sense in laying it out nicely. The software on the far end won't care whether the data is pretty or not, and the added whitespace needed to make the layout look good would add a lot of overhead.

For these cases, and because it's a simple piece of code to start with, we provide a bare-bones compact rendering function:

```
-- file: ch05/Prettify.hs
compact :: Doc -> String
compact x = transform [x]
    where transform [] = ""
          transform (d:ds) =
              case d of
                Empty        -> transform ds
                Char c       -> c : transform ds
                Text s       -> s ++ transform ds
                Line         -> '\n' : transform ds
                a `Concat` b -> transform (a:b:ds)
                _ `Union` b  -> transform (b:ds)
```

The compact function wraps its argument in a list and applies the transform helper function to it. The transform function treats its argument as a stack of items to process, where the first element of the list is the top of the stack.

The transform function's (d:ds) pattern breaks the stack into its head, d, and the remainder, ds. In our case expression, the first several branches recurse on ds, consuming one item from the stack for each recursive application. The last two branches add items in front of ds; the Concat branch adds both elements to the stack, while the Union branch ignores its left element, on which we called flatten, and adds its right element to the stack.

We have now fleshed out enough of our original skeletal definitions that we can try out our compact function in ghci:

```
ghci> let value = renderJValue (JObject [("f", JNumber 1), ("q", JBool True)])
ghci> :type value
value :: Doc
```

```
ghci> putStrLn (compact value)
{"f": 1.0,
"q": true
}
```

To better understand how the code works, let's look at a simpler example in more detail:

```
ghci> char 'f' <> text "oo"
Concat (Char 'f') (Text "oo")
ghci> compact (char 'f' <> text "oo")
"foo"
```

When we apply `compact`, it turns its argument into a list and applies `transform` (the degree of indentation below reflects the depth of recursion):

- The `transform` function receives a one-item list, which matches the `(d:ds)` pattern. Thus d is the value `Concat (Char 'f') (Text "oo")`, and ds is the empty list, `[]`.

  Since d's constructor is `Concat`, the `Concat` pattern matches in the `case` expression. On the righthand side, we add `Char 'f'` and `Text "oo"` to the stack and then apply `transform`, recursively.

- The `transform` function receives a two-item list, again matching the `(d:ds)` pattern. The variable d is bound to `Char 'f'`, and ds to `[Text "oo"]`.

  — The `case` expression matches in the `Char` branch. On the righthand side, we use `(:)` to construct a list whose head is `'f'`, and whose body is the result of a recursive application of `transform`.

    - The recursive invocation receives a one-item list. The variable d is bound to `Text "oo"`, and ds to `[]`.

      The `case` expression matches in the `Text` branch. On the righthand side, we use `(++)` to concatenate `"oo"` with the result of a recursive application of `transform`.

      — In the final invocation, `transform` is invoked with an empty list and returns an empty string.

    - The result is `"oo" ++ ""`.

  - The result is `'f' : "oo" ++ ""`.

True Pretty Printing

While our `compact` function is useful for machine-to-machine communication, its result is not always easy for a human to follow: there's very little information on each line. To generate more readable output, we'll write another function, `pretty`. Compared to `compact`, `pretty` takes one extra argument: the maximum width of a line, in columns (we're assuming that our typeface is of fixed width):

```
-- file: ch05/Prettify.hs
pretty :: Int -> Doc -> String
```

To be more precise, this Int parameter controls the behavior of pretty when it encounters a softline. Only at a softline does pretty have the option of either continuing the current line or beginning a new one. Elsewhere, we must strictly follow the directives set out by the person using our pretty-printing functions.

Here's the core of our implementation:

```
-- file: ch05/Prettify.hs
pretty width x = best 0 [x]
    where best col (d:ds) =
              case d of
                Empty        -> best col ds
                Char c       -> c :  best (col + 1) ds
                Text s       -> s ++ best (col + length s) ds
                Line         -> '\n' : best 0 ds
                a `Concat` b -> best col (a:b:ds)
                a `Union` b  -> nicest col (best col (a:ds))
                                           (best col (b:ds))
          best _ _ = ""

          nicest col a b | (width - least) `fits` a = a
                         | otherwise                = b
                         where least = min width col
```

Our best helper function takes two arguments: the number of columns emitted so far on the current line and the list of remaining Doc values to process.

In the simple cases, best updates the col variable in straightforward ways as it consumes the input. Even the Concat case is obvious: we push the two concatenated components onto our stack/list, and we don't touch col.

The interesting case involves the Union constructor. Recall that we applied flatten to the left element and did nothing to the right. Also, remember that flatten replaces newlines with spaces. Therefore, our job is to see which (if either) of the two layouts —the flattened one or the original—will fit into our width restriction.

To do this, we write a small helper function that determines whether a single line of a rendered Doc value will fit into a given number of columns:

```
-- file: ch05/Prettify.hs
fits :: Int -> String -> Bool
w `fits` _  | w < 0 = False
w `fits` ""         = True
w `fits` ('\n':_)   = True
w `fits` (c:cs)     = (w - 1) `fits` cs
```

Following the Pretty Printer

In order to understand how this code works, let's first consider a simple Doc value:

```
ghci> empty </> char 'a'
Concat (Union (Char ' ') Line) (Char 'a')
```

We'll apply pretty 2 on this value. When we first apply best, the value of col is zero. It matches the Concat case, pushes the values Union (Char ' ') Line and Char 'a' onto the stack, and applies itself recursively. In the recursive application, it matches on Union (Char ' ') Line.

At this point, we're going to ignore Haskell's usual order of evaluation. This keeps our explanation of what's going on simple, without changing the end result. We now have two subexpressions: best 0 [Char ' ', Char 'a'] and best 0 [Line, Char 'a']. The first evaluates to " a", and the second to "\na". We then substitute these into the outer expression to give nicest 0 " a" "\na".

To figure out what the result of nicest is here, we do a little substitution. The values of width and col are 0 and 2, respectively, so least is 0, and width - least is 2. We quickly evaluate 2 `fits` " a" in ghci:

```
ghci> 2 `fits` " a"
True
```

Since this evaluates to True, the result of nicest here is " a".

If we apply our pretty function to the same JSON data that we did earlier, we can see that it produces different output depending on the width that we give it:

```
ghci> putStrLn (pretty 10 value)
{"f": 1.0,
"q": true
}
ghci> putStrLn (pretty 20 value)
{"f": 1.0, "q": true
}
ghci> putStrLn (pretty 30 value)
{"f": 1.0, "q": true }
```

EXERCISES

1. Our current pretty printer is spartan so that it will fit within our space constraints, but there are a number of useful improvements we can make.

   Write a function, fill, with the following type signature:

   ```
   -- file: ch05/Prettify.hs
   fill :: Int -> Doc -> Doc
   ```

   It should add spaces to a document until it is the given number of columns wide. If it is already wider than this value, it should not add any spaces.

2. Our pretty printer does not take nesting into account. Whenever we open parentheses, braces, or brackets, any lines that follow should be indented so that they are aligned with the opening character until a matching closing character is encountered.

   Add support for nesting, with a controllable amount of indentation:

```
-- file: ch05/Prettify.hs
fill :: Int -> Doc -> Doc
```

Creating a Package

The Haskell community has built a standard set of tools, named Cabal, that help with building, installing, and distributing software. Cabal organizes software as a *package*. A package contains one library, and possibly several executable programs.

Writing a Package Description

To do anything with a package, Cabal needs a description of it. This is contained in a text file whose name ends with the suffix *.cabal*. This file belongs in the top-level directory of your project. It has a simple format, which we'll describe next.

A Cabal package must have a name. Usually, the name of the package matches the name of the *.cabal* file. We'll call our package mypretty, so our file is *mypretty.cabal*. Often, the directory that contains a *.cabal* file will have the same name as the package, e.g., mypretty.

A package description begins with a series of global properties, which apply to every library and executable in the package:

```
Name:        mypretty
Version:     0.1

-- This is a comment.  It stretches to the end of the line.
```

Package names must be unique. If you create and install a package that has the same name as a package already present on your system, GHC will get very confused.

The global properties include a substantial amount of information that is intended for human readers, not Cabal itself:

```
Synopsis:    My pretty printing library, with JSON support
Description:
  A simple pretty-printing library that illustrates how to
  develop a Haskell library.
Author:      Real World Haskell
Maintainer:  nobody@realworldhaskell.org
```

As the Description field indicates, a field can span multiple lines, provided they're indented.

Also included in the global properties is license information. Most Haskell packages are licensed under the BSD license, which Cabal calls BSD3.[†] (Obviously, you're free to

---

[†] The "3" in BSD3 refers to the number of clauses in the license. An older version of the BSD license contained 4 clauses, but it is no longer used.

choose whatever license you think is appropriate.) The optional License-File field lets us specify the name of a file that contains the exact text of our package's licensing terms.

The features supported by successive versions of Cabal evolve over time, so it's wise to indicate what versions of Cabal we expect to be compatible with. The features we are describing are supported by versions 1.2 and higher of Cabal:

```
Cabal-Version: >= 1.2
```

To describe an individual library within a package, we write a *library section*. The use of indentation here is significant; the contents of a section must be indented:

```
library
  Exposed-Modules: Prettify
                   PrettyJSON
                   SimpleJSON
  Build-Depends:   base >= 2.0
```

The Exposed-Modules field contains a list of modules that should be available to users of this package. An optional field, Other-Modules, contains a list of *internal* modules. These are required for this library to function, but will not be visible to users.

The Build-Depends field contains a comma-separated list of packages that our library requires to build. For each package, we can optionally specify the range of versions with which this library is known to work. The base package contains many of the core Haskell modules, such as the Prelude, so it's effectively always required.

Figuring out build dependencies

We don't have to guess or do any research to establish which packages we depend on. If we try to build our package without a Build-Depends field, compilation will fail with a useful error message. Here's an example where we commented out the dependency on the base package:

```
$ runghc Setup build
Preprocessing library mypretty-0.1...
Building mypretty-0.1...

PrettyJSON.hs:8:7:
    Could not find module `Data.Bits':
      it is a member of package base, which is hidden
```

The error message makes it clear that we need to add the base package, even though base is already installed. Forcing us to be explicit about every package we need has a practical benefit: a command-line tool named cabal-install will automatically download, build, and install a package and all of the packages it depends on.

GHC's Package Manager

GHC includes a simple package manager that tracks which packages are installed, and what the versions of those packages are. A command-line tool named `ghc-pkg` lets us work with its package databases.

We say *databases* because GHC distinguishes between *system-wide* packages, which are available to every user, and *per-user* packages, which are only visible to the current user. The per-user database lets us avoid the need for administrative privileges to install packages.

The `ghc-pkg` command provides subcommands to address different tasks. Most of the time, we'll need only two of them. The `ghc-pkg list` command lets us see what packages are installed. When we want to uninstall a package, `ghc-pkg unregister` tells GHC that we won't be using a particular package any longer. (We will have to manually delete the installed files ourselves.)

Setting Up, Building, and Installing

In addition to a *.cabal* file, a package must contain a *setup* file. This allows Cabal's build process to be heavily customized (if a package needs it). The simplest setup file looks like this:

```
-- file: ch05/Setup.hs
#!/usr/bin/env runhaskell
import Distribution.Simple
main = defaultMain
```

We save this file under the name *Setup.hs*.

Once we write the *.cabal* and *Setup.hs* files, there are three steps left:

1. To instruct Cabal how to build and where to install a package, we run a simple command:

   ```
   $ runghc Setup configure
   ```

   This ensures that the packages we need are available, and it stores settings to be used later by other Cabal commands.

   If we do not provide any arguments to `configure`, Cabal will install our package in the system-wide package database. To install it into our home directory and our personal package database, we must provide a little more information:

2. We build the package:

   ```
   $ runghc Setup build
   ```

3. If this succeeds, we can install the package. We don't need to indicate where to install to—Cabal will use the settings we provided in the `configure` step. It will install to our own directory and update GHC's per-user package database.

Practical Pointers and Further Reading

GHC already bundles a pretty-printing library, `Text.PrettyPrint.HughesPJ`. It provides the same basic API as our example but a much richer and more useful set of pretty-printing functions. We recommend using it, rather than writing your own.

John Hughes introduced the design of the `HughesPJ` pretty printer "The Design of a Pretty-Printing library" (*http://citeseer.ist.psu.edu/hughes95design.html*). The library was subsequently improved by Simon Peyton Jones, hence the name. Hughes's paper is long, but well worth reading for his discussion of how to design a library in Haskell.

In this chapter, our pretty-printing library is based on a simpler system described by Philip Wadler in "A prettier printer" (*http://citeseerx.ist.psu.edu/viewdoc/summary?doi =10.1.1.19.635*). His library was extended by Daan Leijen; this version is available for download from Hackage as *wl-pprint*. If you use the `cabal` command-line tool, you can download, build, and install it in one step with `cabal install wl-pprint`.

CHAPTER 6

Using Typeclasses

Typeclasses are among the most powerful features in Haskell. They allow us to define generic interfaces that provide a common feature set over a wide variety of types. Typeclasses are at the heart of some basic language features such as equality testing and numeric operators. Before we talk about what exactly typeclasses are, though, we'd like to explain the need for them.

The Need for Typeclasses

Let's imagine that for some unfathomable reason, the designers of the Haskell language neglected to implement the equality test ==. Once you get over your shock at hearing this, you resolve to implement your own equality tests. Your application consists of a simple Color type, and so your first equality test is for this type. Your first attempt might look like this:

```
-- file: ch06/naiveeq.hs
data Color = Red | Green | Blue

colorEq :: Color -> Color -> Bool
colorEq Red   Red   = True
colorEq Green Green = True
colorEq Blue  Blue  = True
colorEq _     _     = False
```

You can test this with ghci:

```
ghci> :load naiveeq.hs
[1 of 1] Compiling Main             ( naiveeq.hs, interpreted )
Ok, modules loaded: Main.
ghci> colorEq Red Red
True
ghci> colorEq Red Green
False
```

Now, let's say that you want to add an equality test for Strings. Since a Haskell String is a list of characters, we can write a simple function to perform that test. For simplicity, we cheat a bit and use the == operator here to illustrate:

```
-- file: ch06/naiveeq.hs
stringEq :: [Char] -> [Char] -> Bool

-- Match if both are empty
stringEq [] [] = True

-- If both start with the same char, check the rest
stringEq (x:xs) (y:ys) = x == y && stringEq xs ys

-- Everything else doesn't match
stringEq _ _ = False
```

You should now be able to see a problem: we have to use a function with a different name for every different type that we want to be able to compare. That's inefficient and annoying. It's much more convenient to be able to just use == to compare anything. It may also be useful to write generic functions such as /= that could be implemented in terms of ==, and valid for almost anything. By having a generic function that can compare anything, we can also make our code generic: if a piece of code needs only to compare things, then it ought to be able to accept any data type that the compiler knows how to compare. What's more, if new data types are added later, the existing code shouldn't have to be modified.

Haskell's typeclasses are designed to address all of these things.

What Are Typeclasses?

Typeclasses define a set of functions that can have different implementations depending on the type of data they are given. Typeclasses may look like the objects of object-oriented programming, but they are truly quite different.

Let's use typeclasses to solve our equality dilemma from the previous section. To begin with, we must define the typeclass itself. We want a function that takes two parameters, both the same type, and returns a Bool indicating whether or not they are equal. We don't care what that type is, but we just want two items of that type. Here's our first definition of a typeclass:

```
-- file: ch06/eqclasses.hs
class BasicEq a where
    isEqual :: a -> a -> Bool
```

This says that we are declaring a typeclass named BasicEq, and we'll refer to instance types with the letter a. An instance type of this typeclass is any type that implements the functions defined in the typeclass. This typeclass defines one function. That function takes two parameters—both corresponding to instance types—and returns a Bool.

When is a class not a class?

The keyword to define a typeclass in Haskell is class. Unfortunately, this may be confusing for those of you coming from an object-oriented background, as we are not really defining the same thing.

On the first line, the name of the parameter a was chosen arbitrarily—we could have used any name. The key is that, when you list the types of your functions, you must use that name to refer to instance types.

Let's look at this in ghci. Recall that you can type :type in ghci to have it show you the type of something. Let's see what it says about isEqual:

```
*Main> :type isEqual
isEqual :: (BasicEq a) => a -> a -> Bool
```

You can read that this way: "For all types a, so long as a is an instance of BasicEq, isEqual takes two parameters of type a and returns a Bool." Let's take a quick look at defining isEqual for a particular type:

```
-- file: ch06/eqclasses.hs
instance BasicEq Bool where
    isEqual True  True  = True
    isEqual False False = True
    isEqual _     _     = False
```

You can also use ghci to verify that we can now use isEqual on Bools but not on any other type:

```
ghci> :load eqclasses.hs
[1 of 1] Compiling Main             ( eqclasses.hs, interpreted )
Ok, modules loaded: Main.
ghci> isEqual False False
True
ghci> isEqual False True
False
ghci> isEqual "Hi" "Hi"

<interactive>:1:0:
    No instance for (BasicEq [Char])
      arising from a use of `isEqual' at <interactive>:1:0-16
    Possible fix: add an instance declaration for (BasicEq [Char])
    In the expression: isEqual "Hi" "Hi"
    In the definition of `it': it = isEqual "Hi" "Hi"
```

Notice that when we tried to compare two strings, ghci recognized that we hadn't provided an instance of BasicEq for String. It therefore didn't know how to compare a String and suggested that we could fix the problem by defining an instance of Basi cEq for [Char], which is the same as String.

We'll go into more detail on defining instances in the next section "Declaring Typeclass Instances" on page 139. First, though, let's continue to look at ways to define typeclasses. In this example, a not-equal-to function might be useful. Here's what we might say to define a typeclass with two functions:

```
-- file: ch06/eqclasses.hs
class BasicEq2 a where
    isEqual2    :: a -> a -> Bool
    isNotEqual2 :: a -> a -> Bool
```

Someone providing an instance of `BasicEq2` will be required to define two functions: `isEqual2` and `isNotEqual2`.

While our definition of `BasicEq2` is fine, it seems that we're making extra work for ourselves. Logically speaking, if we know what `isEqual` or `isNotEqual` would return, we know how to figure out what the other function would return, for all types. Rather than making users of the typeclass define both functions for all types, we can provide default implementations for them. Then, users will only have to implement one function.[*] Here's an example that shows how to do this:

```
-- file: ch06/eqclasses.hs
class BasicEq3 a where
    isEqual3 :: a -> a -> Bool
    isEqual3 x y = not (isNotEqual3 x y)

    isNotEqual3 :: a -> a -> Bool
    isNotEqual3 x y = not (isEqual3 x y)
```

People implementing this class must provide an implementation of at least one function. They can implement both if they wish, but they will not be required to. While we did provide defaults for both functions, each function depends on the presence of the other to calculate an answer. If we don't specify at least one, the resulting code would be an endless loop. Therefore, at least one function must always be implemented.

With `BasicEq3`, we have provided a class that does very much the same thing as Haskell's built-in == and /= operators. In fact, these operators are defined by a typeclass that looks almost identical to `BasicEq3`. The Haskell 98 Report defines a typeclass that implements equality comparison. Here is the code for the built-in `Eq` typeclass. Note how similar it is to our `BasicEq3` typeclass:

```
class  Eq a  where
    (==), (/=) :: a -> a -> Bool

        -- Minimal complete definition:
        --      (==) or (/=)
    x /= y     =  not (x == y)
    x == y     =  not (x /= y)
```

---

[*] We provided a default implementation of both functions, which gives an implementer of instances a choice: he can pick which one he implements. We could have provided a default for only one function, which would force users to implement the other every time. As it is, a user can implement one or both, as he sees fit.

Declaring Typeclass Instances

Now that you know how to define typeclasses, it's time to learn how to define instances of typeclasses. Recall that types are made instances of a particular typeclass by implementing the functions necessary for that typeclass.

Recall our attempt to create a test for equality over a Color type back in "The Need for Typeclasses" on page 135. Now let's see how we could make that same Color type a member of the BasicEq3 class:

```
-- file: ch06/eqclasses.hs
instance BasicEq3 Color where
    isEqual3 Red Red = True
    isEqual3 Green Green = True
    isEqual3 Blue Blue = True
    isEqual3 _ _ = False
```

Notice that we provide essentially the same function as we used in "The Need for Typeclasses" on page 135. In fact, the implementation is identical. However, in this case, we can use isEqual3 on *any* type that we declare is an instance of BasicEq3, not just this one color type. We could define equality tests for anything from numbers to graphics using the same basic pattern. In fact, as you will see in "Equality, Ordering, and Comparisons" on page 148, this is exactly how you can make Haskell's == operator work for your own custom types.

Note also that the BasicEq3 class defined both isEqual3 and isNotEqual3, but we implemented only one of them in the Color instance. That's because of the default implementation contained in BasicEq3. Since we didn't explicitly define isNotEqual3, the compiler automatically uses the default implementation given in the BasicEq3 declaration.

Important Built-in Typeclasses

Now that we've discussed defining your own typeclasses and making your types instances of typeclasses, it's time to introduce you to typeclasses that are a standard part of the Haskell Prelude. As we mentioned at the beginning of this chapter, typeclasses are at the core of some important aspects of the language. We'll cover the most common ones here. For more details, the Haskell library reference is a good resource. It will give you a description of the typeclasses and usually also will tell you which functions you must implement to have a complete definition.

Show

The Show typeclass is used to convert values to Strings. It is perhaps most commonly used to convert numbers to Strings, but it is defined for so many types that it can be used to convert quite a bit more. If you have defined your own types, making them instances of Show will make it easy to display them in ghci or print them out in programs.

The most important function of Show is show. It takes one argument—the data to convert. It returns a String representing that data. ghci reports the type of show like this:

```
ghci> :type show
show :: (Show a) => a -> String
```

Let's look at some examples of converting values to strings:

```
ghci> show 1
"1"
ghci> show [1, 2, 3]
"[1,2,3]"
ghci> show (1, 2)
"(1,2)"
```

Remember that ghci displays results as they would be entered into a Haskell program. So the expression show 1 returns a single-character string containing the digit 1. That is, the quotes are not part of the string itself. We can make that clear by using putStrLn:

```
ghci> putStrLn (show 1)
1
ghci> putStrLn (show [1,2,3])
[1,2,3]
```

You can also use show on Strings:

```
ghci> show "Hello!"
"\"Hello!\""
ghci> putStrLn (show "Hello!")
"Hello!"
ghci> show ['H', 'i']
"\"Hi\""
ghci> putStrLn (show "Hi")
"Hi"
ghci> show "Hi, \"Jane\""
"\"Hi, \\\"Jane\\\"\""
ghci> putStrLn (show "Hi, \"Jane\"")
"Hi, \"Jane\""
```

Running show on Strings can be confusing. Since show generates a result that is suitable for a Haskell literal, it adds quotes and escaping suitable for inclusion in a Haskell program. ghci also uses show to display results, so quotes and escaping get added twice. Using putStrLn can help make this difference clear.

You can define a Show instance for your own types easily. Here's an example:

```
-- file: ch06/eqclasses.hs
instance Show Color where
    show Red   = "Red"
    show Green = "Green"
    show Blue  = "Blue"
```

This example defines an instance of Show for our type Color (see "The Need for Typeclasses" on page 135). The implementation is simple: we define a function show. That's all that's needed.

The Show typeclass

Show is usually used to define a String representation for data that is useful for a machine to parse back with Read. Haskell programmers generally write custom functions to format data attractively for end users, if this representation would be different than expected via Show.

Read

The Read typeclass is essentially the opposite of Show. It defines functions that will take a String, parse it, and return data in any type that is a member of Read. The most useful function in Read is read. You can ask ghci for its type like this:

```
ghci> :type read
read :: (Read a) => String -> a
```

Here's an example illustrating the use of read and show:

```
-- file: ch06/read.hs
main = do
        putStrLn "Please enter a Double:"
        inpStr <- getLine
        let inpDouble = (read inpStr)::Double
        putStrLn ("Twice " ++ show inpDouble ++ " is " ++ show (inpDouble * 2))
```

This is a simple example of read and show together. Notice that we gave an explicit type of Double when processing the read. That's because read returns a value of type Read a => a, and show expects a value of type Show a => a. There are many types that have instances defined for both Read and Show. Without knowing a specific type, the compiler must guess from these many types which one is needed. In situations such as this, it may often choose Integer. If we want to accept floating-point input, this wouldn't work, so we provide an explicit type.

A note about defaulting

In most cases, if the explicit Double type annotation were omitted, the compiler would refuse to guess a common type and simply give an error. The fact that it could default to Integer here is a special case arising from the fact that the literal 2 is treated as an Integer unless a different type is expected for it.

You can see the same effect at work if you try to use read on the ghci command line. ghci uses show internally to display results, meaning that you can encounter this ambiguous typing problem there as well. You'll need to explicitly give types for your read results in ghci as shown here:

```
ghci> read "5"

<interactive>:1:0:
    Ambiguous type variable `a' in the constraint:
```

```
`Read a' arising from a use of `read' at <interactive>:1:0-7
    Probable fix: add a type signature that fixes these type variable(s)
ghci> :type (read "5")
(read "5") :: (Read a) => a
ghci> (read "5")::Integer
5
ghci> (read "5")::Double
5.0
```

Recall the type of read: (Read a) => String -> a. The a here is the type of each instance of Read. The particular parsing function that is called depends upon the type that is expected from the return value of read. Let's see how that works:

```
ghci> (read "5.0")::Double
5.0
ghci> (read "5.0")::Integer
*** Exception: Prelude.read: no parse
```

Notice the error when trying to parse 5.0 as an Integer. The interpreter selects a different instance of Read when the return value was expected to be Integer than it did when a Double was expected. The Integer parser doesn't accept decimal points and caused an exception to be raised.

The Read class provides for some fairly complicated parsers. You can define a simple parser by providing an implementation for the readsPrec function. Your implementation can return a list containing exactly one tuple on a successful parse, or it can return an empty list on an unsuccessful parse. Here's an example implementation:

```
-- file: ch06/eqclasses.hs
instance Read Color where
    -- readsPrec is the main function for parsing input
    readsPrec _ value =
        -- We pass tryParse a list of pairs.  Each pair has a string
        -- and the desired return value.  tryParse will try to match
        -- the input to one of these strings.
        tryParse [("Red", Red), ("Green", Green), ("Blue", Blue)]
        where tryParse [] = []    -- If there is nothing left to try, fail
              tryParse ((attempt, result):xs) =
                      -- Compare the start of the string to be parsed to the
                      -- text we are looking for.
                      if (take (length attempt) value) == attempt
                         -- If we have a match, return the result and the
                         -- remaining input
                         then [(result, drop (length attempt) value)]
                         -- If we don't have a match, try the next pair
                         -- in the list of attempts.
                         else tryParse xs
```

This example handles the known cases for the three colors. It returns an empty list (resulting in a "no parse" message) for others. The function is supposed to return the part of the input that was not parsed so that the system can integrate the parsing of different types together. Here's an example of using this new instance of Read:

```
ghci> (read "Red")::Color
Red
ghci> (read "Green")::Color
Green
ghci> (read "Blue")::Color
Blue
ghci> (read "[Red]")::[Color]
[Red]
ghci> (read "[Red,Red,Blue]")::[Color]
[Red,Red,Blue]
ghci> (read "[Red, Red, Blue]")::[Color]
*** Exception: Prelude.read: no parse
```

Notice the error on the final attempt. That's because our parser is not smart enough to handle leading spaces yet. If we modify it to accept leading spaces, that attempt would work. You could rectify this by changing your Read instance to discard any leading spaces, which is common practice in Haskell programs.

Read is not widely used

While it is possible to build sophisticated parsers using the Read type-class, many people find it easier to do so using Parsec, and rely on Read only for simpler tasks. Parsec is covered in detail in Chapter 16.

Serialization with read and show

You may often have a data structure in memory that you need to store on disk for later retrieval or to send across the network. The process of converting data in memory to a flat series of bits for storage is called *serialization*.

It turns out that read and show make excellent tools for serialization. show produces output that is both human- and machine-readable. Most show output is also syntactically valid Haskell, though it is up to people that write Show instances to make it so.

Parsing large strings

String handling in Haskell is normally lazy, so read and show can be used on quite large data structures without incident. The built-in read and show instances in Haskell are efficient and implemented in pure Haskell. For information on how to handle parsing exceptions, refer to Chapter 19.

Let's try it out in ghci:

```
ghci> let d1 = [Just 5, Nothing, Nothing, Just 8, Just 9]::[Maybe Int]
ghci> putStrLn (show d1)
[Just 5,Nothing,Nothing,Just 8,Just 9]
ghci> writeFile "test" (show d1)
```

First, we assign d1 to be a list. Next, we print out the result of show d1, so we can see what it generates. Then, we write the result of show d1 to a file named test.

Let's try reading it back:

```
ghci> input <- readFile "test"
"[Just 5,Nothing,Nothing,Just 8,Just 9]"
ghci> let d2 = read input

<interactive>:1:9:
    Ambiguous type variable `a' in the constraint:
        `Read a' arising from a use of `read' at <interactive>:1:9-18
    Probable fix: add a type signature that fixes these type variable(s)
ghci> let d2 = (read input)::[Maybe Int]
ghci> print d1
[Just 5,Nothing,Nothing,Just 8,Just 9]
ghci> print d2
[Just 5,Nothing,Nothing,Just 8,Just 9]
ghci> d1 == d2
True
```

First, we ask Haskell to read the file back.[†] Then, we try to assign the result of read input to d2. That generates an error. The reason is that the interpreter doesn't know what type d2 is meant to be, so it doesn't know how to parse the input. If we give it an explicit type, it works, and we can verify that the two sets of data are equal.

Since so many different types are instances of Read and Show by default (and others can be made instances easily; see "Automatic Derivation" on page 148), you can use it for some really complex data structures. Here are a few examples of slightly more complex data structures:

```
ghci> putStrLn $ show [("hi", 1), ("there", 3)]
[("hi",1),("there",3)]
ghci> putStrLn $ show [[1, 2, 3], [], [4, 0, 1], [], [503]]
[[1,2,3],[],[4,0,1],[],[503]]
ghci> putStrLn $ show [Left 5, Right "three", Left 0, Right "nine"]
[Left 5,Right "three",Left 0,Right "nine"]
ghci> putStrLn $ show [Left 0, Right [1, 2, 3], Left 5, Right []]
[Left 0,Right [1,2,3],Left 5,Right []]
```

Numeric Types

Haskell has a powerful set of numeric types. You can use everything from fast 32-bit or 64-bit integers to arbitrary-precision rational numbers. You probably know that operators such as + can work with just about all of these. This feature is implemented using typeclasses. As a side benefit, it allows us to define your own numeric types and make them first-class citizens in Haskell.

[†] As you will see in "Lazy I/O" on page 178, Haskell doesn't actually read the entire file at this point. But for the purposes of this example, we can ignore that distinction.

Let's begin our discussion of the typeclasses surrounding numeric types with an examination of the types themselves. Table 6-1 describes the most commonly used numeric types in Haskell. Note that there are also many more numeric types available for specific purposes such as interfacing to C.

Table 6-1. Selected numeric types

Type	Description
Double	Double-precision floating point. A common choice for floating-point data.
Float	Single-precision floating point. Often used when interfacing with C.
Int	Fixed-precision signed integer; minimum range [-2^29..2^29-1]. Commonly used.
Int8	8-bit signed integer.
Int16	16-bit signed integer.
Int32	32-bit signed integer.
Int64	64-bit signed integer.
Integer	Arbitrary-precision signed integer; range limited only by machine resources. Commonly used.
Rational	Arbitrary-precision rational numbers. Stored as a ratio of two Integers.
Word	Fixed-precision unsigned integer; storage size same as Int.
Word8	8-bit unsigned integer.
Word16	16-bit unsigned integer.
Word32	32-bit unsigned integer.
Word64	64-bit unsigned integer.

These are quite a few different numeric types. There are some operations, such as addition, that work with all of them. There are others, such as asin, that apply only to floating-point types. Table 6-2 summarizes the different functions that operate on numeric types, and Table 6-3 matches the types with their respective typeclasses. As you read Table 6-3, keep in mind that Haskell operators are just functions: you can say either (+) 2 3 or 2 + 3 with the same result. By convention, when referring to an operator as a function, it is written in parentheses as seen in Table 6-2.

Table 6-2. Selected numeric functions and constants

Item	Type	Module	Description
(+)	Num a => a -> a-> a	Prelude	Addition.
(-)	Num a => a -> a -> a	Prelude	Subtraction.
(*)	Num a => a -> a -> a	Prelude	Multiplication.
(/)	Fractional a => a -> a -> a	Prelude	Fractional division.
(**)	Floating a => a -> a -> a	Prelude	Raise to the power of.
(^)	(Num a, Integral b) => a -> b -> a	Prelude	Raise a number to a nonnegative, integral power.

Item	Type	Module	Description
(^^)	(Fractional a, Integral b) => a -> b -> a	Prelude	Raise a fractional number to any integral power.
(%)	Integral a => a -> a -> Ratio a	Data.Ratio	Ratio composition.
(.&.)	Bits a => a -> a -> a	Data.Bits	Bitwise and.
(.|.)	Bits a => a -> a -> a	Data.Bits	Bitwise or.
abs	Num a => a -> a	Prelude	Absolute value
approxRational	RealFrac a => a -> a -> Rational	Data.Ratio	Approximate rational composition based on fractional numerators and denominators.
cos	Floating a => a -> a	Prelude	Cosine. Also provided are acos, cosh, and acosh, with the same type.
div	Integral a => a -> a -> a	Prelude	Integer division always truncated down; see also quot.
fromInteger	Num a => Integer -> a	Prelude	Conversion from an Integer to any numeric type.
fromIntegral	(Integral a, Num b) => a -> b	Prelude	More general conversion from any Integral to any numeric type.
fromRational	Fractional a => Rational -> a	Prelude	Conversion from a Rational. May be lossy.
log	Floating a => a -> a	Prelude	Natural logarithm.
logBase	Floating a => a -> a -> a	Prelude	Log with explicit base.
maxBound	Bounded a => a	Prelude	The maximum value of a bounded type.
minBound	Bounded a => a	Prelude	The minimum value of a bounded type.
mod	Integral a => a -> a -> a	Prelude	Integer modulus.
pi	Floating a => a	Prelude	Mathematical constant pi.
quot	Integral a => a -> a -> a	Prelude	Integer division; fractional part of quotient truncated towards zero.
recip	Fractional a => a -> a	Prelude	Reciprocal.
rem	Integral a => a -> a -> a	Prelude	Remainder of integer division.
round	(RealFrac a, Integral b) => a -> b	Prelude	Rounds to nearest integer.
shift	Bits a => a -> Int -> a	Bits	Shift left by the specified number of bits, which may be negative for a right shift.

Item	Type	Module	Description
sin	Floating a => a -> a	Prelude	Sine. Also provided are asin, sinh, and asinh, with the same type.
sqrt	Floating a => a -> a	Prelude	Square root.
tan	Floating a => a -> a	Prelude	Tangent. Also provided are atan, tanh, and atanh, with the same type.
toInteger	Integral a => a -> Integer	Prelude	Convert any Integral to an Integer.
toRational	Real a => a -> Rational	Prelude	Convert losslessly to Rational.
truncate	(RealFrac a, Integral b) => a -> b	Prelude	Truncates number towards zero.
xor	Bits a => a -> a -> a	Data.Bits	Bitwise exclusive or.

Table 6-3. Typeclass instances for numeric types

Type	Bits	Bounded	Floating	Fractional	Integral	Num	Real	RealFrac
Double			X	X		X	X	X
Float			X	X		X	X	X
Int	X	X			X	X	X	
Int16	X	X			X	X	X	
Int32	X	X			X	X	X	
Int64	X	X			X	X	X	
Integer	X				X	X	X	
Rational or any Ratio				X		X	X	X
Word	X	X			X	X	X	
Word16	X	X			X	X	X	
Word32	X	X			X	X	X	
Word64	X	X			X	X	X	

Converting between numeric types is another common need. Table 6-2 listed many functions that can be used for conversion. However, it is not always obvious how to apply them to convert between two arbitrary types. To help you out, Table 6-4 provides information on converting between different types.

Table 6-4. Conversion between numeric types[a]

Source type	Destination type			
	Double, Float	Int, Word	Integer	Rational
Double, Float	fromRational . toRational	truncate*	truncate*	toRational
Int, Word	fromIntegral	fromIntegral	fromIntegral	fromIntegral
Integer	fromIntegral	fromIntegral	N/A	fromIntegral
Rational	fromRational	truncate*	truncate*	N/A

[a] Instead of **truncate**, you could also use **round**, **ceiling**, or **floor**.

For an extended example demonstrating the use of these numeric typeclasses, see "Extended Example: Numeric Types" on page 307.

Equality, Ordering, and Comparisons

We've already talked about the arithmetic operators such as + that can be used for all sorts of different numbers. But there are some even more widely applied operators in Haskell. The most obvious, of course, are the equality tests: == and /=. These operators are defined in the Eq class.

There are also comparison operators such as >= and <=. These are declared by the Ord typeclass. These are in a separate typeclass because there are some types, such as Handle, where an equality test makes sense, but there is no way to express a particular ordering. Anything that is an instance of Ord can be sorted by Data.List.sort.

Almost all Haskell types are instances of Eq, and nearly as many are instances of Ord.

Automatic Derivation

For many simple data types, the Haskell compiler can automatically derive instances of Read, Show, Bounded, Enum, Eq, and Ord for us. This saves us the effort of having to manually write code to compare or display our own types:

```
-- file: ch06/colorderived.hs
data Color = Red | Green | Blue
    deriving (Read, Show, Eq, Ord)
```

Which types can be automatically derived?

The Haskell standard requires compilers to be able to automatically derive instances of these specific typeclasses. This automation is not available for other typeclasses.

Let's take a look at how these derived instances work for us:

```
ghci> show Red
"Red"
ghci> (read "Red")::Color
Red
ghci> (read "[Red,Red,Blue]")::[Color]
[Red,Red,Blue]
ghci> (read "[Red, Red, Blue]")::[Color]
[Red,Red,Blue]
ghci> Red == Red
True
ghci> Red == Blue
False
ghci> Data.List.sort [Blue,Green,Blue,Red]
[Red,Green,Blue,Blue]
ghci> Red < Blue
True
```

Notice that the sort order for Color was based on the order in which the constructors were defined.

Automatic derivation is not always possible. For instance, if you defined a type data MyType = MyType (Int -> Bool), the compiler will not be able to derive an instance of Show because it doesn't know how to render a function. We will get a compilation error in such a situation.

When we automatically derive an instance of some typeclass, the types that we refer to in our data declaration must also be instances of that typeclass (manually or automatically):

```
-- file: ch06/AutomaticDerivation.hs
data CannotShow = CannotShow
                  deriving (Show)

-- will not compile, since CannotShow is not an instance of Show
data CannotDeriveShow = CannotDeriveShow CannotShow
                        deriving (Show)

data OK = OK

instance Show OK where
    show _ = "OK"

data ThisWorks = ThisWorks OK
                 deriving (Show)
```

Typeclasses at Work: Making JSON Easier to Use

The JValue type that we introduced in "Representing JSON Data in Haskell" on page 111 is not especially easy to work with. Here is a truncated and tidied snippet of some real JSON data, produced by a well-known search engine:

```
{
  "query": "awkward squad haskell",
```

```
  "estimatedCount": 3920,
  "moreResults": true,
  "results":
  [{
    "title": "Simon Peyton Jones: papers",
    "snippet": "Tackling the awkward squad: monadic input/output ...",
    "url": "http://research.microsoft.com/~simonpj/papers/marktoberdorf/",
  },
  {
    "title": "Haskell for C Programmers | Lambda the Ultimate",
    "snippet": "... the best job of all the tutorials I've read ...",
    "url": "http://lambda-the-ultimate.org/node/724",
  }]
}
```

And here's a further slimmed down fragment of that data, represented in Haskell:

```
-- file: ch05/SimpleResult.hs
import SimpleJSON

result :: JValue
result = JObject [
  ("query", JString "awkward squad haskell"),
  ("estimatedCount", JNumber 3920),
  ("moreResults", JBool True),
  ("results", JArray [
    JObject [
      ("title", JString "Simon Peyton Jones: papers"),
      ("snippet", JString "Tackling the awkward ..."),
      ("url", JString "http://.../marktoberdorf/")
    ]])
  ]
```

Because Haskell doesn't natively support lists that contain types of different values, we can't directly represent a JSON object that contains values of different types. Instead, we must wrap each value with a JValue constructor, which limits our flexibility—if we want to change the number 3920 to a string "3,920", we must change the constructor that we use to wrap it from JNumber to JString.

Haskell's typeclasses offer a tempting solution to this problem:

```
-- file: ch06/JSONClass.hs
type JSONError = String

class JSON a where
    toJValue :: a -> JValue
    fromJValue :: JValue -> Either JSONError a

instance JSON JValue where
    toJValue = id
    fromJValue = Right
```

Now, instead of applying a constructor such as JNumber to a value in order to wrap it, we apply the toJValue function. If we change a value's type, the compiler will choose a suitable implementation of toJValue to use with it.

We also provide a fromJValue function, which attempts to convert a JValue into a value of our desired type.

More Helpful Errors

The return type of our fromJValue function uses the Either type. Like Maybe, this type is predefined for us. We'll often use it to represent a computation that could fail.

While Maybe is useful for this purpose, it gives us no information if a failure occurs: we literally have Nothing. The Either type has a similar structure, but instead of Nothing, the "something bad happened" constructor is named Left, and it takes a parameter:

```
-- file: ch06/DataEither.hs
data Maybe a = Nothing
             | Just a
               deriving (Eq, Ord, Read, Show)

data Either a b = Left a
                | Right b
                  deriving (Eq, Ord, Read, Show)
```

Quite often, the type we use for the a parameter value is String, so we can provide a useful description if something goes wrong. To see how we use the Either type in practice, let's look at a simple instance of our typeclass:

```
-- file: ch06/JSONClass.hs
instance JSON Bool where
    toJValue = JBool
    fromJValue (JBool b) = Right b
    fromJValue _ = Left "not a JSON boolean"
```

Making an Instance with a Type Synonym

The Haskell 98 standard does not allow us to write an instance of the following form, even though it seems perfectly reasonable:

```
-- file: ch06/JSONClass.hs
instance JSON String where
    toJValue             = JString

    fromJValue (JString s) = Right s
    fromJValue _           = Left "not a JSON string"
```

Recall that String is a synonym for [Char], which in turn is the type [a] where Char is substituted for the type parameter a. According to Haskell 98's rules, we are not allowed to supply a type in place of a type parameter when we write an instance. In other words, it would be legal for us to write an instance for [a], but not for [Char].

While GHC follows the Haskell 98 standard by default, we can relax this particular restriction by placing a specially formatted comment at the top of our source file:

```
-- file: ch06/JSONClass.hs
{-# LANGUAGE TypeSynonymInstances #-}
```

This comment is a directive to the compiler, called a *pragma*, which tells it to enable a language extension. The TypeSynonymInstances language extension makes the preceding code legal. We'll encounter a few other language extensions in this chapter, and a handful more later in this book.

Living in an Open World

Haskell's typeclasses are intentionally designed to let us create new instances of a typeclass whenever we see fit:

```
-- file: ch06/JSONClass.hs
doubleToJValue :: (Double -> a) -> JValue -> Either JSONError a
doubleToJValue f (JNumber v) = Right (f v)
doubleToJValue _ _ = Left "not a JSON number"

instance JSON Int where
    toJValue = JNumber . realToFrac
    fromJValue = doubleToJValue round

instance JSON Integer where
    toJValue = JNumber . realToFrac
    fromJValue = doubleToJValue round

instance JSON Double where
    toJValue = JNumber
    fromJValue = doubleToJValue id
```

We can add new instances anywhere; they are not confined to the module where we define a typeclass. This feature of the typeclass system is referred to as its *open world assumption*. If we had a way to express a notion of "the following are the only instances of this typeclass that can exist," we would have a *closed* world.

We would like to be able to turn a list into what JSON calls an array. We won't worry about implementation details just yet, so let's use undefined as the bodies of the instance's methods:

```
-- file: ch06/BrokenClass.hs
instance (JSON a) => JSON [a] where
    toJValue = undefined
    fromJValue = undefined
```

It would also be convenient if we could turn a list of name/value pairs into a JSON object:

```
-- file: ch06/BrokenClass.hs
instance (JSON a) => JSON [(String, a)] where
    toJValue = undefined
    fromJValue = undefined
```

When Do Overlapping Instances Cause Problems?

If we put these definitions into a source file and load them into ghci, everything seems fine initially:

```
ghci> :load BrokenClass
[1 of 2] Compiling SimpleJSON        ( ../ch05/SimpleJSON.hs, interpreted )
[2 of 2] Compiling BrokenClass       ( BrokenClass.hs, interpreted )
Ok, modules loaded: BrokenClass, SimpleJSON.
```

However, once we try to *use* the list-of-pairs instance, we run into trouble:

```
ghci> toJValue [("foo","bar")]
```

```
<interactive>:1:0:
    Overlapping instances for JSON [([Char], [Char])]
      arising from a use of `toJValue' at <interactive>:1:0-23
    Matching instances:
      instance (JSON a) => JSON [a]
        -- Defined at BrokenClass.hs:(44,0)-(46,25)
      instance (JSON a) => JSON [(String, a)]
        -- Defined at BrokenClass.hs:(50,0)-(52,25)
    In the expression: toJValue [("foo", "bar")]
    In the definition of `it': it = toJValue [("foo", "bar")]
```

This problem of *overlapping instances* is a consequence of Haskell's open world assumption. Here's a simpler example that makes it clearer what's going on:

```
-- file: ch06/Overlap.hs
class Borked a where
    bork :: a -> String

instance Borked Int where
    bork = show

instance Borked (Int, Int) where
    bork (a, b) = bork a ++ ", " ++ bork b

instance (Borked a, Borked b) => Borked (a, b) where
    bork (a, b) = ">>" ++ bork a ++ " " ++ bork b ++ "<<"
```

We have two instances of the typeclass Borked for pairs: one for a pair of Ints and another for a pair of anything else that's Borked.

Suppose that we want to bork a pair of Int values. To do so, the compiler must choose an instance to use. Because these instances are right next to each other, it may seem that it could simply choose the more specific instance.

However, GHC is conservative by default and insists that there must be only one possible instance that it can use. It will thus report an error if we try to use bork.

When do overlapping instances matter?

As we mentioned earlier, we can scatter instances of a typeclass across several modules. GHC does not complain about the mere existence of overlapping instances. Instead, it complains only when we try to use a method of the affected typeclass, when it is forced to make a decision about which instance to use.

Relaxing Some Restrictions on Typeclasses

Normally, we cannot write an instance of a typeclass for a specialized version of a polymorphic type. The [Char] type is the polymorphic type [a] specialized to the type Char. We are thus prohibited from declaring [Char] to be an instance of a typeclass. This is highly inconvenient, since strings are ubiquitous in real code.

The TypeSynonymInstances language extension removes this restriction, permitting us to write such instances.

GHC supports another useful language extension, OverlappingInstances, which addresses the problem we saw with overlapping instances. When there are multiple overlapping instances to choose from, this extension causes the compiler to pick the most specific one.

We frequently use this extension together with TypeSynonymInstances. Here's an example:

```
-- file: ch06/SimpleClass.hs
{-# LANGUAGE TypeSynonymInstances, OverlappingInstances #-}

import Data.List

class Foo a where
    foo :: a -> String

instance Foo a => Foo [a] where
    foo = concat . intersperse ", " . map foo

instance Foo Char where
    foo c = [c]

instance Foo String where
    foo = id
```

If we apply foo to a String, the compiler will use the String-specific implementation. Even though we have an instance of Foo for [a] and Char, the instance for String is more specific, so GHC chooses it. For other types of list, we will see the behavior specified for [a].

With the OverlappingInstances extension enabled, GHC will still reject code if it finds more than one equally specific instance.

When to use the OverlappingInstances extension

Here's an important point: GHC treats OverlappingInstances as affecting the declaration of an instance, *not* a location where we use the instance. In other words, when we define an instance that we wish to allow to overlap with another instance, we must enable the extension for the module that contains the definition. When it compiles the module, GHC will record that instance as "can be overlapped with other instances."

Once we import this module and use the instance, we *won't* need to enable OverlappingInstances in the importing module. GHC will already know that the instance was marked as "OK to overlap" when it was defined.

This behavior is useful when we are writing a library: we can choose to create overlappable instances, but users of our library do not need to enable any special language extensions.

How Does Show Work for Strings?

The OverlappingInstances and TypeSynonymInstances language extensions are specific to GHC, and by definition were not present in Haskell 98. However, the familiar Show typeclass from Haskell 98 somehow renders a list of Char differently from a list of Int. It achieves this via a clever, but simple, trick.

The Show class defines both a show method, which renders one value, and a showList method, which renders a list of values. The default implementation of showList renders a list using square brackets and commas.

The instance of Show for [a] is implemented using showList. The instance of Show for Char provides a special implementation of showList that uses double quotes and escapes non-ASCII-printable characters.

As a result, if someone applies show to a [Char] value, the implementation of showList will be chosen, and it will correctly render the string using quotes.

At least sometimes, then, we can avoid the need for the OverlappingInstances extension with a little bit of lateral thinking.

How to Give a Type a New Identity

In addition to the familiar data keyword, Haskell provides us with another way to create a new type, using the newtype keyword:

```
-- file: ch06/Newtype.hs
data DataInt = D Int
    deriving (Eq, Ord, Show)
```

```
newtype NewtypeInt = N Int
    deriving (Eq, Ord, Show)
```

The purpose of a `newtype` declaration is to rename an existing type, giving it a distinct identity. As we can see, it is similar in appearance to a type declared using the `data` keyword.

The type and newtype keywords

Although their names are similar, the `type` and `newtype` keywords have different purposes. The `type` keyword gives us another way of referring to a type, like a nickname for a friend. We and the compiler know that `[Char]` and `String` names refer to the same type.

In contrast, the `newtype` keyword exists to *hide* the nature of a type. Consider a `UniqueID` type:

```
-- file: ch06/Newtype.hs
newtype UniqueID = UniqueID Int
    deriving (Eq)
```

The compiler treats `UniqueID` as a different type from `Int`. As a user of a `UniqueID`, we know only that we have a unique identifier; we cannot see that it is implemented as an `Int`.

When we declare a `newtype`, we must choose which of the underlying type's typeclass instances we want to expose. Here, we've elected to make `NewtypeInt` provide `Int`'s instances for `Eq`, `Ord`, and `Show`. As a result, we can compare and print values of type `NewtypeInt`:

```
ghci> N 1 < N 2
True
```

Since we are *not* exposing `Int`'s `Num` or `Integral` instances, values of type `NewtypeInt` are not numbers. For instance, we can't add them:

```
ghci> N 313 + N 37

<interactive>:1:0:
    No instance for (Num NewtypeInt)
      arising from a use of `+' at <interactive>:1:0-11
    Possible fix: add an instance declaration for (Num NewtypeInt)
    In the expression: N 313 + N 37
    In the definition of `it': it = N 313 + N 37
```

As with the `data` keyword, we can use a `newtype`'s value constructor to create a new value or to pattern match on an existing value.

If a `newtype` does not use automatic deriving to expose the underlying type's implementation of a typeclass, we are free to either write a new instance or leave the typeclass unimplemented.

Differences Between Data and Newtype Declarations

The newtype keyword exists to give an existing type a new identity, and it has more restrictions on its uses than the data keyword. Specifically, a newtype can have only one value constructor, which must have exactly one field:

```
-- file: ch06/NewtypeDiff.hs
-- ok: any number of fields and constructors
data TwoFields = TwoFields Int Int

-- ok: exactly one field
newtype Okay = ExactlyOne Int

-- ok: type parameters are no problem
newtype Param a b = Param (Either a b)

-- ok: record syntax is fine
newtype Record = Record {
    getInt :: Int
    }

-- bad: no fields
newtype TooFew = TooFew

-- bad: more than one field
newtype TooManyFields = Fields Int Int

-- bad: more than one constructor
newtype TooManyCtors = Bad Int
                     | Worse Int
```

Beyond this, there's another important difference between data and newtype. A type created with the data keyword has a bookkeeping cost at runtime, for example, in order to track which constructor created a value. A newtype value, on the other hand, can have only one constructor and so does not need this overhead. This makes it more space- and time-efficient at runtime.

Because a newtype's constructor is used only at compile time and does not even exist at runtime, pattern matching on undefined behaves differently for types defined using newtype than for those that use data.

To understand the difference, let's first review what we might expect with a normal data type. We are already familiar with the idea that if undefined is evaluated at runtime, it causes a crash:

```
ghci> undefined
*** Exception: Prelude.undefined
```

Here is a pattern match where we construct a DataInt using the D constructor and put undefined inside:

```
ghci> case D undefined of D _ -> 1
1
```

Since our pattern matches against the constructor but doesn't inspect the payload, undefined remains unevaluated and does not cause an exception to be thrown.

In this example, we're not using the D constructor, so the unprotected undefined is evaluated when the pattern match occurs, and we throw an exception:

```
ghci> case undefined of D _ -> 1
*** Exception: Prelude.undefined
```

When we use the N constructor for the NewtypeInt type, we see the same behavior that we did with the DataInt type's D constructor—no exception:

```
ghci> case N undefined of N _ -> 1
1
```

The crucial difference arises when we get rid of the N constructor from the expression and match against an unprotected undefined:

```
ghci> case undefined of N _ -> 1
1
```

We don't crash! Because there's no constructor present at runtime, matching against N _ is in fact equivalent to matching against the plain wild card (_). Since the wild card always matches, the expression does not need to be evaluated.

Another perspective on newtype constructors

Even though we use the value constructor for a newtype in the same way as that of a type defined using the data keyword, all it does is coerce a value between its "normal" type and its newtype type.

In other words, when we apply the N constructor in an expression, we coerce an expression from type Int to type NewtypeInt as far as we and the compiler are concerned, but absolutely nothing occurs at runtime.

Similarly, when we match on the N constructor in a pattern, we coerce an expression from type NewtypeInt to Int, but again there's no overhead involved at runtime.

Summary: The Three Ways of Naming Types

Here's a brief recap of Haskell's three ways to introduce new names for types:

- The data keyword introduces a truly new algebraic data type.
- The type keyword gives us a synonym to use for an existing type. We can use the type and its synonym interchangeably.
- The newtype keyword gives an existing type a distinct identity. The original type and the new type are *not* interchangeable.

JSON Typeclasses Without Overlapping Instances

Enabling GHC's support for overlapping instances is an effective and quick way to make our JSON code happy. In more complex cases, we will occasionally be faced with several equally good instances for some typeclass, in which case, overlapping instances will not help us and we will need to put some newtype declarations into place. To see what's involved, let's rework our JSON typeclass instances to use newtypes instead of overlapping instances.

Our first task, then, is to help the compiler to distinguish between [a], the representation we use for JSON arrays, and [(String,[a])], which we use for objects. These were the types that gave us problems before we learned about OverlappingInstances. We wrap up the list type so that the compiler will not see it as a list:

```
-- file: ch06/JSONClass.hs
newtype JAry a = JAry {
      fromJAry :: [a]
    } deriving (Eq, Ord, Show)
```

When we export this type from our module, we'll export the complete details of the type. Our module header will look like this:

```
-- file: ch06/JSONClassExport.hs
module JSONClass
    (
      JAry(..)
    ) where
```

The (..) following the JAry name means "export all details of this type."

A Slight Deviation from Normal Use

Usually, when we export a newtype, we will *not* export its data constructor, in order to keep the details of the type abstract. Instead, we would define a function to apply the constructor for us:

```
-- file: ch06/JSONClass.hs
jary :: [a] -> JAry a
jary = JAry
```

We would then export the type constructor, the deconstructor function, and our construction function, but not the data constructor:

```
-- file: ch06/JSONClassExport.hs
module JSONClass
    (
      JAry(fromJAry)
    , jary
    ) where
```

When we don't export a type's data constructor, clients of our library can only use the functions we provide to construct and deconstruct values of that type. This gives us, the library authors, the liberty to change our internal representation if we need to.

If we export the data constructor, clients are likely to start depending on it, for instance by using it in patterns. If we later wish to change the innards of our type, we'll risk breaking any code that uses the constructor.

In our circumstances here, we have nothing to gain by making the array wrapper abstract, so we may as well simply export the entire definition of the type.

We provide another wrapper type that hides our representation of a JSON object:

```
-- file: ch06/JSONClass.hs
newtype JObj a = JObj {
        fromJObj :: [(String, a)]
    } deriving (Eq, Ord, Show)
```

With these types defined, we make small changes to the definition of our JValue type:

```
-- file: ch06/JSONClass.hs
data JValue = JString String
            | JNumber Double
            | JBool Bool
            | JNull
            | JObject (JObj JValue)   -- was [(String, JValue)]
            | JArray (JAry JValue)    -- was [JValue]
              deriving (Eq, Ord, Show)
```

This change doesn't affect the instances of the JSON typeclass that we've already written, but we will want to write instances for our new JAry and JObj types:

```
-- file: ch06/JSONClass.hs
jaryFromJValue :: (JSON a) => JValue -> Either JSONError (JAry a)

jaryToJValue :: (JSON a) => JAry a -> JValue

instance (JSON a) => JSON (JAry a) where
    toJValue = jaryToJValue
    fromJValue = jaryFromJValue
```

Let's take a slow walk through the individual steps of converting a JAry a to a JValue. Given a list where we know that everything inside is a JSON instance, converting it to a list of JValues is easy:

```
-- file: ch06/JSONClass.hs
listToJValues :: (JSON a) => [a] -> [JValue]
listToJValues = map toJValue
```

Taking this and wrapping it to become a JAry JValue is just a matter of applying the newtype's type constructor:

```
-- file: ch06/JSONClass.hs
jvaluesToJAry :: [JValue] -> JAry JValue
jvaluesToJAry = JAry
```

(Remember, this has no performance cost. We're just telling the compiler to hide the fact that we're using a list.) To turn this into a JValue, we apply another type constructor:

```
-- file: ch06/JSONClass.hs
jaryOfJValuesToJValue :: JAry JValue -> JValue
jaryOfJValuesToJValue = JArray
```

Assemble these pieces using function composition, and we get a concise one-liner for converting to a JValue:

```
-- file: ch06/JSONClass.hs
jaryToJValue = JArray . JAry . map toJValue . fromJAry
```

We have more work to do to convert *from* a JValue to a JAry a, but we'll break it into reusable parts. The basic function is straightforward:

```
-- file: ch06/JSONClass.hs
jaryFromJValue (JArray (JAry a)) =
    whenRight JAry (mapEithers fromJValue a)
jaryFromJValue _ = Left "not a JSON array"
```

The whenRight function inspects its argument. It calls a function on the argument if it was created with the Right constructor, and leaves a Left value untouched:

```
-- file: ch06/JSONClass.hs
whenRight :: (b -> c) -> Either a b -> Either a c
whenRight _ (Left err) = Left err
whenRight f (Right a) = Right (f a)
```

More complicated is mapEithers. It acts like the regular map function, but if it ever encounters a Left value, it returns that immediately, instead of continuing to accumulate a list of Right values:

```
-- file: ch06/JSONClass.hs
mapEithers :: (a -> Either b c) -> [a] -> Either b [c]
mapEithers f (x:xs) = case mapEithers f xs of
                        Left err -> Left err
                        Right ys -> case f x of
                                      Left err -> Left err
                                      Right y -> Right (y:ys)
mapEithers _ _ = Right []
```

Because the elements of the list hidden in the JObj type have a little more structure, the code to convert to and from a JValue is a bit more complex. Fortunately, we can reuse the functions that we just defined:

```
-- file: ch06/JSONClass.hs
import Control.Arrow (second)

instance (JSON a) => JSON (JObj a) where
    toJValue = JObject . JObj . map (second toJValue) . fromJObj

    fromJValue (JObject (JObj o)) = whenRight JObj (mapEithers unwrap o)
      where unwrap (k,v) = whenRight ((,) k) (fromJValue v)
    fromJValue _ = Left "not a JSON object"
```

The Dreaded Monomorphism Restriction

The Haskell 98 standard has a subtle feature that can sometimes bite us in unexpected circumstances. Here's a simple function definition that illustrates the issue:

```
-- file: ch06/Monomorphism.hs
myShow = show
```

If we try to load this definition into `ghci`, it issues a peculiar complaint:

```
ghci> :load Monomorphism
[1 of 1] Compiling Main             ( Monomorphism.hs, interpreted )

Monomorphism.hs:2:9:
    Ambiguous type variable `a' in the constraint:
      `Show a' arising from a use of `show' at Monomorphism.hs:2:9-12
    Possible cause: the monomorphism restriction applied to the following:
      myShow :: a -> String (bound at Monomorphism.hs:2:0)
    Probable fix: give these definition(s) an explicit type signature
                  or use -fno-monomorphism-restriction
Failed, modules loaded: none.
```

The *monomorphism restriction* to which the error message refers is a part of the Haskell 98 standard. *Monomorphism* is simply the opposite of polymorphism: it indicates that an expression has exactly one type. The *restriction* lies in the fact that Haskell sometimes forces a declaration to be less polymorphic than we would expect.

We mention the monomorphism restriction here because although it isn't specifically related to typeclasses, they usually provide the circumstances in which it crops up.

 It's possible that you will not run into the monomorphism restriction in real code for a long time. We don't think you need to try to remember the details of this section. It should suffice to make a mental note of its existence, until eventually GHC complains with something such as the just shown error message. If that occurs, simply remember that you read about the error in this chapter, and come back for guidance.

We won't attempt to explain the monomorphism restriction.[‡] The consensus within the Haskell community is that it doesn't arise often, it is tricky to explain, and it provides almost no practical benefit. So, it mostly serves to trip people up. For an example of its trickiness, while the definition provided previously falls afoul of it, the following two compile without problems:

```
-- file: ch06/Monomorphism.hs
myShow2 value = show value

myShow3 :: (Show a) => a -> String
myShow3 = show
```

As these alternative definitions suggest, if GHC complains about the monomorphism restriction, we have three easy ways to address the error:

• Make the function's arguments explicit, instead of leaving them implicit.

• Give the definition an explicit type signature, instead of making the compiler infer its type.

• Leave the code untouched and compile the module with the language extension NoMonomorphismRestriction enabled. This disables the monomorphism restriction.

Because the monomorphism restriction is unwanted and unloved, it will almost certainly be dropped from the next revision of the Haskell standard. This does not quite mean that compiling with NoMonomorphismRestriction is always the right thing to do—some Haskell compilers (including older versions of GHC) do not understand this extension, but they'll accept either of the other approaches to making the error disappear. If this degree of portability isn't a concern to you, then by all means enable the language extension.

Conclusion

In this chapter, you learned about the need for typeclasses and how to use them. We talked about defining our own typeclasses and then covered some of the important typeclasses that are defined in the Haskell library. Finally, we showed how to have the Haskell compiler automatically derive instances of certain typeclasses for your types.

[‡] If you simply *must* read the gory details, see section 4.5.5 (*http://www.haskell.org/onlinereport/decls.html #sect4.5.5*) of the Haskell 98 Report.

CHAPTER 7

I/O

It should be obvious that most, if not all, programs are devoted to gathering data from outside, processing it, and providing results back to the outside world. That is, input and output are key.

Haskell's I/O system is powerful and expressive. It is easy to work with and important to understand. Haskell strictly separates pure code from code that could cause things to occur in the world. That is, it provides a complete isolation from side effects in pure code. Besides helping programmers to reason about the correctness of their code, it also permits compilers to automatically introduce optimizations and parallelism.

We'll begin this chapter with simple, standard-looking I/O in Haskell. Then we'll discuss some of the more powerful options, as well as provide more detail on how I/O fits into the pure, lazy, functional Haskell world.

Classic I/O in Haskell

Let's get started with I/O in Haskell by looking at a program that appears to be surprisingly similar to I/O in other languages such as C or Perl:

```
-- file: ch07/basicio.hs
main = do
       putStrLn "Greetings!  What is your name?"
       inpStr <- getLine
       putStrLn $ "Welcome to Haskell, " ++ inpStr ++ "!"
```

You can compile this program to a standalone executable, run it with runghc, or invoke main from within ghci. Here's a sample session using runghc:

```
$ runghc basicio.hs
Greetings!  What is your name?
John
Welcome to Haskell, John!
```

That's a fairly simple, obvious result. You can see that putStrLn writes out a String, followed by an end-of-line character. getLine reads a line from standard input. The <- syntax may be new to you. Put simply, that binds the result from executing an I/O action to a name.* We use the simple list concatenation operator ++ to join the input string with our own text.

Let's take a look at the types of putStrLn and getLine. You can find that information in the library reference, or just ask ghci:

```
ghci> :type putStrLn
putStrLn :: String -> IO ()
ghci> :type getLine
getLine :: IO String
```

Notice that both of these types have IO in their return value. That is your key to knowing that they may have side effects, or they may return different values even when called with the same arguments, or both. The type of putStrLn looks like a function. It takes a parameter of type String and returns value of type IO (). Just what is an IO () though?

Anything that is type IO *something* is an I/O *action*. You can store it and nothing will happen. I could say writefoo = putStrLn "foo" and nothing happens right then. But if I later use writefoo in the middle of another I/O action, the writefoo action will be executed when its parent action is executed—I/O actions can be glued together to form bigger I/O actions. The () is an empty tuple (pronounced "unit"), indicating that there is no return value from putStrLn. This is similar to void in Java or C.†

Actions can be created, assigned, and passed anywhere. However, they may only be performed (executed) from within another I/O action.

Let's look at this with ghci:

```
ghci> let writefoo = putStrLn "foo"
ghci> writefoo
foo
```

In this example, the output foo is not a return value from putStrLn. Rather, it's the side effect of putStrLn actually writing foo to the terminal.

Notice one other thing: ghci actually executed writefoo. This means that, when given an I/O action, ghci will perform it for you on the spot.

---

* You will later see that it has a more broad application, but it is sufficient to think of it in these terms for now.

† The type of the value () is also ().

What is an I/O action?

Actions:

- Have the type IO t.
- Are first-class values in Haskell and fit seamlessly with Haskell's type system.
- Produce an effect when *performed*, but not when *evaluated*. That is, they produce an effect only when called by something else in an I/O context.
- Any expression may produce an action as its value, but the action will not perform I/O until it is executed inside another I/O action (or it is main).
- Performing (executing) an action of type IO t may perform I/O and will ultimately deliver a result of type t.

The type of getLine may look strange to you. It looks like a value, rather than a function. And in fact, that is one way to look at it: getLine is storing an I/O action. When that action is performed, you get a String. The <- operator is used to "pull out" the result from performing an I/O action and store it in a variable.

main itself is an I/O action with type IO (). You can only perform I/O actions from within other I/O actions. All I/O in Haskell programs is driven from the top at main, which is where execution of every Haskell program begins. This, then, is the mechanism that provides isolation from side effects in Haskell: you perform I/O in your IO actions, and call pure (non-I/O) functions from there. Most Haskell code is pure; the I/O actions perform I/O and call that pure code.

do is a convenient way to define a sequence of actions. As you'll see later, there are other ways. When you use do in this way, indentation is significant; make sure you line up your actions properly.

You need to use do only if you have more than one action that you need to perform. The value of a do block is the value of the last action executed. For a complete description of do syntax, see "Desugaring of do Blocks" on page 344.

Let's consider an example of calling pure code from within an I/O action:

```haskell
-- file: ch07/callingpure.hs
name2reply :: String -> String
name2reply name =
    "Pleased to meet you, " ++ name ++ ".\n" ++
    "Your name contains " ++ charcount ++ " characters."
    where charcount = show (length name)

main :: IO ()
main = do
       putStrLn "Greetings once again.  What is your name?"
       inpStr <- getLine
```

```
let outStr = name2reply inpStr
putStrLn outStr
```

Notice the `name2reply` function in this example. It is a regular Haskell function and obeys all the rules we've told you about: it always returns the same result when given the same input, it has no side effects, and it operates lazily. It uses other Haskell functions: (++), `show`, and `length`.

Down in `main`, we bind the result of `name2reply inpStr` to `outStr`. When you're working in a do block, use `<-` to get results from IO actions and `let` to get results from pure code. When used in a do block, you should not put `in` after your `let` statement.

You can see here how we read the person's name from the keyboard. Then, that data got passed to a pure function, and its result was printed. In fact, the last two lines of `main` could have been replaced with `putStrLn (name2reply inpStr)`. So, while `main` did have side effects—it caused things to appear on the terminal, for instance—`name2reply` did not and could not. That's because `name2reply` is a pure function, not an action.

Let's examine this with `ghci`:

```
ghci> :load callingpure.hs
[1 of 1] Compiling Main             ( callingpure.hs, interpreted )
Ok, modules loaded: Main.
ghci> name2reply "John"
"Pleased to meet you, John.\nYour name contains 4 characters."
ghci> putStrLn (name2reply "John")
Pleased to meet you, John.
Your name contains 4 characters.
```

The \n within the string is the end-of-line (newline) character, which causes the terminal to begin a new line in its output. Just calling `name2reply "John"` in ghci will show you the \n literally, because it is using `show` to display the return value. But using `putStrLn` sends it to the terminal, and the terminal interprets \n to start a new line.

What do you think will happen if you simply type **main** at the ghci prompt? Give it a try.

After looking at these example programs, you may be wondering if Haskell is really imperative rather than pure, lazy, and functional. Some of these examples look like a sequence of actions to be followed in order. There's more to it than that, though. We'll discuss that question later in this chapter in "Is Haskell Really Imperative?" on page 188 and "Lazy I/O" on page 178.

Pure Versus I/O

Table 7-1 is a comparison table to help you understand the differences between pure code and I/O. When we speak of pure code, we are talking about Haskell functions that always return the same result when given the same input and have no side effects. In Haskell, only the execution of I/O actions avoid these rules.

Table 7-1. Pure versus impure

Pure	Impure
Always produces the same result when given the same parameters	May produce different results for the same parameters
Never has side effects	May have side effects
Never alters state	May alter the global state of the program, system, or world

Why Purity Matters

In this section, we've discussed how Haskell, unlike most languages, draws a clear distinction between pure code and I/O actions. In languages such as C or Java, there is no such thing as a function that is guaranteed by the compiler to always return the same result for the same arguments or a function that is guaranteed to never have side effects. The only way to know if a given function has side effects is to read its documentation and hope that it's accurate.

Many bugs in programs are caused by unanticipated side effects. Still more are caused by misunderstanding circumstances in which functions may return different results for the same input. As multithreading and other forms of parallelism grow increasingly common, it becomes more difficult to manage global side effects.

Haskell's method of isolating side effects into I/O actions provides a clear boundary. You can always know which parts of the system may alter state and which won't. You can always be sure that the pure parts of your program aren't having unanticipated results. This helps you to think about the program. It also helps the compiler to think about it. Recent versions of ghc, for instance, can provide a level of automatic parallelism for the pure parts of your code—something of a holy grail for computing.

For more discussion on this topic, refer to "Side Effects with Lazy I/O" on page 188.

Working with Files and Handles

So far, you've seen how to interact with the user at the computer's terminal. Of course, you'll often need to manipulate specific files. That's easy to do, too.

Haskell defines quite a few basic functions for I/O, many of which are similar to functions seen in other programming languages. The library reference for System.IO provides a good summary of all the basic I/O functions, should you need one that we aren't touching upon here.

You will generally begin by using openFile, which will give you a file Handle. That Handle is then used to perform specific operations on the file. Haskell provides functions such as hPutStrLn that work just like putStrLn but take an additional argument, a Handle, that specifies which file to operate upon. When you're done, you'll use hClose to close the Handle. These functions are all defined in System.IO, so you'll need to import that module when working with files. There are "h" functions corresponding to virtually all of the non-"h" functions; for instance, there is `print` for printing to the screen and `hPrint` for printing to a file.

Let's start with an imperative way to read and write files. This should seem similar to a `while` loop that you may find in other languages. This isn't the best way to write it in Haskell; later, you'll see examples of more Haskellish approaches.

```
-- file: ch07/toupper-imp.hs
import System.IO
import Data.Char(toUpper)

main :: IO ()
main = do
       inh <- openFile "input.txt" ReadMode
       outh <- openFile "output.txt" WriteMode
       mainloop inh outh
       hClose inh
       hClose outh

mainloop :: Handle -> Handle -> IO ()
mainloop inh outh =
    do ineof <- hIsEOF inh
       if ineof
           then return ()
           else do inpStr <- hGetLine inh
                   hPutStrLn outh (map toUpper inpStr)
                   mainloop inh outh
```

Like every Haskell program, execution of this program begins with `main`. Two files are opened: *input.txt* is opened for reading, and *output.txt* is opened for writing. Then we call `mainloop` to process the file.

`mainloop` begins by checking to see if we're at the end of file (EOF) for the input. If not, we read a line from the input. We write out the same line to the output, after first converting it to uppercase. Then we recursively call `mainloop` again to continue processing the file.[‡]

Notice that `return` call. This is not really the same as `return` in C or Python. In those languages, `return` is used to terminate execution of the current function immediately, and to return a value to the caller. In Haskell, `return` is the opposite of `<-`. That is, `return` takes a pure value and wraps it inside IO. Since every I/O action must return some IO type, if your result came from pure computation, you must use `return` to wrap it in IO. As an example, if 7 is an `Int`, then `return 7` would create an action stored in a value of type IO `Int`. When executed, that action would produce the result 7. For more details on `return`, see "The True Nature of Return" on page 187.

[‡] Imperative programmers might be concerned that such a recursive call would consume large amounts of stack space. In Haskell, recursion is a common idiom, and the compiler is smart enough to avoid consuming much stack by optimizing tail-recursive functions.

Let's try running the program. We've got a file named *input.txt* that looks like this:

```
This is ch07/input.txt

Test Input
I like Haskell
Haskell is great
I/O is fun

123456789
```

Now, you can use `runghc toupper-imp.hs` and you'll find `output.txt` in your directory. It should look like this:

```
THIS IS CH07/INPUT.TXT

TEST INPUT
I LIKE HASKELL
HASKELL IS GREAT
I/O IS FUN

123456789
```

More on openFile

Let's use `ghci` to check on the type of `openFile`:

```
ghci> :module System.IO
ghci> :type openFile
openFile :: FilePath -> IOMode -> IO Handle
```

`FilePath` is simply another name for `String`. It is used in the types of I/O functions to help clarify that the parameter is being used as a filename, and not as regular data.

`IOMode` specifies how the file is to be managed. The possible values for `IOMode` are listed in Table 7-2.

Table 7-2. Possible IOMode values

IOMode	Can read?	Can write?	Starting position	Notes
ReadMode	Yes	No	Beginning of file	File must exist already.
WriteMode	No	Yes	Beginning of file	File is truncated (completely emptied) if it already existed.
ReadWriteMode	Yes	Yes	Beginning of file	File is created if it didn't exist; otherwise, existing data is left intact.
AppendMode	No	Yes	End of file	File is created if it didn't exist; otherwise, existing data is left intact.

While we are mostly working with text examples in this chapter, binary files can also be used in Haskell. If you are working with a binary file, you should use `openBinaryFile` instead of `openFile`. Operating systems such as Windows process files differently if they are opened as binary instead of as text. On operating systems such as Linux, both openFile and openBinaryFile perform the same operation. Nevertheless, for portability, it is still wise to always use openBinaryFile if you will be dealing with binary data.

Closing Handles

You've already seen that hClose is used to close file handles. Let's take a moment and think about why this is important.

As you'll see in "Buffering" on page 189, Haskell maintains internal buffers for files. This provides an important performance boost. However, it means that until you call hClose on a file that is open for writing, your data may not be flushed out to the operating system.

Another reason to make sure to hClose files is that open files take up resources on the system. If your program runs for a long time, and opens many files but fails to close them, it is conceivable that your program could even crash due to resource exhaustion. All of this is no different in Haskell than in other languages.

When a program exits, Haskell will normally take care of closing any files that remain open. However, there are some circumstances in which this may not happen,[§] so once again, it is best to be responsible and call hClose all the time.

Haskell provides several tools for you to use to easily ensure this happens, regardless of whether errors are present. You can read about finally in "Extended Example: Functional I/O and Temporary Files" on page 175 and bracket in "The Acquire-Use-Release Cycle" on page 221.

Seek and Tell

When reading and writing from a Handle that corresponds to a file on disk, the operating system maintains an internal record of the current position. Each time you do another read, the operating system returns the next chunk of data that begins at the current position, and increments the position to reflect the data that you read.

You can use hTell to find out your current position in the file. When the file is initially created, it is empty and your position will be 0. After you write out 5 bytes, your position will be 5, and so on. hTell takes a Handle and returns an IO Integer with your position.

The companion to hTell is hSeek. hSeek lets you change the file position. It takes three parameters: a Handle, a SeekMode, and a position.

SeekMode can be one of three different values, which specify how the given position is to be interpreted. AbsoluteSeek means that the position is a precise location in the file.

[§] If there was a bug in the C part of a hybrid program, for instance.

This is the same kind of information that hTell gives you. RelativeSeek means to seek from the current position. A positive number requests going forwards in the file, and a negative number means going backwards. Finally, SeekFromEnd will seek to the specified number of bytes before the end of the file. hSeek handle SeekFromEnd 0 will take you to the end of the file. For an example of hSeek, refer to "Extended Example: Functional I/O and Temporary Files" on page 175.

Not all Handles are seekable. A Handle usually corresponds to a file, but it can also correspond to other things such as network connections, tape drives, or terminals. You can use hIsSeekable to see if a given Handle is seekable.

Standard Input, Output, and Error

Earlier, we pointed out that for each non-"h" function, there is usually also a corresponding "h" function that works on any Handle. In fact, the non-"h" functions are nothing more than shortcuts for their "h" counterparts.

There are three predefined Handles in System.IO. These Handles are always available for your use. They are stdin, which corresponds to standard input; stdout for standard output; and stderr for standard error. Standard input normally refers to the keyboard, standard output to the monitor, and standard error also normally goes to the monitor.

Functions such as getLine can thus be trivially defined like this:

```
getLine = hGetLine stdin
putStrLn = hPutStrLn stdout
print = hPrint stdout
```

 We're using partial application here. If this isn't making sense, consult "Partial Function Application and Currying" on page 100 for a refresher.

Earlier, we told you what the three standard file handles "normally" correspond to. That's because some operating systems let you redirect the file handles to come from (or go to) different places—files, devices, or even other programs. This feature is used extensively in shell scripting on POSIX (Linux, BSD, Mac) operating systems, but can also be used on Windows.

It often makes sense to use standard input and output instead of specific files. This lets you interact with a human at the terminal. But it also lets you work with input and output files—or even combine your code with other programs—if that's what's requested.[||]

As an example, we can provide input to callingpure.hs in advance like this:

[||] For more information on interoperating with other programs with pipes, see "Extended Example: Piping" on page 476.

```
$ echo John|runghc callingpure.hs
Greetings once again.  What is your name?
Pleased to meet you, John.
Your name contains 4 characters.
```

While callingpure.hs was running, it did not wait for input at the keyboard; instead it received John from the echo program. Notice also that the output didn't contain the word John on a separate line as it did when this program was run at the keyboard. The terminal normally echoes everything you type back to you, but that is technically input and not included in the output stream.

Deleting and Renaming Files

So far in this chapter, we've discussed the contents of the files. Let's now talk a bit about the files themselves.

System.Directory provides two functions you may find useful. removeFile takes a single argument, a filename, and deletes that file.[#] renameFile takes two filenames: the first is the old name and the second is the new name. If the new filename is in a different directory, you can also think of this as a move. The old filename must exist prior to the call to renameFile. If the new file already exists, it is removed before the rename takes place.

Like many other functions that take a filename, if the "old" name doesn't exist, renameFile will raise an exception. More information on exception handling can be found in Chapter 19.

There are many other functions in System.Directory for doing things such as creating and removing directories, finding lists of files in directories, and testing for file existence. These are discussed in "Directory and File Information" on page 468.

Temporary Files

Programmers frequently need temporary files. These files may be used to store large amounts of data needed for computations, data to be used by other programs, or any number of other uses.

While you could craft a way to manually open files with unique names, the details of doing this in a secure way differ from platform to platform. Haskell provides a convenient function called openTempFile (and a corresponding openBinaryTempFile) to handle the difficult bits for you.

openTempFile takes two parameters: the directory in which to create the file, and a "template" for naming the file. The directory could simply be "." for the current working directory. Or you could use System.Directory.getTemporaryDirectory to find the best place for temporary files on a given machine. The template is used as the basis

---

[#] POSIX programmers may be interested to know that this corresponds to unlink() in C.

for the filename; it will have some random characters added to it to ensure that the result is truly unique. It guarantees that it will be working on a unique filename, in fact.

The return type of openTempFile is IO (FilePath, Handle). The first part of the tuple is the name of the file created, and the second is a Handle opened in ReadWriteMode over that file. When you're done with the file, you'll want to hClose it and then call remove File to delete it. See the following example for a sample function to use.

Extended Example: Functional I/O and Temporary Files

Here's a larger example that puts together some concepts from this chapter, from some earlier chapters, and a few you haven't seen yet. Take a look at the program and see if you can figure out what it does and how it works:

```
-- file: ch07/tempfile.hs
import System.IO
import System.Directory(getTemporaryDirectory, removeFile)
import System.IO.Error(catch)
import Control.Exception(finally)

-- The main entry point.  Work with a temp file in myAction.
main :: IO ()
main = withTempFile "mytemp.txt" myAction

{- The guts of the program.  Called with the path and handle of a temporary
   file.  When this function exits, that file will be closed and deleted
   because myAction was called from withTempFile. -}
myAction :: FilePath -> Handle -> IO ()
myAction tempname temph =
    do -- Start by displaying a greeting on the terminal
       putStrLn "Welcome to tempfile.hs"
       putStrLn $ "I have a temporary file at " ++ tempname

       -- Let's see what the initial position is
       pos <- hTell temph
       putStrLn $ "My initial position is " ++ show pos

       -- Now, write some data to the temporary file
       let tempdata = show [1..10]
       putStrLn $ "Writing one line containing " ++
                  show (length tempdata) ++ " bytes: " ++
                  tempdata
       hPutStrLn temph tempdata

       -- Get our new position.  This doesn't actually modify pos
       -- in memory, but makes the name "pos" correspond to a different
       -- value for the remainder of the "do" block.
       pos <- hTell temph
       putStrLn $ "After writing, my new position is " ++ show pos

       -- Seek to the beginning of the file and display it
       putStrLn $ "The file content is: "
       hSeek temph AbsoluteSeek 0
```

```
        -- hGetContents performs a lazy read of the entire file
        c <- hGetContents temph

        -- Copy the file byte-for-byte to stdout, followed by \n
        putStrLn c

        -- Let's also display it as a Haskell literal
        putStrLn $ "Which could be expressed as this Haskell literal:"
        print c

{- This function takes two parameters: a filename pattern and another
   function.  It will create a temporary file, and pass the name and Handle
   of that file to the given function.

   The temporary file is created with openTempFile.  The directory is the one
   indicated by getTemporaryDirectory, or, if the system has no notion of
   a temporary directory, "." is used.  The given pattern is passed to
   openTempFile.

   After the given function terminates, even if it terminates due to an
   exception, the Handle is closed and the file is deleted. -}
withTempFile :: String -> (FilePath -> Handle -> IO a) -> IO a
withTempFile pattern func =
    do -- The library ref says that getTemporaryDirectory may raise on
       -- exception on systems that have no notion of a temporary directory.
       -- So, we run getTemporaryDirectory under catch.  catch takes
       -- two functions: one to run, and a different one to run if the
       -- first raised an exception.  If getTemporaryDirectory raised an
       -- exception, just use "." (the current working directory).
       tempdir <- catch (getTemporaryDirectory) (\_ -> return ".")
       (tempfile, temph) <- openTempFile tempdir pattern

       -- Call (func tempfile temph) to perform the action on the temporary
       -- file.  finally takes two actions.  The first is the action to run.
       -- The second is an action to run after the first, regardless of
       -- whether the first action raised an exception.  This way, we ensure
       -- the temporary file is always deleted.  The return value from finally
       -- is the first action's return value.
       finally (func tempfile temph)
               (do hClose temph
                   removeFile tempfile)
```

Let's start looking at this program from the end. The `withTempFile` function demonstrates that Haskell doesn't forget its functional nature when I/O is introduced. This function takes a `String` and another function. The function passed to `withTempFile` is invoked with the name and `Handle` of a temporary file. When that function exits, the temporary file is closed and deleted. So even when dealing with I/O, we can still find the idiom of passing functions as parameters to be convenient. Lisp programmers might find our `withTempFile` function similar to Lisp's `with-open-file` function.

There is some exception handling going on to make the program more robust in the face of errors. You normally want the temporary files to be deleted after processing completes, even if something went wrong. So we make sure that happens. For more on exception handling, see Chapter 19.

Let's return to the start of the program. main is defined simply as withTempFile "mytemp.txt" myAction. myAction, then, will be invoked with the name and Handle of the temporary file.

myAction displays some information to the terminal, writes some data to the file, seeks to the beginning of the file, and reads the data back with hGetContents.[*] It then displays the contents of the file byte for byte and also as a Haskell literal via print c. That's the same as putStrLn (show c).

Let's look at the output:

```
$ runhaskell tempfile.hs
Welcome to tempfile.hs
I have a temporary file at /tmp/mytemp8572.txt
My initial position is 0
Writing one line containing 22 bytes: [1,2,3,4,5,6,7,8,9,10]
After writing, my new position is 23
The file content is:
[1,2,3,4,5,6,7,8,9,10]

Which could be expressed as this Haskell literal:
"[1,2,3,4,5,6,7,8,9,10]\n"
```

Every time you run this program, your temporary filename should be slightly different, since it contains a randomly generated component. Looking at this output, there are a few questions that might occur to you:

1. Why is your position 23 after writing a line with 22 bytes?
2. Why is there an empty line after the file content display?
3. Why is there a \n at the end of the Haskell literal display?

You might be able to guess that the answers to all three questions are related. See if you can work out the answers for a moment. If you need some help, here are the explanations:

1. Because we used hPutStrLn instead of hPutStr to write the data. hPutStrLn always terminates the line by writing a \n at the end, which didn't appear in tempdata.
2. We used putStrLn c to display the file contents c. Because the data was written originally with hPutStrLn, c ends with the newline character, and putStrLn adds a second newline character. The result is a blank line.
3. The \n is the newline character from the original hPutStrLn.

---

[*] hGetContents is discussed in "Lazy I/O" on page 178

As a final note, the byte counts may be different on some operating systems. Windows, for instance, uses the two-byte sequence \r\n as the end-of-line marker, so you may see differences on that platform.

Lazy I/O

So far in this chapter, you've seen examples of fairly traditional I/O. Each line, or block of data, is requested and processed individually.

Haskell has another approach available to you as well. Since Haskell is a lazy language, meaning that any given piece of data is only evaluated when its value must be known, there are some novel ways of approaching I/O.

hGetContents

One novel way to approach I/O is with the hGetContents function.[†] hGetContents has the type Handle -> IO String. The String it returns represents all of the data in the file given by the Handle.[‡]

In a strictly evaluated language, using such a function is often a bad idea. It may be fine to read the entire contents of a 2 KB file, but if you try to read the entire contents of a 500 GB file, you are likely to crash due to lack of RAM to store all that data. In these languages, you would traditionally use mechanisms such as loops to process the file's entire data.

But hGetContents is different. The String it returns is evaluated lazily. At the moment you call hGetContents, nothing is actually read. Data is only read from the Handle as the elements (characters) of the list are processed. As elements of the String are no longer used, Haskell's garbage collector automatically frees that memory. All of this happens completely transparently to you. And since you have what looks like (and, really, is) a pure String, you can pass it to pure (non-IO) code.

Let's take a quick look at an example. Back in "Working with Files and Handles" on page 169, you saw an imperative program that converted the entire content of a file to uppercase. Its imperative algorithm was similar to what you'd see in many other languages. Here now is the much simpler algorithm that exploits lazy evaluation:

```
-- file: ch07/toupper-lazy1.hs
import System.IO
import Data.Char(toUpper)

main :: IO ()
main = do
       inh <- openFile "input.txt" ReadMode
```

[†] There is also a shortcut function called getContents that operates on standard input.

[‡] More precisely, it is the entire data from the current position of the file pointer to the end of the file.

```
    outh <- openFile "output.txt" WriteMode
    inpStr <- hGetContents inh
    let result = processData inpStr
    hPutStr outh result
    hClose inh
    hClose outh

processData :: String -> String
processData = map toUpper
```

Notice that hGetContents handled *all* of the reading for us. Also, take a look at processData. It's a pure function since it has no side effects and always returns the same result each time it is called. It has no need to know—and no way to tell—that its input is being read lazily from a file in this case. It can work perfectly well with a 20-character literal or a 500 GB data dump on disk.

You can even verify that with ghci:

```
ghci> :load toupper-lazy1.hs
[1 of 1] Compiling Main                ( toupper-lazy1.hs, interpreted )
Ok, modules loaded: Main.
ghci> processData "Hello, there!  How are you?"
"HELLO, THERE!  HOW ARE YOU?"
ghci> :type processData
processData :: String -> String
ghci> :type processData "Hello!"
processData "Hello!" :: String
```

 If we had tried to hang on to inpStr in the example just shown past the one place where it was used (the call to processData), the program would have lost its memory efficiency. That's because the compiler would have been forced to keep inpStr's value in memory for future use. Here it knows that inpStr will never be reused and frees the memory as soon as it is done with it. Just remember: memory is only freed after its last use.

This program was a bit verbose to make it clear that there was pure code in use. Here's a bit more concise version, which we will build on in the following examples:

```
-- file: ch07/toupper-lazy2.hs
import System.IO
import Data.Char(toUpper)

main = do
       inh <- openFile "input.txt" ReadMode
       outh <- openFile "output.txt" WriteMode
       inpStr <- hGetContents inh
       hPutStr outh (map toUpper inpStr)
       hClose inh
       hClose outh
```

You are not required to ever consume all the data from the input file when using hGetContents. Whenever the Haskell system determines that the entire string hGetContents returned can be garbage collected—which means it will never be used again—the file is closed for you automatically. The same principle applies to data read from the file. Whenever a given piece of data will never again be needed, the Haskell environment releases the memory it was stored within. Strictly speaking, we wouldn't have to call hClose at all in this example program. However, it is still a good practice to get into, as later changes to a program could make the call to hClose important.

 When using hGetContents, it is important to remember that even though you may never again explicitly reference Handle directly in the rest of the program, you must not close the Handle until you have finished consuming its results via hGetContents. Doing so would cause you to miss on some or all of the file's data. Since Haskell is lazy, you generally can assume that you have consumed input only after you have output the result of the computations involving the input.

readFile and writeFile

Haskell programmers use hGetContents as a filter quite often. They read from one file, do something to the data, and write the result out elsewhere. This is so common that there are some shortcuts for doing it. readFile and writeFile are shortcuts for working with files as strings. They handle all the details of opening files, closing files, reading data, and writing data. readFile uses hGetContents internally.

Can you guess the Haskell types of these functions? Let's check with ghci:

```
ghci> :type readFile
readFile :: FilePath -> IO String
ghci> :type writeFile
writeFile :: FilePath -> String -> IO ()
```

Now, here's an example program that uses readFile and writeFile:

```
-- file: ch07/toupper-lazy3.hs
import Data.Char(toUpper)

main = do
       inpStr <- readFile "input.txt"
       writeFile "output.txt" (map toUpper inpStr)
```

Look at that—the guts of the program take up only two lines! readFile returned a lazy String, which we stored in inpStr. We then took that, processed it, and passed it to writeFile for writing.

Neither readFile nor writeFile ever provide a Handle for you to work with, so there is nothing to ever hClose. readFile uses hGetContents internally, and the underlying Handle will be closed when the returned String is garbage-collected or all the input has been consumed. writeFile will close its underlying Handle when the entire String supplied to it has been written.

A Word on Lazy Output

By now, you should understand how lazy input works in Haskell. But what about laziness during output?

As you know, nothing in Haskell is evaluated before its value is needed. Since functions such as `writeFile` and `putStr` write out the entire `String` passed to them, that entire `String` must be evaluated. So you are guaranteed that the argument to `putStr` will be evaluated in full.§

But what does that mean for laziness of the input? In the earlier examples, will the call to `putStr` or `writeFile` force the entire input string to be loaded into memory at once, just to be written out?

The answer is no. `putStr` (and all the similar output functions) write out data as it becomes available. They also have no need for keeping around data already written, so as long as nothing else in the program needs it, the memory can be freed immediately. In a sense, you can think of the `String` between `readFile` and `writeFile` as a pipe linking the two. Data goes in one end, is transformed some way, and flows back out the other.

You can verify this yourself by generating a large `input.txt` for `toupper-lazy3.hs`. It may take a bit to process, but you should see a constant—and low—memory usage while it is being processed.

interact

You learned that `readFile` and `writeFile` address the common situation of reading from one file, making a conversion, and writing to a different file. There's a situation that's even more common than that: reading from standard input, making a conversion, and writing the result to standard output. For that situation, there is a function called `interact`. The type of `interact` is `(String -> String) -> IO ()`. That is, it takes one argument: a function of type `String -> String`. That function is passed the result of `getContents`—that is, standard input read lazily. The result of that function is sent to standard output.

We can convert our example program to operate on standard input and standard output by using `interact`. Here's one way to do that:

```
-- file: ch07/toupper-lazy4.hs
import Data.Char(toUpper)

main = interact (map toUpper)
```

Look at that—*one* line of code to achieve our transformation! To achieve the same effect as with the previous examples, you could run this one like this:

```
$ runghc toupper-lazy4.hs < input.txt > output.txt
```

---

§ Excepting I/O errors such as a full disk, of course.

Or, if you'd like to see the output printed to the screen, you could type:

```
$ runghc toupper-lazy4.hs < input.txt
```

If you want to see that Haskell output truly does write out chunks of data as soon as they are received, run `runghc toupper-lazy4.hs` without any other command-line parameters. You should see each character echoed back out as soon as you type it, but in uppercase. Buffering may change this behavior; see "Buffering" on page 189 for more on buffering. If you see each line echoed as soon as you type it, or even nothing at all for a while, buffering is causing this behavior.

You can also write simple interactive programs using `interact`. Let's start with a simple example—adding a line of text before the uppercase output:

```
-- file: ch07/toupper-lazy5.hs
import Data.Char(toUpper)

main = interact (map toUpper . (++) "Your data, in uppercase, is:\n\n")
```

 If the use of the `.` operator is confusing, you might wish to refer to "Code Reuse Through Composition" on page 104.

Here we add a string at the beginning of the output. Can you spot the problem, though?

Since we're calling `map` on the *result* of `(++)`, that header itself will appear in uppercase. We can fix that in this way:

```
-- file: ch07/toupper-lazy6.hs
import Data.Char(toUpper)

main = interact ((++) "Your data, in uppercase, is:\n\n" .
                 map toUpper)
```

This moved the header outside of the `map`.

Filters with interact

Another common use of `interact` is filtering. Let's say that you want to write a program that reads a file and prints out every line that contains the character "a". Here's how you might do that with `interact`:

```
-- file: ch07/filter.hs
main = interact (unlines . filter (elem 'a') . lines)
```

This may have introduced three functions that you aren't familiar with yet. Let's inspect their types with ghci:

```
ghci> :type lines
lines :: String -> [String]
ghci> :type unlines
unlines :: [String] -> String
```

```
ghci> :type elem
elem :: (Eq a) => a -> [a] -> Bool
```

Can you guess what these functions do just by looking at their types? If not, you can find them explained in "Warming Up: Portably Splitting Lines of Text" on page 72 and "Special String-Handling Functions" on page 84. You'll frequently see lines and unlines used with I/O. Finally, elem takes a element and a list and returns True if that element occurs anywhere in the list.

Try running this over our standard example input:

```
$ runghc filter.hs < input.txt
I like Haskell
Haskell is great
```

Sure enough, you got back the two lines that contain an "a". Lazy filters are a powerful way to use Haskell. When you think about it, a filter—such as the standard Unix program grep—sounds a lot like a function. It takes some input, applies some computation, and generates a predictable output.

The IO Monad

You've seen a number of examples of I/O in Haskell by this point. Let's take a moment to step back and think about how I/O relates to the broader Haskell language.

Since Haskell is a pure language, if you give a certain function a specific argument, the function will return the same result every time you give it that argument. Moreover, the function will not change anything about the program's overall state.

You may be wondering, then, how I/O fits into this picture. Surely if you want to read a line of input from the keyboard, the function to read input can't possibly return the same result every time it is run, right? Moreover, I/O is all about changing state. I/O could cause pixels on a terminal to light up, cause paper to start coming out of a printer, or even to cause a package to be shipped from a warehouse on a different continent. I/O doesn't just change the state of a program. You can think of I/O as changing the state of the world.

Actions

Most languages do not make a distinction between a pure function and an impure one. Haskell has functions in the mathematical sense: they are purely computations that cannot be altered by anything external. Moreover, the computation can be performed at any time—or even never, if its result is never needed.

Clearly, then, we need some other tool to work with I/O. That tool in Haskell is called *actions*. Actions resemble functions. They do nothing when they are defined, but perform some task when they are invoked. I/O actions are defined within the IO monad. Monads are a powerful way of chaining functions together purely and are covered in

Chapter 14. It's not necessary to understand monads in order to understand I/O. Just understand that the result type of actions is "tagged" with IO. Let's take a look at some types:

```
ghci> :type putStrLn
putStrLn :: String -> IO ()
ghci> :type getLine
getLine :: IO String
```

The type of putStrLn is just like any other function. The function takes one parameter and returns an IO (). This IO () is the action. You can store and pass actions in pure code if you wish, though this isn't frequently done. An action doesn't do anything until it is invoked. Let's look at an example of this:

```
-- file: ch07/actions.hs
str2action :: String -> IO ()
str2action input = putStrLn ("Data: " ++ input)

list2actions :: [String] -> [IO ()]
list2actions = map str2action

numbers :: [Int]
numbers = [1..10]

strings :: [String]
strings = map show numbers

actions :: [IO ()]
actions = list2actions strings

printitall :: IO ()
printitall = runall actions

-- Take a list of actions, and execute each of them in turn.
runall :: [IO ()] -> IO ()
runall [] = return ()
runall (firstelem:remainingelems) =
    do firstelem
       runall remainingelems

main = do str2action "Start of the program"
          printitall
          str2action "Done!"
```

str2action is a function that takes one parameter and returns an IO (). As you can see at the end of main, you could use this directly in another action and it will print out a line right away. Or, you can store—but not execute—the action from pure code. You can see an example of that in list2actions—we use map over str2action and return a list of actions, just like we would with other pure data. You can see that everything up through printitall is built up with pure tools.

Although we define `printitall`, it doesn't get executed until its action is evaluated somewhere else. Notice in `main` how we use `str2action` as an I/O action to be executed, but earlier we used it outside of the I/O monad and assembled results into a list.

You could think of it this way: every statement, except `let`, in a do block must yield an I/O action that will be executed.

The call to `printitall` finally executes all those actions. Actually, since Haskell is lazy, the actions aren't generated until here either.

When you run the program, your output will look like this:

```
Data: Start of the program
Data: 1
Data: 2
Data: 3
Data: 4
Data: 5
Data: 6
Data: 7
Data: 8
Data: 9
Data: 10
Data: Done!
```

We can actually write this in a much more compact way. Consider this revision of the example:

```
-- file: ch07/actions2.hs
str2message :: String -> String
str2message input = "Data: " ++ input

str2action :: String -> IO ()
str2action = putStrLn . str2message

numbers :: [Int]
numbers = [1..10]

main = do str2action "Start of the program"
          mapM_ (str2action . show) numbers
          str2action "Done!"
```

Notice in `str2action` the use of the standard function composition operator. In `main`, there's a call to `mapM_`. This function is similar to `map`. It takes a function and a list. The function supplied to `mapM_` is an I/O action that is executed for every item in the list. `mapM_` throws out the result of the function, though you can use `mapM` to return a list of I/O results if you want them. Take a look at their types:

```
ghci> :type mapM
mapM :: (Monad m) => (a -> m b) -> [a] -> m [b]
ghci> :type mapM_
mapM_ :: (Monad m) => (a -> m b) -> [a] -> m ()
```

These functions actually work for more than just I/O; they work for any Monad. For now, wherever you see "M," just think "IO." Also, functions that end with an underscore typically discard their result.

Why a mapM when we already have map? Because map is a pure function that returns a list. It doesn't—and can't—actually execute actions directly. mapM is a utility that lives in the IO monad and thus can actually execute the actions.[||]

Going back to main, mapM_ applies (str2action . show) to every element in numbers. show converts each number to a String and str2action converts each String to an action. mapM_ combines these individual actions into one big action that prints out lines.

Sequencing

do blocks are actually shortcut notations for joining together actions. There are two operators that you can use instead of do blocks: >> and >>=. Let's look at their types in ghci:

```
ghci> :type (>>)
(>>) :: (Monad m) => m a -> m b -> m b
ghci> :type (>>=)
(>>=) :: (Monad m) => m a -> (a -> m b) -> m b
```

The >> operator sequences two actions together: the first action is performed, and then the second. The result of the computation is the result of the second action. The result of the first action is thrown away. This is similar to simply having a line in a do block. You might write putStrLn "line 1" >> putStrLn "line 2" to test this out. It will print out two lines, discard the result from the first putStrLn, and provide the result from the second.

The >>= operator runs an action, and then passes its result to a function that returns an action. That second action is run as well, and the result of the entire expression is the result of that second action. As an example, you could write getLine >>= putStrLn, which would read a line from the keyboard and then display it back out.

Let's rewrite one of our examples to avoid do blocks. Remember this example from the start of the chapter?

```
-- file: ch07/basicio.hs
main = do
        putStrLn "Greetings!  What is your name?"
        inpStr <- getLine
        putStrLn $ "Welcome to Haskell, " ++ inpStr ++ "!"
```

Let's write that without a do block:

[||] Technically speaking, mapM combines a bunch of separate I/O actions into one big action. The separate actions are executed when the big action is.

```
-- file: ch07/basicio-nodo.hs
main =
    putStrLn "Greetings!  What is your name?" >>
    getLine >>=
    (\inpStr -> putStrLn $ "Welcome to Haskell, " ++ inpStr ++ "!")
```

The Haskell compiler internally performs a translation just like this when you define a do block.

Forgetting how to use \ (lambda expressions)? See "Anonymous (lambda) Functions" on page 99.

The True Nature of Return

Earlier in this chapter, we mentioned that return is probably not what it looks like. Many languages have a keyword named return that aborts execution of a function immediately and returns a value to the caller.

The Haskell return function is quite different. In Haskell, return is used to wrap data in a monad. When speaking about I/O, return is used to take pure data and bring it into the IO monad.

Now, why would we want to do that? Remember that anything whose result depends on I/O must be within the IO monad. So if we are writing a function that performs I/O, and then a pure computation, we will need to use return to make this pure computation the proper return value of the function. Otherwise, a type error would occur. Here's an example:

```
-- file: ch07/return1.hs
import Data.Char(toUpper)

isGreen :: IO Bool
isGreen =
    do putStrLn "Is green your favorite color?"
       inpStr <- getLine
       return ((toUpper . head $ inpStr) == 'Y')
```

We have a pure computation that yields a Bool. That computation is passed to return, which puts it into the IO monad. Since it is the last value in the do block, it becomes the return value of isGreen, but this is not because we used the return function.

Here's a version of the same program with the pure computation broken out into a separate function. This helps keep the pure code separate and can also make the intent more clear:

```
-- file: ch07/return2.hs
import Data.Char(toUpper)

isYes :: String -> Bool
```

```
isYes inpStr = (toUpper . head $ inpStr) == 'Y'

isGreen :: IO Bool
isGreen =
    do putStrLn "Is green your favorite color?"
       inpStr <- getLine
       return (isYes inpStr)
```

Finally, here's a contrived example to show that return truly does not have to occur at the end of a do block. In practice, it usually does, but it need not be so.

```
-- file: ch07/return3.hs
returnTest :: IO ()
returnTest =
    do one <- return 1
       let two = 2
       putStrLn $ show (one + two)
```

Notice that we used <- in combination with return, but let in combination with the simple literal. That's because we needed both values to be pure in order to add them, and <- pulls things out of monads, effectively reversing the effect of return. Run this in ghci and you'll see 3 displayed, as expected.

Is Haskell Really Imperative?

These do blocks may look a lot like an imperative language. After all, you're giving commands to run in sequence most of the time.

But Haskell remains a lazy language at its core. While it is sometimes necessary to sequence actions for I/O, this is done using tools that are part of Haskell already. Haskell achieves a nice separation of I/O from the rest of the language through the IO monad as well.

Side Effects with Lazy I/O

Earlier in this chapter, you read about hGetContents. We explained that the String it returns can be used in pure code.

We need to get a bit more specific about what side effects are. When we say Haskell has no side effects, what exactly does that mean?

At a certain level, side effects are always possible. A poorly written loop, even if written in pure code, could cause the system's RAM to be exhausted and the machine to crash. Or it could cause data to be swapped to disk.

When we speak of no side effects, we mean that pure code in Haskell can't run commands that trigger side effects. Pure functions can't modify a global variable, request I/O, or run a command to take down a system.

When you have a String from hGetContents that is passed to a pure function, the function has no idea that this String is backed by a disk file. It will behave just as it always would, but processing that String may cause the environment to issue I/O commands. The pure function isn't issuing them; they are happening as a result of the processing the pure function is doing, just as with the example of swapping RAM to disk.

In some cases, you may need more control over exactly when your I/O occurs. Perhaps you are reading data interactively from the user, or via a pipe from another program, and need to communicate directly with the user. In those cases, hGetContents will probably not be appropriate.

Buffering

The I/O subsystem is one of the slowest parts of a modern computer. Completing a write to disk can take thousands of times as long as a write to memory. A write over the network can be hundreds or thousands of times slower yet. Even if your operation doesn't directly communicate with the disk—perhaps because the data is cached— I/O still involves a system call, which slows things down by itself.

For this reason, modern operating systems and programming languages both provide tools to help programs perform better where I/O is concerned. The operating system typically performs caching—storing frequently used pieces of data in memory for faster access.

Programming languages typically perform buffering. This means that they may request one large chunk of data from the operating system, even if the code underneath is processing data one character at a time. By doing this, they can achieve remarkable performance gains because each request for I/O to the operating system carries a processing cost. Buffering allows us to read the same amount of data with far fewer I/O requests.

Haskell, too, provides buffering in its I/O system. In many cases, it is even on by default. Up until now, we have pretended it isn't there. Haskell usually is good about picking a good default buffering mode, but it is rarely the fastest. If you have speed-critical I/O code, changing buffering could have a significant impact on your program.

Buffering Modes

There are three different buffering modes in Haskell. They are defined as the BufferMode type: NoBuffering, LineBuffering, and BlockBuffering.

NoBuffering does just what it sounds like—no buffering. Data read via functions like hGetLine will be read from the OS one character at a time. Data written will be written immediately, and also often will be written one character at a time. For this reason, NoBuffering is usually a very poor performer and not suitable for general-purpose use.

LineBuffering causes the output buffer to be written whenever the newline character is output, or whenever it gets too large. On input, it will usually attempt to read whatever data is available in chunks until it first sees the newline character. When reading from the terminal, it should return data immediately after each press of Enter. It is often a reasonable default.

BlockBuffering causes Haskell to read or write data in fixed-size chunks when possible. This is the best performer when processing large amounts of data in batch, even if that data is line-oriented. However, it is unusable for interactive programs because it will block input until a full block is read. BlockBuffering accepts one parameter of type Maybe; if Nothing, it will use an implementation-defined buffer size. Or, you can use a setting such as Just 4096 to set the buffer to 4096 bytes.

The default buffering mode is dependent upon the operating system and Haskell implementation. You can ask the system for the current buffering mode by calling hGetBuffering. The current mode can be set with hSetBuffering, which accepts a Handle and BufferMode. You can say hSetBuffering stdin (BlockBuffering Nothing), for example.

Flushing The Buffer

For any type of buffering, you may sometimes want to force Haskell to write out any data that has been saved up in the buffer. There are a few times when this will happen automatically: a call to hClose, for instance. Sometimes you may want to instead call hFlush, which will force any pending data to be written immediately. This could be useful when the Handle is a network socket and you want the data to be transmitted immediately, or when you want to make the data on disk available to other programs that might be reading it concurrently.

Reading Command-Line Arguments

Many command-line programs are interested in the parameters passed on the command line. System.Environment.getArgs returns IO [String] listing each argument. This is the same as argv in C, starting with argv[1]. The program name (argv[0] in C) is available from System.Environment.getProgName.

The System.Console.GetOpt module provides some tools for parsing command-line options. If you have a program with complex options, you may find it useful. You can find an example of its use in "Command-Line Parsing" on page 636.

Environment Variables

If you need to read environment variables, you can use one of two functions in System.Environment: getEnv or getEnvironment. getEnv looks for a specific variable and raises an exception if it doesn't exist. getEnvironment returns the whole environment as a [(String, String)], and then you can use functions such as lookup to find the environment entry you want.

Setting environment variables is not defined in a cross-platform way in Haskell. If you are on a POSIX platform such as Linux, you can use putEnv or setEnv from the System.Posix.Env module. Environment setting is not defined for Windows.

CHAPTER 8

Efficient File Processing, Regular Expressions, and Filename Matching

Efficient File Processing

This simple microbenchmark reads a text file full of numbers and prints their sum:

```
-- file: ch08/SumFile.hs
main = do
    contents <- getContents
    print (sumFile contents)
  where sumFile = sum . map read . words
```

Although the `String` type is the default used for reading and writing files, it is not efficient, so a simple program like this will perform badly.

A `String` is represented as a list of `Char` values; each element of a list is allocated individually and has some bookkeeping overhead. These factors affect the memory consumption and performance of a program that must read or write text or binary data. On simple benchmarks like this, even programs written in interpreted languages such as Python can outperform Haskell code that uses `String` by an order of magnitude.

The `bytestring` library provides a fast, cheap alternative to the `String` type. Code written with `bytestring` can often match or exceed the performance and memory footprint of C, while maintaining Haskell's expressivity and conciseness.

The library supplies two modules—each defines functions that are nearly drop-in replacements for their `String` counterparts:

Data.ByteString
> Defines a *strict* type named `ByteString`. This represents a string of binary or text data in a single array.

Data.ByteString.Lazy
> Provides a *lazy* type, also named `ByteString`. This represents a string of data as a list of *chunks*, arrays of up to 64 KB in size.

Each `ByteString` type performs better under particular circumstances. For streaming a large quantity (hundreds of megabytes to terabytes) of data, the lazy `ByteString` type is usually best. Its chunk size is tuned to be friendly to a modern CPU's L1 cache, and a garbage collector can quickly discard chunks of streamed data that are no longer being used.

The strict `ByteString` type performs best for applications that are less concerned with memory footprint or that need to access data randomly.

Binary I/O and Qualified Imports

Let's develop a small function to illustrate some of the `ByteString` API. We will determine if a file is an ELF object file—this is the format used for executables on almost all modern Unix-like systems.

This is a simple matter of looking at the first four bytes in the file and seeing if they match a specific sequence of bytes. A byte sequence that identifies a file's type is often known as a *magic number*:

```
-- file: ch08/ElfMagic.hs
import qualified Data.ByteString.Lazy as L

hasElfMagic :: L.ByteString -> Bool
hasElfMagic content = L.take 4 content == elfMagic
    where elfMagic = L.pack [0x7f, 0x45, 0x4c, 0x46]
```

We import the `ByteString` modules using Haskell's *qualified import* syntax, the `import qualified` that we just saw. This lets us refer to a module with a name of our choosing.

For instance, when we want to refer to the lazy `ByteString` module's `take` function, we must write `L.take`, since we imported the module under the name `L`. If we are not explicit about which version of, for example, `take` we want, the compiler will report an error.

We will always use qualified import syntax with the `ByteString` modules, because they provide many functions that have the same names as `Prelude` functions.

 Qualified imports make it easy to switch between `ByteString` types. All you should need to do is modify an `import` declaration at the top of your source file; the rest of your code will probably not need any changes. You can thus handily benchmark the two types, to see which is best suited to your application's needs

Whether or not we use qualified imports, we can always use the entire name of a module to identify something unambiguously. Both `Data.ByteString.Lazy.length` and `L.length`, for instance, identify the same function, as do `Prelude.sum` and `sum`.

The lazy and strict `ByteString` modules are intended for binary I/O. The Haskell data type for representing bytes is `Word8`; if we need to refer to it by name, we import it from the `Data.Word` module.

The `L.pack` function takes a list of `Word8` values, and packs them into a lazy `ByteString`. (The `L.unpack` function performs the reverse conversion.) Our `hasElfMagic` function simply compares the first four bytes of a `ByteString` against a magic number.

We are writing in classic Haskell style, where our `hasElfMagic` function does not perform I/O. Here is the function that uses it on a file:

```
-- file: ch08/ElfMagic.hs
isElfFile :: FilePath -> IO Bool
isElfFile path = do
  content <- L.readFile path
  return (hasElfMagic content)
```

The `L.readFile` function is the lazy `ByteString` equivalent of `readFile`. It operates lazily, reading the file as data is demanded. It is also efficient, reading chunks of up to 64 KB at once. The lazy `ByteString` is a good choice for our task: since we only need to read at most the first four bytes of the file, we can safely use this function on a file of any size.

Text I/O

For convenience, the `bytestring` library provides two other modules with limited text I/O capabilities, `Data.ByteString.Char8` and `Data.ByteString.Lazy.Char8`. These expose individual string elements as `Char` instead of `Word8`.

 The functions in these modules only work with byte-sized `Char` values, so they are only suitable for use with ASCII and some European character sets. Values above 255 are truncated.

The character-oriented `bytestring` modules provide useful functions for text processing. Here is a file that contains monthly stock prices for a well-known Internet company from mid-2008:

```
ghci> putStr =<< readFile "prices.csv"
Date,Open,High,Low,Close,Volume,Adj Close
2008-08-01,20.09,20.12,19.53,19.80,19777000,19.80
2008-06-30,21.12,21.20,20.60,20.66,17173500,20.66
2008-05-30,27.07,27.10,26.63,26.76,17754100,26.76
2008-04-30,27.17,27.78,26.76,27.41,30597400,27.41
```

How can we find the highest closing price from a series of entries like this? Closing prices are in the fourth comma-separated column. This function obtains a closing price from one line of data:

```
-- file: ch08/HighestClose.hs
import qualified Data.ByteString.Lazy.Char8 as L

closing = readPrice . (!!4) . L.split ','
```

Since this function is written in point-free style, we read from right to left. The
L.split function splits a lazy ByteString into a list of them, every time it finds a matching character. The (!!) operator retrieves the kth element of a list. Our readPrice function turns a string representing a fractional price into a whole number:

```
-- file: ch08/HighestClose.hs
readPrice :: L.ByteString -> Maybe Int
readPrice str =
    case L.readInt str of
      Nothing              -> Nothing
      Just (dollars,rest) ->
        case L.readInt (L.tail rest) of
          Nothing          -> Nothing
          Just (cents,more) ->
            Just (dollars * 100 + cents)
```

We use the L.readInt function, which parses an integer. It returns both the integer and
the remainder of the string once a run of digits is consumed. Our definition is slightly
complicated by L.readInt returning Nothing if parsing fails.

Our function for finding the highest closing price is straightforward:

```
-- file: ch08/HighestClose.hs
highestClose = maximum . (Nothing:) . map closing . L.lines

highestCloseFrom path = do
    contents <- L.readFile path
    print (highestClose contents)
```

We use one trick to work around the fact that we cannot supply an empty list to the
maximum function:

```
ghci> maximum [3,6,2,9]
9
ghci> maximum []
*** Exception: Prelude.maximum: empty list
```

Since we do not want our code to throw an exception if we have no stock data, the
(Nothing:) expression ensures that the list of Maybe Int values that we supply to
maximum will never be empty:

```
ghci> maximum [Nothing, Just 1]
Just 1
ghci> maximum [Nothing]
Nothing
```

Does our function work?

```
ghci> :load HighestClose
[1 of 1] Compiling Main             ( HighestClose.hs, interpreted )
Ok, modules loaded: Main.
```

```
ghci> highestCloseFrom "prices.csv"
Loading package array-0.1.0.0 ... linking ... done.
Loading package bytestring-0.9.0.1.1 ... linking ... done.
Just 2741
```

Since we have separated our I/O from our logic, we can test the no-data case without having to create an empty file:

```
ghci> highestClose L.empty
Nothing
```

Filename Matching

Many systems-oriented programming languages provide library routines that let us match a filename against a pattern, or that will give a list of files that match the pattern. In other languages, this function is often named fnmatch.) Although Haskell's standard library generally has good systems programming facilities, it doesn't provide these kinds of pattern matching functions. We'll take this as an opportunity to develop our own.

The kinds of patterns we'll be dealing with are commonly referred to as *glob patterns* (the term we'll use), wild card patterns, or shell-style patterns. They have just a few simple rules. You probably already know them, but we'll quickly recap here:

- Matching a string against a pattern starts at the beginning of the string, and finishes at the end.

- Most literal characters match themselves. For example, the text foo in a pattern will match foo, and only foo, in an input string.

- The * (asterisk) character means "match anything"; it will match any text, including the empty string. For instance, the pattern foo* will match any string that begins with foo, such as foo itself, foobar, or foo.c. The pattern quux*.c will match any string that begins with quux and ends in .c, such as quuxbaz.c.

- The ? (question mark) character matches any single character. The pattern pic??.jpg will match names like picaa.jpg or pic01.jpg.

- A [(open square bracket) character begins a *character class*, which is ended by a]. Its meaning is "match any character in this class". A character class can be *negated* by following the opening [with a !, so that it means "match any character *not* in this class".

  As a shorthand, a character followed by a - (dash), followed by another character, denotes a *range*: "match any character within this set."

  Character classes have an added subtlety; they can't be empty. The first character after the opening [or [! is part of the class, so we can write a class containing the] character as []aeiou]. The pattern pic[0-9].[pP][nN][gG] will match a name consisting of the string pic, followed by a single digit, followed by any capitalization of the strig .png.

While Haskell doesn't provide a way to match glob patterns among its standard libraries, it provides a good regular expression matching library. Glob patterns are nothing more than cut-down regular expressions with slightly different syntax. It's easy to convert glob patterns into regular expressions, but to do so, we must first understand how to use regular expressions in Haskell.

Regular Expressions in Haskell

In this section, we assume that you are already familiar with regular expressions by way of some other language, such as Python, Perl, or Java.[*]

For brevity, we will abbreviate "regular expression" as *regexp* from here on.

Rather than introduce regexps as something new, we will focus on what's different about regexp handling in Haskell, compared to other languages. Haskell's regular expression matching libraries are a lot more expressive than those of other languages, so there's plenty to talk about.

To begin our exploration of the regexp libraries, the only module we'll need to work with is `Text.Regex.Posix`. As usual, the most convenient way to explore this module is by interacting with it via `ghci`:

```
ghci> :module +Text.Regex.Posix
```

The only function that we're likely to need for normal use is the regexp matching function, an infix operator named (`=~`) (borrowed from Perl). The first hurdle to overcome is that Haskell's regexp libraries make heavy use of polymorphism. As a result, the type signature of the (`=~`) operator is difficult to understand, so we will not explain it here.

The `=~` operator uses typeclasses for both of its arguments and also for its return type. The first argument (on the left of the `=~`) is the text to match; the second (on the right) is the regular expression to match against. We can pass either a `String` or a `ByteString` as argument.

The Many Types of Result

The `=~` operator is polymorphic in its return type, so the Haskell compiler needs some way to know what type of result we would like. In real code, it may be able to infer the right type, due to the way we subsequently use the result. But such cues are often lacking when we're exploring with `ghci`. If we omit a specific type for the result, we'll get an error from the interpreter, as it does not have enough information to successfuly infer the result type.

---

[*] If you are not acquainted with regular expressions, we recommend Jeffrey Friedl's book *Mastering Regular Expressions* (O'Reilly).

When ghci can't infer the target type, we tell it what we'd like the type to be. If we want a result of type Bool, we'll get a pass/fail answer:

```
ghci> "my left foot" =~ "foo" :: Bool
Loading package array-0.1.0.0 ... linking ... done.
Loading package bytestring-0.9.0.1.1 ... linking ... done.
Loading package regex-base-0.72.0.1 ... linking ... done.
Loading package regex-posix-0.72.0.2 ... linking ... done.
True
ghci> "your right hand" =~ "bar" :: Bool
False
ghci> "your right hand" =~ "(hand|foot)" :: Bool
True
```

In the bowels of the regexp libraries, there's a typeclass named RegexContext that describes how a target type should behave; the base library defines many instances of this typeclass for us. The Bool type is an instance of this typeclass, so we get back a usable result. Another such instance is Int, which gives us a count of the number of times the regexp matches:

```
ghci> "a star called henry" =~ "planet" :: Int
0
ghci> "honorificabilitudinitatibus" =~ "[aeiou]" :: Int
13
```

If we ask for a String result, we'll get the first substring that matches or an empty string if nothing matches:

```
ghci> "I, B. Ionsonii, uurit a lift'd batch" =~ "(uu|ii)" :: String
"ii"
ghci> "hi ludi, F. Baconis nati, tuiti orbi" =~ "Shakespeare" :: String
""
```

Another valid type of result is [String], which returns a list of *all* matching strings:

```
ghci> "I, B. Ionsonii, uurit a lift'd batch" =~ "(uu|ii)" :: [String]
["ii","uu"]
ghci> "hi ludi, F. Baconis nati, tuiti orbi" =~ "Shakespeare" :: [String]
[]
```

Watch out for String results

If you want a result that's a plain String, beware. Since (=~) returns an empty string to signify "no match", this poses an obvious difficulty if the empty string could also be a valid match for the regexp. If such a case arises, you should use a different return type instead, such as [String].

That's about it for "simple" result types, but we're not by any means finished. Before we continue, let's use a single pattern for our remaining examples. We can define this pattern as a variable in ghci, to save a little typing:

```
ghci> let pat = "(foo[a-z]*bar|quux)"
```

We can obtain quite a lot of information about the context in which a match occurs. If we ask for a (String, String, String) tuple, we'll get back the text *before* the first match, the text *of* that match, and the text that *follows* it:

```
ghci> "before foodiebar after" =~ pat :: (String,String,String)
("before ","foodiebar"," after")
```

If the match fails, the entire text is returned as the "before" element of the tuple, with the other two elements left empty:

```
ghci> "no match here" =~ pat :: (String,String,String)
("no match here","","")
```

Asking for a four-element tuple gives us a fourth element that's a list of all groups in the pattern that matched:

```
ghci> "before foodiebar after" =~ pat :: (String,String,String,[String])
("before ","foodiebar"," after",["foodiebar"])
```

We can get numeric information about matches, too. A pair of Ints gives us the starting offset of the first match, and its length. If we ask for a list of these pairs, we'll get this information for all matches:

```
ghci> "before foodiebar after" =~ pat :: (Int,Int)
(7,9)
ghci> "i foobarbar a quux" =~ pat :: [(Int,Int)]
[(2,9),(14,4)]
```

A failed match is represented by the value -1 as the first element of the tuple (the match offset) if we've asked for a single tuple, or an empty list if we've asked for a list of tuples:

```
ghci> "eleemosynary" =~ pat :: (Int,Int)
(-1,0)
ghci> "mondegreen" =~ pat :: [(Int,Int)]
[]
```

This is not a comprehensive list of built-in instances of the RegexContext typeclass. For a complete list, see the documentation for the Text.Regex.Base.Context module.

This ability to make a function polymorphic in its result type is an unusual feature for a statically typed language.

More About Regular Expressions

Mixing and Matching String Types

As we noted earlier, the =~ operator uses typeclasses for its argument types and its return type. We can use either String or strict ByteString values for both the regular expression and the text to match against:

```
ghci> :module +Data.ByteString.Char8
ghci> :type pack "foo"
pack "foo" :: ByteString
```

We can then try using different combinations of String and ByteString:

```
ghci> pack "foo" =~ "bar" :: Bool
False
ghci> "foo" =~ pack "bar" :: Int
0
ghci> pack "foo" =~ pack "o" :: [(Int, Int)]
[(1,1),(2,1)]
```

However, we need to be aware that if we want a string value in the result of a match, the text we're matching against must be the same type of string. Let's see what this means in practice:

```
ghci> pack "good food" =~ ".ood" :: [ByteString]
["good","food"]
```

In the above example, we've used the pack to turn a String into a ByteString. The type checker accepts this because ByteString appears in the result type. But if we try getting a String out, that *won't* work:

```
ghci> "good food" =~ ".ood" :: [ByteString]

<interactive>:1:0:
    No instance for (Text.Regex.Base.RegexLike.RegexContext
                        Regex [Char] [ByteString])
      arising from a use of `=~' at <interactive>:1:0-20
    Possible fix:
      add an instance declaration for
      (Text.Regex.Base.RegexLike.RegexContext Regex [Char] [ByteString])
    In the expression: "good food" =~ ".ood" :: [ByteString]
    In the definition of `it':
        it = "good food" =~ ".ood" :: [ByteString]
```

We can easily fix this problem by making the string types of the lefthand side and the result match once again:

```
ghci> "good food" =~ ".ood" :: [String]
["good","food"]
```

This restriction does *not* apply to the type of the regexp we're matching against. It can be either a String or ByteString, unconstrained by the other types in use.

Other Things You Should Know

When you look through Haskell library documentation, you'll see several regexp-related modules. The modules under Text.Regex.Base define the common API adhered to by all of the other regexp modules. It's possible to have multiple implementations of the regexp API installed at one time. At the time of this writing, GHC is bundled with one implementation, Text.Regex.Posix. As its name suggests, this package provides POSIX regexp semantics.

Perl and POSIX Regular Expressions

If you're coming to Haskell from a language like Perl, Python, or Java, and you've used regular expressions in one of those languages, you should be aware that the POSIX regexps handled by the `Text.Regex.Posix` module are different in some significant ways from Perl-style regexps. Here are a few of the more notable differences.

Perl regexp engines perform left-biased matching when matching alternatives, whereas POSIX engines choose the greediest match. What this means is that given a regexp of (foo|fo*) and a text string of foooooo, a Perl-style engine will give a match of foo (the leftmost match), while a POSIX engine will match the entire string (the greediest match).

POSIX regexps have less uniform syntax than Perl-style regexps. They also lack a number of capabilities provided by Perl-style regexps, such as zero-width assertions and control over greedy matching.

Other Haskell regexp packages are available for download from Hackage. Some provide better performance than the current POSIX engine (e.g., `regex-tdfa`); others provide the Perl-style matching that most programmers are now familiar with (e.g., `regex-pcre`). All follow the standard API that we have covered in this section.

Translating a glob Pattern into a Regular Expression

Now that we've seen the myriad of ways to match text against regular expressions, let's turn our attention back to glob patterns. We want to write a function that will take a glob pattern and return its representation as a regular expression. Both glob patterns and regexps are text strings, so the type that our function ought to have seems clear:

```
-- file: ch08/GlobRegex.hs
module GlobRegex
    (
      globToRegex
    , matchesGlob
    ) where

import Text.Regex.Posix ((=~))

globToRegex :: String -> String
```

The regular expression that we generate must be *anchored* so that it starts matching from the beginning of a string and finishes at the end:

```
-- file: ch08/GlobRegex.hs
globToRegex cs = '^' : globToRegex' cs ++ "$"
```

Recall that the `String` is just a synonym for [Char], a list of Chars. The : operator puts a value (the ^ character in this case) onto the front of a list, where the list is the value returned by the yet-to-be-seen `globToRegex'` function.

Using a value before defining it

Haskell does not require that a value or function be declared or defined in a source file before it's used. It's perfectly normal for a definition to come *after* the first place it's used. The Haskell compiler doesn't care about ordering at this level. This grants us the flexibility to structure our code in the manner that makes most logical sense to us, rather than follow an order that makes the compiler writer's life easiest.

Haskell module writers often use this flexibility to put "more important" code earlier in a source file, relegating "plumbing" to later. This is exactly how we are presenting the globToRegex function and its helpers here.

With the regular expression rooted, the globToRegex' function will do the bulk of the translation work. We'll use the convenience of Haskell's pattern matching to enumerate each of the cases we'll need to cover:

```
-- file: ch08/GlobRegex.hs
globToRegex' :: String -> String
globToRegex' "" = ""

globToRegex' ('*':cs) = ".*" ++ globToRegex' cs

globToRegex' ('?':cs) = '.' : globToRegex' cs

globToRegex' ('[':'!':c:cs) = "[^" ++ c : charClass cs
globToRegex' ('[':c:cs)     = '['  :  c : charClass cs
globToRegex' ('[':_)        = error "unterminated character class"

globToRegex' (c:cs) = escape c ++ globToRegex' cs
```

Our first clause stipulates that if we hit the end of our glob pattern (by which time we'll be looking at the empty string), we return $, the regular expression symbol for "match end-of-line." Following this is a series of clauses that switch our pattern from glob syntax to regexp syntax. The last clause passes every other character through, possibly escaping it first.

The escape function ensures that the regexp engine will not interpret certain characters as pieces of regular expression syntax:

```
-- file: ch08/GlobRegex.hs
escape :: Char -> String
escape c | c `elem` regexChars = '\\' : [c]
         | otherwise = [c]
    where regexChars = "\\+()^$.{}]|"
```

The charClass helper function only checks that a character class is correctly terminated. It passes its input through unmodified until it hits a], when it hands control back to globToRegex':

```
-- file: ch08/GlobRegex.hs
charClass :: String -> String
```

```
charClass (']':cs) = ']' : globToRegex' cs
charClass (c:cs)   = c : charClass cs
charClass []       = error "unterminated character class"
```

Now that we've finished defining globToRegex and its helpers, let's load it into ghci and try it out:

```
ghci> :load GlobRegex.hs
[1 of 1] Compiling GlobRegex        ( GlobRegex.hs, interpreted )
Ok, modules loaded: GlobRegex.
ghci> :module +Text.Regex.Posix
ghci> globToRegex "f??.c"
Loading package array-0.1.0.0 ... linking ... done.
Loading package bytestring-0.9.0.1.1 ... linking ... done.
Loading package regex-base-0.72.0.1 ... linking ... done.
Loading package regex-posix-0.72.0.2 ... linking ... done.
"^f..\\.c$"
```

Sure enough, that looks like a reasonable regexp. Can we use it to match against a string?

```
ghci> "foo.c" =~ globToRegex "f??.c" :: Bool
True
ghci> "test.c" =~ globToRegex "t[ea]s*" :: Bool
True
ghci> "taste.txt" =~ globToRegex "t[ea]s*" :: Bool
True
```

It works! Now let's play around a little with ghci. We can create a temporary definition for fnmatch and try it out:

```
ghci> let fnmatch pat name  =  name =~ globToRegex pat :: Bool
ghci> :type fnmatch
fnmatch :: (Text.Regex.Base.RegexLike.RegexLike Regex source1) =>
           String -> source1 -> Bool
ghci> fnmatch "d*" "myname"
False
```

The name fnmatch doesn't really have the "Haskell nature," though. By far the most common Haskell style is for functions to have descriptive, "camel cased" names. Camel casing concatenates words, capitalizing all but possibly the first word. For instance, the words "filename matches" would become the name fileNameMatches. The name "camel case" comes from the "humps" introduced by the capital letters. In our library, we'll give this function the name matchesGlob:

```
-- file: ch08/GlobRegex.hs
matchesGlob :: FilePath -> String -> Bool
name `matchesGlob` pat = name =~ globToRegex pat
```

You may have noticed that most of the names that we have used for variables so far have been short. As a rule of thumb, descriptive variable names are more useful in longer function definitions, as they aid readability. For a two-line function, a long variable name has less value.

1. Use `ghci` to explore what happens if you pass a malformed pattern, such as [, to `globToRegex`. Write a small function that calls `globToRegex`, and pass it a malformed pattern. What happens?

2. While filesystems on Unix are usually case-sensitive (e.g., "G" vs. "g") in filenames, Windows filesystems are not. Add a parameter to the `globToRegex` and `matchesGlob` functions that allows control over case sensitive matching.

An important Aside: Writing Lazy Functions

In an imperative language, the `globToRegex'` function is one that we'd usually express as a loop. For example, Python's standard `fnmatch` module includes a function named `translate` that does exactly the same job as our `globToRegex` function. It's written as a loop.

If you've been exposed to functional programming through a language such as Scheme or ML, you've probably had drilled into your head the notion that "the way to emulate a loop is via tail recursion."

Looking at the `globToRegex'` function, we can see that it is *not* tail recursive. To see why, examine its final clause again (several of its other clauses are structured similarly):

```
-- file: ch08/GlobRegex.hs
globToRegex' (c:cs) = escape c ++ globToRegex' cs
```

It applies itself recursively, and the result of the recursive application is used as a parameter to the (`++`) function. Since the recursive application *isn't* the last thing the function does, `globToRegex'` is not tail recursive.

Why is our definition of this function not tail recursive? The answer lies with Haskell's nonstrict evaluation strategy. Before we start talking about that, let's quickly talk about why, in a traditional language, we'd try to avoid this kind of recursive definition. Here is a simpler definition of the (`++`) operator. It is recursive, but not tail recursive:

```
-- file: ch08/append.hs
(++) :: [a] -> [a] -> [a]

(x:xs) ++ ys = x : (xs ++ ys)
[]     ++ ys = ys
```

In a strict language, if we evaluate `"foo" ++ "bar"`, the entire list is constructed, and then returned. Non-strict evaluation defers much of the work until it is needed.

If we demand an element of the expression `"foo" ++ "bar"`, the first pattern of the function's definition matches, and we return the expression `x : (xs ++ ys)`. Because the (`:`) constructor is nonstrict, the evaluation of `xs ++ ys` can be deferred: we generate more elements of the result at whatever rate they are demanded. When we generate more of the result, we will no longer be using x, so the garbage collector can reclaim it. Since we generate elements of the result on demand, and do not hold onto parts that we are done with, the compiler can evaluate our code in constant space.

Making Use of Our Pattern Matcher

It's all very well to have a function that can match glob patterns, but we'd like to be able to put this to practical use. On Unix-like systems, the glob function returns the names of all files and directories that match a given glob pattern. Let's build a similar function in Haskell. Following the Haskell norm of descriptive naming, we'll call our function namesMatching:

```
-- file: ch08/Glob.hs
module Glob (namesMatching) where
```

We specify that namesMatching is the only name that users of our Glob module will be able to see.

This function will obviously have to manipulate filesystem paths a lot, splicing and joining them as it goes. We'll need to use a few previously unfamiliar modules along the way.

The System.Directory module provides standard functions for working with directories and their contents:

```
-- file: ch08/Glob.hs
import System.Directory (doesDirectoryExist, doesFileExist,
                         getCurrentDirectory, getDirectoryContents)
```

The System.FilePath module abstracts the details of an operating system's path name conventions. The (</>) function joins two path components:

```
ghci> :m +System.FilePath
ghci> "foo" </> "bar"
Loading package filepath-1.1.0.0 ... linking ... done.
"foo/bar"
```

The name of the dropTrailingPathSeparator function is perfectly descriptive:

```
ghci> dropTrailingPathSeparator "foo/"
"foo"
```

The splitFileName function splits a path at the last slash:

```
ghci> splitFileName "foo/bar/Quux.hs"
("foo/bar/","Quux.hs")
ghci> splitFileName "zippity"
("","zippity")
```

Using System.FilePath together with the System.Directory module, we can write a portable namesMatching function that will run on both Unix-like and Windows systems:

```
-- file: ch08/Glob.hs
import System.FilePath (dropTrailingPathSeparator, splitFileName, (</>))
```

In this module, we'll be emulating a "for" loop; getting our first taste of exception handling in Haskell; and of course using the `matchesGlob` function we just wrote:

```
-- file: ch08/Glob.hs
import Control.Exception (handle)
import Control.Monad (forM)
import GlobRegex (matchesGlob)
```

Since directories and files live in the "real world" of activities that have effects, our globbing function will have to have IO in its result type.

If the string we're passed contains no pattern characters, we simply check that the given name exists in the filesystem. (Notice that we use Haskell's function guard syntax here to write a nice tidy definition. An "if" would do but isn't as aesthetically pleasing.)

```
-- file: ch08/Glob.hs
isPattern :: String -> Bool
isPattern = any (`elem` "[*?]")

namesMatching pat
  | not (isPattern pat) = do
    exists <- doesNameExist pat
    return (if exists then [pat] else [])
```

The name `doesNameExist` refers to a function that we will define shortly.

What if the string *is* a glob pattern? Our function definition continues:

```
-- file: ch08/Glob.hs
  | otherwise = do
    case splitFileName pat of
      ("", baseName) -> do
          curDir <- getCurrentDirectory
          listMatches curDir baseName
      (dirName, baseName) -> do
          dirs <- if isPattern dirName
                  then namesMatching (dropTrailingPathSeparator dirName)
                  else return [dirName]
          let listDir = if isPattern baseName
                        then listMatches
                        else listPlain
          pathNames <- forM dirs $ \dir -> do
                          baseNames <- listDir dir baseName
                          return (map (dir </>) baseNames)
          return (concat pathNames)
```

We use `splitFileName` to split the string into a pair of "everything but the final name" and "the final name." If the first element is empty, we're looking for a pattern in the current directory. Otherwise, we must check the directory name and see if it contains patterns. If it does not, we create a singleton list of the directory name. If it contains a pattern, we list all of the matching directories.

Things to watch out for

The `System.FilePath` module can be a little tricky. The example just shown is a case in point; the `splitFileName` function leaves a trailing slash on the end of the directory name that it returns:

```
ghci> :module +System.FilePath
ghci> splitFileName "foo/bar"
Loading package filepath-1.1.0.0 ... linking ... done.
("foo/","bar")
```

If we didn't remember (or know enough) to remove that slash, we'd recurse endlessly in `namesMatching`, because of the following behavior of `splitFileName`:

```
ghci> splitFileName "foo/"
("foo/","")
```

(You can guess what happened to us that led us to add this note!)

Finally, we collect all matches in every directory, giving us a list of lists, and concatenate them into a single list of names.

The unfamiliar `forM` function above acts a little like a "for" loop: it maps its second argument (an action) over its first (a list), and returns the list of results.

We have a few loose ends to clean up. The first is the definition of the `doesNameExist` function, used above. The `System.Directory` module doesn't let us check to see if a name exists in the filesystem. It forces us to decide whether we want to check for a file or a directory. This API is ungainly, so we roll the two checks into a single function. In the name of performance, we make the check for a file first, since files are far more common than directories:

```
-- file: ch08/Glob.hs
doesNameExist :: FilePath -> IO Bool

doesNameExist name = do
    fileExists <- doesFileExist name
    if fileExists
      then return True
      else doesDirectoryExist name
```

We have two other functions to define, each of which returns a list of names in a directory. The `listMatches` function returns a list of all files matching the given glob pattern in a directory:

```
-- file: ch08/Glob.hs
listMatches :: FilePath -> String -> IO [String]
listMatches dirName pat = do
    dirName' <- if null dirName
                then getCurrentDirectory
                else return dirName
    handle (const (return [])) $ do
        names <- getDirectoryContents dirName'
```

```
            let names' = if isHidden pat
                         then filter isHidden names
                         else filter (not . isHidden) names
            return (filter (`matchesGlob` pat) names')

isHidden ('.':_) = True
isHidden _       = False
```

The listPlain function returns either an empty or singleton list, depending on whether the single name it's passed exists:

```
-- file: ch08/Glob.hs
listPlain :: FilePath -> String -> IO [String]
listPlain dirName baseName = do
    exists <- if null baseName
              then doesDirectoryExist dirName
              else doesNameExist (dirName </> baseName)
    return (if exists then [baseName] else [])
```

If we look closely at the definition of listMatches, we'll see a call to a function named handle. Earlier on, we imported this from the Control.Exception module; as that import implies, this gives us our first taste of exception handling in Haskell. Let's drop into ghci and see what we can find out:

```
ghci> :module +Control.Exception
ghci> :type handle
handle :: (Exception -> IO a) -> IO a -> IO a
```

This is telling us that handle takes two arguments. The first is a function that is passed an exception value, and can have side effects (see the IO type in its return value); this is the handler to run if an exception is thrown. The second argument is the code that might throw an exception.

As for the exception handler, the type of the handle constrains it to return the same type of value as the body of code that threw the exception. So its choices are to either throw an exception or, as in our case, return a list of Strings.

The const function takes two arguments—it always returns its first argument, no matter what its second argument is:

```
ghci> :type const
const :: a -> b -> a
ghci> :type return []
return [] :: (Monad m) => m [a]
ghci> :type handle (const (return []))
handle (const (return [])) :: IO [a] -> IO [a]
```

We use const to write an exception handler that ignores the exception it is passed. Instead, it causes our code to return an empty list if we catch an exception.

We won't have anything more to say about exception handling here. There's plenty more to cover, though, so we'll be returning to the subject of exceptions in Chapter 19.

1. Although we've gone to some lengths to write a portable `namesMatching` function, the function uses our case sensitive `globToRegex` function. Find a way to modify `namesMatching` to be case-sensitive on Unix, and case insensitive on Windows, without modifying its type signature. (*Hint*: consider reading the documentation for `System.FilePath` to look for a variable that tells us whether we're running on a Unix-like system or on Windows.)

2. If you're on a Unix-like system, look through the documentation for the `System.Posix.Files` module, and see if you can find a replacement for the `doesNameExist` function.

3. The * wild card matches names only within a single directory. Many shells have an extended wild card syntax, **, that matches names recursively in all directories. For example, **.c would mean "match a name ending in .c in this directory or any subdirectory at any depth". Implement matching on ** wild cards.

Handling Errors Through API Design

It's not necessarily a disaster if our `globToRegex` is passed a malformed pattern. Perhaps a user mistyped a pattern, in which case, we'd like to be able to report a meaningful error message.

Calling the `error` function when this kind of problem occurs can be a drastic response (exploring its consequences was the focus of "Exercises" on page 210). The `error` throws an exception. Pure Haskell code cannot deal with exceptions, so control is going to rocket out of our pure code into the nearest caller that lives in IO and has an appropriate exception handler installed. If no such handler is installed, the Haskell runtime will default to terminating our program (or print a nasty error message, in `ghci`).

So calling `error` is a little like pulling the handle of a fighter plane's ejection seat. We're bailing out of a catastrophic situation that we can't deal with gracefully, and there's likely to be a lot of flaming wreckage strewn about by the time we hit the ground.

We've established that `error` is for disasters, but we're still using it in `globToRegex`. In that case, malformed input should be rejected, but not turned into a big deal. What would be a better way to handle this?

Haskell's type system and libraries to the rescue! We can encode the possibility of failure in the type signature of `globToRegex` using the predefined `Either` type:

```
-- file: ch08/GlobRegexEither.hs
type GlobError = String

globToRegex :: String -> Either GlobError String
```

A value returned by globToRegex will now be either Left "an error message" or Right "a valid regexp". This return type forces our callers to deal with the possibility of error. (You'll find that this use of the Either type occurs frequently in Haskell code.)

EXERCISES

1. Write a version of globToRegex that uses the type signature shown earlier.

2. Modify the type signature of namesMatching so that it encodes the possibility of a bad pattern, and make it use your rewritten globToRegex function.

 You may find the amount of work involved to be surprisingly large. Don't worry; we will introduce more concise and sophisticated ways of dealing with errors in later chapters.

Putting Our Code to Work

The namesMatching function isn't very exciting by itself, but it's a useful building block. Combine it with a few more functions, and we can start to do interesting things.

Here's one such example. Let's define a renameWith function that, instead of simply renaming a file, applies a function to the file's name, and renames the file to whatever that function returns:

```
-- file: ch08/Useful.hs
import System.FilePath (replaceExtension)
import System.Directory (doesFileExist, renameDirectory, renameFile)
import Glob (namesMatching)

renameWith :: (FilePath -> FilePath)
           -> FilePath
           -> IO FilePath

renameWith f path = do
    let path' = f path
    rename path path'
    return path'
```

Once again, we work around the ungainly file/directory split in System.Directory with a helper function:

```
-- file: ch08/Useful.hs
rename :: FilePath -> FilePath -> IO ()

rename old new = do
    isFile <- doesFileExist old
    let f = if isFile then renameFile else renameDirectory
    f old new
```

The `System.FilePath` module provides many useful functions for manipulating filenames. These functions mesh nicely with our `renameWith` and `namesMatching` functions, so that we can quickly use them to create functions with complex behavior. As an example, this terse function changes the filename suffixing convention for C++ source files:

```
-- file: ch08/Useful.hs
cc2cpp =
  mapM (renameWith (flip replaceExtension ".cpp")) =<< namesMatching "*.cc"
```

The `cc2cpp` function uses a few functions we'll see over and over. The `flip` function takes another function as argument and swaps the order of its arguments (inspect the type of `replaceExtension` in ghci to see why). The `=<<` function feeds the result of the action on its right side to the action on its left.

EXERCISE

1. Glob patterns are simple enough to interpret that it's easy to write a matcher directly in Haskell, rather than going through the regexp machinery. Give it a try.

CHAPTER 9

I/O Case Study: A Library for Searching the Filesystem

The problem of "I know I have this file, but I don't know where it is" has been around for as long as computers have had hierarchical filesystems. The fifth edition of Unix introduced the find command in 1974; it remains indispensable today. The state of the art has come a long way: modern operating systems ship with advanced document indexing and search capabilities.

There's still a valuable place for find-like capability in the programmer's toolbox. In this chapter, we'll develop a library that gives us many of find's capabilities, without leaving Haskell. We'll explore several different approaches to writing this library, each with different strengths.

The find Command

If you don't use a Unix-like operating system, or you're not a heavy shell user, it's quite possible you may not have heard of find. Given a list of directories, it searches each one recursively and prints the name of every entry that matches an expression.

Individual expressions can take such forms as "name matches this glob pattern," "entry is a plain file," "last modified before this date," and many more. They can be stitched together into more complex expressions using "and" and "or" operators.

Starting Simple: Recursively Listing a Directory

Before we plunge into designing our library, let's solve a few smaller issues. Our first problem is to recursively list the contents of a directory and its subdirectories:

```
-- file: ch09/RecursiveContents.hs
module RecursiveContents (getRecursiveContents) where

import Control.Monad (forM)
import System.Directory (doesDirectoryExist, getDirectoryContents)
```

```
import System.FilePath ((</>))

getRecursiveContents :: FilePath -> IO [FilePath]

getRecursiveContents topdir = do
  names <- getDirectoryContents topdir
  let properNames = filter (`notElem` [".", ".."]) names
  paths <- forM properNames $ \name -> do
    let path = topdir </> name
    isDirectory <- doesDirectoryExist path
    if isDirectory
      then getRecursiveContents path
      else return [path]
  return (concat paths)
```

The filter expression ensures that a listing for a single directory won't contain the special directory names . or .., which refer to the current and parent directory, respectively. If we forgot to filter these out, we'd recurse endlessly.

We encountered forM in the previous chapter; it is mapM with its arguments flipped:

```
ghci> :m +Control.Monad
ghci> :type mapM
mapM :: (Monad m) => (a -> m b) -> [a] -> m [b]
ghci> :type forM
forM :: (Monad m) => [a] -> (a -> m b) -> m [b]
```

The body of the loop checks to see whether the current entry is a directory. If it is, it recursively calls getRecursiveContents to list that directory. Otherwise, it returns a single-element list that is the name of the current entry. (Don't forget that the return function has a unique meaning in Haskell: it wraps a value with the monad's type constructor.)

Another thing worth pointing out is the use of the variable isDirectory. In an imperative language such as Python, we'd normally write if os.path.isdir(path). However, the doesDirectoryExist function is an *action*; its return type is IO Bool, not Bool. Since an if expression requires an expression of type Bool, we have to use <- to get the Bool result of the action out of its IO wrapper so that we can use the plain, unwrapped Bool in the if.

Each iteration of the loop body yields a list of names, so the result type of forM here is IO [[FilePath]]. We use concat to flatten it into a single list.

Revisiting Anonymous and Named Functions

In "Anonymous (lambda) Functions" on page 99, we listed some reasons not to use anonymous functions, and yet here we are, using one as the body of a loop. This is one of the most common uses of anonymous functions in Haskell.

We've already seen from their types that forM and mapM take functions as arguments. Most loop bodies are blocks of code that appear only once in a program. Since we're most likely to use a loop body in one place only, why give it a name?

Of course, it sometimes happens that we need to deploy exactly the same code in several different loops. Rather than cutting and pasting the same anonymous function, it makes sense in such cases to give a name to an existing anonymous function.

Why Provide Both mapM and forM?

It might seem a bit odd that there exist two functions that are identical but for the order in which they accept their arguments. However, mapM and forM are convenient in different circumstances.

Consider our previous example, using an anonymous function as a loop body. If we were to use mapM instead of forM, we'd have to place the variable properNames after the body of the function. In order to get the code to parse correctly, we'd have to wrap the entire anonymous function in parentheses, or replace it with a named function that would otherwise be unnecessary. Try it yourself: copy the code just shown, replacing forM with mapM, and see what this does to the readability of the code.

By contrast, if the body of the loop was already a named function, and the list over which we were looping was computed by a complicated expression, we'd have a good case for using mapM instead.

The stylistic rule of thumb to follow here is to use whichever of mapM or forM lets you write the tidiest code. If the loop body and the expression computing the data over which you're looping are both short, it doesn't matter which you use. If the loop is short, but the data is long, use mapM. If the loop is long, but the data short, use forM. And if both are long, use a let or where clause to make one of them short. With just a little practice, it will become obvious which of these approaches is best in every instance.

A Naive Finding Function

We can use our getRecursiveContents function as the basis for a simple-minded file finder:

```
-- file: ch09/SimpleFinder.hs
import RecursiveContents (getRecursiveContents)

simpleFind :: (FilePath -> Bool) -> FilePath -> IO [FilePath]

simpleFind p path = do
  names <- getRecursiveContents path
  return (filter p names)
```

This function takes a predicate that we use to filter the names returned by getRecursiveContents. Each name passed to the predicate is a complete path, so how can we perform a common operation such as "find all files ending in the extension *.c*"?

The System.FilePath module contains numerous invaluable functions that help us to manipulate filenames. In this case, we want takeExtension:

```
ghci> :m +System.FilePath
ghci> :type takeExtension
takeExtension :: FilePath -> String
ghci> takeExtension "foo/bar.c"
Loading package filepath-1.1.0.0 ... linking ... done.
".c"
ghci> takeExtension "quux"
""
```

This gives us a simple matter of writing a function that takes a path, extracts its extension, and compares it with *.c*:

```
ghci> :load SimpleFinder
[1 of 2] Compiling RecursiveContents ( RecursiveContents.hs, interpreted )
[2 of 2] Compiling Main             ( SimpleFinder.hs, interpreted )
Ok, modules loaded: RecursiveContents, Main.
ghci> :type simpleFind (\p -> takeExtension p == ".c")
simpleFind (\p -> takeExtension p == ".c") :: FilePath -> IO [FilePath]
```

While simpleFind works, it has a few glaring problems. The first is that the predicate is not very expressive. It can only look at the name of a directory entry; it cannot, for example, find out whether it's a file or a directory. This means that our attempt to use simpleFind will list directories ending in *.c* as well as files with the same extension.

The second problem is that simpleFind gives us no control over how it traverses the filesystem. To see why this is significant, consider the problem of searching for a source file in a tree managed by the Subversion revision control system. Subversion maintains a private *.svn* directory in every directory that it manages; each one contains many subdirectories and files that are of no interest to us. While we can easily filter out any path containing *.svn*, it's more efficient to simply avoid traversing these directories in the first place. For example, one of us has a Subversion source tree containing 45,000 files, 30,000 of which are stored in 1,200 different *.svn* directories. It's cheaper to avoid traversing those 1,200 directories than to filter out the 30,000 files they contain.

Finally, simpleFind is strict, because it consists of a series of actions executed in the IO monad. If we have a million files to traverse, we encounter a long delay, and then receive one huge result containing a million names. This is bad for both resource usage and responsiveness. We might prefer a lazy stream of results delivered as they arrive.

In the sections that follow, we'll overcome each one of these problems.

Predicates: From Poverty to Riches, While Remaining Pure

Our predicates can only look at filenames. This excludes a wide variety of interesting behaviors—for instance, what if we'd like to list files greater than a given size?

An easy reaction to this is to reach for IO: instead of our predicate being of type `FilePath -> Bool`, why don't we change it to `FilePath -> IO Bool`? This would let us perform arbitrary I/O as part of our predicate. As appealing as this might seem, it's also potentially a problem: such a predicate could have arbitrary side effects, since a function with return type `IO a` can have whatever side effects it pleases.

Let's enlist the type system in our quest to write more predictable, less buggy code; we'll keep predicates pure by avoiding the taint of "IO." This will ensure that they can't have any nasty side effects. We'll feed them more information, too, so that they can gain the expressiveness we want without also becoming potentially dangerous.

Haskell's portable `System.Directory` module provides a useful, albeit limited, set of file metadata:

```
ghci> :m +System.Directory
```

We can use `doesFileExist` and `doesDirectoryExist` to determine whether a directory entry is a file or a directory. There are not yet portable ways to query for other file types that have become widely available in recent years, such as named pipes, hard links, and symbolic links:

```
ghci> :type doesFileExist
doesFileExist :: FilePath -> IO Bool
ghci> doesFileExist "."
Loading package old-locale-1.0.0.0 ... linking ... done.
Loading package old-time-1.0.0.0 ... linking ... done.
Loading package directory-1.0.0.1 ... linking ... done.
False
ghci> :type doesDirectoryExist
doesDirectoryExist :: FilePath -> IO Bool
ghci> doesDirectoryExist "."
True
```

The `getPermissions` function lets us find out whether certain operations on a file or directory are allowed:

```
ghci> :type getPermissions
getPermissions :: FilePath -> IO Permissions
ghci> :info Permissions
data Permissions
  = Permissions {readable :: Bool,
                 writable :: Bool,
                 executable :: Bool,
                 searchable :: Bool}
      -- Defined in System.Directory
instance Eq Permissions -- Defined in System.Directory
instance Ord Permissions -- Defined in System.Directory
instance Read Permissions -- Defined in System.Directory
```

```
instance Show Permissions -- Defined in System.Directory
ghci> getPermissions "."
Permissions {readable = True, writable = True, executable = False, searchable = True}
ghci> :type searchable
searchable :: Permissions -> Bool
ghci> searchable it
True
```

Finally, getModificationTime tells us when an entry was last modified:

```
ghci> :type getModificationTime
getModificationTime :: FilePath -> IO System.Time.ClockTime
ghci> getModificationTime "."
Sat Aug 23 22:28:16 PDT 2008
```

If we stick with portable, standard Haskell code, these functions are all we have at our disposal. (We can also find a file's size using a small hack; see below.) They're also quite enough to let us illustrate the principles we're interested in, without letting us get carried away with an example that's too expansive. If you need to write more demanding code, the System.Posix and System.Win32 module families provide much more detailed file metadata for the two major modern computing platforms. There also exists a unix-compat package on Hackage, which provides a Unix-like API on Windows.

How many pieces of data does our new, richer predicate need to see? Since we can find out whether an entry is a file or a directory by looking at its Permissions, we don't need to pass in the results of doesFileExist or doesDirectoryExist. We thus have four pieces of data that a richer predicate needs to look at:

```
-- file: ch09/BetterPredicate.hs
import Control.Monad (filterM)
import System.Directory (Permissions(..), getModificationTime, getPermissions)
import System.Time (ClockTime(..))
import System.FilePath (takeExtension)
import Control.Exception (bracket, handle)
import System.IO (IOMode(..), hClose, hFileSize, openFile)

-- the function we wrote earlier
import RecursiveContents (getRecursiveContents)

type Predicate =  FilePath       -- path to directory entry
               -> Permissions    -- permissions
               -> Maybe Integer  -- file size (Nothing if not file)
               -> ClockTime      -- last modified
               -> Bool
```

Our Predicate type is just a synonym for a function of four arguments. It will save us a little keyboard work and screen space.

Notice that the return value of this predicate is Bool, not IO Bool: the predicate is pure and cannot perform I/O. With this type in hand, our more expressive finder function is still quite trim:

```
-- file: ch09/BetterPredicate.hs
-- soon to be defined
```

```
getFileSize :: FilePath -> IO (Maybe Integer)

betterFind :: Predicate -> FilePath -> IO [FilePath]

betterFind p path = getRecursiveContents path >>= filterM check
    where check name = do
            perms <- getPermissions name
            size <- getFileSize name
            modified <- getModificationTime name
            return (p name perms size modified)
```

Let's walk through the code. We'll talk about `getFileSize` in some detail soon, so let's skip over it for now.

We can't use `filter` to call our predicate p, as p's purity means it cannot do the I/O needed to gather the metadata it requires.

This leads us to the unfamiliar function `filterM`. It behaves like the normal `filter` function, but in this case it evaluates its predicate in the IO monad, allowing the predicate to perform I/O:

```
ghci> :m +Control.Monad
ghci> :type filterM
filterM :: (Monad m) => (a -> m Bool) -> [a] -> m [a]
```

Our check predicate is an I/O-capable wrapper for our pure predicate p. It does all the "dirty" work of I/O on p's behalf so that we can keep p incapable of unwanted side effects. After gathering the metadata, check calls p, and then uses `return` to wrap p's result with IO.

Sizing a File Safely

Although `System.Directory` doesn't let us find out how large a file is, we can use the similarly portable `System.IO` module to do this. It contains a function named `hFileSize`, which returns the size in bytes of an open file. Here's a simple function that wraps it:

```
-- file: ch09/BetterPredicate.hs
simpleFileSize :: FilePath -> IO Integer

simpleFileSize path = do
  h <- openFile path ReadMode
  size <- hFileSize h
  hClose h
  return size
```

While this function works, it's not yet suitable for us to use. In `betterFind`, we call `getFileSize` unconditionally on any directory entry; it should return `Nothing` if an entry is not a plain file, or it returns the size wrapped by `Just` otherwise. This function instead throws an exception if an entry is not a plain file or could not be opened (perhaps due to insufficient permissions), and returns the size unwrapped.

Here's a safer version of this function:

```
-- file: ch09/BetterPredicate.hs
saferFileSize :: FilePath -> IO (Maybe Integer)

saferFileSize path = handle (\_ -> return Nothing) $ do
  h <- openFile path ReadMode
  size <- hFileSize h
  hClose h
  return (Just size)
```

The body of the function is almost identical, save for the handle clause.

Our exception handler ignores the exception it's passed and returns Nothing. The only change to the body that follows is that it wraps the file size with Just.

The saferFileSize function now has the correct type signature, and it won't throw any exceptions. But it's still not completely well behaved. There are directory entries on which openFile will succeed, but hFileSize will throw an exception. This can happen with, for example, named pipes. Such an exception will be caught by handle, but our call to hClose will never occur.

A Haskell implementation will automatically close the file handle when it notices that the handle is no longer being used. That will not occur until the garbage collector runs, and the delay until the next garbage collection pass is not predictable.

File handles are scarce resources, enforced by the underlying operating system. On Linux, for example, a process is by default allowed to have only 1,024 files open simultaneously.

It's not hard to imagine a scenario in which a program that called a version of betterFind that used saferFileSize could crash due to betterFind exhausting the supply of open file handles before enough garbage file handles could be closed.

This is a particularly pernicious kind of bug: it has several aspects that combine to make it incredibly difficult to track down. It will only be triggered if betterFind visits a sufficiently large number of nonfiles to hit the process's limit on open file handles, and then returns to a caller that tries to open another file before any of the accumulated garbage file handles are closed.

To make matters worse, any subsequent error will be caused by data that is no longer reachable from within the program and has yet to be garbage-collected. Such a bug is thus dependent on the structure of the program, the contents of the filesystem, and how close the current run of the program is to triggering the garbage collector.

This sort of problem is easy to overlook during development, and when it later occurs in the field (as these awkward problems always seem to do), it will be much harder to diagnose.

Fortunately, we can avoid this kind of error very easily, while also making our function *shorter*.

The Acquire-Use-Release Cycle

We need hClose to always be called if openFile succeeds. The Control.Exception module provides the bracket function for exactly this purpose:

```
ghci> :type bracket
bracket :: IO a -> (a -> IO b) -> (a -> IO c) -> IO c
```

The bracket function takes three actions as arguments. The first action acquires a resource. The second releases the resource. The third runs in between, while the resource is acquired; let's call this the "use" action. If the "acquire" action succeeds, the "release" action is *always* called. This guarantees that the resource will always be released. The "use" and "release" actions are each passed the resource acquired by the "acquire" action.

If an exception occurs while the "use" action is executing, bracket calls the "release" action and rethrows the exception. If the "use" action succeeds, bracket calls the "release" action and returns the value returned by the "use" action.

We can now write a function that is completely safe—it will not throw exceptions, neither will it accumulate garbage file handles that could cause spurious failures elsewhere in our program:

```
-- file: ch09/BetterPredicate.hs
getFileSize path = handle (\_ -> return Nothing) $
    bracket (openFile path ReadMode) hClose $ \h -> do
      size <- hFileSize h
      return (Just size)
```

Look again closely at the arguments of bracket. The first opens the file and returns the open file handle. The second closes the handle. The third simply calls hFileSize on the handle and wraps the result in Just.

We need to use both bracket and handle for this function to operate correctly. The former ensures that we don't accumulate garbage file handles, while the latter gets rid of exceptions.

EXERCISE

1. Is the order in which we call bracket and handle important? Why?

A Domain-Specific Language for Predicates

Let's take a stab at writing a predicate that will check for a C++ source file that is over 128 KB in size:

```
-- file: ch09/BetterPredicate.hs
myTest path _ (Just size) _ =
    takeExtension path == ".cpp" && size > 131072
myTest _ _ _ _ = False
```

This isn't especially pleasing. The predicate takes four arguments, always ignores two of them, and requires two equations to define. Surely we can do better. Let's create some code that will help us write more concise predicates.

Sometimes, this kind of library is referred to as an *embedded domain-specific language*: we use our programming language's native facilities (hence *embedded*) to write code that lets us solve some narrow problem (hence *domain-specific*) particularly elegantly.

Our first step is to write a function that returns one of its arguments. This one extracts the path from the arguments passed to a `Predicate`:

```
-- file: ch09/BetterPredicate.hs
pathP path _ _ _ = path
```

If we don't provide a type signature, a Haskell implementation will infer a very general type for this function. This can later lead to error messages that are difficult to interpret, so let's give `pathP` a type:

```
-- file: ch09/BetterPredicate.hs
type InfoP a =  FilePath        -- path to directory entry
             -> Permissions     -- permissions
             -> Maybe Integer   -- file size (Nothing if not file)
             -> ClockTime       -- last modified
             -> a

pathP :: InfoP FilePath
```

We've created a type synonym that we can use as shorthand for writing other, similarly structured functions. Our type synonym accepts a type parameter so that we can specify different result types:

```
-- file: ch09/BetterPredicate.hs
sizeP :: InfoP Integer
sizeP _ _ (Just size) _ = size
sizeP _ _ Nothing     _ = -1
```

(We're being a little sneaky here and returning a size of −1 for entries that are not files or that we couldn't open.)

In fact, a quick glance shows that the `Predicate` type that we defined near the beginning of this chapter is the same type as `InfoP Bool`. (We could thus legitimately get rid of the `Predicate` type.)

What use are `pathP` and `sizeP`? With a little more glue, we can use them in a predicate (the P suffix on each name is intended to suggest "predicate"). This is where things start to get interesting:

```
-- file: ch09/BetterPredicate.hs
equalP :: (Eq a) => InfoP a -> a -> InfoP Bool
equalP f k = \w x y z -> f w x y z == k
```

The type signature of `equalP` deserves a little attention. It takes an `InfoP a` type, which is compatible with both `pathP` and `sizeP`. It next takes an `a` and returns an

InfoP Bool type, which we already observed is a synonym for Predicate. In other words, equalP constructs a predicate.

The equalP function works by returning an anonymous function. That one takes the arguments accepted by a predicate, passes them to f, and compares the result to k.

This equation for equalP emphasizes the fact that we think of it as taking two arguments. Since Haskell curries all functions, writing equalP in this way is not actually necessary. We can omit the anonymous function and rely on currying to work on our behalf, letting us write a function that behaves identically:

```
-- file: ch09/BetterPredicate.hs
equalP' :: (Eq a) => InfoP a -> a -> InfoP Bool
equalP' f k w x y z = f w x y z == k
```

Before we continue with our explorations, let's load our module into ghci:

```
ghci> :load BetterPredicate
[1 of 2] Compiling RecursiveContents ( RecursiveContents.hs, interpreted )
[2 of 2] Compiling Main             ( BetterPredicate.hs, interpreted )
Ok, modules loaded: RecursiveContents, Main.
```

Let's see if a simple predicate constructed from these functions will work:

```
ghci> :type betterFind (sizeP `equalP` 1024)
betterFind (sizeP `equalP` 1024) :: FilePath -> IO [FilePath]
```

Notice that we're not actually calling betterFind, we're merely making sure that our expression typechecks. We now have a more expressive way to list all files that are exactly some size. Our success gives us enough confidence to continue.

Avoiding Boilerplate with Lifting

Besides equalP, we'd like to be able to write other binary functions. We'd prefer not to write a complete definition of each one, because that seems unnecessarily verbose.

To address this, let's put Haskell's powers of abstraction to use. We'll take the definition of equalP, and instead of calling (==) directly, we'll pass in as another argument the binary function that we want to call:

```
-- file: ch09/BetterPredicate.hs
liftP :: (a -> b -> c) -> InfoP a -> b -> InfoP c
liftP q f k w x y z = f w x y z `q` k

greaterP, lesserP :: (Ord a) => InfoP a -> a -> InfoP Bool
greaterP = liftP (>)
lesserP = liftP (<)
```

This act of taking a function, such as (>), and transforming it into another function that operates in a different context (here greaterP) is referred to as *lifting* it into that context. (This explains the presence of lift in the function's name.) Lifting lets us reuse code and reduce boilerplate. We'll be using it a lot, in different guises, throughout the rest of this book.

When we lift a function, we'll often refer to its original and new versions as *unlifted* and *lifted*, respectively.

By the way, our placement of q (the function to lift) as the first argument to liftP was quite deliberate. This made it possible for us to write such concise definitions of greaterP and lesserP. Partial application makes finding the "best" order for arguments a more important part of API design in Haskell than in other languages. In languages without partial application, argument ordering is a matter of taste and convention. Put an argument in the wrong place in Haskell, however, and we lose the concision that partial application gives.

We can recover some of that conciseness via combinators. For instance, forM was not added to the Control.Monad module until 2007. Prior to that, people wrote flip mapM instead:

```
ghci> :m +Control.Monad
ghci> :t mapM
mapM :: (Monad m) => (a -> m b) -> [a] -> m [b]
ghci> :t forM
forM :: (Monad m) => [a] -> (a -> m b) -> m [b]
ghci> :t flip mapM
flip mapM :: (Monad m) => [a] -> (a -> m b) -> m [b]
```

Gluing Predicates Together

If we want to combine predicates, we can, of course, follow the obvious path of doing so by hand:

```
-- file: ch09/BetterPredicate.hs
simpleAndP :: InfoP Bool -> InfoP Bool -> InfoP Bool
simpleAndP f g w x y z = f w x y z && g w x y z
```

Now that we know about lifting, it becomes more natural to reduce the amount of code we must write by lifting our existing Boolean operators:

```
-- file: ch09/BetterPredicate.hs
liftP2 :: (a -> b -> c) -> InfoP a -> InfoP b -> InfoP c
liftP2 q f g w x y z = f w x y z `q` g w x y z

andP = liftP2 (&&)
orP = liftP2 (||)
```

Notice that liftP2 is very similar to our earlier liftP. In fact, it's more general, because we can write liftP in terms of liftP2:

```
-- file: ch09/BetterPredicate.hs
constP :: a -> InfoP a
constP k _ _ _ _ = k

liftP' q f k w x y z = f w x y z `q` constP k w x y z
```

Combinators

In Haskell, we refer to functions that take other functions as arguments and return new functions as *combinators*.

Now that we have some helper functions in place, we can return to the `myTest` function we defined earlier:

```
-- file: ch09/BetterPredicate.hs
myTest path _ (Just size) _ =
    takeExtension path == ".cpp" && size > 131072
myTest _ _ _ _ = False
```

How will this function look if we write it using our new combinators?

```
-- file: ch09/BetterPredicate.hs
liftPath :: (FilePath -> a) -> InfoP a
liftPath f w _ _ = f w

myTest2 = (liftPath takeExtension `equalP` ".cpp") `andP`
          (sizeP `greaterP` 131072)
```

We've added one final combinator, `liftPath`, since manipulating filenames is such a common activity.

Defining and Using New Operators

We can take our domain-specific language further by defining new infix operators:

```
-- file: ch09/BetterPredicate.hs
(==?) = equalP
(&&?) = andP
(>?) = greaterP

myTest3 = (liftPath takeExtension ==? ".cpp") &&? (sizeP >? 131072)
```

We chose names such as (==?) for the lifted functions specifically for their visual similarity to their unlifted counterparts.

The parentheses in our definition are necessary, because we haven't told Haskell about the precedence or associativity of our new operators. The language specifies that operators without fixity declarations should be treated as `infixl 9`, i.e., evaluated from left to right at the highest precedence level. If we were to omit the parentheses, the expression would thus be parsed as `(((liftPath takeExtension) ==? ".cpp") &&? sizeP) >? 131072`, which is horribly wrong.

We can respond by writing fixity declarations for our new operators. Our first step is to find out what the fixities of the unlifted operators are, so that we can mimic them:

```
ghci> :info ==
class Eq a where
  (==) :: a -> a -> Bool
  ...
```

```
      -- Defined in GHC.Base
infix 4 ==
ghci> :info &&
(&&) :: Bool -> Bool -> Bool       -- Defined in GHC.Base
infixr 3 &&
ghci> :info >
class (Eq a) => Ord a where
  ...
  (>) :: a -> a -> Bool
  ...
      -- Defined in GHC.Base
infix 4 >
```

With these in hand, we can now write a parenthesis-free expression that will be parsed identically to myTest3:

```
-- file: ch09/BetterPredicate.hs
infix 4 ==?
infixr 3 &&?
infix 4 >?

myTest4 = liftPath takeExtension ==? ".cpp" &&? sizeP >? 131072
```

Controlling Traversal

When traversing the filesystem, we'd like to give ourselves more control over which directories we enter, and when. An easy way in which we can allow this is to pass in a function that takes a list of subdirectories of a given directory and returns another list. This list can have elements removed, or it can be ordered differently than the original list, or both. The simplest such control function is id, which will return its input list unmodified.

For variety, we're going to change a few aspects of our representation here. Instead of the elaborate function type InfoP a, we'll use a normal algebraic data type to substantially represent the same information:

```
-- file: ch09/ControlledVisit.hs
data Info = Info {
      infoPath :: FilePath
    , infoPerms :: Maybe Permissions
    , infoSize :: Maybe Integer
    , infoModTime :: Maybe ClockTime
    } deriving (Eq, Ord, Show)

getInfo :: FilePath -> IO Info
```

We're using record syntax to give ourselves "free" accessor functions, such as infoPath. The type of our **traverse** function is simple, as we just proposed. To obtain Info about a file or directory, we call the getInfo action:

```
-- file: ch09/ControlledVisit.hs
traverse :: ([Info] -> [Info]) -> FilePath -> IO [Info]
```

The definition of **traverse** is short, but dense:

```
-- file: ch09/ControlledVisit.hs
traverse order path = do
    names <- getUsefulContents path
    contents <- mapM getInfo (path : map (path </>) names)
    liftM concat $ forM (order contents) $ \info -> do
      if isDirectory info && infoPath info /= path
          then traverse order (infoPath info)
          else return [info]

getUsefulContents :: FilePath -> IO [String]
getUsefulContents path = do
    names <- getDirectoryContents path
    return (filter (`notElem` [".", ".."]) names)

isDirectory :: Info -> Bool
isDirectory = maybe False searchable . infoPerms
```

While we're not introducing any new techniques here, this is one of the densest function definitions we've yet encountered. Let's walk through it almost line by line, explaining what is going on.

The first couple of lines hold no mystery, as they're almost verbatim copies of code we've already seen. Things begin to get interesting when we assign to the variable contents. Let's read this line from right to left. We already know that names is a list of directory entries. We make sure that the current directory is prepended to every element of the list and included in the list itself. We use mapM to apply getInfo to the resulting paths.

The line that follows is even more dense. Again reading from right to left, we see that the last element of the line begins the definition of an anonymous function that continues to the end of the paragraph. Given one Info value, this function either visits a directory recursively (there's an extra check to make sure we don't visit path again), or returns that value as a single-element list (to match the result type of **traverse**).

We use forM to apply this function to each element of the list of Info values returned by order, the user-supplied traversal control function.

At the beginning of the line, we use the technique of lifting in a new context. The liftM function takes a regular function, concat, and lifts it into the IO monad. In other words, it takes the result of forM (of type IO [[Info]]) out of the IO monad, applies concat to it (yielding a result of type [Info], which is what we need), and puts the result back into the IO monad.

Finally, we mustn't forget to define our getInfo function:

```
-- file: ch09/ControlledVisit.hs
maybeIO :: IO a -> IO (Maybe a)
maybeIO act = handle (\_ -> return Nothing) (Just `liftM` act)

getInfo path = do
  perms <- maybeIO (getPermissions path)
```

```
size <- maybeIO (bracket (openFile path ReadMode) hClose hFileSize)
modified <- maybeIO (getModificationTime path)
return (Info path perms size modified)
```

The only noteworthy thing here is a useful combinator, `maybeIO`, which turns an `IO` action that might throw an exception into one that wraps its result in `Maybe`.

EXERCISES

1. What should you pass to `traverse` to traverse a directory tree in reverse alphabetic order?

2. Using `id` as a control function, `traverse id` performs a *preorder* traversal of a tree: it returns a parent directory before its children. Write a control function that makes `traverse` perform a *postorder* traversal, in which it returns children before their parent.

3. Take the predicates and combinators from "Gluing Predicates Together" on page 224 and make them work with our new `Info` type.

4. Write a wrapper for `traverse` that lets you control traversal using one predicate and filter results using another.

Density, Readability, and the Learning Process

Code as dense as `traverse` is not unusual in Haskell. The gain in expressiveness is significant, and it requires a relatively small amount of practice to be able to fluently read and write code in this style.

For comparison, here's a less dense presentation of the same code (this might be more typical of a less experienced Haskell programmer):

```
-- file: ch09/ControlledVisit.hs
traverseVerbose order path = do
    names <- getDirectoryContents path
    let usefulNames = filter (`notElem` [".", ".."]) names
    contents <- mapM getEntryName ("" : usefulNames)
    recursiveContents <- mapM recurse (order contents)
    return (concat recursiveContents)
  where getEntryName name = getInfo (path </> name)
        isDirectory info = case infoPerms info of
                             Nothing -> False
                             Just perms -> searchable perms
        recurse info = do
            if isDirectory info && infoPath info /= path
               then traverseVerbose order (infoPath info)
               else return [info]
```

All we've done here is make a few substitutions. Instead of liberally using partial application and function composition, we've defined some local functions in a `where` block. In place of the `maybe` combinator, we're using a `case` expression. And instead of using `liftM`, we're manually lifting `concat` ourselves.

This is not to say that density is a uniformly good property. Each line of the original `traverse` function is short. We introduce a local variable (`usefulNames`) and a local function (`isDirectory`) specifically to keep the lines short and the code clearer. Our names are descriptive. While we use function composition and pipelining, the longest pipeline contains only three elements.

The key to writing maintainable Haskell code is to find a balance between density and readability. Where your code falls on this continuum is likely to be influenced by your level of experience, as detailed here:

- As a beginning Haskell programmer, Andrew doesn't know his way around the standard libraries very well. As a result, he unwittingly duplicates a lot of existing code.

- Zack has been programming for a few months and has mastered the use of (`.`) to compose long pipelines of code. Every time the needs of his program change slightly, he has to construct a new pipeline from scratch; he can't understand the existing pipeline any longer, and it is in any case too fragile to change.

- Monica has been coding for a while. She's familiar enough with Haskell libraries and idioms to write tight code, but she avoids a hyperdense style. Her code is maintainable, and she finds it easy to refactor when faced with changing requirements.

Another Way of Looking at Traversal

While the `traverse` function gives us more control than our original `betterFind` function, it still has a significant failing: we can avoid recursing into directories, but we can't filter other names until after we've generated the entire list of names in a tree. If we are traversing a directory containing 100,000 files of which we care about only 3, we'll allocate a 100,000-element list before we have a chance to trim it down to the 3 we really want.

One approach would be to provide a filter function as a new argument to `traverse`, which we would apply to the list of names as we generate it. This would allow us to allocate a list of only as many elements as we need.

However, this approach also has a weakness. Say we know that we want at most 3 entries from our list, and that those 3 entries happen to be the first 3 of the 100,000 that we traverse. In this case, we'll needlessly visit 99,997 other entries. This is not by any means a contrived example: for instance, the Maildir mailbox format stores a folder of email messages as a directory of individual files. It's common for a single directory representing a mailbox to contain tens of thousands of files.

We can address the weaknesses of our two prior traversal functions by taking a different perspective: what if we think of filesystem traversal as a *fold* over the directory hierarchy?

The familiar folds, `foldr` and `foldl'`, neatly generalize the idea of traversing a list while accumulating a result. It's hardly a stretch to extend the idea of folding from lists to directory trees, but we'd like to add an element of *control* to our fold. We'll represent this control as an algebraic data type:

```
-- file: ch09/FoldDir.hs
data Iterate seed = Done     { unwrap :: seed }
                  | Skip     { unwrap :: seed }
                  | Continue { unwrap :: seed }
                    deriving (Show)

type Iterator seed = seed -> Info -> Iterate seed
```

The `Iterator` type gives us a convenient alias for the function that we fold with. It takes a seed and an `Info` value representing a directory entry, and returns both a new seed and an instruction for our fold function, where the instructions are represented as the constructors of the `Iterate` type:

- If the instruction is `Done`, traversal should cease immediately. The value wrapped by `Done` should be returned as the result.

- If the instruction is `Skip` and the current `Info` type represents a directory, traversal will not recurse into that directory.

- Otherwise, the traversal should continue, using the wrapped value as the input to the next call to the fold function.

Our fold is logically a kind of left fold, because we start folding from the first entry we encounter. The seed for each step is the result of the prior step:

```
-- file: ch09/FoldDir.hs
foldTree :: Iterator a -> a -> FilePath -> IO a

foldTree iter initSeed path = do
    endSeed <- fold initSeed path
    return (unwrap endSeed)
  where
    fold seed subpath = getUsefulContents subpath >>= walk seed

    walk seed (name:names) = do
      let path' = path </> name
      info <- getInfo path'
      case iter seed info of
        done@(Done _) -> return done
        Skip seed'    -> walk seed' names
        Continue seed'
          | isDirectory info -> do
              next <- fold seed' path'
              case next of
                done@(Done _) -> return done
                seed''        -> walk (unwrap seed'') names
          | otherwise -> walk seed' names
    walk seed _ = return (Continue seed)
```

There are a few interesting things about the way this code is written. The first is the use of scoping to avoid having to pass extra parameters around. The top-level `foldTree` function is just a wrapper for `fold` that peels off the constructor of the `fold`'s final result.

Because `fold` is a local function, we don't have to pass `foldTree`'s `iter` variable into it; it can already access it in the outer scope. Similarly, `walk` can see `path` in its outer scope.

Another point to note is that `walk` is a tail recursive loop, instead of an anonymous function called by `forM` as in our earlier functions. By taking the reins ourselves, we can stop early if we need to, which lets us drop out when our iterator returns `Done`.

Although `fold` calls `walk`, `walk` calls `fold` recursively to traverse subdirectories. Each function returns a seed wrapped in an `Iterate`: when `fold` is called by `walk` and returns, `walk` examines its result to see whether it should continue or drop out because it returned `Done`. In this way, a return of `Done` from the caller-supplied iterator immediately terminates all mutually recursive calls between the two functions.

What does an iterator look like in practice? Here's a somewhat complicated example that looks for at most three bitmap images and won't recurse into Subversion metadata directories:

```
-- file: ch09/FoldDir.hs
atMostThreePictures :: Iterator [FilePath]

atMostThreePictures paths info
    | length paths == 3
      = Done paths
    | isDirectory info && takeFileName path == ".svn"
      = Skip paths
    | extension `elem` [".jpg", ".png"]
      = Continue (path : paths)
    | otherwise
      = Continue paths
  where extension = map toLower (takeExtension path)
        path = infoPath info
```

To use this, we'd call `foldTree atMostThreePictures []`, giving us a return value of type `IO [FilePath]`.

Of course, iterators don't have to be this complicated. Here's one that counts the number of directories it encounters:

```
-- file: ch09/FoldDir.hs
countDirectories count info =
    Continue (if isDirectory info
              then count + 1
              else count)
```

Here, the initial seed that we pass to `foldTree` should be the number zero.

1. Modify `foldTree` to allow the caller to change the order of traversal of entries in a directory.

2. The `foldTree` function performs preorder traversal. Modify it to allow the caller to determine the order of traversal.

3. Write a combinator library that makes it possible to express the kinds of iterators that `foldTree` accepts. Does it make the iterators you write any more succinct?

Useful Coding Guidelines

While many good Haskell programming habits come with experience, we have a few general guidelines to offer so that you can write readable code more quickly.

As we already mentioned in "A Note About Tabs Versus Spaces" on page 66, never use tab characters in Haskell source files. Use spaces.

If you find yourself proudly thinking that a particular piece of code is fiendishly clever, stop and consider whether you'll be able to understand it again after you've stepped away from it for a month.

The conventional way of naming types and variables with compound names is to use *camel case*, i.e., `myVariableName`. This style is almost universal in Haskell code. Regardless of your opinion of other naming practices, if you follow a nonstandard convention, your Haskell code will be somewhat jarring to the eyes of other readers.

Until you've been working with Haskell for a substantial amount of time, spend a few minutes searching for library functions before you write small functions. This applies particularly to ubiquitous types such as lists, `Maybe`, and `Either`. If the standard libraries don't already provide exactly what you need, you might be able to combine a few functions to obtain the result you desire.

Long pipelines of composed functions are hard to read, where *long* means a series of more than three or four elements. If you have such a pipeline, use a `let` or `where` block to break it into smaller parts. Give each one of these pipeline elements a meaningful name, and then glue them back together. If you can't think of a meaningful name for an element, ask yourself if you can even describe what it does. If the answer is "no," simplify your code.

Even though it's easy to resize a text editor window far beyond 80 columns, this width is still very common. Wider lines are wrapped or truncated in 80-column text editor windows, which severely hurts readability. Treating lines as no more than 80 characters long limits the amount of code you can cram onto a single line. This helps to keep individual lines less complicated, and therefore easier to understand.

Common Layout Styles

A Haskell implementation won't make a fuss about indentation as long as your code follows the layout rules and can hence be parsed unambiguously. That said, some layout patterns are widely used.

The in keyword is usually aligned directly under the let keyword, with the expression immediately following it:

```
-- file: ch09/Style.hs
tidyLet = let foo = undefined
              bar = foo * 2
          in undefined
```

While it's *legal* to indent the in differently, or to let it "dangle" at the end of a series of equations, the following would generally be considered odd:

```
-- file: ch09/Style.hs
weirdLet = let foo = undefined
               bar = foo * 2
    in undefined

strangeLet = let foo = undefined
                 bar = foo * 2 in
    undefined
```

In contrast, it's usual to let a do dangle at the end of a line, rather than sit at the beginning of one:

```
-- file: ch09/Style.hs
commonDo = do
  something <- undefined
  return ()

-- not seen very often
rareDo =
  do something <- undefined
     return ()
```

Curly braces and semicolons, though legal, are almost never used. There's nothing wrong with them; they just make code look strange due to their rarity. They're really intended to let programs generate Haskell code without having to implement the layout rules and are not meant for human use.

```
-- file: ch09/Style.hs
unusualPunctuation =
    [ (x,y) | x <- [1..a], y <- [1..b] ] where {
                                          b = 7;
  a = 6 }

preferredLayout = [ (x,y) | x <- [1..a], y <- [1..b] ]
    where b = 7
          a = 6
```

If the righthand side of an equation starts on a new line, it's usually indented a small number of spaces relative to the name of the variable or function that it's defining:

```
-- file: ch09/Style.hs
normalIndent =
    undefined

strangeIndent =
                    undefined
```

The actual number of spaces used to indent varies, sometimes within a single file. Depths of two, three, and four spaces are about equally common. A single space is legal but not very visually distinctive, so it's easy to misread.

When indenting a where clause, it's best to make it eye-catching:

```
-- file: ch09/Style.hs
goodWhere = take 5 lambdas
    where lambdas = []

alsoGood =
    take 5 lambdas
  where
    lambdas = []

badWhere =               -- legal, but ugly and hard to read
    take 5 lambdas
    where
    lambdas = []
```

EXERCISES

1. Although the file-finding code we described in this chapter is a good vehicle for learning, it's not ideal for real systems programming tasks, because Haskell's portable I/O libraries don't expose enough information to let us write interesting and complicated queries.

   Port the code from this chapter to your platform's native API, either System.Posix or System.Win32.

2. Add the ability to find out who owns a directory entry to your code. Make this information available to predicates.

CHAPTER 10

Code Case Study: Parsing a Binary Data Format

In this chapter, we'll discuss a common task: parsing a binary file. We will use it for two purposes. Our first is indeed to talk a little about parsing, but our main goal is to talk about program organization, refactoring, and "boilerplate removal." We will demonstrate how you can tidy up repetitious code, and set the stage for our discussion of monads in Chapter 14.

The file formats that we will work with come from the *netpbm suite*, an ancient and venerable collection of programs and file formats for working with bitmap images. These file formats have the dual advantages of being widely used and being fairly easy, though not completely trivial, to parse. Most importantly for our convenience, netpbm files are not compressed.

Grayscale Files

The name of netpbm's grayscale file format is PGM (*portable gray map*). It is actually not one format, but two; the *plain* (or P2) format is encoded as ASCII, while the more common *raw* (P5) format is mostly binary.

A file of either format starts with a header, which in turn begins with a "magic" string describing the format. For a plain file, the string is P2, and for raw, it's P5. The magic string is followed by whitespace, and then by three numbers: the width, height, and maximum gray value of the image. These numbers are represented as ASCII decimal numbers, separated by whitespace.

After the maximum gray value comes the image data. In a raw file, this is a string of binary values. In a plain file, the values are represented as ASCII decimal numbers separated by single-space characters.

A raw file can contain a sequence of images, one after the other, each with its own header. A plain file contains only one image.

Parsing a Raw PGM File

For our first try at a parsing function, we'll only worry about raw PGM files. We'll write our PGM parser as a *pure* function. It's won't be responsible for obtaining the data to parse, just for the actual parsing. This is a common approach in Haskell programs. By separating the reading of the data from what we subsequently do with it, we gain flexibility in where we take the data from.

We'll use the ByteString type to store our graymap data, because it's compact. Since the header of a PGM file is ASCII text but its body is binary, we import both the text- and binary-oriented ByteString modules:

```
-- file: ch10/PNM.hs
import qualified Data.ByteString.Lazy.Char8 as L8
import qualified Data.ByteString.Lazy as L
import Data.Char (isSpace)
```

For our purposes, it doesn't matter whether we use a lazy or strict ByteString, so we've somewhat arbitrarily chosen the lazy kind.

We'll use a straightforward data type to represent PGM images:

```
-- file: ch10/PNM.hs
data Greymap = Greymap {
      greyWidth :: Int
    , greyHeight :: Int
    , greyMax :: Int
    , greyData :: L.ByteString
    } deriving (Eq)
```

Normally, a Haskell Show instance should produce a string representation that we can read back by calling read. However, for a bitmap graphics file, this would potentially produce huge text strings, for example, if we were to show a photo. For this reason, we're not going to let the compiler automatically derive a Show instance for us; we'll write our own and intentionally simplify it:

```
-- file: ch10/PNM.hs
instance Show Greymap where
    show (Greymap w h m _) = "Greymap " ++ show w ++ "x" ++ show h ++
                             " " ++ show m
```

Because our Show instance intentionally avoids printing the bitmap data, there's no point in writing a Read instance, as we can't reconstruct a valid Greymap from the result of show.

Here's an obvious type for our parsing function:

```
-- file: ch10/PNM.hs
parseP5 :: L.ByteString -> Maybe (Greymap, L.ByteString)
```

This will take a ByteString, and if the parse succeeds, it will return a single parsed Greymap, along with the string that remains after parsing. That residual string will be available for future parses.

Our parsing function has to consume a little bit of its input at a time. First, we need to assure ourselves that we're really looking at a raw PGM file; then we need to parse the numbers from the remainder of the header; and then we consume the bitmap data. Here's an obvious way to express this, which we will use as a base for later improvements:

```
-- file: ch10/PNM.hs
matchHeader :: L.ByteString -> L.ByteString -> Maybe L.ByteString

-- "nat" here is short for "natural number"
getNat :: L.ByteString -> Maybe (Int, L.ByteString)

getBytes :: Int -> L.ByteString
         -> Maybe (L.ByteString, L.ByteString)

parseP5 s =
  case matchHeader (L8.pack "P5") s of
    Nothing -> Nothing
    Just s1 ->
      case getNat s1 of
        Nothing -> Nothing
        Just (width, s2) ->
          case getNat (L8.dropWhile isSpace s2) of
            Nothing -> Nothing
            Just (height, s3) ->
              case getNat (L8.dropWhile isSpace s3) of
                Nothing -> Nothing
                Just (maxGrey, s4)
                  | maxGrey > 255 -> Nothing
                  | otherwise ->
                      case getBytes 1 s4 of
                        Nothing -> Nothing
                        Just (_, s5) ->
                          case getBytes (width * height) s5 of
                            Nothing -> Nothing
                            Just (bitmap, s6) ->
                              Just (Greymap width height maxGrey bitmap, s6)
```

This is a very literal piece of code, performing all of the parsing in one long staircase of case expressions. Each function returns the residual ByteString left over after it has consumed all it needs from its input string. We pass each residual string along to the next step. We deconstruct each result in turn, either returning Nothing if the parsing step fails, or building up a piece of the final result as we proceed. Here are the bodies of the functions that we apply during parsing (their types are commented out because we already presented them):

```
-- file: ch10/PNM.hs
-- L.ByteString -> L.ByteString -> Maybe L.ByteString
matchHeader prefix str
    | prefix `L8.isPrefixOf` str
        = Just (L8.dropWhile isSpace (L.drop (L.length prefix) str))
    | otherwise
        = Nothing
```

```
-- L.ByteString -> Maybe (Int, L.ByteString)
getNat s = case L8.readInt s of
             Nothing -> Nothing
             Just (num,rest)
                | num <= 0     -> Nothing
                | otherwise -> Just (fromIntegral num, rest)

-- Int -> L.ByteString -> Maybe (L.ByteString, L.ByteString)
getBytes n str = let count         = fromIntegral n
                     both@(prefix,_) = L.splitAt count str
                 in if L.length prefix < count
                    then Nothing
                    else Just both
```

Getting Rid of Boilerplate Code

While our `parseP5` function works, the style in which we wrote it is somehow not pleasing. Our code marches steadily to the right of the screen, and it's clear that a slightly more complicated function would soon run out of visual real estate. We repeat a pattern of constructing and then deconstructing `Maybe` values, only continuing if a particular value matches `Just`. All of the similar `case` expressions act as *boilerplate code*, busywork that obscures what we're really trying to do. In short, this function is begging for some abstraction and refactoring.

If we step back a little, we can see two patterns. First is that many of the functions that we apply have similar types. Each takes a `ByteString` as its last argument and returns `Maybe` something else. Second, every step in the "ladder" of our `parseP5` function deconstructs a `Maybe` value, and either fails or passes the unwrapped result to a function.

We can quite easily write a function that captures this second pattern:

```
-- file: ch10/PNM.hs
(>>?) :: Maybe a -> (a -> Maybe b) -> Maybe b
Nothing >>? _ = Nothing
Just v  >>? f = f v
```

The (`>>?`) function acts very simply: it takes a value as its left argument, and a function as its right. If the value is not `Nothing`, it applies the function to whatever is wrapped in the `Just` constructor. We have defined our function as an operator so that we can use it to chain functions together. Finally, we haven't provided a fixity declaration for (`>>?`), so it defaults to `infixl 9` (left-associative, strongest operator precedence). In other words, a `>>? b >>? c` will be evaluated from left to right, as `(a >>? b) >>? c`.

With this chaining function in hand, we can take a second try at our parsing function:

```
-- file: ch10/PNM.hs
parseP5_take2 :: L.ByteString -> Maybe (Greymap, L.ByteString)
parseP5_take2 s =
    matchHeader (L8.pack "P5") s        >>?
    \s -> skipSpace ((), s)             >>?
    (getNat . snd)                      >>?
```

```
        skipSpace                        >>?
        \(width, s) ->    getNat s       >>?
        skipSpace                        >>?
        \(height, s) ->  getNat s        >>?
        \(maxGrey, s) -> getBytes 1 s    >>?
        (getBytes (width * height) . snd) >>?
        \(bitmap, s) -> Just (Greymap width height maxGrey bitmap, s)

    skipSpace :: (a, L.ByteString) -> Maybe (a, L.ByteString)
    skipSpace (a, s) = Just (a, L8.dropWhile isSpace s)
```

The key to understanding this function is to think about the chaining. On the left side of each (>>?) is a Maybe value; on the right is a function that returns a Maybe value. Each left-and-right-side expression is thus of type Maybe, suitable for passing to the following (>>?) expression.

The other change that we've made to improve readability is add a skipSpace function. With these changes, we've halved the number of lines of code compared to our original parsing function. By removing the boilerplate case expressions, we've made the code easier to follow.

While we warned against overuse of anonymous functions in "Anonymous (lambda) Functions" on page 99, we use several in our chain of functions here. Because these functions are so small, we wouldn't improve readability by giving them names.

Implicit State

We're not yet out of the woods. Our code explicitly passes pairs around, using one element for an intermediate part of the parsed result and the other for the current residual ByteString. If we want to extend the code, for example, to track the number of bytes we've consumed so that we can report the location of a parse failure, we already have eight different spots that we will need to modify, just to pass a three-tuple around.

This approach makes even a small body of code difficult to change. The problem lies with our use of pattern matching to pull values out of each pair: we have embedded the knowledge that we are always working with pairs straight into our code. As pleasant and helpful as pattern matching is, it can lead us in some undesirable directions if we do not use it carefully.

Let's do something to address the inflexibility of our new code. First, we will change the type of state that our parser uses:

```
-- file: ch10/Parse.hs
data ParseState = ParseState {
      string :: L.ByteString
    , offset :: Int64            -- imported from Data.Int
    } deriving (Show)
```

In our switch to an algebraic data type, we added the ability to track both the current residual string and the offset into the original string since we started parsing. The more important change was our use of record syntax: we can now *avoid* pattern matching on the pieces of state that we pass around and use the accessor functions `string` and `offset` instead.

We have given our parsing state a name. When we name something, it can become easier to reason about. For example, we can now look at parsing as a kind of function: it consumes a parsing state and produces both a new parsing state and some other piece of information. We can directly represent this as a Haskell type:

```
-- file: ch10/Parse.hs
simpleParse :: ParseState -> (a, ParseState)
simpleParse = undefined
```

To provide more help to our users, we would like to report an error message if parsing fails. This requires only a minor tweak to the type of our parser:

```
-- file: ch10/Parse.hs
betterParse :: ParseState -> Either String (a, ParseState)
betterParse = undefined
```

In order to future-proof our code, it is best if we do not expose the implementation of our parser to our users. When we explicitly used pairs for state earlier, we found ourselves in trouble almost immediately, once we considered extending the capabilities of our parser. To stave off a repeat of that difficulty, we will hide the details of our parser type using a `newtype` declaration:

```
-- file: ch10/Parse.hs
newtype Parse a = Parse {
        runParse :: ParseState -> Either String (a, ParseState)
    }
```

Remember that the `newtype` definition is just a compile-time wrapper around a function, so it has no runtime overhead. When we want to use the function, we will apply the `runParser` accessor.

If we do not export the `Parse` value constructor from our module, we can ensure that nobody else will be able to accidentally create a parser, nor will they be able to inspect its internals via pattern matching.

The Identity Parser

Let's try to define a simple parser, the *identity* parser. All it does is turn whatever it is passed into the result of the parse. In this way, it somewhat resembles the `id` function:

```
-- file: ch10/Parse.hs
identity :: a -> Parse a
identity a = Parse (\s -> Right (a, s))
```

This function leaves the parse state untouched and uses its argument as the result of the parse. We wrap the body of the function in our `Parse` type to satisfy the type checker. How can we use this wrapped function to parse something?

The first thing we must do is peel off the Parse wrapper so that we can get at the function inside. We do so using the runParse function. We also need to construct a ParseState, and then run our parsing function on it. Finally, we'd like to separate the result of the parse from the final ParseState:

```
-- file: ch10/Parse.hs
parse :: Parse a -> L.ByteString -> Either String a
parse parser initState
    = case runParse parser (ParseState initState 0) of
        Left err         -> Left err
        Right (result, _) -> Right result
```

Because neither the identity parser nor the parse function examines the parse state, we don't even need to create an input string in order to try our code:

```
ghci> :load Parse
[1 of 2] Compiling PNM              ( PNM.hs, interpreted )
[2 of 2] Compiling Parse            ( Parse.hs, interpreted )
Ok, modules loaded: Parse, PNM.
ghci> :type parse (identity 1) undefined
parse (identity 1) undefined :: (Num t) => Either String t
ghci> parse (identity 1) undefined
Loading package array-0.1.0.0 ... linking ... done.
Loading package bytestring-0.9.0.1.1 ... linking ... done.
Right 1
ghci> parse (identity "foo") undefined
Right "foo"
```

A parser that doesn't even inspect its input might not seem interesting, but we will see shortly that in fact it is useful. Meanwhile, we have gained confidence that our types are correct and that we understand the basic workings of our code.

Record Syntax, Updates, and Pattern Matching

Record syntax is useful for more than just accessor functions—we can use it to copy and partly change an existing value. In use, the notation looks like this:

```
-- file: ch10/Parse.hs
modifyOffset :: ParseState -> Int64 -> ParseState
modifyOffset initState newOffset =
    initState { offset = newOffset }
```

This creates a new ParseState value identical to initState, but with its offset field set to whatever value we specify for newOffset:

```
ghci> let before = ParseState (L8.pack "foo") 0
ghci> let after = modifyOffset before 3
ghci> before
ParseState {string = Chunk "foo" Empty, offset = 0}
ghci> after
ParseState {string = Chunk "foo" Empty, offset = 3}
```

We can set as many fields as we want inside the curly braces, separating them using commas.

A More Interesting Parser

Let's focus now on writing a parser that does something meaningful. We're not going to get too ambitious yet—all we want to do is parse a single byte:

```
-- file: ch10/Parse.hs
-- import the Word8 type from Data.Word
parseByte :: Parse Word8
parseByte =
    getState ==> \initState ->
    case L.uncons (string initState) of
      Nothing ->
          bail "no more input"
      Just (byte,remainder) ->
          putState newState ==> \_ ->
          identity byte
        where newState = initState { string = remainder,
                                     offset = newOffset }
              newOffset = offset initState + 1
```

There are a number of new functions in our definition.

The `L8.uncons` function takes the first element from a `ByteString`:

```
ghci> L8.uncons (L8.pack "foo")
Just ('f',Chunk "oo" Empty)
ghci> L8.uncons L8.empty
Nothing
```

Our `getState` function retrieves the current parsing state, while `putState` replaces it. The `bail` function terminates parsing and reports an error. The `(==>)` function chains parsers together. We will cover each of these functions shortly.

Hanging lambdas

The definition of `parseByte` has a visual style that we haven't discussed before. It contains anonymous functions in which the parameters and `->` sit at the end of a line, with the function's body following on the next line.

This style of laying out an anonymous function doesn't have an official name, so let's call it a "hanging lambda." Its main use is to make room for more text in the body of the function. It also makes it more visually clear that there's a relationship between a function and the one that follows it. Often, for instance, the result of the first function is being passed as a parameter to the second.

Obtaining and Modifying the Parse State

Our `parseByte` function doesn't take the parse state as an argument. Instead, it has to call `getState` to get a copy of the state and `putState` to replace the current state with a new one:

```
-- file: ch10/Parse.hs
getState :: Parse ParseState
getState = Parse (\s -> Right (s, s))

putState :: ParseState -> Parse ()
putState s = Parse (\_ -> Right ((), s))
```

When reading these functions, recall that the left element of the tuple is the result of a
Parse, while the right is the current ParseState. This makes it easier to follow what
these functions are doing.

The getState function extracts the current parsing state so that the caller can access
the string. The putState function replaces the current parsing state with a new one.
This becomes the state that will be seen by the next function in the (==>) chain.

These functions let us move explicit state handling into the bodies of only those functions that need it. Many functions don't need to know what the current state is, and so
they'll never call getState or putState. This lets us write more compact code than our
earlier parser, which had to pass tuples around by hand. We will see the effect in some
of the code that follows.

We've packaged up the details of the parsing state into the ParseState type, and we
work with it using accessors instead of pattern matching. Now that the parsing state is
passed around implicitly, we gain a further benefit. If we want to add more information
to the parsing state, all we need to do is modify the definition of ParseState and the
bodies of whatever functions need the new information. Compared to our earlier parsing code, where all of our state was exposed through pattern matching, this is much
more modular: the only code we affect is code that needs the new information.

Reporting Parse Errors

We carefully defined our Parse type to accommodate the possibility of failure. The
(==>) combinator checks for a parse failure and stops parsing if it runs into a failure.
But we haven't yet introduced the bail function, which we use to report a parse error:

```
-- file: ch10/Parse.hs
bail :: String -> Parse a
bail err = Parse $ \s -> Left $
           "byte offset " ++ show (offset s) ++ ": " ++ err
```

After we call bail, (==>) will successfully pattern match on the Left constructor that it
wraps the error message with, and it will not invoke the next parser in the chain. This
will cause the error message to percolate back through the chain of prior callers.

Chaining Parsers Together

The (==>) function serves a similar purpose to our earlier (>>?) function—it is "glue"
that lets us chain functions together:

```
-- file: ch10/Parse.hs
(==>) :: Parse a -> (a -> Parse b) -> Parse b

firstParser ==> secondParser  =  Parse chainedParser
  where chainedParser initState  =
            case runParse firstParser initState of
              Left errMessage ->
                  Left errMessage
              Right (firstResult, newState) ->
                  runParse (secondParser firstResult) newState
```

The body of (==>) is interesting and ever so slightly tricky. Recall that the Parse type represents really a function inside a wrapper. Since (==>) lets us chain two Parse values to produce a third, it must return a function, in a wrapper.

The function doesn't really "do" much, it just creates a *closure* to remember the values of firstParser and secondParser.

 A closure is simply the pairing of a function with its *environment*, the bound variables that it can see. Closures are commonplace in Haskell. For instance, the section (+5) is a closure. An implementation must record the value 5 as the second argument to the (+) operator so that the resulting function can add 5 to whatever value it is passed.

This closure will not be unwrapped and applied until we apply parse. At that point, it will be applied with a ParseState. It will apply firstParser and inspect its result. If that parse fails, the closure will fail too. Otherwise, it will pass the result of the parse and the new ParseState to secondParser.

This is really quite fancy and subtle stuff. We're effectively passing the ParseState down the chain of Parse values in a hidden argument. (We'll be revisiting this kind of code in a few chapters, so don't fret if this description seems dense.)

Introducing Functors

We're by now thoroughly familiar with the map function, which applies a function to every element of a list, returning a list of possibly a different type:

```
ghci> map (+1) [1,2,3]
[2,3,4]
ghci> map show [1,2,3]
["1","2","3"]
ghci> :type map show
map show :: (Show a) => [a] -> [String]
```

This map-like activity can be useful in other instances. For example, consider a binary tree:

```
-- file: ch10/TreeMap.hs
data Tree a = Node (Tree a) (Tree a)
```

```
      | Leaf a
        deriving (Show)
```

If we want to take a tree of strings and turn it into a tree containing the lengths of those strings, we could write a function to do this:

```
-- file: ch10/TreeMap.hs
treeLengths (Leaf s) = Leaf (length s)
treeLengths (Node l r) = Node (treeLengths l) (treeLengths r)
```

Now that our eyes are attuned to looking for patterns that we can turn into generally useful functions, we can see a possible case of this here:

```
-- file: ch10/TreeMap.hs
treeMap :: (a -> b) -> Tree a -> Tree b
treeMap f (Leaf a)   = Leaf (f a)
treeMap f (Node l r) = Node (treeMap f l) (treeMap f r)
```

As we might hope, `treeLengths` and `treeMap` `length` give the same results:

```
ghci> let tree = Node (Leaf "foo") (Node (Leaf "x") (Leaf "quux"))
ghci> treeLengths tree
Node (Leaf 3) (Node (Leaf 1) (Leaf 4))
ghci> treeMap length tree
Node (Leaf 3) (Node (Leaf 1) (Leaf 4))
ghci> treeMap (odd . length) tree
Node (Leaf True) (Node (Leaf True) (Leaf False))
```

Haskell provides a well-known typeclass to further generalize `treeMap`. This typeclass is named `Functor`, and it defines one function, `fmap`:

```
-- file: ch10/TreeMap.hs
class Functor f where
    fmap :: (a -> b) -> f a -> f b
```

We can think of `fmap` as a kind of *lifting* function, as we introduced in "Avoiding Boilerplate with Lifting" on page 223. It takes a function over ordinary values a -> b, and lifts it to become a function over containers f a -> f b, where f is the container type.

If we substitute `Tree` for the type variable f, for example, then the type of `fmap` is identical to the type of `treeMap`, and in fact we can use `treeMap` as the implementation of `fmap` over `Tree`s:

```
-- file: ch10/TreeMap.hs
instance Functor Tree where
    fmap = treeMap
```

We can also use `map` as the implementation of `fmap` for lists:

```
-- file: ch10/TreeMap.hs
instance Functor [] where
    fmap = map
```

We can now use `fmap` over different container types:

```
ghci> fmap length ["foo","quux"]
[3,4]
```

```
ghci> fmap length (Node (Leaf "Livingstone") (Leaf "I presume"))
Node (Leaf 11) (Leaf 9)
```

The Prelude defines instances of Functor for several common types, notably lists and Maybe:

```
-- file: ch10/TreeMap.hs
instance Functor Maybe where
    fmap _ Nothing  = Nothing
    fmap f (Just x) = Just (f x)
```

The instance for Maybe makes it particularly clear what an fmap implementation needs to do. The implementation must have a sensible behavior for each of a type's constructors. If a value is wrapped in Just, for example, the fmap implementation calls the function on the unwrapped value, then rewraps it in Just.

The definition of Functor imposes a few obvious restrictions on what we can do with fmap. For example, we can only make instances of Functor from types that have exactly one type parameter.

We can't write an fmap implementation for Either a b or (a, b), for example, because these have two type parameters. We also can't write one for Bool or Int, as they have no type parameters.

In addition, we can't place any constraints on our type definition. What does this mean? To illustrate, let's first look at a normal data definition and its Functor instance:

```
-- file: ch10/ValidFunctor.hs
data Foo a = Foo a

instance Functor Foo where
    fmap f (Foo a) = Foo (f a)
```

When we define a new type, we can add a type constraint just after the data keyword as follows:

```
-- file: ch10/ValidFunctor.hs
data Eq a => Bar a = Bar a

instance Functor Bar where
    fmap f (Bar a) = Bar (f a)
```

This says that we can only put a type a into a Foo if a is a member of the Eq typeclass. However, the constraint renders it impossible to write a Functor instance for Bar:

```
ghci> :load ValidFunctor
[1 of 1] Compiling Main             ( ValidFunctor.hs, interpreted )

ValidFunctor.hs:12:12:
    Could not deduce (Eq a) from the context (Functor Bar)
      arising from a use of `Bar' at ValidFunctor.hs:12:12-16
    Possible fix:
      add (Eq a) to the context of the type signature for `fmap'
    In the pattern: Bar a
    In the definition of `fmap': fmap f (Bar a) = Bar (f a)
```

```
    In the definition for method `fmap'

ValidFunctor.hs:12:21:
    Could not deduce (Eq b) from the context (Functor Bar)
      arising from a use of `Bar' at ValidFunctor.hs:12:21-29
    Possible fix:
      add (Eq b) to the context of the type signature for `fmap'
    In the expression: Bar (f a)
    In the definition of `fmap': fmap f (Bar a) = Bar (f a)
    In the definition for method `fmap'
Failed, modules loaded: none.
```

Constraints on Type Definitions Are Bad

Adding a constraint to a type definition is essentially never a good idea. It has the effect of forcing you to add type constraints to *every* function that will operate on values of that type. Let's say that we need a stack data structure that we want to be able to query to see whether its elements obey some ordering. Here's a naive definition of the data type:

```
-- file: ch10/TypeConstraint.hs
data (Ord a) => OrdStack a = Bottom
                          | Item a (OrdStack a)
                          deriving (Show)
```

If we want to write a function that checks the stack to see whether it is increasing (i.e., every element is bigger than the element below it), we'll obviously need an `Ord` constraint to perform the pairwise comparisons:

```
-- file: ch10/TypeConstraint.hs
isIncreasing :: (Ord a) => OrdStack a -> Bool
isIncreasing (Item a rest@(Item b _))
    | a < b     = isIncreasing rest
    | otherwise = False
isIncreasing _  = True
```

However, because we wrote the type constraint on the type definition, that constraint ends up infecting places where it isn't needed. We need to add the `Ord` constraint to `push`, which does not care about the ordering of elements on the stack:

```
-- file: ch10/TypeConstraint.hs
push :: (Ord a) => a -> OrdStack a -> OrdStack a
push a s = Item a s
```

Try removing that `Ord` constraint, and the definition of `push` will fail to typecheck.

This is why our attempt to write a `Functor` instance for `Bar` failed earlier: it would have required an `Eq` constraint to somehow get retroactively added to the signature of `fmap`.

Now that we've tentatively established that putting a type constraint on a type definition is a misfeature of Haskell, what's a more sensible alternative? The answer is simply to omit type constraints from type definitions, and instead place them on the functions that need them.

In this example, we can drop the Ord constraints from OrdStack and push. It needs to stay on isIncreasing, which otherwise couldn't call (<). We now have the constraints where they actually matter. This has the further benefit of making the type signatures better document the true requirements of each function.

Most Haskell container types follow this pattern. The Map type in the Data.Map module requires that its keys be ordered, but the type itself does not have such a constraint. The constraint is expressed on functions such as insert, where it's actually needed, and not on size, where ordering isn't used.

Infix Use of fmap

Quite often, you'll see fmap called as an operator:

```
ghci> (1+) `fmap` [1,2,3] ++ [4,5,6]
[2,3,4,4,5,6]
```

Perhaps strangely, plain old map is almost never used in this way.

One possible reason for the stickiness of the fmap-as-operator meme is that this use lets us omit parentheses from its second argument. Fewer parentheses leads to reduced mental juggling while reading a function:

```
ghci> fmap (1+) ([1,2,3] ++ [4,5,6])
[2,3,4,5,6,7]
```

If you really want to use fmap as an operator, the Control.Applicative module contains an operator (<$>) that is an alias for fmap. The $ in its name appeals to the similarity between applying a function to its arguments (using the ($) operator) and lifting a function into a functor. We will see that this works well for parsing when we return to the code that we have been writing.

Flexible Instances

You might hope that we could write a Functor instance for the type Either Int b, which has one type parameter:

```
-- file: ch10/EitherInt.hs
instance Functor (Either Int) where
    fmap _ (Left n) = Left n
    fmap f (Right r) = Right (f r)
```

However, the type system of Haskell 98 cannot guarantee that checking the constraints on such an instance will terminate. A nonterminating constraint check may send a compiler into an infinite loop, so instances of this form are forbidden:

```
ghci> :load EitherInt
[1 of 1] Compiling Main             ( EitherInt.hs, interpreted )

EitherInt.hs:2:0:
    Illegal instance declaration for `Functor (Either Int)'
        (All instance types must be of the form (T a1 ... an)
```

```
         where a1 ... an are type *variables*,
         and each type variable appears at most once in the instance head.
         Use -XFlexibleInstances if you want to disable this.)
    In the instance declaration for `Functor (Either Int)'
Failed, modules loaded: none.
```

GHC has a more powerful type system than the base Haskell 98 standard. It operates in Haskell 98 compatibility mode by default, for maximal portability. We can instruct it to allow more flexible instances using a special compiler directive:

```
-- file: ch10/EitherIntFlexible.hs
{-# LANGUAGE FlexibleInstances #-}

instance Functor (Either Int) where
    fmap _ (Left n)  = Left n
    fmap f (Right r) = Right (f r)
```

The directive is embedded in the specially formatted LANGUAGE pragma.

With our Functor instance in hand, let's try out fmap on Either Int:

```
ghci> :load EitherIntFlexible
[1 of 1] Compiling Main             ( EitherIntFlexible.hs, interpreted )
Ok, modules loaded: Main.
ghci> fmap (== "cheeseburger") (Left 1 :: Either Int String)
Left 1
ghci> fmap (== "cheeseburger") (Right "fries" :: Either Int String)
Right False
```

Thinking More About Functors

We've made a few implicit assumptions about how functors ought to work. It's helpful to make these explicit and to think of them as rules to follow, because this lets us treat functors as uniform, well-behaved objects. We have only two rules to remember, and they're simple:

- Our first rule is functors must preserve *identity*. That is, applying fmap id to a value should give us back an identical value:

  ```
  ghci> fmap id (Node (Leaf "a") (Leaf "b"))
  Node (Leaf "a") (Leaf "b")
  ```

- Our second rule is functors must be *composable*. That is, composing two uses of fmap should give the same result as one fmap with the same functions composed:

  ```
  ghci> (fmap even . fmap length) (Just "twelve")
  Just True
  ghci> fmap (even . length) (Just "twelve")
  Just True
  ```

Another way of looking at these two rules is that functors must preserve *shape*. The structure of a collection should not be affected by a functor; only the values that it contains should change:

```
ghci> fmap odd (Just 1)
Just True
ghci> fmap odd Nothing
Nothing
```

If you're writing a Functor instance, it's useful to keep these rules in mind, and indeed to test them, because the compiler can't check the rules we've just listed. On the other hand, if you're simply *using* functors, the rules are "natural" enough that there's no need to memorize them. They just formalize a few intuitive notions of "do what I mean." Here is a pseudocode representation of the expected behavior:

```
-- file: ch10/FunctorLaws.hs
fmap id        ==  id
fmap (f . g)   ==  fmap f . fmap g
```

Writing a Functor Instance for Parse

For the types we have surveyed so far, the behavior we ought to expect of fmap has been obvious. This is a little less clear for Parse, due to its complexity. A reasonable guess is that the function we're fmapping should be applied to the current result of a parse, and leave the parse state untouched:

```
-- file: ch10/Parse.hs
instance Functor Parse where
    fmap f parser = parser ==> \result ->
                        identity (f result)
```

This definition is easy to read, so let's perform a few quick experiments to see if we're following our rules for functors.

First, we'll check that identity is preserved. Let's try this first on a parse that ought to fail—parsing a byte from an empty string (remember that (<$>) is fmap):

```
ghci> parse parseByte L.empty
Left "byte offset 0: no more input"
ghci> parse (id <$> parseByte) L.empty
Left "byte offset 0: no more input"
```

Good. Now for a parse that should succeed:

```
ghci> let input = L8.pack "foo"
ghci> L.head input
102
ghci> parse parseByte input
Right 102
ghci> parse (id <$> parseByte) input
Right 102
```

Inspecting these results, we can also see that our Functor instance is obeying our second rule of preserving shape. Failure is preserved as failure, and success as success.

Finally, we'll ensure that composability is preserved:

```
ghci> parse ((chr . fromIntegral) <$> parseByte) input
Right 'f'
ghci> parse (chr <$> fromIntegral <$> parseByte) input
Right 'f'
```

On the basis of this brief inspection, our `Functor` instance appears to be well behaved.

Using Functors for Parsing

All this talk of functors has a purpose: they often let us write tidy, expressive code. Recall the `parseByte` function that we introduced earlier. In recasting our PGM parser to use our new parser infrastructure, we'll often want to work with ASCII characters instead of `Word8` values.

While we could write a `parseChar` function that has a similar structure to `parseByte`, we can now avoid this code duplication by taking advantage of the functor nature of `Parse`. Our functor takes the result of a parse and applies a function to it, so what we need is a function that turns a `Word8` into a `Char`:

```
-- file: ch10/Parse.hs
w2c :: Word8 -> Char
w2c = chr . fromIntegral

-- import Control.Applicative
parseChar :: Parse Char
parseChar = w2c <$> parseByte
```

We can also use functors to write a compact "peek" function. This returns `Nothing` if we're at the end of the input string. Otherwise, it returns the next character without consuming it (i.e., it inspects, but doesn't disturb, the current parsing state):

```
-- file: ch10/Parse.hs
peekByte :: Parse (Maybe Word8)
peekByte = (fmap fst . L.uncons . string) <$> getState
```

The same lifting trick that let us define `parseChar` lets us write a compact definition for `peekChar`:

```
-- file: ch10/Parse.hs
peekChar :: Parse (Maybe Char)
peekChar = fmap w2c <$> peekByte
```

Notice that `peekByte` and `peekChar` each make two calls to `fmap`, one of which is disguised as (`<$>`). This is necessary because the type `Parse (Maybe a)` is a functor within a functor. We thus have to lift a function twice to "get it into" the inner functor.

Finally, we'll write another generic combinator, which is the `Parse` analogue of the familiar `takeWhile`. It consumes its input while its predicate returns `True`:

```
-- file: ch10/Parse.hs
parseWhile :: (Word8 -> Bool) -> Parse [Word8]
parseWhile p = (fmap p <$> peekByte) ==> \mp ->
                 if mp == Just True
                 then parseByte ==> \b ->
                     (b:) <$> parseWhile p
                 else identity []
```

Once again, we're using functors in several places (doubled up, when necessary) to reduce the verbosity of our code. Here's a rewrite of the same function in a more direct style that does not use functors:

```
-- file: ch10/Parse.hs
parseWhileVerbose p =
    peekByte ==> \mc ->
    case mc of
      Nothing -> identity []
      Just c | p c ->
                  parseByte ==> \b ->
                  parseWhileVerbose p ==> \bs ->
                  identity (b:bs)
             | otherwise ->
                  identity []
```

The more verbose definition is likely easier to read when you are less familiar with functors. However, use of functors is sufficiently common in Haskell code that the more compact representation should become second nature (both to read and to write) fairly quickly.

Rewriting Our PGM Parser

With our new parsing code, what does the raw PGM parsing function look like now?

```
-- file: ch10/Parse.hs
parseRawPGM =
    parseWhileWith w2c notWhite ==> \header -> skipSpaces ==>&
    assert (header == "P5") "invalid raw header" ==>&
    parseNat ==> \width -> skipSpaces ==>&
    parseNat ==> \height -> skipSpaces ==>&
    parseNat ==> \maxGrey ->
    parseByte ==>&
    parseBytes (width * height) ==> \bitmap ->
    identity (Greymap width height maxGrey bitmap)
  where notWhite = (`notElem` " \r\n\t")
```

This definition makes use of a few more helper functions that we present here, following a pattern that should be familiar by now:

```
-- file: ch10/Parse.hs
parseWhileWith :: (Word8 -> a) -> (a -> Bool) -> Parse [a]
parseWhileWith f p = fmap f <$> parseWhile (p . f)

parseNat :: Parse Int
parseNat = parseWhileWith w2c isDigit ==> \digits ->
            if null digits
            then bail "no more input"
            else let n = read digits
                  in if n < 0
                     then bail "integer overflow"
                     else identity n

(==>&) :: Parse a -> Parse b -> Parse b
p ==>& f = p ==> \_ -> f

skipSpaces :: Parse ()
skipSpaces = parseWhileWith w2c isSpace ==>& identity ()

assert :: Bool -> String -> Parse ()
assert True  _   = identity ()
assert False err = bail err
```

The (==>&) combinator chains parsers such as (==>), but the righthand side ignores the result from the left. The assert function lets us check a property and abort parsing with a useful error message if the property is False.

Notice how few of the functions that we have written make any reference to the current parsing state. Most notably, where our old parseP5 function explicitly passed two-tuples down the chain of dataflow, all of the state management in parseRawPGM is hidden from us.

Of course, we can't completely avoid inspecting and modifying the parsing state. Here's a case in point, the last of the helper functions needed by parseRawPGM:

```
-- file: ch10/Parse.hs
parseBytes :: Int -> Parse L.ByteString
parseBytes n =
    getState ==> \st ->
    let n' = fromIntegral n
        (h, t) = L.splitAt n' (string st)
        st' = st { offset = offset st + L.length h, string = t }
    in putState st' ==>&
       assert (L.length h == n') "end of input" ==>&
       identity h
```

Future Directions

Our main theme in this chapter has been abstraction. We found passing explicit state down a chain of functions to be unsatisfactory, so we abstracted this detail away. We noticed some recurring needs as we worked out our parsing code, and abstracted those into common functions. Along the way, we introduced the notion of a functor, which offers a generalized way to map over a parameterized type.

We will revisit parsing in Chapter 16, when we discuss `Parsec`, a widely used and flexible parsing library. And in Chapter 14, we will return to our theme of abstraction, where we will find that much of the code that we have developed in this chapter can be further simplified by the use of monads.

For efficiently parsing binary data represented as a `ByteString`, a number of packages are available via the Hackage package database. At the time of this writing, the most popular is `binary`, which is easy to use and offers high performance.

EXERCISES

1. Write a parser for "plain" PGM files.

2. In our description of "raw" PGM files, we omitted a small detail. If the "maximum gray" value in the header is less than 256, each pixel is represented by a single byte. However, it can range up to 65,535, in which case, each pixel will be represented by 2 bytes, in big-endian order (most significant byte first).

   Rewrite the raw PGM parser to accommodate both the single- and double-byte pixel formats.

3. Extend your parser so that it can identify a raw or plain PGM file, and then parse the appropriate file type.

CHAPTER 11

Testing and Quality Assurance

Building real systems means caring about quality control, robustness, and correctness. With the right quality assurance mechanisms in place, well-written code can feel like a precision machine, with all functions performing their tasks exactly as specified. There is no sloppiness around the edges, and the final result can be code that is self-explanatory—and obviously correct—the kind of code that inspires confidence.

In Haskell, we have several tools at our disposal for building such precise systems. The most obvious tool, and one built into the language itself, is the expressive type system, which allows for complicated invariants to be enforced statically—making it impossible to write code violating chosen constraints. In addition, purity and polymorphism encourage a style of code that is modular, refactorable, and testable. This is the kind of code that just doesn't go wrong.

Testing plays a key role in keeping code on the straight-and-narrow path. The main testing mechanisms in Haskell are traditional unit testing (via the HUnit library) and its more powerful descendant, type-based "property" testing, with QuickCheck, an open source testing framework for Haskell. Property-based testing that encourages a high-level approach to testing in the form of abstract invariants functions should satisfy universally, with the actual test data generated for the programmer by the testing library. In this way, code can be hammered with thousands of tests that would be infeasible to write by hand, often uncovering subtle corner cases that wouldn't be found otherwise.

In this chapter, we'll look at how to use QuickCheck to establish invariants in code, and then re-examine the pretty printer developed in previous chapters, testing it with the framework. We'll also see how to guide the testing process with GHC's code coverage tool: HPC.

QuickCheck: Type-Based Testing

To get an overview of how property-based testing works, we'll begin with a simple scenario: you've written a specialized sorting function and want to test its behavior.

First, we import the QuickCheck library,[*] and any other modules we need:

```
-- file: ch11/QC-basics.hs
import Test.QuickCheck
import Data.List
```

And the function we want to test—a custom sort routine:

```
-- file: ch11/QC-basics.hs
qsort :: Ord a => [a] -> [a]
qsort []     = []
qsort (x:xs) = qsort lhs ++ [x] ++ qsort rhs
    where lhs = filter  (< x) xs
          rhs = filter (>= x) xs
```

This is the classic Haskell sort implementation: a study in functional programming elegance, if not efficiency (this isn't an inplace sort). Now, we'd like to check that this function obeys the basic rules a good sort should follow. One useful invariant to start with, and one that comes up in a lot of purely functional code, is *idempotency*—applying a function twice has the same result as applying it only once. For our sort routine—a stable sort algorithm—this should certainly be true, or things have gone horribly wrong! This invariant can be encoded as a property simply, as follows:

```
-- file: ch11/QC-basics.hs
prop_idempotent xs = qsort (qsort xs) == qsort xs
```

We'll use the QuickCheck convention of prefixing test properties with `prop_` in order to distinguish them from normal code. This idempotency property is written simply as a Haskell function stating an equality that must hold for any input data that is sorted. We can check this makes sense for a few simple cases by hand:

```
ghci> prop_idempotent []
True
ghci> prop_idempotent [1,1,1,1]
True
ghci> prop_idempotent [1..100]
True
ghci> prop_idempotent [1,5,2,1,2,0,9]
True
```

Looks good. However, writing out the input data by hand is tedious and violates the moral code of the efficient functional programmer: let the machine do the work! To automate this, the QuickCheck library comes with a set of data generators for all the basic Haskell data types. QuickCheck uses the `Arbitrary` typeclass to present a uniform

---

[*] Throughout this chapter, we'll use QuickCheck 1.0 (classic QuickCheck). It should be kept in mind that some functions may differ in later releases of the library.

interface to (pseudo)random data generation with the type system used to resolve the question of which generator to use. QuickCheck normally hides the data generation plumbing; however, we can also run the generators by hand to get a sense for the distribution of data that QuickCheck produces. For example, to generate a random list of Boolean values:

```
ghci> generate 10 (System.Random.mkStdGen 2) arbitrary :: [Bool]
[False,False,False,False,False,True]
```

QuickCheck generates test data such as this and passes it to the property of our choosing, via the quickCheck function. The type of the property itself determines which data generator is used. quickCheck then checks that for all the test data produced, the property is satisfied. Now, since our idempotency test is polymorphic in the list element type, we need to pick a particular type for which to generate test data, which we write as a type constraint on the property. To run the test, we just call quickCheck with our property function, which is set to the required data type (otherwise, the list element type will default to the uninteresting () type):

```
ghci> :type quickCheck
quickCheck :: (Testable a) => a -> IO ()
ghci> quickCheck (prop_idempotent :: [Integer] -> Bool)
 passed 100 tests.
```

For the 100 different lists generated, our property held—great! When developing tests, it is often useful to see the actual data generated for each test. To do this, we would replace quickCheck with its sibling, verboseCheck, to see (verbose) output for each test. Now, let's look at more sophisticated properties that our function might satisfy.

Testing for Properties

Good libraries consist of a set of orthogonal primitives having sensible relationships to each other. We can use QuickCheck to specify the relationships between functions in our code, helping us find a good library interface by developing functions that are interrelated via useful properties. QuickCheck in this way acts as an API "lint" tool— it provides machine support for ensuring that our library API makes sense.

The list sorting function should certainly have a number of interesting properties that tie it to other list operations. For example, the first element in a sorted list should always be the smallest element of the input list. We might be tempted to specify this intuition in Haskell, using the List library's minimum function:

```
-- file: ch11/QC-basics.hs
prop_minimum xs         = head (qsort xs) == minimum xs
```

Testing this, though, reveals an error:

```
ghci> quickCheck (prop_minimum :: [Integer] -> Bool)
** Exception: Prelude.head: empty list
```

The property failed when sorting an empty list, for which head and minimum aren't defined, as we can see from their definition:

```
-- file: ch11/minimum.hs
head         :: [a] -> a
head (x:_) = x
head []      = error "Prelude.head: empty list"

minimum      :: (Ord a) => [a] -> a
minimum [] = error "Prelude.minimum: empty list"
minimum xs =  foldl1 min xs
```

So this property will only hold for nonempty lists. QuickCheck, thankfully, comes with
a full property writing embedded language, so we can specify more precisely our invariants, filtering out values we don't want to consider. For the empty list case, we
really want to say *if* the list is nonempty, *then* the first element of the sorted result is
the minimum. This is done using the (==>) implication function, which filters out invalid data before running the property:

```
-- file: ch11/QC-basics.hs
prop_minimum' xs          = not (null xs) ==> head (qsort xs) == minimum xs
```

The result is quite clean. By separating out the empty list case, we can now confirm
that the property does in fact hold:

```
ghci> quickCheck (prop_minimum' :: [Integer] -> Property)
passed 100 tests.
```

Note that we had to change the type of the property from being a simple Bool result to
the more general Property type (the property itself is now a function that filters nonempty lists, before testing them, rather than a simple Boolean constant).

We can now complete the basic property set for the sort function with some other
invariants that it should satisfy: the output should be ordered (each element should be
smaller than, or equal to, its successor); the output should be a permutation of the
input (which we achieve via the list difference function, (\\)); the last sorted element
should be the largest element; and if we find the smallest element of two different lists,
that should be the first element if we append and sort those lists. These properties can
be stated as:

```
-- file: ch11/QC-basics.hs
prop_ordered xs = ordered (qsort xs)
    where ordered []        = True
          ordered [x]       = True
          ordered (x:y:xs) = x <= y && ordered (y:xs)

prop_permutation xs = permutation xs (qsort xs)
    where permutation xs ys = null (xs \\ ys) && null (ys \\ xs)

prop_maximum xs          =
    not (null xs) ==>
        last (qsort xs) == maximum xs

prop_append xs ys        =
    not (null xs) ==>
```

```
not (null ys) ==>
    head (qsort (xs ++ ys)) == min (minimum xs) (minimum ys)
```

Testing Against a Model

Another technique for gaining confidence in some code is to test it against a model implementation. We can tie our implementation of list sort to the reference sort function in the standard list library, and, if they behave the same, we gain confidence that our sort does the right thing:

```
-- file: ch11/QC-basics.hs
prop_sort_model xs      = sort xs == qsort xs
```

This kind of model-based testing is extremely powerful. Often, developers will have a reference implementation or prototype that, while inefficient, is correct. This can then be kept around and used to ensure that optimized production code conforms to the reference. By building a large suite of these model-based tests and running them regularly (on every commit, for example), we can cheaply ensure the precision of our code. Large Haskell projects often come bundled with property suites comparable in size to the project itself, with thousands of invariants tested on every change, keeping the code tied to the specification, and ensuring that it behaves as required.

Testing Case Study: Specifying a Pretty Printer

Testing individual functions for their natural properties is one of the basic building blocks that guides development of large systems in Haskell. We'll look now at a more complicated scenario: taking the pretty-printing library developed in earlier chapters and building a test suite for it.

Generating Test Data

Recall that the pretty printer is built around the Doc, an algebraic data type that represents well-formed documents:

```
-- file: ch11/Prettify2.hs

data Doc = Empty
         | Char Char
         | Text String
         | Line
         | Concat Doc Doc
         | Union Doc Doc
           deriving (Show,Eq)
```

The library itself is implemented as a set of functions that build and transform values of this document type, before finally rendering the finished document to a string.

QuickCheck encourages an approach to testing where the developer specifies invariants that should hold for any data we can throw at the code. To test the pretty-printing library, then, we'll need a source of input data. To do this, we take advantage of the small combinator suite for building random data that QuickCheck provides via the `Arbitrary` class. The class provides a function, `arbitrary`, to generate data of each type. With it, we can define our data generator for our custom data types:[†]

```
-- file: ch11/Arbitrary.hs
class Arbitrary a where
  arbitrary   :: Gen a
```

One thing to notice is that the generators run in a `Gen` environment, indicated by the type. This is a simple state-passing monad that is used to hide the random number generator state that is threaded through the code. We'll look thoroughly at monads in later chapters, but for now it suffices to know that, as `Gen` is defined as a monad, we can use `do` syntax to write new generators that access the implicit random number source. To actually write generators for our custom type, we use any of a set of functions defined in the library for introducing new random values and gluing them together to build up data structures of the type we're interested in. The types of the key functions are:

```
-- file: ch11/Arbitrary.hs
elements :: [a] -> Gen a
choose   :: Random a => (a, a) -> Gen a
oneof    :: [Gen a] -> Gen a
```

The function `elements`, for example, takes a list of values and returns a generator of random values from that list. (We'll use `choose` and `oneof` later.) With it, we can start writing generators for simple data types. For example, if we define a new data type for ternary logic:

```
-- file: ch11/Arbitrary.hs
data Ternary
    = Yes
    | No
    | Unknown
    deriving (Eq,Show)
```

we can write an `Arbitrary` instance for the `Ternary` type by defining a function that picks elements from a list of the possible values of the `Ternary` type:

```
-- file: ch11/Arbitrary.hs
instance Arbitrary Ternary where
  arbitrary    = elements [Yes, No, Unknown]
```

Another approach to data generation is to generate values for one of the basic Haskell types and then translate those values into the type we're actually interested in. We could have written the `Ternary` instance by generating integer values from 0 to 2 instead, using `choose`, and then mapping them onto the ternary values:

[†] The class also defines a method, `coarbitrary`, which, given a value of some type, yields a function for new generators. We can disregard for now, as it is only needed for generating random values of function type. One result of disregarding `coarbitrary` is that GHC will warn about it not being defined. However, it is safe to ignore these warnings.

```
-- file: ch11/Arbitrary2.hs
instance Arbitrary Ternary where
  arbitrary     = do
      n <- choose (0, 2) :: Gen Int
      return $ case n of
                   0 -> Yes
                   1 -> No
                   _ -> Unknown
```

For simple *sum* types, this approach works well, as the integers map nicely onto the constructors of the data type. For *product* types (such as structures and tuples), we need to instead generate each component of the product separately (and recursively for nested types), and then combine the components. For example, to generate random pairs of random values:

```
-- file: ch11/Arbitrary.hs
instance (Arbitrary a, Arbitrary b) => Arbitrary (a, b) where
  arbitrary = do
      x <- arbitrary
      y <- arbitrary
      return (x, y)
```

So let's now write a generator for all the different variants of the Doc type. We'll start by breaking the problem down, first generating random constructors for each type, and then, depending on the result, the components of each field. The most complicated case are the union and concatenation variants.

First, though, we need to write an instance for generating random characters—QuickCheck doesn't have a default instance for characters, due to the abundance of different text encodings we might want to use for character tests. We'll write our own, and, as we don't care about the actual text content of the document, a simple generator of alphabetic characters and punctuation will suffice (richer generators are simple extensions of this basic approach):

```
-- file: ch11/QC.hs
instance Arbitrary Char where
    arbitrary = elements (['A'..'Z'] ++ ['a' .. 'z'] ++ " ~!@#$%^&*()")
```

With this in place, we can now write an instance for documents by enumerating the constructors and filling in the fields. We choose a random integer to represent which document variant to generate, and then dispatch based on the result. To generate concat or union document nodes, we just recurse on **arbitrary**, letting type inference determine which instance of **Arbitrary** we mean:

```
-- file: ch11/QC.hs
instance Arbitrary Doc where
    arbitrary = do
        n <- choose (1,6) :: Gen Int
        case n of
            1 -> return Empty

            2 -> do x <- arbitrary
                    return (Char x)
```

```
3 -> do x <- arbitrary
        return (Text x)

4 -> return Line

5 -> do x <- arbitrary
        y <- arbitrary
        return (Concat x y)

6 -> do x <- arbitrary
        y <- arbitrary
        return (Union x y)
```

That was fairly straightforward, and we can clean it up some more by using the oneof function, whose type we saw earlier, to pick between different generators in a list (we can also use the monadic combinator, liftM, in order to avoid naming intermediate results from each generator):

```
-- file: ch11/QC.hs
instance Arbitrary Doc where
    arbitrary =
        oneof [ return Empty
              , liftM  Char    arbitrary
              , liftM  Text    arbitrary
              , return Line
              , liftM2 Concat arbitrary arbitrary
              , liftM2 Union  arbitrary arbitrary ]
```

The latter is more concise—just picking between a list of generators—but they describe the same data either way. We can check that the output makes sense, by generating a list of random documents (seeding the pseudorandom generator with an initial seed of 2):

```
ghci> generate 10 (System.Random.mkStdGen 2) arbitrary :: [Doc]
[Line,Empty,Union Empty Line,Union (Char 'R') (Concat (Union Line (Concat
(Text "i@BmSu") (Char ')'))) (Union (Concat (Concat (Concat (Text "kqV!iN")
Line) Line) Line) Line)),Char 'M',Text "YdwVLrQOQh"]
```

Looking at the output, we see a good mix of simple base cases and some more complicated nested documents. We'll be generating hundreds of these each test run so that should do a pretty good job. We can now write some generic properties for our document functions.

Testing Document Construction

Two of the basic functions on documents are the null document constant (a nullary function), empty, and the append function. Their types are:

```
-- file: ch11/Prettify2.hs
empty :: Doc
(<>)  :: Doc -> Doc -> Doc
```

Together, these should have a nice property: appending or prepending the empty list onto a second list should leave the second list unchanged. We can state this invariant as a property:

```
-- file: ch11/QC.hs
prop_empty_id x =
    empty <> x == x
  &&
    x <> empty == x
```

Confirming that this is indeed true, we're now underway with our testing:

```
ghci> quickCheck prop_empty_id
 passed 100 tests.
```

Use this in order to look at what actual test documents were generated (by replacing quickCheck with verboseCheck). If we look at a good mixture of both simple and complicated cases, we see a good mixture being generated. We can refine the data generation further, with constraints on the proportion of generated data, if desirable.

Other functions in the API are also simple enough to have their behavior fully described via properties. By doing so we can maintain an external, checkable description of the function's behavior, so later changes won't break these basic invariants.

```
-- file: ch11/QC.hs

prop_char c   = char c   == Char c

prop_text s   = text s   == if null s then Empty else Text s

prop_line     = line     == Line

prop_double d = double d == text (show d)
```

These properties are enough to fully test the structure returned by the basic document operators. Testing the rest of the library will require more work.

Using Lists as a Model

Higher order functions are the basic glue of reusable programming, and our pretty-printer library is no exception—a custom fold function is used internally to implement both document concatenation and interleaving separators between document chunks. The fold defined for documents takes a list of document pieces and glues them all together with a supplied combining function:

```
-- file: ch11/Prettify2.hs
fold :: (Doc -> Doc -> Doc) -> [Doc] -> Doc
fold f = foldr f empty
```

We can write tests in isolation for specific instances of fold easily. Horizontal concatenation of documents, for example, is easy to specify by writing a reference implementation on lists:

```
-- file: ch11/QC.hs

prop_hcat xs = hcat xs == glue xs
    where
        glue []     = empty
        glue (d:ds) = d <> glue ds
```

It is a similar story for punctuate, where we can model inserting punctuation with list interspersion (from Data.List, intersperse is a function that takes an element and interleaves it between other elements of a list):

```
-- file: ch11/QC.hs

prop_punctuate s xs = punctuate s xs == intersperse s xs
```

While this looks fine, running it reveals a flaw in our reasoning:

```
ghci> quickCheck prop_punctuate
Falsifiable, after 6 tests:
Empty
[Line,Text "",Line]
```

The pretty-printing library optimizes away redundant empty documents, something the model implementation doesn't do, so we'll need to augment our model to match reality. First, we can intersperse the punctuation text throughout the document list, and then a little loop to clean up the Empty documents scattered through, like so:

```
-- file: ch11/QC.hs
prop_punctuate' s xs = punctuate s xs == combine (intersperse s xs)
    where
        combine []          = []
        combine [x]         = [x]

        combine (x:Empty:ys) = x : combine ys
        combine (Empty:y:ys) = y : combine ys
        combine (x:y:ys)     = x `Concat` y : combine ys
```

Running this in GHCi, we can confirm the result. It is reassuring to have the test framework spot the flaws in our reasoning about the code—exactly what we're looking for:

```
ghci> quickCheck prop_punctuate'
passed 100 tests.
```

Putting It All Together

We can put all these tests together in a single file and run them simply using one of QuickCheck's driver functions. Several exist, including elaborate parallel ones. The basic batch driver is often good enough, however. All we need do is set up some default test parameters, and then list the functions we want to test:

```
-- file: ch11/Run.hs
import Prettify2
import Test.QuickCheck.Batch

options = TestOptions
```

```
        { no_of_tests      = 200
        , length_of_tests   = 1
        , debug_tests       = False }

  main = do
    runTests "simple" options
        [ run prop_empty_id
        , run prop_char
        , run prop_text
        , run prop_line
        , run prop_double
        ]

    runTests "complex" options
        [ run prop_hcat
        , run prop_puncutate'
        ]
```

We've structured the code here as a separate, standalone test script, with instances and properties in their own file, separate from the library source. This is typical for library projects, where the tests are kept apart from the library itself, and where they import the library via the module system. The test script can then be compiled and executed:

```
$ ghc --make Run.hs
$ ./Run
          simple : .....                      (1000)
          complex : ..                        (400)
```

A total of 1,400 individual tests were created, which is comforting. We can increase the depth easily enough, but to find out exactly how well the code is being tested, we should turn to the built-in code coverage tool, HPC, which can state precisely what is going on.

Measuring Test Coverage with HPC

HPC (Haskell Program Coverage) is an extension to the compiler to observe what parts of the code were actually executed during a given program run. This is useful in the context of testing, as it lets us observe exactly which functions, branches, and expressions were evaluated. The result is precise knowledge about the percent of code tested that's easy to obtain. HPC comes with a simple utility to generate useful graphs of program coverage, making it easy to zoom in on weak spots in the test suite.

To obtain test coverage data, all we need to do is add the -fhpc flag to the command line when compiling the tests:

```
$ ghc -fhpc Run.hs --make
```

Then run the tests as normal:

```
$ ./Run
          simple : .....                      (1000)
          complex : ..                        (400)
```

module	Top Level Definitions		Alternatives		Expressions	
	%	covered / total	%	covered / total	%	covered / total
module Prettify2	42%	9/21	23%	8/34	18%	30/158
Program Coverage Total	42%	9/21	23%	8/34	18%	30/158

Figure 11-1. Revised coverage for module Prettify2: 52% of top-level definitions (up from 42%), 23% of alternatives, 18% of expressions

During the test run, the trace of the program is written to *.tix* and *.mix* files in the current directory. Afterwards, these files are used by the command-line tool, hpc, to display various statistics about what happened. The basic interface is textual. To begin, we can get a summary of the code tested during the run using the report flag to hpc. We'll exclude the test programs themselves (using the --exclude flag), so as to concentrate only on code in the pretty-printer library. Entering the following into the console:

```
$ hpc report Run --exclude=Main --exclude=QC
18% expressions used (30/158)
 0% boolean coverage (0/3)
      0% guards (0/3), 3 unevaluated
      100% 'if' conditions (0/0)
      100% qualifiers (0/0)
 23% alternatives used (8/34)
  0% local declarations used (0/4)
 42% top-level declarations used (9/21)
```

we see that, on the last line, 42% of top-level definitions were evaluated during the test run. Not too bad for a first attempt. As we test more and more functions from the library, this figure will rise. The textual version is useful for a quick summary, but to really see what's going on, it is best to look at the marked up output. To generate this, use the markup flag instead:

```
$ hpc markup Run --exclude=Main --exclude=QC
```

This will generate one HTML file for each Haskell source file, and some index files. Loading the file hpc_index.html into a browser, we can see some pretty graphs of the code coverage. See Figure 11-1.

Not too bad. Clicking through to the pretty module itself, we see the actual source of the program (see Figure 11-2). It marked up in bold yellow for code that wasn't tested, and marked simply bold code that was tested.

We forgot to test the Monoid instance, for example, and some of the more complicated functions. HPC helps keep our test suite honest. Let's add a test for the typeclass instance of Monoid, which is the class of types that support appending and empty elements:

```
-- file: ch11/QC.hs
prop_mempty_id x =
    mempty `mappend` x == x
  &&
    x `mappend` mempty == (x :: Doc)
```

```
25   data Doc = Empty
26             | Char Char
27             | Text String
28             | Line
29             | Concat Doc Doc
30             | Union Doc Doc
31             deriving (Show,Eq)
32
33   {-- /snippet Doc --}
34
35   instance Monoid Doc where
36       mempty  = empty
37       mappend = (<>)
38
39   {-- snippet append --}
40   empty :: Doc
41   (<>)  :: Doc -> Doc -> Doc
42   {-- /snippet append --}
43
44   empty = Empty
45
46   Empty <> y = y
47   x <> Empty = x
48   x <> y = x `Concat` y
49
50   char :: Char -> Doc
51   char c = Char c
```

Figure 11-2. Screenshot of annotated coverage output, displaying the Monoid instance for Doc in bold yellow (not tested), and other code nearby in bold (was executed)

Run this property in ghci, to check it is correct:

```
ghci> quickCheck prop_mempty_id
passed 100 tests.
```

We can now recompile and run the test driver. It is important to remove the old *.tix* file first though, or an error will occur as HPC tries to combine the statistics from separate runs:

```
$ ghc -fhpc Run.hs --make -no-recomp
$ ./Run
Hpc failure: inconsistent number of tick boxes
(perhaps remove Run.tix file?)
$ rm *.tix
$ ./Run
                    simple : .....                      (1000)
                   complex : ...                         (600)
```

Another 200 tests were added to the suite, and our coverage statistics improves to 52% of the code base (see Figure 11-3).

module	Top Level Definitions		Alternatives		Expressions	
	%	covered / total	**%**	covered / total	**%**	covered / total
module Prettify2	52%	11/21	23%	8/34	20%	32/158
Program Coverage Total	52%	11/21	23%	8/34	20%	32/158

Figure 11-3. Coverage for module Prettify2: 42% of top-level definitions, 23% of alternatives, 18% of expressions

HPC ensures that we're honest in our testing, as anything less than 100% coverage will be pointed out in glaring color. In particular, it ensures the programmer has to think about error cases, complicated branches with obscure conditions, and all forms of code smell. When combined with a saturating test generation system such as QuickCheck's, testing becomes a rewarding activity and a core part of Haskell development.

CHAPTER 12

Barcode Recognition

In this chapter, we'll make use of the image-parsing library we developed in Chapter 10 to build a barcode recognition application. Given a picture of the back of a book taken with a camera phone, we could use this to extract its ISBN number.

A Little Bit About Barcodes

The vast majority of packaged and mass-produced consumer goods sold have a barcode somewhere on them. Although there are dozens of barcode systems used across a variety of specialized domains, consumer products typically use either UPC-A or EAN-13. UPC-A was developed in the United States, while EAN-13 is European in origin.

EAN-13 was developed after UPC-A and is a superset of UPC-A. (In fact, UPC-A has been officially declared obsolete since 2005, though it's still widely used within the United States.) Any software or hardware that can understand EAN-13 barcodes will automatically handle UPC-A barcodes. This neatly reduces our descriptive problem to one standard.

As the name suggests, EAN-13 describes a 13-digit sequence, which is broken into four groups:

Number system
> The first two digits. This can either indicate the nationality of the manufacturer or describe one of a few other categories, such as ISBN (book identifier) numbers.

Manufacturer ID
> The next five digits. These are assigned by a country's numbering authority.

Product ID
> The next five digits. These are assigned by the manufacturer. (Smaller manufacturers may have a longer manufacturer ID and shorter product ID, but they still add up to 10 digits.)

Check digit
> The last digit. This allows a scanner to validate the digit string it scans.

The only way in which an EAN-13 barcode differs from a UPC-A barcode is that the latter uses a single digit to represent its number system. EAN-13 barcodes retain UPC-A compatibility by setting the first number system digit to zero.

EAN-13 Encoding

Before we worry about decoding an EAN-13 barcode, we need to understand how they are encoded. The system EAN-13 uses is a little involved. We start by computing the check digit, which is the last digit of a string:

```
-- file: ch12/Barcode.hs
checkDigit :: (Integral a) => [a] -> a
checkDigit ds = 10 - (sum products `mod` 10)
    where products = mapEveryOther (*3) (reverse ds)

mapEveryOther :: (a -> a) -> [a] -> [a]
mapEveryOther f = zipWith ($) (cycle [f,id])
```

This is one of those algorithms that is more easily understood via the code than a verbal description. The computation proceeds from the right of the string. Each successive digit is either multiplied by three or left alone (the `cycle` function repeats its input list infinitely). The check digit is the difference between their sum, modulo 10, and the number 10.

A barcode is a series of fixed-width bars, where black represents a binary "one" bit, and white a "zero." A run of the same digits thus looks like a thicker bar.

The sequence of bits in a barcode is as follows:

- The leading guard sequence, encoded as 101.
- A group of six digits, each seven bits wide.
- Another guard sequence, encoded as 01010.
- A group of six more digits.
- The trailing guard sequence, encoded as 101.

The digits in the left and right groups have separate encodings. On the left, digits are encoded with parity bits. The parity bits encode the 13th digit of the barcode.

Introducing Arrays

Before we continue, here are all of the imports that we will be using in the remainder of this chapter:

```
-- file: ch12/Barcode.hs
import Data.Array (Array(..), (!), bounds, elems, indices,
                   ixmap, listArray)

import Control.Applicative ((<$>))
import Control.Monad (forM_)
```

```
import Data.Char (digitToInt)
import Data.Ix (Ix(..))
import Data.List (foldl', group, sort, sortBy, tails)
import Data.Maybe (catMaybes, listToMaybe)
import Data.Ratio (Ratio)
import Data.Word (Word8)
import System.Environment (getArgs)
import qualified Data.ByteString.Lazy.Char8 as L
import qualified Data.Map as M

import Parse                    -- from chapter 11
```

The barcode encoding process can largely be table-driven, in which we use small tables of bit patterns to decide how to encode each digit. Haskell's bread-and-butter—data types, lists, and tuples—are not well-suited to use for tables whose elements may be accessed randomly. A list has to be traversed linearly to reach the kth element. A tuple doesn't have this problem, but Haskell's type system makes it difficult to write a function that takes a tuple and an element offset and returns the element at that offset within the tuple. (We'll explore why in the exercises that follow.)

The usual data type for constant-time random access is of course the array. Haskell provides several array data types. We'll thus represent our encoding tables as arrays of strings.

The simplest array type is in the `Data.Array` module, which we're using here. This presents arrays that can contain values of any Haskell type. Like other common Haskell types, these arrays are *immutable*. An immutable array is populated with values just once, when it is created. Its contents cannot subsequently be modified. (The standard libraries also provide other array types, some of which are mutable, but we won't cover those for a while.)

```
-- file: ch12/Barcode.hs
leftOddList = ["0001101", "0011001", "0010011", "0111101", "0100011",
               "0110001", "0101111", "0111011", "0110111", "0001011"]

rightList = map complement <$> leftOddList
    where complement '0' = '1'
          complement '1' = '0'

leftEvenList = map reverse rightList

parityList = ["111111", "110100", "110010", "110001", "101100",
              "100110", "100011", "101010", "101001", "100101"]

listToArray :: [a] -> Array Int a
listToArray xs = listArray (0,l-1) xs
    where l = length xs

leftOddCodes, leftEvenCodes, rightCodes, parityCodes :: Array Int String

leftOddCodes = listToArray leftOddList
leftEvenCodes = listToArray leftEvenList
```

```
    rightCodes = listToArray rightList
    parityCodes = listToArray parityList
```

The `Data.Array` module's `listArray` function populates an array from a list. It takes as its first parameter the bounds of the array to create; the second is the values with which to populate it.

An unusual feature of the `Array` type is that its type is parameterized over both the data it contains and the index type. For example, the type of a one-dimensional array of `String` is `Array Int String`, but a two-dimensional array would have the type `Array (Int,Int) String`:

```
ghci> :m +Data.Array
ghci> :type listArray
listArray :: (Ix i) => (i, i) -> [e] -> Array i e
```

We can construct an array easily:

```
ghci> listArray (0,2) "foo"
array (0,2) [(0,'f'),(1,'o'),(2,'o')]
```

Notice that we have to specify the lower and upper bounds of the array. These bounds are inclusive, so an array from 0 to 2 has elements 0, 1, and 2:

```
ghci> listArray (0,3) [True,False,False,True,False]
array (0,3) [(0,True),(1,False),(2,False),(3,True)]
ghci> listArray (0,10) "too short"
array (0,10) [(0,'t'),(1,'o'),(2,'o'),(3,' '),(4,'s'),(5,'h'),(6,'o'),
(7,'r'),(8,'t'),(9,*** Exception: (Array.!): undefined array element
```

Once an array is constructed, we can use the `(!)` operator to access its elements by index:

```
ghci> let a = listArray (0,14) ['a'..]
ghci> a ! 2
'c'
ghci> a ! 100
*** Exception: Error in array index
```

Since the array construction function lets us specify the bounds of an array, we don't have to use the zero-based array indexing that is familiar to C programmers. We can choose whatever bounds are convenient for our purposes:

```
ghci> let a = listArray (-9,5) ['a'..]
ghci> a ! (-2)
'h'
```

The index type can be any member of the `Ix` type. This lets us use, for example, `Char` as the index type:

```
ghci> let a = listArray ('a', 'h') [97..]
ghci> a ! 'e'
101
```

To create a higher-dimensioned array, we use a tuple of Ix instances as the index type. The Prelude makes tuples of up to five elements members of the Ix class. To illustrate, here's a small three-dimensional array:

```
ghci> let a = listArray ((0,0,0), (9,9,9)) [0..]
ghci> a ! (4,3,7)
437
```

Arrays and Laziness

The list that we use to populate the array must contain at least as many elements as are in the array. If we do not provide enough elements, we'll get an error at runtime. When the error occurs depends on the nature of the array.

Here, we are using an array type that is nonstrict in its elements. If we provide a list of three values to an array that we specify as containing more than three elements, the remaining elements will undefined. We will not get an error unless we access an element beyond the third:

```
ghci> let a = listArray (0,5) "bar"
ghci> a ! 2
'r'
ghci> a ! 4
*** Exception: (Array.!): undefined array element
```

Haskell also provides strict arrays, which behave differently. We will discuss the trade-offs between the two kinds of arrays in "Unboxing, Lifting, and Bottom" on page 583.

Folding over Arrays

The bounds function returns a tuple describing the bounds that we used to create the array. The indices function returns a list of every index. We can use these to define some useful folds, since the Data.Array module doesn't define any fold functions itself:

```
-- file: ch12/Barcode.hs
-- | Strict left fold, similar to foldl' on lists.
foldA :: Ix k => (a -> b -> a) -> a -> Array k b -> a
foldA f s a = go s (indices a)
    where go s (j:js) = let s' = f s (a ! j)
                        in s' `seq` go s' js
          go s _ = s

-- | Strict left fold using the first element of the array as its
-- starting value, similar to foldl1 on lists.
foldA1 :: Ix k => (a -> a -> a) -> Array k a -> a
foldA1 f a = foldA f (a ! fst (bounds a)) a
```

You might wonder why the array modules don't already provide such useful things as folding functions. There some obvious correspondences between a one-dimensional array and a list. For instance, there are only two natural ways in which we can fold sequentially: left-to-right and right-to-left. Additionally, we can only fold over one element at a time.

This does not translate even to two-dimensional arrays. First of all, there are several kinds of fold that make sense. We might still want to fold over single elements, but we now have the possibility of folding over rows or columns, too. On top of this, for element-at-a-time folding, there are no longer just two sequences for traversal.

In other words, for two-dimensional arrays, there are enough permutations of possibly useful behavior that there aren't many compelling reasons to choose a handful for a standard library. This problem is only compounded for higher dimensions, so it's best to let developers write folds that suit the needs of their applications. As we can see from our examples, this is not hard to do.

Modifying Array Elements

While "modification" functions exist for immutable arrays, they are not very practical. For example, the `accum` function takes an array and a list of (`index, value`) pairs and returns a new array with the values at the given indices replaced.

Since arrays are immutable, modifying even one element requires copying the entire array. This quickly becomes prohibitively expensive on arrays of even modest size.

Another array type, `DiffArray` in the `Data.Array.Diff` module, attempts to offset the cost of small modifications by storing deltas between successive versions of an array. Unfortunately, it is not implemented efficiently at the time of this writing, and it is currently too slow to be of practical use.

Don't lose hope

It *is* in fact possible to modify an array efficiently in Haskell, using the ST monad. We'll return to this subject in Chapter 26.

EXERCISES

Let's briefly explore the suitability of tuples as stand-ins for arrays:

1. Write a function that takes two arguments: a four-element tuple and an integer. With an integer argument of zero, it should return the leftmost element of the tuple. With an argument of one, it should return the next element. And so on. What restrictions do you have to put on the types of the arguments in order to write a function that typechecks correctly?

2. Write a similar function that takes a six-tuple as its first argument.

3. Try refactoring the two functions to share any common code you can identify. How much shared code are you able to find?

Encoding an EAN-13 Barcode

Even though our goal is to *decode* a barcode, it's useful to have an encoder for reference. This will allow us to, for example, ensure that our code is correct by checking that the output of decode . encode is the same as its input:

```
-- file: ch12/Barcode.hs
encodeEAN13 :: String -> String
encodeEAN13 = concat . encodeDigits . map digitToInt

-- | This function computes the check digit; don't pass one in.
encodeDigits :: [Int] -> [String]
encodeDigits s@(first:rest) =
    outerGuard : lefties ++ centerGuard : righties ++ [outerGuard]
  where (left, right) = splitAt 5 rest
        lefties = zipWith leftEncode (parityCodes ! first) left
        righties = map rightEncode (right ++ [checkDigit s])

leftEncode :: Char -> Int -> String
leftEncode '1' = (leftOddCodes !)
leftEncode '0' = (leftEvenCodes !)

rightEncode :: Int -> String
rightEncode = (rightCodes !)

outerGuard = "101"
centerGuard = "01010"
```

The string to encode is 12 digits long, with encodeDigits adding a 13th check digit.

The barcode is encoded as two groups of six digits, with a guard sequence in the middle and "outside" sequences on either side. But if we have two groups of six digits, what happened to the missing digit?

Each digit in the left group is encoded using either odd or even parity, with the parity chosen based on the bits of the first digit in the string. If a bit of the first digit is zero, the corresponding digit in the left group is encoded with even parity. A one bit causes the digit to be encoded with odd parity. This encoding is an elegant hack, chosen to make EAN-13 barcodes backwards-compatible with the older UPC-A standard.

Constraints on Our Decoder

Before we talk about decoding, let's set a few practical limitations on what kinds of barcode images we can work with.

Phone cameras and webcams generally output JPEG images, but writing a JPEG decoder would take us several chapters. We'll simplify our parsing problem by handling the netpbm file format. We will use the parsing combinators we developed earlier in Chapter 10.

Figure 12-1. Barcode image distorted by perspective, due to photo being taken from an angle

We'd like to deal with real images from the kinds of cheap, fixed-focus cameras that come with low-end cell phones. These images tend to be out of focus, noisy, low in contrast, and of poor resolution. Fortunately, it's not hard to write code that can handle noisy, defocused VGA-resolution (640 × 480) images with terrible contrast ratios. We've verified that the code in this chapter captures barcodes from real books, using pictures taken by authentically mediocre cameras.

We will avoid any image-processing heroics, because that's another chapter-consuming subject. We won't correct perspective (such as in Figure 12-1). Neither will we sharpen images taken from too near to the subject (Figure 12-2), which causes narrow bars to fade out; or from too far (Figure 12-3), which causes adjacent bars to blur together.

Divide and Conquer

Our task is to take a camera image and extract a valid barcode from it. Given such a nonspecific description, it can be hard to see how to make progress. However, we can break the big problem into a series of subproblems, each of which is self-contained and more tractable:

- Convert color data into a form we can easily work with.
- Sample a single scan line from the image and extract a set of guesses as to what the encoded digits in this line could be.
- From the guesses, create a list of valid decodings.

Many of these subproblems can be further divided, as we'll see.

You might wonder how closely this approach of subdivision mirrors the actual work we did when writing the code that we present in this chapter. The answer is that we're far from image-processing gurus, and when we started writing this chapter, we didn't know exactly what our solution was going to look like.

Figure 12-2. Barcode image blurred by being taken from inside the focal length of the camera lens, causing bars to run together

Figure 12-3. Barcode image contains insufficient detail, due to poor resolution of camera lens and CCD

We made some early educated guesses as to what a reasonable solution might appear as and came up with the subtasks just listed. We were then able to start tackling those parts that we knew how to solve, using our spare time to think about the bits that we had no prior experience with. We certainly didn't have a preexisting algorithm or master plan in mind.

Dividing the problem up like this helped us in two ways. By making progress on familiar ground, we had the psychological advantage of starting to solve the problem, even when we didn't really know where we were going. And as we started to work on a particular subproblem, we found ourselves able to further subdivide it into tasks of varying familiarity. We continued to focus on easier components, deferring ones we hadn't thought about in enough detail yet, and jumping from one element of the master list to another. Eventually, we ran out of problems that were both unfamiliar and unsolved, and we had a complete idea of our eventual solution.

Turning a Color Image into Something Tractable

Since we want to work with barcodes (which are sequences of black and white stripes) and we want to write a simple decoder, an easy representation to work with will be a monochrome image, in which each pixel is either black or white.

Parsing a Color Image

As we mentioned earlier, we'll work with netpbm images. The netpbm color image format is only slightly more complicated than the grayscale image format that we parsed in Chapter 10. The identifying string in a header is "P6," with the rest of the header layout identical to the grayscale format. In the body of an image, each pixel is represented as three bytes, one each for red, green, and blue.

We'll represent the image data as a two-dimensional array of pixels. We're using arrays here purely to gain experience with them. For this application, we could just as well use a list of lists. The only advantage of an array is slight—we can efficiently extract a row:

```
-- file: ch12/Barcode.hs
type Pixel = Word8
type RGB = (Pixel, Pixel, Pixel)

type Pixmap = Array (Int,Int) RGB
```

We provide a few type synonyms to make our type signatures more readable.

Since Haskell gives us considerable freedom in how we lay out an array, we must choose a representation. We'll play it safe and follow a popular convention: indices begin at zero. We don't need to store the dimensions of the image explicitly, since we can extract them using the bounds function.

The actual parser is mercifully short, thanks to the combinators we developed in Chapter 10:

```
-- file: ch12/Barcode.hs
parseRawPPM :: Parse Pixmap
parseRawPPM =
    parseWhileWith w2c (/= '\n') ==> \header -> skipSpaces ==>&
    assert (header == "P6") "invalid raw header" ==>&
    parseNat ==> \width -> skipSpaces ==>&
    parseNat ==> \height -> skipSpaces ==>&
    parseNat ==> \maxValue ->
    assert (maxValue == 255) "max value out of spec" ==>&
    parseByte ==>&
    parseTimes (width * height) parseRGB ==> \pxs ->
    identity (listArray ((0,0),(width-1,height-1)) pxs)

parseRGB :: Parse RGB
parseRGB = parseByte ==> \r ->
           parseByte ==> \g ->
           parseByte ==> \b ->
```

```
            identity (r,g,b)
parseTimes :: Int -> Parse a -> Parse [a]
parseTimes 0 _ = identity []
parseTimes n p = p ==> \x -> (x:) <$> parseTimes (n-1) p
```

The only function of note here is parseTimes, which calls another parser a given number of times, building up a list of results.

Grayscale Conversion

Now that we have a color image in hand, we need to convert the color data into monochrome. An intermediate step is to convert the data to grayscale. There's a simple, widely used formula[*] for converting an RGB image into a grayscale image, based on the perceived brightness of each color channel:

```
-- file: ch12/Barcode.hs
luminance :: (Pixel, Pixel, Pixel) -> Pixel
luminance (r,g,b) = round (r' * 0.30 + g' * 0.59 + b' * 0.11)
    where r' = fromIntegral r
          g' = fromIntegral g
          b' = fromIntegral b
```

Haskell arrays are members of the Functor typeclass, so we can simply use fmap to turn an entire image, or a single scanline, from color into grayscale:

```
-- file: ch12/Barcode.hs
type Greymap = Array (Int,Int) Pixel

pixmapToGreymap :: Pixmap -> Greymap
pixmapToGreymap = fmap luminance
```

This pixmapToGreymap function is just for illustration. Since we'll only be checking a few rows of an image for possible barcodes, there's no reason to do the extra work of converting data we'll never subsequently use.

Grayscale to Binary and Type Safety

Our next subproblem is to convert the grayscale image into a two-valued image, where each pixel is either on or off.

In an image-processing application, where we're juggling lots of numbers, it would be easy to reuse the same numeric type for several different purposes. For example, we could use the Pixel type to represent on/off states, using the convention that the digit one represents a bit that's "on," and zero represents "off."

However, reusing types for multiple purposes in this way quickly leads to potential confusion. To see whether a particular "Pixel" is a number or an on/off value, we can no longer simply glance at a type signature. We could easily use a value containing

---

[*] The formula originates in ITU-R Recommendation 601.

"the wrong kind of number" in some context, and the compiler wouldn't catch it because the types work out.

We could try to work around this by introducing a type alias. In the same way that we declared Pixel to be a synonym of Word8, we could declare a Bit type as a synonym of Pixel. While this might help readability, type synonyms still don't make the compiler do any useful work on our behalf.

The compiler would treat Pixel and Bit as exactly the same type, so it could not catch a mistake such as using a Pixel value of 253 in a function that expects Bit values of zero or one.

If we define the monochrome type ourselves, the compiler will prevent us from accidentally mixing our types up like this:

```
-- file: ch12/Barcode.hs
data Bit = Zero | One
           deriving (Eq, Show)

threshold :: (Ix k, Integral a) => Double -> Array k a -> Array k Bit
threshold n a = binary <$> a
    where binary i | i < pivot  = Zero
                   | otherwise  = One
          pivot    = round $ least + (greatest - least) * n
          least    = fromIntegral $ choose (<) a
          greatest = fromIntegral $ choose (>) a
          choose f = foldA1 $ \x y -> if f x y then x else y
```

Our threshold function computes the minimum and maximum values in its input array. It takes these and a threshold valued between zero and one, and computes a "pivot" value. Then for each value in the array, if that value is less than the pivot, the result is Zero; otherwise, One. Notice that we use one of the folding functions that we wrote in "Folding over Arrays" on page 273.

What Have We Done to Our Image?

Let's step back for a moment and consider what we did to our image when we converted it from color to monochrome. Figure 12-4 shows an image captured from a VGA-resolution camera. All we've done is crop it down to the barcode.

The encoded digit string, 9780132114677, is printed below the barcode. The left group encodes the digits 780132, with 9 encoded in their parity. The right group encodes the digits 114677, where the final 7 is the check digit. Figure 12-5 shows a clean encoding of this barcode, from one of the many websites that offers barcode image generation for free.

In Figure 12-6, we've chosen a row from the captured image and stretched it out vertically to make it easier to see. We've superimposed this on top of the perfect image and stretched it out so that the two are aligned.

Figure 12-4. Barcode photo, somewhat blurry and dim

Figure 12-5. Automatically generated image of the same barcode

Figure 12-6. Photographic and generated images of barcode juxtaposed to illustrate the variation in bar brightness and resolution

The luminance-converted row from the photo is in the dark gray band. It is low in contrast and poor in quality, with plenty of blurring and noise. The paler band is the same row with the contrast adjusted.

Somewhat below these two bands is another: this shows the effect of thresholding the luminance-converted row. Notice that some bars have gotten thicker, others thinner, and many bars have moved a little to the left or right.

Clearly, any attempt to find exact matches in an image with problems such as these is not going to succeed very often. We must write code that's robust in the face of bars that are too thick, too thin, or not exactly where they're supposed to be. The widths of our bars will depend on how far our book was from the camera, so we can't make any assumptions about widths, either.

Finding Matching Digits

Our first problem is to find the digits that *might* be encoded at a given position. For the next while, we'll make a couple simplifying assumptions. The first is that we're working with a single row. The second is that we know exactly where in a row the left edge of a barcode begins.

Run Length Encoding

How can we overcome the problem of not even knowing how thick our bars are? The answer is to run length encode (instead of repeating a value some number of times, run length encoding presents it once, with a count of the number of consecutive repeats):

```
-- file: ch12/Barcode.hs
type Run = Int
type RunLength a = [(Run, a)]

runLength :: Eq a => [a] -> RunLength a
runLength = map rle . group
    where rle xs = (length xs, head xs)
```

The group function takes sequences of identical elements in a list and groups them into sublists:

```
ghci> group [1,1,2,3,3,3,3]
[[1,1],[2],[3,3,3,3]]
```

Our runLength function represents each group as a pair of its length and first element:

```
ghci> let bits = [0,0,1,1,0,0,1,1,0,0,0,0,0,0,1,1,1,1,0,0,0,0]
ghci> runLength bits
Loading package array-0.1.0.0 ... linking ... done.
Loading package containers-0.1.0.2 ... linking ... done.
Loading package bytestring-0.9.0.1.1 ... linking ... done.
[(2,0),(2,1),(2,0),(2,1),(6,0),(4,1),(4,0)]
```

Since the data we're run length encoding are just ones and zeros, the encoded numbers will simply alternate between one and zero. We can throw the encoded values away without losing any useful information, keeping only the length of each run:

```
-- file: ch12/Barcode.hs
runLengths :: Eq a => [a] -> [Run]
runLengths = map fst . runLength

ghci> runLengths bits
[2,2,2,2,6,4,4]
```

The bit patterns aren't random; they're the left outer guard and first encoded digit of a row from our captured image. If we drop the guard bars, we're left with the run lengths [2,6,4,4]. How do we find matches for these in the encoding tables we wrote in "Introducing Arrays" on page 270?

Scaling Run Lengths, and Finding Approximate Matches

One possible approach is to scale the run lengths so that they sum to one. We'll use the `Ratio Int` type instead of the usual `Double` to manage these scaled values, as Ratios print out more readably in ghci. This makes interactive debugging and development much easier:

```
-- file: ch12/Barcode.hs
type Score = Ratio Int

scaleToOne :: [Run] -> [Score]
scaleToOne xs = map divide xs
    where divide d = fromIntegral d / divisor
          divisor = fromIntegral (sum xs)
-- A more compact alternative that "knows" we're using Ratio Int:
-- scaleToOne xs = map (% sum xs) xs

type ScoreTable = [[Score]]

-- "SRL" means "scaled run length".
asSRL :: [String] -> ScoreTable
asSRL = map (scaleToOne . runLengths)

leftOddSRL = asSRL leftOddList
leftEvenSRL = asSRL leftEvenList
rightSRL = asSRL rightList
paritySRL = asSRL parityList
```

We use the `Score` type synonym so that most of our code won't have to care what the underlying type is. Once we're done developing our code and poking around with ghci, we could, if we wish, go back and turn the `Score` type synonym into `Doubles` without changing any code.

We can use `scaleToOne` to scale a sequence of digits that we're searching for. We've now corrected for variations in bar widths due to distance, as there should be a pretty close match between an entry in a scaled run length encoding table and a run length sequence pulled from an image.

The next question is how we turn the intuitive idea of "pretty close" into a measure of "close enough." Given two scaled run length sequences, we can calculate an approximate "distance" between them as follows:

```
-- file: ch12/Barcode.hs
distance :: [Score] -> [Score] -> Score
distance a b = sum . map abs $ zipWith (-) a b
```

An exact match will give a distance of zero, with weaker matches resulting in larger distances:

```
ghci> let group = scaleToOne [2,6,4,4]
ghci> distance group (head leftEvenSRL)
13%28
ghci> distance group (head leftOddSRL)
17%28
```

Given a scaled run length table, we choose the best few matches in that table for a given input sequence:

```
-- file: ch12/Barcode.hs
bestScores :: ScoreTable -> [Run] -> [(Score, Digit)]
bestScores srl ps = take 3 . sort $ scores
    where scores = zip [distance d (scaleToOne ps) | d <- srl] digits
          digits = [0..9]
```

List Comprehensions

The new notation that we introduced in the previous example is an illustration of a *list comprehension*, which creates a list from one or more other lists:

```
ghci> [ (a,b) | a <- [1,2], b <- "abc" ]
[(1,'a'),(1,'b'),(1,'c'),(2,'a'),(2,'b'),(2,'c')]
```

The expression on the left of the vertical bar is evaluated for each combination of *generator expressions* on the right. A generator expression binds a variable on the left of a <- to an element of the list on the right. As the preceding example shows, the combinations of generators are evaluated in depth first order: for the first element of the first list, we evaluate every element of the second, and so on.

In addition to generators, we can also specify guards on the right of a list comprehension. A guard is a Bool expression. If it evaluates to False, that element is skipped over:

```
ghci> [ (a,b) | a <- [1..6], b <- [5..7], even (a + b ^ 2) ]
[(1,5),(1,7),(2,6),(3,5),(3,7),(4,6),(5,5),(5,7),(6,6)]
```

We can also bind local variables using a let expression:

```
ghci> let vowel = (`elem` "aeiou")
ghci> [ x | a <- "etaoin", b <- "shrdlu", let x = [a,b], all vowel x ]
["eu","au","ou","iu"]
```

If a pattern match fails in a generator expression, no error occurs. Instead, that list element is skipped:

```
ghci> [ a | (3,a) <- [(1,'y'),(3,'e'),(5,'p')] ]
"e"
```

List comprehensions are powerful and concise. As a result, they can be difficult to read, but when used with care, they can make code easier to follow:

```
-- file: ch12/Barcode.hs
-- our original
```

```
zip [distance d (scaleToOne ps) | d <- srl] digits

-- the same expression, expressed without a list comprehension
zip (map (flip distance (scaleToOne ps)) srl) digits

-- the same expression, written entirely as a list comprehension
[(distance d (scaleToOne ps), n) | d <- srl, n <- digits]
```

Remembering a Match's Parity

For each match in the left group, we have to remember whether we found it in the even parity table or the odd table:

```
-- file: ch12/Barcode.hs
data Parity a = Even a | Odd a | None a
                deriving (Show)

fromParity :: Parity a -> a
fromParity (Even a) = a
fromParity (Odd a) = a
fromParity (None a) = a

parityMap :: (a -> b) -> Parity a -> Parity b
parityMap f (Even a) = Even (f a)
parityMap f (Odd a) = Odd (f a)
parityMap f (None a) = None (f a)

instance Functor Parity where
    fmap = parityMap
```

We wrap a value in the parity with which it was encoded, and then make it a Functor instance so that we can easily manipulate parity-encoded values.

We would like to be able to sort parity-encoded values based on the values they contain. The Data.Function module provides a lovely combinator that we can use for this, named on:

```
-- file: ch12/Barcode.hs
on :: (a -> a -> b) -> (c -> a) -> c -> c -> b
on f g x y = g x `f` g y

compareWithoutParity = compare `on` fromParity
```

In case it's unclear, try thinking of on as a function of two arguments, f and g, which return a function of two arguments, x and y. It applies g to x and to y, then f on the two results (hence the name on).

Wrapping a match in a parity value is straightforward:

```
-- file: ch12/Barcode.hs
type Digit = Word8

bestLeft :: [Run] -> [Parity (Score, Digit)]
bestLeft ps = sortBy compareWithoutParity
                ((map Odd (bestScores leftOddSRL ps)) ++
                 (map Even (bestScores leftEvenSRL ps)))

bestRight :: [Run] -> [Parity (Score, Digit)]
bestRight = map None . bestScores rightSRL
```

Once we have the best lefthand matches from the even and odd tables, we sort them based only on the quality of each match.

Another kind of laziness, of the keyboarding variety

In our definition of the Parity type, we could have used Haskell's record syntax to avoid the need to write a fromParity function. In other words, we could have written it as follows:

```
-- file: ch12/Barcode.hs
data AltParity a = AltEven {fromAltParity :: a}
                 | AltOdd  {fromAltParity :: a}
                 | AltNone {fromAltParity :: a}
                   deriving (Show)
```

Why did we not do this? The answer is slightly shameful and has to do with interactive debugging in ghci. When we tell GHC to automatically derive a Show instance for a type, it produces different code depending on whether or not we declare the type with record syntax:

```
ghci> show $ Even 1
"Even 1"
ghci> show $ AltEven 1
"AltEven {fromAltParity = 1}"
ghci> length . show $ Even 1
6
ghci> length . show $ AltEven 1
27
```

The Show instance for the variant that uses record syntax is considerably more verbose. This creates much more noise that we must scan through when we're trying to read, say, a list of parity-encoded values output by ghci.

Of course, we could write our own, less noisy, Show instance. It's simply less effort to avoid record syntax and write our own fromParity function instead, letting GHC derive a more terse Show instance for us. This isn't an especially satisfying rationale, but programmer laziness can lead in odd directions at times.

Chunking a List

A common aspect of working with lists is needing to "chunk" them. For example, each digit in a barcode is encoded using a run of four digits. We can turn the flat list that represents a row into a list of four-element lists as follows:

```
-- file: ch12/Barcode.hs
chunkWith :: ([a] -> ([a], [a])) -> [a] -> [[a]]
chunkWith _ [] = []
chunkWith f xs = let (h, t) = f xs
                 in h : chunkWith f t

chunksOf :: Int -> [a] -> [[a]]
chunksOf n = chunkWith (splitAt n)
```

It's somewhat rare that we need to write generic list manipulation functions such as this. Often, a glance through the Data.List module will find us a function that does exactly or close enough to what we need.

Generating a List of Candidate Digits

With our small army of helper functions deployed, the function that generates lists of candidate matches for each digit group is easy to write. First of all, we take care of a few early checks to determine whether matching even makes sense. A list of runs must start on a black (Zero) bar, and contain enough bars. Here are the first few equations of our function:

```
-- file: ch12/Barcode.hs
candidateDigits :: RunLength Bit -> [[Parity Digit]]
candidateDigits ((_, One):_) = []
candidateDigits rle | length rle < 59 = []
```

If any application of bestLeft or bestRight results in an empty list, we can't possibly have a match. Otherwise, we throw away the scores, and return a list of lists of parity-encoded candidate digits. The outer list is 12 elements long, 1 per digit in the barcode. The digits in each sublist are ordered by match quality.

Here is the remainder of the definition of our function:

```
-- file: ch12/Barcode.hs
candidateDigits rle
    | any null match = []
    | otherwise      = map (map (fmap snd)) match
  where match = map bestLeft left ++ map bestRight right
        left = chunksOf 4 . take 24 . drop 3 $ runLengths
        right = chunksOf 4 . take 24 . drop 32 $ runLengths
        runLengths = map fst rle
```

Let's take a glance at the candidate digits chosen for each group of bars, from a row taken from Figure 12-5:

```
ghci> :type input
input :: [(Run, Bit)]
```

```
ghci> take 7 input
[(2,Zero),(2,One),(2,Zero),(2,One),(6,Zero),(4,One),(4,Zero)]
ghci> mapM_ print $ candidateDigits input
[Even 1,Even 5,Odd 7,Odd 1,Even 2,Odd 5]
[Even 8,Even 7,Odd 1,Odd 2,Odd 0,Even 6]
[Even 0,Even 1,Odd 8,Odd 2,Odd 4,Even 9]
[Odd 1,Odd 0,Even 8,Odd 2,Even 2,Even 4]
[Even 3,Odd 4,Odd 5,Even 7,Even 0,Odd 2]
[Odd 2,Odd 4,Even 7,Even 0,Odd 1,Even 1]
[None 1,None 5,None 0]
[None 1,None 5,None 2]
[None 4,None 5,None 2]
[None 6,None 8,None 2]
[None 7,None 8,None 3]
[None 7,None 3,None 8]
```

Life Without Arrays or Hash Tables

In an imperative language, the array is as much a "bread and butter" type as a list or tuple in Haskell. We take it for granted that an array in an imperative language is usually mutable; we can change an element of an array whenever it suits us.

As we mentioned in "Modifying Array Elements" on page 274, Haskell arrays are *not* mutable. This means that to "modify" a single array element, a copy of the entire array is made, with that single element set to its new value. Clearly, this approach is not a winner for performance.

The mutable array is a building block for another ubiquitous imperative data structure, the hash table. In the typical implementation, an array acts as the "spine" of the table, with each element containing a list of elements. To add an element to a hash table, we hash the element to find the array offset and modify the list at that offset to add the element to it.

If arrays aren't mutable for updating a hash table, we must create a new one. We copy the array, putting a new list at the offset indicated by the element's hash. We don't need to copy the lists at other offsets, but we've already dealt performance a fatal blow simply by having to copy the spine.

At a single stroke, then, immutable arrays have eliminated *two* canonical imperative data structures from our toolbox. Arrays are somewhat less useful in pure Haskell code than in many other languages. Still, many array codes update an array only during a build phase, and subsequently use it in a read-only manner.

A Forest of Solutions

This is not the calamitous situation that it might seem, though. Arrays and hash tables are often used as collections indexed by a key, and in Haskell we use *trees* for this purpose.

Implementing a naive tree type is particularly easy in Haskell. Beyond that, more useful tree types are also unusually easy to implement. Self-balancing structures, such as red-black trees, have struck fear into generations of undergraduate computer science students, because the balancing algorithms are notoriously hard to get right.

Haskell's combination of algebraic data types, pattern matching, and guards reduce even the hairiest of balancing operations to a few lines of code. We'll bite back our enthusiasm for building trees, however, and focus on why they're particularly useful in a pure functional language.

The attraction of a tree to a functional programmer is *cheap modification*. We don't break the immutability rule: trees are immutable just like everything else. However, when we modify a tree, thus creating a new tree, we can share most of the structure between the old and new versions. For example, in a tree containing 10,000 nodes, we might expect that the old and new versions will share about 9,985 elements when we add or remove one. In other words, the number of elements modified per update depends on the height of the tree or the logarithm of the size of the tree.

Haskell's standard libraries provide two collection types that are implemented using balanced trees behind the scenes: `Data.Map` for key/value pairs and `Data.Set` for sets of values. As we'll be using `Data.Map` in the sections that follow, we'll give a quick introduction to it next. `Data.Set` is sufficiently similar that you should be able to pick it up quickly.

A word about performance

Compared to a hash table, a well-implemented purely functional tree data structure will perform competitively. You should not approach trees with the assumption that your code will pay a performance penalty.

A Brief Introduction to Maps

The `Data.Map` module provides a parameterized type, `Map k a`, that maps from a key type `k` to a value type `a`. Although it is internally a size-balanced binary tree, the implementation is not visible to us.

`Map` is strict in its keys, but nonstrict in its values. In other words, the *spine*, or structure, of the map is always kept up-to-date, but values in the map aren't evaluated unless we force them to be.

It is very important to remember this, as `Map`'s laziness over values is a frequent source of space leaks among coders who are not expecting it.

Because the `Data.Map` module contains a number of names that clash with `Prelude` names, it's usually imported in qualified form. Earlier in this chapter, we imported it using the prefix `M`.

Type constraints

The Map type doesn't place any explicit constraints on its key type, but most of the module's useful functions require that keys be instances of Ord. This is noteworthy, as it's an example of a common design pattern in Haskell code: type constraints are pushed out to where they're actually needed, not necessarily applied at the point where they'd result in the least typing for a library's author.

Neither the Map type nor any functions in the module constrain the types that can be used as values.

Partial application awkwardness

For some reason, the type signatures of the functions in Data.Map are not generally friendly to partial application. The map parameter always comes last, whereas it would be easier to partially apply if it were first. As a result, code that uses partially applied map functions almost always contains adapter functions to fiddle with argument ordering.

Getting started with the API

The Data.Map module has a large "surface area": it exports dozens of functions. Just a handful of these comprise the most frequently used core of the module.

To create an empty map, we use empty. For a map containing one key/value pair, we use singleton:

```
ghci> M.empty
Loading package array-0.1.0.0 ... linking ... done.
Loading package containers-0.1.0.2 ... linking ... done.
fromList []
ghci> M.singleton "foo" True
fromList [("foo",True)]
```

Since the implementation is abstract, we can't pattern match on Map values. Instead, it provides a number of lookup functions, of which two are particularly widely used. The lookup function has a slightly tricky type signature,[†] but don't worry—all will become clear in Chapter 14:

```
ghci> :type M.lookup
M.lookup :: (Ord k, Monad m) => k -> M.Map k a -> m a
```

Most often, the type parameter m in the result is Maybe. In other words, if the map contains a value for the given key, lookup will return the value wrapped in Just. Otherwise, it will return Nothing:

```
ghci> let m = M.singleton "foo" 1 :: M.Map String Int
ghci> case M.lookup "bar" m of { Just v -> "yay"; Nothing -> "boo" }
"boo"
```

[†] Starting with GHC 6.10.1, the type of this function has been simplified to k -> M.Map k a -> Maybe a.

The findWithDefault function takes a value to return if the key isn't in the map.

Beware the partial functions!

There exists a (!) operator that performs a lookup and returns the un-adorned value associated with a key (i.e., not wrapped in Maybe or whatever). Unfortunately, it is not a total function: it calls error if the key is not present in the map.

To add a key/value pair to the map, the most useful functions are insert and insertWith'. The insert function simply inserts a value into the map, overwriting any matching value that may already have been present.

```
ghci> :type M.insert
M.insert :: (Ord k) => k -> a -> M.Map k a -> M.Map k a
ghci> M.insert "quux" 10 m
fromList [("foo",1),("quux",10)]
ghci> M.insert "foo" 9999 m
fromList [("foo",9999)]
```

The insertWith' function takes a further *combining function* as its argument. If no matching key was present in the map, the new value is inserted verbatim. Otherwise, the combining function is called on the new and old values, and its result is inserted into the map:

```
ghci> :type M.insertWith'
M.insertWith' :: (Ord k) => (a -> a -> a) -> k -> a -> M.Map k a -> M.Map k a
ghci> M.insertWith' (+) "zippity" 10 m
fromList [("foo",1),("zippity",10)]
ghci> M.insertWith' (+) "foo" 9999 m
fromList [("foo",10000)]
```

As the tick at the end of its name suggests, insertWith' evaluates the combining function strictly, allowing us to avoid space leaks. While there exists a lazy variant (insertWith without the trailing tick in the name), it's rarely what we'll actually want.

The delete function deletes the given key from the map. It returns the map unmodified if the key is not present:

```
ghci> :type M.delete
M.delete :: (Ord k) => k -> M.Map k a -> M.Map k a
ghci> M.delete "foo" m
fromList []
```

Finally, there are several efficient functions for performing set-like operations on maps. Of these, we'll be using union. This function is *left-biased*—if two maps contain the same key, the result will contain the value from the left map:

```
ghci> m `M.union` M.singleton "quux" 1
fromList [("foo",1),("quux",1)]
ghci> m `M.union` M.singleton "foo" 0
fromList [("foo",1)]
```

We have barely covered ten percent of the `Data.Map` API. We will cover maps and similar data structures in greater detail in Chapter 13. For further inspiration, we encourage you to browse the module documentation. The module is impressively thorough.

Further Reading

Purely Functional Data Structures by Chris Okasaki (Cambridge University Press) gives a wonderful and thorough implementor's tour of many pure functional data structures, including several kinds of balanced trees. It also provides valuable insight into reasoning about the performance of purely functional data structures and lazy evaluation.

We recommend Okasaki's book as essential reading for functional programmers. If you're not convinced, Okasaki's Ph.D. thesis, *Purely Functional Data Structures* (see *http://www.cs.cmu.edu/~rwh/theses/okasaki.pdf*), is a less complete and polished version of the book, and it is available for free online.

Turning Digit Soup into an Answer

We've got yet another problem to solve. We have many candidates for the last 12 digits of the barcode. In addition, we need to use the parities of the first six digits to figure out what the first digit is. Finally, we need to ensure that our answer's check digit makes sense.

This seems quite challenging! We have a lot of uncertain data; what should we do? It's reasonable to ask if we could perform a brute-force search. Given the candidates we saw in th preceding `ghci` session, how many combinations would we have to examine?

```
ghci> product . map length . candidateDigits $ input
34012224
```

So much for that idea. Once again, we'll initially focus on a subproblem that we know how to solve and postpone worrying about the rest.

Solving for Check Digits in Parallel

Let's abandon the idea of searching for now, and focus on computing a check digit. The check digit for a barcode can assume 1 of 12 possible values. For a given parity digit, which input sequences can cause that digit to be computed?

```
-- file: ch12/Barcode.hs
type Map a = M.Map Digit [a]
```

In this map, the key is a check digit, and the value is a sequence that evaluates to this check digit. We have two further map types based on this definition:

```
-- file: ch12/Barcode.hs
type DigitMap = Map Digit
type ParityMap = Map (Parity Digit)
```

We'll generically refer to these as *solution maps*, because they show us the digit sequence that "solves for" each check digit.

Given a single digit, here's how we can update an existing solution map:

```
-- file: ch12/Barcode.hs
updateMap :: Parity Digit       -- ^ new digit
         -> Digit               -- ^ existing key
         -> [Parity Digit]      -- ^ existing digit sequence
         -> ParityMap           -- ^ map to update
         -> ParityMap
updateMap digit key seq = insertMap key (fromParity digit) (digit:seq)

insertMap :: Digit -> Digit -> [a] -> Map a -> Map a
insertMap key digit val m = val `seq` M.insert key' val m
    where key' = (key + digit) `mod` 10
```

With an existing check digit drawn from the map, the sequence that solves for it, and a new input digit, this function updates the map with the new sequence that leads to the new check digit.

This might seem a bit much to digest, but an example will make it clear. Let's say the check digit we're looking at is 4, the sequence leading to it is [1,3], and the digit we want to add to the map is 8. The sum of 4 and 8, modulo 10, is 2, so this is the key we'll be inserting into the map. The sequence that leads to the new check digit 2 is thus [8,1,3], so this is what we'll insert as the value.

For each digit in a sequence, we'll generate a new solution map, using that digit and an older solution map:

```
-- file: ch12/Barcode.hs
useDigit :: ParityMap -> ParityMap -> Parity Digit -> ParityMap
useDigit old new digit =
    new `M.union` M.foldWithKey (updateMap digit) M.empty old
```

Once again, let's illustrate what this code is doing using some examples. This time, we'll use ghci:

```
ghci> let single n = M.singleton n [Even n] :: ParityMap
ghci> useDigit (single 1) M.empty (Even 1)
fromList [(2,[Even 1,Even 1])]
ghci> useDigit (single 1) (single 2) (Even 2)
fromList [(2,[Even 2]),(3,[Even 2,Even 1])]
```

The new solution map that we feed to useDigits starts out empty. We populate it completely by folding useDigits over a sequence of input digits:

```
-- file: ch12/Barcode.hs
incorporateDigits :: ParityMap -> [Parity Digit] -> ParityMap
incorporateDigits old digits = foldl' (useDigit old) M.empty digits
```

This generates a complete new solution map from an old one:

```
ghci> incorporateDigits (M.singleton 0 []) [Even 1, Even 5]
fromList [(1,[Even 1]),(5,[Even 5])]
```

Finally, we must build the complete solution map. We start out with an empty map, then fold over each digit position from the barcode in turn. For each position, we create a new map from our guesses at the digits in that position. This becomes the old map for the next round of the fold:

```
-- file: ch12/Barcode.hs
finalDigits :: [[Parity Digit]] -> ParityMap
finalDigits = foldl' incorporateDigits (M.singleton 0 [])
            . mapEveryOther (map (fmap (*3)))
```

(From the checkDigit function that we defined in "EAN-13 Encoding" on page 270, we remember that the check digit computation requires that we multiply every other digit by 3.)

How long is the list with which we call finalDigits? We don't yet know what the first digit of our sequence is, so obviously we can't provide that. And we don't want to include our guess at the check digit, so the list must be 11 elements long.

Once we've returned from finalDigits, our solution map is necessarily incomplete, because we haven't yet figured out what the first digit is.

Completing the Solution Map with the First Digit

We haven't yet discussed how we should extract the value of the first digit from the parities of the left group of digits. This is a straightforward matter of reusing code that we've already written:

```
-- file: ch12/Barcode.hs
firstDigit :: [Parity a] -> Digit
firstDigit = snd
           . head
           . bestScores paritySRL
           . runLengths
           . map parityBit
           . take 6
    where parityBit (Even _) = Zero
          parityBit (Odd _) = One
```

Each element of our partial solution map now contains a reversed list of digits and parity data. Our next task is to create a completed solution map, by computing the first digit in each sequence, and using it to create that last solution map:

```
-- file: ch12/Barcode.hs
addFirstDigit :: ParityMap -> DigitMap
addFirstDigit = M.foldWithKey updateFirst M.empty

updateFirst :: Digit -> [Parity Digit] -> DigitMap -> DigitMap
updateFirst key seq = insertMap key digit (digit:renormalize qes)
```

```
      where renormalize = mapEveryOther (`div` 3) . map fromParity
            digit = firstDigit qes
            qes = reverse seq
```

Along the way, we get rid of the Parity type and reverse our earlier multiplications by three. Our last step is to complete the check digit computation:

```
-- file: ch12/Barcode.hs
buildMap :: [[Parity Digit]] -> DigitMap
buildMap = M.mapKeys (10 -)
         . addFirstDigit
         . finalDigits
```

Finding the Correct Sequence

We now have a map of all possible checksums and the sequences that lead to each. All that remains is to take our guesses at the check digit, and then see if we have a corresponding solution map entry:

```
-- file: ch12/Barcode.hs
solve :: [[Parity Digit]] -> [[Digit]]
solve [] = []
solve xs = catMaybes $ map (addCheckDigit m) checkDigits
    where checkDigits = map fromParity (last xs)
          m = buildMap (init xs)
          addCheckDigit m k = (++[k]) <$> M.lookup k m
```

Let's try this out on the row we picked from our photo and see if we get a sensible answer:

```
ghci> listToMaybe . solve . candidateDigits $ input
Just [9,7,8,0,1,3,2,1,1,4,6,7,7]
```

Excellent! This is exactly the string encoded in the barcode that we photographed.

Working with Row Data

We've mentioned repeatedly that we are taking a single row from our image. Here's how:

```
-- file: ch12/Barcode.hs
withRow :: Int -> Pixmap -> (RunLength Bit -> a) -> a
withRow n greymap f = f . runLength . elems $ posterized
    where posterized = threshold 0.4 . fmap luminance . row n $ greymap
```

The withRow function takes a row, converts it to monochrome, and then calls another function on the run length encoded row data. To get the row data, it calls row:

```
-- file: ch12/Barcode.hs
row :: (Ix a, Ix b) => b -> Array (a,b) c -> Array a c
row j a = ixmap (l,u) project a
    where project i = (i,j)
          ((l,_), (u,_)) = bounds a
```

This function takes a bit of explaining. Whereas fmap transforms the *values* in an array, ixmap transforms the *indices* of an array. It's a very powerful function that lets us "slice" an array however we please.

The first argument to ixmap is the bounds of the new array. These bounds can be of a different dimension than the source array. In row, for example, we're extracting a one-dimensional array from a two-dimensional array.

The second argument is a *projection* function. This takes an index from the new array and returns an index into the source array. The value at that projected index then becomes the value in the new array at the original index. For example, if we pass 2 into the projection function and it returns (2,2), the element at index 2 of the new array will be taken from element (2,2) of the source array.

Pulling It All Together

Our candidateDigits function gives an empty result unless we call it at the beginning of a barcode sequence. We can easily scan across a row until we get a match as follows:

```
-- file: ch12/Barcode.hs
findMatch :: [(Run, Bit)] -> Maybe [[Digit]]
findMatch = listToMaybe
          . filter (not . null)
          . map (solve . candidateDigits)
          . tails
```

Here, we're taking advantage of lazy evaluation. The call to map over tails will only be evaluated until it results in a nonempty list.

Next, we choose a row from an image and try to find a barcode in it:

```
-- file: ch12/Barcode.hs
findEAN13 :: Pixmap -> Maybe [Digit]
findEAN13 pixmap = withRow center pixmap (fmap head . findMatch)
  where (_, (maxX, _)) = bounds pixmap
        center = (maxX + 1) `div` 2
```

Finally, here's a very simple wrapper that prints barcodes from whatever netpbm image files we pass into our program on the command line:

```
-- file: ch12/Barcode.hs
main :: IO ()
main = do
  args <- getArgs
  forM_ args $ \arg -> do
    e <- parse parseRawPPM <$> L.readFile arg
    case e of
      Left err ->    print $ "error: " ++ err
      Right pixmap -> print $ findEAN13 pixmap
```

Notice that, of the more than 30 functions we've defined in this chapter, main is the only one that lives in IO.

A Few Comments on Development Style

You may have noticed that many of the functions we presented in this chapter were short functions at the top level of the source file. This is no accident. As we mentioned earlier, when we started writing this chapter, we didn't know what form our solution was going to take.

Quite often, then, we had to explore a problem space in order to figure out where we were going. To do this, we spent a lot of time fiddling about in ghci, performing tiny experiments on individual functions. This kind of exploration requires that a function be declared at the top level of a source file; otherwise, ghci won't be able to see it.

Once we were satisfied that individual functions were behaving themselves, we started to glue them together, again investigating the consequences in ghci. This is where our devotion to writing type signatures paid back, as we immediately discovered when a particular composition of functions couldn't possibly work.

At the end of this process, we were left with a large number of very small top-level functions, each with a type signature. This isn't the most compact representation possible; we could have hoisted many of those functions into let or where blocks when we were done with them. However, we find that the added vertical space, small function bodies, and type signatures make the code far more readable, so we generally avoided "golfing" functions after we wrote them.[‡]

Working in a language with strong, static typing does not at all interfere with incrementally and fluidly developing a solution to a problem. We find the turnaround between writing a function and getting useful feedback from ghci to be very rapid; it greatly assists us in writing good code quickly.

[‡] Our use of the word *golf* comes from a game originally played by Perl hackers, in which programmers try to create the smallest piece of code for some purpose. The code with the fewest (key)strokes wins.

CHAPTER 13

Data Structures

Association Lists

Often, we have to deal with data that is unordered but is indexed by a key. For instance, a Unix administrator might have a list of numeric *UIDs* (user IDs) and the textual usernames that they correspond to. The value of this list lies in being able to look up a textual username for a given UID, not in the order of the data. In other words, the UID is a key into a database.

In Haskell, there are several ways to handle data that is structured in this way. The two most common are association lists and the `Map` type provided by `Data.Map` module. Association lists are handy because they are simple. They are standard Haskell lists, so all the familiar list functions work with them. However, for large data sets, `Map` will have a considerable performance advantage over association lists. We'll use both in this chapter.

An association list is just a normal list containing (key, value) tuples. The type of a list of mappings from UID to username might be `[(Integer, String)]`. We could use just about any type* for both the key and the value.

We can build association lists just like we do any other list. Haskell comes with one built-in function called `Data.List.lookup` to look up data in an association list. Its type is `Eq a => a -> [(a, b)] -> Maybe b`. Can you guess how it works from that type? Let's take a look in ghci:

```
ghci> let al = [(1, "one"), (2, "two"), (3, "three"), (4, "four")]
ghci> lookup 1 al
Just "one"
ghci> lookup 5 al
Nothing
```

The lookup function is really simple. Here's one way we could write it:

```
-- file: ch13/lookup.hs
myLookup :: Eq a => a -> [(a, b)] -> Maybe b
```

---

* The type we use for the key must be a member of the `Eq` typeclass.

```
myLookup _ [] = Nothing
myLookup key ((thiskey,thisval):rest) =
    if key == thiskey
        then Just thisval
        else myLookup key rest
```

This function returns Nothing if passed the empty list. Otherwise, it compares the key
with the key we're looking for. If a match is found, the corresponding value is returned;
otherwise, it searches the rest of the list.

Let's take a look at a more complex example of association lists. On Unix/Linux machines, there is a file called */etc/passwd* that stores usernames, UIDs, home directories,
and various other data. We will write a program that parses such a file, creates an
association list, and lets the user look up a username with a UID:

```
-- file: ch13/passwd-al.hs
import Data.List
import System.IO
import Control.Monad(when)
import System.Exit
import System.Environment(getArgs)

main = do
    -- Load the command-line arguments
    args <- getArgs

    -- If we don't have the right amount of args, give an error and abort
    when (length args /= 2) $ do
        putStrLn "Syntax: passwd-al filename uid"
        exitFailure

    -- Read the file lazily
    content <- readFile (args !! 0)

    -- Compute the username in pure code
    let username = findByUID content (read (args !! 1))

    -- Display the result
    case username of
        Just x -> putStrLn x
        Nothing -> putStrLn "Could not find that UID"

-- Given the entire input and a UID, see if we can find a username.
findByUID :: String -> Integer -> Maybe String
findByUID content uid =
    let al = map parseline . lines $ content
        in lookup uid al

-- Convert a colon-separated line into fields
parseline :: String -> (Integer, String)
parseline input =
    let fields = split ':' input
        in (read (fields !! 2), fields !! 0)

{- | Takes a delimiter and a list.  Break up the list based on the
```

```
  -  delimiter. -}
split :: Eq a => a -> [a] -> [[a]]

-- If the input is empty, the result is a list of empty lists.
split _ [] = [[]]
split delim str =
    let -- Find the part of the list before delim and put it in "before".
        -- The rest of the list, including the leading delim, goes
        -- in "remainder".
        (before, remainder) = span (/= delim) str
    in
        before : case remainder of
                    [] -> []
                    x -> -- If there is more data to process,
                        -- call split recursively to process it
                        split delim (tail x)
```

Let's look at this program. The heart of it is `findByUID`, which is a simple function that parses the input one line at a time, then calls `lookup` over the result. The remaining program is concerned with parsing the input. The input file looks like this:

```
root:x:0:0:root:/root:/bin/bash
daemon:x:1:1:daemon:/usr/sbin:/bin/sh
bin:x:2:2:bin:/bin:/bin/sh
sys:x:3:3:sys:/dev:/bin/sh
sync:x:4:65534:sync:/bin:/bin/sync
games:x:5:60:games:/usr/games:/bin/sh
man:x:6:12:man:/var/cache/man:/bin/sh
lp:x:7:7:lp:/var/spool/lpd:/bin/sh
mail:x:8:8:mail:/var/mail:/bin/sh
news:x:9:9:news:/var/spool/news:/bin/sh
jgoerzen:x:1000:1000:John Goerzen,,,:/home/jgoerzen:/bin/bash
```

Its fields are separated by colons and include a username, numeric user ID, numeric group ID, full name, home directory, and shell. No field may contain an internal colon.

Maps

The `Data.Map` module provides a `Map` type with behavior that is similar to association lists but has much better performance.

Maps give us the same capabilities as hash tables do in other languages. Internally, a map is implemented as a balanced binary tree. Compared to a hash table, this is a much more efficient representation in a language with immutable data. This is the most visible example of how deeply pure functional programming affects how we write code: we choose data structures and algorithms that we can express cleanly and that perform efficiently, but our choices for specific tasks are often different from their counterparts in imperative languages.

Some functions in the `Data.Map` module have the same names as those in the `Prelude`. Therefore, we will import it with `import qualified Data.Map as Map` and use

Map.*name* to refer to names in that module. Let's start our tour of `Data.Map` by taking a look at some ways to build a map:

```
-- file: ch13/buildmap.hs
import qualified Data.Map as Map

-- Functions to generate a Map that represents an association list
-- as a map

al = [(1, "one"), (2, "two"), (3, "three"), (4, "four")]

{- | Create a map representation of 'al' by converting the association
 -  list using Map.fromList -}
mapFromAL =
    Map.fromList al

{- | Create a map representation of 'al' by doing a fold -}
mapFold =
    foldl (\map (k, v) -> Map.insert k v map) Map.empty al

{- | Manually create a map with the elements of 'al' in it -}
mapManual =
    Map.insert 2 "two" .
    Map.insert 4 "four" .
    Map.insert 1 "one" .
    Map.insert 3 "three" $ Map.empty
```

Functions such as `Map.insert` work in the usual Haskell way: they return a copy of the input data, with the requested change applied. This is quite handy with maps. It means that you can use `foldl` to build up a map as in the `mapFold` example. Or, you can chain together calls to `Map.insert` as in the `mapManual` example. Let's use ghci to verify that all of these maps are as expected:

```
ghci> :l buildmap.hs
[1 of 1] Compiling Main             ( buildmap.hs, interpreted )
Ok, modules loaded: Main.
ghci> al
Loading package array-0.1.0.0 ... linking ... done.
Loading package containers-0.1.0.2 ... linking ... done.
[(1,"one"),(2,"two"),(3,"three"),(4,"four")]
ghci> mapFromAL
fromList [(1,"one"),(2,"two"),(3,"three"),(4,"four")]
ghci> mapFold
fromList [(1,"one"),(2,"two"),(3,"three"),(4,"four")]
ghci> mapManual
fromList [(1,"one"),(2,"two"),(3,"three"),(4,"four")]
```

Notice that the output from `mapManual` differs from the order of the list we used to construct the map. Maps do not guarantee that they will preserve the original ordering.

Maps operate similarly in concept to association lists. The `Data.Map` module provides functions for adding and removing data from maps. It also lets us filter them, modify them, fold over them, and convert to and from association lists. The library documentation for this module is good, so instead of going into detail on each function, we will present an example that ties together many of the concepts we've discussed in this chapter.

Functions Are Data, Too

Part of Haskell's power is the ease with which it lets us create and manipulate functions. Let's take a look at a record that stores a function as one of its fields:

```
-- file: ch13/funcrecs.hs
{- | Our usual CustomColor type to play with -}
data CustomColor =
  CustomColor {red :: Int,
               green :: Int,
               blue :: Int}
  deriving (Eq, Show, Read)

{- | A new type that stores a name and a function.

The function takes an Int, applies some computation to it, and returns
an Int along with a CustomColor -}
data FuncRec =
    FuncRec {name :: String,
             colorCalc :: Int -> (CustomColor, Int)}

plus5func color x = (color, x + 5)

purple = CustomColor 255 0 255

plus5 = FuncRec {name = "plus5", colorCalc = plus5func purple}
always0 = FuncRec {name = "always0", colorCalc = \_ -> (purple, 0)}
```

Notice the type of the colorCalc field: it's a function. It takes an Int and returns a tuple of (CustomColor, Int). We create two FuncRec records: plus5 and always0. Notice that the colorCalc for both of them will always return the color purple. FuncRec itself has no field to store the color in, yet that value somehow becomes part of the function itself. This is called a *closure*. Let's play with this a bit:

```
ghci> :l funcrecs.hs
[1 of 1] Compiling Main             ( funcrecs.hs, interpreted )
Ok, modules loaded: Main.
ghci> :t plus5
plus5 :: FuncRec
ghci> name plus5
"plus5"
ghci> :t colorCalc plus5
colorCalc plus5 :: Int -> (CustomColor, Int)
ghci> (colorCalc plus5) 7
(CustomColor {red = 255, green = 0, blue = 255},12)
ghci> :t colorCalc always0
colorCalc always0 :: Int -> (CustomColor, Int)
ghci> (colorCalc always0) 7
(CustomColor {red = 255, green = 0, blue = 255},0)
```

That worked well enough, but you might wonder how to do something more advanced, such as making a piece of data available in multiple places. A type construction function can be helpful. Here's an example:

```
-- file: ch13/funcrecs2.hs
data FuncRec =
    FuncRec {name :: String,
             calc :: Int -> Int,
             namedCalc :: Int -> (String, Int)}

mkFuncRec :: String -> (Int -> Int) -> FuncRec
mkFuncRec name calcfunc =
    FuncRec {name = name,
             calc = calcfunc,
             namedCalc = \x -> (name, calcfunc x)}

plus5 = mkFuncRec "plus5" (+ 5)
always0 = mkFuncRec "always0" (\_ -> 0)
```

Here we have a function called mkFuncRec that takes a String and another function as parameters, and then returns a new FuncRec record. Notice how both parameters to mkFuncRec are used in multiple places. Let's try it out:

```
ghci> :l funcrecs2.hs
[1 of 1] Compiling Main             ( funcrecs2.hs, interpreted )
Ok, modules loaded: Main.
ghci> :t plus5
plus5 :: FuncRec
ghci> name plus5
"plus5"
ghci> (calc plus5) 5
10
ghci> (namedCalc plus5) 5
("plus5",10)
ghci> let plus5a = plus5 {name = "PLUS5A"}
ghci> name plus5a
"PLUS5A"
ghci> (namedCalc plus5a) 5
("plus5",10)
```

Notice the creation of plus5a. We changed the name field, but not the namedCalc field. That's why name has the new name, but namedCalc still returns the name that was passed to mkFuncRec; it doesn't change unless we explicitly change it.

Extended Example: /etc/passwd

In order to illustrate the usage of a number of different data structures together, we've prepared an extended example. This example parses and stores entries from files in the format of a typical /etc/passwd file:

```
-- file: ch13/passwdmap.hs
import Data.List
import qualified Data.Map as Map
import System.IO
import Text.Printf(printf)
import System.Environment(getArgs)
import System.Exit
import Control.Monad(when)

{- | The primary piece of data this program will store.
   It represents the fields in a POSIX /etc/passwd file -}
data PasswdEntry = PasswdEntry {
    userName :: String,
    password :: String,
    uid :: Integer,
    gid :: Integer,
    gecos :: String,
    homeDir :: String,
    shell :: String}
    deriving (Eq, Ord)

{- | Define how we get data to a 'PasswdEntry'. -}
instance Show PasswdEntry where
    show pe = printf "%s:%s:%d:%d:%s:%s:%s"
                (userName pe) (password pe) (uid pe) (gid pe)
                (gecos pe) (homeDir pe) (shell pe)

{- | Converting data back out of a 'PasswdEntry'. -}
instance Read PasswdEntry where
    readsPrec _ value =
        case split ':' value of
             [f1, f2, f3, f4, f5, f6, f7] ->
                -- Generate a 'PasswdEntry' the shorthand way:
                -- using the positional fields.  We use 'read' to convert
                -- the numeric fields to Integers.
                [(PasswdEntry f1 f2 (read f3) (read f4) f5 f6 f7, [])]
             x -> error $ "Invalid number of fields in input: " ++ show x
        where
        {- | Takes a delimiter and a list.  Break up the list based on the
        -  delimiter. -}
        split :: Eq a => a -> [a] -> [[a]]

        -- If the input is empty, the result is a list of empty lists.
        split _ [] = [[]]
        split delim str =
            let -- Find the part of the list before delim and put it in
                -- "before".  The rest of the list, including the leading
                -- delim, goes in "remainder".
                (before, remainder) = span (/= delim) str
                in
                before : case remainder of
                            [] -> []
                            x -> -- If there is more data to process,
                                 -- call split recursively to process it
                                 split delim (tail x)
```

```
-- Convenience aliases; we'll have two maps: one from UID to entries
-- and the other from username to entries
type UIDMap = Map.Map Integer PasswdEntry
type UserMap = Map.Map String PasswdEntry

{- | Converts input data to maps.  Returns UID and User maps. -}
inputToMaps :: String -> (UIDMap, UserMap)
inputToMaps inp =
    (uidmap, usermap)
    where
    -- fromList converts a [(key, value)] list into a Map
    uidmap = Map.fromList . map (\pe -> (uid pe, pe)) $ entries
    usermap = Map.fromList .
              map (\pe -> (userName pe, pe)) $ entries
    -- Convert the input String to [PasswdEntry]
    entries = map read (lines inp)

main = do
    -- Load the command-line arguments
    args <- getArgs

    -- If we don't have the right number of args,
    -- give an error and abort

    when (length args /= 1) $ do
        putStrLn "Syntax: passwdmap filename"
        exitFailure

    -- Read the file lazily
    content <- readFile (head args)
    let maps = inputToMaps content
    mainMenu maps

mainMenu maps@(uidmap, usermap) = do
    putStr optionText
    hFlush stdout
    sel <- getLine
    -- See what they want to do.  For every option except 4,
    -- return them to the main menu afterwards by calling
    -- mainMenu recursively
    case sel of
        "1" -> lookupUserName >> mainMenu maps
        "2" -> lookupUID >> mainMenu maps
        "3" -> displayFile >> mainMenu maps
        "4" -> return ()
        _ -> putStrLn "Invalid selection" >> mainMenu maps

    where
    lookupUserName = do
        putStrLn "Username: "
        username <- getLine
        case Map.lookup username usermap of
            Nothing -> putStrLn "Not found."
            Just x -> print x
```

```
lookupUID = do
    putStrLn "UID: "
    uidstring <- getLine
    case Map.lookup (read uidstring) uidmap of
        Nothing -> putStrLn "Not found."
        Just x -> print x
displayFile =
    putStr . unlines . map (show . snd) . Map.toList $ uidmap
optionText =
    "\npasswdmap options:\n\
    \\n\
    \1   Look up a user name\n\
    \2   Look up a UID\n\
    \3   Display entire file\n\
    \4   Quit\n\n\
    \Your selection: "
```

This example maintains two maps: one from username to PasswdEntry and another one from UID to PasswdEntry. Database developers may find it convenient to think of this as having two different indices into the data to speed searching on different fields.

Take a look at the Show and Read instances for PasswdEntry. There is already a standard format for rendering data of this type as a string: the colon-separated version the system already uses. So our Show function displays a PasswdEntry in the format, and Read parses that format.

Extended Example: Numeric Types

We've told you how powerful and expressive Haskell's type system is. We've shown you a lot of ways to use that power. Here's a chance to really see that in action.

Back in "Numeric Types" on page 144, we showed the numeric typeclasses that come with Haskell. Let's see what we can do by defining new types and utilizing the numeric typeclasses to integrate them with basic mathematics in Haskell.

To begin let's think through what we'd like to see out of ghci when we interact with our new types. To start with, it might be nice to render numeric expressions as strings, making sure to indicate proper precedence. Perhaps we could create a function called prettyShow to do that. We'll show you how to write it in a bit, but first we'll look at how we might use it:

```
ghci> :l num.hs
[1 of 1] Compiling Main               ( num.hs, interpreted )
Ok, modules loaded: Main.
ghci> 5 + 1 * 3
8
ghci> prettyShow $ 5 + 1 * 3
"5+(1*3)"
ghci> prettyShow $ 5 * 1 + 3
"(5*1)+3"
```

That looks nice, but it wasn't all that smart. We could easily simplify out the 1 * part of the expression. How about a function to do some very basic simplification?

```
ghci> prettyShow $ simplify $ 5 + 1 * 3
"5+3"
```

How about converting a numeric expression to *Reverse Polish Notation* (RPN)? RPN is a postfix notation that never requires parentheses and is commonly found on HP calculators. RPN is a stack-based notation. We push numbers onto the stack, and when we enter operations, they pop the most recent numbers off the stack and place the result on the stack:

```
ghci> rpnShow $ 5 + 1 * 3
"5 1 3 * +"
ghci> rpnShow $ simplify $ 5 + 1 * 3
"5 3 +"
```

Maybe it would be nice to be able to represent simple expressions with symbols for the unknowns:

```
ghci> prettyShow $ 5 + (Symbol "x") * 3
"5+(x*3)"
```

It's often important to track units of measure when working with numbers. For instance, when you see the number 5, does it mean 5 meters, 5 feet, or 5 bytes? Of course, if you divide 5 meters by 2 seconds, the system ought to be able to figure out the appropriate units. Moreover, it should stop you from adding 2 seconds to 5 meters:

```
ghci> 5 / 2
2.5
ghci> (units 5 "m") / (units 2 "s")
2.5_m/s
ghci> (units 5 "m") + (units 2 "s")
*** Exception: Mis-matched units in add or subtract
ghci> (units 5 "m") + (units 2 "m")
7_m
ghci> (units 5 "m") / 2
2.5_m
ghci> 10 * (units 5 "m") / (units 2 "s")
25.0_m/s
```

If we define an expression or a function that is valid for all numbers, we should be able to calculate the result, or render the expression. For instance, if we define test to have type Num a => a—and, say, test = 2 * 5 + 3, then we ought to be able to do this:

```
ghci> test
13
ghci> rpnShow test
"2 5 * 3 +"
ghci> prettyShow test
"(2*5)+3"
ghci> test + 5
18
ghci> prettyShow (test + 5)
"((2*5)+3)+5"
```

```
ghci> rpnShow (test + 5)
"2 5 * 3 + 5 +"
```

Since we have units, we should be able to handle some basic trigonometry as well. Many of these operations operate on angles. Let's make sure that we can handle both degrees and radians:

```
ghci> sin (pi / 2)
1.0
ghci> sin (units (pi / 2) "rad")
1.0_1.0
ghci> sin (units 90 "deg")
1.0_1.0
ghci> (units 50 "m") * sin (units 90 "deg")
50.0_m
```

Finally, we ought to be able to put all this together and combine different kinds of expressions:

```
ghci> ((units 50 "m") * sin (units 90 "deg")) :: Units (SymbolicManip Double)
50.0*sin(((2.0*pi)*90.0)/360.0)_m
ghci> prettyShow $ dropUnits $ (units 50 "m") * sin (units 90 "deg")
"50.0*sin(((2.0*pi)*90.0)/360.0)"
ghci> rpnShow $ dropUnits $ (units 50 "m") * sin (units 90 "deg")
"50.0 2.0 pi * 90.0 * 360.0 / sin *"
ghci> (units (Symbol "x") "m") * sin (units 90 "deg")
x*sin(((2.0*pi)*90.0)/360.0)_m
```

Everything you've just seen is possible with Haskell types and classes. In fact, you've been reading a real ghci session demonstrating *num.hs*, which you'll see shortly.

First Steps

Let's think about how we would accomplish everything just shown. To start with, we might use ghci to check the type of (+), which is Num a => a -> a -> a. If we want to make some custom behavior for the plus operator possible, then we will have to define a new type and make it an instance of Num. This type will need to store an expression symbolically. We can start by thinking of operations such as addition. To store that, we will need to store the operation itself, its left and right sides. The left and right sides could themselves be expressions.

We can therefore think of an expression as a sort of tree. Let's start with some simple types:

```
-- file: ch13/numsimple.hs
-- The "operators" that we're going to support
data Op = Plus | Minus | Mul | Div | Pow
          deriving (Eq, Show)

{- The core symbolic manipulation type -}
data SymbolicManip a =
            Number a            -- Simple number, such as 5
          | Arith Op (SymbolicManip a) (SymbolicManip a)
            deriving (Eq, Show)

{- SymbolicManip will be an instance of Num.  Define how the Num
operations are handled over a SymbolicManip.  This will implement things
like (+) for SymbolicManip. -}
instance Num a => Num (SymbolicManip a) where
    a + b = Arith Plus a b
    a - b = Arith Minus a b
    a * b = Arith Mul a b
    negate a = Arith Mul (Number (-1)) a
    abs a = error "abs is unimplemented"
    signum _ = error "signum is unimplemented"
    fromInteger i = Number (fromInteger i)
```

First, we define a type called Op, which simply represents some of the operations we will support. Next, there is a definition for SymbolicManip a. Because of the Num a constraint, any Num can be used for the a. So a full type may be something like SymbolicManip Int.

A SymbolicManip type can be a plain number or some arithmetic operation. The type for the Arith constructor is recursive, which is perfectly legal in Haskell. Arith creates a SymbolicManip out of an Op and two other SymbolicManip items. Let's look at an example:

```
ghci> :l numsimple.hs
[1 of 1] Compiling Main               ( numsimple.hs, interpreted )
Ok, modules loaded: Main.
ghci> Number 5
Number 5
ghci> :t Number 5
Number 5 :: (Num t) => SymbolicManip t
ghci> :t Number (5::Int)
Number (5::Int) :: SymbolicManip Int
ghci> Number 5 * Number 10
Arith Mul (Number 5) (Number 10)
ghci> (5 * 10)::SymbolicManip Int
Arith Mul (Number 5) (Number 10)
ghci> (5 * 10 + 2)::SymbolicManip Int
Arith Plus (Arith Mul (Number 5) (Number 10)) (Number 2)
```

You can see that we already have a very basic representation of expressions working. Notice how Haskell "converted" 5 * 10 + 2 into a SymbolicManip, and even handled order of evaluation properly. This wasn't really a true conversion; SymbolicManip is a first-class number now. Integer numeric literals are internally treated as being wrapped in `fromInteger` anyway, so 5 is just as valid as a `SymbolicManip Int` as it as an `Int`.

From here, then, our task is simple: extend the `SymbolicManip` type to be able to represent all the operations we will want to perform, implement instances of it for the other numeric typeclasses, and implement our own instance of `Show` for `SymbolicManip` that renders this tree in a more accessible fashion.

Completed Code

Here is the completed *num.hs*, which was used with the `ghci` examples at the beginning of this chapter. Let's look at this code one piece at a time:

```
-- file: ch13/num.hs
import Data.List

----------------------------------------------------
-- Symbolic/units manipulation
----------------------------------------------------

-- The "operators" that we're going to support
data Op = Plus | Minus | Mul | Div | Pow
          deriving (Eq, Show)

{- The core symbolic manipulation type.  It can be a simple number,
a symbol, a binary arithmetic operation (such as +), or a unary
arithmetic operation (such as cos)

Notice the types of BinaryArith and UnaryArith: it's a recursive
type.  So, we could represent a (+) over two SymbolicManips. -}
data SymbolicManip a =
          Number a            -- Simple number, such as 5
        | Symbol String       -- A symbol, such as x
        | BinaryArith Op (SymbolicManip a) (SymbolicManip a)
        | UnaryArith String (SymbolicManip a)
          deriving (Eq)
```

In this section of code, we define an `Op` that is identical to the one we used earlier. We also define `SymbolicManip`, which is similar to what we used before. In this version, we now support unary arithmetic operations (those which take only one parameter) such as `abs` or `cos`. Next we define our instance of `Num`:

```
-- file: ch13/num.hs
{- SymbolicManip will be an instance of Num.  Define how the Num
operations are handled over a SymbolicManip.  This will implement things
like (+) for SymbolicManip. -}
instance Num a => Num (SymbolicManip a) where
    a + b = BinaryArith Plus a b
    a - b = BinaryArith Minus a b
    a * b = BinaryArith Mul a b
    negate a = BinaryArith Mul (Number (-1)) a
    abs a = UnaryArith "abs" a
```

```
            signum _ = error "signum is unimplemented"
            fromInteger i = Number (fromInteger i)
```

This is pretty straightforward and also similar to our earlier code. Note that earlier we weren't able to properly support abs, but now with the UnaryArith constructor, we can. Next we define some more instances:

```
-- file: ch13/num.hs
{- Make SymbolicManip an instance of Fractional -}
instance (Fractional a) => Fractional (SymbolicManip a) where
    a / b = BinaryArith Div a b
    recip a = BinaryArith Div (Number 1) a
    fromRational r = Number (fromRational r)

{- Make SymbolicManip an instance of Floating -}
instance (Floating a) => Floating (SymbolicManip a) where
    pi = Symbol "pi"
    exp a = UnaryArith "exp" a
    log a = UnaryArith "log" a
    sqrt a = UnaryArith "sqrt" a
    a ** b = BinaryArith Pow a b
    sin a = UnaryArith "sin" a
    cos a = UnaryArith "cos" a
    tan a = UnaryArith "tan" a
    asin a = UnaryArith "asin" a
    acos a = UnaryArith "acos" a
    atan a = UnaryArith "atan" a
    sinh a = UnaryArith "sinh" a
    cosh a = UnaryArith "cosh" a
    tanh a = UnaryArith "tanh" a
    asinh a = UnaryArith "asinh" a
    acosh a = UnaryArith "acosh" a
    atanh a = UnaryArith "atanh" a
```

This section of code defines some fairly straightforward instances of Fractional and Floating. Now let's work on converting our expressions to strings for display:

```
-- file: ch13/num.hs
{- Show a SymbolicManip as a String, using conventional
algebraic notation -}
prettyShow :: (Show a, Num a) => SymbolicManip a -> String

-- Show a number or symbol as a bare number or serial
prettyShow (Number x) = show x
prettyShow (Symbol x) = x

prettyShow (BinaryArith op a b) =
    let pa = simpleParen a
        pb = simpleParen b
        pop = op2str op
        in pa ++ pop ++ pb
prettyShow (UnaryArith opstr a) =
    opstr ++ "(" ++ show a ++ ")"

op2str :: Op -> String
op2str Plus = "+"
```

```
op2str Minus = "-"
op2str Mul = "*"
op2str Div = "/"
op2str Pow = "**"

{- Add parentheses where needed.  This function is fairly conservative
and will add parenthesis when not needed in some cases.

Haskell will have already figured out precedence for us while building
up the SymbolicManip. -}
simpleParen :: (Show a, Num a) => SymbolicManip a -> String
simpleParen (Number x) = prettyShow (Number x)
simpleParen (Symbol x) = prettyShow (Symbol x)
simpleParen x@(BinaryArith _ _ _) = "(" ++ prettyShow x ++ ")"
simpleParen x@(UnaryArith _ _) = prettyShow x

{- Showing a SymbolicManip calls the prettyShow function on it -}
instance (Show a, Num a) => Show (SymbolicManip a) where
    show a = prettyShow a
```

We start by defining a function prettyShow. It renders an expression using conventional style. The algorithm is fairly simple: bare numbers and symbols are rendered bare; binary arithmetic is rendered with the two sides plus the operator in the middle, and, of course, we handle the unary operators as well. op2str simply converts an Op to a String. In simpleParen, we have a quite conservative algorithm that adds parentheses to keep precedence clear in the result. Finally, we make SymbolicManip an instance of Show, using prettyShow to accomplish that. Now let's implement an algorithm that converts an expression to a string in RPN format:

```
-- file: ch13/num.hs
{- Show a SymbolicManip using RPN.  HP calculator users may
find this familiar. -}
rpnShow :: (Show a, Num a) => SymbolicManip a -> String
rpnShow i =
    let toList (Number x) = [show x]
        toList (Symbol x) = [x]
        toList (BinaryArith op a b) = toList a ++ toList b ++
            [op2str op]
        toList (UnaryArith op a) = toList a ++ [op]
        join :: [a] -> [[a]] -> [a]
        join delim l = concat (intersperse delim l)
    in join " " (toList i)
```

Fans of RPN will note how much simpler this algorithm is compared to the algorithm used to render with conventional notation. In particular, we didn't have to worry about where to add parentheses, because RPN can, by definition, be evaluated only one way. Next, let's see how we might implement a function to do some rudimentary simplification on expressions:

```
-- file: ch13/num.hs
{- Perform some basic algebraic simplifications on a SymbolicManip. -}
simplify :: (Num a) => SymbolicManip a -> SymbolicManip a
simplify (BinaryArith op ia ib) =
```

```
      let sa = simplify ia
          sb = simplify ib
          in
          case (op, sa, sb) of
                  (Mul, Number 1, b) -> b
                  (Mul, a, Number 1) -> a
                  (Mul, Number 0, b) -> Number 0
                  (Mul, a, Number 0) -> Number 0
                  (Div, a, Number 1) -> a
                  (Plus, a, Number 0) -> a
                  (Plus, Number 0, b) -> b
                  (Minus, a, Number 0) -> a
                  _ -> BinaryArith op sa sb
    simplify (UnaryArith op a) = UnaryArith op (simplify a)
    simplify x = x
```

This function is pretty simple. For certain binary arithmetic operations—for instance, multiplying any value by 1—we are able to easily simplify the situation. First, we obtain simplified versions of both sides of the calculation (this is where recursion hits) and then simplify the result. We have little to do with unary operators, so we just simplify the expression they act upon.

From here on, we will add support for units of measure to our established library. This will let us represent quantities such as "5 meters." We start, as before, by defining a type:

```
-- file: ch13/num.hs
{- New data type: Units.  A Units type contains a number
and a SymbolicManip, which represents the units of measure.
A simple label would be something like (Symbol "m") -}
data Num a => Units a = Units a (SymbolicManip a)
              deriving (Eq)
```

So, Units contains a number and a label that is itself a SymbolicManip. Next, it will probably come as no surprise to see an instance of Num for Units:

```
-- file: ch13/num.hs
{- Implement Units for Num.  We don't know how to convert between
arbitrary units, so we generate an error if we try to add numbers with
different units.  For multiplication, generate the appropriate
new units. -}
instance (Num a) => Num (Units a) where
    (Units xa ua) + (Units xb ub)
        | ua == ub = Units (xa + xb) ua
        | otherwise = error "Mis-matched units in add or subtract"
    (Units xa ua) - (Units xb ub) = (Units xa ua) + (Units (xb * (-1)) ub)
    (Units xa ua) * (Units xb ub) = Units (xa * xb) (ua * ub)
    negate (Units xa ua) = Units (negate xa) ua
    abs (Units xa ua) = Units (abs xa) ua
    signum (Units xa _) = Units (signum xa) (Number 1)
    fromInteger i = Units (fromInteger i) (Number 1)
```

Now it may be clear why we use a SymbolicManip instead of a String to store the unit of measure. As calculations such as multiplication occur, the unit of measure also changes. For instance, if we multiply 5 meters by 2 meters, we obtain 10 square meters.

We force the units for addition to match and implement subtraction in terms of addition. Let's look at more typeclass instances for Units:

```
-- file: ch13/num.hs
{- Make Units an instance of Fractional -}
instance (Fractional a) => Fractional (Units a) where
    (Units xa ua) / (Units xb ub) = Units (xa / xb) (ua / ub)
    recip a = 1 / a
    fromRational r = Units (fromRational r) (Number 1)

{- Floating implementation for Units.

Use some intelligence for angle calculations: support deg and rad
-}
instance (Floating a) => Floating (Units a) where
    pi = (Units pi (Number 1))
    exp _ = error "exp not yet implemented in Units"
    log _ = error "log not yet implemented in Units"
    (Units xa ua) ** (Units xb ub)
        | ub == Number 1 = Units (xa ** xb) (ua ** Number xb)
        | otherwise = error "units for RHS of ** not supported"
    sqrt (Units xa ua) = Units (sqrt xa) (sqrt ua)
    sin (Units xa ua)
        | ua == Symbol "rad" = Units (sin xa) (Number 1)
        | ua == Symbol "deg" = Units (sin (deg2rad xa)) (Number 1)
        | otherwise = error "Units for sin must be deg or rad"
    cos (Units xa ua)
        | ua == Symbol "rad" = Units (cos xa) (Number 1)
        | ua == Symbol "deg" = Units (cos (deg2rad xa)) (Number 1)
        | otherwise = error "Units for cos must be deg or rad"
    tan (Units xa ua)
        | ua == Symbol "rad" = Units (tan xa) (Number 1)
        | ua == Symbol "deg" = Units (tan (deg2rad xa)) (Number 1)
        | otherwise = error "Units for tan must be deg or rad"
    asin (Units xa ua)
        | ua == Number 1 = Units (rad2deg $ asin xa) (Symbol "deg")
        | otherwise = error "Units for asin must be empty"
    acos (Units xa ua)
        | ua == Number 1 = Units (rad2deg $ acos xa) (Symbol "deg")
        | otherwise = error "Units for acos must be empty"
    atan (Units xa ua)
        | ua == Number 1 = Units (rad2deg $ atan xa) (Symbol "deg")
        | otherwise = error "Units for atan must be empty"
    sinh = error "sinh not yet implemented in Units"
    cosh = error "cosh not yet implemented in Units"
    tanh = error "tanh not yet implemented in Units"
    asinh = error "asinh not yet implemented in Units"
    acosh = error "acosh not yet implemented in Units"
    atanh = error "atanh not yet implemented in Units"
```

We didn't supply implementations for every function, but quite a few have been defined. Now let's define a few utility functions for working with units:

```
-- file: ch13/num.hs
{- A simple function that takes a number and a String and returns an
appropriate Units type to represent the number and its unit of measure -}
```

```
units :: (Num z) => z -> String -> Units z
units a b = Units a (Symbol b)

{- Extract the number only out of a Units type -}
dropUnits :: (Num z) => Units z -> z
dropUnits (Units x _) = x

{- Utilities for the Unit implementation -}
deg2rad x = 2 * pi * x / 360
rad2deg x = 360 * x / (2 * pi)
```

First, we have units, which makes it easy to craft simple expressions. It's faster to say units 5 "m" than Units 5 (Symbol "m"). We also have a corresponding dropUnits, which discards the unit of measure and returns the embedded bare Num. Finally, we define some functions for use by our earlier instances to convert between degrees and radians. Next, we just define a Show instance for Units:

```
-- file: ch13/num.hs
{- Showing units: we show the numeric component, an underscore,
then the prettyShow version of the simplified units -}
instance (Show a, Num a) => Show (Units a) where
    show (Units xa ua) = show xa ++ "_" ++ prettyShow (simplify ua)
```

That was simple. For one last piece, we define a variable test to experiment with:

```
-- file: ch13/num.hs
test :: (Num a) => a
test = 2 * 5 + 3
```

So, looking back over all this code, we have done what we set out to accomplish: implement more instances for SymbolicManip. We have also introduced another type called Units, which stores a number and a unit of measure. We employed several show-like functions, which render the SymbolicManip or Units in different ways.

There is one other point that this example drives home: every language—even those with objects and overloading—has parts that are special in some way. In Haskell, the "special" bits are extremely small. We just developed a new representation for something as fundamental as a number, and it was really quite easy. Our new type is first-class, and the compiler knows what functions to use with it at compile time. Haskell takes code reuse and interchangeability to the extreme. It is easy to make code generic and work on things of many different types. It's also easy to create new types and automatically make them first-class features of the system.

Remember our ghci examples at the beginning of the chapter? All of them were made with the code in this example. You might want to try them out for yourself and see how they work.

EXERCISE

1. Extend the prettyShow function to remove unnecessary parentheses.

Taking Advantage of Functions as Data

In an imperative language, appending two lists is cheap and easy. Here's a simple C structure in which we maintain a pointer to the head and tail of a list:

```
struct list {
    struct node *head, *tail;
};
```

When we have one list and want to append another list onto its end, we modify the last node of the existing list to point to its head node, and then update its tail pointer to point to its tail node.

Obviously, this approach is off limits to us in Haskell if we want to stay pure. Since pure data is immutable, we can't go around modifying lists in place. Haskell's (++) operator appends two lists by creating a new one:

```
-- file: ch13/Append.hs
(++) :: [a] -> [a] -> [a]
(x:xs) ++ ys = x : xs ++ ys
_      ++ ys = ys
```

From inspecting the code, we can see that the cost of creating a new list depends on the length of the initial one.[†]

We often need to append lists over and over in order to construct one big list. For instance, we might be generating the contents of a web page as a String, emitting a chunk at a time as we traverse some data structure. Each time we have a chunk of markup to add to the page, we will naturally want to append it onto the end of our existing String.

If a single append has a cost proportional to the length of the initial list, and each repeated append makes the initial list longer, we end up in an unhappy situation: the cost of all of the repeated appends is proportional to the *square* of the length of the final list.

To understand this, let's dig in a little. The (++) operator is right-associative:

```
ghci> :info (++)
(++) :: [a] -> [a] -> [a]      -- Defined in GHC.Base
infixr 5 ++
```

This means that a Haskell implementation will evaluate the expression "a" ++ "b" ++ "c" as though we had put parentheses around it as follows: "a" ++ ("b" ++ "c"). This makes good performance sense, because it keeps the left operand as short as possible.

When we repeatedly append onto the end of a list, we defeat this associativity. Let's say we start with the list "a" and append "b", and save the result as our new list. If we

---

[†] Nonstrict evaluation makes the cost calculation more subtle. We pay for an append only if we actually use the resulting list. Even then, we pay only for as much as we actually use.

later append "c" onto this new list, our left operand is now "ab". In this scheme, every time we append, our left operand gets longer.

Meanwhile, the imperative programmers are cackling with glee, because the cost of *their* repeated appends depends only on the number that they perform. They have linear performance; ours is quadratic.

When something as common as repeated appending of lists imposes such a performance penalty, it's time to look at the problem from another angle.

The expression ("a"++) is a section, a partially applied function. What is its type?

```
ghci> :type ("a" ++)
("a" ++) :: [Char] -> [Char]
```

Since this is a function, we can use the (.) operator to compose it with another section, let's say ("b"++):

```
ghci> :type ("a" ++) . ("b" ++)
("a" ++) . ("b" ++) :: [Char] -> [Char]
```

Our new function has the same type. What happens if we stop composing functions, and instead provide a String to the function we've created?

```
ghci> let f = ("a" ++) . ("b" ++)
ghci> f []
"ab"
```

We've appended the strings! We're using these partially applied functions to store data, which we can retrieve by providing an empty list. Each partial application of (++) and (.) *represents* an append, but it doesn't actually *perform* the append.

There are two very interesting things about this approach. The first is that the cost of a partial application is constant, so the cost of many partial applications is linear. The second is that when we finally provide a [] value to unlock the final list from its chain of partial applications, application proceeds from right to left. This keeps the left operand (++) small, and so the overall cost of all of these appends is linear, not quadratic.

By choosing an unfamiliar data representation, we've avoided a nasty performance quagmire, while gaining a new perspective on the usefulness of treating functions as data. By the way, this is an old trick, and it's usually called a *difference list*.

We're not yet finished, though. As appealing as difference lists are in theory, ours won't be very pleasant in practice if we leave all the plumbing of (++), (.), and partial applications exposed. We need to turn this mess into something pleasant to work with.

Turning Difference Lists into a Proper Library

Our first step is to use a newtype declaration to hide the underlying type from our users. We'll create a new type and call it DList, and like a regular list, it will be a parameterized type:

```
-- file: ch13/DList.hs
newtype DList a = DL {
      unDL :: [a] -> [a]
    }
```

The unDL function is our deconstructor, which removes the DL constructor. When we go back and decide what we want to export from our module, we will omit our data constructor and deconstruction function, so the DList type will be completely opaque to our users. They'll only be able to work with the type using the other functions we export:

```
-- file: ch13/DList.hs
append :: DList a -> DList a -> DList a
append xs ys = DL (unDL xs . unDL ys)
```

Our append function may seem a little complicated, but it's just performing some book-keeping around the same use of the (.) operator that we demonstrated earlier. To compose our functions, we must first unwrap them from their DL constructor—hence the use of unDL. We then re-wrap the resulting function with the DL constructor so that it will have the right type.

Here's another way of writing the same function, in which we perform the unwrapping of xs and ys via pattern matching:

```
-- file: ch13/DList.hs
append' :: DList a -> DList a -> DList a
append' (DL xs) (DL ys) = DL (xs . ys)
```

Our DList type won't be much use if we can't convert back and forth between the DList representation and a regular list:

```
-- file: ch13/DList.hs
fromList :: [a] -> DList a
fromList xs = DL (xs ++)

toList :: DList a -> [a]
toList (DL xs) = xs []
```

Once again, compared to the original versions of these functions that we wrote, all we're doing is a little bookkeeping to hide the plumbing.

If we want to make DList useful as a substitute for regular lists, we need to provide some more of the common list operations:

```
-- file: ch13/DList.hs
empty :: DList a
empty = DL id

-- equivalent of the list type's (:) operator
cons :: a -> DList a -> DList a
cons x (DL xs) = DL ((x:) . xs)
infixr `cons`

dfoldr :: (a -> b -> b) -> b -> DList a -> b
dfoldr f z xs = foldr f z (toList xs)
```

Although the DList approach makes appends cheap, not all list-like operations are easily available. The head function has constant cost for lists. Our DList equivalent requires that we convert the entire DList to a regular list, so it is much more expensive than its list counterpart—its cost is linear in the number of appends we have performed to construct the DList:

```
-- file: ch13/DList.hs
safeHead :: DList a -> Maybe a
safeHead xs = case toList xs of
                (y:_) -> Just y
                _ -> Nothing
```

To support an equivalent of map, we can make our DList type a functor:

```
-- file: ch13/DList.hs
dmap :: (a -> b) -> DList a -> DList b
dmap f = dfoldr go empty
    where go x xs = cons (f x) xs

instance Functor DList where
    fmap = dmap
```

Once we decide that we have written enough equivalents of list functions, we go back to the top of our source file and add a module header:

```
-- file: ch13/DList.hs
module DList
    (
      DList
    , fromList
    , toList
    , empty
    , append
    , cons
    , dfoldr
    ) where
```

Lists, Difference Lists, and Monoids

In abstract algebra, there is a simple abstract structure called a *monoid*. Many mathematical objects are monoids, because the "bar to entry" is very low. In order to be considered a monoid, an object must have two properties:

An associative binary operator
  Let's call it (*): the expression a * (b * c) must give the same result as (a * b) * c.

An identity value
  If we call this e, it must obey two rules: a * e == a and e * a == a.

The rules for monoids don't say what the binary operator must do, merely that such an operator must exist. Because of this, lots of mathematical objects are monoids. If we take addition as the binary operator and zero as the identity value, integers form a monoid. With multiplication as the binary operator and one as the identity value, integers form a different monoid.

Monoids are ubiquitous in Haskell.[‡] The `Monoid` typeclass is defined in the `Data.Monoid` module:

```
-- file: ch13/Monoid.hs
class Monoid a where
    mempty  :: a              -- the identity
    mappend :: a -> a -> a    -- associative binary operator
```

If we take (++) as the binary operator and [] as the identity, `lists` forms a monoid:

```
-- file: ch13/Monoid.hs
instance Monoid [a] where
    mempty  = []
    mappend = (++)
```

Since lists and `DLists` are so closely related, it follows that our `DList` type must be a monoid, too:

```
-- file: ch13/DList.hs
instance Monoid (DList a) where
    mempty = empty
    mappend = append
```

Let's try our the methods of the `Monoid` typeclass in ghci:

```
ghci> "foo" `mappend` "bar"
"foobar"
ghci> toList (fromList [1,2] `mappend` fromList [3,4])
[1,2,3,4]
ghci> mempty `mappend` [1]
[1]
```

Writing Multiple Monoid Instances

Although from a mathematical perspective, integers can be monoids in two different ways, we can't write two differing `Monoid` instances for `Int` in Haskell—the compiler would complain about duplicate instances.

In those rare cases where we really need several `Monoid` instances for the same type, we can use some `newtype` trickery to create distinct types for the purpose:

```
-- file: ch13/Monoid.hs
{-# LANGUAGE GeneralizedNewtypeDeriving #-}

newtype AInt = A { unA :: Int }
    deriving (Show, Eq, Num)

-- monoid under addition
instance Monoid AInt where
    mempty = 0
```

[‡] Indeed, monoids are ubiquitous throughout programming. The difference is that in Haskell, we recognize, and talk about them.

```
        mappend = (+)

    newtype MInt = M { unM :: Int }
        deriving (Show, Eq, Num)

    -- monoid under multiplication
    instance Monoid MInt where
        mempty = 1
        mappend = (*)
```

We'll then get different behavior depending on the type we use:

```
ghci> 2 `mappend` 5 :: MInt
M {unM = 10}
ghci> 2 `mappend` 5 :: AInt
A {unA = 7}
```

We will have more to say about difference lists and their monoidal nature in "The Writer Monad and Lists" on page 380.

Enforcing the monoid rules

As with the rules for functors, Haskell cannot check the rules for monoids on our behalf. If we're defining a Monoid instance, we can easily write QuickCheck properties to give us high statistical confidence that our code is following the monoid rules.

General-Purpose Sequences

Both Haskell's built-in list type and the DList type that we defined earlier have poor performance characteristics under some circumstances. The Data.Sequence module defines a Seq container type that gives good performance for a wider variety of operations.

As with other modules, Data.Sequence is intended to be used via qualified import:

```
-- file: ch13/DataSequence.hs
import qualified Data.Sequence as Seq
```

We can construct an empty Seq using empty and a single-element container using singleton:

```
ghci> Seq.empty
Loading package array-0.1.0.0 ... linking ... done.
Loading package containers-0.1.0.2 ... linking ... done.
fromList []
ghci> Seq.singleton 1
fromList [1]
```

We can create a Seq from a list using fromList:

```
ghci> let a = Seq.fromList [1,2,3]
```

The Data.Sequence module provides some constructor functions in the form of operators. When we perform a qualified import, we must qualify the name of an operator in our code (which is ugly):

```
ghci> 1 Seq.<| Seq.singleton 2
fromList [1,2]
```

If we import the operators explicitly, we can avoid the need to qualify them:

```
-- file: ch13/DataSequence.hs
import Data.Sequence ((><), (<|), (|>))
```

By removing the qualification from the operator, we improve the readability of our code:

```
ghci> Seq.singleton 1 |> 2
fromList [1,2]
```

A useful way to remember the (<|) and (|>) functions is that the "arrow" points to the element we're adding to the Seq. The element will be added on the side to which the arrow points: (<|) adds on the left, (|>) on the right.

Both adding on the left and adding on the right are constant-time operations. Appending two Seqs is also cheap, occurring in time proportional to the logarithm of whichever is shorter. To append, we use the (><) operator:

```
ghci> let left = Seq.fromList [1,3,3]
ghci> let right = Seq.fromList [7,1]
ghci> left >< right
fromList [1,3,3,7,1]
```

If we want to create a list from a Seq, we must use the Data.Foldable module, which is best imported qualified:

```
-- file: ch13/DataSequence.hs
import qualified Data.Foldable as Foldable
```

This module defines a typeclass, Foldable, which Seq implements:

```
ghci> Foldable.toList (Seq.fromList [1,2,3])
[1,2,3]
```

If we want to fold over a Seq, we use the fold functions from the Data.Foldable module:

```
ghci> Foldable.foldl' (+) 0 (Seq.fromList [1,2,3])
6
```

The Data.Sequence module provides a number of other useful list-like functions. Its documentation is very thorough, giving time bounds for each operation.

If Seq has so many desirable characteristics, why is it not the default sequence type? Lists are simpler and have less overhead, and so quite often they are good enough for the task at hand. They are also well suited to a lazy setting, whereas Seq does not fare well.

CHAPTER 14

Monads

In Chapter 7, we talked about the IO monad, but we intentionally kept the discussion narrowly focused on how to communicate with the outside world. We didn't discuss what a monad *is*.

We've already seen in Chapter 7 that the IO monad is easy to work with. Notational differences aside, writing code in the IO monad isn't much different from coding in any other imperative language.

When we had practical problems to solve in earlier chapters, we introduced structures that, as we will soon see, are actually monads. We aim to show you that a monad is often an *obvious* and *useful* tool to help solve a problem. We'll define a few monads in this chapter, to show how easy it is.

Revisiting Earlier Code Examples

Maybe Chaining

Let's take another look at the parseP5 function that we wrote in Chapter 10:

```
-- file: ch10/PNM.hs
matchHeader :: L.ByteString -> L.ByteString -> Maybe L.ByteString

-- "nat" here is short for "natural number"
getNat :: L.ByteString -> Maybe (Int, L.ByteString)

getBytes :: Int -> L.ByteString
        -> Maybe (L.ByteString, L.ByteString)

parseP5 s =
  case matchHeader (L8.pack "P5") s of
    Nothing -> Nothing
    Just s1 ->
      case getNat s1 of
        Nothing -> Nothing
        Just (width, s2) ->
```

```
             case getNat (L8.dropWhile isSpace s2) of
               Nothing -> Nothing
               Just (height, s3) ->
                 case getNat (L8.dropWhile isSpace s3) of
                   Nothing -> Nothing
                   Just (maxGrey, s4)
                     | maxGrey > 255 -> Nothing
                     | otherwise ->
                         case getBytes 1 s4 of
                           Nothing -> Nothing
                           Just (_, s5) ->
                             case getBytes (width * height) s5 of
                               Nothing -> Nothing
                               Just (bitmap, s6) ->
                                 Just (Greymap width height maxGrey bitmap, s6)
```

When we introduced this function, it threatened to march off the right side of the page
if it got much more complicated. We brought the staircasing under control using the
(>>?) function:

```
-- file: ch10/PNM.hs
(>>?) :: Maybe a -> (a -> Maybe b) -> Maybe b
Nothing >>? _ = Nothing
Just v  >>? f = f v
```

We carefully chose the type of (>>?) to let us chain together functions that return a
Maybe value. So long as the result type of one function matches the parameter of the
next, we can chain functions returning Maybe together indefinitely. The body of (>>?)
hides the details of whether the chain of functions we build is short-circuited somewhere, due to one returning Nothing, or whenever it is completely evaluated.

Implicit State

Useful as (>>?) was for cleaning up the structure of parseP5, we had to incrementally
consume pieces of a string as we parsed it. This forced us to pass the current value of
the string down our chain of Maybes, wrapped up in a tuple. Each function in the chain
put a result into one element of the tuple and the unconsumed remainder of the string
into the other:

```
-- file: ch10/PNM.hs
parseP5_take2 :: L.ByteString -> Maybe (Greymap, L.ByteString)
parseP5_take2 s =
    matchHeader (L8.pack "P5") s        >>?
    \s -> skipSpace ((), s)             >>?
    (getNat . snd)                      >>?
    skipSpace                           >>?
    \(width, s) ->   getNat s           >>?
    skipSpace                           >>?
    \(height, s) ->  getNat s           >>?
    \(maxGrey, s) -> getBytes 1 s       >>?
    (getBytes (width * height) . snd)   >>?
    \(bitmap, s) -> Just (Greymap width height maxGrey bitmap, s)
```

```
skipSpace :: (a, L.ByteString) -> Maybe (a, L.ByteString)
skipSpace (a, s) = Just (a, L8.dropWhile isSpace s)
```

Once again, we were faced with a pattern of repeated behavior: consume some string, return a result, and return the remaining string for the next function to consume. However, this pattern was more insidious. If we wanted to pass another piece of information down the chain, we'd have to modify nearly every element of the chain, turning each two-tuple into a three-tuple!

We addressed this by moving the responsibility for managing the current piece of string out of the individual functions in the chain, and into the function that we used to chain them together:

```
-- file: ch10/Parse.hs
(==>) :: Parse a -> (a -> Parse b) -> Parse b

firstParser ==> secondParser  =  Parse chainedParser
  where chainedParser initState   =
          case runParse firstParser initState of
            Left errMessage ->
                Left errMessage
            Right (firstResult, newState) ->
                runParse (secondParser firstResult) newState
```

We also hid the details of the parsing state in the ParseState type. Even the getState and putState functions don't inspect the parsing state, so any modification to ParseState will have no effect on any existing code.

Looking for Shared Patterns

When we look at the preceding examples in detail, they don't seem to have much in common. Obviously, they're both concerned with chaining functions together and hiding details to let us write tidier code. However, let's take a step back and consider them in *less* detail.

First, let's look at the type definitions:

```
-- file: ch14/Maybe.hs
data Maybe a = Nothing
             | Just a

-- file: ch10/Parse.hs
newtype Parse a = Parse {
      runParse :: ParseState -> Either String (a, ParseState)
    }
```

The common feature of these two types is that each has a single type parameter on the left of the definition, which appears somewhere on the right. These are thus generic types, which know nothing about their payloads.

Next, we'll examine the chaining functions that we wrote for the two types:

```
ghci> :type (>>?)
(>>?) :: Maybe a -> (a -> Maybe b) -> Maybe b

ghci> :type (==>)
(==>) :: Parse a -> (a -> Parse b) -> Parse b
```

These functions have strikingly similar types. If we were to turn those type constructors into a type variable, we'd end up with a single more abstract type:

```
-- file: ch14/Maybe.hs
chain :: m a -> (a -> m b) -> m b
```

Finally, in each case, we have a function that takes a "plain" value and "injects" it into the target type. For Maybe, this function is simply the value constructor Just, but the injector for Parse is more complicated:

```
-- file: ch10/Parse.hs
identity :: a -> Parse a
identity a = Parse (\s -> Right (a, s))
```

Again, it's not the details or complexity that we're interested in, it's the fact that each of these types has an "injector" function, which looks like this:

```
-- file: ch14/Maybe.hs
inject :: a -> m a
```

It is *exactly* these three properties, and a few rules about how we can use them together, that define a monad in Haskell. Let's revisit the preceding list in condensed form:

- A type constructor m.
- A function of type m a -> (a -> m b) -> m b for chaining the output of one function into the input of another.
- A function of type a -> m a for injecting a normal value into the chain, that is, it wraps a type a with the type constructor m.

The properties that make the Maybe type a monad are its type constructor Maybe a, our chaining function (>>?), and the injector function Just.

For Parse, the corresponding properties are the type constructor Parse a, the chaining function (==>), and the injector function identity.

We intentionally have said nothing about how the chaining and injection functions of a monad should behave, because this almost doesn't matter. In fact, monads are ubiquitous in Haskell code precisely because they are so simple. Many common programming patterns have a monadic structure: passing around implicit data or short-circuiting a chain of evaluations if one fails, to choose but two.

The Monad Typeclass

We can capture the notions of chaining and injection, and the types that we want them to have, in a Haskell typeclass. The standard `Prelude` already defines just such a typeclass, named `Monad`:

```
-- file: ch14/Maybe.hs
class Monad m where
    -- chain
    (>>=)  :: m a -> (a -> m b) -> m b
    -- inject
    return :: a -> m a
```

Here, `(>>=)` is our chaining function. We've already been introduced to it in "Sequencing" on page 186. It's often referred to as *bind*, as it binds the result of the computation on the left to the parameter of the one on the right.

Our injection function is `return`. As we noted in "The True Nature of Return" on page 187, the choice of the name `return` is a little unfortunate. That name is widely used in imperative languages, where it has a fairly well-understood meaning. In Haskell, its behavior is much less constrained. In particular, calling `return` in the middle of a chain of functions won't cause the chain to exit early. A useful way to link its behavior to its name is that it *returns* a pure value (of type `a`) into a monad (of type `m a`). But really, "inject" would be a better name.

While `(>>=)` and `return` are the core functions of the `Monad` typeclass, it also defines two other functions. The first is `(>>)`. Like `(>>=)`, it performs chaining, but it ignores the value on the left:

```
-- file: ch14/Maybe.hs
    (>>) :: m a -> m b -> m b
    a >> f = a >>= \_ -> f
```

We use this function when we want to perform actions in a certain order, but don't care what the result of one is. This might seem pointless: why would we not care what a function's return value is? Recall, though, that we defined a `(==>&)` combinator earlier to express exactly this. Alternatively, consider a function such as `print`, which provides a placeholder result that we do not need to inspect:

```
ghci> :type print "foo"
print "foo" :: IO ()
```

If we use plain `(>>=)`, we have to provide, as its righthand side, a function that ignores its argument:

```
ghci> print "foo" >>= \_ -> print "bar"
"foo"
"bar"
```

But if we use (>>), we can omit the needless function:

```
ghci> print "baz" >> print "quux"
"baz"
"quux"
```

As we just showed, the default implementation of (>>) is defined in terms of (>>=).

The second noncore Monad function is fail, which takes an error message and does something to make the chain of functions fail:

```
-- file: ch14/Maybe.hs
    fail :: String -> m a
    fail = error
```

Beware of fail

Many Monad instances don't override the default implementation of fail that we show here, so in those monads, fail uses error. Calling error is usually highly undesirable, since it throws an exception that callers either cannot catch or will not expect.

Even if you know that right now you're executing in a monad that has fail do something more sensible, we still recommend avoiding it. It's far too easy to cause yourself a problem later when you refactor your code and forget that a previously safe use of fail might be dangerous in its new context.

To revisit the parser that we developed in Chapter 10, here is its Monad instance:

```
-- file: ch10/Parse.hs
instance Monad Parse where
    return = identity
    (>>=) = (==>)
    fail = bail
```

And Now, a Jargon Moment

There are a few terms of art around monads that you may not be familiar with. These aren't formal, but they're commonly used, so it's helpful to know about them:

- *Monadic* simply means "pertaining to monads." A monadic *type* is an instance of the Monad typeclass; a monadic *value* has a monadic type.

- When we say that a type "is a monad," this is really a shorthand way of saying that it's an instance of the Monad typeclass. Being an instance of Monad gives us the necessary monadic triple of type constructor, injection function, and chaining function.

- In the same way, a reference to "the Foo monad" implies that we're talking about the type named Foo and that it's an instance of Monad.

- An *action* is another name for a monadic value. This use of the word probably originated with the introduction of monads for I/O, where a monadic value such as `print "foo"` can have an observable side effect. A function with a monadic return type might also be referred to as an action, though this is a little less common.

Using a New Monad: Show Your Work!

In our introduction to monads, we showed how some preexisting code was already monadic in form. Now that we are beginning to grasp what a monad is and have seen the Monad typeclass, let's build a monad with foreknowledge of what we're doing. We'll start out by defining its interface, and then we'll put it to use. Once we have those out of the way, we'll finally build it.

Pure Haskell code is wonderfully clean to write, but, of course, it can't perform I/O. Sometimes, we'd like to have a record of decisions we made, without writing log information to a file. Let's develop a small library to help with this.

Recall the `globToRegex` function that we developed in "Translating a glob Pattern into a Regular Expression" on page 202. We will modify it so that it keeps a record of each of the special pattern sequences that it translates. We are revisiting familiar territory for a reason: it lets us compare nonmonadic and monadic versions of the same code.

To start off, we'll wrap our result type with a Logger type constructor:

```
-- file: ch14/Logger.hs
globToRegex :: String -> Logger String
```

Information Hiding

We'll intentionally keep the internals of the Logger module abstract:

```
-- file: ch14/Logger.hs
module Logger
    (
      Logger
    , Log
    , runLogger
    , record
    ) where
```

Hiding the details like this has two benefits: it grants us considerable flexibility in how we implement our monad, and more importantly, it gives users a simple interface.

Our Logger type is purely a *type* constructor. We don't export the *value* constructor that a user would need to create a value of this type. All they can use Logger for is writing type signatures.

The Log type is just a synonym for a list of strings, to make a few signatures more readable. We use a list of strings to keep the implementation simple:

```
-- file: ch14/Logger.hs
type Log = [String]
```

Instead of giving our users a value constructor, we provide them with a function, runLogger, that evaluates a logged action. This returns both the result of an action and whatever was logged while the result was being computed:

```
-- file: ch14/Logger.hs
runLogger :: Logger a -> (a, Log)
```

Controlled Escape

The Monad typeclass doesn't provide any means for values to escape their monadic shackles. We can inject a value into a monad using return. We can extract a value from a monad using (>>=) but the function on the right, which can see an unwrapped value, has to wrap its own result back up again.

Most monads have one or more runLogger-like functions. The notable exception is of course IO, which we usually escape from simply by exiting a program.

A monad execution function runs the code inside the monad and unwraps its result. Such functions are usually the only means provided for a value to escape from its monadic wrapper. The author of a monad thus has complete control over how whatever happens inside the monad gets out.

Some monads have several execution functions. In our case, we can imagine a few alternatives to runLogger: one might return only the log messages, whereas another might return just the result and drop the log messages.

Leaving a Trace

When executing inside a Logger action, the user code calls record to record something:

```
-- file: ch14/Logger.hs
record :: String -> Logger ()
```

Since recording occurs in the plumbing of our monad, our action's result supplies no information.

Usually, a monad will provide one or more helper functions such as our record. These are our means for accessing the special behaviors of that monad.

Our module also defines the Monad instance for the Logger type. These definitions are all that a client module needs in order to be able to use this monad.

Here is a preview, in ghci, of how our monad will behave:

```
ghci> let simple = return True :: Logger Bool
ghci> runLogger simple
(True,[])
```

When we run the logged action using runLogger, we get back a pair. The first element is the result of our code; the second is the list of items logged while the action executed. We haven't logged anything, so the list is empty. Let's fix that:

```
ghci> runLogger (record "hi mom!" >> return 3.1337)
(3.1337,["hi mom!"])
```

Using the Logger Monad

Here's how we kick off our glob-to-regexp conversion inside the Logger monad:

```
-- file: ch14/Logger.hs
globToRegex cs =
    globToRegex' cs >>= \ds ->
    return ('^':ds)
```

There are a few coding style issues worth mentioning here. The body of the function starts on the line after its name. This gives us some horizontal whitespace. We've also "hung" the parameter of the anonymous function at the end of the line. This is common practice in monadic code.

Remember the type of (>>=): it extracts the value on the left from its Logger wrapper, and passes the unwrapped value to the function on the right. The function on the right must, in turn, wrap *its* result with the Logger wrapper. This is exactly what return does. It takes a pure value, and wraps it in the monad's type constructor:

```
ghci> :type (>>=)
(>>=) :: (Monad m) => m a -> (a -> m b) -> m b
ghci> :type (globToRegex "" >>=)
(globToRegex "" >>=) :: (String -> Logger b) -> Logger b
```

Even when we write a function that does almost nothing, we must call return to wrap the result with the correct type:

```
-- file: ch14/Logger.hs
globToRegex' :: String -> Logger String
globToRegex' "" = return "$"
```

When we call record to save a log entry, we use (>>) instead of (>>=) to chain it with the following action:

```
-- file: ch14/Logger.hs
globToRegex' ('?':cs) =
    record "any" >>
    globToRegex' cs >>= \ds ->
    return ('.':ds)
```

Recall that this is a variant of (>>=) that ignores the result on the left. We know that the result of record will always be (), so there's no point in capturing it.

We can use do notation, which we first encountered in "Sequencing" on page 186, to tidy up our code somewhat:

```
-- file: ch14/Logger.hs
globToRegex' ('*':cs) = do
    record "kleene star"
    ds <- globToRegex' cs
    return (".*" ++ ds)
```

The choice of do notation versus explicit (>>=) with anonymous functions is mostly a matter of taste, although almost everyone's taste is to use do notation for anything longer than about two lines. There is one significant difference between the two styles, though, which we'll return to in "Desugaring of do Blocks" on page 344.

Parsing a character class mostly follows the same pattern that we've already seen:

```
-- file: ch14/Logger.hs
globToRegex' ('[':'!':c:cs) =
    record "character class, negative" >>
    charClass cs >>= \ds ->
    return ("[^" ++ c : ds)
globToRegex' ('[':c:cs) =
    record "character class" >>
    charClass cs >>= \ds ->
    return ("[" ++ c : ds)
globToRegex' ('[':_) =
    fail "unterminated character class"
```

Mixing Pure and Monadic Code

Based on the code we've seen so far, monads seem to have a substantial shortcoming: the type constructor that wraps a monadic value makes it tricky to use a normal, pure function on a value trapped inside a monadic wrapper. Here's a simple illustration of the apparent problem. Let's say we have a trivial piece of code that runs in the Logger monad and returns a string:

```
ghci> let m = return "foo" :: Logger String
```

If we want to find out the length of that string, we can't simply call length. The string is wrapped, so the types don't match up:

```
ghci> length m

<interactive>:1:7:
    Couldn't match expected type `[a]'
            against inferred type `Logger String'
    In the first argument of `length', namely `m'
    In the expression: length m
    In the definition of `it': it = length m
```

So far, to work around this, we've something like the following:

```
ghci> :type   m >>= \s -> return (length s)
m >>= \s -> return (length s) :: Logger Int
```

We use (>>=) to unwrap the string, and then write a small anonymous function that calls length and rewraps the result using return.

This need crops up often in Haskell code. You won't be surprised to learn that a shorthand already exists: we use the *lifting* technique that we introduced for functors in "Introducing Functors" on page 244. Lifting a pure function into a functor usually involves unwrapping the value inside the functor, calling the function on it, and rewrapping the result with the same constructor.

We do exactly the same thing with a monad. Because the Monad typeclass already provides the (>>=) and return functions that know how to unwrap and wrap a value, the liftM function doesn't need to know any details of a monad's implementation:

```
-- file: ch14/Logger.hs
liftM :: (Monad m) => (a -> b) -> m a -> m b
liftM f m = m >>= \i ->
            return (f i)
```

When we declare a type to be an instance of the Functor typeclass, we have to write our own version of fmap specially tailored to that type. By contrast, liftM doesn't need to know anything of a monad's internals, because they're abstracted by (>>=) and return. We need to write it only once, with the appropriate type constraint.

The liftM function is predefined for us in the standard Control.Monad module.

To see how liftM can help readability, we'll compare two otherwise identical pieces of code. First, we'll look at the familiar kind that does not use liftM:

```
-- file: ch14/Logger.hs
charClass_wordy (']':cs) =
    globToRegex' cs >>= \ds ->
    return (']':ds)
charClass_wordy (c:cs) =
    charClass_wordy cs >>= \ds ->
    return (c:ds)
```

Now we can eliminate the (>>=) and anonymous function cruft with liftM:

```
-- file: ch14/Logger.hs
charClass (']':cs) = (']':) `liftM` globToRegex' cs
charClass (c:cs) = (c:) `liftM` charClass cs
```

As with fmap, we often use liftM in infix form. An easy way to read such an expression is "apply the pure function on the left to the result of the monadic action on the right."

The liftM function is so useful that Control.Monad defines several variants, which combine longer chains of actions. We can see one in the last clause of our globToRegex' function:

```
-- file: ch14/Logger.hs
globToRegex' (c:cs) = liftM2 (++) (escape c) (globToRegex' cs)

escape :: Char -> Logger String
escape c
    | c `elem` regexChars = record "escape" >> return ['\\',c]
    | otherwise           = return [c]
  where regexChars = "\\+()^$.{}]|"
```

The liftM2 function that we use here is defined as follows:

```
-- file: ch14/Logger.hs
liftM2 :: (Monad m) => (a -> b -> c) -> m a -> m b -> m c
liftM2 f m1 m2 =
    m1 >>= \a ->
    m2 >>= \b ->
    return (f a b)
```

It executes the first action, then the second, and then combines their results using the pure function f, and wraps that result. In addition to liftM2, the variants in Control.Monad go up to liftM5.

Putting a Few Misconceptions to Rest

We've now seen enough examples of monads in action to have some feel for what's going on. Before we continue, there are a few oft-repeated myths about monads that we're going to address. You're bound to encounter these assertions "in the wild," so you might as well be prepared with a few good retorts:

Monads can be hard to understand
> We've already shown that monads "fall out naturally" from several problems. We've found that the best key to understanding them is to explain several concrete examples, and then talk about what they have in common.

Monads are only useful for I/O and imperative coding
> While we use monads for I/O in Haskell, they're valuable for many other purposes as well. We've already used them for short-circuiting a chain of computations, hiding complicated state, and logging. Even so, we've barely scratched the surface.

Monads are unique to Haskell
> Haskell is probably the language that makes the most explicit use of monads, but people write them in other languages, too, ranging from C++ to OCaml. They happen to be particularly tractable in Haskell, due to do notation, the power and inference of the type system, and the language's syntax.

Monads are for controlling the order of evaluation

Building the Logger Monad

The definition of our Logger type is very simple:

```
-- file: ch14/Logger.hs
newtype Logger a = Logger { execLogger :: (a, Log) }
```

It's a pair, where the first element is the result of an action, and the second is a list of messages logged while that action was run.

We've wrapped the tuple in a newtype to make it a distinct type. The runLogger function extracts the tuple from its wrapper. The function that we're exporting to execute a logged action, runLogger, is just a synonym for execLogger:

```
-- file: ch14/Logger.hs
runLogger = execLogger
```

Our record helper function creates a singleton list of the message that we pass it:

```
-- file: ch14/Logger.hs
record s = Logger ((), [s])
```

The result of this action is (), so that's the value we put in the result slot.

Let's begin our Monad instance with return, which is trivial. It logs nothing and stores its input in the result slot of the tuple:

```
-- file: ch14/Logger.hs
instance Monad Logger where
    return a = Logger (a, [])
```

Slightly more interesting is (>>=), which is the heart of the monad. It combines an action and a monadic function to give a new result and a new log:

```
-- file: ch14/Logger.hs
    -- (>>=) :: Logger a -> (a -> Logger b) -> Logger b
    m >>= k = let (a, w) = execLogger m
                  n      = k a
                  (b, x) = execLogger n
              in Logger (b, w ++ x)
```

Let's spell out explicitly what is going on. We use runLogger to extract the result a from the action m, and we pass it to the monadic function k. We extract the result b from that in turn, and put it into the result slot of the final action. We concatenate the logs w and x to give the new log.

Sequential Logging, Not Sequential Evaluation

Our definition of (>>=) ensures that messages logged on the left will appear in the new log before those on the right. However, it says nothing about when the values a and b are evaluated: (>>=) is lazy.

Like most other aspects of a monad's behavior, strictness is under the control of the its implementor. It is not a constant shared by all monads. Indeed, some monads come in multiple flavors, each with different levels of strictness.

The Writer Monad

Our Logger monad is a specialized version of the standard Writer monad, which can be found in the Control.Monad.Writer module of the mtl package. We will present a Writer example in "Using Typeclasses" on page 378.

The Maybe Monad

The Maybe type is very nearly the simplest instance of Monad. It represents a computation that might not produce a result:

```
-- file: ch14/Maybe.hs
instance Monad Maybe where
    Just x >>= k    =  k x
    Nothing >>= _   =  Nothing

    Just _ >> k     =  k
    Nothing >> _    =  Nothing

    return x        =  Just x

    fail _          =  Nothing
```

If, when we chain together a number of computations over Maybe using (>>=) or (>>), any of them returns Nothing, we don't evaluate any of the remaining computations.

Note, though, that the chain is not completely short-circuited. Each (>>=) or (>>) in the chain will still match a Nothing on its left and produce a Nothing on its right, all the way to the end. It's easy to forget this point: when a computation in the chain fails, the subsequent production, chaining, and consumption of Nothing values are cheap at runtime, but they're not free.

Executing the Maybe Monad

A function suitable for executing the Maybe monad is maybe. (Remember that "executing" a monad involves evaluating it and returning a result that's had the monad's type wrapper removed.)

```
-- file: ch14/Maybe.hs
maybe :: b -> (a -> b) -> Maybe a -> b
maybe n _ Nothing  = n
maybe _ f (Just x) = f x
```

Its first parameter is the value to return if the result is Nothing. The second is a function to apply to a result wrapped in the Just constructor; the result of that application is then returned.

Since the Maybe type is so simple, it's about as common to simply pattern match on a Maybe value as it is to call maybe. Each one is more readable in different circumstances.

Maybe at Work, and Good API Design

Here's an example of Maybe in use as a monad. Given a customer's name, we want to find the billing address of her mobile phone carrier:

```
-- file: ch14/Carrier.hs
import qualified Data.Map as M

type PersonName = String
type PhoneNumber = String
type BillingAddress = String
data MobileCarrier = Honest_Bobs_Phone_Network
                   | Morrisas_Marvelous_Mobiles
                   | Petes_Plutocratic_Phones
                     deriving (Eq, Ord)

findCarrierBillingAddress :: PersonName
                          -> M.Map PersonName PhoneNumber
                          -> M.Map PhoneNumber MobileCarrier
                          -> M.Map MobileCarrier BillingAddress
                          -> Maybe BillingAddress
```

Our first version is the dreaded ladder of code marching off the right of the screen, with many boilerplate case expressions:

```
-- file: ch14/Carrier.hs
variation1 person phoneMap carrierMap addressMap =
    case M.lookup person phoneMap of
      Nothing -> Nothing
      Just number ->
          case M.lookup number carrierMap of
            Nothing -> Nothing
            Just carrier -> M.lookup carrier addressMap
```

The Data.Map module's lookup function has a monadic return type:

```
ghci> :module +Data.Map
ghci> :type Data.Map.lookup
Data.Map.lookup :: (Ord k, Monad m) => k -> Map k a -> m a
```

In other words, if the given key is present in the map, lookup injects it into the monad using return. Otherwise, it calls fail. This is an interesting piece of API design, though one that we think was a poor choice:

- On the positive side, the behaviors of success and failure are automatically customized to our needs, based on the monad from which we're calling lookup. Better yet, lookup itself doesn't know or care what those behaviors are.

  The case expressions just shown typecheck because we're comparing the result of lookup against values of type Maybe.

- The hitch is, of course, that using fail in the wrong monad throws a bothersome exception. We have already warned against the use of fail, so we will not repeat ourselves here.

In practice, *everyone* uses Maybe as the result type for lookup. The result type of such a conceptually simple function provides generality where it is not needed: lookup should have been written to return Maybe.

Let's set aside the API question and deal with the ugliness of our code. We can make more sensible use of Maybe's status as a monad:

```
-- file: ch14/Carrier.hs
variation2 person phoneMap carrierMap addressMap = do
  number <- M.lookup person phoneMap
  carrier <- M.lookup number carrierMap
  address <- M.lookup carrier addressMap
  return address
```

If any of these lookups fails, the definitions of (>>=) and (>>) mean that the result of the function as a whole will be Nothing, just as it was for our first attempt that used case explicitly.

This version is much tidier, but the return isn't necessary. Stylistically, it makes the code look more regular, and perhaps more familiar to the eyes of an imperative programmer, but behaviorally it's redundant. Here's an equivalent piece of code:

```
-- file: ch14/Carrier.hs
variation2a person phoneMap carrierMap addressMap = do
  number <- M.lookup person phoneMap
  carrier <- M.lookup number carrierMap
  M.lookup carrier addressMap
```

When we introduced maps, we mentioned in "Partial application awkwardness" on page 290 that the type signatures of functions in the Data.Map module often make them awkward to partially apply. The lookup function is a good example. If we flip its arguments, we can write the function body as a one-liner:

```
-- file: ch14/Carrier.hs
variation3 person phoneMap carrierMap addressMap =
    lookup phoneMap person >>= lookup carrierMap >>= lookup addressMap
  where lookup = flip M.lookup
```

The List Monad

While the Maybe type can represent either no value or one, there are many situations where we might want to return some number of results that we do not know in advance. Obviously, a list is well suited to this purpose. The type of a list suggests that we might be able to use it as a monad, because its type constructor has one free variable. And sure enough, we can use a list as a monad.

Rather than simply present the Prelude's Monad instance for the list type, let's try to figure out what an instance *ought* to look like. This is easy to do: we'll look at the types of (>>=) and return, perform some substitutions, and see if we can use a few familiar list functions.

The more obvious of the two functions is return. We know that it takes a type a, and wraps it in a type constructor m to give the type m a. We also know that the type constructor here is [ ]. Substituting this type constructor for the type variable m gives us the type [] a (yes, this really is valid notation!), which we can rewrite in more familiar form as [a].

We now know that return for lists should have the type a -> [a]. There are only a few sensible possibilities for an implementation of this function. It might return the empty list, a singleton list, or an infinite list. The most appealing behavior, based on what we know so far about monads, is the singleton list—it doesn't throw away information, nor does it repeat it infinitely:

```
-- file: ch14/ListMonad.hs
returnSingleton :: a -> [a]
returnSingleton x = [x]
```

If we perform the same substitution trick on the type of (>>=) as we did with return, we discover that it should have the type [a] -> (a -> [b]) -> [b]. This seems close to the type of map:

```
ghci> :type (>>=)
(>>=) :: (Monad m) => m a -> (a -> m b) -> m b
ghci> :type map
map :: (a -> b) -> [a] -> [b]
```

The ordering of the types in map's arguments doesn't match, but that's easy to fix:

```
ghci> :type (>>=)
(>>=) :: (Monad m) => m a -> (a -> m b) -> m b
ghci> :type flip map
flip map :: [a] -> (a -> b) -> [b]
```

We've still got a problem: the second argument of flip map has the type a -> b, whereas the second argument of (>>=) for lists has the type a -> [b]. What do we do about this?

Let's do a little more substitution and see what happens with the types. The function flip map can return any type b as its result. If we substitute [b] for b in both places where it appears in flip map's type signature, its type signature reads as a -> (a -> [b]) -> [[b]]. In other words, if we map a function that returns a list over a list, we get a list of lists back:

```
ghci> flip map [1,2,3] (\a -> [a,a+100])
[[1,101],[2,102],[3,103]]
```

Interestingly, we haven't really changed how closely our type signatures match. The type of (>>=) is [a] -> (a -> [b]) -> [b], while that of flip map when the mapped function returns a list is [a] -> (a -> [b]) -> [[b]]. There's still a mismatch in one type term—we've just moved that term from the middle of the type signature to the end. However, our juggling wasn't in vain—we now need a function that takes a [[b]] and returns a [b], and one readily suggests itself in the form of concat:

```
ghci> :type concat
concat :: [[a]] -> [a]
```

The types suggest that we should flip the arguments to map, and then concat the results to give a single list:

```
ghci> :type \xs f -> concat (map f xs)
\xs f -> concat (map f xs) :: [a] -> (a -> [a1]) -> [a1]
```

This is exactly the definition of (>>=) for lists:

```
-- file: ch14/ListMonad.hs
instance Monad [] where
    return x = [x]
    xs >>= f = concat (map f xs)
```

It applies f to every element in the list xs, and concatenates the results to return a single list.

With our two core Monad definitions in hand, the implementations of the noncore definitions that remain, (>>) and fail, ought to be obvious:

```
-- file: ch14/ListMonad.hs
    xs >> f = concat (map (\_ -> f) xs)
    fail _ = []
```

Understanding the List Monad

The list monad is similar to a familiar Haskell tool, the list comprehension. We can illustrate this similarity by computing the Cartesian product of two lists. First, we'll write a list comprehension:

```
-- file: ch14/CartesianProduct.hs
comprehensive xs ys = [(x,y) | x <- xs, y <- ys]
```

For once, we'll use bracketed notation for the monadic code instead of layout notation. This will highlight how structurally similar the monadic code is to the list comprehension:

```
-- file: ch14/CartesianProduct.hs
monadic xs ys = do { x <- xs; y <- ys; return (x,y) }
```

The only real difference is that the value we're constructing comes at the end of the sequence of expressions, instead of at the beginning as in the list comprehension. Also, the results of the two functions are identical:

```
ghci> comprehensive [1,2] "bar"
[(1,'b'),(1,'a'),(1,'r'),(2,'b'),(2,'a'),(2,'r')]
ghci> comprehensive [1,2] "bar" == monadic [1,2] "bar"
True
```

It's easy to be baffled by the list monad early on, so let's walk through our monadic Cartesian product code again in more detail. This time, we'll rearrange the function to use layout instead of brackets:

```
-- file: ch14/CartesianProduct.hs
blockyDo xs ys = do
    x <- xs
```

```
    y <- ys
    return (x, y)
```

For every element in the list xs, the rest of the function is evaluated once, with x bound to a different value from the list each time. Then for every element in the list ys, the remainder of the function is evaluated once, with y bound to a different value from the list each time.

What we really have here is a doubly nested loop! This highlights an important fact about monads: you *cannot* predict how a block of monadic code will behave unless you know what monad it will execute in.

We'll now walk through the code even more explicitly, but first let's get rid of the do notation to make the underlying structure clearer. We've indented the code a little unusually to make the loop nesting more obvious:

```
-- file: ch14/CartesianProduct.hs
blockyPlain xs ys =
    xs >>=
    \x -> ys >>=
    \y -> return (x, y)

blockyPlain_reloaded xs ys =
    concat (map (\x ->
                  concat (map (\y ->
                               return (x, y))
                         ys))
           xs)
```

If xs has the value [1,2,3], the two lines that follow are evaluated with x bound to 1, then to 2, and finally to 3. If ys has the value [True, False], the final line is evaluated *six* times: once with x as 1 and y as True; again with x as 1 and y as False; and so on. The return expression wraps each tuple in a single-element list.

Putting the List Monad to Work

Here is a simple brute-force constraint solver. Given an integer, it finds all pairs of positive integers that, when multiplied, give that value (this is the constraint being solved):

```
-- file: ch14/MultiplyTo.hs
guarded :: Bool -> [a] -> [a]
guarded True  xs = xs
guarded False _  = []

multiplyTo :: Int -> [(Int, Int)]
multiplyTo n = do
  x <- [1..n]
  y <- [x..n]
  guarded (x * y == n) $
    return (x, y)
```

Let's try this in ghci:

```
ghci> multiplyTo 8
[(1,8),(2,4)]
ghci> multiplyTo 100
[(1,100),(2,50),(4,25),(5,20),(10,10)]
ghci> multiplyTo 891
[(1,891),(3,297),(9,99),(11,81),(27,33)]
```

Desugaring of do Blocks

Haskell's do syntax is an example of *syntactic sugar*: it provides an alternative way of writing monadic code, without using (>>=) and anonymous functions. *Desugaring* is the translation of syntactic sugar back to the core language.

The rules for desugaring a do block are easy to follow. We can think of a compiler as applying these rules mechanically and repeatedly to a do block until no more do keywords remain.

A do keyword followed by a single action is translated to that action by itself:

```
-- file: ch14/Do.hs          -- file: ch14/Do.hs
doNotation1 =                 translated1 =
    do act                        act
```

A do keyword followed by more than one action is translated to the first action, then (>>), followed by a do keyword and the remaining actions. When we apply this rule repeatedly, the entire do block ends up chained together by applications of (>>):

```
-- file: ch14/Do.hs          -- file: ch14/Do.hs
doNotation2 =                 translated2 =
    do act1                       act1 >>
       act2                       do act2
       {- ... etc. -}                {- ... etc. -}
       actN                          actN

                              finalTranslation2 =
                                  act1 >>
                                  act2 >>
                                  {- ... etc. -}
                                  actN
```

The <- notation has a translation that's worth paying close attention to. On the left of the <- is a normal Haskell pattern. This can be a single variable or something more complicated, but a guard expression is not allowed:

```
-- file: ch14/Do.hs          -- file: ch14/Do.hs
doNotation3 =                 translated3 =
    do pattern <- act1            let f pattern = do act2
       act2                                 let f pattern = do act2
       {- ... etc. -}                       actN
       actN                          f _      = fail "..."
                                  in act1 >>= f
```

This pattern is translated into a `let` binding that declares a local function with a unique name (we're just using f as an example). The action on the right of the <- is then chained with this function using (>>=).

What's noteworthy about this translation is that if the pattern match fails, the local function calls the monad's `fail` implementation. Here's an example using the Maybe monad:

```
-- file: ch14/Do.hs
robust :: [a] -> Maybe a
robust xs = do (_:x:_) <- Just xs
               return x
```

The `fail` implementation in the Maybe monad simply returns Nothing. If the pattern match in the preceding function fails, we thus get Nothing as our result:

```
ghci> robust [1,2,3]
Just 2
ghci> robust [1]
Nothing
```

Finally, when we write a `let` expression in a do block, we can omit the usual in keyword. Subsequent actions in the block must be lined up with the let keyword:

```
-- file: ch14/Do.hs
doNotation4 =
    do let val1 = expr1
           val2 = expr2
           {- ... etc. -}
           valN = exprN
       act1
       act2
       {- ... etc. -}
       actN
```

```
-- file: ch14/Do.hs
translated4 =
    let val1 = expr1
        val2 = expr2
        valN = exprN
    in do act1
          act2
          {- ... etc. -}
          actN
```

Monads as a Programmable Semicolon

Earlier in "The Offside Rule Is Not Mandatory" on page 66, we mentioned that layout is the norm in Haskell, but it's not *required*. We can write a do block using explicit structure instead of layout:

```
-- file: ch14/Do.hs
semicolon = do
  {
    act1;
    val1 <- act2;
    let { val2 = expr1 };
    actN;
  }
```

```
-- file: ch14/Do.hs
semicolonTranslated =
        act1 >>
        let f val1 = let val2 = expr1
                     in actN
            f _ = fail "..."
        in act2 >>= f
```

Even though this use of explicit structure is rare, the fact that it uses semicolons to separate expressions has given rise to an apt slogan: monads are a kind of "programmable semicolon," because the behaviors of (>>) and (>>=) are different in each monad.

Why Go Sugar-Free?

When we write (>>=) explicitly in our code, it reminds us that we're stitching functions together using combinators, not simply sequencing actions.

As long as you feel like a novice with monads, we think you should prefer to explicitly write (>>=) over the syntactic sugar of do notation. The repeated reinforcement of what's really happening seems, for many programmers, to help keep things clear. (It can be easy for an imperative programmer to relax a little too much from exposure to the IO monad and assume that a do block means nothing more than a simple sequence of actions.)

Once you're feeling more familiar with monads, you can choose whichever style seems more appropriate for writing a particular function. Indeed, when you read other people's monadic code, you'll see that it's unusual, but by no means rare, to mix *both* do notation and (>>=) in a single function.

The (=<<) function shows up frequently whether or not we use do notation. It is a flipped version of (>>=):

```
ghci> :type (>>=)
(>>=) :: (Monad m) => m a -> (a -> m b) -> m b
ghci> :type (=<<)
(=<<) :: (Monad m) => (a -> m b) -> m a -> m b
```

It comes in handy if we want to compose monadic functions in the usual Haskell right-to-left style:

```
-- file: ch14/CartesianProduct.hs
wordCount = print . length . words =<< getContents
```

The State Monad

We discovered earlier in this chapter that Parse from Chapter 10 was a monad. It has two logically distinct aspects. One is the idea of a parse failing and providing a message with the details (we represented this using the Either type). The other involves carrying around a piece of implicit state, in our case, the partially consumed ByteString.

This need for a way to read and write state is common enough in Haskell programs that the standard libraries provide a monad named State that is dedicated to this purpose. This monad lives in the Control.Monad.State module.

Where our Parse type carried around a ByteString as its piece of state, the State monad can carry any type of state. We'll refer to the state's unknown type as s.

What's an obvious and general thing we might want to do with a state? Given a state value, we inspect it, and then produce a result and a new state value. Let's say the result can be of any type a. A type signature that captures this idea is s -> (a, s). Take a state s, do something with it, and return a result a and possibly a new state s.

Almost a State Monad

Let's develop some simple code that's *almost* the State monad, and then take a look at the real thing. We'll start with our type definition, which has exactly the obvious type that we just described:

```
-- file: ch14/SimpleState.hs
type SimpleState s a = s -> (a, s)
```

Our monad is a function that transforms one state into another, yielding a result when it does so. Because of this, the State monad is sometimes called the state transformer monad.

Yes, this is a type synonym, not a new type, and so we're cheating a little. Bear with us for now; this simplifies the description that follows.

Earlier in this chapter, we said that a monad has a type constructor with a single type variable, and yet here we have a type with two parameters. The key is to understand that we can partially apply a *type* just as we can partially apply a normal function. This is easiest to follow with an example:

```
-- file: ch14/SimpleState.hs
type StringState a = SimpleState String a
```

Here, we've bound the type variable s to String. The type StringState still has a type parameter a, though. It's now more obvious that we have a suitable type constructor for a monad. In other words, our monad's type constructor is SimpleState s, not SimpleState alone.

The next ingredient we need to make a monad is a definition for the return function:

```
-- file: ch14/SimpleState.hs
returnSt :: a -> SimpleState s a
returnSt a = \s -> (a, s)
```

All this does is take the result and the current state and "tuple them up." You may now be used to the idea that a Haskell function with multiple parameters is just a chain of single-parameter functions, but just in case you're not, here's a more familiar way of writing returnSt that makes it more obvious how simple this function is:

```
-- file: ch14/SimpleState.hs
returnAlt :: a -> SimpleState s a
returnAlt a s = (a, s)
```

Our final piece of the monadic puzzle is a definition for (>>=). Here it is, using the actual variable names from the standard library's definition of (>>=) for State:

```
-- file: ch14/SimpleState.hs
bindSt :: (SimpleState s a) -> (a -> SimpleState s b) -> SimpleState s b
```

```
bindSt m k = \s -> let (a, s') = m s
                   in (k a) s'
```

Those single-letter variable names aren't exactly a boon to readability, so let's see if we can substitute some more meaningful names:

```
-- file: ch14/SimpleState.hs
-- m == step
-- k == makeStep
-- s == oldState

bindAlt step makeStep oldState =
    let (result, newState) = step oldState
    in  (makeStep result) newState
```

To understand this definition, remember that `step` is a function with the type `s -> (a, s)`. When we evaluate this, we get a tuple, which we have to use to return a new function of type `s -> (a, s)`. This is perhaps easier to follow if we get rid of the `SimpleState` type synonyms from `bindAlt`'s type signature, and then examine the types of its parameters and result:

```
-- file: ch14/SimpleState.hs
bindAlt :: (s -> (a, s))          -- step
        -> (a -> s -> (b, s))     -- makeStep
        -> (s -> (b, s))          -- (makeStep result) newState
```

Reading and Modifying the State

The definitions of (>>=) and `return` for the `State` monad simply act as plumbing: they move a piece of state around, but they don't touch it in any way. We need a few other simple functions to actually do useful work with the state:

```
-- file: ch14/SimpleState.hs
getSt :: SimpleState s s
getSt = \s -> (s, s)

putSt :: s -> SimpleState s ()
putSt s = \_ -> ((), s)
```

The `getSt` function simply takes the current state and returns it as the result, while `putSt` ignores the current state and replaces it with a new one.

Will the Real State Monad Please Stand Up?

The only simplifying trick we played in the previous section was to use a type synonym instead of a type definition for `SimpleState`. If we had introduced a `newtype` wrapper at the same time, the extra wrapping and unwrapping would have made our code harder to follow.

In order to define a `Monad` instance, we have to provide a proper type constructor as well as definitions for (>>=) and `return`. This leads us to the *real* definition of `State`:

```
-- file: ch14/State.hs
newtype State s a = State {
    runState :: s -> (a, s)
    }
```

All we've done is wrap our s -> (a, s) type in a State constructor. We're automatically given a runState function that will unwrap a State value from its constructor when we use Haskell's record syntax to define the type. The type of runState is State s a -> s -> (a, s).

The definition of return is almost the same as for SimpleState, except we wrap our function with a State constructor:

```
-- file: ch14/State.hs
returnState :: a -> State s a
returnState a = State $ \s -> (a, s)
```

The definition of (>>=) is a little more complicated, because it has to use runState to remove the State wrappers:

```
-- file: ch14/State.hs
bindState :: State s a -> (a -> State s b) -> State s b
bindState m k = State $ \s -> let (a, s') = runState m s
                              in runState (k a) s'
```

This function differs from our earlier bindSt only in adding the wrapping and unwrapping of a few values. By separating the "real work" from the bookkeeping, we've hopefully made it clearer what's really happening.

We modify the functions for reading and modifying the state in the same way, by adding a little wrapping:

```
-- file: ch14/State.hs
get :: State s s
get = State $ \s -> (s, s)

put :: s -> State s ()
put s = State $ \_ -> ((), s)
```

Using the State Monad: Generating Random Values

We've already used Parse, our precursor to the State monad, to parse binary data. In that case, we wired the type of the state we were manipulating directly into the Parse type.

The State monad, by contrast, accepts any type of state as a parameter. We supply the type of the state to give, for example, State ByteString.

The State monad will probably feel more familiar to you than many other monads if you have a background in imperative languages. After all, imperative languages are all about carrying around some implicit state, reading some parts, and modifying others through assignment, which is just what the State monad is for.

So instead of unnecessarily cheerleading for the idea of using the State monad, we'll begin by demonstrating how to use it for something simple: *pseudorandom value generation*. In an imperative language, there's usually an easily available source of uniformly distributed pseudorandom numbers. For example, in C, there's a standard rand function that generates a pseudorandom number, using a global state that it updates.

Haskell's standard random value generation module is named System.Random. It allows the generation of random values of any type, not just numbers. The module contains several handy functions that live in the IO monad. For example, a rough equivalent of C's rand function would be the following:

```
-- file: ch14/Random.hs
import System.Random

rand :: IO Int
rand = getStdRandom (randomR (0, maxBound))
```

(The randomR function takes an inclusive range within which the generated random value should lie.)

The System.Random module provides a typeclass, RandomGen, that lets us define new sources of random Int values. The type StdGen is the standard RandomGen instance. It generates pseudorandom values. If we had an external source of truly random data, we could make it an instance of RandomGen and get truly random, instead of merely pseudorandom, values.

Another typeclass, Random, indicates how to generate random values of a particular type. The module defines Random instances for all of the usual simple types.

Incidentally, the definition of rand here reads and modifies a built-in global random generator that inhabits the IO monad.

A First Attempt at Purity

After all of our emphasis so far on avoiding the IO monad wherever possible, it would be a shame if we were dragged back into it just to generate some random values. Indeed, System.Random contains pure random number generation functions.

The traditional downside of purity is that we have to get or create a random number generator, and then ship it from the point we created it to the place where it's needed. When we finally call it, it returns a *new* random number generator—we're in pure code, remember, so we can't modify the state of the existing generator.

If we forget about immutability and reuse the same generator within a function, we get back exactly the same "random" number every time:

```
-- file: ch14/Random.hs
twoBadRandoms :: RandomGen g => g -> (Int, Int)
twoBadRandoms gen = (fst $ random gen, fst $ random gen)
```

Needless to say, this has unpleasant consequences:

```
ghci> twoBadRandoms `fmap` getStdGen
Loading package old-locale-1.0.0.0 ... linking ... done.
Loading package old-time-1.0.0.0 ... linking ... done.
Loading package random-1.0.0.0 ... linking ... done.
Loading package mtl-1.1.0.1 ... linking ... done.
(639600350314210417,639600350314210417)
```

The random function uses an implicit range instead of the user-supplied range employed by randomR. The getStdGen function retrieves the current value of the global standard number generator from the IO monad.

Unfortunately, correctly passing around and using successive versions of the generator does not make for palatable reading. Here's a simple example:

```
-- file: ch14/Random.hs
twoGoodRandoms :: RandomGen g => g -> ((Int, Int), g)
twoGoodRandoms gen = let (a, gen') = random gen
                         (b, gen'') = random gen'
                     in ((a, b), gen'')
```

Now that we know about the State monad, though, it looks like a fine candidate to hide the generator. The State monad lets us manage our mutable state tidily, while guaranteeing that our code will be free of other unexpected side effects, such as modifying files or making network connections. This makes it easier to reason about the behavior of our code.

Random Values in the State Monad

Here's a State monad that carries around a StdGen as its piece of state:

```
-- file: ch14/Random.hs
type RandomState a = State StdGen a
```

The type synonym is, of course, not necessary, but it's handy. It saves a little keyboarding, and if we want to swap another random generator for StdGen, it would reduce the number of type signatures we'd need to change.

Generating a random value is now a matter of fetching the current generator, using it, then modifying the state to replace it with the new generator:

```
-- file: ch14/Random.hs
getRandom :: Random a => RandomState a
getRandom =
  get >>= \gen ->
  let (val, gen') = random gen in
  put gen' >>
  return val
```

We can now use some of the monadic machinery that we saw earlier to write a much more concise function for giving us a pair of random numbers:

```
-- file: ch14/Random.hs
getTwoRandoms :: Random a => RandomState (a, a)
getTwoRandoms = liftM2 (,) getRandom getRandom
```

EXERCISE

1. Rewrite getRandom to use do notation.

Running the State Monad

As we've already mentioned, each monad has its own specialized evaluation functions. In the case of the State monad, we have several to choose from:

runState
Returns both the result and the final state

evalState
Returns only the result, throwing away the final state

execState
Throws the result away, returning only the final state

The evalState and execState functions are simply compositions of fst and snd with runState, respectively. Thus, of the three, runState is the one most worth remembering.

Here's a complete example of how to implement our getTwoRandoms function:

```
-- file: ch14/Random.hs
runTwoRandoms :: IO (Int, Int)
runTwoRandoms = do
  oldState <- getStdGen
  let (result, newState) = runState getTwoRandoms oldState
  setStdGen newState
  return result
```

The call to runState follows a standard pattern: we pass it a function in the State monad and an initial state. It returns the result of the function and the final state.

The code surrounding the call to runState merely obtains the current global StdGen value, and then replaces it afterwards so that subsequent calls to runTwoRandoms or other random generation functions will pick up the updated state.

What About a Bit More State?

It's a little hard to imagine writing much interesting code in which there's only a single state value to pass around. When we want to track multiple pieces of state at once, the usual trick is to maintain them in a data type. The following is an example of keeping track of how many of random numbers we are handing out:

```
-- file: ch14/Random.hs
data CountedRandom = CountedRandom {
      crGen :: StdGen
    , crCount :: Int
    }

type CRState = State CountedRandom

getCountedRandom :: Random a => CRState a
getCountedRandom = do
  st <- get
  let (val, gen') = random (crGen st)
  put CountedRandom { crGen = gen', crCount = crCount st + 1 }
  return val
```

This example happens to consume both elements of the state, and it constructs a completely new state, every time we call into it. More frequently, we're likely to read or modify only part of a state. This function gets the number of random values generated so far:

```
-- file: ch14/Random.hs
getCount :: CRState Int
getCount = crCount `liftM` get
```

This example illustrates why we used record syntax to define our CountedRandom state. It gives us accessor functions that we can glue together with **get** to read specific pieces of the state.

If we want to partially update a state, the code doesn't come out quite so appealingly:

```
-- file: ch14/Random.hs
putCount :: Int -> CRState ()
putCount a = do
  st <- get
  put st { crCount = a }
```

Here, instead of a function, we're using record update syntax. The expression st { crCount = a } creates a new value that's an identical copy of st, except in its crCount field, which is given the value a. Because this is a syntactic hack, we don't get the same kind of flexibility as with a function. Record syntax may not exhibit Haskell's usual elegance, but it at least gets the job done.

There is a function named **modify** that combines the **get** and **put** steps. It takes as argument a state transformation function, but it's hardly more satisfactory—we still can't escape from the clumsiness of record update syntax:

```
-- file: ch14/Random.hs
putCountModify :: Int -> CRState ()
putCountModify a = modify $ \st -> st { crCount = a }
```

Monads and Functors

Functors and monads are closely related. The terms are borrowed from a branch of mathematics called *category theory*, but they did not make the transition to Haskell completely unscathed.

In category theory, a monad is built from a functor. You might expect that in Haskell, the Monad typeclass would thus be a subclass of Functor, but it isn't defined as such in the standard Prelude—an unfortunate oversight.

However, authors of Haskell libraries use a workaround: when programmers define an instance of Monad for a type, they almost always write a Functor instance for it, too. You can expect that you'll be able to use the Functor typeclass's fmap function with any monad.

If we compare the type signature of fmap with those of some of the standard monad functions that we've already seen, we get a hint as to what fmap on a monad does:

```
ghci> :type fmap
fmap :: (Functor f) => (a -> b) -> f a -> f b
ghci> :module +Control.Monad
ghci> :type liftM
liftM :: (Monad m) => (a1 -> r) -> m a1 -> m r
```

Sure enough, fmap lifts a pure function into the monad, just as liftM does.

Another Way of Looking at Monads

Now that we know about the relationship between functors and monads, if we look back at the list monad, we can see something interesting. Specifically, take a look at the definition of (>>=) for lists:

```
-- file: ch14/ListMonad.hs
instance Monad [] where
    return x = [x]
    xs >>= f = concat (map f xs)
```

Recall that f has type a -> [a]. When we call map f xs, we get back a value of type [[a]], which we have to "flatten" using concat.

Consider what we could do if Monad was a subclass of Functor. Since fmap for lists is defined to be map, we could replace map with fmap in the definition of (>>=). This is not very interesting by itself, but suppose we go further.

The concat function is of type [[a]] -> [a]. As we mentioned, it flattens the nesting of lists. We could generalize this type signature from lists to monads, giving us the "remove a level of nesting" type m (m a) -> m a. The function that has this type is conventionally named join.

If we had definitions of join and fmap, we wouldn't need to write a definition of (>>=) for every monad, because it would be completely generic. Here's what an alternative definition of the Monad typeclass might look like, along with a definition of (>>=):

```
-- file: ch14/AltMonad.hs
import Prelude hiding ((>>=), return)

class Functor m => AltMonad m where
    join :: m (m a) -> m a
    return :: a -> m a

(>>=) :: AltMonad m => m a -> (a -> m b) -> m b
xs >>= f = join (fmap f xs)
```

Neither definition of a monad is "better," because if we have join we can write (>>=) and vice versa, but the different perspectives can be refreshing.

Removing a layer of monadic wrapping can, in fact, be useful in realistic circumstances. We can find a generic definition of join in the Control.Monad module:

```
-- file: ch14/MonadJoin.hs
join :: Monad m => m (m a) -> m a
join x = x >>= id
```

Here are some examples of what it does:

```
ghci> join (Just (Just 1))
Just 1
ghci> join Nothing
Nothing
ghci> join [[1],[2,3]]
[1,2,3]
```

The Monad Laws and Good Coding Style

In "Thinking More About Functors" on page 249, we introduced two rules for how functors should always behave:

```
-- file: ch14/MonadLaws.hs
fmap id        ==    id
fmap (f . g)   ==    fmap f . fmap g
```

There are also rules for how monads ought to behave. The three laws described in the following paragraphs are referred to as the monad laws. A Haskell implementation doesn't enforce these laws—it's up to the author of a Monad instance to follow them.

The monad laws are simply formal ways of saying "a monad shouldn't surprise me." In principle, we could probably get away with skipping over them entirely. It would be a shame if we did, however, because the laws contain gems of wisdom that we might otherwise overlook.

Reading the laws

You can read each of the following laws as "the expression on the left of the == is equivalent to that on the right."

The first law states that `return` is a *left identity* for (`>>=`):

```
-- file: ch14/MonadLaws.hs
return x >>= f            ===    f x
```

Another way to phrase this is that there's no reason to use `return` to wrap up a pure value if all you're going to do is unwrap it again with (`>>=`). It's actually a common style error among programmers new to monads to wrap a value with `return`, and then unwrap it with (`>>=`) a few lines later in the same function. Here's the same law written with `do` notation:

```
-- file: ch14/MonadLaws.hs
do y <- return x
   f y                   ===    f x
```

This law has practical consequences for our coding style: we don't want to write unnecessary code, and the law lets us assume that the terse code will be identical in its effect to the more verbose version.

The second monad law states that `return` is a *right identity* for (`>>=`):

```
-- file: ch14/MonadLaws.hs
m >>= return             ===    m
```

This law also has style consequences in real programs, particularly if you're coming from an imperative language: there's no need to use `return` if the last action in a block would otherwise be returning the correct result. Let's look at this law in `do` notation:

```
-- file: ch14/MonadLaws.hs
do y <- m
   return y              ===    m
```

Once again, if we assume that a monad obeys this law, we can write the shorter code with the knowledge that it will have the same effect as the longer code.

The final law is concerned with associativity:

```
-- file: ch14/MonadLaws.hs
m >>= (\x -> f x >>= g)   ===   (m >>= f) >>= g
```

This law can be a little more difficult to follow, so let's look at the contents of the parentheses on each side of the equation. We can rewrite the expression on the left as follows:

```
-- file: ch14/MonadLaws.hs
m >>= s
  where s x = f x >>= g
```

On the right, we can also rearrange things:

```
-- file: ch14/MonadLaws.hs
t >>= g
  where t = m >>= f
```

We're now claiming that the following two expressions are equivalent:

```
-- file: ch14/MonadLaws.hs
m >>= s                    ===    t >>= g
```

This means that if we want to break up an action into smaller pieces, it doesn't matter which subactions we hoist out to make new actions, provided we preserve their ordering. If we have three actions chained together, we can substitute the first two and leave the third in place, or we can replace the second two and leave the first in place.

Even this more complicated law has a practical consequence. In the terminology of software refactoring, the *extract method* technique is a fancy term for snipping out a piece of inline code, turning it into a function, and calling the function from the site of the snipped code. This law essentially states that this technique can be applied to monadic Haskell code.

We've now seen how each of the monad laws offers us an insight into writing better monadic code. The first two laws show us how to avoid any unnecessary use of return. The third suggests that we can safely refactor a complicated action into several simpler ones. We can now safely let the details fade, with the knowledge that our "do what I mean" intuitions won't be violated when we use properly written monads.

Incidentally, a Haskell compiler cannot guarantee that a monad actually follows the monad laws. It is the responsibility of a monad's author to satisfy—or, preferably, prove to—himself that his code follows the laws.

CHAPTER 15

Programming with Monads

Golfing Practice: Association Lists

Web clients and servers often pass information around as a simple textual list of key-value pairs:

```
name=Attila+%42The+Hun%42&occupation=Khan
```

The encoding is named `application/x-www-form-urlencoded`, and it's easy to understand. Each key-value pair is separated by an & character. Within a pair, a key is a series of characters, followed by an =, followed by a value.

We can obviously represent a key as a `String`, but the HTTP specification is not clear about whether a key must be followed by a value. We can capture this ambiguity by representing a value as a `Maybe String`. If we use `Nothing` for a value, then there is no value present. If we wrap a string in `Just`, then there is a value. Using `Maybe` lets us distinguish between "no value" and "empty value."

Haskell programmers use the name *association list* for the type `[(a, b)]`, where we can think of each element as an association between a key and a value. The name originates in the Lisp community, where it's usually abbreviated as an *alist*. We could thus represent the preceding string as the following Haskell value:

```haskell
-- file: ch15/MovieReview.hs
    [("name",      Just "Attila \"The Hun\""),
     ("occupation", Just "Khan")]
```

In "Parsing a URL-Encoded Query String" on page 393, we'll parse an `application/x-www-form-urlencoded` string, and we will represent the result as an alist of `[(String, Maybe String)]`. Let's say we want to use one of these alists to fill out a data structure:

```haskell
-- file: ch15/MovieReview.hs
data MovieReview = MovieReview {
      revTitle :: String
    , revUser :: String
    , revReview :: String
    }
```

We'll begin by belaboring the obvious with a naive function:

```
-- file: ch15/MovieReview.hs
simpleReview :: [(String, Maybe String)] -> Maybe MovieReview
simpleReview alist =
  case lookup "title" alist of
    Just (Just title@(_:_)) ->
      case lookup "user" alist of
        Just (Just user@(_:_)) ->
          case lookup "review" alist of
            Just (Just review@(_:_)) ->
                Just (MovieReview title user review)
            _ -> Nothing -- no review
        _ -> Nothing -- no user
    _ -> Nothing -- no title
```

It returns a `MovieReview` only if the alist contains all of the necessary values, and they're all nonempty strings. However, the fact that it validates its inputs is its only merit. It suffers badly from the "staircasing" that we've learned to be wary of, and it knows the intimate details of the representation of an alist.

Since we're now well acquainted with the `Maybe` monad, we can tidy up the staircasing:

```
-- file: ch15/MovieReview.hs
maybeReview alist = do
    title <- lookup1 "title" alist
    user <- lookup1 "user" alist
    review <- lookup1 "review" alist
    return (MovieReview title user review)

lookup1 key alist = case lookup key alist of
                      Just (Just s@(_:_)) -> Just s
                      _ -> Nothing
```

Although this is much neater, we're still repeating ourselves. We can take advantage of the fact that the `MovieReview` constructor acts as a normal, pure function by *lifting* it into the monad, as we discussed in "Mixing Pure and Monadic Code" on page 334:

```
-- file: ch15/MovieReview.hs
liftedReview alist =
    liftM3 MovieReview (lookup1 "title" alist)
                       (lookup1 "user" alist)
                       (lookup1 "review" alist)
```

We still have some repetition here, but it is dramatically reduced and also more difficult to remove.

Generalized Lifting

Although using `liftM3` tidies up our code, we can't use a `liftM`-family function to solve this sort of problem in general, because the standard libraries define them only up to `liftM5`. We could write variants up to whatever number we pleased, but that would amount to drudgery.

If we had a constructor or pure function that takes, say, 10 parameters, and decided to stick with the standard libraries, you might think we'd be out of luck.

Of course, our toolbox isn't empty yet. In Control.Monad, there's a function named ap with an interesting type signature:

```
ghci> :m +Control.Monad
ghci> :type ap
ap :: (Monad m) => m (a -> b) -> m a -> m b
```

You might wonder who would put a single-argument pure function inside a monad, and why. Recall, however, that *all* Haskell functions really take only one argument, and you'll begin to see how this might relate to the MovieReview constructor:

```
ghci> :type MovieReview
MovieReview :: String -> String -> String -> MovieReview
```

We can just as easily write that type as:

```
String -> (String -> (String -> MovieReview))
```

If we use plain old liftM to lift MovieReview into the Maybe monad, we'll have a value of type:

```
Maybe (String -> (String -> (String -> MovieReview)))
```

We can now see that this type is suitable as an argument for ap, in which case, the result type will be:

```
Maybe (String -> (String -> MovieReview))
```

We can pass this, in turn, to ap, and continue to chain until we end up with this definition:

```
-- file: ch15/MovieReview.hs
apReview alist =
    MovieReview `liftM` lookup1 "title" alist
                   `ap` lookup1 "user" alist
                   `ap` lookup1 "review" alist
```

We can chain applications of ap such as this as many times as we need to, thereby bypassing the liftM family of functions.

Another helpful way to look at ap is that it's the monadic equivalent of the familiar ($) operator; think of pronouncing ap as *apply*. We can see this clearly when we compare the type signatures of the two functions:

```
ghci> :type ($)
($) :: (a -> b) -> a -> b
ghci> :type ap
ap :: (Monad m) => m (a -> b) -> m a -> m b
```

In fact, ap is usually defined as either liftM2 id or liftM2 ($).

Looking for Alternatives

Here's a simple representation of a person's phone numbers:

```
-- file: ch15/VCard.hs
data Context = Home | Mobile | Business
               deriving (Eq, Show)

type Phone = String

albulena = [(Home, "+355-652-55512")]

nils = [(Mobile, "+47-922-55-512"), (Business, "+47-922-12-121"),
        (Home, "+47-925-55-121"), (Business, "+47-922-25-551")]

twalumba = [(Business, "+260-02-55-5121")]
```

Suppose we want to get in touch with someone to make a personal call. We don't want his business number, and we'd prefer to use his home number (if he has one) instead of their mobile number:

```
-- file: ch15/VCard.hs
onePersonalPhone :: [(Context, Phone)] -> Maybe Phone
onePersonalPhone ps = case lookup Home ps of
                        Nothing -> lookup Mobile ps
                        Just n -> Just n
```

Of course, if we use Maybe as the result type, we can't accommodate the possibility that someone might have more than one number that meets our criteria. For that, we switch to a list:

```
-- file: ch15/VCard.hs
allBusinessPhones :: [(Context, Phone)] -> [Phone]
allBusinessPhones ps = map snd numbers
    where numbers = case filter (contextIs Business) ps of
                      [] -> filter (contextIs Mobile) ps
                      ns -> ns

contextIs a (b, _) = a == b
```

Notice that these two functions structure their case expressions similarly—one alternative handles the case where the first lookup returns an empty result, while the other handles the nonempty case:

```
ghci> onePersonalPhone twalumba
Nothing
ghci> onePersonalPhone albulena
Just "+355-652-55512"
ghci> allBusinessPhones nils
["+47-922-12-121","+47-922-25-551"]
```

Haskell's Control.Monad module defines a typeclass, MonadPlus, that lets us abstract the common pattern out of our case expressions:

```
-- file: ch15/VCard.hs
class Monad m => MonadPlus m where
    mzero :: m a
    mplus :: m a -> m a -> m a
```

The value `mzero` represents an empty result, while `mplus` combines two results into one. Here are the standard definitions of `mzero` and `mplus` for `Maybe` and lists:

```
-- file: ch15/VCard.hs
instance MonadPlus [] where
    mzero = []
    mplus = (++)

instance MonadPlus Maybe where
    mzero = Nothing

    Nothing `mplus` ys  = ys
    xs      `mplus` _  = xs
```

We can now use `mplus` to get rid of our `case` expressions entirely. For variety, let's fetch one business and all personal phone numbers:

```
-- file: ch15/VCard.hs
oneBusinessPhone :: [(Context, Phone)] -> Maybe Phone
oneBusinessPhone ps = lookup Business ps `mplus` lookup Mobile ps

allPersonalPhones :: [(Context, Phone)] -> [Phone]
allPersonalPhones ps = map snd $ filter (contextIs Home) ps `mplus`
                                  filter (contextIs Mobile) ps
```

In these functions, because we know that `lookup` returns a value of type `Maybe`, and `filter` returns a list, it's obvious which version of `mplus` is going to be used in each case.

What's more interesting is that we can use `mzero` and `mplus` to write functions that will be useful for *any* MonadPlus instance. As an example, here's the standard `lookup` function, which returns a value of type `Maybe`:

```
-- file: ch15/VCard.hs
lookup :: (Eq a) => a -> [(a, b)] -> Maybe b
lookup _ []           = Nothing
lookup k ((x,y):xys) | x == k    = Just y
                     | otherwise = lookup k xys
```

We can easily generalize the result type to any instance of `MonadPlus` as follows:

```
-- file: ch15/VCard.hs
lookupM :: (MonadPlus m, Eq a) => a -> [(a, b)] -> m b
lookupM _ []      = mzero
lookupM k ((x,y):xys)
    | x == k    = return y `mplus` lookupM k xys
    | otherwise = lookupM k xys
```

This lets us get either no result or one, if our result type is `Maybe`; all results, if our result type is a list; or something more appropriate for some other exotic instance of `MonadPlus`.

For small functions, such as those we present here, there's little benefit to using `mplus`. The advantage lies in more complex code and in code that is independent of the monad in which it executes. Even if you don't find yourself needing `MonadPlus` for your own code, you are likely to encounter it in other people's projects.

The Name mplus Does Not Imply Addition

Even though the `mplus` function contains the text "plus," you should not think of it as necessarily implying that we're trying to add two values.

Depending on the monad we're working in, `mplus` *may* implement an operation that looks like addition. For example, `mplus` in the list monad is implemented as the (++) operator:

```
ghci> [1,2,3] `mplus` [4,5,6]
[1,2,3,4,5,6]
```

However, if we switch to another monad, the obvious similarity to addition falls away:

```
ghci> Just 1 `mplus` Just 2
Just 1
```

Rules for Working with MonadPlus

Instances of the `MonadPlus` typeclass must follow a few simple rules in addition to the usual monad rules.

An instance must short-circuit if `mzero` appears on the left of a bind expression. In other words, an expression `mzero >>= f` must evaluate to the same result as `mzero` alone:

```
-- file: ch15/MonadPlus.hs
    mzero >>= f == mzero
```

An instance must short-circuit if `mzero` appears on the *right* of a sequence expression:

```
-- file: ch15/MonadPlus.hs
    v >> == mzero
```

Failing Safely with MonadPlus

When we introduced the `fail` function in "The Monad Typeclass" on page 329, we took pains to warn against its use: in many monads, it's implemented as a call to `error`, which has unpleasant consequences.

The `MonadPlus` typeclass gives us a gentler way to fail a computation, without `fail` or `error` blowing up in our faces. The rules that we just introduced allow us to introduce an `mzero` into our code wherever we need to, and computation will short-circuit at that point.

In the `Control.Monad` module, the standard function `guard` packages up this idea in a convenient form:

```
-- file: ch15/MonadPlus.hs
guard        :: (MonadPlus m) => Bool -> m ()
guard True   = return ()
guard False  = mzero
```

As a simple example, here's a function that takes a number `x` and computes its value modulo some other number `n`. If the result is zero, it returns `x`; otherwise, the current monad's `mzero`:

```
-- file: ch15/MonadPlus.hs
x `zeroMod` n = guard ((x `mod` n) == 0) >> return x
```

Adventures in Hiding the Plumbing

In "Using the State Monad: Generating Random Values" on page 349, we showed how to use the `State` monad to give ourselves access to random numbers in a way that is easy to use.

A drawback of the code we developed is that it's *leaky*: Users know that they're executing inside the `State` monad. This means that they can inspect and modify the state of the random number generator just as easily as we, the authors, can.

Human nature dictates that if we leave our internal workings exposed, someone will surely come along and monkey with them. For a sufficiently small program, this may be fine, but in a larger software project, when one consumer of a library modifies its internals in a way that other consumers are not prepared for, the resulting bugs can be among the most difficult to track down. These bugs occur at a level where we're unlikely to question our basic assumptions about a library until long after we've exhausted all other avenues of inquiry.

Even worse, once we leave our implementation exposed for a while, and some well-intentioned person inevitably bypasses our APIs and uses the implementation directly, we have a nasty quandary if we need to fix a bug or make an enhancement. Either we can modify our internals and break code that depends on them; or we're stuck with our existing internals and must try to find some other way to make the change that we need.

How can we revise our random number monad so that the fact that we're using the `State` monad is hidden? We need to somehow prevent our users from being able to call `get` or `put`. This is not difficult to do, and it introduces some tricks that we'll reuse often in day-to-day Haskell programming.

To widen our scope, we'll move beyond random numbers and implement a monad that supplies unique values of *any* kind. The name we'll give to our monad is `Supply`. We'll provide the execution function, `runSupply`, with a list of values (it will be up to us to ensure that each one is unique):

```
-- file: ch15/Supply.hs
runSupply :: Supply s a -> [s] -> (a, [s])
```

The monad won't care what the values are. They might be random numbers, or names for temporary files, or identifiers for HTTP cookies.

Within the monad, every time a consumer asks for a value, the next action will take the next one from the list and give it to the consumer. Each value is wrapped in a Maybe constructor in case the list isn't long enough to satisfy the demand:

```
-- file: ch15/Supply.hs
next :: Supply s (Maybe s)
```

To hide our plumbing, in our module declaration, we export only the type constructor, the execution function, and the next action:

```
-- file: ch15/Supply.hs
module Supply
    (
      Supply
    , next
    , runSupply
    ) where
```

Since a module that imports the library can't see the internals of the monad, it can't manipulate them.

Our plumbing is exceedingly simple. We use a newtype declaration to wrap the existing State monad:

```
-- file: ch15/Supply.hs
import Control.Monad.State

newtype Supply s a = S (State [s] a)
```

The s parameter is the type of the unique values we are going to supply, and a is the usual type parameter that we must provide in order to make our type a monad.

Our use of newtype for the Supply type and our module header join forces to prevent our clients from using the State monad's get and set actions. Because our module does not export the S data constructor, clients have no programmatic way to see that we're wrapping the State monad, or to access it.

At this point, we've got a type, Supply, that we need to make an instance of the Monad typeclass. We could follow the usual pattern of defining (>>=) and return, but this would be pure boilerplate code. All we'd be doing is wrapping and unwrapping the State monad's versions of (>>=) and return using our S value constructor. Here is how such code would look:

```
-- file: ch15/AltSupply.hs
unwrapS :: Supply s a -> State [s] a
unwrapS (S s) = s

instance Monad (Supply s) where
```

```
    s >>= m = S (unwrapS s >>= unwrapS . m)
    return = S . return
```

Haskell programmers are not fond of boilerplate, and sure enough, GHC has a lovely language extension that eliminates the work. To use it, we add the following directive to the top of our source file, before the module header:

```
-- file: ch15/Supply.hs
{-# LANGUAGE GeneralizedNewtypeDeriving #-}
```

Usually, we can only automatically derive instances of a handful of standard type-classes, such as Show and Eq. As its name suggests, the GeneralizedNewtypeDeriving extension broadens our ability to derive typeclass instances, and it is specific to newtype declarations. If the type we're wrapping is an instance of any typeclass, the extensions can automatically make our new type an instance of that typeclass as follows:

```
-- file: ch15/Supply.hs
    deriving (Monad)
```

This takes the underlying type's implementations of (>>=) and return, adds the necessary wrapping and unwrapping with our S data constructor, and uses the new versions of those functions to derive a Monad instance for us.

What we gain here is very useful beyond just this example. We can use newtype to wrap any underlying type; we selectively expose only those typeclass instances that we want; and we expend almost no effort to create these narrower, more specialized types.

Now that we've seen the GeneralizedNewtypeDeriving technique, all that remains is to provide definitions of next and runSupply:

```
-- file: ch15/Supply.hs
next = S $ do st <- get
              case st of
                [] -> return Nothing
                (x:xs) -> do put xs
                             return (Just x)

runSupply (S m) xs = runState m xs
```

If we load our module into ghci, we can try it out in a few simple ways:

```
ghci> :load Supply
[1 of 1] Compiling Supply            ( Supply.hs, interpreted )
Ok, modules loaded: Supply.
ghci> runSupply next [1,2,3]
Loading package mtl-1.1.0.1 ... linking ... done.
(Just 1,[2,3])
ghci> runSupply (liftM2 (,) next next) [1,2,3]
((Just 1,Just 2),[3])
ghci> runSupply (liftM2 (,) next next) [1]
((Just 1,Nothing),[])
```

We can also verify that the State monad has not somehow leaked out:

```
ghci> :browse Supply
data Supply s a
next :: Supply s (Maybe s)
runSupply :: Supply s a -> [s] -> (a, [s])
ghci> :info Supply
data Supply s a      -- Defined at Supply.hs:17:8-13
instance Monad (Supply s) -- Defined at Supply.hs:17:8-13
```

Supplying Random Numbers

If we want to use our Supply monad as a source of random numbers, we have a small difficulty to face. Ideally, we'd like to be able to provide it with an infinite stream of random numbers. We can get a StdGen in the IO monad, but we must "put back" a different StdGen when we're done. If we don't, the next piece of code to get a StdGen will get the same state as we did. This means it will generate the same random numbers as we did, which is potentially catastrophic.

From the parts of the System.Random module we've seen so far, it's difficult to reconcile these demands. We can use getStdRandom, whose type ensures that when we get a StdGen, we put one back:

```
ghci> :type getStdRandom
getStdRandom :: (StdGen -> (a, StdGen)) -> IO a
```

We can use random to get back a new StdGen when they give us a random number. And we can use randoms to get an infinite list of random numbers. But how do we get both an infinite list of random numbers *and* a new StdGen?

The answer lies with the RandomGen typeclass's split function, which takes one random number generator and turns it into two generators. Splitting a random generator such as this is a most unusual thing to be able to do: it's obviously tremendously useful in a pure functional setting, but it is essentially either never necessary an impure language, or the language doesn't provide for it.

With the split function, we can use one StdGen to generate an infinite list of random numbers to feed to runSupply, while we give the other back to the IO monad:

```
-- file: ch15/RandomSupply.hs
import Supply
import System.Random hiding (next)

randomsIO :: Random a => IO [a]
randomsIO =
    getStdRandom $ \g ->
        let (a, b) = split g
        in (randoms a, b)
```

If we've written this function properly, our example ought to print a different random number on each invocation:

```
ghci> :load RandomSupply
[1 of 2] Compiling Supply           ( Supply.hs, interpreted )
```

```
[2 of 2] Compiling RandomSupply    ( RandomSupply.hs, interpreted )
Ok, modules loaded: RandomSupply, Supply.
ghci> (fst . runSupply next) `fmap` randomsIO

<interactive>:1:17:
    Ambiguous occurrence `next'
    It could refer to either `Supply.next', imported from Supply at RandomSupply.hs:4:
                                        (defined at Supply.hs:32:0)
                      or `System.Random.next', imported from System.Random
ghci> (fst . runSupply next) `fmap` randomsIO

<interactive>:1:17:
    Ambiguous occurrence `next'
    It could refer to either `Supply.next', imported from Supply at RandomSupply.hs:4:
                                        (defined at Supply.hs:32:0)
                      or `System.Random.next', imported from System.Random
```

Recall that our runSupply function returns both the result of executing the monadic action and the unconsumed remainder of the list. Since we passed it an infinite list of random numbers, we compose with fst to ensure that we don't get drowned in random numbers when ghci tries to print the result.

Another Round of Golf

The pattern of applying a function to one element of a pair and constructing a new pair with the other original element untouched is common enough in Haskell code that it has been turned into standard code.

Two functions, first and second, perform this operation in the Control.Arrow module:

```
ghci> :m +Control.Arrow
ghci> first (+3) (1,2)
(4,2)
ghci> second odd ('a',1)
('a',True)
```

(Indeed, we already encountered second in "JSON Typeclasses Without Overlapping Instances" on page 159.) We can use first to golf our definition of randomsIO, turning it into a one-liner:

```
-- file: ch15/RandomGolf.hs
import Control.Arrow (first)

randomsIO_golfed :: Random a => IO [a]
randomsIO_golfed = getStdRandom (first randoms . split)
```

Separating Interface from Implementation

In the previous section, we saw how to hide the fact that we're using a State monad to hold the state for our Supply monad.

Another important way to make code more modular involves separating its *interface* (what the code can do) from its *implementation*—how it does it.

The standard random number generator in `System.Random` is known to be quite slow. If we use our `randomsIO` function to provide it with random numbers, then our `next` action will not perform well.

One simple and effective way that we could deal with this is to provide `Supply` with a better source of random numbers. Let's set this idea aside, though, and consider an alternative approach, one that is useful in many settings. We will separate the actions we can perform with the monad from how it works using a typeclass:

```
-- file: ch15/SupplyClass.hs
class (Monad m) => MonadSupply s m | m -> s where
    next :: m (Maybe s)
```

This typeclass defines the interface that any supply monad must implement. It bears careful inspection, since it uses several unfamiliar Haskell language extensions. We will cover each one in the sections that follow.

Multiparameter Typeclasses

How should we read the snippet `MonadSupply s m` in the typeclass? If we add parentheses, an equivalent expression is `(MonadSupply s) m`, which is a little clearer. In other words, given some type variable `m` that is a `Monad`, we can make it an instance of the typeclass `MonadSupply s`. Unlike a regular typeclass, this one has a *parameter*.

As this language extension allows a typeclass to have more than one parameter, its name is `MultiParamTypeClasses`. The parameter `s` serves the same purpose as the `Supply` type's parameter of the same name: it represents the type of the values handed out by the `next` function.

Notice that we don't need to mention (`>>=`) or `return` in the definition of `MonadSupply` `s`, since the typeclass's context (superclass) requires that a `MonadSupply s` must already be a `Monad`.

Functional Dependencies

To revisit a snippet that we ignored earlier, `| m -> s` is a *functional dependency*, often called a *fundep*. We can read the vertical bar `|` as "such that," and the arrow `->` as "uniquely determines." Our functional dependency establishes a *relationship* between `m` and `s`.

The `FunctionalDependencies` language pragma governs the availability of functional dependencies.

The purpose behind us declaring a relationship is to help the type checker. Recall that a Haskell type checker is essentially a theorem prover, and that it is conservative in how it operates: it insists that its proofs must terminate. A nonterminating proof results in the compiler either giving up or getting stuck in an infinite loop.

With our functional dependency, we are telling the type checker that every time it sees some monad m being used in the context of a MonadSupply s, the type s is the only acceptable type to use with it. If we were to omit the functional dependency, the type checker would simply give up with an error message.

It's hard to picture what the relationship between m and s really means, so let's look at an instance of this typeclass:

```
-- file: ch15/SupplyClass.hs
import qualified Supply as S

instance MonadSupply s (S.Supply s) where
    next = S.next
```

Here, the type variable m is replaced by the type S.Supply s. Thanks to our functional dependency, the type checker now knows that when it sees a type S.Supply s, the type can be used as an instance of the typeclass MonadSupply s.

If we didn't have a functional dependency, the type checker would not be able to figure out the relationship between the type parameter of the class MonadSupply s and that of the type Supply s, and it would abort compilation with an error. The definition itself would compile; the type error would not arise until the first time we tried to use it.

To strip away one final layer of abstraction, consider the type S.Supply Int. Without a functional dependency, we could declare this an instance of MonadSupply s. However, if we try to write code using this instance, the compiler would not be able to figure out that the type's Int parameter needs to be the same as the typeclass's s parameter, and it would report an error.

Functional dependencies can be tricky to understand, and once we move beyond simple uses, they often prove difficult to work with in practice. Fortunately, the most frequent use of functional dependencies is in situations as simple as ours, where they cause little trouble.

Rounding Out Our Module

If we save our typeclass and instance in a source file named *SupplyClass.hs*, we'll need to add a module header such as the following:

```
-- file: ch15/SupplyClass.hs
{-# LANGUAGE FlexibleInstances, FunctionalDependencies,
             MultiParamTypeClasses #-}

module SupplyClass
    (
      MonadSupply(..)
    , S.Supply
```

```
    , S.runSupply
    ) where
```

The `FlexibleInstances` extension is necessary so that the compiler will accept our instance declaration. This extension relaxes the normal rules for writing instances in some circumstances, in a way that still lets the compiler's type checker guarantee that it will terminate. Our need for `FlexibleInstances` here is caused by our use of functional dependencies, but the details are unfortunately beyond the scope of this book.

How to know when a language extension is needed

If GHC cannot compile a piece of code because it would require some language extension to be enabled, it will tell us which extension we should use. For example, if it decides that our code needs flexible instance support, it will suggest that we try compiling with the `-XFlexibleInstances` option. A `-X` option has the same effect as a `LANGUAGE` directive: it enables a particular extension.

Finally, notice that we're re-exporting the `runSupply` and `Supply` names from this module. It's perfectly legal to export a name from one module even though it's defined in another. In our case, it means that client code needs only to import the `SupplyClass` module, without also importing the `Supply` module. This reduces the number of "moving parts" that a user of our code needs to keep in mind.

Programming to a Monad's Interface

Here is a simple function that fetches two values from our `Supply` monad, formats them as a string, and returns them:

```
-- file: ch15/Supply.hs
showTwo :: (Show s) => Supply s String
showTwo = do
  a <- next
  b <- next
  return (show "a: " ++ show a ++ ", b: " ++ show b)
```

This code is tied by its result type to our `Supply` monad. We can easily generalize to any monad that implements our `MonadSupply` interface by modifying our function's type. Notice that the body of the function remains unchanged:

```
-- file: ch15/SupplyClass.hs
showTwo_class :: (Show s, Monad m, MonadSupply s m) => m String
showTwo_class = do
  a <- next
  b <- next
  return (show "a: " ++ show a ++ ", b: " ++ show b)
```

The Reader Monad

The `State` monad lets us plumb a piece of mutable state through our code. Sometimes, we would like to be able to pass some *immutable* state around, such as a program's configuration data. We could use the `State` monad for this purpose, but we might then find ourselves accidentally modifying data that should remain unchanged.

Let's forget about monads for a moment and think about what a *function* with our desired characteristics ought to do. It should accept a value of some type `e` (for environment) that represents the data that we're passing in, and return a value of some other type `a` as its result. The overall type we want is `e -> a`.

To turn this type into a convenient `Monad` instance, we'll wrap it in a `newtype`:

```
-- file: ch15/SupplyInstance.hs
newtype Reader e a = R { runReader :: e -> a }
```

Making this into a `Monad` instance doesn't take much work:

```
-- file: ch15/SupplyInstance.hs
instance Monad (Reader e) where
    return a = R $ \_ -> a
    m >>= k  = R $ \r -> runReader (k (runReader m r)) r
```

We can think of our value of type `e` as an environment in which we're evaluating some expression. The `return` action should have the same effect no matter what the environment is, so our version ignores its environment.

Our definition of (`>>=`) is a little more complicated, but only because we have to make the environment—here the variable `r`—available both in the current computation and in the computation we're chaining into.

How does a piece of code executing in this monad find out what's in its environment? It simply has to `ask`:

```
-- file: ch15/SupplyInstance.hs
ask :: Reader e e
ask = R id
```

Within a given chain of actions, every invocation of `ask` will return the same value, since the value stored in the environment doesn't change. Our code is easy to test in `ghci`:

```
ghci> runReader (ask >>= \x -> return (x * 3)) 2
Loading package old-locale-1.0.0.0 ... linking ... done.
Loading package old-time-1.0.0.0 ... linking ... done.
Loading package random-1.0.0.0 ... linking ... done.
6
```

The `Reader` monad is included in the standard `mtl` library, which is usually bundled with GHC. You can find it in the `Control.Monad.Reader` module. The motivation for this monad may initially seem a little thin, because it is most often useful in complicated code. We'll often need to access a piece of configuration information deep in the bowels of a program; passing that information in as a normal parameter would require a painful restructuring of our code. By hiding this information in our monad's plumbing, intermediate functions that don't care about the configuration information don't need to see it.

The clearest motivation for the Reader monad will come in Chapter 18, when we discuss combining several monads to build a new monad. There, we'll see how to gain finer control over state, so that our code can modify some values via the State monad, while other values remain immutable, courtesy of the Reader monad.

A Return to Automated Deriving

Now that we know about the Reader monad, let's use it to create an instance of our MonadSupply typeclass. To keep our example simple, we'll violate the spirit of MonadSupply here: our next action will always return the same value, instead of always returning a different one.

It would be a bad idea to directly make the Reader type an instance of the MonadSupply class, because then *any* Reader could act as a MonadSupply. This would usually not make any sense.

Instead, we create a newtype based on Reader. The newtype hides the fact that we're using Reader internally. We must now make our type an instance of both of the typeclasses we care about. With the GeneralizedNewtypeDeriving extension enabled, GHC will do most of the hard work for us:

```
-- file: ch15/SupplyInstance.hs
newtype MySupply e a = MySupply { runMySupply :: Reader e a }
    deriving (Monad)

instance MonadSupply e (MySupply e) where
    next = MySupply $ do
             v <- ask
             return (Just v)

    -- more concise:
    -- next = MySupply (Just `liftM` ask)
```

Notice that we must make our type an instance of MonadSupply e, not MonadSupply. If we omit the type variable, the compiler will complain.

To try out our MySupply type, we'll first create a simple function that should work with any MonadSupply instance:

```
-- file: ch15/SupplyInstance.hs
xy :: (Num s, MonadSupply s m) => m s
xy = do
  Just x <- next
  Just y <- next
  return (x * y)
```

If we use this with our Supply monad and randomsIO function, we get a different answer every time, as we expect:

```
ghci> (fst . runSupply xy) `fmap` randomsIO
31552680085335616051042450476861213 54
ghci> (fst . runSupply xy) `fmap` randomsIO
17642207677028922600348220634 50517650
```

Because our MySupply monad has two layers of newtype wrapping, we can write a custom execution function for it to make it easier to use:

```
-- file: ch15/SupplyInstance.hs
runMS :: MySupply i a -> i -> a
runMS = runReader . runMySupply
```

When we apply our xy action using this execution function, we get the same answer every time. Our code remains the same, but because we are executing it in a different implementation of MonadSupply, its behavior has changed:

```
ghci> runMS xy 2
4
ghci> runMS xy 2
4
```

Like our MonadSupply typeclass and Supply monad, almost all of the common Haskell monads are built with a split between interface and implementation. For example, the get and put functions that we introduced as "belonging to" the State monad are actually methods of the MonadState typeclass; the State type is an instance of this class.

Similarly, the standard Reader monad is an instance of the MonadReader typeclass, which specifies the ask method.

While the separation of interface and implementation that we discussed is appealing for its architectural cleanliness, it has important practical applications that will become clearer later. When we start combining monads in Chapter 18, we will save a lot of effort through the use of GeneralizedNewtypeDeriving and typeclasses.

Hiding the IO Monad

The blessing and curse of the IO monad is that it is extremely powerful. If we believe that careful use of types helps us to avoid programming mistakes, then the IO monad should be a great source of unease. Because the IO monad imposes no restrictions on what we can do, it leaves us vulnerable to all kinds of accidents.

How can we tame its power? Let's say that we would like guarantee to ourselves that a piece of code can read and write files on the local filesystem, but it will not access the network. We can't use the plain IO monad, because it won't restrict us.

Using a newtype

Let's create a module that provides a small set of functionality for reading and writing files:

```
-- file: ch15/HandleIO.hs
{-# LANGUAGE GeneralizedNewtypeDeriving #-}

module HandleIO
    (
      HandleIO
    , Handle
    , IOMode(..)
    , runHandleIO
    , openFile
    , hClose
    , hPutStrLn
    ) where

import System.IO (Handle, IOMode(..))
import qualified System.IO
```

Our first approach to creating a restricted version of IO is to wrap it with a newtype:

```
-- file: ch15/HandleIO.hs
newtype HandleIO a = HandleIO { runHandleIO :: IO a }
    deriving (Monad)
```

We do the by now familiar trick of exporting the type constructor and the runHandleIO execution function from our module, but not the data constructor. This will prevent code running within the HandleIO monad from getting hold of the IO monad that it wraps.

All that remains is for us to wrap each of the actions that we want our monad to allow. This is a simple matter of wrapping each IO with a HandleIO data constructor:

```
-- file: ch15/HandleIO.hs
openFile :: FilePath -> IOMode -> HandleIO Handle
openFile path mode = HandleIO (System.IO.openFile path mode)

hClose :: Handle -> HandleIO ()
hClose = HandleIO . System.IO.hClose

hPutStrLn :: Handle -> String -> HandleIO ()
hPutStrLn h s = HandleIO (System.IO.hPutStrLn h s)
```

We can now use our restricted HandleIO monad to perform I/O:

```
-- file: ch15/HandleIO.hs
safeHello :: FilePath -> HandleIO ()
safeHello path = do
  h <- openFile path WriteMode
  hPutStrLn h "hello world"
  hClose h
```

To run this action, we use runHandleIO:

```
ghci> :load HandleIO
[1 of 1] Compiling HandleIO        ( HandleIO.hs, interpreted )
Ok, modules loaded: HandleIO.
ghci> runHandleIO (safeHello "hello_world_101.txt")
Loading package old-locale-1.0.0.0 ... linking ... done.
Loading package old-time-1.0.0.0 ... linking ... done.
Loading package filepath-1.1.0.0 ... linking ... done.
Loading package directory-1.0.0.1 ... linking ... done.
Loading package mtl-1.1.0.1 ... linking ... done.
ghci> :m +System.Directory
ghci> removeFile "hello_world_101.txt"
```

If we try to sequence an action that runs in the HandleIO monad with one that is not
permitted, the type system will forbid it:

```
ghci> runHandleIO (safeHello "goodbye" >> removeFile "goodbye")

<interactive>:1:36:
    Couldn't match expected type `HandleIO a'
           against inferred type `IO ()'
    In the second argument of `(>>)', namely `removeFile "goodbye"'
    In the first argument of `runHandleIO', namely
        `(safeHello "goodbye" >> removeFile "goodbye")'
    In the expression:
        runHandleIO (safeHello "goodbye" >> removeFile "goodbye")
```

Designing for Unexpected Uses

There's one small, but significant, problem with our HandleIO monad: it doesn't take
into account the possibility that we might occasionally need an escape hatch. If we
define a monad such as this, it is likely that we will occasionally need to perform an
I/O action that isn't allowed for by the design of our monad.

Our purpose in defining a monad like this is to make it easier for us to write solid code
in the common case, not to make corner cases impossible. Let's give ourselves a way out.

The Control.Monad.Trans module defines a "standard escape hatch," the MonadIO typeclass. This defines a single function, liftIO, which lets us embed an IO action in another
monad:

```
ghci> :m +Control.Monad.Trans
ghci> :info MonadIO
class (Monad m) => MonadIO m where liftIO :: IO a -> m a
    -- Defined in Control.Monad.Trans
instance MonadIO IO -- Defined in Control.Monad.Trans
```

Our implementation of this typeclass is trivial; we just wrap IO with our data
constructor:

```
-- file: ch15/HandleIO.hs
import Control.Monad.Trans (MonadIO(..))

instance MonadIO HandleIO where
    liftIO = HandleIO
```

With judicious use of liftIO, we can escape our shackles and invoke IO actions where necessary:

```
-- file: ch15/HandleIO.hs
tidyHello :: FilePath -> HandleIO ()
tidyHello path = do
  safeHello path
  liftIO (removeFile path)
```

Automatic derivation and MonadIO

We could have had the compiler automatically derive an instance of MonadIO for us by adding the typeclass to the deriving clause of HandleIO. In fact, in production code, this would be our usual strategy. We avoided that here simply to separate the presentation of the earlier material from that of MonadIO.

Using Typeclasses

The disadvantage of hiding IO in another monad is that we're still tied to a concrete implementation. If we want to swap HandleIO for some other monad, we must change the type of every action that uses HandleIO.

As an alternative, we can create a typeclass that specifies the interface we want from a monad that manipulates files:

```
-- file: ch15/MonadHandle.hs
{-# LANGUAGE FunctionalDependencies, MultiParamTypeClasses #-}

module MonadHandle (MonadHandle(..)) where

import System.IO (IOMode(..))

class Monad m => MonadHandle h m | m -> h where
    openFile :: FilePath -> IOMode -> m h
    hPutStr :: h -> String -> m ()
    hClose :: h -> m ()
    hGetContents :: h -> m String

    hPutStrLn :: h -> String -> m ()
    hPutStrLn h s = hPutStr h s >> hPutStr h "\n"
```

Here, we've chosen to abstract away both the type of the monad and the type of a file handle. To satisfy the type checker, we've added a functional dependency: for any instance of MonadHandle, there is exactly one handle type that we can use. When we make the IO monad an instance of this class, we use a regular Handle:

```
-- file: ch15/MonadHandleIO.hs
{-# LANGUAGE FunctionalDependencies, MultiParamTypeClasses #-}

import MonadHandle
import qualified System.IO
```

```
import System.IO (IOMode(..))
import Control.Monad.Trans (MonadIO(..), MonadTrans(..))
import System.Directory (removeFile)

import SafeHello

instance MonadHandle System.IO.Handle IO where
    openFile = System.IO.openFile
    hPutStr = System.IO.hPutStr
    hClose = System.IO.hClose
    hGetContents = System.IO.hGetContents
    hPutStrLn = System.IO.hPutStrLn
```

Because any MonadHandle must also be a Monad, we can write code that manipulates files using normal do notation, without caring what monad it will finally execute in:

```
-- file: ch15/SafeHello.hs
safeHello :: MonadHandle h m => FilePath -> m ()
safeHello path = do
  h <- openFile path WriteMode
  hPutStrLn h "hello world"
  hClose h
```

Because we made IO an instance of this typeclass, we can execute this action from ghci:

```
ghci> safeHello "hello to my fans in domestic surveillance"
Loading package old-locale-1.0.0.0 ... linking ... done.
Loading package old-time-1.0.0.0 ... linking ... done.
Loading package filepath-1.1.0.0 ... linking ... done.
Loading package directory-1.0.0.1 ... linking ... done.
Loading package mtl-1.1.0.1 ... linking ... done.
ghci> removeFile "hello to my fans in domestic surveillance"
```

The beauty of the typeclass approach is that we can swap one underlying monad for another without touching much code, as most of our code doesn't know or care about the implementation. For instance, we could replace IO with a monad that compresses files as it writes them out.

Defining a monad's interface through a typeclass has a further benefit. It lets another user hide our implementation in a newtype wrapper and automatically derive instances of just the typeclasses she wants to expose.

Isolation and Testing

In fact, because our safeHello function doesn't use the IO type, we can even use a monad that *can't* perform I/O. This allows us to test code that would normally have side effects in a completely pure, controlled environment.

To do this, we will create a monad that doesn't perform I/O but instead logs every file-related event for later processing:

```
-- file: ch15/WriterIO.hs
data Event = Open FilePath IOMode
```

```
                        | Put String String
                        | Close String
                        | GetContents String
                          deriving (Show)
```

Although we already developed a `Logger` type in "Using a New Monad: Show Your Work!" on page 331, here we'll use the standard, and more general, `Writer` monad. Like other `mtl` monads, the API provided by `Writer` is defined in a typeclass—in this case, `MonadWriter`. Its most useful method is `tell`, which logs a value:

```
ghci> :m +Control.Monad.Writer
ghci> :type tell
tell :: (MonadWriter w m) => w -> m ()
```

The values we log can be of any `Monoid` type. Since the list type is a `Monoid`, we'll log to a list of `Event`.

We could make `Writer [Event]` an instance of `MonadHandle`, but it's cheap, easy, and safer to make a special-purpose monad:

```
-- file: ch15/WriterIO.hs
newtype WriterIO a = W { runW :: Writer [Event] a }
    deriving (Monad, MonadWriter [Event])
```

Our execution function simply removes the `newtype` wrapper we added, and then calls the normal `Writer` monad's execution function:

```
-- file: ch15/WriterIO.hs
runWriterIO :: WriterIO a -> (a, [Event])
runWriterIO = runWriter . runW
```

When we try this code out in ghci, it gives us a log of the function's file activities:

```
ghci> :load WriterIO
[1 of 3] Compiling MonadHandle      ( MonadHandle.hs, interpreted )
[2 of 3] Compiling SafeHello        ( SafeHello.hs, interpreted )
[3 of 3] Compiling WriterIO         ( WriterIO.hs, interpreted )
Ok, modules loaded: MonadHandle, SafeHello, WriterIO.
ghci> runWriterIO (safeHello "foo")
((),[Open "foo" WriteMode,Put "foo" "hello world",Put "foo" "\n",Close "foo"])
```

The Writer Monad and Lists

The `Writer` monad uses the `Monoid`'s `mappend` function every time we use `tell`. Because `mappend` for lists is (`++`), lists are not a good practical choice for use with `Writer`: repeated appends are expensive. We used lists previously purely for simplicity.

In production code, if you want to use the `Writer` monad and you need list-like behavior, use a type with better append characteristics. One such type is the difference list, which we introduced in "Taking Advantage of Functions as Data" on page 317. You don't need to roll your own difference list implementation: a well-tuned library is available for download from Hackage, the Haskell package database. Alternatively, you can use the Seq type from the Data.Sequence module, which we introduced in "General-Purpose Sequences" on page 322.

Arbitrary I/O Revisited

If we use the typeclass approach to restricting IO, we may still want to retain the ability to perform arbitrary I/O actions. We might try adding MonadIO as a constraint on our typeclass:

```
-- file: ch15/MonadHandleIO.hs
class (MonadHandle h m, MonadIO m) => MonadHandleIO h m | m -> h

instance MonadHandleIO System.IO.Handle IO

tidierHello :: (MonadHandleIO h m) => FilePath -> m ()
tidierHello path = do
  safeHello path
  liftIO (removeFile path)
```

This approach has a problem, though: the added MonadIO constraint strips us of the ability to test our code in a pure environment, because we can no longer tell whether a test might have damaging side effects. The alternative is to move this constraint from the typeclass—where it "infects" all functions—to only those functions that really need to perform I/O:

```
-- file: ch15/MonadHandleIO.hs
tidyHello :: (MonadIO m, MonadHandle h m) => FilePath -> m ()
tidyHello path = do
  safeHello path
  liftIO (removeFile path)
```

We can use pure property tests on the functions that lack MonadIO constraints and traditional unit tests on the rest.

Unfortunately, we've substituted one problem for another: we can't invoke code with both MonadIO and MonadHandle constraints from code that has the MonadHandle constraint alone. If we find that somewhere deep in our MonadHandle-only code that we really need the MonadIO constraint, we must add it to all the code paths that lead to this point.

Allowing arbitrary I/O is risky, and it has a profound effect on how we develop and test our code. When we have to choose between being permissive on the one hand, and easier reasoning and testing on the other, we usually opt for the latter.

1. Using QuickCheck, write a test for an action in the MonadHandle monad, in order to see if it tries to write to a file handle that is not open. Try it out on safeHello.

2. Write an action that tries to write to a file handle that it has closed. Does your test catch this bug?

3. In a form-encoded string, the same key may appear several times, with or without values, e.g., key&key=1&key=2. What type might you use to represent the values associated with a key in this sort of string? Write a parser that correctly captures all of the information.

CHAPTER 16

Using Parsec

Parsing a file, or data of various types, is a common task for programmers. We already learned about Haskell's support for regular expressions back in "Regular Expressions in Haskell" on page 198. Regular expressions are nice for many tasks, but they rapidly become unwieldy, or cannot be used at all, when dealing with a complex data format. For instance, we cannot use regular expressions to parse source code from most programming languages.

Parsec is a useful parser combinator library, with which we combine small parsing functions to build more sophisticated parsers. Parsec provides some simple parsing functions, as well as functions to tie them all together. It should come as no surprise that this parser library for Haskell is built around the notion of functions.

It's helpful to know where Parsec fits compared to the tools used for parsing in other languages. Parsing is sometimes divided into two stages: lexical analysis (the domain of tools such as `flex`) and parsing itself (performed by programs such as `bison`). Parsec can perform both lexical analysis and parsing.

First Steps with Parsec: Simple CSV Parsing

Let's jump right in and write some code for parsing a CSV file. CSV files are often used as a plain-text representation of spreadsheets or databases. Each line is a record, and each field in the record is separated from the next by a comma. There are ways of dealing with fields that contain commas, but we won't worry about that now.

This first example is much longer than it really needs to be. We will soon introduce more Parsec features that will shrink the parser down to only four lines!

```
-- file: ch16/csv1.hs
import Text.ParserCombinators.Parsec

{- A CSV file contains 0 or more lines, each of which is terminated
   by the end-of-line character (eol). -}
csvFile :: GenParser Char st [[String]]
csvFile =
```

```
      do result <- many line
         eof
         return result

-- Each line contains 1 or more cells, separated by a comma
line :: GenParser Char st [String]
line =
    do result <- cells
       eol                     -- end of line
       return result

-- Build up a list of cells.  Try to parse the first cell, then figure out
-- what ends the cell.
cells :: GenParser Char st [String]
cells =
    do first <- cellContent
       next <- remainingCells
       return (first : next)

-- The cell either ends with a comma, indicating that 1 or more cells follow,
-- or it doesn't, indicating that we're at the end of the cells for this line
remainingCells :: GenParser Char st [String]
remainingCells =
    (char ',' >> cells)            -- Found comma?  More cells coming
    <|> (return [])                -- No comma?  Return [], no more cells

-- Each cell contains 0 or more characters, which must not be a comma or
-- EOL
cellContent :: GenParser Char st String
cellContent =
    many (noneOf ",\n")


-- The end of line character is \n
eol :: GenParser Char st Char
eol = char '\n'

parseCSV :: String -> Either ParseError [[String]]
parseCSV input = parse csvFile "(unknown)" input
```

Let's take a look at the code for this example. We didn't use many shortcuts here, so remember that this will get shorter and simpler!

We've built it from the top down, so our first function is csvFile. The type of this function is GenParser Char st [[String]]. This means that the type of the input is a sequence of characters, which is exactly what a Haskell string is, since String is the same as [Char]. It also means that we will return a value of type [[String]]: a list of a list of strings. The st can be ignored for now.

Parsec programmers often omit type declarations, since we write so many small functions. Haskell's type inference can figure it out. We've listed the types for the first example, here so you can get a better idea of what's going on. You can always use :t in ghci to inspect types as well.

The csvFile uses a do block. As this implies, Parsec is a monadic library: it defines its own special parsing monad,[*] GenParser.

We start by running many line. many is a function that takes a function as an argument. It tries to repeatedly parse the input using the function passed to it. It gathers up the results from all that repeated parsing and returns a list of them. So, here, we are storing the results of parsing all lines in result. Then we look for the end-of-file indicator, called eof. Finally, we return the result. So, a CSV file is made up of many lines, and then the end of file. We can often read out Parsec functions in plain English just like this.

Now we must answer the question: what is a line? We define the line function to do just that. Reading the function, we can see that a line consists of cells followed by the end-of-line character.

So what are cells? We defined them in the cells function. The cells of a line start with the content of the first cell, and then continue with the content of the remaining cells, if any. The result is simply the first cell and the remaining cells assembled into a list.

Let's skip over remainingCells for a minute and look at cellContent. A cell contains any number of characters, but each character must not be a comma or end-of-line character. The noneOf function matches one item, so long as it isn't in the list of items that we pass. So, saying many (noneOf ",\n") defines a cell the way we want it.

Back in remainingCells, we have the first example of a choice in Parsec. The choice operator is <|>. This operator behaves like this: it will try the parser on the left, and if it consumes no input,[†] it will try the parser on the right.

So, in remainingCells, our task is to come up with all the cells after the first. Recall that cellContent uses noneOf ",\n". So it will not consume the comma or end-of-line character from the input. If we see a comma after parsing a cell, it means that at least one more cell follows. Otherwise, we're done. So, our first choice in remainingCells is char ','. This parser simply matches the passed character in the input. If we find a comma, we want this function to return the remaining cells on the line. At this point, the "remaining cells" looks exactly like the start of the line, so we call cells recursively to parse them. If we don't find a comma, we return the empty list, signifying no remaining cells on the line.

Finally, we must define what the end-of-line indicator is. We set it to char '\n', which will suit our purposes fine for now.

At the very end of the program, we define a function parseCSV that takes a String and parses it as a CSV file. This function is just a shortcut that calls Parsec's parse function, filling in a few parameters. parse returns Either ParseError [[String]] for the CSV

---

[*] For more on monads, refer to Chapter 14.

[†] For information on dealing with choices that may consume some input before failing, see "Lookahead" on page 389.

file. If there is an error, the return value will be Left with the error; otherwise, it will be Right with the result.

Now that we understand this code, let's play with it a bit and see what it does:

```
ghci> :l csv1.hs
[1 of 1] Compiling Main             ( csv1.hs, interpreted )
Ok, modules loaded: Main.
ghci> parseCSV ""
Loading package parsec-2.1.0.1 ... linking ... done.
Right []
```

That makes sense—parsing the empty string returns an empty list. Let's try parsing a single cell:

```
ghci> parseCSV "hi"
Left "(unknown)" (line 1, column 3):
unexpected end of input
expecting "," or "\n"
```

Look at that. Recall how we defined that each line must end with the end-of-line character, and we didn't give it. Parsec's error message helpfully indicated the line number and column number of the problem, and even told us what it was expecting! Let's give it an end-of-line character and continue experimenting:

```
ghci> parseCSV "hi\n"
Right [["hi"]]
ghci> parseCSV "line1\nline2\nline3\n"
Right [["line1"],["line2"],["line3"]]
ghci> parseCSV "cell1,cell2,cell3\n"
Right [["cell1","cell2","cell3"]]
ghci> parseCSV "l1c1,l1c2\nl2c1,l2c2\n"
Right [["l1c1","l1c2"],["l2c1","l2c2"]]
ghci> parseCSV "Hi,\n\n,Hello\n"
Right [["Hi",""],[""],["","Hello"]]
```

You can see that parseCSV is doing exactly what we want it to do. It's even handling empty cells and empty lines properly.

The sepBy and endBy Combinators

We promised you earlier that we could simplify our CSV parser significantly by using a few Parsec helper functions. There are two that will dramatically simplify this code.

The first tool is the sepBy function. This function takes two functions as arguments: the first parses some sort of content, while the second parses a separator. sepBy starts by trying to parse content, and then separators, and alternates back and forth until it can't parse a separator. It returns a list of all the content that it was able to parse.

The second tool is endBy. It's similar to sepBy, but expects the very last item to be followed by the separator. That is, it continues parsing until it can't parse any more content.

So, we can use endBy to parse lines, since every line must end with the end-of-line character. We can use sepBy to parse cells, since the last cell will not end with a comma. Take a look at how much simpler our parser is now:

```
-- file: ch16/csv2.hs
import Text.ParserCombinators.Parsec

csvFile = endBy line eol
line = sepBy cell (char ',')
cell = many (noneOf ",\n")
eol = char '\n'

parseCSV :: String -> Either ParseError [[String]]
parseCSV input = parse csvFile "(unknown)" input
```

This program behaves exactly the same as the first one. We can verify this by using ghci to rerun our examples from the earlier example. We'll get the same result from every one. Yet the program is much shorter and more readable. It won't be long before you can translate Parsec code such as this into a file format definition in plain English. As you read over this code, you can see that:

- A CSV file contains zero or more lines, each of which is terminated by the end-of-line character.
- A line contains one or more cells, separated by a comma.
- A cell contains zero or more characters, which must be neither the comma nor the end-of-line character.
- The end-of-line character is the newline, \n.

Choices and Errors

Different operating systems use different characters to mark the end of line. Unix/Linux systems, and Windows in text mode, use simply "\n". DOS and Windows systems use "\r\n", and Macs traditionally use "\r". We could add support for "\n\r" too, just in case anybody uses that.

We could easily adapt our example to be able to handle all these types of line endings in a single file. We would need to make two modifications: adjust eol to recognize the different endings, and adjust the noneOf pattern in cell to ignore \r.

This must be done carefully. Recall that our earlier definition of eol was simply char '\n'. There is a parser called string that we can use to match the multicharacter patterns. Let's start by thinking of how we would add support for \n\r.

Our first attempt might look like this:

```
-- file: ch16/csv3.hs
-- This function is not correct!
eol = string "\n" <|> string "\n\r"
```

This isn't quite right. Recall that the <|> operator always tries the left alternative first. Looking for the single character \n will match both types of line endings, so it will look to the system that the following line begins with \r. Not what we want. Try it in ghci:

```
ghci> :m Text.ParserCombinators.Parsec
ghci> let eol = string "\n" <|> string "\n\r"
Loading package parsec-2.1.0.1 ... linking ... done.
ghci> parse eol "" "\n"
Right "\n"
ghci> parse eol "" "\n\r"
Right "\n"
```

It may seem like the parser worked for both endings, but actually looking at it this way, we can't tell. If it left something unparsed, we don't know, because we're not trying to consume anything else from the input. So let's look for the end of file after our end of line:

```
ghci> parse (eol >> eof) "" "\n\r"
Left (line 2, column 1):
unexpected "\r"
expecting end of input
ghci> parse (eol >> eof) "" "\n"
Right ()
```

As expected, we got an error from the \n\r ending. So the next temptation may be to try it this way:

```
-- file: ch16/csv4.hs
-- This function is not correct!
eol = string "\n\r" <|> string "\n"
```

This also isn't right. Recall that <|> attempts the option on the right only if the option on the left consumes no input. But by the time we are able to see if there is a \r after the \n, we've already consumed the \n. This time, we fail on the other case in ghci:

```
ghci> :m Text.ParserCombinators.Parsec
ghci> let eol = string "\n\r" <|> string "\n"
Loading package parsec-2.1.0.1 ... linking ... done.
ghci> parse (eol >> eof) "" "\n\r"
Right ()
ghci> parse (eol >> eof) "" "\n"
Left (line 1, column 1):
unexpected end of input
expecting "\n\r"
```

We've stumbled upon the lookahead problem. It turns out that, when writing parsers, it's often very convenient to be able to "look ahead" at the data that's coming in. Parsec supports this, but before showing you how to use it, let's see how you would have to write this to get along without it. You'd have to manually expand all the options after the \n like this:

```
-- file: ch16/csv5.hs
eol =
    do char '\n'
       char '\r' <|> return '\n'
```

This function first looks for \n. If it finds it, then it will look for \r, consuming it if possible. Since the return type of char '\r' is a Char, the alternative action is to simply return a Char without attempting to parse anything. Parsec has a function option that can also express this idiom as option '\n' (char '\r'). Let's test this with ghci:

```
ghci> :l csv5.hs
[1 of 1] Compiling Main             ( csv5.hs, interpreted )
Ok, modules loaded: Main.
ghci> parse (eol >> eof) "" "\n\r"
Loading package parsec-2.1.0.1 ... linking ... done.
Right ()
ghci> parse (eol >> eof) "" "\n"
Right ()
```

This time, we got the right result! But we could have done it easier with Parsec's look-ahead support.

Lookahead

Parsec has a function called try that is used to express lookaheads. try takes one function, a parser, and applies it. If the parser doesn't succeed, try behaves as if it hadn't consumed any input at all. So, when you use try on the left side of <|>, Parsec will try the option on the right even if the left side failed after consuming some input. try has an effect only if it is on the left of a <|>. Keep in mind, though, that many functions use <|> internally. Here's a way to add expanded end-of-line support to our CSV parser using try:

```
-- file: ch16/csv6.hs
import Text.ParserCombinators.Parsec

csvFile = endBy line eol
line = sepBy cell (char ',')
cell = many (noneOf ",\n\r")

eol =   try (string "\n\r")
    <|> try (string "\r\n")
    <|> string "\n"
    <|> string "\r"

parseCSV :: String -> Either ParseError [[String]]
parseCSV input = parse csvFile "(unknown)" input
```

Here we put both of the two-character endings first, and run both tests under try. Both of them occur to the left of a <|>, so they will do the right thing. We could have put string "\n" within a try, but it wouldn't have altered any behavior since they look at only one character anyway. We can load this up and test the eol function in ghci:

```
ghci> :l csv6.hs
[1 of 1] Compiling Main             ( csv6.hs, interpreted )
Ok, modules loaded: Main.
ghci> parse (eol >> eof) "" "\n\r"
Loading package parsec-2.1.0.1 ... linking ... done.
```

```
Right ()
ghci> parse (eol >> eof) "" "\n"
Right ()
ghci> parse (eol >> eof) "" "\r\n"
Right ()
ghci> parse (eol >> eof) "" "\r"
Right ()
```

All four endings were handled properly. You can also test the full CSV parser with some different endings like this:

```
ghci> parseCSV "line1\r\nline2\nline3\n\rline4\rline5\n"
Right [["line1"],["line2"],["line3"],["line4"],["line5"]]
```

As you can see, this program even supports different line endings within a single file.

Error Handling

At the beginning of this chapter, you saw how Parsec could generate error messages that list the location where the error occurred as well as what was expected. As parsers get more complex, the list of what was expected can become cumbersome. Parsec provides a way for you to specify custom error messages in the event of parse failures.

Let's look at what happens when our current CSV parser encounters an error:

```
ghci> parseCSV "line1"
Left "(unknown)" (line 1, column 6):
unexpected end of input
expecting ",", "\n\r", "\r\n", "\n" or "\r"
```

That's a pretty long, and technical, error message. We could make an attempt to resolve this using the monad `fail` function, like so:

```
-- file: ch16/csv7.hs
eol =    try (string "\n\r")
     <|> try (string "\r\n")
     <|> string "\n"
     <|> string "\r"
     <|> fail "Couldn't find EOL"
```

Under ghci, we can see the result:

```
ghci> :l csv7.hs
[1 of 1] Compiling Main             ( csv7.hs, interpreted )
Ok, modules loaded: Main.
ghci> parseCSV "line1"
Loading package parsec-2.1.0.1 ... linking ... done.
Left "(unknown)" (line 1, column 6):
unexpected end of input
expecting ",", "\n\r", "\r\n", "\n" or "\r"
Couldn't find EOL
```

We added to the error result but didn't really help clean up the output. Parsec has an `<?>` operator that is designed for just these situations. It is similar to `<|>` in that it first tries the parser on its left. Instead of trying another parser in the event of a failure, it presents an error message. Here's how we'd use it:

```
-- file: ch16/csv8.hs
eol =   try (string "\n\r")
    <|> try (string "\r\n")
    <|> string "\n"
    <|> string "\r"
    <?> "end of line"
```

Now, when you generate an error, you'll get more helpful output:

```
ghci> :l csv8.hs
[1 of 1] Compiling Main              ( csv8.hs, interpreted )
Ok, modules loaded: Main.
ghci> parseCSV "line1"
Loading package parsec-2.1.0.1 ... linking ... done.
Left "(unknown)" (line 1, column 6):
unexpected end of input
expecting "," or end of line
```

That's pretty helpful! The general rule of thumb is that you put a human description of what you're looking for to the right of <?>.

Extended Example: Full CSV Parser

Our earlier CSV examples have had an important flaw—they weren't able to handle cells that contain a comma. CSV generating programs typically put quotation marks around such data. But then you have another problem: what to do if a cell contains a quotation mark and a comma. In these cases, the embedded quotation marks are doubled up.

Here is a full CSV parser. You can use this from ghci, or if you compile it to a standalone program, it will parse a CSV file on standard input and convert it to a different format on output:

```
-- file: ch16/csv9.hs
import Text.ParserCombinators.Parsec

csvFile = endBy line eol
line = sepBy cell (char ',')
cell = quotedCell <|> many (noneOf ",\n\r")

quotedCell =
    do char '"'
        content <- many quotedChar
        char '"' <?> "quote at end of cell"
        return content

quotedChar =
        noneOf "\""
    <|> try (string "\"\"" >> return '"')
```

```
eol =   try (string "\n\r")
    <|> try (string "\r\n")
    <|> string "\n"
    <|> string "\r"
    <?> "end of line"

parseCSV :: String -> Either ParseError [[String]]
parseCSV input = parse csvFile "(unknown)" input

main =
    do c <- getContents
       case parse csvFile "(stdin)" c of
            Left e -> do putStrLn "Error parsing input:"
                         print e
            Right r -> mapM_ print r
```

That's a full-featured CSV parser in just 21 lines of code, plus an additional 10 lines for the parseCSV and main utility functions.

Let's look at the changes in this program from the previous versions. First, a cell may now be either a bare cell or a *quoted* cell. We give the quotedCell option first, because we want to follow that path if the first character in a cell is the quote mark.

The quotedCell begins and ends with a quote mark and contains zero or more characters. These characters can't be copied directly, though, because they may contain embedded, doubled-up quote marks themselves, so we define a custom quotedChar to process them.

When we're processing characters inside a quoted cell, we first say noneOf "\"". This will match and return any single character as long as it's not the quote mark. Otherwise, if it is the quote mark, we see if we have two in a row. If so, we return a single quote mark to go on our result string.

Notice that try in quotedChar is on the *right* side of <|>. Recall that we said that try has an effect only if it is on the left side of <|>. This try does occur on the left side of a <|>, but on the left of one that must be within the implementation of many.

This try is important. Let's say we are parsing a quoted cell and are getting towards the end of it. There will be another cell following. So we will expect to see a quote to end the current cell, followed by a comma. When we hit quotedChar, we will fail the noneOf test and proceed to the test that looks for two quotes in a row. We'll also fail that one because we'll have a quote, and then a comma. If we hadn't used try, we'd crash with an error at this point, saying that it was expecting the second quote, because the first quote was already consumed. Since we use try, this is properly recognized as not part of the cell, so it terminates the many quotedChar expression as expected. Lookahead has once again proven very useful, and the fact that it is so easy to add makes it a remarkable tool in Parsec.

We can test this program with ghci over some quoted cells:

```
ghci> :l csv9.hs
[1 of 1] Compiling Main             ( csv9.hs, interpreted )
Ok, modules loaded: Main.
ghci> parseCSV "\"This, is, one, big, cell\"\n"
Loading package parsec-2.1.0.1 ... linking ... done.
Right [["This, is, one, big, cell"]]
ghci> parseCSV "\"Cell without an end\n"
Left "(unknown)" (line 2, column 1):
unexpected end of input
expecting "\"\"" or quote at end of cell
```

Let's run it over a real CSV file. Here's one generated by a spreadsheet program:

```
"Product","Price"
"O'Reilly Socks",10
"Shirt with ""Haskell"" text",20
"Shirt, ""O'Reilly"" version",20
"Haskell Caps",15
```

Now, we can run this under our test program and watch:

```
$ runhaskell csv9.hs < test.csv
["Product","Price"]
["O'Reilly Socks","10"]
["Shirt with \"Haskell\" text","20"]
["Shirt, \"O'Reilly\" version","20"]
["Haskell Caps","15"]
```

Parsec and MonadPlus

Parsec's `GenParser` monad is an instance of the `MonadPlus` typeclass that we introduced in "Looking for Alternatives" on page 362. The value `mzero` represents a parse failure, while `mplus` combines two alternative parses into one, using (`<|>`):

```
-- file: ch16/ParsecPlus.hs
instance MonadPlus (GenParser tok st) where
    mzero = fail "mzero"
    mplus = (<|>)
```

Parsing a URL-Encoded Query String

When we introduced application/x-www-form-urlencoded text in "Golfing Practice: Association Lists" on page 359, we mentioned that we'd write a parser for these strings. We can quickly and easily do this using Parsec.

Each key-value pair is separated by the & character:

```
-- file: ch16/FormParse.hs
p_query :: CharParser () [(String, Maybe String)]
p_query = p_pair `sepBy` char '&'
```

Notice that in the type signature, we're using `Maybe` to represent a value: the HTTP specification is unclear about whether a key *must* have an associated value, and we'd like to be able to distinguish between "no value" and "empty value":

```
-- file: ch16/FormParse.hs
p_pair :: CharParser () (String, Maybe String)
p_pair = do
  name <- many1 p_char
  value <- optionMaybe (char '=' >> many p_char)
  return (name, value)
```

The `many1` function is similar to `many`: it applies its parser repeatedly, returning a list of results. While `many` will succeed and return an empty list if its parser never succeeds, `many1` will fail if its parser never succeeds and will otherwise return a list of at least one element.

The `optionMaybe` function modifies the behavior of a parser. If the parser fails, `optionMaybe` doesn't: it returns `Nothing`. Otherwise, it wraps the parser's successful result with `Just`. This gives us the ability to distinguish between "no value" and "empty value," as we mentioned earlier.

Individual characters can be encoded in one of several ways:

```
-- file: ch16/FormParse.hs
p_char :: CharParser () Char
p_char = oneOf urlBaseChars
      <|> (char '+' >> return ' ')
      <|> p_hex

urlBaseChars = ['a'..'z']++['A'..'Z']++['0'..'9']++"$-_.!*'(),"

p_hex :: CharParser () Char
p_hex = do
  char '%'
  a <- hexDigit
  b <- hexDigit
  let ((d, _):_) = readHex [a,b]
  return . toEnum $ d
```

Some characters can be represented literally. Spaces are treated specially, using a + character. Other characters must be encoded as a % character followed by two hexadecimal digits. The `Numeric` module's `readHex` parses a hex string as a number:

```
ghci> parseTest p_query "foo=bar&a%21=b+c"
Loading package parsec-2.1.0.1 ... linking ... done.
[("foo",Just "bar"),("a!",Just "b c")]
```

As appealing and readable as this parser is, we can profit from stepping back and taking another look at some of our building blocks.

Supplanting Regular Expressions for Casual Parsing

In many popular languages, people tend to put regular expressions to work for "casual" parsing. They're notoriously tricky for this purpose: hard to write, difficult to debug, nearly incomprehensible after a few months of neglect, and they provide no error messages on failure.

If we can write compact Parsec parsers, we'll gain in readability, expressiveness, and error reporting. Our parsers won't be as short as regular expressions, but they'll be close enough to negate much of the temptation of regexps.

Parsing Without Variables

A few of our parsers just shown use do notation and bind the result of an intermediate parse to a variable for later use. One such function is p_pair:

```
-- file: ch16/FormParse.hs
p_pair :: CharParser () (String, Maybe String)
p_pair = do
  name <- many1 p_char
  value <- optionMaybe (char '=' >> many p_char)
  return (name, value)
```

We can get rid of the need for explicit variables by using the liftM2 combinator from Control.Monad:

```
-- file: ch16/FormParse.hs
p_pair_app1 =
    liftM2 (,) (many1 p_char) (optionMaybe (char '=' >> many p_char))
```

This parser has exactly the same type and behavior as p_pair, but it's one line long. Instead of writing our parser in a "procedural" style, we've simply switched to a programming style that emphasizes that we're *applying* parsers and *combining* their results.

We can take this applicative style of writing a parser much further. In most cases, the extra compactness that we will gain will *not* come at any cost in readability, beyond the initial effort of coming to grips with the idea.

Applicative Functors for Parsing

The standard Haskell libraries include a module named Control.Applicative, which we already encountered in "Infix Use of fmap" on page 248. This module defines a typeclass named Applicative, which represents an *applicative functor*. This is a little bit more structured than a functor, but a little bit less than a monad. It also defines Alternative, which is similar to MonadPlus.

As usual, we think that the best way to introduce applicative functors is to put them to work. In theory, every monad is an applicative functor, but not every applicative functor is a monad. Because applicative functors were added to the standard Haskell libraries long after monads, we often don't get an `Applicative` instance for free; frequently, we have to declare the monad we're using to be `Applicative` or `Alternative`.

To do this for `Parsec`, we'll write a small module that we can import instead of the normal `Parsec` module:

```
-- file: ch16/ApplicativeParsec.hs
module ApplicativeParsec
    (
      module Control.Applicative
    , module Text.ParserCombinators.Parsec
    ) where

import Control.Applicative
import Control.Monad (MonadPlus(..), ap)
-- Hide a few names that are provided by Applicative.
import Text.ParserCombinators.Parsec hiding (many, optional, (<|>))

-- The Applicative instance for every Monad looks like this.
instance Applicative (GenParser s a) where
    pure  = return
    (<*>) = ap

-- The Alternative instance for every MonadPlus looks like this.
instance Alternative (GenParser s a) where
    empty = mzero
    (<|>) = mplus
```

For convenience, our module's export section exports all the names we imported from both the `Applicative` and `Parsec` modules. Because we hid Parsec's version of (<|>) when importing, the one that will be exported is from `Control.Applicative`—as we would like.

Applicative Parsing by Example

We'll start by rewriting our existing form parser from the bottom up, beginning with p_hex, which parses a hexadecimal escape sequence. Here's the code in normal do-notation style:

```
-- file: ch16/FormApp.hs
p_hex :: CharParser () Char
p_hex = do
  char '%'
  a <- hexDigit
  b <- hexDigit
  let ((d, _):_) = readHex [a,b]
  return . toEnum $ d
```

And here's our applicative version:

```
-- file: ch16/FormApp.hs
a_hex = hexify <$> (char '%' *> hexDigit) <*> hexDigit
    where hexify a b = toEnum . fst . head . readHex $ [a,b]
```

Although the individual parsers are mostly untouched, the combinators that we're gluing them together with have changed. The only familiar one is (<$>), which we already know is a synonym for fmap.

From our definition of Applicative, we know that (<*>) is ap.

The remaining unfamiliar combinator is (*>), which applies its first argument, throws away its result, and then applies the second and returns its result. In other words, it's similar to (>>).

A handy tip about angle brackets

Before we continue, here's a useful aid for remembering what all the angle brackets are for in the combinators from Control.Applicative: if there's an angle bracket pointing to a side, the result from that side should be used.

For example, (*>) returns the result on its right; (<*>) returns results from both sides; and (<*)—which we have not seen yet—returns the result on its left.

Although the concepts here should mostly be familiar from our earlier coverage of functors and monads, we'll walk through this function to explain what's happening. First, to get a grip on our types, we'll hoist hexify to the top level and give it a signature:

```
-- file: ch16/FormApp.hs
hexify :: Char -> Char -> Char
hexify a b = toEnum . fst . head . readHex $ [a,b]
```

Parsec's hexDigit parser parses a single hexadecimal digit:

```
ghci> :type hexDigit
hexDigit :: CharParser st Char
```

Therefore, char '%' *> hexDigit has the same type, since (*>) returns the result on its right. (The CharParser type is nothing more than a synonym for GenParser Char.)

```
ghci> :type char '%' *> hexDigit
char '%' *> hexDigit :: GenParser Char st Char
```

The expression hexify <$> (char '%' *> hexDigit) is a parser that matches a % character followed by hexDigit, and whose result is a function:

```
ghci> :type hexify <$> (char '%' *> hexDigit)
hexify <$> (char '%' *> hexDigit) :: GenParser Char st (Char -> Char)
```

Finally, (<*>) applies the parser on its left, and then the parser on its right, and then applies the function that's the result of the left parse to the value that's the result of the right.

If you've been able to follow this, you understand the (<*>) and ap combinators—(<*>) is plain old ($) lifted to applicative functors, and ap is the same thing lifted to monads:

```
ghci> :type ($)
($) :: (a -> b) -> a -> b
ghci> :type (<*>)
(<*>) :: (Applicative f) => f (a -> b) -> f a -> f b
ghci> :type ap
ap :: (Monad m) => m (a -> b) -> m a -> m b
```

Next, we'll consider the p_char parser:

```
-- file: ch16/FormApp.hs
p_char :: CharParser () Char
p_char = oneOf urlBaseChars
     <|> (char '+' >> return ' ')
     <|> p_hex

urlBaseChars = ['a'..'z']++['A'..'Z']++['0'..'9']++"$-_.!*'(),"
```

This remains almost the same in an applicative style, save for one piece of convenient notation:

```
-- file: ch16/FormApp.hs
a_char = oneOf urlBaseChars
     <|> (' ' <$ char '+')
     <|> a_hex
```

Here, the (<$) combinator uses the value on the left if the parser on the right succeeds.

Finally, the equivalent of p_pair_app1 is almost identical:

```
-- file: ch16/FormParse.hs
p_pair_app1 =
    liftM2 (,) (many1 p_char) (optionMaybe (char '=' >> many p_char))
```

All we've changed is the combinator we use for lifting—the liftA functions act in the same way as their liftM cousins:

```
-- file: ch16/FormApp.hs
a_pair :: CharParser () (String, Maybe String)
a_pair = liftA2 (,) (many1 a_char) (optionMaybe (char '=' *> many a_char))
```

Parsing JSON Data

To give ourselves a better feel for parsing with applicative functors, and to explore a few more corners of Parsec, we'll write a JSON parser that follows the definition in RFC 4627.

At the top level, a JSON value must be either an object or an array:

```
-- file: ch16/JSONParsec.hs
p_text :: CharParser () JValue
p_text = spaces *> text
     <?> "JSON text"
```

```
            where text = JObject <$> p_object
                      <|> JArray <$> p_array
```

These are structurally similar, with an opening character, followed by one or more items separated by commas, followed by a closing character. We capture this similarity by writing a small helper function:

```
-- file: ch16/JSONParsec.hs
p_series :: Char -> CharParser () a -> Char -> CharParser () [a]
p_series left parser right =
    between (char left <* spaces) (char right) $
            (parser <* spaces) `sepBy` (char ',' <* spaces)
```

Here, we finally have a use for the (<*) combinator that we introduced earlier. We use it to skip over any whitespace that might follow certain tokens. With this p_series function, parsing an array is simple:

```
-- file: ch16/JSONParsec.hs
p_array :: CharParser () (JAry JValue)
p_array = JAry <$> p_series '[' p_value ']'
```

Dealing with a JSON object is hardly more complicated, requiring just a little additional effort to produce a name/value pair for each of the object's fields:

```
-- file: ch16/JSONParsec.hs
p_object :: CharParser () (JObj JValue)
p_object = JObj <$> p_series '{' p_field '}'
    where p_field = (,) <$> (p_string <* char ':' <* spaces) <*> p_value
```

Parsing an individual value is a matter of calling an existing parser, and then wrapping its result with the appropriate JValue constructor:

```
-- file: ch16/JSONParsec.hs
p_value :: CharParser () JValue
p_value = value <* spaces
  where value = JString <$> p_string
            <|> JNumber <$> p_number
            <|> JObject <$> p_object
            <|> JArray <$> p_array
            <|> JBool <$> p_bool
            <|> JNull <$ string "null"
            <?> "JSON value"

p_bool :: CharParser () Bool
p_bool = True <$ string "true"
     <|> False <$ string "false"
```

The choice combinator allows us to represent this kind of ladder-of-alternatives as a list. It returns the result of the first parser to succeed:

```
-- file: ch16/JSONParsec.hs
p_value_choice = value <* spaces
  where value = choice [ JString <$> p_string
                       , JNumber <$> p_number
                       , JObject <$> p_object
                       , JArray <$> p_array
```

```
                    , JBool <$> p_bool
                    , JNull <$ string "null"
                    ]
              <?> "JSON value"
```

This leads us to the two most interesting parsers, for numbers and strings. We'll deal with numbers first, since they're simpler:

```
-- file: ch16/JSONParsec.hs
p_number :: CharParser () Double
p_number = do s <- getInput
              case readSigned readFloat s of
                [(n, s')] -> n <$ setInput s'
                _         -> empty
```

Our trick here is to take advantage of Haskell's standard number parsing library functions, which are defined in the `Numeric` module. The `readFloat` function reads an unsigned floating-point number; `readSigned` takes a parser for an unsigned number and turns it into a parser for possibly signed numbers.

Since these functions know nothing about Parsec, we have to work with them specially. Parsec's `getInput` function gives us direct access to Parsec's unconsumed input stream. If `readSigned readFloat` succeeds, it returns both the parsed number and the rest of the unparsed input. We then use `setInput` to give this back to Parsec as its new unconsumed input stream.

Parsing a string isn't difficult, merely detailed:

```
-- file: ch16/JSONParsec.hs
p_string :: CharParser () String
p_string = between (char '"') (char '"') (many jchar)
    where jchar = char '\\' *> (p_escape <|> p_unicode)
              <|> satisfy (`notElem` "\"\\")
```

We can parse and decode an escape sequence with the help of the `choice` combinator that we just met:

```
-- file: ch16/JSONParsec.hs
p_escape = choice (zipWith decode "bnfrt\\\"/" "\b\n\f\r\t\\\"/")
    where decode c r = r <$ char c
```

Finally, JSON lets us encode a Unicode character in a string as \u, followed by four hexadecimal digits:

```
-- file: ch16/JSONParsec.hs
p_unicode :: CharParser () Char
p_unicode = char 'u' *> (decode <$> count 4 hexDigit)
    where decode x = toEnum code
              where ((code,_):_) = readHex x
```

The only piece of functionality that applicative functors are missing, compared to monads, is the ability to bind a value to a variable, which we need here in order to be able to validate the value we're trying to decode.

This is the one place in our parser that we've needed to use a monadic function. This pattern extends to more complicated parsers, too—only infrequently do we need the extra bit of power that monads offer.

As of this writing, applicative functors are still quite new to Haskell, and people are only beginning to explore the possible uses for them beyond the realm of parsing.

Parsing a HTTP Request

As another example of applicative parsing, we will develop a basic parser for HTTP requests:

```
-- file: ch16/HttpRequestParser.hs
module HttpRequestParser
    (
      HttpRequest(..)
    , Method(..)
    , p_request
    , p_query
    ) where

import ApplicativeParsec
import Numeric (readHex)
import Control.Monad (liftM4)
import System.IO (Handle)
```

An HTTP request consists of a method, an identifier, a series of headers, and an optional body. For simplicity, we'll focus on just two of the six method types specified by the HTTP 1.1 standard. A POST method has a body; a GET has none:

```
-- file: ch16/HttpRequestParser.hs
data Method = Get | Post
          deriving (Eq, Ord, Show)

data HttpRequest = HttpRequest {
      reqMethod :: Method
    , reqURL :: String
    , reqHeaders :: [(String, String)]
    , reqBody :: Maybe String
    } deriving (Eq, Show)
```

Because we're writing in an applicative style, our parser can be both brief and readable. Readable, that is, if you're becoming used to the applicative parsing notation:

```
-- file: ch16/HttpRequestParser.hs
p_request :: CharParser () HttpRequest
p_request = q "GET" Get (pure Nothing)
        <|> q "POST" Post (Just <$> many anyChar)
  where q name ctor body = liftM4 HttpRequest req url p_headers body
          where req = ctor <$ string name <* char ' '
        url = optional (char '/') *>
              manyTill notEOL (try $ string " HTTP/1." <* oneOf "01")
              <* crlf
```

Briefly, the q helper function accepts a method name, the type constructor to apply to it, and a parser for a request's optional body. The url helper does not attempt to validate a URL, because the HTTP specification does not state what characters a URL contain. The function just consumes input until either the line ends or it reaches an HTTP version identifier.

Backtracking and Its Discontents

The try combinator has to hold onto input in case it needs to restore it so that an alternative parser can be used. This practice is referred to as *backtracking*. Because try must save input, it is expensive to use. Sprinkling a parser with unnecessary uses of try is a very effective way to slow it down, sometimes to the point of unacceptable performance.

The standard way to avoid the need for backtracking is to tidy up a parser so that we can decide whether it will succeed or fail using only a single token of input. In this case, the two parsers consume the same initial tokens, so we turn them into a single parser:

```
ghci> let parser = (++) <$> string "HT" <*> (string "TP" <|> string "ML")
ghci> parseTest parser "HTTP"
"HTTP"
ghci> parseTest parser "HTML"
"HTML"
```

Even better, Parsec gives us an improved error message if we feed it nonmatching input:

```
ghci> parseTest parser "HTXY"
parse error at (line 1, column 3):
unexpected "X"
expecting "TP" or "ML"
```

Parsing Headers

Following the first line of a HTTP request is a series of zero or more headers. A header begins with a field name, followed by a colon, followed by the content. If the lines that follow begin with spaces, they are treated as *continuations* of the current content:

```
-- file: ch16/HttpRequestParser.hs
p_headers :: CharParser st [(String, String)]
p_headers = header `manyTill` crlf
  where header = liftA2 (,) fieldName (char ':' *> spaces *> contents)
        contents = liftA2 (++) (many1 notEOL <* crlf)
                               (continuation <|> pure [])
        continuation = liftA2 (:) (' ' <$ many1 (oneOf " \t")) contents
        fieldName = (:) <$> letter <*> many fieldChar
        fieldChar = letter <|> digit <|> oneOf "-_"

crlf :: CharParser st ()
crlf = (() <$ string "\r\n") <|> (() <$ newline)
```

```
notEOL :: CharParser st Char
notEOL = noneOf "\r\n"
```

EXERCISES

1. Our HTTP request parser is too simple to be useful in real deployments. It is missing vital functionality and is not resistant to even the most basic denial-of-service attacks.

   Make the parser honor the `Content-Length` field properly, if it is present.

2. A popular denial-of-service attack against naive web servers is simply to send unreasonably long headers. A single header might contain 10s or 100s of megabytes of garbage text, causing a server to run out of memory.

   Restructure the header parser so that it will fail if any line is longer than 4,096 characters. It must fail immediately when this occurs; it cannot wait until the end of a line eventually shows up.

3. Add the ability to honor the `Transfer-Encoding: chunked` header if it is present. See section 3.6.1 of RFC 2616 (*http://www.w3.org/Protocols/rfc2616/rfc2616-sec3 .html#sec3.6.1*) for details.

4. Another popular attack is to open a connection and either leave it idle or send data extremely slowly.

   Write a wrapper in the `IO` monad that will invoke the parser. Use the `System.Timeout` module to close the connection if the parser does not complete within 30 seconds.

CHAPTER 17

Interfacing with C: The FFI

Programming languages do not exist in perfect isolation. They inhabit an ecosystem of tools and libraries, built up over decades, and often written in a range of programming languages. Good engineering practice suggests we reuse that effort. The *Haskell Foreign Function Interface* (the FFI) is the means by which Haskell code can use, and be used by, code written in other languages. In this chapter, we'll look at how the FFI works and how to produce a Haskell binding to a C library, including how to use an FFI preprocessor to automate much of the work. The challenge: take PCRE, the standard Perl-compatible regular expression library, and make it usable from Haskell in an efficient and functional way. Throughout, we'll seek to abstract out manual effort required by the C implementation, delegating that work to Haskell to make the interface more robust, yielding a clean, high-level binding. We assume only some basic familiarity with regular expressions.

Binding one language to another is a nontrivial task. The binding language needs to understand the calling conventions, type system, data structures, memory allocation mechanisms, and linking strategy of the target language, just to get things working. The task is to carefully align the semantics of both languages so that both can understand the data that passes between them.

For Haskell, this technology stack is specified by FFI (*http://www.cse.unsw.edu.au/~chak/haskell/ffi/*) to the Haskell report. The FFI report describes how to correctly bind Haskell and C together and how to extend bindings to other languages. The standard is designed to be portable so that FFI bindings will work reliably across Haskell implementations, operating systems, and C compilers.

All implementations of Haskell support the FFI, and it is a key technology when using Haskell in a new field. Instead of reimplementing the standard libraries in a domain, we just bind to existing ones written in languages other than Haskell.

The FFI adds a new dimension of flexibility to the language: if we need to access raw hardware for some reason (say we're programming new hardware or implementing an operating system), the FFI lets us get access to that hardware. It also gives us a performance escape hatch: if we can't get a code hot spot fast enough, there's always the option of trying again in C. So let's look at what the FFI actually means for writing code.

Foreign Language Bindings: The Basics

The most common operation we'll want to do, unsurprisingly, is call a C function from Haskell. So let's do that, by binding to some functions from the standard C math library. We'll put the binding in a source file, and then compile it into a Haskell binary that makes use of the C code.

To start with, we need to enable the FFI extension, as the FFI addendum support isn't enabled by default. We do this, as always, via a LANGUAGE pragma at the top of our source file:

```
-- file: ch17/SimpleFFI.hs
{-# LANGUAGE ForeignFunctionInterface #-}
```

The LANGUAGE pragmas indicate which extensions to Haskell 98 a module uses. We bring just the FFI extension in play this time. It is important to track which extensions to the language you need. Fewer extensions generally means more portable, more robust code. Indeed, it is common for Haskell programs written more than a decade ago to compile perfectly well today, thanks to standardization, despite changes to the language's syntax, type system, and core libraries.

The next step is to import the Foreign modules, which provide useful types (such as pointers, numerical types, and arrays) and utility functions (such as malloc and alloca) for writing bindings to other languages:

```
-- file: ch17/SimpleFFI.hs
import Foreign
import Foreign.C.Types
```

For extensive work with foreign libraries, a good knowledge of the Foreign module is essential. Other useful modules include Foreign.C.String, Foreign.Ptr, and Foreign.Marshal.Array.

Now we can get down to work calling C functions. To do this, we need to know three things: the name of the C function, its type, and its associated header file. Additionally, for code that isn't provided by the standard C library, we'll need to know the C library's name for linking purposes. The actual binding work is done with a foreign import declaration, like so:

```
-- file: ch17/SimpleFFI.hs
foreign import ccall "math.h sin"
    c_sin :: CDouble -> CDouble
```

This defines a new Haskell function, `c_sin`, whose concrete implementation is in C, via the `sin` function. When `c_sin` is called, a call to the actual `sin` will be made (using the standard C calling convention, indicated by `ccall`). The Haskell runtime passes control to C, which returns its results back to Haskell. The result is then wrapped up as a Haskell value of type `CDouble`.

A common idiom when writing FFI bindings is to expose the C function with the prefix `c_`, distinguishing it from more user-friendly, higher-level functions. The raw C function is specified by the `math.h` header, where it is declared to have the type:

```
double sin(double x);
```

When writing the binding, the programmer has to translate C type signatures such as this into their Haskell FFI equivalents, making sure that the data representations match up. For example, `double` in C corresponds to `CDouble` in Haskell. We need to be careful here, since if a mistake is made, the Haskell compiler will happily generate incorrect code to call C! The poor Haskell compiler doesn't know anything about what types the C function actually requires, so if instructed to, it will call the C function with the wrong arguments. At best this will lead to C compiler warnings, and more likely, it will end with with a runtime crash. At worst the error will silently go unnoticed until some critical failure occurs. So make sure you use the correct FFI types, and don't be wary of using QuickCheck to test your C code via the bindings.[*]

The most important primitive C types are represented in Haskell with the somewhat intuitive names (for signed and unsigned types) `CChar`, `CUChar`, `CInt`, `CUInt`, `CLong`, `CULong`, `CSize`, `CFloat`, and `CDouble`. More are defined in the FFI standard and can be found in the Haskell base library under `Foreign.C.Types`. It is also possible to define your own Haskell-side representation types for C, as we'll see later.

Be Careful of Side Effects

One point to note is that we bound `sin` as a pure function in Haskell, one with no side effects. That's fine in this case, since the `sin` function in C is referentially transparent. By binding pure C functions to pure Haskell functions, the Haskell compiler is taught something about the C code—namely, that it has no side effects, making optimizations easier. Pure code is also more flexible for the Haskell programmer, as it yields naturally persistent data structures and threadsafe functions. However, while pure Haskell code is always threadsafe, this is harder to guarantee of C. Even if the documentation indicates the function is likely to expose no side effects, there's little to ensure it is also threadsafe, unless explicitly documented as "reentrant." Pure, threadsafe C code, while rare, is a valuable commodity. It is the easiest flavor of C to use from Haskell.

---

[*] Some more advanced binding tools provide greater degrees of type checking. For example, `c2hs` is able to parse the C header, and generate the binding definition for you, and it is especially suited for large projects where the full API is specified.

Of course, code with side effects is more common in imperative languages, where the explicit sequencing of statements encourages the use of effects. It is much more common in C for functions to return different values, given the same arguments, due to changes in global or local state, or to have other side effects. Typically, this is signalled in C by the function returning only a status value or some void type, rather than a useful result value. This indicates that the real work of the function was in its side effects. For such functions, we'll need to capture those side effects in the IO monad (by changing the return type to IO CDouble, for example). We also need to be very careful with pure C functions that aren't also reentrant, as multiple threads are extremely common in Haskell code, in comparison to C. We might need to moderate access to the FFI binding with a transactional lock, or by duplicating the underlying C state to make nonreentrant code safe for use.

A High-Level Wrapper

With the foreign imports out of the way, the next step is to convert the C types we pass to and receive from the foreign language call into native Haskell types, wrapping the binding so that it appears as a normal Haskell function:

```
-- file: ch17/SimpleFFI.hs
fastsin :: Double -> Double
fastsin x = realToFrac (c_sin (realToFrac x))
```

The main thing to remember when writing convenient wrappers over bindings such as this is to correctly convert input and output back to normal Haskell types. To convert between floating-point values, we can use `realToFrac`, which lets us translate different floating-point values to each other (and these conversions, such as from CDouble to Double, are usually free, as the underlying representations are unchanged). For integer values, `fromIntegral` is available. For other common C data types, such as arrays, we may need to unpack the data to a more workable Haskell type (such as a list), or possibly leave the C data opaque and operate on it indirectly only (perhaps via a ByteString). The choice depends on how costly the transformation is and the functions that are available on the source and destination types.

We can now proceed to use the bound function in a program. For example, we can apply the C sin function to a Haskell list of 10ths:

```
-- file: ch17/SimpleFFI.hs
main = mapM_ (print . fastsin) [0/10, 1/10 .. 10/10]
```

This simple program prints each result as it is computed. Putting the complete binding in the file *SimpleFFI.hs* allows us to run it in ghci:

```
$ ghci SimpleFFI.hs
*Main> main
0.0
9.983341664682815e-2
0.19866933079506122
0.2955202066613396
```

```
0.3894183423086505
0.479425538604203
0.5646424733950354
0.644217687237691
0.7173560908995227
0.7833269096274833
0.8414709848078964
```

Alternatively, we can compile the code to an executable, dynamically linked against the corresponding C library:

```
$ ghc -O --make SimpleFFI.hs
[1 of 1] Compiling Main                  ( SimpleFFI.hs, SimpleFFI.o )
Linking SimpleFFI ...
```

and then run that:

```
$ ./SimpleFFI
0.0
9.983341664682815e-2
0.19866933079506122
0.2955202066613396
0.3894183423086505
0.479425538604203
0.5646424733950354
0.644217687237691
0.7173560908995227
0.7833269096274833
0.8414709848078964
```

We're well on our way now, with a full program, statically linked against C, which interleaves C and Haskell code and passes data across the language boundary. Simple bindings such as the one just shown are almost trivial, as the standard `Foreign` library provides convenient aliases for common types such as `CDouble`. In the next section, we'll look at a larger engineering task: binding to the PCRE library, which brings up issues of memory management and type safety.

Regular Expressions for Haskell: A Binding for PCRE

As we've seen in previous sections, Haskell programs have something of a bias towards lists as a foundational data structure. List functions are a core part of the base library, and convenient syntax for constructing and taking apart list structures is wired into the language. Strings are, of course, simply lists of characters (rather than, for example, flat arrays of characters). This flexibility is all well and good, but it results in a tendency for the standard library to favor polymorphic list operations at the expense of string-specific operations.

Indeed, many common tasks can be solved via regular-expression-based string processing, yet support for regular expressions isn't part of the Haskell `Prelude`. So let's look at how we'd take an off-the-shelf regular expression library, PCRE, and provide a natural, convenient Haskell binding to it, giving us useful regular expressions for Haskell.

PCRE itself is a ubiquitous C library implementing Perl-style regular expressions. It is widely available and preinstalled on many systems. You can find it at *http://www.pcre.org/*. In the following sections, we'll assume the PCRE library and headers are available on the machine.

Simple Tasks: Using the C Preprocessor

The simplest task when setting out to write a new FFI binding from Haskell to C is to bind constants defined in C headers to equivalent Haskell values. For example, PCRE provides a set of flags for modifying how the core pattern matching system works (such as ignoring case or allowing matching on newlines). These flags appear as numeric constants in the PCRE header files:

```
/* Options */

#define PCRE_CASELESS           0x00000001
#define PCRE_MULTILINE          0x00000002
#define PCRE_DOTALL             0x00000004
#define PCRE_EXTENDED           0x00000008
```

To export these values to Haskell, we need to insert them into a Haskell source file somehow. One obvious way to do this is by using the C preprocessor to substitute definitions from C into the Haskell source, which we then compile as a normal Haskell source file. Using the preprocessor, we can even declare simple constants, via textual substitutions on the Haskell source file:

```haskell
-- file: ch17/Enum1.hs
{-# LANGUAGE CPP #-}

#define N 16

main = print [ 1 .. N ]
```

The file is processed with the preprocessor in a similar manner to C source (with CPP run for us by the Haskell compiler, when it spots the LANGUAGE pragma), resulting in program output:

```
$ runhaskell Enum.hs
[1,2,3,4,5,6,7,8,9,10,11,12,13,14,15,16]
```

However, relying on CPP is a rather fragile approach. The C preprocessor isn't aware it is processing a Haskell source file and will happily include text, or transform source, in such a way as to make our Haskell code invalid. We need to be careful not to confuse CPP. If we were to include C headers, we risk substituting unwanted symbols, or inserting C type information and prototypes into the Haskell source, resulting in a broken mess.

To solve these problems, the binding preprocessor hsc2hs is distributed with GHC. It provides a convenient syntax for including C binding information in Haskell, as well as letting us safely operate with headers. It is the tool of choice for the majority of Haskell FFI bindings.

Binding Haskell to C with hsc2hs

To use hsc2hs as an intelligent binding tool for Haskell, we need to create an *.hsc* file, *Regex.hsc*, which will hold the Haskell source for our binding, along with hsc2hs processing rules, C headers, and C type information. To start off, we need some pragmas and imports:

```
-- file: ch17/Regex-hsc.hs
{-# LANGUAGE CPP, ForeignFunctionInterface #-}

module Regex where

import Foreign
import Foreign.C.Types

#include <pcre.h>
```

The module begins with a typical preamble for an FFI binding: enable CPP, enable the FFI syntax, declare a module name, and then import some things from the base library. The unusual item is the final line, where we include the C header for PCRE. This wouldn't be valid in a *.hs* source file, but is fine in *.hsc* code.

Adding Type Safety to PCRE

Next we need a type to represent PCRE compile-time flags. In C, these are integer flags to the compile function, so we could just use CInt to represent them. All we know about the flags is that they're C numeric constants, so CInt is the appropriate representation.

As a Haskell library writer though, this feels sloppy. The type of values that can be used as regex flags contains fewer values than CInt allows for. Nothing would prevent the end user from passing illegal integer values as arguments, or mixing up flags that should be passed only at regex compile time, with runtime flags. It is also possible to do arbitrary math on flags or to make other mistakes where integers and flags are confused. We really need to more precisely specify that the type of flags is distinct from its runtime representation as a numeric value. If we can do this, we can statically prevent a class of bugs relating to misuse of flags.

Adding such a layer of type safety is relatively easy, and a great use case for newtype, the type introduction declaration. newtype lets us create a type with an identical runtime representation type to another type, but which is treated as a separate type at compile time. We can represent flags as CInt values, but at compile time they'll be tagged distinctly for the type checker. This makes it a type error to use invalid flag values (as we specify only those valid flags and prevent access to the data constructor), or to pass flags to functions expecting integers. We get to use the Haskell type system to introduce a layer of type safety to the C PCRE API.

To do this, we define a `newtype` for PCRE compile-time options, whose representation is actually that of a `CInt` value, like so:

```
-- file: ch17/Regex-hsc.hs
-- | A type for PCRE compile-time options. These are newtyped CInts,
-- which can be bitwise-or'd together, using '(Data.Bits..|.)'
--
newtype PCREOption = PCREOption { unPCREOption :: CInt }
    deriving (Eq,Show)
```

The type name is `PCREOption`, and it has a single constructor, also named `PCREOption`, which lifts a `CInt` value into a new type by wrapping it in a constructor. We can also happily define an accessor, `unPCREOption`, using the Haskell record syntax to access the underlying `CInt`. That's a lot of convenience in one line. While we're here, we can also derive some useful typeclass operations for flags (equality and printing). We need to remember to export the data constructor abstractly from the source module, ensuring that users can't construct their own `PCREOption` values.

Binding to Constants

Now that we've pulled in the required modules, turned on the language features we need, and defined a type to represent PCRE options, we need to actually define some Haskell values corresponding to those PCRE constants.

We can do this in two ways with `hsc2hs`. The first is to use the `#const` keyword `hsc2hs` provides. This lets us name constants to be provided by the C preprocessor. We can bind to the constants manually by listing the CPP symbols for them using the `#const` keyword:

```
-- file: ch17/Regex-hsc-const.hs
caseless       :: PCREOption
caseless       = PCREOption #const PCRE_CASELESS

dollar_endonly :: PCREOption
dollar_endonly = PCREOption #const PCRE_DOLLAR_ENDONLY

dotall         :: PCREOption
dotall         = PCREOption #const PCRE_DOTALL
```

This introduces three new constants on the Haskell side, `caseless`, `dollar_endonly`, and `dotall`, corresponding to the similarly named C definitions. We immediately wrap the constants in a `newtype` constructor, so they're exposed to the programmer as abstract `PCREOption` types only.

Creating a *.hsc* file is the first step. We now need to actually create a Haskell source file, with the C preprocessing done. Time to run `hsc2hs` over the *.hsc* file:

```
$ hsc2hs Regex.hsc
```

This creates a new output file, *Regex.hs*, where the CPP variables have been expanded, yielding valid Haskell code:

```
-- file: ch17/Regex-hsc-const-generated.hs
caseless        :: PCREOption
caseless        = PCREOption 1
{-# LINE 21 "Regex.hsc" #-}

dollar_endonly :: PCREOption
dollar_endonly = PCREOption 32
{-# LINE 24 "Regex.hsc" #-}

dotall          :: PCREOption
dotall          = PCREOption 4
{-# LINE 27 "Regex.hsc" #-}
```

Notice how the original line in the *.hsc* file is listed next to each expanded definition via the LINE pragma. The compiler uses this information to report errors in terms of their source, in the original file, rather than in the generated one. We can load this generated *.hs* file into the interpreter and play with the results:

```
$ ghci Regex.hs
*Regex> caseless
PCREOption {unPCREOption = 1}
*Regex> unPCREOption caseless
1
*Regex> unPCREOption caseless + unPCREOption caseless
2
*Regex> caseless + caseless
interactive>:1:0:
    No instance for (Num PCREOption)
```

So things are working as expected. The values are opaque, we get type errors if we try to break the abstraction, and we can unwrap them and operate on them if needed. The unPCREOption accessor is used to unwrap the boxes. That's a good start, but let's see how we can simplify this task further.

Automating the Binding

Clearly, manually listing all the C defines and wrapping them is tedious and error prone. Wrapping all the literals in newtype constructors is also annoying. This kind of binding is such a common task that hsc2hs provides convenient syntax to automate it: the #enum construct.

We can replace our list of top-level bindings with the equivalent:

```
-- file: ch17/Regex-hsc.hs
-- PCRE compile options
#{enum PCREOption, PCREOption
  , caseless              = PCRE_CASELESS
  , dollar_endonly        = PCRE_DOLLAR_ENDONLY
  , dotall                = PCRE_DOTALL
  }
```

This is much more concise! The #enum construct gives us three fields to work with. The first is the name of the type we'd like the C defines to be treated as. This lets us pick something other than just CInt for the binding. We chose PCREOption's to construct.

The second field is an optional constructor to place in front of the symbols. This is specifically for the case we want to construct newtype values, and where much of the grunt work is saved. The final part of the #enum syntax is self-explanatory: it just defines Haskell names for constants to be filled in via CPP.

Running this code through hsc2hs, as before, generates a Haskell file with the following binding code produced (with LINE pragmas removed for brevity):

```
-- file: ch17/Regex.hs
caseless              :: PCREOption
caseless              = PCREOption 1
dollar_endonly        :: PCREOption
dollar_endonly        = PCREOption 32
dotall                :: PCREOption
dotall                = PCREOption 4
```

Perfect. Now we can do something in Haskell with these values. Our aim here is to treat flags as abstract types, not as bit fields in integers in C. Passing multiple flags in C would be done by bitwise or-ing multiple flags together. For an abstract type though, that would expose too much information. In order to preserve the abstraction and give it a Haskell flavor, we'd prefer that users pass in flags in a list that the library itself combined. This is achievable with a simple fold:

```
-- file: ch17/Regex.hs
-- | Combine a list of options into a single option, using bitwise (.|.)
combineOptions :: [PCREOption] -> PCREOption
combineOptions = PCREOption . foldr ((.|.) . unPCREOption) 0
```

This simple loop starts with an initial value of 0, unpacks each flag, and uses bitwise-or—(.|.)—on the underlying CInt, to combine each value with the loop accumulator. The final accumulated state is then wrapped up in the PCREOption constructor.

Let's turn now to actually compiling some regular expressions.

Passing String Data Between Haskell and C

The next task is to write a binding to the PCRE regular expression compile function. Let's look at its type, straight from the *pcre.h* header file:

```
pcre *pcre_compile(const char *pattern,
                   int options,
                   const char **errptr,
                   int *erroffset,
                   const unsigned char *tableptr);
```

This function compiles a regular expression pattern into some internal format, taking the pattern as an argument, along with some flags and some variables for returning status information.

We need to work out what Haskell types to represent each argument with. Most of these types are covered by equivalents defined for us by the FFI standard and are available in `Foreign.C.Types`. The first argument, the regular expression itself, is passed as a null-terminated `char` pointer to C, equivalent to the Haskell `CString` type. We've already chosen PCRE compile-time options to represent the abstract `PCREOption` newtype, whose runtime representation is a `CInt`. As the representations are guaranteed to be identical, we can pass the `newtype` safely. The other arguments are a little more complicated and require some work to construct and take apart.

The third argument, a pointer to a C string, will be used as a reference to any error message generated when compiling the expression. The value of the pointer will be modified by the C function to point to a custom error string. We can represent this with a `Ptr CString` type. Pointers in Haskell are heap-allocated containers for raw addresses and can be created and operated on with a number of allocation primitives in the FFI library. For example, we can represent a pointer to a C int as `Ptr CInt`, and a pointer to an unsigned char as `Ptr Word8`.

A note about pointers

Once we have a Haskell `Ptr` value handy, we can do various pointer-like things with it. We can compare it for equality with the null pointer, represented with the special `nullPtr` constant. We can cast a pointer from one type to a pointer to another, or we can advance a pointer by an offset in bytes with `plusPtr`. We can even modify the value pointed to, using `poke`, and, of course, dereference a pointer yielding that which it points to, with `peek`. In the majority of circumstances, a Haskell programmer doesn't need to operate on pointers directly, but when they are needed, these tools come in handy.

The question then is how to represent the abstract `pcre` pointer returned when we compile the regular expression. We need to find a Haskell type that is as abstract as the C type. Since the C type is treated abstractly, we can assign any heap-allocated Haskell type to the data, as long as it has few or no operations on it. This is a common trick for arbitrarily typed foreign data. The idiomatic simple type to use to represent unknown foreign data is a pointer to the () type. We can use a type synonym to remember the binding:

```
-- file: ch17/PCRE-compile.hs
type PCRE = ()
```

That is, the foreign data is some unknown, opaque object, and we'll just treat it as a pointer to (), knowing full well that we'll never actually dereference that pointer. This gives us the following foreign import binding for `pcre_compile`, which must be in IO, as the pointer returned will vary on each call, even if the returned object is functionally equivalent:

```
-- file: ch17/PCRE-compile.hs
foreign import ccall unsafe "pcre.h pcre_compile"
    c_pcre_compile  :: CString
                    -> PCREOption
                    -> Ptr CString
                    -> Ptr CInt
                    -> Ptr Word8
                    -> IO (Ptr PCRE)
```

Typed Pointers

We can increase safety in the binding futher by using a *typed* pointer, instead of using the () type. That is, a unique type, distinct from the unit type, that has no meaningful runtime representation. A type for which no data can be constructed, making dereferencing it a type error. One good way to build such provably uninspectable data types is with a nullary data type:

```
-- file: ch17/PCRE-nullary.hs
data PCRE
```

A note about safety

When making a foreign import declaration, we can optionally specify a *safety* level to use when making the call, using either the `safe` or `unsafe` keyword. A safe call is less efficient but guarantees that the Haskell system can be safely called into from C. An unsafe call has far less overhead, but the C code that is called must not call back into Haskell. By default, foreign imports are safe, but in practice it is rare for C code to call back into Haskell, so for efficiency we mostly use unsafe calls.

This requires the `EmptyDataDecls` language extension. This type clearly contains no values! We can only ever construct pointers to such values, as there are no concrete values (other than bottom) that have this type.

We can also achieve the same thing, without requiring a language extension, using a recursive `newtype`:

```
-- file: ch17/PCRE-recursive.hs
newtype PCRE = PCRE (Ptr PCRE)
```

Again, we can't really do anything with a value of this type, as it has no runtime representation. Using typed pointers in these ways is just another way to add safety to a Haskell layer over what C provides. What would require discipline on the part of the C programmer (remembering never to dereference a PCRE pointer) can be enforced statically in the type system of the Haskell binding. If this code compiles, the type checker has given us a proof that the PCRE objects returned by C are never dereferenced on the Haskell side.

We have the foreign import declaration sorted out now, and the next step is to marshal data into the right form so that we can finally call the C code.

Memory Management: Let the Garbage Collector Do the Work

One question that isn't resolved yet is how to manage the memory associated with the abstract PCRE structure returned by the C library. The caller didn't have to allocate it—the library took care of that by allocating memory on the C side. At some point, though, we'll need to deallocate it. This, again, is an opportunity to abstract the tedium of using the C library by hiding the complexity inside the Haskell binding.

We'll use the Haskell garbage collector to automatically deallocate the C structure once it is no longer in use. To do this, we'll make use of Haskell garbage collector finalizers and the ForeignPtr type.

We don't want users to have to manually deallocate the Ptr PCRE value returned by the foreign call. The PCRE library specifically states that structures are allocated on the C side with malloc and need to be freed when no longer in use, or we risk leaking memory. The Haskell garbage collector already goes to great lengths to automate the task of managing memory for Haskell values. Cleverly, we can also assign our hardworking garbage collector the task of looking after C's memory for us. The trick is to associate a piece of Haskell data with the foreign allocator data and to give the Haskell garbage collector an arbitrary function that is to deallocate the C resource once it notices that the Haskell data is finished.

We have two tools at our disposal here—the opaque ForeignPtr data type and the newForeignPtr function, which has type:

```
-- file: ch17/ForeignPtr.hs
newForeignPtr :: FinalizerPtr a -> Ptr a -> IO (ForeignPtr a)
```

The function takes two arguments: a finalizer to run when the data goes out of scope and a pointer to the associated C data. It returns a new managed pointer, which will have its finalizer run once the garbage collector decides the data is no longer in use. What a lovely abstraction!

These finalizable pointers are appropriate whenever a C library requires the user to explicitly deallocate, or otherwise clean up a resource, when it is no longer in use. It is a simple piece of equipment that goes a long way towards making the C library binding more natural, more functional, and in flavor.

So with this in mind, we can hide the manually managed Ptr PCRE type inside an automatically managed data structure. This yields us the data type used to represent regular expressions that users will see:

```
-- file: ch17/PCRE-compile.hs
data Regex = Regex !(ForeignPtr PCRE)
                   !ByteString
         deriving (Eq, Ord, Show)
```

This new Regex data type consists of two parts. The first is an abstract ForeignPtr, which we'll use to manage the underlying PCRE data allocated in C. The second component is a strict ByteString, which is the string representation of the regular expression that we compiled. By keeping the user-level representation of the regular expression handy inside the Regex type, it'll be easier to print friendly error messages and show the Regex itself in a meaningful way.

A High-Level Interface: Marshaling Data

The challenge when writing FFI bindings, once the Haskell types have been decided upon, is to convert regular data types that a Haskell programmer will be familiar with into low-level pointers to arrays and other C types. What would an ideal Haskell interface to regular expression compilation look like? We have some design intuitions to guide us.

For starters, the act of compilation should be a referentially transparent operation: passing the same regex string will yield functionally the same compiled pattern each time, although the C library will give us observably different pointers to functionally identical expressions. If we can hide these memory management details, we should be able to represent the binding as a pure function. The ability to represent a C function in Haskell as a pure operation is a key step towards flexibility, and an indicator that the interface will be easy to use (as it won't require complicated state to be initialized before it can be used).

Despite being pure, the function can still fail. If the regular expression input the user provides is ill-formed, an error string is returned. A good data type to represent optional failure with an error value is Either. That is, either we return a valid compiled regular expression or we return an error string. Encoding the results of a C function in a familiar, foundational Haskell type such as this is another useful step to make the binding more idiomatic.

For the user-supplied parameters, we've already decided to pass compilation flags in as a list. We can choose to pass the input regular expression either as an efficient ByteString or as a regular String. An appropriate type signature, then, for referentially transparent compilation success with a value or failure with an error string would be:

```
-- file: ch17/PCRE-compile.hs
compile :: ByteString -> [PCREOption] -> Either String Regex
```

The input is a ByteString, available from the Data.ByteString.Char8 module (and we'll import this qualified to avoid name clashes), containing the regular expression and a list of flags (or the empty list if there are no flags to pass). The result is either an error string, or a new, compiled regular expression.

Marshaling ByteStrings

Given this type, we can sketch out the compile function: the high-level interface to the raw C binding. At its heart, it will call c_pcre_compile. Before it does that, it has to marshal the input ByteString into a CString. This is done with the ByteString library's useAsCString function, which copies the input ByteString into a null-terminated C array (there is also an unsafe, zero copy variant, which assumes the ByteString is already null-terminated):

```
-- file: ch17/ForeignPtr.hs
useAsCString :: ByteString -> (CString -> IO a) -> IO a
```

This function takes a ByteString as input. The second argument is a user-defined function that will run with the resulting CString. We see here another useful idiom: data marshaling functions that are naturally scoped via closures. Our useAsCString function will convert the input data to a C string, which we can then pass to C as a pointer. Our burden then is to supply it with a chunk of code to call C.

Code in this style is often written in a dangling do-block notation. The following pseudocode illustrates this structure:

```
-- file: ch17/DoBlock.hs
useAsCString str $ \cstr -> do
    ... operate on the C string
    ... return a result
```

The second argument here is an anonymous function, a lambda, with a monadic do block for a body. It is common to use the simple ($) application operator to avoid the need for parentheses when delimiting the code block argument. This is a useful idiom to remember when dealing with code block parameters such as this.

Allocating Local C Data: The Storable Class

We can happily marshal ByteString data to C-compatible types, but the pcre_compile function also needs some pointers and arrays in which to place its other return values. These should only exist briefly, so we don't need complicated allocation strategies. Such short-lifetime C data can be created with the alloca function:

```
-- file: ch17/ForeignPtr.hs
alloca :: Storable a => (Ptr a -> IO b) -> IO b
```

This function takes a code block accepting a pointer to some C type as an argument and arranges to call that function with the unitialized data of the right shape, allocated freshly. The allocation mechanism mirrors local stack variables in other languages. The allocated memory is released once the argument function exits. In this way, we get lexically scoped allocation of low-level data types, which are guaranteed to be released once the scope is exited. We can use it to allocate any data types that have an instance of the Storable typeclass. An implication of overloading the allocation operator such as this is that the data type allocated can be inferred from type information, based on use! Haskell will know what to allocate based on the functions we use on that data.

To allocate a pointer to a CString, for example, which will be updated to point to a particular CString by the called function, we would call alloca, in pseudocode as:

```
-- file: ch17/DoBlock.hs
alloca $ \stringptr -> do
   ... call some Ptr CString function
   peek stringptr
```

This locally allocates a Ptr CString and applies the code block to that pointer, which then calls a C function to modify the pointer contents. Finally, we dereference the pointer with the Storable class peek function, yielding a CString.

We can now put it all together, to complete our high-level PCRE compilation wrapper.

Putting It All Together

We've decided what Haskell type to represent the C function with, what the result data will be represented by, and how its memory will be managed. We've chosen a representation for flags to the pcre_compile function and worked out how to get C strings to and from code inspecting it. So let's write the complete function for compiling PCRE regular expressions from Haskell:

```
-- file: ch17/PCRE-compile.hs
compile :: ByteString -> [PCREOption] -> Either String Regex
compile str flags = unsafePerformIO $
  useAsCString str $ \pattern -> do
    alloca $ \errptr      -> do
    alloca $ \erroffset   -> do
        pcre_ptr <- c_pcre_compile pattern (combineOptions flags) errptr
        erroffset nullPtr
        if pcre_ptr == nullPtr
            then do
                err <- peekCString =<< peek errptr
                return (Left err)
            else do
                reg <- newForeignPtr finalizerFree pcre_ptr -- release with free()
                return (Right (Regex reg str))
```

That's it! Let's carefully walk through the details here, since it is rather dense. The first thing that stands out is the use of unsafePerformIO, a rather infamous function, with a very unusual type, imported from the ominous System.IO.Unsafe:

```
-- file: ch17/ForeignPtr.hs
unsafePerformIO :: IO a -> a
```

This function does something odd. It takes an IO value and converts it to a pure one! After warning about the danger of effects for so long, here we have the very enabler of dangerous effects in one line. Used unwisely, this function lets us sidestep all safety guarantees that the Haskell type system provides, inserting arbitrary side effects into a

Haskell program, anywhere. The dangers in doing this are significant. We can break optimizations, modify arbitrary locations in memory, remove files on the user's machine, or launch nuclear missiles from our Fibonacci sequences. So why does this function exist at all?

It exists precisely to enable Haskell to bind to C code that we know to be referentially transparent, but can't prove the case to the Haskell type system. It lets us say to the compiler, "I know what I'm doing—this code really is pure." For regular expression compilation, we know this to be the case: given the same pattern, we should get the same regular expression matcher every time. However, proving that to the compiler is beyond the Haskell type system, so we're forced to assert that this code is pure. Using unsafePerformIO allows us to do just that.

However, if we know the C code is pure, why don't we just declare it as such, by giving it a pure type in the import declaration? We don't because we have to allocate local memory for the C function to work with, which must be done in the IO monad, as it is a local side effect. Those effects won't escape the code surrounding the foreign call, though, so when wrapped, we use unsafePerformIO to reintroduce purity.

The argument to unsafePerformIO is the actual body of our compilation function, which consists of four parts: marshaling Haskell data to C form; calling into the C library; checking the return values; and finally, constructing a Haskell value from the results.

We marshal with useAsCString and alloca, setting up the data we need to pass to C, and use combineOptions, developed previously, to collapse the list of flags into a single CInt. Once that's all in place, we can finally call c_pcre_compile with the pattern, flags, and pointers for the results. We use nullPtr for the character-encoding table, which is unused in this case.

The result returned from the C call is a pointer to the abstract PCRE structure. We then test this against the nullPtr. If there is a problem with the regular expression, we have to dereference the error pointer, yielding a CString. We then unpack that to a normal Haskell list with the library function, peekCString. The final result of the error path is a value of Left err, indicating failure to the caller.

If the call succeeds, however, we allocate a new storage-managed pointer, with the C function using a ForeignPtr. The special value finalizerFree is bound as the finalizer for this data, which uses the standard C free to deallocate the data. This is then wrapped as an opaque Regex value. The successful result is tagged as such with Right, and then returned to the user. And now we're done!

We need to process our source file with hsc2hs, and then load the function in ghci. However, doing this results in an error on the first attempt:

```
$ hsc2hs Regex.hsc
$ ghci Regex.hs

During interactive linking, GHCi couldn't find the following symbol:
  pcre_compile
```

```
This may be due to you not asking GHCi to load extra object files,
archives, or DLLs needed by your current session.  Restart GHCi, specifying
the missing library using the -L/path/to/object/dir and -lmissinglibname
flags, or simply by naming the relevant files on the GHCi command line.
```

A little scary. However, this is just because we didn't link the C library we wanted to call to the Haskell code. Assuming the PCRE library has been installed on the system in the default library location, we can let ghci know about it by adding -lpcre to the ghci command line. Now we can try out the code on some regular expressions, looking at the success and error cases:

```
$ ghci Regex.hs -lpcre
*Regex> :m + Data.ByteString.Char8
*Regex Data.ByteString.Char8> compile (pack "a.*b") []
Right (Regex 0x00000000028882a0 "a.*b")
*Regex Data.ByteString.Char8> compile (pack "a.*b[xy]+(foo?)") []
Right (Regex 0x0000000002888860 "a.*b[xy]+(foo?)")
*Regex Data.ByteString.Char8> compile (pack "*") []
Left "nothing to repeat"
```

The regular expressions are packed into byte strings and marshaled to C, where they are compiled by the PCRE library. The result is then handed back to Haskell, where we display the structure using the default Show instance. Our next step is to pattern match some strings with these compiled regular expressions.

Matching on Strings

The second part of a good regular expression library is the matching function. Given a compiled regular expression, this function does the matching of the compiled regex against some input, indicating whether it matched, and if so, what parts of the string matched. In PCRE, this function is pcre_exec, which has type:

```
int pcre_exec(const pcre *code,
              const pcre_extra *extra,
              const char *subject,
              int length,
              int startoffset,
              int options,
              int *ovector,
              int ovecsize);
```

The most important arguments are the input pcre pointer structure (which we obtained from pcre_compile) and the subject string. The other flags let us provide bookkeeping structures and space for return values. We can directly translate this type to the Haskell import declaration:

```
-- file: ch17/RegexExec.hs
foreign import ccall "pcre.h pcre_exec"
    c_pcre_exec     :: Ptr PCRE
                    -> Ptr PCREExtra
                    -> Ptr Word8
                    -> CInt
```

```
                  -> CInt
                  -> PCREExecOption
                  -> Ptr CInt
                  -> CInt
                  -> IO CInt
```

We use the same method as before to create typed pointers for the PCREExtra structure, and a newtype to represent flags passed at regex execution time. This lets us ensure that users don't pass compile-time flags incorrectly at regex runtime.

Extracting Information About the Pattern

The main complication involved in calling pcre_exec is the array of int pointers used to hold the offsets of matching substrings found by the pattern matcher. These offsets are held in an offset vector, whose required size is determined by analyzing the input regular expression to determine the number of captured patterns it contains. PCRE provides a function, pcre_fullinfo, for determining much information about the regular expression, including the number of patterns. We'll need to call this, and now, we can directly write down the Haskell type for binding to pcre_fullinfo as:

```
-- file: ch17/RegexExec.hs
foreign import ccall "pcre.h pcre_fullinfo"
    c_pcre_fullinfo :: Ptr PCRE
                    -> Ptr PCREExtra
                    -> PCREInfo
                    -> Ptr a
                    -> IO CInt
```

The most important arguments to this function are the compiled regular expression and the PCREInfo flag, which indicates which information we're interested in. In this case, we care about the captured pattern count. The flags are encoded in numeric constants, and we need to use specifically the PCRE_INFO_CAPTURECOUNT value. There is a range of other constants that determine the result type of the function, which we can bind to using the #enum construct as before. The final argument is a pointer to a location to store the information about the pattern (whose size depends on the flag argument passed in!).

Calling pcre_fullinfo to determine the captured pattern count is pretty easy:

```
-- file: ch17/RegexExec.hs
capturedCount :: Ptr PCRE -> IO Int
capturedCount regex_ptr =
    alloca $ \n_ptr -> do
        c_pcre_fullinfo regex_ptr nullPtr info_capturecount n_ptr
        return . fromIntegral =<< peek (n_ptr :: Ptr CInt)
```

This takes a raw PCRE pointer and allocates space for the CInt count of the matched patterns. We then call the information function and peek into the result structure, finding a CInt. Finally, we convert this to a normal Haskell Int and pass it back to the user.

Pattern Matching with Substrings

Let's now write the regex matching function. The Haskell type for matching is similar to that for compiling regular expressions:

```
-- file: ch17/RegexExec.hs
match :: Regex -> ByteString -> [PCREExecOption] -> Maybe [ByteString]
```

This function is how users will match strings against compiled regular expressions. Again, the main design point is that it is a pure function. Matching is a pure function: given the same input regular expression and subject string, it will always return the same matched substrings. We convey this information to the user via the type signature, indicating no side effects will occur when you call this function.

The arguments are a compiled `Regex`, a strict `ByteString` (containing the input data), and a list of flags that modify the regular expression engine's behavior at runtime. The result is either no match at all, indicated by a `Nothing` value, or just a list of matched substrings. We use the `Maybe` type to clearly indicate in the type that matching may fail. Using strict `ByteStrings` for the input data, we can extract matched substrings in constant time, without copying, which makes the interface rather efficient. If substrings are matched in the input, the offset vector is populated with pairs of integer offsets into the subject string. We'll need to loop over this result vector, reading offsets, and building `ByteString` slices as we go.

The implementation of the match wrapper can be broken into three parts. At the top level, our function takes apart the compiled `Regex` structure, yielding the underlying PCRE pointer:

```
-- file: ch17/RegexExec.hs
match :: Regex -> ByteString -> [PCREExecOption] -> Maybe [ByteString]
match (Regex pcre_fp _) subject os = unsafePerformIO $ do
  withForeignPtr pcre_fp $ \pcre_ptr -> do
    n_capt <- capturedCount pcre_ptr

    let ovec_size = (n_capt + 1) * 3
        ovec_bytes = ovec_size * sizeOf (undefined :: CInt)
```

As it is pure, we can use `unsafePerformIO` to hide any allocation effects internally. After pattern matching on the PCRE type, we need to take apart the `ForeignPtr` that hides our C-allocated raw PCRE data. We can use `withForeignPtr`. This holds onto the Haskell data associated with the PCRE value while the call is being made, preventing it from being collected for at least the time it is used by this call. We then call the information function and use that value to compute the size of the offset vector (the formula for which is given in the PCRE documentation). The number of bytes we need is the number of elements multiplied by the size of a `CInt`. To portably compute C type sizes, the `Storable` class provides a `sizeOf` function, which takes some arbitrary value of the required type (and we can use the `undefined` value here to do our type dispatch).

The next step is to allocate an offset vector of the size we computed, in order to convert the input ByteString into a pointer to a C char array. Finally, we call pcre_exec with all the required arguments:

```
-- file: ch17/RegexExec.hs
    allocaBytes ovec_bytes $ \ovec -> do

        let (str_fp, off, len) = toForeignPtr subject
        withForeignPtr str_fp $ \cstr -> do
            r <- c_pcre_exec
                        pcre_ptr
                        nullPtr
                        (cstr `plusPtr` off)
                        (fromIntegral len)
                        0
                        (combineExecOptions os)
                        ovec
                        (fromIntegral ovec_size)
```

For the offset vector, we use allocaBytes to control exactly the size of the allocated array. It is like alloca, but rather than using the Storable class to determine the required size, it takes an explicit size in bytes to allocate. Taking apart ByteStrings, yielding the underlying pointer to memory that the Bytestrings contain, is done with toForeignPtr, which converts our nice ByteString type into a managed pointer. Using withForeignPtr on the result gives us a raw Ptr CChar, which is exactly what we need to pass the input string to C. Programming in Haskell is often just solving a type puzzle!

We then just call c_pcre_exec with the raw PCRE pointer, the input string pointer at the correct offset, its length, and the result vector pointer. A status code is returned, and, finally, we analyze the result:

```
-- file: ch17/RegexExec.hs
            if r < 0
                then return Nothing
                else let loop n o acc =
                            if n == r
                              then return (Just (reverse acc))
                              else do
                                  i <- peekElemOff ovec o
                                  j <- peekElemOff ovec (o+1)
                                  let s = substring i j subject
                                  loop (n+1) (o+2) (s : acc)
                     in loop 0 0 []

    where
      substring :: CInt -> CInt -> ByteString -> ByteString
      substring x y _ | x == y = empty
      substring a b s = end
          where
              start = unsafeDrop (fromIntegral a) s
              end   = unsafeTake (fromIntegral (b-a)) start
```

If the result value is less than zero, there was an error, or no match, so we return Nothing to the user. Otherwise, we need a loop peeking pairs of offsets from the offset vector (via peekElemOff). Those offsets are used to find the matched substrings. To build substrings, we use a helper function that, given a start and end offset, drops the surrounding portions of the subject string, yielding just the matched portion. The loop runs until it has extracted the number of substrings we were told the matcher found.

The substrings are accumulated in a tail recursive loop, building up a reverse list of each string. Before returning the substrings of the user, we need to flip that list around and wrap it in a successful Just tag. Let's try it out!

The Real Deal: Compiling and Matching Regular Expressions

If we take this function and its surrounding hsc2hs definitions and data wrappers, and process it with hsc2hs, we can load the resulting Haskell file in GHCi and try out our code (we need to import Data.ByteString.Char8 so we can build ByteStrings from string literals):

```
$ hsc2hs Regex.hsc
$ ghci Regex.hs -lpcre
*Regex> :t compile
compile :: ByteString -> [PCREOption] -> Either String Regex
*Regex> :t match
match :: Regex -> ByteString -> Maybe [ByteString]
```

Things seem to be in order. Now let's try some compilation and matching. First, something easy:

```
*Regex> :m + Data.ByteString.Char8
*Regex Data.ByteString.Char8> let Right r = compile (pack "the quick brown fox") []
*Regex Data.ByteString.Char8> match r (pack "the quick brown fox") []
Just ["the quick brown fox"]
*Regex Data.ByteString.Char8> match r (pack "The Quick Brown Fox") []
Nothing
*Regex Data.ByteString.Char8> match r (pack "What
  do you know about the quick brown fox?") []
Just ["the quick brown fox"]
```

(We could also avoid the pack calls by using the OverloadedStrings extensions). Or we can be more adventurous:

```
*Regex Data.ByteString.Char8> let Right r = compile
(pack "a*abc?xyz+pqr{3}ab{2,}xy{4,5}pq{0,6}AB{0,}zz") []
*Regex Data.ByteString.Char8> match r (pack "abxyzpqrrabbxyyyypqAzz") []
Just ["abxyzpqrrabbxyyyypqAzz"]
*Regex Data.ByteString.Char8> let Right r = compile
(pack "^([^!]+)!(.+)=apquxz\\.ixr\\.zzz\\.ac\\.uk$") []
*Regex Data.ByteString.Char8> match r (pack "abc!pqr=apquxz.ixr.zzz.ac.uk") []
Just ["abc!pqr=apquxz.ixr.zzz.ac.uk","abc","pqr"]
```

That's pretty awesome. The full power of Perl regular expressions in Haskell, at your fingertips.

In this chapter, we've looked at how to declare bindings that let Haskell code call C functions, how to marshal different data types between the two languages, how to allocate memory at a low level (by allocating locally or via C's memory management), and how to exploit the Haskell type system and garbage collector to automate much of the hard work of dealing with C. Finally, we looked at how FFI preprocessors can ease much of the labor of constructing new bindings. The result is a natural Haskell API that is actually implemented primarily in C.

The majority of FFI tasks fall into these categories. Other advanced techniques that we are unable to cover include linking Haskell into C programs, registering callbacks from one language to another, and the c2hs preprocessing tool. You can find more information about these topics online.

CHAPTER 18

Monad Transformers

Motivation: Boilerplate Avoidance

Monads provide a powerful way to build computations with effects. Each of the standard monads is specialized to do exactly one thing. In real code, we often need to be able to use several effects at once.

Recall the `Parse` type that we developed in Chapter 10, for instance. When we introduced monads, we mentioned that this type was a `State` monad in disguise. Our monad is more complex than the standard `State` monad, because it uses the `Either` type to allow the possibility of a parsing failure. In our case, if a parse fails early on, we want to stop parsing, not continue in some broken state. Our monad combines the effect of carrying state around with the effect of early exit.

The normal `State` monad doesn't let us escape in this way; it carries state only. It uses the default implementation of `fail`: this calls `error`, which throws an exception that we can't catch in pure code. The `State` monad thus *appears* to allow for failure, without that capability actually being any use. (Once again, we recommend that you almost always avoid using `fail`!)

It would be ideal if we could somehow take the standard `State` monad and add failure handling to it, without resorting to the wholesale construction of custom monads by hand. The standard monads in the `mtl` library don't allow us to combine them. Instead, the library provides a set of *monad transformers*[*] to achieve the same result.

A monad transformer is similar to a regular monad, but it's not a standalone entity. Instead, it modifies the behavior of an underlying monad. Most of the monads in the `mtl` library have transformer equivalents. By convention, the transformer version of a monad has the same name, with a T stuck on the end. For example, the transformer equivalent of `State` is `StateT`; it adds mutable state to an underlying monad. The

---

[*] The name `mtl` stands for "monad transformer library."

`WriterT` monad transformer makes it possible to write data when stacked on top of another monad.

A Simple Monad Transformer Example

Before we introduce monad transformers, let's look at a function written using techniques we are already familiar with. The function that follows recurses into a directory tree and returns a list of the number of entries it finds at each level of the tree:

```
-- file: ch18/CountEntries.hs
module CountEntries (listDirectory, countEntriesTrad) where

import System.Directory (doesDirectoryExist, getDirectoryContents)
import System.FilePath ((</>))
import Control.Monad (forM, liftM)

listDirectory :: FilePath -> IO [String]
listDirectory = liftM (filter notDots) . getDirectoryContents
    where notDots p = p /= "." && p /= ".."

countEntriesTrad :: FilePath -> IO [(FilePath, Int)]
countEntriesTrad path = do
  contents <- listDirectory path
  rest <- forM contents $ \name -> do
            let newName = path </> name
            isDir <- doesDirectoryExist newName
            if isDir
              then countEntriesTrad newName
              else return []
  return $ (path, length contents) : concat rest
```

We'll now look at using the `Writer` monad to achieve the same goal. Since this monad lets us record a value wherever we want, we don't need to explicitly build up a result.

As our function must execute in the `IO` monad so that it can traverse directories, we can't use the `Writer` monad directly. Instead, we use `WriterT` to add the recording capability to `IO`. We will find the going easier if we look at the types involved.

The normal `Writer` monad has two type parameters, so it's more properly written `Writer w a`. The first parameter `w` is the type of the values to be recorded, and a is the usual type that the `Monad` typeclass requires. Thus `Writer [(FilePath, Int)] a` is a writer monad that records a list of directory names and sizes.

The `WriterT` transformer has a similar structure, but it adds another type parameter `m`: this is the underlying monad whose behavior we are augmenting. The full signature of `WriterT` is `WriterT w m a`.

Because we need to traverse directories, which requires access to the `IO` monad, we'll stack our writer on top of the `IO` monad. Our combination of monad transformer and underlying monad will thus have the type `WriterT [(FilePath, Int)] IO a`. This stack of monad transformer and monad is itself a monad:

```
-- file: ch18/CountEntriesT.hs
module CountEntriesT (listDirectory, countEntries) where

import CountEntries (listDirectory)
import System.Directory (doesDirectoryExist)
import System.FilePath ((</>))
import Control.Monad (forM_, when)
import Control.Monad.Trans (liftIO)
import Control.Monad.Writer (WriterT, tell)

countEntries :: FilePath -> WriterT [(FilePath, Int)] IO ()
countEntries path = do
  contents <- liftIO . listDirectory $ path
  tell [(path, length contents)]
  forM_ contents $ \name -> do
    let newName = path </> name
    isDir <- liftIO . doesDirectoryExist $ newName
    when isDir $ countEntries newName
```

This code is not terribly different from our earlier version. We use liftIO to expose the IO monad where necessary and use tell to record a visit to a directory.

To run our code, we must use one of WriterT's execution functions:

```
ghci> :type runWriterT
runWriterT :: WriterT w m a -> m (a, w)
ghci> :type execWriterT
execWriterT :: (Monad m) => WriterT w m a -> m w
```

These functions execute the action, and then remove the WriterT wrapper and give a result that is wrapped in the underlying monad. The runWriterT function gives both the result of the action and whatever was recorded as it ran, while execWriterT throws away the result and just gives us what was recorded:

```
ghci> :type countEntries ".."
countEntries ".." :: WriterT [(FilePath, Int)] IO ()
ghci> :type execWriterT (countEntries "..")
execWriterT (countEntries "..") :: IO [(FilePath, Int)]
ghci> take 4 `liftM` execWriterT (countEntries "..")
[("..",30),("../ch05",28),("../ch05/dist",3),("../ch05/dist/build",9)]
```

We use a WriterT on top of IO because there is no IOT monad transformer. Whenever we use the IO monad with one or more monad transformers, IO will always be at the bottom of the stack.

Common Patterns in Monads and Monad Transformers

Most of the monads and monad transformers in the mtl library follow a few common patterns around naming and typeclasses.

To illustrate these rules, we will focus on a single straightforward monad: the reader monad. The reader monad's API is detailed by the MonadReader typeclass. Most mtl monads have similarly named typeclasses. `MonadWriter` defines the API of the writer monad, and so on:

```
-- file: ch18/Reader.hs
class (Monad m) => MonadReader r m | m -> r where
    ask   :: m r
    local :: (r -> r) -> m a -> m a
```

The type variable `r` represents the immutable state that the reader monad carries around. The `Reader r` monad is an instance of the `MonadReader` class, as is the `ReaderT r m` monad transformer. Again, this pattern is repeated by other `mtl` monads: there usually exist both a concrete monad and a transformer, each of which are instances of the typeclass that defines the monad's API.

Returning to the specifics of the reader monad, we haven't touched upon the `local` function before. It temporarily modifies the current environment using the `r -> r` function, and then executes its action in the modified environment. To make this idea more concrete, here is a simple example:

```
-- file: ch18/LocalReader.hs
import Control.Monad.Reader

myName step = do
  name <- ask
  return (step ++ ", I am " ++ name)

localExample :: Reader String (String, String, String)
localExample = do
  a <- myName "First"
  b <- local (++"dy") (myName "Second")
  c <- myName "Third"
  return (a, b, c)
```

If we execute the `localExample` action in ghci, we can see that the effect of modifying the environment is confined to one place:

```
ghci> runReader localExample "Fred"
Loading package mtl-1.1.0.1 ... linking ... done.
("First, I am Fred","Second, I am Freddy","Third, I am Fred")
```

When the underlying monad `m` is an instance of `MonadIO`, the `mtl` library provides an instance for `ReaderT r m` and also for a number of other typeclasses. Here are a few:

```
-- file: ch18/Reader.hs
instance (Monad m) => Functor (ReaderT r m) where
    ...

instance (MonadIO m) => MonadIO (ReaderT r m) where
    ...

instance (MonadPlus m) => MonadPlus (ReaderT r m) where
    ...
```

Once again, most `mtl` monad transformers define instances such as these, in order to make it easier for us to work with them.

Stacking Multiple Monad Transformers

As we have already mentioned, when we stack a monad transformer on a normal monad, the result is another monad. This suggests the possibility that we can again stack a monad transformer on top of our combined monad, in order to get a new monad and in fact, this is a common thing to do. Under what circumstances might we want to create such a stack?

- If we need to talk to the outside world, we'll have IO at the base of the stack. Otherwise, we will have some normal monad.
- If we add a ReaderT layer, we give ourselves access to read-only configuration information.
- Add a StateT layer, and we gain a global state that we can modify.
- Should we need the ability to log events, we can add a WriterT layer.

The power of this approach is that we can customize the stack to our exact needs, specifying which kinds of effects we want to support.

As a small example of stacked monad transformers in action, here is a reworking of the countEntries function we developed earlier. We will modify it to recurse no deeper into a directory tree than a given amount and to record the maximum depth it reaches:

```
-- file: ch18/UglyStack.hs
import System.Directory
import System.FilePath
import Control.Monad.Reader
import Control.Monad.State

data AppConfig = AppConfig {
    cfgMaxDepth :: Int
    } deriving (Show)

data AppState = AppState {
    stDeepestReached :: Int
    } deriving (Show)
```

We use ReaderT to store configuration data, in the form of the maximum depth of recursion we will perform. We also use StateT to record the maximum depth we reach during an actual traversal:

```
-- file: ch18/UglyStack.hs
type App = ReaderT AppConfig (StateT AppState IO)
```

Our transformer stack has IO on the bottom, then StateT, with ReaderT on top. In this particular case, it doesn't matter whether we have ReaderT or WriterT on top, but IO must be on the bottom.

Even a small stack of monad transformers quickly develops an unwieldy type name. We can use a type alias to reduce the lengths of the type signatures that we write.

The execution function for our monad stack is simple:

```
-- file: ch18/UglyStack.hs
runApp :: App a -> Int -> IO (a, AppState)
runApp k maxDepth =
    let config = AppConfig maxDepth
        state = AppState 0
    in runStateT (runReaderT k config) state
```

Our application of `runReaderT` removes the `ReaderT` transformer wrapper, while `runStateT` removes the `StateT` wrapper, leaving us with a result in the IO monad.

Compared to earlier versions, the only complications we added to our traversal function are slight. We track our current depth, and record the maximum depth we reach:

```
-- file: ch18/UglyStack.hs
constrainedCount :: Int -> FilePath -> App [(FilePath, Int)]
constrainedCount curDepth path = do
  contents <- liftIO . listDirectory $ path
  cfg <- ask
  rest <- forM contents $ \name -> do
            let newPath = path </> name
            isDir <- liftIO $ doesDirectoryExist newPath
            if isDir && curDepth < cfgMaxDepth cfg
              then do
                let newDepth = curDepth + 1
                st <- get
                when (stDeepestReached st < newDepth) $
                  put st { stDeepestReached = newDepth }
                constrainedCount newDepth newPath
              else return []
  return $ (path, length contents) : concat rest
```

Our use of monad transformers here is admittedly a little contrived. Because we're writing a single straightforward function, we're not really winning anything. What's useful about this approach, though, is that it *scales* to bigger programs.

We can write most of an application's imperative-style code in a monad stack similar to our App monad. In a real program, we'd carry around more complex configuration data, but we'd still use ReaderT to keep it read-only and hidden except when needed. We'd have more mutable state to manage, but we'd still use StateT to encapsulate it.

Hiding Our Work

We can use the usual newtype technique to erect a solid barrier between the implementation of our custom monad and its interface:

```
-- file: ch18/UglyStack.hs
newtype MyApp a = MyA {
      runA :: ReaderT AppConfig (StateT AppState IO) a
    } deriving (Monad, MonadIO, MonadReader AppConfig,
                MonadState AppState)

runMyApp :: MyApp a -> Int -> IO (a, AppState)
runMyApp k maxDepth =
    let config = AppConfig maxDepth
        state = AppState 0
    in runStateT (runReaderT (runA k) config) state
```

If we export the MyApp type constructor and the runMyApp execution function from a module, client code will not be able to tell that the internals of our monad is a stack of monad transformers.

The large deriving clause requires the GeneralizedNewtypeDeriving language pragma. It seems somehow magical that the compiler can derive all of these instances for us. How does this work?

Earlier, we mentioned that the mtl library provides instances of a number of typeclasses for each monad transformer. For example, the IO monad implements MonadIO. If the underlying monad is an instance of MonadIO, mtl makes StateT an instance, too, and likewise for ReaderT.

There is thus no magic going on: the top-level monad transformer in the stack is an instance of all of the typeclasses that we're rederiving with our deriving clause. This is a consequence of mtl providing a carefully coordinated set of typeclasses and instances that fit together well. There is nothing more going on than the usual automatic derivation that we can perform with newtype declarations.

Moving Down the Stack

So far, our uses of monad transformers have been simple, and the plumbing of the `mtl` library has allowed us to avoid the details of how a stack of monads is constructed. Indeed, we already know enough about monad transformers to simplify many common programming tasks.

There are a few useful ways in which we can depart from the comfort of `mtl`. Most often, a custom monad sits at the bottom of the stack, or a custom monad transformer lies somewhere within the stack. To understand the potential difficulty, let's look at an example.

Suppose we have a custom monad transformer, `CustomT`:

```
-- file: ch18/CustomT.hs
newtype CustomT m a = ...
```

In the framework that `mtl` provides, each monad transformer in the stack makes the API of a lower level available by providing instances of a host of typeclasses. We could follow this pattern and write a number of boilerplate instances:

```
-- file: ch18/CustomT.hs
instance MonadReader r m => MonadReader r (CustomT m) where
    ...

instance MonadIO m => MonadIO (CustomT m) where
    ...
```

If the underlying monad was an instance of `MonadReader`, we would write a `MonadReader` instance for `CustomT` in which each function in the API passes through to the corresponding function in the underlying instance. This would allow higher-level code to only care that the stack as a whole is an instance of `MonadReader`, without knowing or caring about which layer provides the *real* implementation.

Instead of relying on all of these typeclass instances to work for us behind the scenes, we can be explicit. The `MonadTrans` typeclass defines a useful function named `lift`:

```
ghci> :m +Control.Monad.Trans
ghci> :info MonadTrans
```

```
class MonadTrans t where lift :: (Monad m) => m a -> t m a
    -- Defined in Control.Monad.Trans
```

This function takes a monadic action from one layer down the stack, and turns it—in other words, *lifts* it—into an action in the current monad transformer. Every monad transformer is an instance of MonadTrans.

We use the name lift based on its similarity of purpose to fmap and liftM. In each case, we hoist something from a lower level of the type system to the level we're currently working in. The different options are described here:

fmap
    Elevates a pure function to the level of functors

liftM
    Takes a pure function to the level of monads

lift
    Raises a monadic action from one level beneath in the transformer stack to the current one

Let's revisit the App monad stack we defined earlier (before we wrapped it with a newtype):

```
-- file: ch18/UglyStack.hs
type App = ReaderT AppConfig (StateT AppState IO)
```

If we want to access the AppState carried by the StateT, we would usually rely on mtl's typeclasses and instances to handle the plumbing for us:

```
-- file: ch18/UglyStack.hs
implicitGet :: App AppState
implicitGet = get
```

The lift function lets us achieve the same effect, by lifting get from StateT into ReaderT:

```
-- file: ch18/UglyStack.hs
explicitGet :: App AppState
explicitGet = lift get
```

Obviously, when we can let mtl do this work for us, we end up with cleaner code, but this is not always possible.

When Explicit Lifting Is Necessary

One case in which we *must* use lift is when we create a monad transformer stack in which instances of the same typeclass appear at multiple levels:

```
-- file: ch18/StackStack.hs
type Foo = StateT Int (State String)
```

If we try to use the put action of the MonadState typeclass, the instance we will get is that of StateT Int, because it's at the top of the stack:

```
-- file: ch18/StackStack.hs
outerPut :: Int -> Foo ()
outerPut = put
```

In this case, the only way we can access the underlying `State` monad's `put` is through use of `lift`:

```
-- file: ch18/StackStack.hs
innerPut :: String -> Foo ()
innerPut = lift . put
```

Sometimes, we need to access a monad more than one level down the stack, in which case we must compose calls to `lift`. Each composed use of `lift` gives us access to one deeper level:

```
-- file: ch18/StackStack.hs
type Bar = ReaderT Bool Foo

barPut :: String -> Bar ()
barPut = lift . lift . put
```

When we need to use `lift`, it can be good style to write wrapper functions that do the lifting for us, as just shown, and to use those. The alternative of sprinkling explicit uses of `lift` throughout our code tends to look messy. Worse, it hardwires the details of the layout of our monad stack into our code, which will complicate any subsequent modifications.

Understanding Monad Transformers by Building One

To give ourselves some insight into how monad transformers in general work, we will create one and describe its machinery as we go. Our target is simple and useful: `MaybeT`. Surprisingly, though, it is missing from the `mtl` library.

This monad transformer modifies the behavior of an underlying monad `m a` by wrapping its type parameter with `Maybe`, in order to get `m (Maybe a)`. As with the `Maybe` monad, if we call `fail` in the `MaybeT` monad transformer, execution terminates early.

In order to turn `m (Maybe a)` into a `Monad` instance, we must make it a distinct type, via a `newtype` declaration:

```
-- file: ch18/MaybeT.hs
newtype MaybeT m a = MaybeT {
    runMaybeT :: m (Maybe a)
  }
```

We now need to define the three standard monad functions. The most complex is (`>>=`), and its innards shed the most light on what we are actually doing. Before we delve into its operation, let us first take a look at its type:

```
-- file: ch18/MaybeT.hs
bindMT :: (Monad m) => MaybeT m a -> (a -> MaybeT m b) -> MaybeT m b
```

To understand this type signature, hark back to our discussion of multiparameter typeclasses in "Multiparameter Typeclasses" on page 370. The thing that we intend to make a Monad instance is the *partial type* MaybeT m; this has the usual single type parameter, a, that satisfies the requirements of the Monad typeclass.

The trick to understanding the body of our (>>=) implementation is that everything inside the do block executes in the *underlying* monad m, whatever that is:

```
-- file: ch18/MaybeT.hs
x `bindMT` f = MaybeT $ do
                 unwrapped <- runMaybeT x
                 case unwrapped of
                   Nothing -> return Nothing
                   Just y -> runMaybeT (f y)
```

Our runMaybeT function unwraps the result contained in x. Next, recall that the <- symbol desugars to (>>=): a monad transformer's (>>=) must use the underlying monad's (>>=). The final bit of case analysis determines whether we short-circuit or chain our computation. Finally, look back at the top of the body. Here, we must wrap the result with the MaybeT constructor, in order to once again hide the underlying monad.

The do notation just shown might be pleasant to read, but it hides the fact that we are relying on the underlying monad's (>>=) implementation. Here is a more idiomatic version of (>>=) for MaybeT that makes this clearer:

```
-- file: ch18/MaybeT.hs
x `altBindMT` f =
    MaybeT $ runMaybeT x >>= maybe (return Nothing) (runMaybeT . f)
```

Now that we understand what (>>=) is doing, our implementations of return and fail need no explanation, and neither does our Monad instance:

```
-- file: ch18/MaybeT.hs
returnMT :: (Monad m) => a -> MaybeT m a
returnMT a = MaybeT $ return (Just a)

failMT :: (Monad m) => t -> MaybeT m a
failMT _ = MaybeT $ return Nothing

instance (Monad m) => Monad (MaybeT m) where
  return = returnMT
  (>>=) = bindMT
  fail = failMT
```

Creating a Monad Transformer

To turn our type into a monad transformer, we must provide an instance of the MonadTrans class so that a user can access the underlying monad:

```
-- file: ch18/MaybeT.hs
instance MonadTrans MaybeT where
    lift m = MaybeT (Just `liftM` m)
```

The underlying monad starts out with a type parameter of a: we "inject" the Just constructor so that it will acquire the type that we need, Maybe a. We then hide the monad with our MaybeT constructor.

More Typeclass Instances

Once we have an instance for MonadTrans defined, we can use it to define instances for the umpteen other mtl typeclasses:

```
-- file: ch18/MaybeT.hs
instance (MonadIO m) => MonadIO (MaybeT m) where
  liftIO m = lift (liftIO m)

instance (MonadState s m) => MonadState s (MaybeT m) where
  get = lift get
  put k = lift (put k)

-- ... and so on for MonadReader, MonadWriter, etc ...
```

Because several of the mtl typeclasses use functional dependencies, some of our instance declarations require us to considerably relax GHC's usual strict type checking rules. (If we were to forget any of these directives, the compiler would helpfully advise us which ones we needed in its error messages.)

```
-- file: ch18/MaybeT.hs
{-# LANGUAGE FlexibleInstances, MultiParamTypeClasses,
             UndecidableInstances #-}
```

Is it better to use lift explicitly or to spend time writing these boilerplate instances? That depends on what we expect to do with our monad transformer. If we're going to use it in just a few restricted situations, we can get away with providing an instance for MonadTrans alone. In this case, a few more instances might still make sense, such as MonadIO. On the other hand, if our transformer is going to pop up in diverse situations throughout a body of code, spending a dull hour to write those instances might be a good investment.

Replacing the Parse Type with a Monad Stack

Now that we have developed a monad transformer that can exit early, we can use it to bail if, for example, a parse fails partway through. We could thus replace the Parse type that we developed in "Implicit State" on page 239 with a monad customized to our needs:

```
-- file: ch18/MaybeTParse.hs
{-# LANGUAGE GeneralizedNewtypeDeriving #-}

module MaybeTParse
    (
      Parse
    , evalParse
    ) where
```

```
import MaybeT
import Control.Monad.State
import Data.Int (Int64)
import qualified Data.ByteString.Lazy as L

data ParseState = ParseState {
      string :: L.ByteString
    , offset :: Int64
    } deriving (Show)

newtype Parse a = P {
      runP :: MaybeT (State ParseState) a
    } deriving (Monad, MonadState ParseState)

evalParse :: Parse a -> L.ByteString -> Maybe a
evalParse m s = evalState (runMaybeT (runP m)) (ParseState s 0)
```

Transformer Stacking Order Is Important

From our early examples using monad transformers such as ReaderT and StateT, it might be easy to conclude that the order in which we stack monad transformers doesn't matter.

When we stack StateT on top of State, it should be clearer that order can indeed make a difference. The types StateT Int (State String) and StateT String (State Int) might carry around the same information, but we can't use them interchangeably. The ordering determines when we need to use lift to get at one or the other piece of state.

Here's a case that more dramatically demonstrates the importance of ordering. Suppose we have a computation that might fail, and we want to log the circumstances under which it does so:

```
-- file: ch18/MTComposition.hs
{-# LANGUAGE FlexibleContexts #-}
import Control.Monad.Writer
import MaybeT

problem :: MonadWriter [String] m => m ()
problem = do
  tell ["this is where i fail"]
  fail "oops"
```

Which of these monad stacks will give us the information we need?

```
-- file: ch18/MTComposition.hs
type A = WriterT [String] Maybe

type B = MaybeT (Writer [String])

a :: A ()
a = problem

b :: B ()
b = problem
```

Let's try the alternatives in ghci:

```
ghci> runWriterT a
Loading package mtl-1.1.0.1 ... linking ... done.
Nothing
ghci> runWriter $ runMaybeT b
(Nothing,["this is where i fail"])
```

This difference in results should not come as a surprise—just look at the signatures of the execution functions:

```
ghci> :t runWriterT
runWriterT :: WriterT w m a -> m (a, w)
ghci> :t runWriter . runMaybeT
runWriter . runMaybeT :: MaybeT (Writer w) a -> (Maybe a, w)
```

Our WriterT-on-Maybe stack has Maybe as the underlying monad, so runWriterT must give us back a result of type Maybe. In our test case, we get to see only the log of what happened if nothing actually went wrong!

Stacking monad transformers is analogous to composing functions. If we change the order in which we apply functions and then get different results, we won't be surprised. So it is with monad transformers, too.

Putting Monads and Monad Transformers into Perspective

It's useful to step back from details for a few moments and look at the weaknesses and strengths of programming with monads and monad transformers.

Interference with Pure Code

Probably the biggest practical irritation of working with monads is that a monad's type constructor often gets in our way when we'd like to use pure code. Many useful pure functions need monadic counterparts, simply to tack on a placeholder parameter m for some monadic type constructor:

```
ghci> :t filter
filter :: (a -> Bool) -> [a] -> [a]
ghci> :i filterM
filterM :: (Monad m) => (a -> m Bool) -> [a] -> m [a]
      -- Defined in Control.Monad
```

However, the coverage is incomplete: the standard libraries don't always provide monadic versions of pure functions.

The reason for this lies in history. Eugenio Moggi introduced the idea of using monads for programming in 1988, around the time the Haskell 1.0 standard was being developed. Many of the functions in today's Prelude date back to Haskell 1.0, which was released in 1990. In 1991, Philip Wadler started writing for a wider functional programming audience about the potential of monads, at which point, they began to be put in use.

Not until 1996 and the release of Haskell 1.3 did the standard acquire support for monads. By this time, the language designers were already constrained by backwards compatibility: they couldn't change the signatures of functions in the Prelude, because it would have broken existing code.

Since then, the Haskell community has learned a lot about creating suitable abstractions, so that we can write code that is less affected by the pure/monadic divide. You can find modern distillations of these ideas in the Data.Traversable and Data.Foldable modules. As appealing as those modules are, we do not cover them in this book. This is in part for want of space, but also because if you're still following us at this point, you won't have trouble figuring them out for yourself.

In an ideal world, would we make a break from the past and switch over Prelude to use Traversable and Foldable types? Probably not. Learning Haskell is already a stimulating enough adventure for newcomers. The Foldable and Traversable abstractions are easy to pick up when we already understand functors and monads, but they would put early learners on too pure a diet of abstraction. For teaching the language, it's *good* that map operates on lists, not on functors.

Overdetermined Ordering

One of the principal reasons that we use monads is that they let us specify an ordering for effects. Look again at a small snippet of code we wrote earlier:

```
-- file: ch18/MTComposition.hs
{-# LANGUAGE FlexibleContexts #-}
import Control.Monad.Writer
import MaybeT

problem :: MonadWriter [String] m => m ()
problem = do
  tell ["this is where i fail"]
  fail "oops"
```

Because we are executing in a monad, we are guaranteed that the effect of the `tell` will occur before the effect of `fail`. The problem is that we get this guarantee of ordering even when we don't necessarily want it: the compiler is not free to rearrange monadic code, even if doing so would make it more efficient.

Runtime Overhead

Finally, when we use monads and monad transformers, we can pay an efficiency tax. For instance, the `State` monad carries its state around in a closure. Closures might be cheap in a Haskell implementation, but they're not free.

A monad transformer adds its own overhead to that of whatever is underneath. Our `MaybeT` transformer has to wrap and unwrap `Maybe` values every time we use `(>>=)`. A stack of `MaybeT` on top of `StateT` over `ReaderT` thus has a lot of bookkeeping to do for each `(>>=)`.

A sufficiently smart compiler might make some or all of these costs vanish, but that degree of sophistication is not yet widely available.

There are relatively simple techniques to avoid some of these costs, though we lack space to do more than mention them by name. For instance, using a continuation monad, we can avoid the constant wrapping and unwrapping in `(>>=)`, paying only for effects when we use them. Much of the complexity of this approach has already been packaged up in libraries. This area of work is still under lively development as of this writing. If you want to make your use of monad transformers more efficient, we recommend looking on Hackage or asking for directions on a mailing list or IRC.

Unwieldy Interfaces

If we use the `mtl` library as a black box, all of its components mesh quite nicely. However, once we start developing our own monads and monad transformers, and also using them with those provided by `mtl`, some deficiencies start to show.

For example, if we create a new monad transformer `FooT` and want to follow the same pattern as `mtl`, we'll have it implement a typeclass `MonadFoo`. If we really want to integrate it cleanly into the `mtl`, we'll have to provide instances for each of the dozen or so `mtl` typeclasses.

On top of that, we'll have to declare instances of `MonadFoo` for each of the `mtl` transformers. Most of those instances will be almost identical, and quite dull to write. If we want to keep integrating new monad transformers into the `mtl` framework, the number of moving parts we must deal with increases with the *square* of the number of new transformers!

In fairness, this problem matters to a tiny number of people only. Most users of `mtl` don't need to develop new transformers at all, so they are not affected.

This weakness of `mtl`'s design lies with the fact that it was the first library of monad transformers that was developed. Given that its designers were plunging into the unknown, they did a remarkable job of producing a powerful library that is easy for most users to understand and work with.

A newer library of monads and transformers, `monadLib`, corrects many of the design flaws in `mtl`. If at some point you turn into a hardcore hacker of monad transformers, it is well worth looking at.

The quadratic instances definition is actually a problem with the approach of using monad transformers. There have been many other approaches put forward for composing monads that don't have this problem, but none of them seem as convenient to the end user as monad transformers. Fortunately, there simply aren't that many foundational, generically useful monad transformers.

Pulling It All Together

Monads are not by any means the end of the road when it comes to working with effects and types. What they are is the most practical resting point we have reached so far. Language researchers are always working on systems that try to provide similar advantages, without the same compromises.

Although we must make compromises when we use them, monads and monad transformers still offer a degree of flexibility and control that has no precedent in an imperative language. With just a few declarations, we can rewire something as fundamental as the semicolon to give it a new meaning.

CHAPTER 19

Error Handling

Error handling is one of the most important—and overlooked—topics for programmers, regardless of the language used. In Haskell, you will find two major types of error handling employed: *pure error handling* and *exceptions*.

When we speak of pure error handling, we are referring to algorithms that do not require anything from the IO monad. We can often implement error handling for them simply by using Haskell's expressive data type system to our advantage. Haskell also has an exception system. Due to the complexities of lazy evaluation, exceptions in Haskell can be thrown anywhere, but caught only within the IO monad. In this chapter, we'll consider both.

Error Handling with Data Types

Let's begin our discussion of error handling with a very simple function. Let's say that we wish to perform division on a series of numbers. We have a constant numerator but wish to vary the denominator. We might come up with a function like this:

```
-- file: ch19/divby1.hs
divBy :: Integral a => a -> [a] -> [a]
divBy numerator = map (numerator `div`)
```

Very simple, right? We can play around with this a bit in ghci:

```
ghci> divBy 50 [1,2,5,8,10]
[50,25,10,6,5]
ghci> take 5 (divBy 100 [1..])
[100,50,33,25,20]
```

This behaves as expected: 50 / 1 is 50, 50 / 2 is 25, and so forth.[*] This even worked with the infinite list [1..]. What happens if we sneak a 0 into our list somewhere?

---

[*] We're using integral division here, so 50 / 8 shows as 6 instead of 6.25. We're not using floating-point arithmetic in this example because division by zero with a Double produces the special value Infinity rather than an error.

```
ghci> divBy 50 [1,2,0,8,10]
[50,25,*** Exception: divide by zero
```

Isn't that interesting? ghci started displaying the output, and then stopped with an exception when it got to the zero. That's lazy evaluation at work—it calculated results as needed.

As we will see later in this chapter, in the absence of an explicit exception handler, this exception will crash the program. That's obviously not desirable, so let's consider better ways we could indicate an error in this pure function.

Use of Maybe

One immediately recognizable and easy way to indicate failure is to use Maybe.[†] Instead of just returning a list and throwing an exception on failure, we can return Nothing if the input list contains a zero anywhere, or return Just with the results otherwise. Here's an implementation of such an algorithm:

```
-- file: ch19/divby2.hs
divBy :: Integral a => a -> [a] -> Maybe [a]
divBy _ [] = Just []
divBy _ (0:_) = Nothing
divBy numerator (denom:xs) =
    case divBy numerator xs of
      Nothing -> Nothing
      Just results -> Just ((numerator `div` denom) : results)
```

If you try it out in ghci, you'll see that it works:

```
ghci> divBy 50 [1,2,5,8,10]
Just [50,25,10,6,5]
ghci> divBy 50 [1,2,0,8,10]
Nothing
```

The function that calls divBy can now use a case statement to see if the call was successful, just as divBy does when it calls itself.

You may note that you could use a monadic implementation of the preceding example, like so:

```
-- file: ch19/divby2m.hs
divBy :: Integral a => a -> [a] -> Maybe [a]
divBy numerator denominators =
    mapM (numerator `safeDiv`) denominators
    where safeDiv _ 0 = Nothing
          safeDiv x y = x `div` y
```

We will avoid the monadic implementation in this chapter for simplicity but wanted to point out that it exists.

[†] For an introduction to Maybe, refer to "A More Controlled Approach" on page 61.

Loss and preservation of laziness

The use of `Maybe` is convenient, but it has come at a cost. `divBy` can no longer handle infinite lists as input. Since the result is `Maybe [a]`, the entire input list must be examined before we can be sure that we won't be returning `Nothing` due to a zero somewhere in it. You can verify this is the case by attempting one of our earlier examples:

```
ghci> divBy 100 [1..]
*** Exception: stack overflow
```

Note that you don't start seeing partial output here; you get *no* output. Notice that at each step in `divBy` (except for the case of an empty input list or a zero at the start of the list), the results from every subsequent element must be known before the results from the current element can be known. Thus this algorithm can't work on infinite lists, and it is also not very space-efficient for large finite lists.

Having said all that, `Maybe` is often a fine choice. In this particular case, we don't know whether there will be a problem until we get into evaluating the entire input. Sometimes we know of a problem up front—for instance, `tail []` in ghci produces an exception. We could easily write an infinite-capable `tail` that doesn't have this problem:

```
-- file: ch19/safetail.hs
safeTail :: [a] -> Maybe [a]
safeTail [] = Nothing
safeTail (_:xs) = Just xs
```

This simply returns `Nothing` if given an empty input list or `Just` with the result for anything else. Since we have only to make sure the list is nonempty before knowing whether or not we have an error, using `Maybe` here doesn't reduce our laziness. We can test this out in ghci and see how it compares with regular `tail`:

```
ghci> tail [1,2,3,4,5]
[2,3,4,5]
ghci> safeTail [1,2,3,4,5]
Just [2,3,4,5]
ghci> tail []
*** Exception: Prelude.tail: empty list
ghci> safeTail []
Nothing
```

Here, we can see our `safeTail` performed as expected. But what about infinite lists? We don't want to print out an infinite number of results, so we can test with `take 5 (tail [1..])` and a similar construction with `safeTail`:

```
ghci> take 5 (tail [1..])
[2,3,4,5,6]
ghci> case safeTail [1..] of {Nothing -> Nothing; Just x -> Just (take 5 x)}
Just [2,3,4,5,6]
ghci> take 5 (tail [])
*** Exception: Prelude.tail: empty list
ghci> case safeTail [] of {Nothing -> Nothing; Just x -> Just (take 5 x)}
Nothing
```

Here you can see that both `tail` and `safeTail` handled infinite lists just fine. Note that we were able to deal better with an empty input list; instead of throwing an exception, we decided to return `Nothing` in that situation. We were able to achieve error handling at no expense to laziness.

But how do we apply this to our `divBy` example? Let's consider the situation there. Failure is a property of an individual bad input, not of the input list itself. How about making failure a property of an individual output element, rather than the output list itself? That is, instead of a function of type a -> [a] -> Maybe [a], we will have a -> [a] -> [Maybe a]. This will have the benefit of preserving laziness, plus the caller will be able to determine exactly where in the list the problem is—or even just filter out the problem results if desired. Here's an implementation:

```
-- file: ch19/divby3.hs
divBy :: Integral a => a -> [a] -> [Maybe a]
divBy numerator denominators =
    map worker denominators
    where worker 0 = Nothing
          worker x = Just (numerator `div` x)
```

Take a look at this function. We're back to using `map`, which is a good thing for both laziness and simplicity. We can try it out in `ghci` and see that it works for finite and infinite lists just fine:

```
ghci> divBy 50 [1,2,5,8,10]
[Just 50,Just 25,Just 10,Just 6,Just 5]
ghci> divBy 50 [1,2,0,8,10]
[Just 50,Just 25,Nothing,Just 6,Just 5]
ghci> take 5 (divBy 100 [1..])
[Just 100,Just 50,Just 33,Just 25,Just 20]
```

We hope that you can take from this discussion the point that there is a distinction between the input not being well-formed (as in the case of `safeTail`) and the input potentially containing some bad data, as in the case of `divBy`. These two cases can often justify different handling of the results.

Usage of the Maybe monad

Back in "Use of Maybe" on page 448, we had an example program named *divby2.hs*. This example didn't preserve laziness but returned a value of type `Maybe [a]`. The exact same algorithm could be expressed using a monadic style. For more information and important background on monads, please refer to Chapter 14. Here's our new monadic-style algorithm:

```
-- file: ch19/divby4.hs
divBy :: Integral a => a -> [a] -> Maybe [a]
divBy _ [] = return []
divBy _ (0:_) = fail "division by zero in divBy"
divBy numerator (denom:xs) =
    do next <- divBy numerator xs
       return ((numerator `div` denom) : next)
```

The Maybe monad makes the expression of this algorithm look nicer. For the Maybe monad, return is the same as Just, and fail _ = Nothing, so our error explanation string is never actually seen anywhere. We can test this algorithm with the same tests we used against *divby2.hs* if we want:

```
ghci> divBy 50 [1,2,5,8,10]
Just [50,25,10,6,5]
ghci> divBy 50 [1,2,0,8,10]
Nothing
ghci> divBy 100 [1..]
*** Exception: stack overflow
```

The code we wrote actually isn't specific to the Maybe monad. By simply changing the type, we can make it work for *any* monad. Let's try it:

```
-- file: ch19/divby5.hs
divBy :: Integral a => a -> [a] -> Maybe [a]
divBy = divByGeneric

divByGeneric :: (Monad m, Integral a) => a -> [a] -> m [a]
divByGeneric _ [] = return []
divByGeneric _ (0:_) = fail "division by zero in divByGeneric"
divByGeneric numerator (denom:xs) =
    do next <- divByGeneric numerator xs
       return ((numerator `div` denom) : next)
```

The divByGeneric function contains the same code as divBy did before; we just gave it a more general type. This is, in fact, the type that ghci infers if no type is given. We also defined a convenience function divBy with a more specific type.

Let's try this out in ghci:

```
ghci> :l divby5.hs
[1 of 1] Compiling Main             ( divby5.hs, interpreted )
Ok, modules loaded: Main.
ghci> divBy 50 [1,2,5,8,10]
Just [50,25,10,6,5]
ghci> (divByGeneric 50 [1,2,5,8,10])::(Integral a => Maybe [a])
Just [50,25,10,6,5]
ghci> divByGeneric 50 [1,2,5,8,10]
[50,25,10,6,5]
ghci> divByGeneric 50 [1,2,0,8,10]
*** Exception: user error (division by zero in divByGeneric)
```

The first two inputs both produce the same output that we saw earlier. Since divByGeneric doesn't have a specific return type, we must either give one or let the interpreter infer one from the environment. If we don't give a specific return type, ghci infers the IO monad. You can see that in the third and fourth examples. The IO monad converts fail into an exception, as you can see with the fourth example.

The Control.Monad.Error module in the mtl package makes Either String into a monad as well. If you use Either, you can get a pure result that preserves the error message, like so:

```
ghci> :m +Control.Monad.Error
ghci> (divByGeneric 50 [1,2,5,8,10])::(Integral a => Either String [a])
Loading package mtl-1.1.0.1 ... linking ... done.
Right [50,25,10,6,5]
ghci> (divByGeneric 50 [1,2,0,8,10])::(Integral a => Either String [a])
Left "division by zero in divByGeneric"
```

This leads us into our next topic of discussion: using Either for returning error information.

Use of Either

The Either type is similar to the Maybe type, with one key difference: it can carry attached data both for an error and a success ("the Right answer").[‡] Although the language imposes no restrictions, by convention, a function returning an Either uses a Left return value to indicate an error, and it uses Right to indicate success. If it helps you remember, you can think of getting the Right answer. We can start with our *divby2.hs* example from the earlier section on Maybe and adapt it to work with Either:

```
-- file: ch19/divby6.hs
divBy :: Integral a => a -> [a] -> Either String [a]
divBy _ [] = Right []
divBy _ (0:_) = Left "divBy: division by 0"
divBy numerator (denom:xs) =
    case divBy numerator xs of
        Left x -> Left x
        Right results -> Right ((numerator `div` denom) : results)
```

This code is almost identical to the Maybe code; we've substituted Right for every Just. Left compares to Nothing, but now it can carry a message. Let's check it out in ghci:

```
ghci> divBy 50 [1,2,5,8,10]
Right [50,25,10,6,5]
ghci> divBy 50 [1,2,0,8,10]
Left "divBy: division by 0"
```

Custom data types for errors

While a String indicating the cause of an error may be useful to humans down the road, it's often helpful to define a custom error type that we can use to programmatically decide on a course of action based upon exactly what the problem was. For instance, let's say that for some reason, besides 0, we also don't want to divide by 10 or 20. We could define a custom error type like so:

```
-- file: ch19/divby7.hs
data DivByError a = DivBy0
                  | ForbiddenDenominator a
                    deriving (Eq, Read, Show)

divBy :: Integral a => a -> [a] -> Either (DivByError a) [a]
```

[‡] For more information on Either, refer to "Handling Errors Through API Design" on page 210.

```
divBy _ []  = Right []
divBy _ (0:_) = Left DivBy0
divBy _ (10:_) = Left (ForbiddenDenominator 10)
divBy _ (20:_) = Left (ForbiddenDenominator 20)
divBy numerator (denom:xs) =
    case divBy numerator xs of
      Left x -> Left x
      Right results -> Right ((numerator `div` denom) : results)
```

Now, in the event of an error, the Left data could be inspected to find the exact cause. Or, it could simply be printed out with show, which will generate a reasonable idea of the problem as well. Here's this function in action:

```
ghci> divBy 50 [1,2,5,8]
Right [50,25,10,6]
ghci> divBy 50 [1,2,5,8,10]
Left (ForbiddenDenominator 10)
ghci> divBy 50 [1,2,0,8,10]
Left DivBy0
```

 All of these Either examples suffer from the lack of laziness that our early Maybe examples suffered from. We address that in an exercise question at the end of this chapter.

Monadic use of Either

Back in "Usage of the Maybe monad" on page 450, we showed you how to use Maybe in a monad. Either can be used in a monad too, but it can be slightly more complicated. The reason is that fail is hardcoded to accept only a String as the failure code, so we have to have a way to map such a string into whatever type we used for Left. As you saw earlier, Control.Monad.Error provides built-in support for Either String a, which involves no mapping for the argument to fail. Here's how we can set up our example to work with Either in the monadic style:

```
-- file: ch19/divby8.hs
{-# LANGUAGE FlexibleContexts #-}

import Control.Monad.Error

data Show a =>
    DivByError a = DivBy0
                 | ForbiddenDenominator a
                 | OtherDivByError String
                   deriving (Eq, Read, Show)

instance Error (DivByError a) where
    strMsg x = OtherDivByError x

divBy :: Integral a => a -> [a] -> Either (DivByError a) [a]
divBy = divByGeneric

divByGeneric :: (Integral a, MonadError (DivByError a) m) =>
                a -> [a] -> m [a]
```

```
divByGeneric _ [] = return []
divByGeneric _ (0:_) = throwError DivBy0
divByGeneric _ (10:_) = throwError (ForbiddenDenominator 10)
divByGeneric _ (20:_) = throwError (ForbiddenDenominator 20)
divByGeneric numerator (denom:xs) =
    do next <- divByGeneric numerator xs
       return ((numerator `div` denom) : next)
```

Here, we needed to turn on the FlexibleContexts language extension in order to provide the type signature for divByGeneric. The divBy function works exactly the same as before. For divByGeneric, we make divByError a member of the Error class by defining what happens when someone calls fail (the strMsg function). We also convert Right to return and Left to throwError to enable this to be generic.

Exceptions

 Version 6.10.1 of GHC was released as this book went to press. It introduces an extensible extension system. In the sections that follow, we document the older exception system. The two are similar, but not completely compatible.

Exception handling is found in many programming languages, including Haskell. It can be useful because, when a problem occurs, exception handling can provide an easy way of handling it, even if it occurs several layers down through a chain of function calls. With exceptions, it's not necessary to check the return value of every function call for errors, and we must take care to produce a return value that reflects the error, as C programmers must do. In Haskell, thanks to monads and the Either and Maybe types, we can often achieve the same effects in pure code without the need to use exceptions and exception handling.

Some problems—especially those involving I/O—call for working with exceptions. In Haskell, exceptions may be thrown from any location in the program. However, due to the unspecified evaluation order, they can only be caught in the IO monad. Haskell exception handling doesn't involve special syntax as it does in Python or Java. Rather, the mechanisms to catch and handle exceptions are—surprise—functions.

First Steps with Exceptions

In the Control.Exception module, various functions and types relating to exceptions are defined. There is an Exception type defined there; all exceptions are of type Exception. There are also functions for catching and handling exceptions. Let's start by looking at try, which has type IO a -> IO (Either Exception a). This wraps an IO action with exception handling. If an exception is thrown, it will return a Left value with the exception; otherwise, it returns a Right value with the original result. Let's try this out in ghci. We'll first trigger an unhandled exception, and then try to catch it:

```
ghci> :m Control.Exception
ghci> let x = 5 `div` 0
ghci> let y = 5 `div` 1
ghci> print x
*** Exception: divide by zero
ghci> print y
5
ghci> try (print x)
Left divide by zero
ghci> try (print y)
5
Right ()
```

Notice that no exception was thrown by the let statements. That's to be expected due to lazy evaluation; the division by zero won't be attempted until it is demanded by the attempt to print out x. Also, notice that there were two lines of output from try (print y). The first line was produced by print, which displayed the digit 5 on the terminal. The second was produced by ghci and shows us that print y returned () and didn't throw an exception.

Laziness and Exception Handling

Now that you know how try works, let's try another experiment. Let's say we want to catch the result of try for future evaluation, so we can handle the result of division. Perhaps we would do it like this:

```
ghci> result <- try (return x)
Right *** Exception: divide by zero
```

What happened here? Let's try to piece it together, and illustrate with another attempt:

```
ghci> let z = undefined
ghci> try (print z)
Left Prelude.undefined
ghci> result <- try (return z)
Right *** Exception: Prelude.undefined
```

As before, assigning undefined to z was not a problem. The key to this puzzle, and to the division puzzle, lies with lazy evaluation. Specifically, it lies with return, which does not force the evaluation of its argument; it only wraps it up. So, the result of try (return undefined) would be Right undefined. Now, ghci wants to display this result on the terminal. It gets as far as printing out "Right ", but we can't print out undefined (or the result of division by zero). So when we see the exception message, it's coming from ghci, not your program.

This is a key point. Let's think about why our earlier example worked and this one didn't. Earlier, we put print x inside try. Printing the value of something, of course, requires it to be evaluated, so the exception was detected at the right place. But simply using return does not force evaluation. To solve this problem, the Control.Exception module defines the evaluate function. It behaves just like return but forces its argument to be evaluated immediately. Let's try it:

```
ghci> let z = undefined
ghci> result <- try (evaluate z)
Left Prelude.undefined
ghci> result <- try (evaluate x)
Left divide by zero
```

There, that's what was expected. This worked for both undefined and our division by zero example.

 Remember: whenever you are trying to catch exceptions thrown by pure code, use evaluate instead of return inside your exception-catching function.

Using handle

Often, you may wish to perform one action if a piece of code completes without an exception, and perform a different action otherwise. For situations such as this, there's a function called handle. This function has type (Exception -> IO a) -> IO a -> IO a. That is, it takes two parameters. The first is a function to call in the event where there is an exception while performing the second. Here's one way we could use it:

```
ghci> :m Control.Exception
ghci> let x = 5 `div` 0
ghci> let y = 5 `div` 1
ghci> handle (\_ -> putStrLn "Error calculating result") (print x)
Error calculating result
ghci> handle (\_ -> putStrLn "Error calculating result") (print y)
5
```

This way, we can print out a nice message if there is an error in the calculations. It's nicer than having the program crash with a division by zero error, for sure.

Selective Handling of Exceptions

One problem with the previous example is that it prints "Error calculating result" for *any* exception. There may have been an exception other than a division by zero exception. For instance, there may have been an error displaying the output, or some other exception could have been thrown by the pure code.

There's a function handleJust for these situations. It lets you specify a test to see whether you are interested in a given exception. Let's take a look:

```
-- file: ch19/hj1.hs
import Control.Exception

catchIt :: Exception -> Maybe ()
catchIt (ArithException DivideByZero) = Just ()
catchIt _ = Nothing

handler :: () -> IO ()
```

```
    handler _ = putStrLn "Caught error: divide by zero"

    safePrint :: Integer -> IO ()
    safePrint x = handleJust catchIt handler (print x)
```

catchIt defines a function that decides whether or not we're interested in a given exception. It returns Just if so, and Nothing if not. Also, the value attached to Just will be passed to our handler. We can now use safePrint nicely:

```
ghci> :l hj1.hs
[1 of 1] Compiling Main                ( hj1.hs, interpreted )
Ok, modules loaded: Main.
ghci> let x = 5 `div` 0
ghci> let y = 5 `div` 1
ghci> safePrint x
Caught error: divide by zero
ghci> safePrint y
5
```

The Control.Exception module also presents a number of functions that we can use as part of the test in handleJust to narrow down the kinds of exceptions we care about. For instance, there is a function arithExceptions of type Exception -> Maybe ArithException that will pick out any ArithException, but ignore any other one. We could use it like this:

```
-- file: ch19/hj2.hs
import Control.Exception

handler :: ArithException -> IO ()
handler e = putStrLn $ "Caught arithmetic error: " ++ show e

safePrint :: Integer -> IO ()
safePrint x = handleJust arithExceptions handler (print x)
```

In this way, we can catch all types of ArithException, but still let other exceptions pass through unmodified and uncaught. We can see it work like so:

```
ghci> :l hj2.hs
[1 of 1] Compiling Main                ( hj2.hs, interpreted )
Ok, modules loaded: Main.
ghci> let x = 5 `div` 0
ghci> let y = 5 `div` 1
ghci> safePrint x
Caught arithmetic error: divide by zero
ghci> safePrint y
5
```

Of particular interest is the ioErrors test, which corresponds to the large class of I/O-related exceptions.

I/O Exceptions

Perhaps the largest source of exceptions in any program is I/O. All sorts of things can go wrong when dealing with the outside world: disks can be full, networks can go down, or files can be empty when you expect them to have data. In Haskell, an I/O exception is just like any other exception in that the Exception data type can represent it. On the other hand, because there are so many types of I/O exceptions, a special module, System.IO.Error, exists for dealing with them.

System.IO.Error defines two functions, catch and try, that, like their counterparts in Control.Exception, are used to deal with exceptions. Unlike the Control.Exception functions, however, these functions will trap only I/O errors and will pass all other exceptions through uncaught. In Haskell, I/O errors all have type IOError, which is defined as the same as IOException.

Be careful which names you use

Because both System.IO.Error and Control.Exception define functions with the same names, if you import both in your program, you will get an error message about an ambiguous reference to a function. You can import one or the other module qualified, or hide the symbols from one module or the other.

Note that Prelude exports System.IO.Error's version of catch, *not* the version provided by Control.Exception. Remember that the former can catch only I/O errors, while the latter can catch all exceptions. In other words, the catch in Control.Exception is almost always the one you will want, but it is *not* the one you will get by default.

Let's take a look at one approach to using exceptions in the I/O system to our benefit. Back in "Working with Files and Handles" on page 169, we presented a program that used an imperative style to read lines from a file one by one. Although we subsequently demonstrated more compact, "Haskelly" ways to solve that problem, let's revisit that example here. In the mainloop function, we had to explicitly test if we were at the end of the input file before each attempt to read a line from it. Instead, we could check if the attempt to read a line resulted in an EOF error, like so:

```
-- file: ch19/toupper-impch20.hs
import System.IO
import System.IO.Error
import Data.Char(toUpper)

main :: IO ()
main = do
       inh <- openFile "input.txt" ReadMode
       outh <- openFile "output.txt" WriteMode
       mainloop inh outh
       hClose inh
       hClose outh

mainloop :: Handle -> Handle -> IO ()
mainloop inh outh =
    do input <- try (hGetLine inh)
       case input of
         Left e ->
```

```
            if isEOFError e
                then return ()
                else ioError e
        Right inpStr ->
            do hPutStrLn outh (map toUpper inpStr)
               mainloop inh outh
```

Here, we use the System.IO.Error version of try to check whether hGetLine threw an
IOError. If it did, we use isEOFError (defined in System.IO.Error) to see if the thrown
exception indicated that we reached the end of the file. If it did, we exit the loop. If the
exception was something else, we call ioError to rethrow it.

There are many such tests and ways to extract information from IOError defined in
System.IO.Error. We recommend that you consult that page in the library reference
when you need to know about them.

Throwing Exceptions

Thus far, we have talked in detail about handling exceptions. There is another piece to
the puzzle: throwing exceptions.[§] In the examples we have visited so far in this chapter,
the Haskell system throws exceptions for you. However, it is possible to throw any
exception yourself. We'll show you how.

You'll notice that most of these functions appear to return a value of type a or IO a.
This means that the function can appear to return a value of any type. In fact, because
these functions throw exceptions, they never "return" anything in the normal sense.
These return values let you use these functions in various contexts where various different types are expected.

Let's start our tour of ways to throw exceptions with the functions in
Control.Exception. The most generic function is throw, which has type Exception ->
a. This function can throw any Exception, and can do so in a pure context. There is a
companion function—throwIO with type Exception -> IO a—that throws an exception
in the IO monad. Both functions require an Exception to throw. You can craft an
Exception by hand or reuse an Exception that was previously created.

There is also a function ioError, which is defined identically in Control.Exception and
System.IO.Error with type IOError -> IO a. This is used when you want to generate
an arbitrary I/O-related exception.

Dynamic Exceptions

Dynamic Exceptions make use of two little-used Haskell modules: Data.Dynamic and
Data.Typeable. We will not go into a great level of detail on those modules here, but
we will give you the tools you need to craft and use your own dynamic exception type.

[§] In some other languages, throwing an exception is referred to as *raising* it.

In Chapter 21, you will see that the HDBC database library uses dynamic exceptions to indicate errors from SQL databases back to applications. Errors from database engines often have three components: an integer that represents an error code, a state, and a human-readable error message. We will build up our own implementation of the HDBC `SqlError` type here. Let's start with the data structure representing the error itself:

```
-- file: ch19/dynexc.hs
{-# LANGUAGE DeriveDataTypeable #-}

import Data.Dynamic
import Control.Exception

data SqlError = SqlError {seState :: String,
                          seNativeError :: Int,
                          seErrorMsg :: String}
                 deriving (Eq, Show, Read, Typeable)
```

By deriving the `Typeable` typeclass, we've made this type available for dynamically typed programming. In order for GHC to automatically generate a `Typeable` instance, we had to enable the `DeriveDataTypeable` language extension.[||]

Now, let's define a `catchSql` and a `handleSql` that can be used to catch an exception that is an `SqlError` (note that the regular `catch` and `handle` functions cannot catch our `SqlError`, because it is not a type of `Exception`):

```
-- file: ch19/dynexc.hs
{- | Execute the given IO action.

If it raises a 'SqlError', then execute the supplied
handler and return its return value.  Otherwise, proceed
as normal. -}
catchSql :: IO a -> (SqlError -> IO a) -> IO a
catchSql = catchDyn

{- | Like 'catchSql', with the order of arguments reversed. -}
handleSql :: (SqlError -> IO a) -> IO a -> IO a
handleSql = flip catchSql
```

These functions are simply thin wrappers around `catchDyn`, which has type `Typeable exception => IO a -> (exception -> IO a) -> IO a`. We simply restrict the type of this here so that it catches only SQL exceptions.

Normally, when an exception is thrown but not caught anywhere, the program will crash and display the exception to standard error. With a dynamic exception, however, the system will not know how to display this, so we will simply see an unhelpful "unknown exception" message. We can provide a utility so that application writers can simply say `main = handleSqlError $ do ...` and have confidence that any exceptions thrown (in that thread) will be displayed. Here's how to write `handleSqlError`:

[||] It is possible to derive `Typeable` instances by hand, but that is cumbersome.

```
-- file: ch19/dynexc.hs
{- | Catches 'SqlError's, and re-raises them as IO errors with fail.
Useful if you don't care to catch SQL errors, but want to see a sane
error message if one happens.  One would often use this as a
high-level wrapper around SQL calls. -}
handleSqlError :: IO a -> IO a
handleSqlError action =
    catchSql action handler
    where handler e = fail ("SQL error: " ++ show e)
```

Finally, here's an example of how to throw an SqlError as an exception. Here's a function that will do just that:

```
-- file: ch19/dynexc.hs
throwSqlError :: String -> Int -> String -> a
throwSqlError state nativeerror errormsg =
    throwDyn (SqlError state nativeerror errormsg)

throwSqlErrorIO :: String -> Int -> String -> IO a
throwSqlErrorIO state nativeerror errormsg =
    evaluate (throwSqlError state nativeerror errormsg)
```

 As a reminder, evaluate is like return but forces the evaluation of its argument.

This completes our dynamic exception support. That was a lot of code, and you may not have needed that much, but we wanted to give you an example of the dynamic exception itself and the utilities that often go with it. In fact, these examples reflect almost exactly what is present in the HDBC library. Let's play with these in ghci for a bit:

```
ghci> :l dynexc.hs
[1 of 1] Compiling Main             ( dynexc.hs, interpreted )
Ok, modules loaded: Main.
ghci> throwSqlErrorIO "state" 5 "error message"
*** Exception: (unknown)
ghci> handleSqlError $ throwSqlErrorIO "state" 5 "error message"
*** Exception: user error (SQL error: SqlError {seState = "state", seNativeError = 5,
seErrorMsg = "error message"})
ghci> handleSqlError $ fail "other error"
*** Exception: user error (other error)
```

From this, you can see that ghci doesn't know how to display an SQL error by itself. However, you can also see that our handleSqlError function helped out with that but also passed through other errors unmodified. Let's finally try out a custom handler:

```
ghci> handleSql (fail . seErrorMsg) (throwSqlErrorIO "state" 5 "my error")
*** Exception: user error (my error)
```

Here, we defined a custom error handler that threw a new exception, consisting of the message in the seErrorMsg field of the SqlError. You can see that it worked as intended.

1. Take the `Either` example and made it work with laziness in the style of the `Maybe` example.

Error Handling in Monads

Because we must catch exceptions in the IO monad, if we try to use them inside a monad, or in a stack of monad transformers, we'll get bounced out to the IO monad. This is almost never what we would actually like.

We defined a `MaybeT` transformer in "Understanding Monad Transformers by Building One" on page 438, but it is more useful as an aid to understanding than a programming tool. Fortunately, a dedicated—and more useful—monad transformer already exists: `ErrorT`, which is defined in the `Control.Monad.Error` module.

The `ErrorT` transformer lets us add exceptions to a monad, but it uses its own special exception machinery, separate from that provided the `Control.Exception` module. It gives us some interesting capabilities:

- If we stick with the `ErrorT` interfaces, we can both throw and catch exceptions within this monad.
- Following the naming pattern of other monad transformers, the execution function is named `runErrorT`. An uncaught `ErrorT` exception will stop propagating upwards when it reaches `runErrorT`. We will not be kicked out to the IO monad.
- We control the type that our exceptions will have.

Do not confuse ErrorT with regular exceptions

If we use the `throw` function from `Control.Exception` inside `ErrorT` (or if we use `error` or `undefined`), we will *still* be bounced out to the IO monad.

As with other `mtl` monads, the interface that `ErrorT` provides is defined by a typeclass:

```
-- file: ch19/MonadError.hs
class (Monad m) => MonadError e m | m -> e where
    throwError :: e              -- error to throw
                 -> m a

    catchError :: m a           -- action to execute
                 -> (e -> m a)  -- error handler
                 -> m a
```

The type variable e represents the error type that we want to use. Whatever our error type is, we must make it an instance of the `Error` typeclass:

```
-- file: ch19/MonadError.hs
class Error a where
    -- create an exception with no message
    noMsg  :: a

    -- create an exception with a message
    strMsg :: String -> a
```

ErrorT's implementation of fail uses the strMsg function. It throws strMsg as an exception, passing it the string argument that it received. As for noMsg, it is used to provide an mzero implementation for the MonadPlus typeclass.

To support the strMsg and noMsg functions, our ParseError type will have a Chatty constructor. This will be used as the constructor if, for example, someone calls fail in our monad.

One last piece of plumbing that we need to know about is the type of the execution function runErrorT:

```
ghci> :t runErrorT
runErrorT :: ErrorT e m a -> m (Either e a)
```

A Tiny Parsing Framework

To illustrate the use of ErrorT, let's develop the bare bones of a parsing library similar to Parsec:

```
-- file: ch19/ParseInt.hs
{-# LANGUAGE GeneralizedNewtypeDeriving #-}

import Control.Monad.Error
import Control.Monad.State
import qualified Data.ByteString.Char8 as B

data ParseError = NumericOverflow
                | EndOfInput
                | Chatty String
                  deriving (Eq, Ord, Show)

instance Error ParseError where
    noMsg  = Chatty "oh noes!"
    strMsg = Chatty
```

For our parser's state, we will create a very small monad transformer stack. A State monad carries around the ByteString to parse, and ErrorT is stacked on top to provide error handling:

```
-- file: ch19/ParseInt.hs
newtype Parser a = P {
      runP :: ErrorT ParseError (State B.ByteString) a
    } deriving (Monad, MonadError ParseError)
```

As usual, we have wrapped our monad stack in a newtype. This costs us nothing in performance but adds type safety. We deliberately avoided deriving an instance of

`MonadState B.ByteString`. This means that users of the `Parser` monad will not be able to use `get` or `put` to query or modify the parser's state. As a result, we force ourselves to do some manual lifting to get at the `State` monad in our stack. This is, however, very easy to do:

```
-- file: ch19/ParseInt.hs
liftP :: State B.ByteString a -> Parser a
liftP m = P (lift m)

satisfy :: (Char -> Bool) -> Parser Char
satisfy p = do
  s <- liftP get
  case B.uncons s of
    Nothing         -> throwError EndOfInput
    Just (c, s')
        | p c       -> liftP (put s') >> return c
        | otherwise -> throwError (Chatty "satisfy failed")
```

The `catchError` function is useful for tasks beyond simple error handling. For instance, we can easily defang an exception, turning it into a more friendly form:

```
-- file: ch19/ParseInt.hs
optional :: Parser a -> Parser (Maybe a)
optional p = (Just `liftM` p) `catchError` \_ -> return Nothing
```

Our execution function merely plugs together the various layers and rearranges the result into a tidier form:

```
-- file: ch19/ParseInt.hs
runParser :: Parser a -> B.ByteString
          -> Either ParseError (a, B.ByteString)
runParser p bs = case runState (runErrorT (runP p)) bs of
                   (Left err, _) -> Left err
                   (Right r, bs) -> Right (r, bs)
```

If we load this into ghci, we can put it through its paces:

```
ghci> :m +Data.Char
ghci> let p = satisfy isDigit
Loading package array-0.1.0.0 ... linking ... done.
Loading package bytestring-0.9.0.1.1 ... linking ... done.
Loading package mtl-1.1.0.1 ... linking ... done.
ghci> runParser p (B.pack "x")
Left (Chatty "satisfy failed")
ghci> runParser p (B.pack "9abc")
Right ('9',"abc")
ghci> runParser (optional p) (B.pack "x")
Right (Nothing,"x")
ghci> runParser (optional p) (B.pack "9a")
Right (Just '9',"a")
```

1. Write a `many` parser, with type `Parser a -> Parser [a]`. It should apply a parser until it fails.

2. Use `many` to write an `int` parser, with type `Parser Int`. It should accept negative and positive integers.

3. Modify your `int` parser to throw a `NumericOverflow` exception if it detects a numeric overflow while parsing.

CHAPTER 20

Systems Programming in Haskell

So far, we've been talking mostly about high-level concepts. Haskell can also be used for lower-level systems programming. It is quite possible to write programs that interface with the operating system at a low level using Haskell.

In this chapter, we are going to attempt something ambitious: a Perl-like "language" that is valid Haskell, implemented in pure Haskell, that makes shell scripting easy. We are going to implement piping, easy command invocation, and some simple tools to handle tasks that might otherwise be performed with grep or sed.

Specialized modules exist for different operating systems. In this chapter, we will use generic OS-independent modules as much as possible. However, we will be focusing on the POSIX environment for much of the chapter. POSIX is a standard for Unix-like operating systems such as Linux, FreeBSD, MacOS X, or Solaris. Windows does not support POSIX by default, but the Cygwin environment provides a POSIX compatibility layer for Windows.

Running External Programs

It is possible to invoke external commands from Haskell. To do that, we suggest using rawSystem from the System.Cmd module. This will invoke a specified program, with the specified arguments, and return the exit code from that program. You can play with it in ghci:

```
ghci> :module System.Cmd
ghci> rawSystem "ls" ["-l", "/usr"]
Loading package old-locale-1.0.0.0 ... linking ... done.
Loading package old-time-1.0.0.0 ... linking ... done.
Loading package filepath-1.1.0.0 ... linking ... done.
Loading package directory-1.0.0.1 ... linking ... done.
Loading package unix-2.3.0.1 ... linking ... done.
Loading package process-1.0.0.1 ... linking ... done.
total 408
drwxr-xr-x   2 root root   94208 2008-08-22 04:51 bin
drwxr-xr-x   2 root root    4096 2008-04-07 14:44 etc
drwxr-xr-x   2 root root    4096 2008-04-07 14:44 games
```

```
drwxr-xr-x 155 root root  16384 2008-08-20 20:54 include
drwxr-xr-x   4 root root   4096 2007-11-01 21:31 java
drwxr-xr-x   6 root root   4096 2008-03-18 11:38 kerberos
drwxr-xr-x  70 root root  36864 2008-08-21 04:52 lib
drwxr-xr-x 212 root root 126976 2008-08-21 04:53 lib64
drwxr-xr-x  23 root root  12288 2008-08-21 04:53 libexec
drwxr-xr-x  15 root root   4096 2008-04-07 14:44 local
drwxr-xr-x   2 root root  20480 2008-08-21 04:53 sbin
drwxr-xr-x 347 root root  12288 2008-08-21 11:01 share
drwxr-xr-x   5 root root   4096 2008-04-07 14:44 src
lrwxrwxrwx   1 root root     10 2008-05-16 15:01 tmp -> ../var/tmp
drwxr-xr-x   2 root root   4096 2007-04-10 11:01 X11R6
ExitSuccess
```

Here, we run the equivalent of the shell command ls -l /usr. rawSystem does not parse arguments from a string or expand wild cards.[*] Instead, it expects every argument to be contained in a list. If you don't want to pass any arguments, you can simply pass an empty list like this:

```
ghci> rawSystem "ls" []
calendartime.ghci  modtime.ghci    rp.ghci        RunProcessSimple.hs
cmd.ghci           posixtime.hs    rps.ghci       timediff.ghci
dir.ghci           rawSystem.ghci  RunProcess.hs  time.ghci
ExitSuccess
```

Directory and File Information

The System.Directory module contains quite a few functions that can be used to obtain information from the filesystem. You can get a list of files in a directory, rename or delete files, copy files, change the current working directory, or create new directories. System.Directory is portable and works on any platform where GHC itself works.

The library reference for System.Directory (*http://www.haskell.org/ghc/docs/latest/ html/libraries/base/System-Directory.html*) provides a comprehensive list of the functions available. Let's use ghci to demonstrate a few of them. Most of these functions are straightforward equivalents to C library calls or shell commands:

```
ghci> :module System.Directory
ghci> setCurrentDirectory "/etc"
Loading package old-locale-1.0.0.0 ... linking ... done.
Loading package old-time-1.0.0.0 ... linking ... done.
Loading package filepath-1.1.0.0 ... linking ... done.
Loading package directory-1.0.0.1 ... linking ... done.
ghci> getCurrentDirectory
"/etc"
ghci> setCurrentDirectory ".."
ghci> getCurrentDirectory
"/"
```

---

[*] There is also a function system that takes only a single string and passes it through the shell to parse. We recommend using rawSystem instead, because the shell attaches special meaning to certain characters, which could lead to security issues or unexpected behavior.

Here we saw commands to change the current working directory and obtain the current working directory from the system. These are similar to the `cd` and `pwd` commands in the POSIX shell:

```
ghci> getDirectoryContents "/"
["dev",".vmware","mnt","var","etc","net","..","lib","srv","media","lib64","opt",
".ccache","bin","selinux",".","lost+found","proc",".autorelabel",".autofsck",
"sys","misc","home","tmp","boot",".bash_history","root","sbin","usr"]
```

`getDirectoryContents` returns a list for every item in a given directory. Note that on POSIX systems, this list normally includes the special values "." and "..". You will usually want to filter these out when processing the content of the directory, perhaps like this:

```
ghci> getDirectoryContents "/" >>= return . filter (`notElem` [".", ".."])
["dev",".vmware","mnt","var","etc","net","lib","srv","media","lib64","opt",
".ccache","bin","selinux","lost+found","proc",".autorelabel",".autofsck",
"sys","misc","home","tmp","boot",".bash_history","root","sbin","usr"]
```

For a more detailed discussion of filtering the results of `getDirectory Contents`, refer to Chapter 8.

Is the `filter (`notElem` [".", ".."])` part confusing? That could got also be written as `filter (\c -> not $ elem c [".", ".."])`. The backticks in this case effectively let us pass the second argument to `notElem`; see "Infix Functions" on page 76 for more information on backticks.

You can also query the system about the location of certain directories. This query will ask the underlying operating system for the information:

```
ghci> getHomeDirectory
"/home/bos"
ghci> getAppUserDataDirectory "myApp"
"/home/bos/.myApp"
ghci> getUserDocumentsDirectory
"/home/bos"
```

Program Termination

Developers often write individual programs to accomplish particular tasks. These individual parts may be combined to accomplish larger tasks. A shell script or another program may execute them. The calling script often needs a way to discover whether the program was able to complete its task successfully. Haskell automatically indicates a nonsuccessful exit whenever a program is aborted by an exception.

However, you may need more fine-grained control over the exit code than that. Perhaps you need to return different codes for different types of errors. The `System.Exit` module provides a way to exit the program and return a specific exit status code to the caller.

You can call `exitWith ExitSuccess` to return a code indicating a successful termination (0 on POSIX systems). Or, you can call something like `exitWith (ExitFailure 5)`, which will return code 5 to the calling program.

Dates and Times

Everything from file timestamps to business transactions involve dates and times. Haskell provides ways for manipulating dates and times, as well as features for obtaining date and time information from the system.

ClockTime and CalendarTime

In Haskell, the `System.Time` module is primarily responsible for date and time handling. It defines two types: `ClockTime` and `CalendarTime`.

`ClockTime` is the Haskell version of the traditional POSIX epoch. A `ClockTime` represents a time relative to midnight the morning of January 1, 1970, Coordinated Universal Time (UTC). A negative `ClockTime` represents a number of seconds prior to that date, while a positive number represents a count of seconds after it.

`ClockTime` is convenient for computations. Since it tracks UTC, it doesn't have to adjust for local time zones, daylight saving time, or other special cases in time handling. Every day is exactly (60 * 60 * 24) or 86,400 seconds,[†] which makes time interval calculations simple. You can, for instance, check the `ClockTime` at the start of a long task, again at the end, and simply subtract the start time from the end time to determine how much time elapsed. You can then divide by 3,600 and display the elapsed time as a count of hours if you wish.

`ClockTime` is ideal for answering questions such as these:

- How much time has elapsed?
- What will be the `ClockTime` 14 days ahead of this precise instant?
- When was the file last modified?
- What is the precise time right now?

These are good uses of `ClockTime` because they refer to precise, unambiguous moments in time. However, `ClockTime` is not as easily used for questions such as:

- Is today Monday?
- What day of the week will May 1 fall on next year?

[†] Some will note that UTC defines leap seconds at irregular intervals. The POSIX standard, which Haskell follows, states that every day is exactly 86,400 seconds in length in its representation, so you need not be concerned about leap seconds when performing routine calculations. The exact manner of handling leap seconds is system-dependent and complex, though usually it can be explained as having a "long second." This nuance is generally only of interest when performing precise subsecond calculations.

- What is the current time in my local time zone, taking the potential presence of Daylight Saving Time (DST) into account?

CalendarTime stores time the way humans do: with a year, month, day, hour, minute, second, time zone, and DST information. It's easy to convert this into a conveniently displayable string, or to answer questions about the local time.

You can convert between ClockTime and CalendarTime at will. Haskell includes functions to convert a ClockTime to a CalendarTime in the local time zone or to a CalendarTime representing UTC.

Using ClockTime

ClockTime is defined in System.Time like this:

```
data ClockTime = TOD Integer Integer
```

The first Integer represents the number of seconds since the epoch. The second Integer represents an additional number of picoseconds. Because ClockTime in Haskell uses the unbounded Integer type, it can effectively represent a date range limited only by computational resources.

Let's look at some ways to use ClockTime. First, there is the getClockTime function that returns the current time according to the system's clock:

```
ghci> :module System.Time
ghci> getClockTime
Loading package old-locale-1.0.0.0 ... linking ... done.
Loading package old-time-1.0.0.0 ... linking ... done.
Sat Aug 23 22:30:03 PDT 2008
```

If you wait a second and run getClockTime again, it will return an updated time. Notice that the output from this command is a nice-looking string, complete with day-of-week information. That's due to the Show instance for ClockTime. Let's look at the ClockTime at a lower level:

```
ghci> TOD 1000 0
Wed Dec 31 16:16:40 PST 1969
ghci> getClockTime >>= (\(TOD sec _) -> return sec)
1219555803
```

Here we first construct a ClockTime representing the point in time 1,000 seconds after midnight on January 1, 1970, UTC. That moment in time is known as the *epoch*. Depending on your time zone, this moment in time may correspond to the evening of December 31, 1969, in your local time zone.

In the second example we pull the number of seconds out of the value returned by getClockTime. We can now manipulate it, like so:

```
ghci> getClockTime >>= (\(TOD sec _) -> return (TOD (sec + 86400) 0))
Sun Aug 24 22:30:03 PDT 2008
```

This will display what the time will be exactly 24 hours from now in your local time zone, since there are 86,400 seconds in 24 hours.

Using CalendarTime

As its name implies, CalendarTime represents time like we would on a calendar. It has fields for information such as year, month, and day. CalendarTime and its associated types are defined like this:

```
data CalendarTime = CalendarTime
    {ctYear :: Int,        -- Year (post-Gregorian)
     ctMonth :: Month,
     ctDay :: Int,         -- Day of the month (1 to 31)
     ctHour :: Int,        -- Hour of the day (0 to 23)
     ctMin :: Int,         -- Minutes (0 to 59)
     ctSec :: Int,         -- Seconds (0 to 61, allowing for leap seconds)
     ctPicosec :: Integer, -- Picoseconds
     ctWDay :: Day,        -- Day of the week
     ctYDay :: Int,        -- Day of the year (0 to 364 or 365)
     ctTZName :: String,   -- Name of timezone
     ctTZ :: Int,          -- Variation from UTC in seconds
     ctIsDST :: Bool       -- True if Daylight Saving Time in effect
    }

data Month = January | February | March | April | May | June
             | July | August | September | October | November | December

data Day = Sunday | Monday | Tuesday | Wednesday
           | Thursday | Friday | Saturday
```

There are a few things about these structures that should be highlighted:

- ctWDay, ctYDay, and ctTZName are generated by the library functions that create a CalendarTime but are not used in calculations. If you are creating a CalendarTime by hand, it is not necessary to put accurate values into these fields, unless your later calculations will depend upon them.

- All of these three types are members of the Eq, Ord, Read, and Show typeclasses. In addition, Month and Day are declared as members of the Enum and Bounded typeclasses. For more information on these typeclasses, refer to "Important Built-in Typeclasses" on page 139.

  You can generate CalendarTime values several ways. You could start by converting a ClockTime to a CalendarTime such as this:

```
ghci> :module System.Time
ghci> now <- getClockTime
Loading package old-locale-1.0.0.0 ... linking ... done.
Loading package old-time-1.0.0.0 ... linking ... done.
Sat Aug 23 22:29:59 PDT 2008
ghci> nowCal <- toCalendarTime now
CalendarTime {ctYear = 2008, ctMonth = August, ctDay = 23, ctHour = 22,
ctMin = 29,ctSec = 59, ctPicosec = 877577000000, ctWDay = Saturday,
ctYDay = 235, ctTZName ="PDT", ctTZ = -25200, ctIsDST = True}
```

```
ghci> let nowUTC = toUTCTime now
ghci> nowCal
CalendarTime {ctYear = 2008, ctMonth = August, ctDay = 23, ctHour = 22,
ctMin = 29, ctSec = 59, ctPicosec = 877577000000, ctWDay = Saturday,
ctYDay = 235, ctTZName = "PDT", ctTZ = -25200, ctIsDST = True}
ghci> nowUTC
CalendarTime {ctYear = 2008, ctMonth = August, ctDay = 24, ctHour = 5,
ctMin = 29, ctSec = 59, ctPicosec = 877577000000, ctWDay = Sunday,
ctYDay = 236, ctTZName = "UTC", ctTZ = 0, ctIsDST = False}
```

We used getClockTime to obtain the current ClockTime from the system's clock. Next, toCalendarTime converts the ClockTime to a CalendarTime representing the time in the local time zone. toUTCtime performs a similar conversion, but its result is in the UTC time zone instead of the local time zone.

Notice that toCalendarTime is an IO function, but toUTCTime is not. The reason is that toCalendarTime returns a different result depending upon the locally configured time zone, but toUTCTime will return the exact same result whenever it is passed the same source ClockTime.

It's easy to modify a CalendarTime value:

```
ghci> nowCal {ctYear = 1960}
CalendarTime {ctYear = 1960, ctMonth = August, ctDay = 23,
ctHour = 22, ctMin = 29, ctSec = 59, ctPicosec = 877577000000,
ctWDay = Saturday, ctYDay = 235, ctTZName = "PDT",
ctTZ = -25200, ctIsDST = True}
ghci> (\(TOD sec _) -> sec) (toClockTime nowCal)
1219555799
ghci> (\(TOD sec _) -> sec) (toClockTime (nowCal {ctYear = 1960}))
-295209001
```

In this example, we first took the CalendarTime value from earlier and simply switched its year to 1960. Then, we used toClockTime to convert the unmodified value to a ClockTime, and then the modified value, so you can see the difference. Notice that the modified value shows a negative number of seconds once converted to ClockTime. That's to be expected, since a ClockTime is an offset from midnight on January 1, 1970, UTC, and this value is in 1960.

You can also create CalendarTime values manually:

```
ghci> let newCT = CalendarTime 2010 January 15 12 30 0 0 Sunday 0 "UTC" 0 False
ghci> newCT
CalendarTime {ctYear = 2010, ctMonth = January, ctDay = 15, ctHour = 12,
ctMin = 30, ctSec = 0, ctPicosec = 0, ctWDay = Sunday, ctYDay = 0,
ctTZName = "UTC", ctTZ = 0, ctIsDST = False}
ghci> (\(TOD sec _) -> sec) (toClockTime newCT)
1263558600
```

Note that even though January 15, 2010, isn't a Sunday—and isn't day 0 in the year—the system was able to process this just fine. In fact, if we convert the value to a ClockTime and then back to a CalendarTime, you'll find those fields properly filled in:

```
ghci> toUTCTime . toClockTime $ newCT
CalendarTime {ctYear = 2010, ctMonth = January, ctDay = 15, ctHour = 12,
ctMin = 30, ctSec = 0, ctPicosec = 0, ctWDay = Friday, ctYDay = 14,
ctTZName = "UTC", ctTZ = 0, ctIsDST = False}
```

TimeDiff for ClockTime

Because it can be difficult to manage differences between ClockTime values in a human-friendly way, the System.Time module includes a TimeDiff type. TimeDiff can be used, where convenient, to handle these differences. It is defined like this:

```
data TimeDiff = TimeDiff
    {tdYear :: Int,
     tdMonth :: Int,
     tdDay :: Int,
     tdHour :: Int,
     tdMin :: Int,
     tdSec :: Int,
     tdPicosec :: Integer}
```

Functions such as diffClockTimes and addToClockTime take a ClockTime and a TimeDiff and handle the calculations internally by converting to a CalendarTime in UTC, applying the differences, and converting back to a ClockTime.

Let's see how it works:

```
ghci> :module System.Time
ghci> let feb5 = toClockTime $ CalendarTime 2008 February 5 0 0 0 0 Sunday 0
"UTC" 0 False
Loading package old-locale-1.0.0.0 ... linking ... done.
Loading package old-time-1.0.0.0 ... linking ... done.
ghci> feb5
Mon Feb  4 16:00:00 PST 2008
ghci> addToClockTime (TimeDiff 0 1 0 0 0 0 0) feb5
Tue Mar  4 16:00:00 PST 2008
ghci> toUTCTime $ addToClockTime (TimeDiff 0 1 0 0 0 0 0) feb5
CalendarTime {ctYear = 2008, ctMonth = March, ctDay = 5, ctHour = 0,
ctMin = 0, ctSec = 0, ctPicosec = 0, ctWDay = Wednesday, ctYDay = 64,
ctTZName = "UTC", ctTZ = 0, ctIsDST = False}
ghci> let jan30 = toClockTime $ CalendarTime 2009 January 30 0 0 0 0
Sunday 0 "UTC" 0 False
ghci> jan30
Thu Jan 29 16:00:00 PST 2009
ghci> addToClockTime (TimeDiff 0 1 0 0 0 0 0) jan30
Sun Mar  1 16:00:00 PST 2009
ghci> toUTCTime $ addToClockTime (TimeDiff 0 1 0 0 0 0 0) jan30
CalendarTime {ctYear = 2009, ctMonth = March, ctDay = 2, ctHour = 0, ctMin = 0,
ctSec = 0, ctPicosec = 0, ctWDay = Monday, ctYDay = 60, ctTZName = "UTC", ctTZ =
0, ctIsDST = False}
ghci> diffClockTimes jan30 feb5
TimeDiff {tdYear = 0, tdMonth = 0, tdDay = 0, tdHour = 0, tdMin = 0, tdSec = 31104000,
tdPicosec = 0}
ghci> normalizeTimeDiff $ diffClockTimes jan30 feb5
TimeDiff {tdYear = 0, tdMonth = 12, tdDay = 0, tdHour = 0, tdMin = 0, tdSec = 0,
tdPicosec = 0}
```

We started by generating a ClockTime representing midnight February 5, 2008 in UTC. Note that, unless your time zone is the same as UTC, when this time is printed out on the display, it may show up as the evening of February 4 because it is formatted for your local time zone.

Next, we add one month to it by calling addToClockTime. 2008 is a leap year, but the system handled that properly and we get a result that has the same date and time in March. Using toUTCTime, we can see the effect on this in the original UTC time zone.

For a second experiment, we set up a time representing midnight on January 30, 2009 in UTC. 2009 is not a leap year, so we might wonder what will happen when trying to add one month to it. We can see that, since neither February 29 or 30 exist in 2009, we wind up with March 2.

Finally, we can see how diffClockTimes turns two ClockTime values into a TimeDiff, though only the seconds and picoseconds are filled in. The normalizeTimeDiff function takes such a TimeDiff and reformats it as a human might expect to see it.

File Modification Times

Many programs need to find out when particular files were last modified. Programs such as ls or graphical file managers typically display the modification time of files. The System.Directory module contains a cross-platform getModificationTime function. It takes a filename and returns a ClockTime representing the time the file was last modified. For instance:

```
ghci> :module System.Directory
ghci> getModificationTime "/etc/passwd"
Loading package old-locale-1.0.0.0 ... linking ... done.
Loading package old-time-1.0.0.0 ... linking ... done.
Loading package filepath-1.1.0.0 ... linking ... done.
Loading package directory-1.0.0.1 ... linking ... done.
Mon Jul 14 04:06:29 PDT 2008
```

POSIX platforms maintain not just a modification time (known as mtime), but also the time of last read or write access (atime) and the time of last status change (ctime). Since this information is POSIX-specific, the cross-platform System.Directory module does not provide access to it. Instead, you will need to use functions in System.Posix.Files. Here is an example function to do that:

```
-- file: ch20/posixtime.hs
-- posixtime.hs

import System.Posix.Files
import System.Time
import System.Posix.Types

-- | Given a path, returns (atime, mtime, ctime)
getTimes :: FilePath -> IO (ClockTime, ClockTime, ClockTime)
getTimes fp =
    do stat <- getFileStatus fp
```

```
        return (toct (accessTime stat),
                toct (modificationTime stat),
                toct (statusChangeTime stat))

-- | Convert an EpochTime to a ClockTime
toct :: EpochTime -> ClockTime
toct et =
    TOD (truncate (toRational et)) 0
```

Notice that call to getFileStatus. That call maps directly to the C function stat(). Its return value stores a vast assortment of information, including file type, permissions, owner, group, and the three time values we're interested in. System.Posix.Files provides various functions, such as accessTime, that extract the information we're interested out of the opaque FileStatus type returned by getFileStatus.

The functions such as accessTime return data in a POSIX-specific type called EpochTime, which converts to a ClockTime using the toct function. System.Posix.Files also provides a setFileTimes function to set the atime and mtime for a file.[‡]

Extended Example: Piping

We've just seen how to invoke external programs. Sometimes we need more control than that. Perhaps we need to obtain the output from those programs, provide input, or even chain together multiple external programs. Piping can help with all of these needs. Piping is often used in shell scripts. When you set up a pipe in the shell, you run multiple programs. The output of the first program is sent to the input of the second. Its output is sent to the third as input, and so on. The last program's output normally goes to the terminal, or it could go to a file. Here's an example session with the POSIX shell to illustrate piping:

```
$ ls /etc | grep 'm.*ap' | tr a-z A-Z
IDMAPD.CONF
MAILCAP
MAILCAP.ORDER
MEDIAPRM
TERMCAP
```

This command runs three programs, piping data between them. It starts with ls /etc, which outputs a list of all files or directories in /etc. The output of ls is sent as input to grep. We gave grep a regular expression that will cause it to output only the lines that start with 'm' and then contain "ap" somewhere in the line. Finally, the result of that is sent to tr. We gave tr options to convert everything to uppercase. The output of tr isn't set anywhere in particular, so it is displayed on the screen.

In this situation, the shell handles setting up all the pipelines between programs. By using some of the POSIX tools in Haskell, we can accomplish the same thing.

[‡] It is not normally possible to set the ctime on POSIX systems.

Before describing how to do this, we should first warn you that the System.Posix modules expose a very low-level interface to Unix systems. The interfaces can be complex and their interactions can be complex as well, regardless of the programming language you use to access them. The full nature of these low-level interfaces has been the topic of entire books themselves, so we will just scratch the surface in this chapter.

Using Pipes for Redirection

POSIX defines a function that creates a pipe. This function returns two file descriptors (FDs), which are similar in concept to a Haskell Handle. One FD is the reading end of the pipe, and the other is the writing end. Anything that is written to the writing end can be read by the reading end. The data is "shoved through a pipe." In Haskell, you call createPipe to access this interface.

Having a pipe is the first step to being able to pipe data between external programs. We must also be able to redirect the output of a program to a pipe and the input of another program from a pipe. The Haskell function dupTo accomplishes this. It takes an FD and makes a copy of it at another FD number. POSIX FDs for standard input, standard output, and standard error have the predefined FD numbers of 0, 1, and 2, respectively. By renumbering an endpoint of a pipe to one of those numbers, we effectively can cause programs to have their input or output redirected.

There is another piece of the puzzle, however. We can't just use dupTo before a call such as rawSystem because that would mess up the standard input or output of our main Haskell process. Moreover, rawSystem blocks until the invoked program executes, leaving us no way to start multiple processes running in parallel. To make this happen, we must use forkProcess. This is a very special function. It actually makes a copy of the program currently running and we wind up with two copies of the program running at the same time. Haskell's forkProcess function takes a function to execute in the new process (known as the child). We have that function call dupTo. After it has done that, it calls executeFile to actually invoke the command. This is also a special function: if all goes well, it *never returns*. That's because executeFile replaces the running process with a different program. Eventually, the original Haskell process will call getProcess Status to wait for the child processes to terminate and learn of their exit codes.

Whenever you run a command on POSIX systems, whether you've just typed ls on the command line or used rawSystem in Haskell, under the hood, forkProcess, executeFile, and getProcessStatus (or their C equivalents) are always being used. To set up pipes, we duplicate the process that the system uses to start up programs, and add a few steps involving piping and redirection along the way.

There are a few other housekeeping things we must be careful about. When you call forkProcess, just about everything about your program is cloned.[§] That includes the set of open file descriptors (handles). Programs detect when they're done receiving

---

[§] The main exception is threads, which are not cloned.

input from a pipe by checking the end-of-file indicator. When the process at the writing end of a pipe closes the pipe, the process at the reading end will receive an end-of-file indication. However, if the writing file descriptor exists in more than one process, the end-of-file indicator won't be sent until all processes have closed that particular FD. Therefore, we must keep track of which FDs are opened so that we can close them all in the child processes. We must also close the child ends of the pipes in the parent process as soon as possible.

Here is an initial implementation of a system of piping in Haskell:

```haskell
-- file: ch20/RunProcessSimple.hs
{-# OPTIONS_GHC -fglasgow-exts #-}
-- RunProcessSimple.hs

module RunProcessSimple where

import System.Process
import Control.Concurrent
import Control.Concurrent.MVar
import System.IO
import System.Exit
import Text.Regex
import System.Posix.Process
import System.Posix.IO
import System.Posix.Types

{- | The type for running external commands.  The first part
of the tuple is the program name.  The list represents the
command-line parameters to pass to the command. -}
type SysCommand = (String, [String])

{- | The result of running any command -}
data CommandResult = CommandResult {
    cmdOutput :: IO String,            -- ^ IO action that yields the output
    getExitStatus :: IO ProcessStatus  -- ^ IO action that yields exit result
    }

{- | The type for handling global lists of FDs to always close in the clients
-}
type CloseFDs = MVar [Fd]

{- | Class representing anything that is a runnable command -}
class CommandLike a where
    {- | Given the command and a String representing input,
         invokes the command.  Returns a String
         representing the output of the command. -}
    invoke :: a -> CloseFDs -> String -> IO CommandResult

-- Support for running system commands
instance CommandLike SysCommand where
    invoke (cmd, args) closefds input =
        do -- Create two pipes: one to handle stdin and the other
           -- to handle stdout.  We do not redirect stderr in this program.
           (stdinread, stdinwrite) <- createPipe
```

```
    (stdoutread, stdoutwrite) <- createPipe

    -- We add the parent FDs to this list because we always need
    -- to close them in the clients.
    addCloseFDs closefds [stdinwrite, stdoutread]

    -- Now, grab the closed FDs list and fork the child.
    childPID <- withMVar closefds (\fds ->
                    forkProcess (child fds stdinread stdoutwrite))

    -- Now, on the parent, close the client-side FDs.
    closeFd stdinread
    closeFd stdoutwrite

    -- Write the input to the command.
    stdinhdl <- fdToHandle stdinwrite
    forkIO $ do hPutStr stdinhdl input
                hClose stdinhdl

    -- Prepare to receive output from the command
    stdouthdl <- fdToHandle stdoutread

    -- Set up the function to call when ready to wait for the
    -- child to exit.
    let waitfunc =
        do status <- getProcessStatus True False childPID
           case status of
               Nothing -> fail $ "Error: Nothing from getProcessStatus"
               Just ps -> do removeCloseFDs closefds
                                    [stdinwrite, stdoutread]
                             return ps
    return $ CommandResult {cmdOutput = hGetContents stdouthdl,
                            getExitStatus = waitfunc}

    -- Define what happens in the child process
    where child closefds stdinread stdoutwrite =
            do -- Copy our pipes over the regular stdin/stdout FDs
               dupTo stdinread stdInput
               dupTo stdoutwrite stdOutput

               -- Now close the original pipe FDs
               closeFd stdinread
               closeFd stdoutwrite

               -- Close all the open FDs we inherited from the parent
               mapM_ (\fd -> catch (closeFd fd) (\_ -> return ())) closefds

               -- Start the program
               executeFile cmd True args Nothing

-- Add FDs to the list of FDs that must be closed post-fork in a child
addCloseFDs :: CloseFDs -> [Fd] -> IO ()
addCloseFDs closefds newfds =
    modifyMVar_ closefds (\oldfds -> return $ oldfds ++ newfds)
```

```
-- Remove FDs from the list
removeCloseFDs :: CloseFDs -> [Fd] -> IO ()
removeCloseFDs closefds removethem =
    modifyMVar_ closefds (\fdlist -> return $ procfdlist fdlist removethem)

    where
    procfdlist fdlist [] = fdlist
    procfdlist fdlist (x:xs) = procfdlist (removefd fdlist x) xs

    -- We want to remove only the first occurance ot any given fd
    removefd [] _ = []
    removefd (x:xs) fd
        | fd == x = xs
        | otherwise = x : removefd xs fd

{- | Type representing a pipe.  A 'PipeCommand' consists of a source
and destination part, both of which must be instances of
'CommandLike'. -}
data (CommandLike src, CommandLike dest) =>
    PipeCommand src dest = PipeCommand src dest

{- | A convenient function for creating a 'PipeCommand'. -}
(-|-) :: (CommandLike a, CommandLike b) => a -> b -> PipeCommand a b
(-|-) = PipeCommand

{- | Make 'PipeCommand' runnable as a command -}
instance (CommandLike a, CommandLike b) =>
        CommandLike (PipeCommand a b) where
    invoke (PipeCommand src dest) closefds input =
        do res1 <- invoke src closefds input
           output1 <- cmdOutput res1
           res2 <- invoke dest closefds output1
           return $ CommandResult (cmdOutput res2) (getEC res1 res2)

{- | Given two 'CommandResult' items, evaluate the exit codes for
both and then return a "combined" exit code.  This will be ExitSuccess
if both exited successfully.  Otherwise, it will reflect the first
error encountered. -}
getEC :: CommandResult -> CommandResult -> IO ProcessStatus
getEC src dest =
    do sec <- getExitStatus src
       dec <- getExitStatus dest
       case sec of
            Exited ExitSuccess -> return dec
            x -> return x

{- | Execute a 'CommandLike'. -}
runIO :: CommandLike a => a -> IO ()
runIO cmd =
    do -- Initialize our closefds list
       closefds <- newMVar []

       -- Invoke the command
       res <- invoke cmd closefds []
```

```
    -- Process its output
    output <- cmdOutput res
    putStr output

    -- Wait for termination and get exit status
    ec <- getExitStatus res
    case ec of
        Exited ExitSuccess -> return ()
        x -> fail $ "Exited: " ++ show x
```

Let's experiment with this in ghci a bit before looking at how it works:

```
ghci> :load RunProcessSimple.hs
[1 of 1] Compiling RunProcessSimple ( RunProcessSimple.hs, interpreted )
Ok, modules loaded: RunProcessSimple.
ghci> runIO $ ("pwd", []::[String])
Loading package array-0.1.0.0 ... linking ... done.
Loading package bytestring-0.9.0.1.1 ... linking ... done.
Loading package old-locale-1.0.0.0 ... linking ... done.
Loading package old-time-1.0.0.0 ... linking ... done.
Loading package filepath-1.1.0.0 ... linking ... done.
Loading package directory-1.0.0.1 ... linking ... done.
Loading package unix-2.3.0.1 ... linking ... done.
Loading package process-1.0.0.1 ... linking ... done.
Loading package regex-base-0.72.0.1 ... linking ... done.
Loading package regex-posix-0.72.0.2 ... linking ... done.
Loading package regex-compat-0.71.0.1 ... linking ... done.
/home/bos/src/darcs/book/examples/ch20
ghci> runIO $ ("ls", ["/usr"])
bin
etc
games
include
java
kerberos
lib
lib64
libexec
local
sbin
share
src
tmp
X11R6
ghci> runIO $ ("ls", ["/usr"]) -|- ("grep", ["^l"])
lib
lib64
libexec
local
ghci> runIO $ ("ls", ["/etc"]) -|- ("grep", ["m.*ap"]) -|- ("tr", ["a-z", "A-Z"])
IDMAPD.CONF
MAILCAP
PM-UTILS-HD-APM-RESTORE.CONF
```

We start by running a simple command, pwd, which just prints the name of the current working directory. We pass [] for the list of arguments, because pwd doesn't need any arguments. Due to the typeclasses used, Haskell can't infer the type of [], so we specifically mention that it's a `String`.

Then we get into more complex commands. We run `ls`, sending it through `grep`. At the end, we set up a pipe to run the exact same command that we ran via a shell-built pipe at the start of this section. It's not yet as pleasant as it was in the shell, but then again our program is still relatively simple when compared to the shell.

Let's look at the program. The very first line has a special `OPTIONS_GHC` clause. This is the same as passing `-fglasgow-exts` to `ghc` or `ghci`. We are using a GHC extension that permits us to use a (`String, [String]`) type as an instance of a typeclass.[||] Putting it in the source file means we don't have to remember to specify it every time we use this module.

After the `import` lines, we define a few types. First, we define `type SysCommand = (String, [String])` as an alias. This is the type a command to be executed by the system will take. We used data of this type for each command in the example execution above. The `CommandResult` type represents the result from executing a given command, and the `CloseFDs` type represents the list of FDs that we must close upon forking a new child process.

Next, we define a class named `CommandLike`, which will be used to run "things," where a "thing" might be a standalone program, a pipe set up between two or more programs, or in the future, even pure Haskell functions. To be a member of this class, only one function—`invoke`—needs to be present for a given type. This will let us use `runIO` to start either a standalone command or a pipeline. It will also be useful for defining a pipeline, since we may have a whole stack of commands on one or both sides of a given command.

Our piping infrastructure is going to use strings as the way of sending data from one process to another. We can take advantage of Haskell's support for lazy reading via `hGetContents` while reading data, and use `forkIO` to let writing occur in the background. This will work well, although not as fast as connecting the endpoints of two processes directly together.[#] It makes implementation quite simple, however. We need only take care to do nothing that would require the entire `String` to be buffered, and let Haskell's laziness do the rest.

Next, we define an instance of `CommandLike` for `SysCommand`. We create two pipes: one to use for the new process's standard input, and the other for its standard output. This creates four endpoints, and thus four file descriptors. We add the parent file descriptors

---

[||] This extension is well-supported in the Haskell community; Hugs users can access the same thing with `hugs -98 +o`.

[#] The Haskell library HSH provides a similar API to that presented here, but it uses a more efficient (and much more complex) mechanism of connecting pipes directly between external processes without the data needing to pass through Haskell. This is the same approach that the shell takes, and it reduces the CPU load of handling piping.

to the list of those that must be closed in all children. These would be the write end of the child's standard input, and the read end of the child's standard output. Next, we fork the child process. In the parent, we can then close the file descriptors that correspond to the child. We can't do that before the fork, because they wouldn't be available to the child. We obtain a handle for the `stdinwrite` file descriptor, and start a thread via `forkIO` to write the input data to it. We then define `waitfunc`, which is the action that the caller will invoke when it is ready to wait for the called process to terminate. Meanwhile, the child uses `dupTo`, closes the file descriptors it doesn't need, and executes the command.

Next, we define some utility functions to manage the list of file descriptors. After that, we define the tools that help set up pipelines. First, we define a new type `PipeCommand` that has a source and destination. Both the source and destination must be members of `CommandLike`. We also define the `-|-` convenience operator. Then, we make `PipeCommand` an instance of `CommandLike`. Its `invoke` implementation starts the first command with the given input, obtains its output, and passes that output to the invocation of the second command. It then returns the output of the second command and causes the `getExitStatus` function to wait for and check the exit statuses from both commands.

We finish by defining `runIO`. This function establishes the list of FDs that must be closed in the client, starts the command, displays its output, and checks its exit status.

Better Piping

Our previous example solved the basic need of letting us set up shell-like pipes. There are some other features that it would be nice to have though:

- Support more shell-like syntax
- The ability to let people pipe data into external programs or regular Haskell functions, freely mixing and matching the two
- The ability to return the final output and exit code in a way that Haskell programs can readily use

Fortunately, we already have most of the pieces to support this in place. We need only to add a few more instances of `CommandLike` to support this and a few more functions similar to `runIO`. Here is a revised example that implements all of these features:

```
-- file: ch20/RunProcess.hs
{-# OPTIONS_GHC -fglasgow-exts #-}

module RunProcess where

import System.Process
import Control.Concurrent
import Control.Concurrent.MVar
import Control.Exception(evaluate)
import System.Posix.Directory
import System.Directory(setCurrentDirectory)
```

```
import System.IO
import System.Exit
import Text.Regex
import System.Posix.Process
import System.Posix.IO
import System.Posix.Types
import Data.List
import System.Posix.Env(getEnv)

{- | The type for running external commands.  The first part
of the tuple is the program name.  The list represents the
command-line parameters to pass to the command. -}
type SysCommand = (String, [String])

{- | The result of running any command -}
data CommandResult = CommandResult {
    cmdOutput :: IO String,             -- ^ IO action that yields the output
    getExitStatus :: IO ProcessStatus   -- ^ IO action that yields exit result
    }

{- | The type for handling global lists of FDs to always close in the clients
-}
type CloseFDs = MVar [Fd]

{- | Class representing anything that is a runnable command -}
class CommandLike a where
    {- | Given the command and a String representing input,
         invokes the command.  Returns a String
         representing the output of the command. -}
    invoke :: a -> CloseFDs -> String -> IO CommandResult

-- Support for running system commands
instance CommandLike SysCommand where
    invoke (cmd, args) closefds input =
        do -- Create two pipes: one to handle stdin and the other
           -- to handle stdout.  We do not redirect stderr in this program.
           (stdinread, stdinwrite) <- createPipe
           (stdoutread, stdoutwrite) <- createPipe

           -- We add the parent FDs to this list because we always need
           -- to close them in the clients.
           addCloseFDs closefds [stdinwrite, stdoutread]

           -- Now, grab the closed FDs list and fork the child.
           childPID <- withMVar closefds (\fds ->
                           forkProcess (child fds stdinread stdoutwrite))

           -- Now, on the parent, close the client-side FDs.
           closeFd stdinread
           closeFd stdoutwrite

           -- Write the input to the command.
           stdinhdl <- fdToHandle stdinwrite
           forkIO $ do hPutStr stdinhdl input
                       hClose stdinhdl
```

```
                    -- Prepare to receive output from the command
                    stdouthdl <- fdToHandle stdoutread

                    -- Set up the function to call when ready to wait for the
                    -- child to exit.
                    let waitfunc =
                            do status <- getProcessStatus True False childPID
                               case status of
                                   Nothing -> fail $ "Error: Nothing from getProcessStatus"
                                   Just ps -> do removeCloseFDs closefds
                                                     [stdinwrite, stdoutread]
                                                 return ps
                    return $ CommandResult {cmdOutput = hGetContents stdouthdl,
                                            getExitStatus = waitfunc}

            -- Define what happens in the child process
            where child closefds stdinread stdoutwrite =
                    do -- Copy our pipes over the regular stdin/stdout FDs
                       dupTo stdinread stdInput
                       dupTo stdoutwrite stdOutput

                       -- Now close the original pipe FDs
                       closeFd stdinread
                       closeFd stdoutwrite

                       -- Close all the open FDs we inherited from the parent
                       mapM_ (\fd -> catch (closeFd fd) (\_ -> return ())) closefds

                       -- Start the program
                       executeFile cmd True args Nothing

{- | An instance of 'CommandLike' for an external command.  The String is
passed to a shell for evaluation and invocation. -}
instance CommandLike String where
    invoke cmd closefds input =
        do -- Use the shell given by the environment variable SHELL,
           -- if any.  Otherwise, use /bin/sh
           esh <- getEnv "SHELL"
           let sh = case esh of
                        Nothing -> "/bin/sh"
                        Just x -> x
           invoke (sh, ["-c", cmd]) closefds input

-- Add FDs to the list of FDs that must be closed post-fork in a child
addCloseFDs :: CloseFDs -> [Fd] -> IO ()
addCloseFDs closefds newfds =
    modifyMVar_ closefds (\oldfds -> return $ oldfds ++ newfds)

-- Remove FDs from the list
removeCloseFDs :: CloseFDs -> [Fd] -> IO ()
removeCloseFDs closefds removethem =
    modifyMVar_ closefds (\fdlist -> return $ procfdlist fdlist removethem)

    where
```

```
    procfdlist fdlist [] = fdlist
    procfdlist fdlist (x:xs) = procfdlist (removefd fdlist x) xs

    -- We want to remove only the first occurance ot any given fd
    removefd [] _ = []
    removefd (x:xs) fd
        | fd == x = xs
        | otherwise = x : removefd xs fd

-- Support for running Haskell commands
instance CommandLike (String -> IO String) where
    invoke func _ input =
        return $ CommandResult (func input) (return (Exited ExitSuccess))

-- Support pure Haskell functions by wrapping them in IO
instance CommandLike (String -> String) where
    invoke func = invoke iofunc
        where iofunc :: String -> IO String
              iofunc = return . func

-- It's also useful to operate on lines.  Define support for line-based
-- functions both within and without the IO monad.

instance CommandLike ([String] -> IO [String]) where
    invoke func _ input =
            return $ CommandResult linedfunc (return (Exited ExitSuccess))
        where linedfunc = func (lines input) >>= (return . unlines)

instance CommandLike ([String] -> [String]) where
    invoke func = invoke (unlines . func . lines)

{- | Type representing a pipe.  A 'PipeCommand' consists of a source
and destination part, both of which must be instances of
'CommandLike'. -}
data (CommandLike src, CommandLike dest) =>
    PipeCommand src dest = PipeCommand src dest

{- | A convenient function for creating a 'PipeCommand'. -}
(-|-) :: (CommandLike a, CommandLike b) => a -> b -> PipeCommand a b
(-|-) = PipeCommand

{- | Make 'PipeCommand' runnable as a command -}
instance (CommandLike a, CommandLike b) =>
        CommandLike (PipeCommand a b) where
    invoke (PipeCommand src dest) closefds input =
        do res1 <- invoke src closefds input
           output1 <- cmdOutput res1
           res2 <- invoke dest closefds output1
           return $ CommandResult (cmdOutput res2) (getEC res1 res2)

{- | Given two 'CommandResult' items, evaluate the exit codes for
both and then return a "combined" exit code.  This will be ExitSuccess
if both exited successfully.  Otherwise, it will reflect the first
error encountered. -}
getEC :: CommandResult -> CommandResult -> IO ProcessStatus
```

```
getEC src dest =
    do sec <- getExitStatus src
       dec <- getExitStatus dest
       case sec of
           Exited ExitSuccess -> return dec
           x -> return x

{- | Different ways to get data from 'run'.

 * IO () runs, throws an exception on error, and sends stdout to stdout.

 * IO String runs, throws an exception on error, reads stdout into
   a buffer, and returns it as a string.

 * IO [String] is same as IO String, but returns the results as lines.

 * IO ProcessStatus runs and returns a ProcessStatus with the exit
   information.  stdout is sent to stdout.  Exceptions are not thrown.

 * IO (String, ProcessStatus) is like IO ProcessStatus, but also
   includes a description of the last command in the pipe to have
   an error (or the last command, if there was no error).

 * IO Int returns the exit code from a program directly.  If a signal
   caused the command to be reaped, returns 128 + SIGNUM.

 * IO Bool returns True if the program exited normally (exit code 0,
   not stopped by a signal) and False otherwise.

-}
class RunResult a where
    {- | Runs a command (or pipe of commands), with results presented
       in any number of different ways. -}
    run :: (CommandLike b) => b -> a

-- | Utility function for use by 'RunResult' instances
setUpCommand :: CommandLike a => a -> IO CommandResult
setUpCommand cmd =
    do -- Initialize our closefds list
       closefds <- newMVar []

       -- Invoke the command
       invoke cmd closefds []

instance RunResult (IO ()) where
    run cmd = run cmd >>= checkResult

instance RunResult (IO ProcessStatus) where
    run cmd =
        do res <- setUpCommand cmd

           -- Process its output
           output <- cmdOutput res
           putStr output
```

```
              getExitStatus res

instance RunResult (IO Int) where
    run cmd = do rc <- run cmd
                 case rc of
                     Exited (ExitSuccess) -> return 0
                     Exited (ExitFailure x) -> return x
                     Terminated x -> return (128 + (fromIntegral x))
                     Stopped x -> return (128 + (fromIntegral x))

instance RunResult (IO Bool) where
    run cmd = do rc <- run cmd
                 return ((rc::Int) == 0)

instance RunResult (IO [String]) where
    run cmd = do r <- run cmd
                 return (lines r)

instance RunResult (IO String) where
    run cmd =
        do res <- setUpCommand cmd

           output <- cmdOutput res

           -- Force output to be buffered
           evaluate (length output)

           ec <- getExitStatus res
           checkResult ec
           return output

checkResult :: ProcessStatus -> IO ()
checkResult ps =
    case ps of
         Exited (ExitSuccess) -> return ()
         x -> fail (show x)

{- | A convenience function.  Refers only to the version of 'run'
that returns @IO ()@.  This prevents you from having to cast to it
all the time when you do not care about the result of 'run'.
-}
runIO :: CommandLike a => a -> IO ()
runIO = run


----------------------------------------------------------------
-- Utility Functions
----------------------------------------------------------------
cd :: FilePath -> IO ()
cd = setCurrentDirectory

{- | Takes a string and sends it on as standard output.
The input to this function is never read. -}
echo :: String -> String -> String
echo inp _ = inp
```

```
-- | Search for the regexp in the lines.  Return those that match.
grep :: String -> [String] -> [String]
grep pat = filter (ismatch regex)
    where regex = mkRegex pat
          ismatch r inp = case matchRegex r inp of
                                Nothing -> False
                                Just _ -> True

{- | Creates the given directory.  A value of 0o755 for mode would be typical.
An alias for System.Posix.Directory.createDirectory. -}
mkdir :: FilePath -> FileMode -> IO ()
mkdir = createDirectory

{- | Remove duplicate lines from a file (like Unix uniq).
Takes a String representing a file or output and plugs it through
lines and then nub to uniqify on a line basis. -}
uniq :: String -> String
uniq = unlines . nub . lines

-- | Count number of lines.  wc -l
wcL, wcW :: [String] -> [String]
wcL inp = [show (genericLength inp :: Integer)]

-- | Count number of words in a file (like wc -w)
wcW inp = [show ((genericLength $ words $ unlines inp) :: Integer)]

sortLines :: [String] -> [String]
sortLines = sort

-- | Count the lines in the input
countLines :: String -> IO String
countLines = return . (++) "\n" . show . length . lines
```

Here's what has changed:

- A new CommandLike instance for String that uses the shell to evaluate and invoke the string.

- New CommandLike instances for String -> IO String and various other types that are implemented in terms of this one. These process Haskell functions as commands.

- A new RunResult typeclass that defines a function run that returns information about the command in many different ways. See the comments in the source for more information. runIO is now just an alias for one particular RunResult instance.

- A few utility functions providing Haskell implementations of familiar Unix shell commands.

Let's try out the new shell features. First, let's make sure that the command we used in the previous example still works. Then, let's try it using a more shell-like syntax.

```
ghci> :load RunProcess.hs
[1 of 1] Compiling RunProcess      ( RunProcess.hs, interpreted )
Ok, modules loaded: RunProcess.
ghci> runIO $ ("ls", ["/etc"]) -|- ("grep", ["m.*ap"]) -|- ("tr", ["a-z", "A-Z"])
Loading package array-0.1.0.0 ... linking ... done.
Loading package bytestring-0.9.0.1.1 ... linking ... done.
Loading package old-locale-1.0.0.0 ... linking ... done.
Loading package old-time-1.0.0.0 ... linking ... done.
Loading package filepath-1.1.0.0 ... linking ... done.
Loading package directory-1.0.0.1 ... linking ... done.
Loading package unix-2.3.0.1 ... linking ... done.
Loading package process-1.0.0.1 ... linking ... done.
Loading package regex-base-0.72.0.1 ... linking ... done.
Loading package regex-posix-0.72.0.2 ... linking ... done.
Loading package regex-compat-0.71.0.1 ... linking ... done.
IDMAPD.CONF
MAILCAP
PM-UTILS-HD-APM-RESTORE.CONF
ghci> runIO $ "ls /etc" -|- "grep 'm.*ap'" -|- "tr a-z A-Z"
IDMAPD.CONF
MAILCAP
PM-UTILS-HD-APM-RESTORE.CONF
```

That was a lot easier to type. Let's try substituting our native Haskell implementation of grep and try out some other new features as well:

```
ghci> runIO $ "ls /etc" -|- grep "m.*ap" -|- "tr a-z A-Z"
IDMAPD.CONF
MAILCAP
PM-UTILS-HD-APM-RESTORE.CONF
ghci> run $ "ls /etc" -|- grep "m.*ap" -|- "tr a-z A-Z" :: IO String
"IDMAPD.CONF\nMAILCAP\nPM-UTILS-HD-APM-RESTORE.CONF\n"
ghci> run $ "ls /etc" -|- grep "m.*ap" -|- "tr a-z A-Z" :: IO [String]
["IDMAPD.CONF","MAILCAP","PM-UTILS-HD-APM-RESTORE.CONF"]
ghci> run $ "ls /nonexistant" :: IO String
ls: cannot access /nonexistant: No such file or directory
*** Exception: user error (Exited (ExitFailure 2))
ghci> run $ "ls /nonexistant" :: IO ProcessStatus
ls: cannot access /nonexistant: No such file or directory
Exited (ExitFailure 2)
ghci> run $ "ls /nonexistant" :: IO Int
ls: cannot access /nonexistant: No such file or directory
2
ghci> runIO $ echo "Line1\nHi, test\n" -|- "tr a-z A-Z" -|- sortLines
HI, TEST
LINE1
```

Final Words on Pipes

We have developed a sophisticated system here. We warned you earlier that POSIX can be complex. One other thing we need to highlight: you must always make sure to evaluate the String returned by these functions before you attempt to evaluate the exit code of the child process. The child process will often not exit until it can write all of its data, and if you do this in the wrong order, your program will hang.

In this chapter, we developed, from the ground up, a simplified version of HSH. If you wish to use these shell-like capabilities in your own programs, we recommend HSH instead of the example developed here due to optimizations present in HSH. HSH also comes with a larger set of utility functions and more capabilities, but the source code behind the library is much more complex and large. Some of the utility functions presented here, in fact, were copied verbatim from HSH. HSH is available at *http://software .complete.org/hsh.*

CHAPTER 21

Using Databases

Everything from web forums to podcatchers or even backup programs frequently use databases for persistent storage. SQL-based databases are often quite convenient: they are fast, can scale from tiny to massive sizes, can operate over the network, often help handle locking and transactions, and can even provide failover and redundancy improvements for applications. Databases come in many different shapes: the large commercial databases such as Oracle, open source engines such as PostgreSQL or MySQL, and even embeddable engines such as Sqlite.

Because databases are so important, Haskell support for them is important as well. In this chapter, we will introduce you to one of the Haskell frameworks for working with databases. We will also use this framework to begin building a podcast downloader, which we will further develop in Chapter 22.

Overview of HDBC

At the bottom of the database stack is the *database engine*, which is responsible for actually storing data on disk. Well-known database engines include PostgreSQL, MySQL, and Oracle.

Most modern database engines support the Structured Query Language (SQL) as a standard way of getting data into and out of relational databases. This book will not provide a tutorial on SQL or relational database management.[*]

Once you have a database engine that supports SQL, you need a way to communicate with it. Each database has its own protocol. Since SQL is reasonably constant across databases, it is possible to make a generic interface that uses drivers for each individual protocol.

---

[*] Alan Beaulieu's *Learning SQL* and Kevin Kline et al.'s *SQL in a Nutshell* (both O'Reilly) may be useful if you don't have experience with SQL.

Haskell has several different database frameworks available, some providing high-level layers atop others. For this chapter, we will concentrate on the Haskell DataBase Connectivity system (HDBC). HDBC is a database abstraction library. That is, you can write code that uses HDBC and can access data stored in almost any SQL database with little or no modification.[†] Even if you never need to switch underlying database engines, the HDBC system of drivers makes a large number of choices available to you with a single interface.

Another database abstraction library for Haskell is HSQL, which shares a similar purpose with HDBC. There is also a higher-level framework called HaskellDB, which sits atop either HDBC or HSQL and is designed to help insulate the programmer from the details of working with SQL. However, it does not have as broad appeal because its design limits it to certain—albeit quite common—database access patterns. Finally, Takusen is a framework that uses a "left fold" approach to reading data from the database.

Installing HDBC and Drivers

To connect to a given database with HDBC, you need at least two packages: the generic interface and a driver for your specific database. You can obtain the generic HDBC package, and all of the other drivers, from Hackage (*http://hackage.haskell.org/*).[‡] For this chapter, we will use HDBC version 1.1.3.

You'll also need a database backend and a backend driver. For this chapter, we'll use Sqlite version 3. Sqlite is an embedded database, so it doesn't require a separate server and is easy to set up. Many operating systems already ship with Sqlite version 3. If yours doesn't, you can download it from *http://www.sqlite.org/*. The HDBC home page has a link to known HDBC backend drivers. The specific driver for Sqlite version 3 can be obtained from Hackage.

If you want to use HDBC with other databases, check out the HDBC Known Drivers page at *http://software.complete.org/hdbc/wiki/KnownDrivers*. There you will find a link to the ODBC binding, which lets you connect to virtually any database on virtually any platform (Windows, POSIX, and others). You will also find a PostgreSQL binding. MySQL is supported via the ODBC binding, and specific information for MySQL users can be found in the HDBC-ODBC API documentation (*http://software.complete.org/static/hdbc-odbc/doc/HDBC-odbc/*).

[†] This assumes that you restrict yourself to using standard SQL.

[‡] For more information on installing Haskell software, please refer to "Installing Haskell Software" on page 646.

Connecting to Databases

To connect to a database, you will use a connection function from a database backend driver. Each database has its own unique method of connecting. The initial connection is generally the only time you will call anything from a backend driver module directly.

The database connection function will return a database handle. The precise type of this handle may vary from one driver to the next, but it will always be an instance of the IConnection typeclass. All of the functions you will use to operate on databases will work with any type that is an instance of IConnection. When you're done talking to the database, call the disconnect function to disconnect from it. Here's an example of making a connection to an Sqlite database:

```
ghci> :module Database.HDBC Database.HDBC.Sqlite3
ghci> conn <- connectSqlite3 "test1.db"
Loading package array-0.1.0.0 ... linking ... done.
Loading package containers-0.1.0.2 ... linking ... done.
Loading package bytestring-0.9.0.1.1 ... linking ... done.
Loading package old-locale-1.0.0.0 ... linking ... done.
Loading package old-time-1.0.0.0 ... linking ... done.
Loading package mtl-1.1.0.1 ... linking ... done.
Loading package HDBC-1.1.4 ... linking ... done.
Loading package HDBC-sqlite3-1.1.4.0 ... linking ... done.
ghci> :type conn
conn :: Connectionghci> disconnect conn
```

Transactions

Most modern SQL databases have a notion of transactions. A transaction is designed to ensure that all components of a modification get applied, or that none of them do. Furthermore, transactions help prevent other processes accessing the same database from seeing partial data from modifications that are in progress.

Many databases require you to either explicitly commit all your changes before they appear on disk, or to run in an *autocommit* mode. Autocommit mode runs an implicit commit after every statement. This may make the adjustment to transactional databases easier for programmers not accustomed to them, but it is just a hindrance to people who actually want to use multistatement transactions.

HDBC intentionally does not support autocommit mode. When you modify data in your databases, you must explicitly cause it to be committed to disk. There are two ways to do that in HDBC: you can call commit when you're ready to write the data to disk, or you can use the withTransaction function to wrap around your modification code. withTransaction will cause data to be committed upon successful completion of your function.

Sometimes a problem will occur while you are working on writing data to the database. Perhaps you get an error from the database or discover a problem with the data. In these instances, you can "roll back" your changes. This will cause all changes you made since your last commit or rollback to be forgotten. In HDBC, you can call the rollback function to do this. If you are using withTransaction, any uncaught exception will cause a rollback to be issued.

Note that a roll back operation rolls back only the changes since the last commit, rollback, or withTransaction. A database does not maintain an extensive history like a version-control system. You will see examples of commit later in this chapter.

 One popular database, MySQL, does not support transactions with its default table type. In its default configuration, MySQL will silently ignore calls to commit or rollback and will commit all changes to disk immediately. The HDBC ODBC driver has instructions for configuring MySQL to indicate to HDBC that it does not support transactions, which will cause commit and rollback to generate errors. Alternatively, you can use InnoDB tables with MySQL, which do support transactions. InnoDB tables are recommended for use with HDBC.

Simple Queries

Some of the simplest queries in SQL involve statements that don't return any data. These queries can be used to create tables, insert data, delete data, and set database parameters.

The most basic function for sending queries to a database is run. This function takes an IConnection, a String representing the query itself, and a list of parameters. Let's use it to set up some things in our database:

```
ghci> :module Database.HDBC Database.HDBC.Sqlite3
ghci> conn <- connectSqlite3 "test1.db"
Loading package array-0.1.0.0 ... linking ... done.
Loading package containers-0.1.0.2 ... linking ... done.
Loading package bytestring-0.9.0.1.1 ... linking ... done.
Loading package old-locale-1.0.0.0 ... linking ... done.
Loading package old-time-1.0.0.0 ... linking ... done.
Loading package mtl-1.1.0.1 ... linking ... done.
Loading package HDBC-1.1.4 ... linking ... done.
Loading package HDBC-sqlite3-1.1.4.0 ... linking ... done.
ghci> run conn "CREATE TABLE test (id INTEGER NOT NULL, desc VARCHAR(80))" []
0
ghci> run conn "INSERT INTO test (id) VALUES (0)" []
1
ghci> commit conn
ghci> disconnect conn
```

In this example, after connecting to the database, we first created a table called test. Then we inserted one row of data into the table. Finally, we committed the changes and disconnected from the database. Note that if we hadn't called commit, no final change would have been written to the database at all.

The run function returns the number of rows that each query modified. For the first query, which created a table, no rows were modified. The second query inserted a single row, so run returned 1.

SqlValue

Before proceeding, we need to discuss a data type introduced in HDBC: SqlValue. Since both Haskell and SQL are strongly typed systems, HDBC tries to preserve type information as much as possible. At the same time, Haskell and SQL types don't exactly mirror each other. Furthermore, different databases have different ways of representing things such as dates or special characters in strings.

SqlValue is a data type that has a number of constructors such as SqlString, SqlBool, SqlNull, SqlInteger, and more. This lets you represent various types of data in argument lists to the database and see various types of data in the results coming back, and still store it all in a list. There are convenience functions, toSql and fromSql, that you will normally use. If you care about the precise representation of data, you can still manually construct SqlValue data if you need to.

Query Parameters

HDBC, like most databases, supports a notion of replaceable parameters in queries. There are three primary benefits of using replaceable parameters: they prevent SQL injection attacks or trouble when the input contains quote characters, they improve performance when executing similar queries repeatedly, and they permit easy and portable insertion of data into queries.

Let's say you want to add thousands of rows into our new table test. You could issue queries that look like INSERT INTO test VALUES (0, 'zero') and INSERT INTO test VALUES (1, 'one'). This forces the database server to parse each SQL statement individually. If you could replace the two values with a placeholder, the server could parse the SQL query once and just execute it multiple times with the different data.

A second problem involves escaping characters. What if you want to insert the string "I don't like 1"? SQL uses the single quote character to show the end of the field. Most SQL databases would require you to write this as 'I don''t like 1'. But rules for other special characters such as backslashes differ between databases. Rather than trying to code this yourself, HDBC can handle it all for you. Let's look at an example:

```
ghci> conn <- connectSqlite3 "test1.db"
ghci> run conn "INSERT INTO test VALUES (?, ?)" [toSql 0, toSql "zero"]
1
ghci> commit conn
ghci> disconnect conn
```

The question marks in the INSERT query in this example are the placeholders. We then pass the parameters that are going to go there. run takes a list of SqlValue, so we use toSql to convert each item into an SqlValue. HDBC automatically handles conversion of the String "zero" into the appropriate representation for the database in use.

This approach won't actually achieve any performance benefits when inserting large amounts of data. For that, we need more control over the process of creating the SQL query. We'll discuss that in the next section.

Using replaceable parameters

Replaceable parameters work only for parts of the queries where the server is expecting a value, such as a WHERE clause in a SELECT statement or a value for an INSERT statement. You cannot say `run "SELECT * from ?" [toSql "tablename"]` and expect it to work. A table name is not a value, and most databases will not accept this syntax. That's not a big problem in practice, because there is rarely a call for replacing things in this way that aren't values.

Prepared Statements

HDBC defines a function `prepare` that will prepare a SQL query, but it does not yet bind the parameters to the query. `prepare` returns a `Statement` representing the compiled query.

Once you have a `Statement`, you can do a number of things with it. You can call `execute` on it one or more times. After calling `execute` on a query that returns data, you can use one of the fetch functions to retrieve that data. Functions such as `run` and `quickQuery'` use statements and `execute` internally; they are simply shortcuts to let you perform common tasks quickly. When you need more control over what's happening, you can use a `Statement` instead of a function such as `run`.

Let's look at using statements to insert multiple values with a single query. Here's an example:

```
ghci> conn <- connectSqlite3 "test1.db"
ghci> stmt <- prepare conn "INSERT INTO test VALUES (?, ?)"
ghci> execute stmt [toSql 1, toSql "one"]
1
ghci> execute stmt [toSql 2, toSql "two"]
1
ghci> execute stmt [toSql 3, toSql "three"]
1
ghci> execute stmt [toSql 4, SqlNull]
1
ghci> commit conn
ghci> disconnect conn
```

Here, we create a prepared statement and call it stmt. We then execute that statement four times and pass different parameters each time. These parameters are used, in order, to replace the question marks in the original query string. Finally, we commit the changes and disconnect the database.

HDBC also provides a function, executeMany, that can be useful in situations such as this. executeMany simply takes a list of rows of data to call the statement with. Here's an example:

```
ghci> conn <- connectSqlite3 "test1.db"
ghci> stmt <- prepare conn "INSERT INTO test VALUES (?, ?)"
ghci> executeMany stmt [[toSql 5, toSql "five's nice"], [toSql 6, SqlNull]]
ghci> commit conn
ghci> disconnect conn
```

More efficient execution

On the server, most databases will have an optimization that they can apply to executeMany so that they only have to compile this query string once, rather than twice.[§] This can lead to a dramatic performance gain when inserting large amounts of data at one time. Some databases can also apply this optimization to execute, but not all.

Reading Results

So far, we have discussed queries that insert or change data. Let's now go over getting data back out of the database. The type of the function quickQuery' looks very similar to run, but it returns a list of results instead of a count of changed rows. quickQuery' is normally used with SELECT statements. Let's see an example:

```
ghci> conn <- connectSqlite3 "test1.db"
ghci> quickQuery' conn "SELECT * from test where id < 2" []
[[SqlString "0",SqlNull],[SqlString "0",SqlString "zero"],
[SqlString "1",SqlString "one"],[SqlString "0",SqlNull],
[SqlString "0",SqlString "zero"],[SqlString "1",SqlString "one"]]
ghci> disconnect conn
```

quickQuery' works with replaceable parameters, as we just discussed. In this case, we aren't using any, so the set of values to replace is the empty list at the end of the quickQuery' call. quickQuery' returns a list of rows, where each row is itself represented as [SqlValue]. The values in the row are listed in the order returned by the database. You can use fromSql to convert them into regular Haskell types as needed.

It's a bit hard to read that output. Let's extend this example to format the results nicely. Here's some code to do that:

```
-- file: ch21/query.hs
import Database.HDBC.Sqlite3 (connectSqlite3)
import Database.HDBC
```

[§] HDBC emulates this behavior for databases that do not provide it, offering programmers a unified API for running queries repeatedly.

```
{- | Define a function that takes an integer representing the maximum
id value to look up.  Will fetch all matching rows from the test database
and print them to the screen in a friendly format. -}
query :: Int -> IO ()
query maxId =
    do -- Connect to the database
       conn <- connectSqlite3 "test1.db"

       -- Run the query and store the results in r
       r <- quickQuery' conn
           "SELECT id, desc from test where id <= ? ORDER BY id, desc"
           [toSql maxId]

       -- Convert each row into a String
       let stringRows = map convRow r

       -- Print the rows out
       mapM_ putStrLn stringRows

       -- And disconnect from the database
       disconnect conn

    where convRow :: [SqlValue] -> String
          convRow [sqlId, sqlDesc] =
              show intid ++ ": " ++ desc
              where intid = (fromSql sqlId)::Integer
                    desc = case fromSql sqlDesc of
                             Just x -> x
                             Nothing -> "NULL"
          convRow x = fail $ "Unexpected result: " ++ show x
```

This program does mostly the same thing as our example with ghci but with a new addition: the convRow function. This function takes a row of data from the database and converts it to a String. This string can then be easily printed out.

Notice how we took intid from fromSql directly but processed fromSql sqlDesc as a Maybe String type. If you recall, we declared that the first column in this table can never contain a NULL value but that the second column could. Therefore, we can safely ignore the potential for a NULL in the first column but not in the second. It is possible to use fromSql to convert the second column to a String directly, and it would even work—until a row with a NULL in that position is encountered. This would cause a runtime exception. So, we convert a SQL NULL value into the string "NULL". When printed, this will be indistinguishable from a SQL string 'NULL', but that's acceptable for this example. Let's try calling this function in ghci:

```
ghci> :load query.hs
[1 of 1] Compiling Main             ( query.hs, interpreted )
Ok, modules loaded: Main.
ghci> query 2
0: NULL
0: NULL
0: zero
```

```
0: zero
1: one
1: one
2: two
2: two
```

Reading with Statements

As we discussed in "Prepared Statements" on page 498, you can use statements for reading. There are a number of ways of reading data from statements that can be useful in certain situations. Like run, quickQuery' is a convenience function that in fact uses statements to accomplish its task.

To create a statement for reading, we use prepare just as we would for a statement that will be used to write data. You also use execute to execute it on the database server. Then, we can use various functions to read data from the Statement. The fetchAll Rows' function returns [[SqlValue]], just like quickQuery'. There is also a function called sFetchAllRows', which converts every column's data to Maybe String before returning it. Finally, there is fetchAllRowsAL', which returns (String, SqlValue) pairs for each column. The String is the column name as returned by the database; see "Database Metadata" on page 502 for other ways to obtain column names.

You can also read data one row at a time by calling fetchRow, which returns IO (Maybe [SqlValue]). It will be Nothing if all the results have already been read, or one row otherwise.

Lazy Reading

Back in "Lazy I/O" on page 178, we talked about lazy I/O from files. It is also possible to read data lazily from databases. This can be particularly useful when dealing with queries that return an exceptionally large amount of data. By reading data lazily, you can still use convenient functions such as fetchAllRows instead of having to manually read each row as it comes in. If we are careful in our use of the data, we can avoid having to buffer all of the results in memory.

Lazy reading from a database, however, is more complex than reading from a file. When we're done reading data lazily from a file, the file is closed—which is generally fine. When we're done reading data lazily from a database, the database connection is still open—you may be submitting other queries with it, for instance. Some databases can even support multiple simultaneous queries, so HDBC can't just close the connection when we're done.

When using lazy reading, it is critically important that we finish reading the entire data set before we attempt to close the connection or execute a new query. We encourage you to use the strict functions, or row-by-row processing, wherever possible to minimize complex interactions with lazy reading.

If you are new to HDBC or the concept of lazy reading but have lots of data to read, repeated calls to fetchRow may be easier to understand. Lazy reading is a powerful and useful tool, but must be used correctly.

To read lazily from a database, we use the same functions we used before, without the apostrophe. For instance, use fetchAllRows instead of fetchAllRows'. The types of the lazy functions are the same as their strict cousins. Here's an example of lazy reading:

```
ghci> conn <- connectSqlite3 "test1.db"
ghci> stmt <- prepare conn "SELECT * from test where id < 2"
ghci> execute stmt []
0
ghci> results <- fetchAllRowsAL stmt
[[("id",SqlString "0"),("desc",SqlNull)],[("id",SqlString "0"),
("desc",SqlString "zero")],[("id",SqlString "1"),("desc",SqlString "one")]
,[("id",SqlString "0"),("desc",SqlNull)],[("id",SqlString "0"),
("desc",SqlString "zero")],[("id",SqlString "1"),("desc",SqlString "one")]]
ghci> mapM_ print results
[("id",SqlString "0"),("desc",SqlNull)]
[("id",SqlString "0"),("desc",SqlString "zero")]
[("id",SqlString "1"),("desc",SqlString "one")]
[("id",SqlString "0"),("desc",SqlNull)]
[("id",SqlString "0"),("desc",SqlString "zero")]
[("id",SqlString "1"),("desc",SqlString "one")]ghci> disconnect conn
```

Note that you could have used fetchAllRowsAL' here as well. However, if you had a large data set to read, it would consume a lot of memory. By reading the data lazily, we can print out extremely large result sets using a constant amount of memory. With the lazy version, results will be evaluated in chunks; with the strict version, all results are read up front, stored in RAM, and then printed.

Database Metadata

Sometimes it can be useful for a program to learn information about the database itself. For instance, a program may want to see what tables exist so that it can automatically create missing tables or upgrade the database schema. In some cases, a program may need to alter its behavior depending on the database backend in use.

First, there is a getTables function that will obtain a list of defined tables in a database. You can also use the describeTable function, which will provide information about the defined columns in a given table.

You can learn about the database server in use by calling dbServerVer and proxiedClientName, for instance. The dbTransactionSupport function can be used to determine whether or not a given database supports transactions. Let's look at an example of some of these items:

```
ghci> conn <- connectSqlite3 "test1.db"
ghci> getTables conn
```

```
["test"]
ghci> proxiedClientName conn
"sqlite3"
ghci> dbServerVer conn
"3.5.6"
ghci> dbTransactionSupport conn
Trueghci> disconnect conn
```

You can also learn about the results of a specific query by obtaining information from its statement. The describeResult function returns [(String, SqlColDesc)], a list of pairs. The first item gives the column name, and the second provides information about the column: the type, the size, and whether it may be NULL. The full specification is given in the HDBC API reference.

 Some databases may not be able to provide all this metadata. In these circumstances, an exception will be raised. Sqlite3, for instance, does not support describeResult or describeTable as of this writing.

Error Handling

HDBC will raise exceptions when errors occur. The exceptions have type SqlError. They convey information from the underlying SQL engine, such as the database's state, the error message, and the database's numeric error code, if any.

ghci does not know how to display an SqlError on the screen when it occurs. While the exception will cause the program to terminate, it will not display a useful message. Here's an example:

```
ghci> conn <- connectSqlite3 "test1.db"
ghci> quickQuery' conn "SELECT * from test2" []
*** Exception: (unknown)
ghci> disconnect conn
```

Here we tried to SELECT data from a table that didn't exist. The error message we got wasn't helpful. There's a utility function, handleSqlError, that will catch an SqlError and re-raise it as an IOError. In this form, it will be printable onscreen, but it will be more difficult to extract specific pieces of information programmatically. Let's look at its usage:

```
ghci> conn <- connectSqlite3 "test1.db"
ghci> handleSqlError $ quickQuery' conn "SELECT * from test2" []
*** Exception: user error (SQL error: SqlError {seState = "", seNativeError = 1,
seErrorMsg = "prepare 20: SELECT * from test2: no such table: test2"})
ghci> disconnect conn
```

Here we got more information, including a message saying that there is no such table as test2. This is much more helpful. Many HDBC programmers make it a standard practice to start their programs with `main = handleSqlError $ do`, which will ensure that every uncaught `SqlError` will be printed in a helpful manner.

There are also `catchSql` and `handleSql`—similar to the standard `catch` and `handle` functions. `catchSql` and `handleSql` will intercept HDBC errors only. For more information on error handling, refer to Chapter 19.

CHAPTER 22

Extended Example: Web Client Programming

By this point, you've seen how to interact with a database, parse things, and handle errors. Let's now take this a step farther and introduce a web client library to the mix.

We'll develop a real application in this chapter: a podcast downloader, or *podcatcher*. The idea of a podcatcher is simple. It is given a list of URLs to process. Downloading each of these URLs results in an XML file in the RSS format. Inside this XML file, we'll find references to URLs for audio files to download.

Podcatchers usually let the user subscribe to podcasts by adding RSS URLs to their configuration. Then, the user can periodically run an update operation. The podcatcher will download the RSS documents, examine them for audio file references, and download any audio files that haven't already been downloaded on behalf of this user.

 Users often call the RSS document a podcast or the podcast feed, and call each individual audio file an episode.

To make this happen, we need to have several things:

- An HTTP client library to download files
- An XML parser
- A way to specify and persistently store which podcasts we're interested in
- A way to persistently store which podcast episodes we've already downloaded

The last two items can be accommodated via a database that we'll set up using HDBC. The first two can be accommodated via other library modules we'll introduce in this chapter.

The code in this chapter was written specifically for this book, but is based on code written for hpodder, an existing podcatcher written in Haskell. hpodder has many more features than the examples presented here, which make it too long and complex to cover in this book. If you are interested in studying hpodder, its source code is freely available at *http://software.complete.org/hpodder*.

We'll write the code for this chapter in pieces. Each piece will be its own Haskell module. You'll be able to play with each piece by itself in `ghci`. At the end, we'll write the final code that ties everything together into a finished application. We'll start with the basic types that we'll need to use.

Basic Types

The first thing to do is have some idea of the basic information that will be important to the application. This will generally be information about the podcasts the user is interested in, plus information about episodes that we have seen and processed. It's easy enough to change this later if needed, but since we'll be importing it just about everywhere, we'll define it first:

```
-- file: ch22/PodTypes.hs
module PodTypes where

data Podcast =
    Podcast {castId :: Integer, -- ^ Numeric ID for this podcast
             castURL :: String   -- ^ Its feed URL
            }
    deriving (Eq, Show, Read)

data Episode =
    Episode {epId :: Integer,      -- ^ Numeric ID for this episode
             epCast :: Podcast,    -- ^ The ID of the podcast it came from
             epURL :: String,      -- ^ The download URL for this episode
             epDone :: Bool        -- ^ Whether or not we are done with this ep
            }
    deriving (Eq, Show, Read)
```

We'll be storing this information in a database. Having a unique identifier for both a podcast and an episode makes it easy to find which episodes belong to a particular podcast, load information for a particular podcast or episode, or handle future cases such as changing URLs for podcasts.

The Database

Next, we'll write the code to make possible persistent storage in a database. We'll primarily be interested in moving data between the Haskell structures that we defined in *PodTypes.hs* and the database on disk. Also, the first time the user runs the program, the user will need to create the database tables that he will use to store our data.

We'll use HDBC (see Chapter 21) to interact with a Sqlite database. Sqlite is lightweight and self-contained, which makes it perfect for this project. For information on installing HDBC and Sqlite, consult "Installing HDBC and Drivers" on page 494:

```
-- file: ch22/PodDB.hs
module PodDB where

import Database.HDBC
import Database.HDBC.Sqlite3
import PodTypes
import Control.Monad(when)
import Data.List(sort)

-- | Initialize DB and return database Connection
connect :: FilePath -> IO Connection
connect fp =
    do dbh <- connectSqlite3 fp
       prepDB dbh
       return dbh

{- | Prepare the database for our data.

We create two tables and ask the database engine to verify some pieces
of data consistency for us:

* castid and epid both are unique primary keys and must never be duplicated
* castURL also is unique
* In the episodes table, for a given podcast (epcast), there must be only
  one instance of each given URL or episode ID
-}
prepDB :: IConnection conn => conn -> IO ()
prepDB dbh =
    do tables <- getTables dbh
       when (not ("podcasts" `elem` tables)) $
           do run dbh "CREATE TABLE podcasts (\
                      \castid INTEGER NOT NULL PRIMARY KEY AUTOINCREMENT,\
                      \castURL TEXT NOT NULL UNIQUE)" []
              return ()
       when (not ("episodes" `elem` tables)) $
           do run dbh "CREATE TABLE episodes (\
                      \epid INTEGER NOT NULL PRIMARY KEY AUTOINCREMENT,\
                      \epcastid INTEGER NOT NULL,\
                      \epurl TEXT NOT NULL,\
                      \epdone INTEGER NOT NULL,\
                      \UNIQUE(epcastid, epurl),\
                      \UNIQUE(epcastid, epid))" []
              return ()
       commit dbh

{- | Adds a new podcast to the database.  Ignores the castid on the
incoming podcast, and returns a new object with the castid populated.
```

```
An attempt to add a podcast that already exists is an error. -}
addPodcast :: IConnection conn => conn -> Podcast -> IO Podcast
addPodcast dbh podcast =
    handleSql errorHandler $
        do -- Insert the castURL into the table.  The database
           -- will automatically assign a cast ID.
           run dbh "INSERT INTO podcasts (castURL) VALUES (?)"
               [toSql (castURL podcast)]
           -- Find out the castID for the URL we just added.
           r <- quickQuery' dbh "SELECT castid FROM podcasts WHERE castURL = ?"
               [toSql (castURL podcast)]
           case r of
             [[x]] -> return $ podcast {castId = fromSql x}
             y -> fail $ "addPodcast: unexpected result: " ++ show y
    where errorHandler e =
              do fail $ "Error adding podcast; does this URL already exist?\n"
                     ++ show e

{- | Adds a new episode to the database.

Since this is done by automation instead of by user request, we will
simply ignore requests to add duplicate episodes.  This way, when we are
processing a feed, each URL encountered can be fed to this function,
without having to first look it up in the DB.

Also, we generally won't care about the new ID here, so don't bother
fetching it. -}
addEpisode :: IConnection conn => conn -> Episode -> IO ()
addEpisode dbh ep =
    run dbh "INSERT OR IGNORE INTO episodes (epCastId, epURL, epDone) \
            \VALUES (?, ?, ?)"
            [toSql (castId . epCast $ ep), toSql (epURL ep),
             toSql (epDone ep)]
    >> return ()

{- | Modifies an existing podcast.  Looks up the given podcast by
ID and modifies the database record to match the passed Podcast. -}
updatePodcast :: IConnection conn => conn -> Podcast -> IO ()
updatePodcast dbh podcast =
    run dbh "UPDATE podcasts SET castURL = ? WHERE castId = ?"
            [toSql (castURL podcast), toSql (castId podcast)]
    >> return ()

{- | Modifies an existing episode.  Looks it up by ID and modifies the
database record to match the given episode. -}
updateEpisode :: IConnection conn => conn -> Episode -> IO ()
updateEpisode dbh episode =
    run dbh "UPDATE episodes SET epCastId = ?, epURL = ?, epDone = ? \
            \WHERE epId = ?"
            [toSql (castId . epCast $ episode),
             toSql (epURL episode),
             toSql (epDone episode),
             toSql (epId episode)]
    >> return ()
```

```
{- | Remove a podcast.  First removes any episodes that may exist
for this podcast. -}
removePodcast :: IConnection conn => conn -> Podcast -> IO ()
removePodcast dbh podcast =
    do run dbh "DELETE FROM episodes WHERE epcastid = ?"
          [toSql (castId podcast)]
       run dbh "DELETE FROM podcasts WHERE castid = ?"
          [toSql (castId podcast)]
       return ()

{- | Gets a list of all podcasts. -}
getPodcasts :: IConnection conn => conn -> IO [Podcast]
getPodcasts dbh =
    do res <- quickQuery' dbh
              "SELECT castid, casturl FROM podcasts ORDER BY castid" []
       return (map convPodcastRow res)

{- | Get a particular podcast.  Nothing if the ID doesn't match, or
Just Podcast if it does. -}
getPodcast :: IConnection conn => conn -> Integer -> IO (Maybe Podcast)
getPodcast dbh wantedId =
    do res <- quickQuery' dbh
              "SELECT castid, casturl FROM podcasts WHERE castid = ?"
              [toSql wantedId]
       case res of
         [x] -> return (Just (convPodcastRow x))
         [] -> return Nothing
         x -> fail $ "Really bad error; more than one podcast with ID"

{- | Convert the result of a SELECT into a Podcast record -}
convPodcastRow :: [SqlValue] -> Podcast
convPodcastRow [svId, svURL] =
    Podcast {castId = fromSql svId,
             castURL = fromSql svURL}
convPodcastRow x = error $ "Can't convert podcast row " ++ show x

{- | Get all episodes for a particular podcast. -}
getPodcastEpisodes :: IConnection conn => conn -> Podcast -> IO [Episode]
getPodcastEpisodes dbh pc =
    do r <- quickQuery' dbh
            "SELECT epId, epURL, epDone FROM episodes WHERE epCastId = ?"
            [toSql (castId pc)]
       return (map convEpisodeRow r)
    where convEpisodeRow [svId, svURL, svDone] =
              Episode {epId = fromSql svId, epURL = fromSql svURL,
                       epDone = fromSql svDone, epCast = pc}
```

In the PodDB module, we have defined functions to connect to the database, create the needed tables for it, add data to it, query it, and remove data from it. Here is an example ghci session demonstrating interacting with the database. It will create a database file named *poddbtest.db* in the current working directory and add a podcast and an episode to it:

```
ghci> :load PodDB.hs
[1 of 2] Compiling PodTypes        ( PodTypes.hs, interpreted )
[2 of 2] Compiling PodDB           ( PodDB.hs, interpreted )
Ok, modules loaded: PodDB, PodTypes.
ghci> dbh <- connect "poddbtest.db"
ghci> :type dbh
dbh :: Connection
ghci> getTables dbh
["episodes","podcasts","sqlite_sequence"]
ghci> let url = "http://feeds.thisamericanlife.org/talpodcast"
ghci> pc <- addPodcast dbh (Podcast {castId=0, castURL=url})
Podcast {castId = 1, castURL = "http://feeds.thisamericanlife.org/talpodcast"}
ghci> getPodcasts dbh
[Podcast {castId = 1, castURL = "http://feeds.thisamericanlife.org/talpodcast"}]
ghci> addEpisode dbh (Episode {epId = 0, epCast = pc, epURL =
"http://www.example.com/foo.mp3", epDone = False})
ghci> getPodcastEpisodes dbh pc
[Episode {epId = 1, epCast = Podcast {castId = 1, castURL =
"http://feeds.thisamericanlife.org/talpodcast"}, epURL = "http://www.example.com/foo.mp3",
epDone = False}]
ghci> commit dbh
ghci> disconnect dbh
```

The Parser

Now that we have the database component, we need to have code to parse the podcast
feeds. These are XML files that contain various information. Here's an example XML
file to show you what they look like:

```
<?xml version="1.0" encoding="UTF-8"?>
<rss xmlns:itunes="http://www.itunes.com/DTDs/Podcast-1.0.dtd" version="2.0">
  <channel>
    <title>Haskell Radio</title>
    <link>http://www.example.com/radio/</link>
    <description>Description of this podcast</description>
    <item>
      <title>Episode 2: Lambdas</title>
      <link>http://www.example.com/radio/lambdas</link>
      <enclosure url="http://www.example.com/radio/lambdas.mp3"
       type="audio/mpeg" length="10485760"/>
    </item>
    <item>
      <title>Episode 1: Parsec</title>
      <link>http://www.example.com/radio/parsec</link>
      <enclosure url="http://www.example.com/radio/parsec.mp3"
       type="audio/mpeg" length="10485150"/>
    </item>
  </channel>
</rss>
```

Out of these files, we are mainly interested in two things: the podcast title and the
enclosure URLs. We use the HaXml toolkit (*http://www.cs.york.ac.uk/fp/HaXml/*) to
parse the XML file. Here's the source code for this component:

```
-- file: ch22/PodParser.hs
module PodParser where

import PodTypes
import Text.XML.HaXml
import Text.XML.HaXml.Parse
import Text.XML.HaXml.Html.Generate(showattr)
import Data.Char
import Data.List

data PodItem = PodItem {itemtitle :: String,
                        enclosureurl :: String
                       }
           deriving (Eq, Show, Read)

data Feed = Feed {channeltitle :: String,
                  items :: [PodItem]}
            deriving (Eq, Show, Read)

{- | Given a podcast and an PodItem, produce an Episode -}
item2ep :: Podcast -> PodItem -> Episode
item2ep pc item =
    Episode {epId = 0,
             epCast = pc,
             epURL = enclosureurl item,
             epDone = False}

{- | Parse the data from a given string, with the given name to use
in error messages. -}
parse :: String -> String -> Feed
parse content name =
    Feed {channeltitle = getTitle doc,
          items = getEnclosures doc}

    where parseResult = xmlParse name (stripUnicodeBOM content)
          doc = getContent parseResult

          getContent :: Document -> Content
          getContent (Document _ _ e _) = CElem e

          {- | Some Unicode documents begin with a binary sequence;
             strip it off before processing. -}
          stripUnicodeBOM :: String -> String
          stripUnicodeBOM ('\xef':'\xbb':'\xbf':x) = x
          stripUnicodeBOM x = x

{- | Pull out the channel part of the document.

Note that HaXml defines CFilter as:

> type CFilter = Content -> [Content]
-}
channel :: CFilter
channel = tag "rss" /> tag "channel"
```

```
getTitle :: Content -> String
getTitle doc =
    contentToStringDefault "Untitled Podcast"
        (channel /> tag "title" /> txt $ doc)

getEnclosures :: Content -> [PodItem]
getEnclosures doc =
    concatMap procPodItem $ getPodItems doc
    where procPodItem :: Content -> [PodItem]
          procPodItem item = concatMap (procEnclosure title) enclosure
              where title = contentToStringDefault "Untitled Episode"
                                (keep /> tag "title" /> txt $ item)
                    enclosure = (keep /> tag "enclosure") item

          getPodItems :: CFilter
          getPodItems = channel /> tag "item"

          procEnclosure :: String -> Content -> [PodItem]
          procEnclosure title enclosure =
              map makePodItem (showattr "url" enclosure)
              where makePodItem :: Content -> PodItem
                    makePodItem x = PodItem {itemtitle = title,
                                             enclosureurl = contentToString [x]}

{- | Convert [Content] to a printable String, with a default if the
passed-in [Content] is [], signifying a lack of a match. -}
contentToStringDefault :: String -> [Content] -> String
contentToStringDefault msg [] = msg
contentToStringDefault _ x = contentToString x

{- | Convert [Content] to a printable string, taking care to unescape it.

An implementation without unescaping would simply be:

> contentToString = concatMap (show . content)

Because HaXml's unescaping works only on Elements, we must make sure that
whatever Content we have is wrapped in an Element, then use txt to
pull the insides back out. -}
contentToString :: [Content] -> String
contentToString =
    concatMap procContent
    where procContent x =
              verbatim $ keep /> txt $ CElem (unesc (fakeElem x))

          fakeElem :: Content -> Element
          fakeElem x = Elem "fake" [] [x]

          unesc :: Element -> Element
          unesc = xmlUnEscape stdXmlEscaper
```

Let's look at this code. First, we declare two types: PodItem and Feed. We will be transforming the XML document into a Feed, which then contains items. We also provide a function to convert an PodItem into an Episode as defined in *PodTypes.hs*.

Next, it is on to parsing. The parse function takes a String representing the XML content as well as a String representing a name to use in error messages, and then returns a Feed.

HaXml is designed as a "filter" converting data of one type to another. It can be a simple straightforward conversion of XML to XML, or of XML to Haskell data, or of Haskell data to XML. HaXml has a data type called CFilter, which is defined like this:

```
type CFilter = Content -> [Content]
```

That is, a CFilter takes a fragment of an XML document and returns 0 or more fragments. A CFilter might be asked to find all children of a specified tag, all tags with a certain name, the literal text contained within a part of an XML document, or any of a number of other things. There is also an operator (/>) that chains CFilter functions together. All of the data that we're interested in occurs within the <channel> tag, so first we want to get at that. We define a simple CFilter:

```
channel = tag "rss" /> tag "channel"
```

When we pass a document to channel, it will search the top level for the tag named rss. Then, within that, it will look for the channel tag.

The rest of the program follows this basic approach. txt extracts the literal text from a tag, and by using CFilter functions, we can get at any part of the document.

Downloading

The next part of our program is a module to download data. We'll need to download two different types of data: the content of a podcast and the audio for each episode. In the former case, we'll parse the data and update our database. For the latter, we'll write the data out to a file on disk.

We'll be downloading from HTTP servers, so we'll use a Haskell see HTTP library (*http://www.haskell.org/http/*). For downloading podcast feeds, we'll download the document, parse it, and update the database. For episode audio, we'll download the file, write it to disk, and mark it downloaded in the database. Here's the code:

```
-- file: ch22/PodDownload.hs
module PodDownload where
import PodTypes
import PodDB
import PodParser
import Network.HTTP
import System.IO
import Database.HDBC
import Data.Maybe
import Network.URI

{- | Download a URL.  (Left errorMessage) if an error,
(Right doc) if success. -}
downloadURL :: String -> IO (Either String String)
```

```
downloadURL url =
    do resp <- simpleHTTP request
       case resp of
         Left x -> return $ Left ("Error connecting: " ++ show x)
         Right r ->
             case rspCode r of
               (2,_,_) -> return $ Right (rspBody r)
               (3,_,_) -> -- A HTTP redirect
                 case findHeader HdrLocation r of
                   Nothing -> return $ Left (show r)
                   Just url -> downloadURL url
               _ -> return $ Left (show r)
    where request = Request {rqURI = uri,
                             rqMethod = GET,
                             rqHeaders = [],
                             rqBody = ""}
          uri = fromJust $ parseURI url

{- | Update the podcast in the database. -}
updatePodcastFromFeed :: IConnection conn => conn -> Podcast -> IO ()
updatePodcastFromFeed dbh pc =
    do resp <- downloadURL (castURL pc)
       case resp of
         Left x -> putStrLn x
         Right doc -> updateDB doc

    where updateDB doc =
                do mapM_ (addEpisode dbh) episodes
                   commit dbh
                where feed = parse doc (castURL pc)
                      episodes = map (item2ep pc) (items feed)

{- | Downloads an episode, returning a String representing
the filename it was placed into, or Nothing on error. -}
getEpisode :: IConnection conn => conn -> Episode -> IO (Maybe String)
getEpisode dbh ep =
    do resp <- downloadURL (epURL ep)
       case resp of
         Left x -> do putStrLn x
                      return Nothing
         Right doc ->
             do file <- openBinaryFile filename WriteMode
                hPutStr file doc
                hClose file
                updateEpisode dbh (ep {epDone = True})
                commit dbh
                return (Just filename)
          -- This function ought to apply an extension based on the file type
    where filename = "pod." ++ (show . castId . epCast $ ep) ++ "." ++
                     (show (epId ep)) ++ ".mp3"
```

This module defines three functions: downloadURL, which simply downloads a URL and
returns it as a String; updatePodcastFromFeed, which downloads an XML feed file, parses it, and updates the database; and getEpisode, which downloads a given episode and
marks it done in the database.

The HTTP library used here does not read the HTTP result lazily. As a result, it can result in the consumption of a large amount of RAM when downloading large files such as podcasts. Other libraries are available that do not have this limitation. We used this one because it is stable, easy to install, and reasonably easy to use. We suggest mini-http, available from Hackage, for serious HTTP needs.

Main Program

Finally, we need a main program to tie it all together. Here's our main module:

```
-- file: ch22/PodMain.hs
module Main where

import PodDownload
import PodDB
import PodTypes
import System.Environment
import Database.HDBC
import Network.Socket(withSocketsDo)

main = withSocketsDo $ handleSqlError $
    do args <- getArgs
       dbh <- connect "pod.db"
       case args of
         ["add", url] -> add dbh url
         ["update"] -> update dbh
         ["download"] -> download dbh
         ["fetch"] -> do update dbh
                         download dbh
         _ -> syntaxError
       disconnect dbh

add dbh url =
    do addPodcast dbh pc
       commit dbh
    where pc = Podcast {castId = 0, castURL = url}

update dbh =
    do pclist <- getPodcasts dbh
       mapM_ procPodcast pclist
    where procPodcast pc =
              do putStrLn $ "Updating from " ++ (castURL pc)
                 updatePodcastFromFeed dbh pc

download dbh =
    do pclist <- getPodcasts dbh
       mapM_ procPodcast pclist
    where procPodcast pc =
              do putStrLn $ "Considering " ++ (castURL pc)
                 episodelist <- getPodcastEpisodes dbh pc
                 let dleps = filter (\ep -> epDone ep == False)
                             episodelist
                 mapM_ procEpisode dleps
```

```
          procEpisode ep =
              do putStrLn $ "Downloading " ++ (epURL ep)
                 getEpisode dbh ep

syntaxError = putStrLn
  "Usage: pod command [args]\n\
  \\n\
  \pod add url      Adds a new podcast with the given URL\n\
  \pod download     Downloads all pending episodes\n\
  \pod fetch        Updates, then downloads\n\
  \pod update       Downloads podcast feeds, looks for new episodes\n"
```

We have a very simple command-line parser with a function to indicate a command-line syntax error, plus small functions to handle the different command-line arguments.

You can compile this program with a command like this:

```
ghc --make -O2 -o pod -package HTTP -package HaXml -package network \
    -package HDBC -package HDBC-sqlite3 PodMain.hs
```

Alternatively, you could use a Cabal file as documented in "Creating a Package" on page 131 to build this project:

```
-- ch23/pod.cabal
Name: pod
Version: 1.0.0
Build-type: Simple
Build-Depends: HTTP, HaXml, network, HDBC, HDBC-sqlite3, base

Executable: pod
Main-Is: PodMain.hs
GHC-Options: -O2
```

Also, you'll want a simple *Setup.hs* file:

```
import Distribution.Simple
main = defaultMain
```

Now, to build with Cabal, you just run the following:

```
runghc Setup.hs configure
runghc Setup.hs build
```

And you'll find a *dist* directory containing your output. To install the program system-wide, run `runghc Setup.hs install`.

CHAPTER 23

GUI Programming with gtk2hs

Throughout this book, we have been developing simple text-based tools. While these are often ideal interfaces, sometimes a graphical user interface (GUI) is required. There are several GUI toolkits available for Haskell. In this chapter, we will look at one of them, gtk2hs.[*]

Installing gtk2hs

Before we dive in to working with gtk2hs, you'll need to get it installed. On most Linux, BSD, or other POSIX platforms, you will find ready-made gtk2hs packages. You will generally need to install the GTK+ development environment, Glade, and gtk2hs. The specifics of doing so vary by distribution.

Windows and Mac developers should consult the gtk2hs downloads site at *http://www .haskell.org/gtk2hs/download/*. Begin by downloading gtk2hs from there. Then you will also need Glade version 3. Mac developers can find this at *http://www.macports.org/*, while Windows developers should consult *http://sourceforge.net/projects/gladewin32*.

Overview of the GTK+ Stack

Before examining the code, let's pause a brief moment and consider the architecture of the system we are going to use. First off, we have GTK+. GTK+ is a cross-platform GUI-building toolkit, implemented in C. It runs on Windows, Mac, Linux, BSDs, and more. It is also the toolkit beneath the GNOME desktop environment.

Next, we have Glade. Glade is a user-interface designer, which lets you graphically lay out your application's windows and dialogs. Glade saves the interface in XML files, which your application will load at runtime.

---

[*] Several alternatives also exist. Alongside gtk2hs, wxHaskell is also a prominent cross-platform GUI toolkit.

The last piece of this puzzle is gtk2hs. This is the Haskell binding for GTK+, Glade, and several related libraries. It is one of many language bindings available for GTK+.

User Interface Design with Glade

In this chapter, we are going to develop a GUI for the podcast downloader we first developed in Chapter 22. Our first task is to design the user interface in Glade. Once we have accomplished that, we will write the Haskell code to integrate it with the application.

Because this is a Haskell book, rather than a GUI design book, we will move fast through some of these early parts. For more information on interface design with Glade, you may wish to refer to one of these resources:

The Glade homepage
 Contains documentation for Glade; see *http://glade.gnome.org/*.

The GTK+ homepage
 Contains information about the different widgets. Refer to the documentation section, and then the stable GTK documentation area; see *http://www.gtk.org/*.

The gtk2hs homepage
 Also has a useful documentation section, which contains an API reference to gtk2hs as well as a glade tutorial; see *http://www.haskell.org/gtk2hs/documentation/*.

Glade Concepts

Glade is a user-interface design tool. It lets us use a graphical interface to design our graphical interface. We could build up the window components using a bunch of calls to GTK+ functions, but it is usually easier to do this with Glade.

The fundamental "thing" we work with in GTK+ is the *widget*. A widget represents any part of the GUI, and may contain other widgets. Some examples of widgets include a window, dialog box, button, and text within the button.

Glade, then, is a widget layout tool. We set up a whole tree of widgets, with top-level windows at the top of the tree. You can think of Glade and widgets in somewhat the same terms as HTML: you can arrange widgets in a table-like layout, set up padding rules, and structure the entire description in a hierarchical way.

Glade saves the widget descriptions into an XML file. Our program loads this XML file at runtime. We load the widgets by asking the Glade runtime library to load a widget with a specific name.

Figure 23-1 shows a screenshot of an example working with Glade to design our application's main screen.

In the downloadable material available for this book, you can find the full Glade XML file as *podresources.glade*. You can load this file in Glade and edit it if you wish.

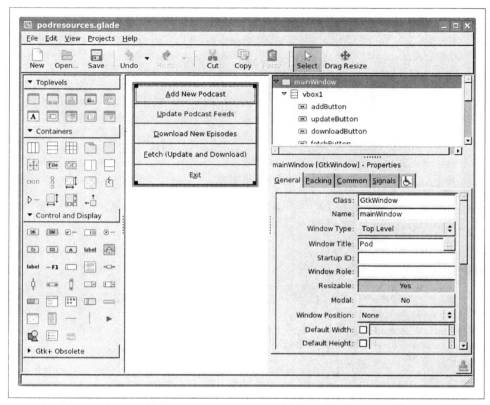

Figure 23-1. Screenshot of Glade, showing components of the graphical user interface

Event-Driven Programming

GTK+, like many GUI toolkits, is an *event-driven* toolkit. That means that instead of, say, displaying a dialog box and waiting for the user to click on a button, we instead tell gtk2hs what function to call if a certain button is clicked, but don't sit there waiting for a click in the dialog box.

This is different from the model traditionally used for console programs. When you think about it, though, it almost has to be. A GUI program could have multiple windows open, and writing code to sit there waiting for input in the particular combination of open windows could be a complicated proposition.

Event-driven programming complements Haskell nicely. As we've discussed over and over in this book, functional languages thrive on passing around functions. So we'll be passing functions to gtk2hs that get called when certain events occur. These are known as *callback functions*.

At the core of a GTK+ program is the *main loop*. This is the part of the program that waits for actions from the user or commands from the program and carries them out.

The GTK+ main loop is handled entirely by GTK+. To us, it looks like an I/O action that we execute, which doesn't return until the GUI has been disposed of.

Since the main loop is responsible for doing everything from handling clicks of a mouse to redrawing a window when it has been uncovered, it must always be available. We can't just run a long-running task—such as downloading a podcast episode—from within the main loop. This would make the GUI unresponsive, and actions such as clicking a Cancel button wouldn't be processed in a timely manner.

Therefore, we will be using multithreading to handle these long-running tasks. More information on multithreading can be found in Chapter 24. For now, just know that we will use forkIO to create new threads for long-running tasks such as downloading podcast feeds and episodes. For very quick tasks, such as adding a new podcast to the database, we will not bother with a separate thread since it will be executed so fast that the user will never notice.

Initializing the GUI

Our first steps are going to involve initializing the GUI for our program. For reasons that we'll explain later in this chapter in "Using Cabal" on page 528, we're going to have a small file called *PodLocalMain.hs* that loads PodMain and passes to it the path to *podresources.glade*, which is the XML file saved by Glade that gives the information about our GUI widgets:

```
-- file: ch23/PodLocalMain.hs
module Main where

import qualified PodMainGUI

main = PodMainGUI.main "podresources.glade"
```

Now, let's consider *PodMainGUI.hs*. This file is the only Haskell source file that we had to modify from the example in Chapter 22 to make it work as a GUI. Let's begin by looking at the start of our new *PodMainGUI.hs* file—we've renamed it from *PodMain.hs* for clarity:

```
-- file: ch23/PodMainGUI.hs
module PodMainGUI where

import PodDownload
import PodDB
import PodTypes
import System.Environment
import Database.HDBC
import Network.Socket(withSocketsDo)

-- GUI libraries

import Graphics.UI.Gtk hiding (disconnect)
import Graphics.UI.Gtk.Glade
```

```
-- Threading

import Control.Concurrent
```

This first part of *PodMainGUI.hs* is similar to our non-GUI version. We import three additional components, however. First, we have `Graphics.UI.Gtk`, which provides most of the GTK+ functions we will be using. Both this module and `Database.HDBC` provide a function named `disconnect`. Since we'll be using the HDBC version, but not the GTK+ version, we don't import that function from `Graphics.UI.Gtk`. `Graphics.UI.Gtk.Glade` contains functions needed for loading and working with our Glade file.

We also import `Control.Concurrent`, which has the basics needed for multithreaded programming. We'll use a few functions from here as just described once we get into the guts of the program. Next, let's define a type to store information about our GUI:

```
-- file: ch23/PodMainGUI.hs
-- | Our main GUI type
data GUI = GUI {
    mainWin :: Window,
    mwAddBt :: Button,
    mwUpdateBt :: Button,
    mwDownloadBt :: Button,
    mwFetchBt :: Button,
    mwExitBt :: Button,
    statusWin :: Dialog,
    swOKBt :: Button,
    swCancelBt :: Button,
    swLabel :: Label,
    addWin :: Dialog,
    awOKBt :: Button,
    awCancelBt :: Button,
    awEntry :: Entry}
```

Our new GUI type stores all the widgets we will care about in the entire program. Large programs may not wish to have a monolithic type like this. For this small example, it makes sense because it can be easily passed around to different functions, and we'll know that we always have the information we need available.

Within this record, we have fields for a `Window` (a top-level window), `Dialog` (dialog window), `Button` (clickable button), `Label` (piece of text), and `Entry` (place for the user to enter text). Let's now look at our `main` function:

```
-- file: ch23/PodMainGUI.hs
main :: FilePath -> IO ()
main gladepath = withSocketsDo $ handleSqlError $
    do initGUI                     -- Initialize GTK+ engine

       -- Every so often, we try to run other threads.
       timeoutAddFull (yield >> return True)
                 priorityDefaultIdle 100
```

```
-- Load the GUI from the Glade file
gui <- loadGlade gladepath

-- Connect to the database
dbh <- connect "pod.db"

-- Set up our events
connectGui gui dbh

-- Run the GTK+ main loop; exits after GUI is done
mainGUI

-- Disconnect from the database at the end
disconnect dbh
```

Remember that the type of this `main` function is a little different than usual because it is being called by `main` in *PodLocalMain.hs*. We start by calling `initGUI`, which initializes the GTK+ system. Next, we have a call to `timeoutAddFull`. This call is only needed for multithreaded GTK+ programs. It tells the GTK+ main loop to pause to give other threads a chance to run every so often.

After that, we call our `loadGlade` function (see the following code) to load the widgets from our Glade XML file. Next, we connect to our database and call our `connectGui` function to set up our callback functions. Then, we fire up the GTK+ main loop. We expect it could be minutes, hours, or even days before `mainGUI` returns. When it does, it means the user has closed the main window or clicked the Exit button. After that, we disconnect from the database and close the program. Now, let's look at our `loadGlade` function:

```
-- file: ch23/PodMainGUI.hs
loadGlade gladepath =
    do -- Load XML from glade path.
       -- Note: crashes with a runtime error on console if fails!
       Just xml <- xmlNew gladepath

       -- Load main window
       mw <- xmlGetWidget xml castToWindow "mainWindow"

       -- Load all buttons

       [mwAdd, mwUpdate, mwDownload, mwFetch, mwExit, swOK, swCancel,
        auOK, auCancel] <-
           mapM (xmlGetWidget xml castToButton)
           ["addButton", "updateButton", "downloadButton",
            "fetchButton", "exitButton", "okButton", "cancelButton",
            "auOK", "auCancel"]

       sw <- xmlGetWidget xml castToDialog "statusDialog"
       swl <- xmlGetWidget xml castToLabel "statusLabel"

       au <- xmlGetWidget xml castToDialog "addDialog"
       aue <- xmlGetWidget xml castToEntry "auEntry"
```

```
          return $ GUI mw mwAdd mwUpdate mwDownload mwFetch mwExit
              sw swOK swCancel swl au auOK auCancel aue
```

This function starts by calling `xmlNew`, which loads the Glade XML file. It returns `Nothing` on error. Here we are using pattern matching to extract the result value on success. If it fails, there will be a console (not graphical) exception displayed; one of the exercises at the end of this chapter addresses this.

Now that we have Glade's XML file loaded, you will see a bunch of calls to `xmlGetWidget`. This Glade function is used to load the XML definition of a widget and return a GTK+ widget type for that widget. We have to pass along to that function a value indicating what GTK+ type we expect—we'll get a runtime error if these don't match.

We start by creating a widget for the main window. It is loaded from the XML widget defined with name `"mainWindow"` and stored in the `mw` variable. We then use pattern matching and `mapM` to load up all the buttons. Then, we have two dialogs, a label, and an entry to load. Finally, we use all of these to build up the GUI type and return it. Next, we need to set up our callback functions as event handlers:

```
-- file: ch23/PodMainGUI.hs
connectGui gui dbh =
    do -- When the close button is clicked, terminate the GUI loop
       -- by calling GTK mainQuit function
       onDestroy (mainWin gui) mainQuit

       -- Main window buttons
       onClicked (mwAddBt gui) (guiAdd gui dbh)
       onClicked (mwUpdateBt gui) (guiUpdate gui dbh)
       onClicked (mwDownloadBt gui) (guiDownload gui dbh)
       onClicked (mwFetchBt gui) (guiFetch gui dbh)
       onClicked (mwExitBt gui) mainQuit

       -- We leave the status window buttons for later
```

We start out the `connectGui` function by calling `onDestroy`. This means that when somebody clicks on the operating system's close button (typically an X in the titlebar on Windows or Linux, or a red circle on Mac OS X), we call the `mainQuit` function on the main window. `mainQuit` closes all GUI windows and terminates the GTK+ main loop.

Next, we call `onClicked` to register event handlers for clicking on our five different buttons. For buttons, these handlers are also called if the user selects the button via the keyboard. Clicking on these buttons will call our functions such as `guiAdd`, passing along the GUI record as well as a database handle.

At this point, we have completely defined the main window for the GUI podcatcher. It looks like the screenshot in Figure 23-2.

Figure 23-2. Screenshot of the main window of the podcatcher application

The Add Podcast Window

Now that we've covered the main window, let's talk about the other windows that our application presents, starting with the Add Podcast window. When the user clicks the button to add a new podcast, we need to pop up a dialog box to prompt for the URL of the podcast. We have defined this dialog box in Glade, so all we need to do is set it up:

```
-- file: ch23/PodMainGUI.hs
guiAdd gui dbh =
    do -- Initialize the add URL window
       entrySetText (awEntry gui) ""
       onClicked (awCancelBt gui) (widgetHide (addWin gui))
       onClicked (awOKBt gui) procOK

       -- Show the add URL window
       windowPresent (addWin gui)
    where procOK =
              do url <- entryGetText (awEntry gui)
                 widgetHide (addWin gui) -- Remove the dialog
                 add dbh url             -- Add to the DB
```

We start by calling `entrySetText` to set the contents of the entry box (the place where the user types in the URL) to the empty string. That's because the same widget gets reused over the lifetime of the program, and we don't want the last URL the user entered to remain there. Next, we set up actions for the two buttons in the dialog. If the user clicks on the cancel button, we simply remove the dialog box from the screen by calling `widgetHide` on it. If the user clicks the OK button, we call `procOK`.

`procOK` starts by retrieving the supplied URL from the entry widget. Next, it uses `widgetHide` to get rid of the dialog box. Finally, it calls `add` to add the URL to the database. This `add` is exactly the same function as we had in the non-GUI version of the program.

The last thing we do in `guiAdd` is actually display the pop-up window. That's done by calling `windowPresent`, which is the opposite of `widgetHide`.

Figure 23-3. Screenshot of the add-a-podcast window

Note that the guiAdd function returns almost immediately. It just sets up the widgets and causes the box to be displayed; at no point does it block waiting for input. Figure 23-3 shows what the dialog box looks like.

Long-Running Tasks

As we think about the buttons available in the main window, three of them correspond to tasks that could take a while to complete: update, download, and fetch. While these operations take place, we'd like to do two things with our GUI: provide the user with the status of the operation and the ability to cancel the operation as it is in progress.

Since all three of these things are very similar operations, it makes sense to provide a generic way to handle this interaction. We have defined a single status window widget in the Glade file that will be used by all three of these. In our Haskell source code, we'll define a generic statusWindow function that will be used by all three of these operations as well.

statusWindow takes four parameters: the GUI information, the database information, a String giving the title of the window, and a function that will perform the operation. This function will itself be passed a function that it can call to report its progress. Here's the code:

```
-- file: ch23/PodMainGUI.hs
statusWindow :: IConnection conn =>
                GUI
             -> conn
             -> String
             -> ((String -> IO ()) -> IO ())
             -> IO ()
statusWindow gui dbh title func =
    do -- Clear the status text
       labelSetText (swLabel gui) ""

       -- Disable the OK button, enable Cancel button
       widgetSetSensitivity (swOKBt gui) False
       widgetSetSensitivity (swCancelBt gui) True

       -- Set the title
       windowSetTitle (statusWin gui) title
```

```
        -- Start the operation
        childThread <- forkIO childTasks

        -- Define what happens when clicking on Cancel
        onClicked (swCancelBt gui) (cancelChild childThread)

        -- Show the window
        windowPresent (statusWin gui)
    where childTasks =
              do updateLabel "Starting thread..."
                 func updateLabel
                 -- After the child task finishes, enable OK
                 -- and disable Cancel
                 enableOK

          enableOK =
              do widgetSetSensitivity (swCancelBt gui) False
                 widgetSetSensitivity (swOKBt gui) True
                 onClicked (swOKBt gui) (widgetHide (statusWin gui))
                 return ()

          updateLabel text =
              labelSetText (swLabel gui) text
          cancelChild childThread =
              do killThread childThread
                 yield
                 updateLabel "Action has been cancelled."
                 enableOK
```

This function starts by clearing the label text from the last run. Next, we disable (gray out) the OK button and enable the Cancel button. While the operation is in progress, clicking OK doesn't make much sense. And when it's done, clicking Cancel also doesn't make much sense.

Next, we set the title of the window. The title is the part that is displayed by the system in the title bar of the window. Finally, we start off the new thread (represented by childTasks) and save off its thread ID. Then, we define what to do if the user clicks Cancel—we call cancelChild, passing along the thread ID. Finally, we call windowPresent to show the status window.

In childTasks, we display a message saying that we're starting the thread. Then we call the actual worker function, passing updateLabel as the function to use for displaying status messages. Note that a command-line version of the program could pass putStrLn here.

Finally, after the worker function exits, we call enableOK. This function disables the Cancel button, enables the OK button, and defines that a click on the OK button causes the status window to go away.

updateLabel simply calls labelSetText on the label widget to update it with the displayed text. Finally, cancelChild kills the thread that is processing the task, updates the label, and enables the OK button.

We now have the infrastructure in place to define our three GUI functions. They look like this:

```
-- file: ch23/PodMainGUI.hs
guiUpdate :: IConnection conn => GUI -> conn -> IO ()
guiUpdate gui dbh =
    statusWindow gui dbh "Pod: Update" (update dbh)

guiDownload gui dbh =
    statusWindow gui dbh "Pod: Download" (download dbh)

guiFetch gui dbh =
    statusWindow gui dbh "Pod: Fetch"
                 (\logf -> update dbh logf >> download dbh logf)
```

For brevity, we have given the type for only the first one, but all three have the same type, and Haskell can work them out via type inference. Notice our implementation of guiFetch. We don't call statusWindow twice, but rather combine functions in its action.

The final piece of the puzzle consists of the three functions that do our work. add is unmodified from the command-line chapter. update and download are modified only to take a logging function instead of calling putStrLn for status updates.

```
-- file: ch23/PodMainGUI.hs
add dbh url =
    do addPodcast dbh pc
       commit dbh
    where pc = Podcast {castId = 0, castURL = url}

update :: IConnection conn => conn -> (String -> IO ()) -> IO ()
update dbh logf =
    do pclist <- getPodcasts dbh
       mapM_ procPodcast pclist
       logf "Update complete."
    where procPodcast pc =
              do logf $ "Updating from " ++ (castURL pc)
                 updatePodcastFromFeed dbh pc

download dbh logf =
    do pclist <- getPodcasts dbh
       mapM_ procPodcast pclist
       logf "Download complete."
    where procPodcast pc =
              do logf $ "Considering " ++ (castURL pc)
                 episodelist <- getPodcastEpisodes dbh pc
                 let dleps = filter (\ep -> epDone ep == False)
                                 episodelist
                 mapM_ procEpisode dleps
          procEpisode ep =
              do logf $ "Downloading " ++ (epURL ep)
                 getEpisode dbh ep
```

Figure 23-4 shows what the final result looks like after running an update.

Figure 23-4. Screenshot of a dialog box displaying the words "Update complete"

Using Cabal

We presented a Cabal file to build this project for the command-line version in "Main Program" on page 515. We need to make a few tweaks for it to work with our GUI version. First, there's the obvious need to add the gtk2hs packages to the list of build dependencies. There is also the matter of the Glade XML file.

Earlier, we wrote a *PodLocalMain.hs* file that simply assumed this file is named *podresources.glade* and stored in the current working directory. For a real, system-wide installation, we can't make that assumption. Moreover, different systems may place the file in different locations.

Cabal provides a way around this problem. It automatically generates a module that exports functions that can interrogate the environment. We must add a `Data-files` line to our Cabal description file. This file names all data files that will be part of a system-wide installation. Then, Cabal will export a `Paths_pod` module (the "pod" part comes from the `Name` line in the Cabal file) that we can interrogate for the location at runtime. Here's our new Cabal description file:

```
-- ch24/pod.cabal
Name: pod
Version: 1.0.0
Build-type: Simple
Build-Depends: HTTP, HaXml, network, HDBC, HDBC-sqlite3, base,
               gtk, glade
Data-files: podresources.glade

Executable: pod
Main-Is: PodCabalMain.hs
GHC-Options: -O2
```

And, to go with it, here's *PodCabalMain.hs*:

```
-- file: ch23/PodCabalMain.hs
module Main where

import qualified PodMainGUI
import Paths_pod(getDataFileName)

main =
    do gladefn <- getDataFileName "podresources.glade"
       PodMainGUI.main gladefn
```

EXERCISES

1. Present a helpful GUI error message if the call to `xmlNew` returns `Nothing`.

2. Modify the podcatcher to be able to run with either the GUI or the command-line interface from a single code base. Hint: move common code out of *PodMain GUI.hs*, then have two different `Main` modules—one for the GUI, and one for the command line.

3. Why does `guiFetch` combine worker functions instead of calling `statusWindow` twice?

CHAPTER 24

Concurrent and Multicore Programming

As we write this book, the landscape of CPU architecture is changing more rapidly than it has in decades.

Defining Concurrency and Parallelism

A *concurrent* program needs to perform several possibly unrelated tasks at the same time. Consider the example of a game server: it is typically composed of dozens of components, each of which has complicated interactions with the outside world. One component might handle multiuser chat; several more will process players' inputs and also feed state updates back to them; while yet another performs physics calculations.

The correct operation of a concurrent program does not require multiple cores, though they may improve performance and responsiveness.

In contrast, a *parallel* program solves a single problem. Consider a financial model that attempts to predict the next minute of fluctuations in the price of a single stock. If we want to apply this model to every stock listed on an exchange—for example, to estimate which ones we should buy and sell—we hope to get an answer more quickly if we run the model on 500 cores than if we use just 1. As this suggests, a parallel program does not usually depend on the presence of multiple cores to work correctly.

Another useful distinction between concurrent and parallel programs lies in their interaction with the outside world. By definition, a concurrent program deals continuously with networking protocols, databases, and the like. A typical parallel program is likely to be more focused: it streams in data, crunches it for a while (with little further I/O), and then streams data back out.

Many traditional languages further blur the already indistinct boundary between concurrent and parallel programming, because they force programmers to use the same primitives to construct both kinds of programs.

In this chapter, we will concern ourselves with concurrent and parallel programs that operate within the boundaries of a single operating system process.

Concurrent Programming with Threads

As a building block for concurrent programs, most programming languages provide a way of creating multiple independent *threads of control*. Haskell is no exception, though programming with threads in Haskell looks somewhat different than in other languages.

In Haskell, a thread is an IO action that executes independently from other threads. To create a thread, we import the `Control.Concurrent` module and use the `forkIO` function:

```
ghci> :m +Control.Concurrent
ghci> :t forkIO
forkIO :: IO () -> IO ThreadId
ghci> :m +System.Directory
ghci> forkIO (writeFile "xyzzy" "seo craic nua!") >> doesFileExist "xyzzy"
False
```

The new thread starts to execute almost immediately, and the thread that created it continues to execute concurrently. The thread will stop executing when it reaches the end of its IO action.

Threads Are Nondeterministic

The runtime component of GHC does not specify an order in which it executes threads. As a result, in the preceding example, the file *xyzzy* created by the new thread *may or may not* have been created by the time the original thread checks for its existence. If we try this example once, and then remove *xyzzy* and try again, we may get a different result the second time.

Hiding Latency

Suppose we have a large file to compress and write to disk, but we want to handle a user's input quickly enough that she will perceive our program as responding immediately. If we use `forkIO` to write the file out in a separate thread, we can do both simultaneously:

```
-- file: ch24/Compressor.hs
import Control.Concurrent (forkIO)
import Control.Exception (handle)
import Control.Monad (forever)
```

```
import qualified Data.ByteString.Lazy as L
import System.Console.Readline (readline)

-- Provided by the 'zlib' package on http://hackage.haskell.org/
import Codec.Compression.GZip (compress)

main = do
    maybeLine <- readline "Enter a file to compress> "
    case maybeLine of
      Nothing -> return ()      -- user entered EOF
      Just "" -> return ()      -- treat no name as "want to quit"
      Just name -> do
            handle print $ do
              content <- L.readFile name
              forkIO (compressFile name content)
              return ()
            main
  where compressFile path = L.writeFile (path ++ ".gz") . compress
```

Because we're using lazy `ByteString` I/O here, all we really do in the main thread is open the file. The actual reading occurs on demand in the other thread.

The use of `handle print` gives us a cheap way to print an error message if the user enters the name of a file that does not exist.

Simple Communication Between Threads

The simplest way to share information between two threads is to let them both use a variable. In our file compression example, the `main` thread shares both the name of a file and its contents with the other thread. Because Haskell data is immutable by default, this poses no risks: neither thread can modify the other's view of the file's name or contents.

We often need to have threads actively communicate with each other. For example, GHC does not provide a way for one thread to find out whether another is still executing, has completed, or has crashed.[*] However, it provides a *synchronizing variable* type, the `MVar`, which we can use to create this capability for ourselves.

An `MVar` acts like a single-element box: it can be either full or empty. We can put something into the box, making it full, or take something out, making it empty:

```
ghci> :t putMVar
putMVar :: MVar a -> a -> IO ()
ghci> :t takeMVar
takeMVar :: MVar a -> IO a
```

---

[*] As we will show later, GHC threads are extraordinarily lightweight. If the runtime were to provide a way to check the status of every thread, the overhead of every thread would increase, even if this information were never used.

If we try to put a value into an MVar that is already full, our thread is put to sleep until another thread takes the value out. Similarly, if we try to take a value from an empty MVar, our thread is put to sleep until some other thread puts a value in:

```
-- file: ch24/MVarExample.hs
import Control.Concurrent

communicate = do
  m <- newEmptyMVar
  forkIO $ do
    v <- takeMVar m
    putStrLn ("received " ++ show v)
  putStrLn "sending"
  putMVar m "wake up!"
```

The newEmptyMVar function has a descriptive name. To create an MVar that starts out nonempty, we'd use newMVar:

```
ghci> :t newEmptyMVar
newEmptyMVar :: IO (MVar a)
ghci> :t newMVar
newMVar :: a -> IO (MVar a)
```

Let's run our example in ghci:

```
ghci> :load MVarExample
[1 of 1] Compiling Main             ( MVarExample.hs, interpreted )
Ok, modules loaded: Main.
ghci> communicate
sending
received "wake up!"
```

If you're coming from a background of concurrent programming in a traditional language, you can think of an MVar as being useful for two familiar purposes:

• Sending a message from one thread to another, for example, a notification.

• Providing *mutual exclusion* for a piece of mutable data that is shared among threads. We put the data into the MVar when it is not being used by any thread. One thread then takes it out temporarily to read or modify it.

The Main Thread and Waiting for Other Threads

GHC's runtime system treats the program's original thread of control differently from other threads. When this thread finishes executing, the runtime system considers the program as a whole to have completed. If any other threads are executing at the time, they are terminated.

As a result, when we have long-running threads that must not be killed, we need to make special arrangements to ensure that the main thread doesn't complete until the others do. Let's develop a small library that makes this easy to do:

```
-- file: ch24/NiceFork.hs
import Control.Concurrent
import Control.Exception (Exception, try)
import qualified Data.Map as M

data ThreadStatus = Running
                  | Finished        -- terminated normally
                  | Threw Exception  -- killed by uncaught exception
                    deriving (Eq, Show)

-- | Create a new thread manager.
newManager :: IO ThreadManager

-- | Create a new managed thread.
forkManaged :: ThreadManager -> IO () -> IO ThreadId

-- | Immediately return the status of a managed thread.
getStatus :: ThreadManager -> ThreadId -> IO (Maybe ThreadStatus)

-- | Block until a specific managed thread terminates.
waitFor :: ThreadManager -> ThreadId -> IO (Maybe ThreadStatus)

-- | Block until all managed threads terminate.
waitAll :: ThreadManager -> IO ()
```

We keep our ThreadManager type abstract using the usual recipe: we wrap it in a newtype and prevent clients from creating values of this type. Among our module's exports, we list the type constructor and the IO action that constructs a manager, but we do not export the data constructor:

```
-- file: ch24/NiceFork.hs
module NiceFork
    (
      ThreadManager
    , newManager
    , forkManaged
    , getStatus
    , waitFor
    , waitAll
    ) where
```

For the implementation of ThreadManager, we maintain a map from thread ID to thread state. We'll refer to this as the *thread map*:

```
-- file: ch24/NiceFork.hs
newtype ThreadManager =
    Mgr (MVar (M.Map ThreadId (MVar ThreadStatus)))
    deriving (Eq)

newManager = Mgr `fmap` newMVar M.empty
```

We have two levels of MVar at use here. We keep the Map in an MVar. This lets us "modify" the Map by replacing it with a new version. We also ensure that any thread that uses the Map will see a consistent view of it.

For each thread that we manage, we maintain an MVar. A per-thread MVar starts off empty, which indicates that the thread is executing. When the thread finishes or is killed by an uncaught exception, we put this information into the MVar.

To create a thread and watch its status, we must perform a little bit of bookkeeping:

```
-- file: ch24/NiceFork.hs
forkManaged (Mgr mgr) body =
    modifyMVar mgr $ \m -> do
      state <- newEmptyMVar
      tid <- forkIO $ do
        result <- try body
        putMVar state (either Threw (const Finished) result)
      return (M.insert tid state m, tid)
```

Safely Modifying an MVar

The modifyMVar function that we used in forkManaged in the preceding code is very useful. It's a safe combination of takeMVar and putMVar:

```
ghci> :t modifyMVar
modifyMVar :: MVar a -> (a -> IO (a, b)) -> IO b
```

It takes the value from an MVar and passes it to a function. This function can both generate a new value and return a result. If the function throws an exception, modifyMVar puts the original value back into the MVar; otherwise, it puts in the new value. It returns the other element of the function as its own result.

When we use modifyMVar instead of manually managing an MVar with takeMVar and putMVar, we avoid two common kinds of concurrency bugs:

- Forgetting to put a value back into an MVar. This can result in *deadlock*, in which some thread waits forever on an MVar that will never have a value put into it.

- Failure to account for the possibility that an exception might be thrown, disrupting the flow of a piece of code. This can result in a call to putMVar that *should* occur, but doesn't actually happen, again leading to deadlock.

Because of these nice safety properties, it's wise to use modifyMVar whenever possible.

Safe Resource Management: A Good Idea, and Easy Besides

We can the take the pattern that modifyMVar follows and apply it to many other resource management situations. Here are the steps of the pattern:

1. Acquire a resource.
2. Pass the resource to a function that will do something with it.
3. Always release the resource, even if the function throws an exception. If that occurs, rethrow the exception so application code can catch it.

Safety aside, this approach has another benefit: it can make our code shorter and easier to follow. As we can see from looking at forkManaged in the previous code listing, Haskell's lightweight syntax for anonymous functions makes this style of coding visually unobtrusive.

Here's the definition of modifyMVar so that you can see a specific form of this pattern:

```
-- file: ch24/ModifyMVar.hs
import Control.Concurrent (MVar, putMVar, takeMVar)
import Control.Exception (block, catch, throw, unblock)
import Prelude hiding (catch) -- use Control.Exception's version

modifyMVar :: MVar a -> (a -> IO (a,b)) -> IO b
modifyMVar m io =
  block $ do
    a <- takeMVar m
    (b,r) <- unblock (io a) `catch` \e ->
               putMVar m a >> throw e
    putMVar m b
    return r
```

You should easily be able to adapt this to your particular needs, whether you're working with network connections, database handles, or data managed by a C library.

Finding the Status of a Thread

Our getStatus function tells us the current state of a thread. If the thread is no longer managed (or was never managed in the first place), it returns Nothing:

```
-- file: ch24/NiceFork.hs
getStatus (Mgr mgr) tid =
  modifyMVar mgr $ \m ->
    case M.lookup tid m of
      Nothing -> return (m, Nothing)
      Just st -> tryTakeMVar st >>= \mst -> case mst of
                   Nothing -> return (m, Just Running)
                   Just sth -> return (M.delete tid m, Just sth)
```

If the thread is still running, it returns Just Running. Otherwise, it indicates why the thread terminated *and* stops managing the thread.

If the tryTakeMVar function finds that the MVar is empty, it returns Nothing immediately instead of blocking:

```
ghci> :t tryTakeMVar
tryTakeMVar :: MVar a -> IO (Maybe a)
```

Otherwise, it extracts the value from the MVar as usual.

The waitFor function behaves similarly, but instead of returning immediately, it blocks until the given thread terminates before returning:

```
-- file: ch24/NiceFork.hs
waitFor (Mgr mgr) tid = do
  maybeDone <- modifyMVar mgr $ \m ->
```

```
        return $ case M.updateLookupWithKey (\_ _ -> Nothing) tid m of
          (Nothing, _) -> (m, Nothing)
          (done, m') -> (m', done)
      case maybeDone of
        Nothing -> return Nothing
        Just st -> Just `fmap` takeMVar st
```

It first extracts the MVar that holds the thread's state, if it exists. The Map type's updateLookupWithKey function is useful—it combines looking up a key with modifying or removing the value:

```
ghci> :m +Data.Map
ghci> :t updateLookupWithKey
updateLookupWithKey :: (Ord k) =>
                       (k -> a -> Maybe a) -> k -> Map k a -> (Maybe a, Map k a)
```

In this case, we want to always remove the MVar holding the thread's state if it is present so that our thread manager will no longer be managing the thread. If there is a value to extract, we take the thread's exit status from the MVar and return it.

Our final useful function simply waits for all currently managed threads to complete and ignores their exit statuses:

```
-- file: ch24/NiceFork.hs
waitAll (Mgr mgr) = modifyMVar mgr elems >>= mapM_ takeMVar
    where elems m = return (M.empty, M.elems m)
```

Writing Tighter Code

Our definition of waitFor is a little unsatisfactory, because we're performing more or less the same case analysis in two places: inside the function called by modifyMVar, and again on its return value.

Sure enough, we can apply a function that we came across earlier to eliminate this duplication. The function in question is join, from the Control.Monad module:

```
ghci> :m +Control.Monad
ghci> :t join
join :: (Monad m) => m (m a) -> m a
```

The trick here is to see that we can get rid of the second case expression by having the first one return the IO action that we should perform once we return from modifyMVar. We'll use join to execute the action:

```
-- file: ch24/NiceFork.hs
waitFor2 (Mgr mgr) tid =
  join . modifyMVar mgr $ \m ->
    return $ case M.updateLookupWithKey (\_ _ -> Nothing) tid m of
      (Nothing, _) -> (m, return Nothing)
      (Just st, m') -> (m', Just `fmap` takeMVar st)
```

This is an interesting idea: we can create a monadic function or action in pure code, and then pass it around until we end up in a monad where we can use it. This can be a nimble way to write code, once you develop an eye for when it makes sense.

Communicating over Channels

For one-shot communications between threads, an MVar is perfectly good. Another type, Chan, provides a one-way communication channel. Here is a simple example of its use:

```
-- file: ch24/Chan.hs
import Control.Concurrent
import Control.Concurrent.Chan

chanExample = do
  ch <- newChan
  forkIO $ do
    writeChan ch "hello world"
    writeChan ch "now i quit"
  readChan ch >>= print
  readChan ch >>= print
```

If a Chan is empty, readChan blocks until there is a value to read. The writeChan function never blocks; it writes a new value into a Chan immediately.

Useful Things to Know About

MVar and Chan Are Nonstrict

Like most Haskell container types, both MVar and Chan are nonstrict: neither evaluates its contents. We mention this not because it's a problem but because it's a common blind spot. People tend to assume that these types are strict, perhaps because they're used in the IO monad.

As for other container types, the upshot of a mistaken guess about the strictness of an MVar or Chan type is often a space or performance leak. Here's a plausible scenario to consider.

We fork off a thread to perform some expensive computation on another core:

```
-- file: ch24/Expensive.hs
import Control.Concurrent

notQuiteRight = do
  mv <- newEmptyMVar
  forkIO $ expensiveComputation_stricter mv
  someOtherActivity
  result <- takeMVar mv
  print result
```

It *seems* to do something and puts its result back into the MVar:

```
-- file: ch24/Expensive.hs
expensiveComputation mv = do
  let a = "this is "
      b = "not really "
```

```
        c = "all that expensive"
    putMVar mv (a ++ b ++ c)
```

When we take the result from the MVar in the parent thread and attempt to do something with it, our thread starts computing furiously, because we never forced the computation to actually occur in the other thread!

As usual, the solution is straightforward, once we know there's a potential for a problem: we add strictness to the forked thread, in order to ensure that the computation occurs there. This strictness is best added in one place, in order to avoid the possibility that we might forget to add it:

```
-- file: ch24/ModifyMVarStrict.hs
{-# LANGUAGE BangPatterns #-}

import Control.Concurrent (MVar, putMVar, takeMVar)
import Control.Exception (block, catch, throw, unblock)
import Prelude hiding (catch) -- use Control.Exception's version

modifyMVar_strict :: MVar a -> (a -> IO a) -> IO ()
modifyMVar_strict m io = block $ do
  a <- takeMVar m
  !b <- unblock (io a) `catch` \e ->
        putMVar m a >> throw e
  putMVar m b
```

It's always worth checking Hackage

In the Hackage package database, you will find a library, strict-concurrency, that provides strict versions of the MVar and Chan types.

The ! pattern in the preceding code is simple to use, but it is not always sufficient to ensure that our data is evaluated. For a more complete approach, see "Separating Algorithm from Evaluation" on page 552.

Chan Is Unbounded

Because writeChan always succeeds immediately, there is a potential risk to using a Chan. If one thread writes to a Chan more often than another thread reads from it, the Chan will grow in an unchecked manner: unread messages will pile up as the reader falls further and further behind.

Shared-State Concurrency Is Still Hard

Although Haskell has different primitives for sharing data between threads than other languages, it still suffers from the same fundamental problem: writing correct concurrent programs is fiendishly difficult. Indeed, several pitfalls of concurrent programming in other languages apply equally to Haskell. Two of the better-known problems are *deadlock* and *starvation*.

Deadlock

In a *deadlock* situation, two or more threads get stuck forever in a clash over access to shared resources. One classic way to make a multithreaded program deadlock is to forget the order in which we must acquire locks. This kind of bug is so common, it has a name: *lock order inversion*. While Haskell doesn't provide locks, the MVar type is prone to the order inversion problem. Here's a simple example:

```
-- file: ch24/LockHierarchy.hs
import Control.Concurrent

nestedModification outer inner = do
  modifyMVar_ outer $ \x -> do
    yield  -- force this thread to temporarily yield the CPU
    modifyMVar_ inner $ \y -> return (y + 1)
    return (x + 1)
  putStrLn "done"

main = do
  a <- newMVar 1
  b <- newMVar 2
  forkIO $ nestedModification a b
  forkIO $ nestedModification b a
```

If we run this in ghci, it will usually—but not always—print nothing, indicating that both threads have gotten stuck.

The problem with the nestedModification function is easy to spot. In the first thread, we take the MVar a, then b. In the second, we take b, then a. If the first thread succeeds in taking a and the second takes b, both threads will block; each tries to take an MVar that the other has already emptied, so neither can make progress.

Across languages, the usual way to solve an order inversion problem is to always follow a consistent order when acquiring resources. Since this approach requires manual adherence to a coding convention, it is easy to miss in practice.

To make matters more complicated, these kinds of inversion problems can be difficult to spot in real code. The taking of MVars is often spread across several functions in different files, making visual inspection more tricky. Worse, these problems are often *intermittent*, which makes them tough to even reproduce, never mind isolate and fix.

Starvation

Concurrent software is also prone to *starvation*, in which one thread "hogs" a shared resource, preventing another from using it. It's easy to imagine how this might occur: one thread calls modifyMVar with a body that executes for 100 milliseconds, while another calls modifyMVar on the same MVar with a body that executes for 1 millisecond.

The second thread cannot make progress until the first puts a value back into the MVar.

The nonstrict nature of the MVar type can either cause or exacerbate a starvation problem. If we put a thunk into an MVar that will be expensive to evaluate, and then take it out of the MVar in a thread that otherwise looks like it *ought* to be cheap, that thread could suddenly become computationally expensive if it has to evaluate the thunk. This makes the advice we gave in "MVar and Chan Are Nonstrict" on page 539 particularly relevant.

Is There Any Hope?

Fortunately, the APIs for concurrency that we have covered here are by no means the end of the story. A more recent addition to Haskell, software transactional memory (STM), is both easier and safer to work with. We will discuss it in Chapter 28.

EXERCISES

1. The Chan type is implemented using MVars. Use MVars to develop a BoundedChan library.

   Your newBoundedChan function should accept an Int parameter, limiting the number of unread items that can be present in a BoundedChan at once.

   If this limit is hit, a call to your writeBoundedChan function must block until a reader uses readBoundedChan to consume a value.

2. Although we've already mentioned the existence of the strict-concurrency package in the Hackage repository, try developing your own, as a wrapper around the built-in MVar type. Following classic Haskell practice, make your library type safe, so that users cannot accidentally mix uses of strict and nonstrict MVars.

Using Multiple Cores with GHC

By default, GHC generates programs that use just one core, even when we write explicitly concurrent code. To use multiple cores, we must explicitly choose to do so. We make this choice at *link time*, when we are generating an executable program:

- The *nonthreaded* runtime library runs all Haskell threads in a single operating system thread. This runtime is highly efficient for creating threads and passing data around in MVars.

- The *threaded* runtime library uses multiple operating system threads to run Haskell threads. It has somewhat more overhead for creating threads and using MVars.

If we pass the -threaded option to the compiler, it will link our program against the threaded runtime library. We do not need to use -threaded when we are compiling libraries or source files—only when we are finally generating an executable.

Even when we select the threaded runtime for our program, it will still default to using only one core when we run it. We must explicitly tell the runtime how many cores to use.

Runtime Options

We can pass options to GHC's runtime system on the command line of our program. Before handing control to our code, the runtime scans the program's arguments for the special command-line option +RTS. It interprets everything that follows (until the special option -RTS) as an option for the runtime system, not our program. It hides all of these options from our code. When we use the System.Environment module's getArgs function to obtain our command-line arguments, we will not find any runtime options in the list.

The threaded runtime accepts an option -N.[†] This takes one argument, which specifies the number of cores that GHC's runtime system should use. The option parser is picky: there cannot be any spaces between -N and the number that follows it. The option -N4 is acceptable, but -N 4 is not.

Finding the Number of Available Cores from Haskell

The module GHC.Conc exports a variable, numCapabilities, that tells us how many cores the runtime system has been given with the -N RTS option:

```
-- file: ch24/NumCapabilities.hs
import GHC.Conc (numCapabilities)
import System.Environment (getArgs)

main = do
  args <- getArgs
  putStrLn $ "command line arguments: " ++ show args
  putStrLn $ "number of cores: " ++ show numCapabilities
```

If we compile and run this program, we can see that the options to the runtime system are not visible to the program, but we can see how many cores it can run on:

```
$ ghc -c NumCapabilities.hs
$ ghc -threaded -o NumCapabilities NumCapabilities.o
$ ./NumCapabilities +RTS -N4 -RTS foo
command line arguments: ["foo"]
number of cores: 4
```

[†] The nonthreaded runtime does not understand this option and will reject it with an error message.

Choosing the Right Runtime

The decision of which runtime to use is not completely clear cut. While the threaded runtime can use multiple cores, it has a cost: threads and sharing data between them are more expensive than with the nonthreaded runtime.

Furthermore, the garbage collector used by GHC as of version 6.8.3 is single-threaded: it pauses all other threads while it runs and executes on one core. This limits the performance improvement we can hope to see from using multiple cores.[‡] In many real-world concurrent programs, an individual thread will spend most of its time waiting for a network request or response. In these cases, if a single Haskell program serves tens of thousands of concurrent clients, the lower overhead of the nonthreaded runtime may be helpful. For example, instead of having a single server program use the threaded runtime on four cores, we might see better performance if we design our server so that we can run four copies of it simultaneously and use the nonthreaded runtime.

Our purpose here is not to dissuade you from using the threaded runtime. It is not much more expensive than the nonthreaded runtime—threads remain amazingly cheap compared to the runtimes of most other programming languages. We merely want to make it clear that switching to the threaded runtime will not necessarily result in an automatic win.

Parallel Programming in Haskell

We will now switch our focus to parallel programming. For many computationally expensive problems, we could calculate a result more quickly if we could divide the solution and evaluate it on many cores at once. Computers with multiple cores are already ubiquitous, but few programs can take advantage of the computing power of even a modern laptop.

In large part, this is because parallel programming is traditionally seen as very difficult. In a typical programming language, we would use the same libraries and constructs that we apply to concurrent programs to develop a parallel program. This forces us to contend with the familiar problems of deadlocks, race conditions, starvation, and sheer complexity.

While we could certainly use Haskell's concurrency features to develop parallel code, there is a much simpler approach available to us. We can take a normal Haskell function, apply a few simple transformations to it, and have it evaluated in parallel.

[‡] As of this writing, the garbage collector is being retooled to use multiple cores, but we cannot yet predict its future effect.

Normal Form and Head Normal Form

The familiar seq function evaluates an expression to what we call *head normal form* (HNF). It stops once it reaches the outermost constructor (the *head*). This is distinct from *normal form* (NF), in which an expression is completely evaluated.

You will also hear Haskell programmers refer to *weak* head normal form (WHNF). For normal data, weak head normal form is the same as head normal form. The difference arises only for functions and is too abstruse to concern us here.

Sequential Sorting

Here is a normal Haskell function that sorts a list using a divide-and-conquer approach:

```
-- file: ch24/Sorting.hs
sort :: (Ord a) => [a] -> [a]
sort (x:xs) = lesser ++ x:greater
    where lesser  = sort [y | y <- xs, y < x]
          greater = sort [y | y <- xs, y >= x]
sort _ = []
```

This function is inspired by the well-known Quicksort algorithm, and it is a classic among Haskell programmers. It is often presented as a one-liner early in a Haskell tutorial to tease the reader with an example of Haskell's expressiveness. Here, we've split the code over a few lines, in order to make it easier to compare the serial and parallel versions.

Here is a very brief description of how sort operates:

1. It chooses an element from the list. This is called the *pivot*. Any element would do as the pivot; the first is merely the easiest to pattern match on.

2. It creates a sublist of all elements less than the pivot and recursively sorts them.

3. It creates a sublist of all elements greater than or equal to the pivot and recursively sorts them.

4. It appends the two sorted sublists.

Transforming Our Code into Parallel Code

The parallel version of the function is only a little more complicated than the initial version:

```
-- file: ch24/Sorting.hs
module Sorting where

import Control.Parallel (par, pseq)

parSort :: (Ord a) => [a] -> [a]
parSort (x:xs)    = force greater `par` (force lesser `pseq`
                                         (lesser ++ x:greater))
    where lesser  = parSort [y | y <- xs, y <  x]
```

```
            greater = parSort [y | y <- xs, y >= x]
    parSort _         = []
```

We have barely perturbed the code—all we have added are three functions: par, pseq, and force.

The par function is provided by the Control.Parallel module. It serves a similar purpose to seq. It evaluates its left argument to WHNF and returns its right. As its name suggests, par can evaluate its left argument in parallel with whatever other evaluations are occurring.

As for pseq, it is similar to seq: it evaluates the expression on the left to WHNF before returning the expression on the right. The difference between the two is subtle but important for parallel programs: the compiler does not *promise* to evaluate the left argument of seq if it can see that evaluating the right argument first would improve performance. This flexibility is fine for a program executing on one core, but it is not strong enough for code running on multiple cores. In contrast, the compiler *guarantees* that pseq will evaluate its left argument before its right.

These changes to our code are remarkable for all the things we have *not* needed to say:

- How many cores to use
- What threads do to communicate with each other
- How to divide up work among the available cores
- Which data are shared between threads, and which are private
- How to determine when all the participants are finished

Knowing What to Evaluate in Parallel

The key to getting decent performance out of parallel Haskell code is to find meaningful chunks of work to perform in parallel. Nonstrict evaluation can get in the way of this, which is why we use the force function in our parallel sort. To best explain what the force function is for, we will first look at a mistaken example:

```
-- file: ch24/Sorting.hs
sillySort (x:xs) = greater `par` (lesser `pseq`
                                    (lesser ++ x:greater))
    where lesser  = sillySort [y | y <- xs, y <  x]
          greater = sillySort [y | y <- xs, y >= x]
sillySort _       = []
```

Take a look at the small changes in each use of par. Instead of force lesser and force greater, here we evaluate lesser and greater.

Remember that evaluation to WHNF computes only enough of an expression to see its *outermost* constructor. In this mistaken example, we evaluate each sorted sublist to WHNF. Since the outermost constructor in each case is just a single list constructor, we are in fact forcing only the evaluation of the first element of each sorted sublist!

Every other element of each list remains unevaluated. In other words, we do almost no useful work in parallel: our sillySort is nearly completely sequential.

We avoid this with our force function by forcing the entire spine of a list to be evaluated before we give back a constructor:

```
-- file: ch24/Sorting.hs
force :: [a] -> ()
force xs = go xs `pseq` ()
    where go (_:xs) = go xs
          go [] = 1
```

Notice that we don't care what's in the list; we walk down its spine to the end, and then use pseq once. There is clearly no magic involved here—we are just using our usual understanding of Haskell's evaluation model. And because we will be using force on the lefthand side of par or pseq, we don't need to return a meaningful value.

Of course, in many cases, we will need to force the evaluation of individual elements of the list, too. Below, we will discuss a typeclass-based solution to this problem.

What Promises Does par Make?

The par function does not actually promise to evaluate an expression in parallel with another. Instead, it undertakes to do so if it "makes sense." This wishy-washy non-promise is actually more useful than a guarantee to always evaluate an expression in parallel. It gives the runtime system the freedom to act intelligently when it encounters par.

For instance, the runtime could decide that an expression is too cheap to be worth evaluating in parallel. Or it might notice that all cores are currently busy so that "sparking" a new parallel evaluation would lead to more runnable threads than there are cores available to execute them.

This lax specification in turn affects how we write parallel code. Since par may be somewhat intelligent at runtime, we can use it almost wherever we like, on the assumption that performance will not be bogged down by threads contending for busy cores.

Running Our Code and Measuring Performance

To try our code out, let's save sort, parSort, and parSort2 to a module named Sorting.hs. We create a small driver program that we can use to time the performance of one of those sorting functions:

```
-- file: ch24/SortMain.hs

module Main where

import Data.Time.Clock (diffUTCTime, getCurrentTime)
import System.Environment (getArgs)
```

```
import System.Random (StdGen, getStdGen, randoms)

import Sorting

-- testFunction = sort
-- testFunction = seqSort
testFunction = parSort
-- testFunction = parSort2 2

randomInts :: Int -> StdGen -> [Int]
randomInts k g = let result = take k (randoms g)
                 in force result `seq` result

main = do
  args <- getArgs
  let count | null args = 500000
            | otherwise = read (head args)
  input <- randomInts count `fmap` getStdGen
  putStrLn $ "We have " ++ show (length input) ++ " elements to sort."
  start <- getCurrentTime
  let sorted = testFunction input
  putStrLn $ "Sorted all " ++ show (length sorted) ++ " elements."
  end <- getCurrentTime
  putStrLn $ show (end `diffUTCTime` start) ++ " elapsed."
```

For simplicity, we choose the sorting function to benchmark at compilation time, via the testFunction variable.

Our program accepts a single, optional command-line argument, the length of the random list to generate.

Nonstrict evaluation can turn performance measurement and analysis into something of a minefield. Here are some potential problems that we specifically work to avoid in our driver program:

Measuring several things when we think we are looking at just one
> Haskell's default pseudorandom number generator (PRNG) is slow, and the randoms function generates random numbers on demand.

> Before we record our starting time, we force every element of the input list to be evaluated, and we print the length of the list. This ensures that we create all of the random numbers that we will need in advance.

> If we were to omit this step, we would interleave the generation of random numbers with attempts to work with them in parallel. We would thus be measuring both the cost of sorting the numbers and, less obviously, the cost of generating them.

Invisible data dependencies
> When we generate the list of random numbers, simply printing the length of the list would not perform enough evaluation. This would evaluate the *spine* of the list, but not its elements. The actual random numbers would not be evaluated until the sort compares them.

This can have serious consequences for performance. The value of a random number depends on the value of the preceding random number in the list, but we have scattered the list elements randomly among our processor cores. If we did not evaluate the list elements prior to sorting, we would suffer a terrible "ping pong" effect: not only would evaluation bounce from one core to another, performance would suffer.

Try snipping out the application of force from the body of main. You should find that the parallel code can easily end up three times *slower* than the nonparallel code.

Benchmarking a thunk when we believe that the code is performing meaningful work
To force the sort to take place, we print the length of the result list before we record the ending time. Without putStrLn demanding the length of the list in order to print it, the sort would not occur at all.

When we build the program, we enable optimization and ghc's threaded runtime:

```
$ ghc -threaded -O2 --make SortMain
[1 of 2] Compiling Sorting           ( Sorting.hs, Sorting.o )
[2 of 2] Compiling Main              ( SortMain.hs, SortMain.o )
Linking SortMain ...
```

When we run the program, we must tell ghc's runtime how many cores to use. Initially, we try the original sort, in order to establish a performance baseline:

```
$ ./Sorting +RTS -N1 -RTS 700000
We have 700000 elements to sort.
Sorted all 700000 elements.
3.178941s elapsed.
```

Enabling a second core ought to have no effect on performance:

```
$ ./Sorting +RTS -N2 -RTS 700000
We have 700000 elements to sort.
Sorted all 700000 elements.
3.259869s elapsed.
```

If we recompile and test the performance of parSort, the results are less than stellar:

```
$ ./Sorting +RTS -N1 -RTS 700000
We have 700000 elements to sort.
Sorted all 700000 elements.
3.915818s elapsed.
$ ./Sorting +RTS -N2 -RTS 700000
We have 700000 elements to sort.
Sorted all 700000 elements.
4.029781s elapsed.
```

We have gained nothing in performance. It seems that this could be due to one of two factors: either par is intrinsically expensive or we are using it too much. To help us to distinguish between the two possibilities, here is a sort that is identical to parSort, but it uses pseq instead of par:

```
-- file: ch24/Sorting.hs
seqSort :: (Ord a) => [a] -> [a]
seqSort (x:xs) = lesser `pseq` (greater `pseq`
                                 (lesser ++ x:greater))
    where lesser  = seqSort [y | y <- xs, y <  x]
          greater = seqSort [y | y <- xs, y >= x]
seqSort _ = []
```

We also drop the use of force, so compared to our original sort, we should only be measuring the cost of using pseq. What effect does pseq alone have on performance?

```
$ ./Sorting +RTS -N1 -RTS 700000
We have 700000 elements to sort.
Sorted all 700000 elements.
3.848295s elapsed.
```

This suggests that par and pseq have similar costs. What can we do to improve performance?

Tuning for Performance

In our parSort, we perform twice as many applications of par as there are elements to sort. While par is *cheap*, as we have seen, it is not *free*. When we recursively apply parSort, we eventually apply par to individual list elements. At this fine granularity, the cost of using par outweighs any possible usefulness. To reduce this effect, we switch to our nonparallel sort after passing some threshold:

```
-- file: ch24/Sorting.hs
parSort2 :: (Ord a) => Int -> [a] -> [a]
parSort2 d list@(x:xs)
  | d <= 0    = sort list
  | otherwise = force greater `par` (force lesser `pseq`
                                      (lesser ++ x:greater))
      where lesser      = parSort2 d' [y | y <- xs, y <  x]
            greater     = parSort2 d' [y | y <- xs, y >= x]
            d' = d - 1
parSort2 _ _              = []
```

Here, we stop recursing and sparking new parallel evaluations at a controllable depth. If we knew the size of the data we were dealing with, we could stop subdividing and switch to the nonparallel code once we reached a sufficiently small amount of remaining work:

```
$ ./Sorting +RTS -N2 -RTS 700000
We have 700000 elements to sort.
Sorted all 700000 elements.
2.947872s elapsed.
```

On a dual core system, this gives us roughly a 25% speedup. This is not a huge number, but consider that we had to change only a few annotations in return for this performance improvement.

This sorting function is particularly resistant to good parallel performance. The amount of memory allocation it performs forces the garbage collector to run frequently. We can see the effect by running our program with the `-sstderr` RTS option, which prints garbage collection statistics to the screen. This indicates that our program spends roughly 40% of its time collecting garbage. Since the garbage collector in GHC 6.8 stops all threads and runs on a single core, it acts as a bottleneck.

You can expect more impressive performance improvements from less allocation-heavy code when you use `par` annotations. We have seen some simple numerical benchmarks run 1.8 times faster on a dual core system than with a single core. As of this writing, a parallel garbage collector is under development for GHC, which should help considerably with the performance of allocation-heavy code on multicore systems.

Beware a GC bug in GHC 6.8.2

The garbage collector in release 6.8.2 of GHC has a bug that can cause programs using `par` to crash. If you want to use `par` and you are using 6.8.2, we suggest upgrading to at least 6.8.3.

EXERCISES

1. It can be difficult to determine when to switch from `parSort2` to `sort`. An alternative approach to the one we outline previously would be to decide based on the length of a sublist. Rewrite `parList2` so that it switches to `sort` if the list contains more than some number of elements.

2. Measure the performance of the length-based approach and compare it with the depth approach. Which gives better performance results?

Parallel Strategies and MapReduce

Within the programming community, one of the most famous software systems to credit functional programming for inspiration is Google's MapReduce infrastructure for parallel processing of bulk data.

We can easily construct a greatly simplified, but still useful, Haskell equivalent. To focus our attention, we will look at processing web server logfiles, which tend to be both huge and plentiful.[§] As an example, here is a log entry for a page visit recorded by the Apache Web Server. The entry originally filled one line—we split it across several lines to fit:

```
201.49.94.87 - - [08/Jun/2008:07:04:20 -0500] "GET / HTTP/1.1"
200 2097 "http://en.wikipedia.org/wiki/Mercurial_(software)"
"Mozilla/5.0 (Windows; U; Windows XP 5.1; en-GB; rv:1.8.1.12)
Gecko/20080201 Firefox/2.0.0.12" 0 hgbook.red-bean.com
```

[§] The genesis of this idea came from Tim Bray.

While we could create a straightforward implementation without much effort, we will resist the temptation to dive in. If we think about solving a *class* of problems instead of a single one, we may end up with more widely applicable code.

When we develop a parallel program, we always face a few "bad penny" problems, which turn up regardless of the underlying programming language. A few are described here:

- Our algorithm quickly becomes obscured by the details of partitioning and communication. This makes it difficult to understand code, which in turn makes modifying it risky.

- Choosing a *grain size*—the smallest unit of work parceled out to a core—can be difficult. If the grain size is too small, cores spend so much of their time on bookkeeping that a parallel program can easily become slower than a serial counterpart. If the grain size is too large, some cores may lie idle due to poor load balancing.

Separating Algorithm from Evaluation

In parallel Haskell code, the clutter that would arise from communication code in a traditional language is replaced with the clutter of `par` and `pseq` annotations. As an example, this function operates similarly to `map`, but evaluates each element to WHNF in parallel as it goes:

```
-- file: ch24/ParMap.hs
import Control.Parallel (par)

parallelMap :: (a -> b) -> [a] -> [b]
parallelMap f (x:xs) = let r = f x
                       in r `par` r : parallelMap f xs
parallelMap _ _      = []
```

The type b might be a list or some other type for which evaluation to WHNF doesn't do a useful amount of work. We'd prefer not to have to write a special `parallelMap` for lists and every other type that needs special handling.

To address this problem, we will begin by considering a simpler problem: how to force a value to be evaluated. Here is a function that forces every element of a list to be evaluated to WHNF:

```
-- file: ch24/ParMap.hs
forceList :: [a] -> ()
forceList (x:xs) = x `pseq` forceList xs
forceList _      = ()
```

Our function performs no computation on the list. (In fact, from examining its type signature, we can tell that it *cannot* perform any computation, since it knows nothing about the elements of the list.) Its only purpose is to ensure that the spine of the list is evaluated to head normal form. The only place that it makes any sense to apply this function is in the first argument of `seq` or `par`, as follows:

```
-- file: ch24/ParMap.hs
stricterMap :: (a -> b) -> [a] -> [b]
stricterMap f xs = forceList xs `seq` map f xs
```

This still leaves us with the elements of the list evaluated only to WHNF. We address
this by adding a function as parameter that can force an element to be evaluated more
deeply:

```
-- file: ch24/ParMap.hs
forceListAndElts :: (a -> ()) -> [a] -> ()
forceListAndElts forceElt (x:xs) =
    forceElt x `seq` forceListAndElts forceElt xs
forceListAndElts _         _       = ()
```

The `Control.Parallel.Strategies` module generalizes this idea into something we can
use as a library. It introduces the idea of an *evaluation strategy*:

```
-- file: ch24/Strat.hs
type Done = ()

type Strategy a = a -> Done
```

An evaluation strategy performs no computation; it simply ensures that a value is evaluated to some extent. The simplest strategy is named r0, and does nothing at all:

```
-- file: ch24/Strat.hs
r0 :: Strategy a
r0 _ = ()
```

Next is `rwhnf`, which evaluates a value to WHNF:

```
-- file: ch24/Strat.hs
rwhnf :: Strategy a
rwhnf x = x `seq` ()
```

To evaluate a value to normal form, the module provides a typeclass with a method
named `rnf`:

```
-- file: ch24/Strat.hs
class NFData a where
  rnf :: Strategy a
  rnf = rwhnf
```

Remembering those names

If the names of these functions and types are not sticking in your head,
look at them as acronyms. The name `rwhnf` expands to reduce to weak
head normal form; NFData becomes normal form data; and so on.

For the basic types, such as Int, weak head normal form and normal form are the same
thing, which is why the `NFData` typeclass uses `rwhnf` as the default implementation of
`rnf`. For many common types, the `Control.Parallel.Strategies` module provides instances of `NFData`:

```
-- file: ch24/Strat.hs
instance NFData Char
instance NFData Int

instance NFData a => NFData (Maybe a) where
    rnf Nothing  = ()
    rnf (Just x) = rnf x

{- ... and so on ... -}
```

From these examples, it should be clear how you might write an NFData instance for a type of your own. Your implementation of rnf must handle every constructor and apply rnf to every field of a constructor.

Separating Algorithm from Strategy

From these strategy building blocks, we can construct more elaborate strategies. Many are already provided by Control.Parallel.Strategies. For instance, parList applies an evaluation strategy in parallel to every element of a list:

```
-- file: ch24/Strat.hs
parList :: Strategy a -> Strategy [a]
parList strat []     = ()
parList strat (x:xs) = strat x `par` (parList strat xs)
```

The module uses this to define a parallel map function:

```
-- file: ch24/Strat.hs
parMap :: Strategy b -> (a -> b) -> [a] -> [b]
parMap strat f xs = map f xs `using` parList strat
```

This is where the code becomes interesting. On the left of using, we have a normal application of map. On the right, we have an evaluation strategy. The using combinator tells us how to apply a strategy to a value, allowing us to keep the code separate from how we plan to evaluate it:

```
-- file: ch24/Strat.hs
using :: a -> Strategy a -> a
using x s = s x `seq` x
```

The Control.Parallel.Strategies module provides many other functions that enable fine control over evaluation. For instance, parZipWith that applies zipWith in parallel, using an evaluation strategy:

```
-- file: ch24/Strat.hs
vectorSum' :: (NFData a, Num a) => [a] -> [a] -> [a]
vectorSum' = parZipWith rnf (+)
```

Writing a Simple MapReduce Definition

We can quickly suggest a type for a mapReduce function by considering what it must do. We need a *map* component, to which we will give the usual type a -> b. And we need a *reduce*; this term is a synonym for *fold*. Rather than commit ourselves to using a specific kind of fold, we'll use a more general type, [b] -> c. This type lets us use a left or right fold, so we can choose the one that suits our data and processing needs.

If we plug these types together, the complete type looks like this:

```
-- file: ch24/MapReduce.hs
simpleMapReduce
    :: (a -> b)        -- map function
    -> ([b] -> c)      -- reduce function
    -> [a]             -- list to map over
    -> c
```

The code that goes with the type is extremely simple:

```
-- file: ch24/MapReduce.hs
simpleMapReduce mapFunc reduceFunc = reduceFunc . map mapFunc
```

MapReduce and Strategies

Our definition of simpleMapReduce is too simple to really be interesting. To make it useful, we want to be able to specify that some of the work should occur in parallel. We'll achieve this using strategies, passing in a strategy for the map phase and one for the reduction phase:

```
-- file: ch24/MapReduce.hs
mapReduce
    :: Strategy b      -- evaluation strategy for mapping
    -> (a -> b)        -- map function
    -> Strategy c      -- evaluation strategy for reduction
    -> ([b] -> c)      -- reduce function
    -> [a]             -- list to map over
    -> c
```

Both the type and the body of the function must grow a little in size to accommodate the strategy parameters.

```
-- file: ch24/MapReduce.hs
mapReduce mapStrat mapFunc reduceStrat reduceFunc input =
    mapResult `pseq` reduceResult
  where mapResult    = parMap mapStrat mapFunc input
        reduceResult = reduceFunc mapResult `using` reduceStrat
```

Sizing Work Appropriately

To achieve decent performance, we must ensure that the work that we do per application of par substantially outweighs its bookkeeping costs. If we are processing a huge file, splitting it on line boundaries gives us far too little work compared to overhead.

We will develop a way to process a file in larger chunks in a later section. What should those chunks consist of? Because a web server logfile ought to contain only ASCII text, we will see excellent performance with a lazy ByteString. This type is highly efficient and consumes little memory when we stream it from a file:

```
-- file: ch24/LineChunks.hs
module LineChunks
    (
      chunkedReadWith
    ) where

import Control.Exception (bracket, finally)
import Control.Monad (forM, liftM)
import Control.Parallel.Strategies (NFData, rnf)
import Data.Int (Int64)
import qualified Data.ByteString.Lazy.Char8 as LB
import GHC.Conc (numCapabilities)
import System.IO

data ChunkSpec = CS {
      chunkOffset :: !Int64
    , chunkLength :: !Int64
    } deriving (Eq, Show)

withChunks :: (NFData a) =>
              (FilePath -> IO [ChunkSpec])
           -> ([LB.ByteString] -> a)
           -> FilePath
           -> IO a
withChunks chunkFunc process path = do
  (chunks, handles) <- chunkedRead chunkFunc path
  let r = process chunks
  (rnf r `seq` return r) `finally` mapM_ hClose handles

chunkedReadWith :: (NFData a) =>
                   ([LB.ByteString] -> a) -> FilePath -> IO a
chunkedReadWith func path =
    withChunks (lineChunks (numCapabilities * 4)) func path
```

We consume each chunk in parallel, taking careful advantage of lazy I/O to ensure that we can stream these chunks safely.

Mitigating the risks of lazy I/O

Lazy I/O poses a few well-known hazards that we would like to avoid:

- We may invisibly keep a file handle open for longer than necessary by not forcing the computation that pulls data from it to be evaluated. Since an operating system will typically place a small, fixed limit on the number of files we can have open at once, if we do not address this risk, we can accidentally starve some other part of our program of file handles.
- If we do not explicitly close a file handle, the garbage collector will automatically close it for us, but it may take a long time to notice that it should close the file handle. This poses the same starvation risk mentioned earlier.

- We can avoid starvation by explicitly closing a file handle. If we do so too early, though, we can cause a lazy computation to fail if it expects to be able to pull more data from a closed file handle.

On top of these well-known risks, we cannot use a single file handle to supply data to multiple threads. A file handle has a single *seek pointer* that tracks the position from which it should be reading, but when we want to read multiple chunks, each needs to consume data from a different position in the file.

With these ideas in mind, let's fill out the lazy I/O picture:

```
-- file: ch24/LineChunks.hs
chunkedRead :: (FilePath -> IO [ChunkSpec])
            -> FilePath
            -> IO ([LB.ByteString], [Handle])
chunkedRead chunkFunc path = do
  chunks <- chunkFunc path
  liftM unzip . forM chunks $ \spec -> do
    h <- openFile path ReadMode
    hSeek h AbsoluteSeek (fromIntegral (chunkOffset spec))
    chunk <- LB.take (chunkLength spec) `liftM` LB.hGetContents h
    return (chunk, h)
```

We avoid the starvation problem by explicitly closing file handles. We allow multiple threads to read different chunks at once by supplying each one with a distinct file handle, all reading the same file.

The final problem that we try to mitigate is that of a lazy computation having a file handle closed behind its back. We use `rnf` to force all of our processing to complete before we return from `withChunks`. We can then close our file handles explicitly, as they should no longer be read from. If you must use lazy I/O in a program, it is often best to "firewall" it like this so that it cannot cause problems in unexpected parts of your code.

Processing chunks via a fold

We can adapt the fold-with-early-termination technique from "Another Way of Looking at Traversal" on page 229 to stream-based file processing. While this requires more work than the lazy I/O approach, it nicely avoids the problems just discussed.

Efficiently Finding Line-Aligned Chunks

Since a server logfile is line-oriented, we need an efficient way to break a file into large chunks, while making sure that each chunk ends on a line boundary. Since a chunk might be tens of megabytes in size, we don't want to scan all of the data in a chunk to determine where its final boundary should be.

Our approach works whether we choose a fixed chunk size or a fixed number of chunks. Here, we opt for the latter. We begin by seeking to the approximate position of the end of a chunk, and then scan forwards until we reach a newline character. We next start the following chunk after the newline, and repeat the procedure:

```haskell
-- file: ch24/LineChunks.hs
lineChunks :: Int -> FilePath -> IO [ChunkSpec]
lineChunks numChunks path = do
  bracket (openFile path ReadMode) hClose $ \h -> do
    totalSize <- fromIntegral `liftM` hFileSize h
    let chunkSize = totalSize `div` fromIntegral numChunks
        findChunks offset = do
          let newOffset = offset + chunkSize
          hSeek h AbsoluteSeek (fromIntegral newOffset)
          let findNewline off = do
                eof <- hIsEOF h
                if eof
                  then return [CS offset (totalSize - offset)]
                  else do
                    bytes <- LB.hGet h 4096
                    case LB.elemIndex '\n' bytes of
                      Just n -> do
                        chunks@(c:_) <- findChunks (off + n + 1)
                        let coff = chunkOffset c
                        return (CS offset (coff - offset):chunks)
                      Nothing -> findNewline (off + LB.length bytes)
          findNewline newOffset
    findChunks 0
```

The last chunk will end up a little shorter than its predecessors, but this difference will be insignificant in practice.

Counting Lines

This simple example illustrates how to use the scaffolding we built:

```haskell
-- file: ch24/LineCount.hs
module Main where

import Control.Monad (forM_)
import Data.Int (Int64)
import qualified Data.ByteString.Lazy.Char8 as LB
import System.Environment (getArgs)

import LineChunks (chunkedReadWith)
import MapReduce (mapReduce, rnf)

lineCount :: [LB.ByteString] -> Int64
lineCount = mapReduce rnf (LB.count '\n')
                      rnf sum

main :: IO ()
main = do
  args <- getArgs
  forM_ args $ \path -> do
    numLines <- chunkedReadWith lineCount path
    putStrLn $ path ++ ": " ++ show numLines
```

If we compile this program with ghc -O2 --make -threaded, it should perform well after an initial run to "warm" the filesystem cache. On a dual-core laptop processing a logfile 248 megabytes (1.1 million lines) in size, this program runs in 0.576 seconds using a single core, and in 0.361 using two (using +RTS -N2).

Finding the Most Popular URLs

In this example, we count the number of times each URL is accessed. This example comes from "MapReduce: simplified data processing on large clusters" by Jeffrey Dean and Sanjay Ghemawat (*http://labs.google.com/papers/mapreduce.html*), Google's original paper discussing MapReduce. In the *map* phase, for each chunk, we create a Map from a URL using the number of times it was accessed. In the *reduce* phase, we union-merge these maps into one:

```
-- file: ch24/CommonURLs.hs
module Main where

import Control.Parallel.Strategies (NFData(..), rwhnf)
import Control.Monad (forM_)
import Data.List (foldl', sortBy)
import qualified Data.ByteString.Lazy.Char8 as L
import qualified Data.ByteString.Char8 as S
import qualified Data.Map as M
import Text.Regex.PCRE.Light (compile, match)

import System.Environment (getArgs)
import LineChunks (chunkedReadWith)
import MapReduce (mapReduce)

countURLs :: [L.ByteString] -> M.Map S.ByteString Int
countURLs = mapReduce rwhnf (foldl' augment M.empty . L.lines)
                      rwhnf (M.unionsWith (+))
  where augment map line =
            case match (compile pattern []) (strict line) [] of
              Just (_:url:_) -> M.insertWith' (+) url 1 map
              _ -> map
        strict = S.concat . L.toChunks
        pattern = S.pack "\"(?:GET|POST|HEAD) ([^ ]+) HTTP/"
```

To pick a URL out of a line of the logfile, we use the bindings to the PCRE regular expression library that we developed in Chapter 17.

Our driver function prints the 10 most popular URLs. As with the line-counting example, this program runs about 1.8 times faster with two cores than with one, taking 1.7 seconds to process the a logfile containing 1.1 million entries.

Conclusions

Given a problem that fits its model well, the MapReduce programming model lets us write "casual" parallel programs in Haskell with good performance and minimal additional effort. We can easily extend the idea to use other data sources, such as collections of files or data sourced over the network.

In many cases, the performance bottleneck will be streaming data at a rate high enough to keep up with a core's processing capacity. For instance, if we try to use either of the sample programs just shown on a file that is not cached in memory or streamed from a high-bandwidth storage array, we will spend most of our time waiting for disk I/O, gaining no benefit from multiple cores.

CHAPTER 25

Profiling and Optimization

Haskell is a high-level language. A really high-level language. We can spend our days programming entirely in abstractions, in monoids, functors, and hylomorphisms, far removed from any specific hardware model of computation. The language specification goes to great lengths to avoid prescribing any particular evaluation model. These layers of abstraction let us treat Haskell as a notation for computation itself, letting us concentrate on the essence of the problem without getting bogged down in low-level implementation decisions. We get to program in pure thought.

However, this is a book about real-world programming, and in the real world, code runs on stock hardware with limited resources. Our programs will have time and space requirements that we may need to enforce. As such, we need a good knowledge of how our program data is represented, the precise consequences of using lazy or strict evaluation strategies, and techniques for analyzing and controlling space and time behavior.

In this chapter, we'll look at typical space and time problems a Haskell programmer might encounter and how to methodically analyze, understand, and address them. To do this, we'll use a range of techniques: time and space profiling, runtime statistics, and reasoning about strict and lazy evaluation. We'll also look at the impact of compiler optimizations on performance and the use of advanced optimization techniques that become feasible in a purely functional language. So let's begin with a challenge: squashing unexpected memory usage in some inocuous-looking code.

Profiling Haskell Programs

Let's consider the following list manipulating program, which naively computes the mean of some large list of values. While only a program fragment (and we'll stress that the particular algorithm we're implementing is irrelevant here), it is representative of real code that we might find in any Haskell program: typically concise list manipulation code and heavy use of standard library functions. It also illustrates several common performance trouble spots that can catch the unwary:

```
-- file: ch25/A.hs
import System.Environment
import Text.Printf

main = do
    [d] <- map read `fmap` getArgs
    printf "%f\n" (mean [1..d])

mean :: [Double] -> Double
mean xs = sum xs / fromIntegral (length xs)
```

This program is very simple. We import functions for accessing the system's environment (in particular, getArgs), and the Haskell version of printf, for formatted text output. The program then reads a numeric literal from the command line, using that to build a list of floating-point values, whose mean value we compute by dividing the list sum by its length. The result is printed as a string. Let's compile this source to native code (with optimizations on) and run it with the time command to see how it performs:

```
$ ghc --make -O2 A.hs
[1 of 1] Compiling Main             ( A.hs, A.o )
Linking A ...
$ time ./A 1e5
50000.5
./A 1e5   0.05s user 0.01s system 102% cpu 0.059 total
$ time ./A 1e6
500000.5
./A 1e6   0.26s user 0.04s system 99% cpu 0.298 total
$ time ./A 1e7
5000000.5
./A 1e7   63.80s user 0.62s system 99% cpu 1:04.53 total
```

It worked well for small numbers, but the program really started to struggle with a list size of 10 million. From this alone, we know something's not quite right, but it's unclear what resources are being used. Let's investigate.

Collecting Runtime Statistics

To get access to that kind of information, GHC lets us pass flags directly to the Haskell runtime, using the special +RTS and -RTS flags to delimit arguments reserved for the runtime system. The application itself won't see those flags, as they're immediately consumed by the Haskell runtime system.

In particular, we can ask the runtime system to gather memory and garbage collector performance numbers with the -s flag (as well as control the number of OS threads with -N or tweak the stack and heap sizes). We'll also use runtime flags to enable different varieties of profiling. The complete set of flags the Haskell runtime accepts is documented in the GHC User's Guide (*http://www.haskell.org/ghc/docs/latest/html/users_guide/*).

So let's run the program with statistic reporting enabled, via +RTS -sstderr, yielding this result:

```
$ ./A 1e7 +RTS -sstderr
./A 1e7 +RTS -sstderr
5000000.5
1,689,133,824 bytes allocated in the heap
  697,882,192 bytes copied during GC (scavenged)
  465,051,008 bytes copied during GC (not scavenged)
  382,705,664 bytes maximum residency (10 sample(s))

        3222 collections in generation 0 (  0.91s)
          10 collections in generation 1 ( 18.69s)

         742 Mb total memory in use

  INIT  time    0.00s  (  0.00s elapsed)
  MUT   time    0.63s  (  0.71s elapsed)
  GC    time   19.60s  ( 20.73s elapsed)
  EXIT  time    0.00s  (  0.00s elapsed)
  Total time   20.23s  ( 21.44s elapsed)

  %GC time      96.9%  (96.7% elapsed)

  Alloc rate    2,681,318,018 bytes per MUT second

  Productivity   3.1% of total user, 2.9% of total elapsed
```

When using `-sstderr`, our program's performance numbers are printed to the standard error stream, giving us a lot of information about what our program is doing. In particular, it tells us how much time was spent in garbage collection and what the maximum live memory usage was. It turns out that to compute the mean of a list of 10 million elements, our program used a maximum of 742 megabytes on the heap, and spent 96.9% of its time doing garbage collection! In total, only 3.1% of the program's running time was spent doing productive work.

So why is our program behaving so badly, and what can we do to improve it? After all, Haskell is a lazy language—shouldn't it be able to process the list in constant space?

Time Profiling

Thankfully, GHC comes with several tools to analyze a program's time and space usage. In particular, we can compile a program with profiling enabled, which, when run yields useful information about what resources each function is using. Profiling proceeds in three steps: compile the program for profiling, run it with particular profiling modes enabled, and inspect the resulting statistics.

To compile our program for basic time and allocation profiling, we use the `-prof` flag. We also need to tell the profiling code which functions we're interested in profiling, by adding *cost centers* to them. A cost center is a location in the program we'd like to collect statistics about. GHC will generate code to compute the cost of evaluating the expression at each location. Cost centers can be added manually to instrument any expression, using the SCC pragma:

```
-- file: ch25/SCC.hs
mean :: [Double] -> Double
mean xs = {-# SCC "mean" #-} sum xs / fromIntegral (length xs)
```

Alternatively, we can have the compiler insert the cost centers on all top-level functions for us by compiling with the -auto-all flag. Manual cost centers are a useful addition to automated cost-center profiling, as once a hot spot is been identified, we can precisely pin down the expensive subexpressions of a function.

One complication to be aware of is that in a lazy, pure language such as Haskell, values with no arguments need only be computed once (for example, the large list in our example program), and the result shared for later uses. Such values are not really part of the call graph of a program, as they're not evaluated on each call, but we would of course still like to know how expensive their one-off cost of evaluation was. To get accurate numbers for these values, known as *constant applicative forms* (CAFs), we use the -caf-all flag.

Compiling our example program for profiling then (using the -fforce-recomp flag to force full recompilation):

```
$ ghc -O2 --make A.hs -prof -auto-all -caf-all -fforce-recomp
[1 of 1] Compiling Main             ( A.hs, A.o )
Linking A ...
```

We can now run this annotated program with time profiling enabled (and we'll use a smaller input size for the time being, as the program now has additional profiling overhead):

```
$ time ./A  1e6 +RTS -p
Stack space overflow: current size 8388608 bytes.
Use `+RTS -Ksize' to increase it.
./A 1e6 +RTS -p  1.11s user 0.15s system 95% cpu 1.319 total
```

The program ran out of stack space! This is the main complication to be aware of when using profiling: adding cost centers to a program modifies how it is optimized, possibly changing its runtime behavior, as each expression now has additional code associated with it to track the evaluation steps. In a sense, observing the program that is executing modifies how it executes. In this case, it is simple to proceed—we use the GHC runtime flag, -K, to set a larger stack limit for our program (with the usual suffixes to indicate magnitude):

```
$ time ./A 1e6 +RTS -p -K100M
500000.5
./A 1e6 +RTS -p -K100M  4.27s user 0.20s system 99% cpu 4.489 total
```

The runtime will dump its profiling information into a file, *A.prof* (named after the binary that was executed), which contains the following information:

```
Time and Allocation Profiling Report  (Final)

        A +RTS -p -K100M -RTS 1e6

    total time  =        0.28 secs   (14 ticks @ 20 ms)
```

```
        total alloc = 224,041,656 bytes   (excludes profiling overheads)

COST CENTRE   MODULE              %time %alloc

CAF:sum       Main                78.6   25.0
CAF           GHC.Float           21.4   75.0

                                          individual      inherited
COST CENTRE MODULE         no.    entries  %time %alloc   %time %alloc

MAIN         MAIN           1         0    0.0    0.0    100.0  100.0
  main       Main          166        2    0.0    0.0      0.0    0.0
   mean      Main          168        1    0.0    0.0      0.0    0.0
  CAF:sum    Main          160        1   78.6   25.0     78.6   25.0
  CAF:lvl    Main          158        1    0.0    0.0      0.0    0.0
   main      Main          167        0    0.0    0.0      0.0    0.0
  CAF        Numeric       136        1    0.0    0.0      0.0    0.0
  CAF        Text.Read.Lex 135        9    0.0    0.0      0.0    0.0
  CAF        GHC.Read      130        1    0.0    0.0      0.0    0.0
  CAF        GHC.Float     129        1   21.4   75.0     21.4   75.0
  CAF        GHC.Handle    110        4    0.0    0.0      0.0    0.0
```

This gives us a view into the program's runtime behavior. We can see the program's name and the flags we ran it with. The *total time* is time actually spent executing code from the runtime system's point of view, and the *total allocation* is the number of bytes allocated during the entire program run (not the maximum live memory, which is around 700 MB).

The second section of the profiling report is the proportion of time and space each function was responsible for. The third section is the cost center report, structured as a call graph (for example, we can see that mean was called from main). The "individual" and "inherited" columns give us the resources a cost center was responsible for on its own, and what it and its children were responsible for. Additionally, we see the one-off costs of evaluating constants (such as the floating-point values in the large list and the list itself) assigned to top-level CAFs.

What conclusions can we draw from this information? We can see that the majority of time is spent in two CAFs, one related to computing the sum and another for floating-point numbers. These alone account for nearly all allocations that occurred during the program run. Combined with our earlier observation about garbage collector stress, it begins to look like the list node allocations, containing floating-point values, are causing a problem.

For simple performance hot spot identification, particularly in large programs where we might have little idea where time is being spent, the initial time profile can highlight a particular problematic module and top-level function, which is often enough to reveal the trouble spot. Once we've narrowed down the code to a problematic section, such as our example here, we can use more sophisticated profiling tools to extract more information.

Space Profiling

Beyond basic time and allocation statistics, GHC is able to generate graphs of memory usage of the heap, over the program's lifetime. This is perfect for revealing *space leaks*, where memory is retained unnecessarily, leading to the kind of heavy garbage collector activity we see in our example.

Constructing a heap profile follows the same procedure as constructing a normal time profile—namely, compile with `-prof -auto-all -caf-all`. But, when we execute the program, we'll ask the runtime system to gather more detailed heap use statistics. We can break down the heap use information in several ways: via cost center, via module, by constructor, or by data type. Each has its own insights. Heap profiling *A.hs* logs to a file *A.hp*, with raw data that is in turn processed by the tool hp2ps, which generates a PostScript-based, graphical visualization of the heap over time.

To extract a standard heap profile from our program, we run it with the `-hc` runtime flag:

```
$ time ./A 1e6 +RTS -hc -p -K100M
500000.5
./A 1e6 +RTS -hc -p -K100M  4.15s user 0.27s system 99% cpu 4.432 total
```

A heap profiling log, *A.hp*, was created, with the content in the following form:

```
JOB "A 1e6 +RTS -hc -p -K100M"
SAMPLE_UNIT "seconds"
VALUE_UNIT "bytes"
BEGIN_SAMPLE 0.00
END_SAMPLE 0.00
BEGIN_SAMPLE 0.24
(167)main/CAF:lvl    48
(136)Numeric.CAF     112
(166)main   8384
(110)GHC.Handle.CAF 8480
(160)CAF:sum     10562000
(129)GHC.Float.CAF   10562080
END_SAMPLE 0.24
```

Samples are taken at regular intervals during the program run. We can increase the heap sampling frequency using `-iN`, where N is the number of seconds (e.g., 0.01) between heap size samples. Obviously, the more we sample, the more accurate the results, but the slower our program will run. We can now render the heap profile as a graph, using the hp2ps tool:

```
$ hp2ps -e8in -c A.hp
```

This produces the graph, in the file *A.ps* shown in Figure 25-1.

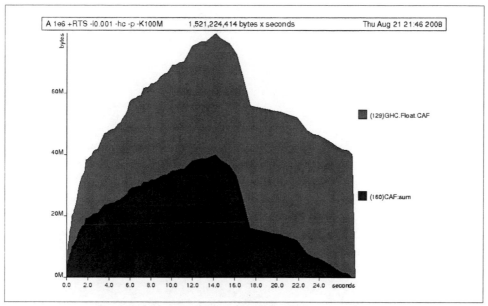

Figure 25-1. The heap profile graph rises in a gently decreasing curve in the first half of the program's run, drops abruptly, then trails off during the remaining third.

What does this graph tell us? For one, the program runs in two phases, spending its first half allocating increasingly large amounts of memory while summing values, and the second half cleaning up those values. The initial allocation also coincides with sum, doing some work, allocating a lot of data. We get a slightly different presentation if we break down the allocation by type, using -hy profiling:

```
$ time ./A 1e6 +RTS -hy -p -K100M
500000.5
./A 1e6 +RTS -i0.001 -hy -p -K100M  34.96s user 0.22s system 99% cpu 35.237 total
$ hp2ps -e8in -c A.hp
```

This yields the graph shown in Figure 25-2.

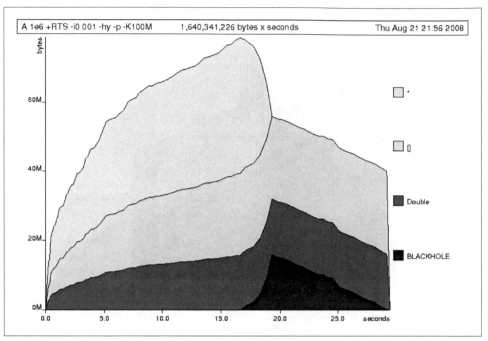

Figure 25-2. Heap profiling curve, broken down by data type. Values of unknown type account for half of the first phase, with Double and lists split. The second phase is one third black holes, the rest split between Double and lists.

The most interesting things to notice here are large parts of the heap devoted to values of list type (the [] band) and heap-allocated `Double` values. There's also some heap-allocated data of unknown type (represented as data of type *). Finally, let's break it down by what constructors are being allocated, using the -hd flag:

```
$ time ./A 1e6 +RTS -hd -p -K100M
$ time ./A 1e6 +RTS -i0.001 -hd -p -K100M
500000.5
./A 1e6 +RTS -i0.001 -hd -p -K100M  27.85s user 0.31s system 99% cpu 28.222 total
```

Our final graphic reveals the full story of what is going on. See Figure 25-3.

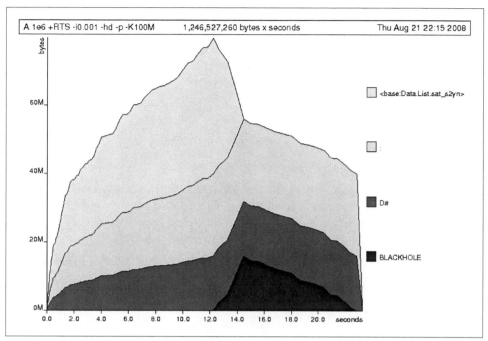

Figure 25-3. The graph is similar in shape but reveals the unknown values to be lists.

A lot of work is going into allocating list nodes containing double-precision floating-point values. Haskell lists are lazy, so the full million element list is built up over time. Crucially, though, it is not being deallocated as it is traversed, leading to increasingly large resident memory use. Finally, a bit over halfway through the program run, the program finally finishes summing the list and starts calculating the length. If we look at the original fragment for mean, we can see exactly why that memory is being retained:

```
-- file: ch25/Fragment.hs
mean :: [Double] -> Double
mean xs = sum xs / fromIntegral (length xs)
```

At first we sum our list, which triggers the allocation of list nodes, but we're unable to release the list nodes once we're done, as the entire list is still needed by length. As soon as sum is done though, and length starts consuming the list, the garbage collector can chase it along, deallocating the list nodes, until we're done. These two phases of evaluation give two strikingly different phases of allocation and deallocation, and point at exactly what we need to do: traverse the list once only, summing and averaging it as we go.

Controlling Evaluation

We have a number of options if we want to write our loop to traverse the list only once. For example, we can write the loop as a fold over the list or via explicit recursion on the list structure. Sticking to the high-level approaches, we'll try a fold first:

```
-- file: ch25/B.hs
mean :: [Double] -> Double
mean xs = s / fromIntegral n
  where
    (n, s)     = foldl k (0, 0) xs
    k (n, s) x = (n+1, s+x)
```

Now, instead of taking the sum of the list and retaining the list until we can take its length, we left-fold over the list, accumulating the intermediate sum and length values in a pair (and we must left-fold, since a right-fold would take us to the end of the list and work backwards, which is exactly what we're trying to avoid).

The body of our loop is the k function, which takes the intermediate loop state and the current element and returns a new state with the length increased by one and the sum increased by the current element. When we run this, however, we get a stack overflow:

```
$ ghc -O2 --make B.hs -fforce-recomp
$ time ./B 1e6
Stack space overflow: current size 8388608 bytes.
Use `+RTS -Ksize' to increase it.
./B 1e6  0.44s user 0.10s system 96% cpu 0.565 total
```

We traded wasted heap for wasted stack! In fact, if we increase the stack size to the size of the heap in our previous implementation, using the -K runtime flag, the program runs to completion and has similar allocation figures:

```
$ ghc -O2 --make B.hs -prof -auto-all -caf-all -fforce-recomp
[1 of 1] Compiling Main             ( B.hs, B.o )
Linking B ...
$ time ./B 1e6 +RTS -i0.001 -hc -p -K100M
500000.5
./B 1e6 +RTS -i0.001 -hc -p -K100M  38.70s user 0.27s system 99% cpu 39.241 total
```

Generating the heap profile, we see all the allocation is now in mean. See Figure 25-4.

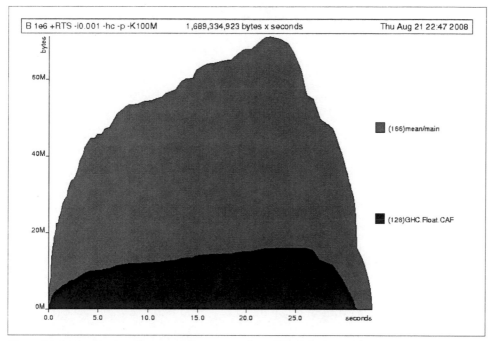

Figure 25-4. Graph of stack usage. The curve is shaped like a hump, with mean representing 80%, and GHC.Real.CAF the other 20%.

The question is: why are we building up more and more allocated state, when all we are doing is folding over the list? This, it turns out, is a classic space leak due to excessive laziness.

Strictness and Tail Recursion

The problem is that our left-fold, `foldl`, is too lazy. What we want is a tail-recursive loop, which can be implemented effectively as a `goto`, with no state left on the stack. In this case though, rather than fully reducing the tuple state at each step, a long chain of thunks is being created, which is evaluated only towards the end of the program. At no point do we demand reduction of the loop state, so the compiler is unable to infer any strictness and must reduce the value purely lazily.

What we need to do is tune the evaluation strategy slightly—lazily unfolding the list, but strictly accumulating the fold state. The standard approach here is to replace `foldl` with `foldl'`, from the `Data.List` module:

```
-- file: ch25/C.hs
mean :: [Double] -> Double
mean xs = s / fromIntegral n
  where
    (n, s)      = foldl' k (0, 0) xs
    k (n, s) x = (n+1, s+x)
```

However, if we run this implementation, we see that we still haven't quite got it right:

```
$ ghc -O2 --make C.hs
[1 of 1] Compiling Main             ( C.hs, C.o )
Linking C ...
$ time ./C 1e6
Stack space overflow: current size 8388608 bytes.
Use `+RTS -Ksize' to increase it.
./C 1e6  0.44s user 0.13s system 94% cpu 0.601 total
```

Still not strict enough! Our loop is continuing to accumulate unevaluated state on the stack. The problem here is that `foldl'` is only outermost strict:

```
-- file: ch25/Foldl.hs
foldl' :: (a -> b -> a) -> a -> [b] -> a
foldl' f z xs = lgo z xs
    where lgo z []     = z
          lgo z (x:xs) = let z' = f z x in z' `seq` lgo z' xs
```

This loop uses `seq` to reduce the accumulated state at each step, but only to the outermost constructor on the loop state. That is, `seq` reduces an expression to weak head normal form (WHNF). Evaluation stops on the loop state once the first constructor is reached. In this case, the outermost constructor is the tuple wrapper, (,), which isn't deep enough. The problem is still the unevaluated numeric state inside the tuple.

Adding Strictness

There are a number of ways to make this function fully strict. We can, for example, add our own strictness hints to the internal state of the tuple, yielding a truly tail-recursive loop:

```
-- file: ch25/D.hs
mean :: [Double] -> Double
mean xs = s / fromIntegral n
  where
    (n, s)      = foldl' k (0, 0) xs
    k (n, s) x = n `seq` s `seq` (n+1, s+x)
```

In this variant, we step inside the tuple state and explicitly tell the compiler that each state component should be reduced on each step. This gives us a version that does, at last, run in constant space:

```
$ ghc -O2 D.hs --make
[1 of 1] Compiling Main             ( D.hs, D.o )
Linking D ...
```

If we run this, with allocation statistics enabled, we get the satisfying result:

```
$ time ./D 1e6 +RTS -sstderr
./D 1e6 +RTS -sstderr
500000.5
256,060,848 bytes allocated in the heap
     43,928 bytes copied during GC (scavenged)
     23,456 bytes copied during GC (not scavenged)
```

```
      45,056 bytes maximum residency (1 sample(s))

         489 collections in generation 0 (   0.00s)
           1 collections in generation 1 (   0.00s)

           1 Mb total memory in use

   INIT  time    0.00s  (  0.00s elapsed)
   MUT   time    0.12s  (  0.13s elapsed)
   GC    time    0.00s  (  0.00s elapsed)
   EXIT  time    0.00s  (  0.00s elapsed)
   Total time    0.13s  (  0.13s elapsed)

   %GC time       2.6%  (2.6% elapsed)

   Alloc rate    2,076,309,329 bytes per MUT second

   Productivity  97.4% of total user, 94.8% of total elapsed

 ./D 1e6 +RTS -sstderr   0.13s user 0.00s system 95% cpu 0.133 total
```

Unlike our first version, this program is 97.4% efficient, spending only 2.6% of its time doing garbage collection, and it runs in a constant 1 megabyte of space. It illustrates a nice balance between mixed strict and lazy evaluation, with the large list unfolded lazily, while we walk over it strictly. The result is a program that runs in constant space, and does so quickly.

Normal form reduction

There are a number of other ways we could have addressed the strictness issue here. For deep strictness, we can use the rnf function, part of the parallel strategies library (along with using), which unlike seq reduces to the fully evaluated "normal form" (hence its name). We can write as such a *deep seq* fold:

```
-- file: ch25/E.hs
import System.Environment
import Text.Printf
import Control.Parallel.Strategies

main = do
    [d] <- map read `fmap` getArgs
    printf "%f\n" (mean [1..d])

foldl'rnf :: NFData a => (a -> b -> a) -> a -> [b] -> a
foldl'rnf f z xs = lgo z xs
    where
        lgo z []     = z
        lgo z (x:xs) = lgo z' xs
            where
                z' = f z x `using` rnf

mean :: [Double] -> Double
mean xs = s / fromIntegral n
  where
```

```
(n, s)      = foldl'rnf k (0, 0) xs
k (n, s) x = (n+1, s+x) :: (Int, Double)
```

We change the implementation of `foldl'` to reduce the state to normal form, using the `rnf` strategy. This also raises an issue that we avoided earlier: the type inferred for the loop accumulator state. Previously, we relied on type defaulting to infer a numeric, integral type for the length of the list in the accumulator, but switching to `rnf` introduces the `NFData` class constraint, and we can no longer rely on defaulting to set the length type.

Bang patterns

Perhaps the cheapest way, syntactically, to add required strictness to code that's excessively lazy is via bang patterns (whose name comes from pronunciation of the "!" character as "bang"), a language extension introduced with the following pragma:

```
-- file: ch25/F.hs
{-# LANGUAGE BangPatterns #-}
```

With bang patterns, we can hint at strictness on any binding form, making the function strict in that variable. Much as explicit type annotations can guide type inference, bang patterns can help guide strictness inference. Bang patterns are a language extension and are enabled with the **BangPatterns** language pragma. We can now rewrite the loop state to be simply:

```
-- file: ch25/F.hs
mean :: [Double] -> Double
mean xs = s / fromIntegral n
  where
    (n, s)       = foldl' k (0, 0) xs
    k (!n, !s) x = (n+1, s+x)
```

The intermediate values in the loop state are now strict, and the loop runs in constant space:

```
$ ghc -O2 F.hs --make
$ time ./F 1e6 +RTS -sstderr
./F 1e6 +RTS -sstderr
500000.5
256,060,848 bytes allocated in the heap
     43,928 bytes copied during GC (scavenged)
     23,456 bytes copied during GC (not scavenged)
     45,056 bytes maximum residency (1 sample(s))

       489 collections in generation 0 (  0.00s)
         1 collections in generation 1 (  0.00s)

         1 Mb total memory in use

  INIT  time    0.00s  (  0.00s elapsed)
  MUT   time    0.14s  (  0.15s elapsed)
  GC    time    0.00s  (  0.00s elapsed)
  EXIT  time    0.00s  (  0.00s elapsed)
```

```
Total time     0.14s  (  0.15s elapsed)

%GC time       0.0%  (2.3% elapsed)

Alloc rate     1,786,599,833 bytes per MUT second

Productivity 100.0% of total user, 94.6% of total elapsed

./F 1e6 +RTS -sstderr  0.14s user 0.01s system 96% cpu 0.155 total
```

In large projects, when we are investigating memory allocation hot spots, bang patterns are the cheapest way to speculatively modify the strictness properties of some code, as they're syntactically less invasive than other methods.

Strict data types

Strict data types are another effective way to provide strictness information to the compiler. By default, Haskell data types are lazy, but it is easy enough to add strictness information to the fields of a data type that then propagate through the program. We can declare a new strict pair type, for example:

```
-- file: ch25/G.hs
data Pair a b = Pair !a !b
```

This creates a pair type whose fields will always be kept in WHNF. We can now rewrite our loop as:

```
-- file: ch25/G.hs
mean :: [Double] -> Double
mean xs = s / fromIntegral n
  where
    Pair n s      = foldl' k (Pair 0 0) xs
    k (Pair n s) x = Pair (n+1) (s+x)
```

This implementation again has the same efficient, constant space behavior. At this point, to squeeze the last drops of performance out of this code, though, we have to dive a bit deeper.

Understanding Core

Besides looking at runtime profiling data, one sure way to determine exactly what your program is doing is to look at the final program source after the compiler is done optimizing it, particularly in the case of Haskell compilers, which can perform very aggressive transformations on the code. GHC uses what is humorously referred to as "a simple functional language"—known as Core—as the compiler intermediate representation. It is essentially a subset of Haskell, augmented with unboxed data types (raw machine types, directly corresponding to primitive data types in languages such as C), suitable for code generation. GHC optimizes Haskell by transformation, repeatedly rewriting the source into more and more efficient forms. The Core representation is the final functional version of your program, before translation to low-level imperative code. In other words, Core has the final say, and if all-out performance is your goal, it is worth understanding.

To view the Core version of our Haskell program, we compile with the `-ddump-simpl` flag, or use the `ghc-core` tool, a third-party utility that lets us view Core in a pager. So let's look at the representation of our final `fold` using strict data types, in Core form:

```
$ ghc -O2 -ddump-simpl G.hs
```

A screenful of text is generated. If we look carefully at it, we'll see a loop (here, cleaned up slightly for clarity):

```
lgo :: Integer -> [Double] -> Double# -> (# Integer, Double #)

lgo = \ n xs s ->
    case xs of
      []        -> (# n, D# s #);
      (:) x ys ->
        case plusInteger n 1 of
          n' -> case x of
            D# y -> lgo n' ys (+## s y)
```

This is the final version of our `foldl'`, and it tells us a lot about the next steps for optimization. The fold itself has been entirely inlined, yielding an explicit recursive loop over the list. The loop state, our strict pair, has disappeared entirely, and the function now takes its length and sum accumulators as direct arguments along with the list.

The sum of the list elements is represented with an unboxed `Double#` value, a raw machine `double` kept in a floating-point register. This is ideal, as there will be no memory traffic involved in keeping the sum on the heap. However, the length of the list—since we gave no explicit type annotation—has been inferred to be a heap-allocated `Integer`, which requires a nonprimitive `plusInteger` to perform addition. If it is algorithmically sound to use a `Int` instead, we can replace `Integer` with it, via a type annotation, and GHC will then be able to use a raw machine `Int#` for the length. We can hope for an improvement in time and space by ensuring that both loop components are unboxed and kept in registers.

The base case of the loop, its end, yields an unboxed pair (a pair allocated only in registers), storing the final length of the list and the accumulated sum. Notice that the return type is a heap-allocated `Double` value, indicated by the `D#` constructor, which lifts a raw double value onto the heap. Again this has implications for performance, as GHC will need to check that there is sufficient heap space available before it can allocate and return from the loop.

We can use a custom pair type in the loop to make `ghc` return an unboxed `Double#` value, which avoids this final heap check. In addition, `ghc` provides an optimization that unboxes the strict fields of a data type, ensuring that the fields of the new pair type will be stored in registers. This optimization is turned on with `-funbox-strict-fields`.

We can make both representation changes by replacing the polymorphic strict pair type with one whose fields are fixed as `Int` and `Double`:

```
-- file: ch25/H.hs
data Pair = Pair !Int !Double

mean :: [Double] -> Double
mean xs = s / fromIntegral n
  where
    Pair n s       = foldl' k (Pair 0 0) xs
    k (Pair n s) x = Pair (n+1) (s+x)
```

Compiling this with optimizations on and -funbox-strict-fields -ddump-simpl, we get a tighter inner loop in Core:

```
lgo :: Int# -> Double# -> [Double] -> (# Int#, Double# #)
lgo = \ n s xs ->
    case xs of
      []          -> (# n, s #)
      (:) x ys ->
        case x of
            D# y -> lgo (+# n 1) (+## s y) ys
```

Now the pair we use to represent the loop state is represented and returned as unboxed primitive types and will be kept in registers. The final version now allocates heap memory for the list nodes only, as the list is lazily demanded. If we compile and run this tuned version, we can compare the allocation and time performance against our original program:

```
$ time ./H 1e7 +RTS -sstderr
./H 1e7 +RTS -sstderr
5000000.5
1,689,133,824 bytes allocated in the heap
    284,432 bytes copied during GC (scavenged)
         32 bytes copied during GC (not scavenged)
     45,056 bytes maximum residency (1 sample(s))

      3222 collections in generation 0 (  0.01s)
         1 collections in generation 1 (  0.00s)

        1 Mb total memory in use

  INIT  time    0.00s  (  0.00s elapsed)
  MUT   time    0.63s  (  0.63s elapsed)
  GC    time    0.01s  (  0.02s elapsed)
  EXIT  time    0.00s  (  0.00s elapsed)
  Total time    0.64s  (  0.64s elapsed)

  %GC time       1.0%  (2.4% elapsed)

  Alloc rate    2,667,227,478 bytes per MUT second

  Productivity  98.4% of total user, 98.2% of total elapsed

./H 1e7 +RTS -sstderr  0.64s user 0.00s system 99% cpu 0.644 total
```

Our original program, when operating on a list of 10 million elements, took more than a minute to run and allocated more than 700 megabytes of memory. The final version, using a simple higher order fold and a strict data type, however runs in around half a second and allocates a total of 1 megabyte. Quite an improvement!

The general rules we can learn from the profiling and optimization process are:

- Compile to native code, with optimizations on.
- When in doubt, use runtime statistics and time profiling.
- If you suspect allocation problems, use heap profiling.
- A careful mixture of strict and lazy evaluation can yield the best results.
- Prefer strict fields for atomic data types (`Int`, `Double`, and similar types).
- Use data types with simpler machine representations (prefer `Int` over `Integer`).

These simple strategies are enough to identify and squash untoward memory use issues, and when used wisely, can keep them from occurring in the first place.

Advanced Techniques: Fusion

The final bottleneck in our program is the lazy list itself. While we can avoid allocating it all at once, there is still memory traffic each time around the loop, as we demand the next cons cell in the list, allocate it to the heap, operate on it, and continue. The list type is also polymorphic, so the elements of the list will be represented as heap-allocated `Double` values.

What we'd like to do is eliminate the list entirely, keeping just the next element we need in a register. Perhaps surprisingly, GHC is able to transform the list program into a listless version, using an optimization known as deforestation, which refers to a general class of optimizations that involve eliminating intermediate data structures. Due to the absence of side effects, a Haskell compiler can be extremely aggressive when rearranging code, reordering and transforming wholesale at times. The specific deforestation optimization we will use here is stream fusion.

This optimization transforms recursive list generation and transformation functions into nonrecursive `unfold`s. When an `unfold` appears next to a `fold`, the structure between them is then eliminated entirely, yielding a single, tight loop with no heap allocation. The optimization isn't enabled by default, and it can radically change the complexity of a piece of code, but it is enabled by a number of data structure libraries, which provide *rewrite rules*, custom optimizations, that the compiler applies to functions that the library exports.

We'll use the `uvector` library, which provides a suite of list-like operations that use stream fusion to remove intermediate data structures. Rewriting our program to use streams is straightforward:

```
-- file: ch25/I.hs
import System.Environment
import Text.Printf
import Data.Array.Vector
```

```
main = do
    [d] <- map read `fmap` getArgs
    printf "%f\n" (mean (enumFromToFracU 1 d))

data Pair = Pair !Int !Double

mean :: UArr Double -> Double
mean xs = s / fromIntegral n
  where
    Pair n s      = foldlU k (Pair 0 0) xs
    k (Pair n s) x = Pair (n+1) (s+x)
```

After installing the uvector library from Hackage, we can build our program, with -O2 -funbox-strict-fields, and then inspect the Core that results:

```
fold :: Int# -> Double# -> Double# -> (# Int#, Double# #)
fold = \ n s t ->
    case >## t limit of {
      False -> fold (+# n 1) (+## s t) (+## t 1.0)
      True  -> (# n, s #)
```

This is really the optimal result! Our lists have been entirely fused away, yielding a tight loop where list generation is interleaved with accumulation, and all input and output variables are kept in registers. Running this, we see another improvement bump in performance, with runtime falling by another order of magnitude:

```
$ time ./I 1e7
5000000.5
./I 1e7  0.06s user 0.00s system 72% cpu 0.083 total
```

Tuning the Generated Assembly

Given that our Core is now optimal, the only step left to take this program further is to look directly at the assembly. Of course, there are only small gains left to make at this point. To view the generated assembly, we can use a tool such as ghc-core or generate assembly to standard output with the -ddump-asm flag to GHC. We have few levers available to adjust the generated assembly, but we may choose between the C and native code backends to GHC. And, if we then choose the C backend, which optimization flags to pass to GCC. Particularly with floating-point code, it is sometimes useful to compile via C, and enable specific high-performance C compiler optimizations.

For example, we can squeeze out the last drops of performance from our final fused loop code by using -funbox-strict-fields -fvia-C -optc-O2, which cuts the running time in half again (as the C compiler is able to optimize away some redundant move instructions in the program's inner loop):

```
$ ghc -fforce-recomp --make -O2 -funbox-strict-fields -fvia-C -optc-O2 I.hs
[1 of 1] Compiling Main             ( I.hs, I.o )
Linking I ...
$ time ./I 1e7
```

```
5000000.5
./I 1e7  0.04s user 0.00s system 98% cpu 0.047 total
```

Inspecting the final x86_64 assembly (via `-keep-tmp-files`), we see the generated loop contains only six instructions:

```
go:
    ucomisd     5(%rbx), %xmm6
    ja  .L31
    addsd       %xmm6, %xmm5
    addq        $1, %rsi
    addsd       .LC0(%rip), %xmm6
    jmp go
```

We've effectively massaged the program through multiple source-level optimizations, all the way to the final assembly. There's nowhere else to go from here. Optimizing code to this level is very rarely necessary, of course, and typically makes sense only when writing low-level libraries or optimizing particularly important code, where all algorithm choices have already been determined. For day-to-day code, choosing better algorithms is always a more effective strategy, but it's useful to know we can optimize down to the metal if necessary.

Conclusions

In this chapter, we've looked at a suite of tools and techniques you can use to track down and identify problematic areas of your code, along with a variety of conventions that can go a long way towards keeping your code lean and efficient. The goal is really to program in such a way that you have good knowledge of what your code is doing at all levels from source through the compiler to the metal, and to be able to focus in on particular levels when requirements demand.

By sticking to simple rules, choosing the right data structures, and avoiding the traps of the unwary, it is perfectly possible to reliably achieve high performance from your Haskell code, while being able to develop at a very high level. The result is a sweet balance of productivity and ruthless efficiency.

CHAPTER 26

Advanced Library Design: Building a Bloom Filter

Introducing the Bloom Filter

A Bloom filter is a set-like data structure that is highly efficient in its use of space. It supports two operations only: insertion and membership querying. Unlike a normal set data structure, a Bloom filter can give incorrect answers. If we query it to see whether an element that we have inserted is present, it will answer affirmatively. If we query for an element that we have *not* inserted, it *might* incorrectly claim that the element is present.

For many applications, a low rate of false positives is tolerable. For instance, the job of a network traffic shaper is to throttle bulk transfers (e.g., BitTorrent) so that interactive sessions (such as ssh sessions or games) see good response times. A traffic shaper might use a Bloom filter to determine whether a packet belonging to a particular session is bulk or interactive. If it misidentifies 1 in 10,000 bulk packets as interactive and fails to throttle it, nobody will notice.

The attraction of a Bloom filter is its space efficiency. If we want to build a spell checker and have a dictionary of 500,000 words, a set data structure might consume 20 megabytes of space. A Bloom filter, in contrast, would consume about half a megabyte, at the cost of missing perhaps 1% of misspelled words.

Behind the scenes, a Bloom filter is remarkably simple. It consists of a bit array and a handful of hash functions. We'll use k for the number of hash functions. If we want to insert a value into the Bloom filter, we compute k hashes of the value and turn on those bits in the bit array. If we want to see whether a value is present, we compute k hashes and check all of those bits in the array to see if they are turned on.

To see how this works, let's say we want to insert the strings `"foo"` and `"bar"` into a Bloom filter that is 8 bits wide, and we have two hash functions:

1. Compute the two hashes of `"foo"`, and get the values 1 and 6.
2. Set bits 1 and 6 in the bit array.
3. Compute the two hashes of `"bar"`, and get the values 6 and 3.
4. Set bits 6 and 3 in the bit array.

This example should make it clear why we cannot remove an element from a Bloom filter: both `"foo"` and `"bar"` resulted in bit 6 being set.

Suppose we now want to query the Bloom filter to see whether the values `"quux"` and `"baz"` are present:

1. Compute the two hashes of `"quux"`, and get the values 4 and 0.
2. Check bit 4 in the bit array. It is not set, so `"quux"` cannot be present. We do not need to check bit 0.
3. Compute the two hashes of `"baz"` and get the values 1 and 3.
4. Check bit 1 in the bit array. It is set, as is bit 3, so we say that `"baz"` is present even though it is not. We have reported a false positive.

For a survey of some of the uses of Bloom filters in networking, see "Network Applications of Bloom Filters: A Survey" by Andrei Broder and Michael Mitzenmacher (see *http://www.eecs.harvard.edu/~michaelm/postscripts/im2005b.pdf*).

Use Cases and Package Layout

Not all users of Bloom filters have the same needs. In some cases, it suffices to create a Bloom filter in one pass, and only query it afterwards. For other applications, we may need to continue to update the Bloom filter after we create it. To accommodate these needs, we will design our library with mutable and immutable APIs.

We will segregate the mutable and immutable APIs that we publish by placing them in different modules: `BloomFilter` for the immutable code and `BloomFilter.Mutable` for the mutable code.

In addition, we will create several "helper" modules that won't provide parts of the public API but will keep the internal code cleaner.

Finally, we will ask our API's users to provide a function that can generate a number of hashes of an element. This function will have the type `a -> [Word32]`. We will use all of the hashes that this function returns, so the list must not be infinite!

Basic Design

The data structure that we use for our Haskell Bloom filter is a direct translation of the simple description we gave earlier—a bit array and a function that computes hashes:

```
-- file: BloomFilter/Internal.hs
module BloomFilter.Internal
    (
      Bloom(..)
    , MutBloom(..)
    ) where

import Data.Array.ST (STUArray)
import Data.Array.Unboxed (UArray)
import Data.Word (Word32)

data Bloom a = B {
      blmHash  :: (a -> [Word32])
    , blmArray :: UArray Word32 Bool
    }
```

When we create our Cabal package, we will not be exporting this BloomFilter.Internal module. It exists purely to let us control the visibility of names. We will import BloomFilter.Internal into both the mutable and immutable modules, but we will re-export from each module only the type that is relevant to that module's API.

Unboxing, Lifting, and Bottom

Unlike other Haskell arrays, a UArray contains *unboxed* values.

For a normal Haskell type, a value can be either fully evaluated, an unevaluated thunk, or the special value $\perp$, pronounced (and sometimes written) *bottom*. The value $\perp$ is a placeholder for a computation that does not succeed. Such a computation could take any of several forms. It could be an infinite loop, an application of error, or the special value undefined.

A type that can contain $\perp$ is referred to as *lifted*. All normal Haskell types are lifted. In practice, this means that we can always write error "eek!" or undefined in place of a normal expression.

This ability to store thunks or $\perp$ comes with a performance cost: it adds an extra layer of indirection. To see why we need this indirection, consider the Word32 type. A value of this type is a full 32 bits wide, so on a 32-bit system, there is no way to directly encode the value $\perp$ within 32 bits. The runtime system has to maintain, and check, some extra data to track whether the value is $\perp$ or not.

An unboxed value does away with this indirection. In doing so, it gains performance but sacrifices the ability to represent a thunk or $\perp$. Since it can be denser than a normal

Haskell array, an array of unboxed values is an excellent choice for numeric data and bits.

GHC implements a `UArray` of `Bool` values by packing eight array elements into each byte, so this type is perfect for our needs.

Boxing and lifting

The counterpart of an unboxed type is a *boxed* type, which uses indirection. All lifted types are boxed, but a few low-level boxed types are not lifted. For instance, GHC's runtime system has a low-level array type for which it uses boxing (i.e., it maintains a pointer to the array). If it has a reference to such an array, it knows that the array must exist, so it does not need to account for the possibility of ⊥. This array type is thus boxed, but not lifted. Boxed but unlifted types show up only at the lowest level of runtime hacking. We will never encounter them in normal use.

The ST Monad

Back in "Modifying Array Elements" on page 274, we mentioned that modifying an immutable array is prohibitively expensive, as it requires copying the entire array. Using a `UArray` does not change this, so what can we do to reduce the cost to bearable levels?

In an imperative language, we would simply modify the elements of the array in place —this will be our approach in Haskell, too.

Haskell provides a special monad, named `ST`,[*] which lets us work safely with mutable state. Compared to the `State` monad, it has some powerful added capabilities:

- We can *thaw* an immutable array to give a mutable array; modify the mutable array in place; and *freeze* a new immutable array when we are done.
- We have the ability to use *mutable references*. This lets us implement data structures that we can modify after construction, as in an imperative language. This ability is vital for some imperative data structures and algorithms, for which similarly efficient, purely functional alternatives have not yet been discovered.

The `IO` monad also provides these capabilities. The major difference between the two is that the `ST` monad is intentionally designed so that we can *escape* from it back into pure Haskell code. We enter the `ST` monad via the execution function `runST` (in the same way as most other Haskell monads do—except `IO`, of course), and we escape by returning from `runST`.

When we apply a monad's execution function, we expect it to behave repeatably: given the same body and arguments, we must get the same results every time. This also applies

---

[*] The name `ST` is an acronym for *state thread*.

to runST. To achieve this repeatability, the ST monad is more restrictive than the IO monad. We cannot read or write files, create global variables, or fork threads. Indeed, although we can create and work with mutable references and arrays, the type system prevents them from escaping to the caller of runST. A mutable array must be frozen into an immutable array before we can return it, and a mutable reference cannot escape at all.

Designing an API for Qualified Import

The public interfaces that we provide for working with Bloom filters are worth a little discussion:

```
-- file: BloomFilter/Mutable.hs
module BloomFilter.Mutable
    (
      MutBloom
    , elem
    , notElem
    , insert
    , length
    , new
    ) where

import Control.Monad (liftM)
import Control.Monad.ST (ST)
import Data.Array.MArray (getBounds, newArray, readArray, writeArray)
import Data.Word (Word32)
import Prelude hiding (elem, length, notElem)

import BloomFilter.Internal (MutBloom(..))
```

We export several names that clash with names the Prelude exports. This is deliberate: we expect users of our modules to import them with qualified names. This reduces the burden on the memory of our users, as they should already be familiar with the Prelude's elem, notElem, and length functions.

When we use a module written in this style, we might often import it with a single-letter prefix—for instance, as import qualified BloomFilter.Mutable as M. This would allow us to write M.length, which stays compact and readable.

Alternatively, we could import the module unqualified and import the Prelude while hiding the clashing names with import Prelude hiding (length). This is much less useful, as it gives a reader skimming the code no local cue that she is *not* actually seeing the Prelude's length.

Of course, we seem to be violating this precept in our own module's header: we import the Prelude and hide some of the names it exports. There is a practical reason for this. We define a function named length. If we export this from our module without first hiding the Prelude's length, the compiler will complain that it cannot tell whether to export our version of length or the Prelude's.

While we could export the fully qualified name `BloomFilter.Mutable.length` to eliminate the ambiguity, that seems uglier in this case. This decision has no consequences
for someone using our module, just for ourselves as the authors of what ought to be a
"black box," so there is little chance of confusion here.

Creating a Mutable Bloom Filter

We put type declaration for our mutable Bloom filter in the `BloomFilter.Internal`
module, along with the immutable `Bloom` type:

```
-- file: BloomFilter/Internal.hs
data MutBloom s a = MB {
      mutHash :: (a -> [Word32])
    , mutArray :: STUArray s Word32 Bool
    }
```

The `STUArray` type gives us a mutable unboxed array that we can work with in the ST
monad. To create an `STUArray`, we use the `newArray` function. The `new` function belongs
in the `BloomFilter.Mutable` function:

```
-- file: BloomFilter/Mutable.hs
new :: (a -> [Word32]) -> Word32 -> ST s (MutBloom s a)
new hash numBits = MB hash `liftM` newArray (0,numBits-1) False
```

Most of the methods of `STUArray` are actually implementations of the `MArray` typeclass,
which is defined in the `Data.Array.MArray` module.

Our `length` function is slightly complicated by two factors. We are relying on our bit
array's record of its own bounds, and an `MArray` instance's `getBounds` function has a
monadic type. We also have to add one to the answer, as the upper bound of the array
is one less than its actual length:

```
-- file: BloomFilter/Mutable.hs
length :: MutBloom s a -> ST s Word32
length filt = (succ . snd) `liftM` getBounds (mutArray filt)
```

To add an element to the Bloom filter, we set all of the bits indicated by the hash
function. We use the `mod` function to ensure that all of the hashes stay within the bounds
of our array, and isolate our code that computes offsets into the bit array in one function:

```
-- file: BloomFilter/Mutable.hs
insert :: MutBloom s a -> a -> ST s ()
insert filt elt = indices filt elt >>=
                    mapM_ (\bit -> writeArray (mutArray filt) bit True)

indices :: MutBloom s a -> a -> ST s [Word32]
indices filt elt = do
  modulus <- length filt
  return $ map (`mod` modulus) (mutHash filt elt)
```

Testing for membership is no more difficult. If every bit indicated by the hash function
is set, we consider an element to be present in the Bloom filter:

```
-- file: BloomFilter/Mutable.hs
elem, notElem :: a -> MutBloom s a -> ST s Bool

elem elt filt = indices filt elt >>=
                allM (readArray (mutArray filt))

notElem elt filt = not `liftM` elem elt filt
```

We need to write a small supporting function—a monadic version of `all`, which we will call `allM`:

```
-- file: BloomFilter/Mutable.hs
allM :: Monad m => (a -> m Bool) -> [a] -> m Bool
allM p (x:xs) = do
  ok <- p x
  if ok
    then allM p xs
    else return False
allM _ [] = return True
```

The Immutable API

Our interface to the immutable Bloom filter has the same structure as the mutable API:

```
-- file: ch26/BloomFilter.hs
module BloomFilter
    (
      Bloom
    , length
    , elem
    , notElem
    , fromList
    ) where

import BloomFilter.Internal
import BloomFilter.Mutable (insert, new)
import Data.Array.ST (runSTUArray)
import Data.Array.IArray ((!), bounds)
import Data.Word (Word32)
import Prelude hiding (elem, length, notElem)

length :: Bloom a -> Int
length = fromIntegral . len

len :: Bloom a -> Word32
len = succ . snd . bounds . blmArray

elem :: a -> Bloom a -> Bool
elt `elem` filt   = all test (blmHash filt elt)
  where test hash = blmArray filt ! (hash `mod` len filt)

notElem :: a -> Bloom a -> Bool
elt `notElem` filt = not (elt `elem` filt)
```

We provide an easy-to-use means to create an immutable Bloom filter, via a `fromList` function. This hides the ST monad from our users so that they see only the immutable type:

```
-- file: ch26/BloomFilter.hs
fromList :: (a -> [Word32])    -- family of hash functions to use
            -> Word32          -- number of bits in filter
            -> [a]             -- values to populate with
            -> Bloom a
fromList hash numBits values =
    B hash . runSTUArray $
      do mb <- new hash numBits
         mapM_ (insert mb) values
         return (mutArray mb)
```

The key to this function is `runSTUArray`. We mentioned earlier that in order to return an immutable array from the ST monad, we must freeze a mutable array. The `runSTUArray` function combines execution with freezing. Given an action that returns an `STUArray`, it executes the action using `runST`; freezes the `STUArray` that it returns; and returns that as a `UArray`.

The `MArray` typeclass provides a `freeze` function that we could use instead, but `runSTUArray` is both more convenient and more efficient. The efficiency lies in the fact that `freeze` must copy the underlying data from the `STUArray` to the new `UArray`, in order to ensure that subsequent modifications of the `STUArray` cannot affect the contents of the `UArray`. Thanks to the type system, `runSTUArray` can guarantee that an `STUArray` is no longer accessible when it uses it to create a `UArray`. It can thus share the underlying contents between the two arrays, avoiding the copy.

Creating a Friendly Interface

Although our immutable Bloom filter API is straightforward to use once we have created a `Bloom` value, the `fromList` function leaves some important decisions unresolved. We still have to choose a function that can generate many hash values and determine what the capacity of a Bloom filter should be:

```
-- file: BloomFilter/Easy.hs
easyList :: (Hashable a)
         => Double        -- false positive rate (between 0 and 1)
         -> [a]           -- values to populate the filter with
         -> Either String (B.Bloom a)
```

Here is a possible "friendlier" way to create a Bloom filter. It leaves responsibility for hashing values in the hands of a typeclass, `Hashable`. It lets us configure the Bloom filter based on a parameter that is easier to understand—namely the rate of false positives that we are willing to tolerate. And it chooses the size of the filter for us, based on the desired false positive rate and the number of elements in the input list.

This function will, of course, not always be usable—for example, it will fail if the length of the input list is too long. However, its simplicity rounds out the other interfaces we provide. It lets us offer our users a range of control over creation, from entirely imperative to completely declarative.

Re-Exporting Names for Convenience

In the export list for our module, we re-export some names from the base `BloomFilter` module. This allows casual users to import only the `BloomFilter.Easy` module and have access to all of the types and functions they are likely to need.

If we import both `BloomFilter.Easy` and `BloomFilter`, you might wonder what will happen if we try to use a name exported by both. We already know that if we import `BloomFilter` unqualified and try to use `length`, GHC will issue an error about ambiguity, because the `Prelude` also makes the name `length` available.

The Haskell standard requires an implementation to be able to tell when several names refer to the same "thing." For instance, the `Bloom` type is exported by `BloomFilter` and `BloomFilter.Easy`. If we import both modules and try to use `Bloom`, GHC will be able to see that the `Bloom` re-exported from `BloomFilter.Easy` is the same as the one exported from `BloomFilter`, and it will not report an ambiguity.

Hashing Values

A Bloom filter depends on fast, high-quality hashes for good performance and a low false positive rate. It is surprisingly difficult to write a general purpose hash function that has both of these properties.

Luckily for us, a fellow named Bob Jenkins developed some hash functions that have exactly these properties, and he placed the code in the public domain at *http://burtle burtle.net/bob/hash/doobs.html*.[†] He wrote his hash functions in C, so we can easily use the FFI to create bindings to them. The specific source file that we need from that site is named *lookup3.c* (*http://burtleburtle.net/bob/c/lookup3.c*). We create a *cbits* directory and download it to there.

A little editing

On line 36 of the copy of *lookup3.c* that you just downloaded, there is a macro named `SELF_TEST` defined. To use this source file as a library, you *must* delete this line or comment it out. If you forget to do so, the `main` function defined near the bottom of the file will supersede the `main` of any Haskell program you link this library against.

There remains one hitch: we will frequently need 7 or even 10 hash functions. We really don't want to scrape together that many different functions, and fortunately we do not

---

[†] Jenkins's hash functions have *much* better mixing properties than some other popular noncryptographic hash functions that you might be familiar with, such as `FNV` and `hashpjw`, so we recommend avoiding them.

need to. In most cases, we can get away with just two. We will see how shortly. The Jenkins hash library includes two functions, `hashword2` and `hashlittle2`, that compute two hash values. Here is a C header file that describes the APIs of these two functions. We save this to *cbits/lookup3.h*:

```
/* save this file as lookup3.h */

#ifndef _lookup3_h
#define _lookup3_h

#include <stdint.h>
#include <sys/types.h>

/* only accepts uint32_t aligned arrays of uint32_t */
void hashword2(const uint32_t *key,  /* array of uint32_t */
            size_t length,           /* number of uint32_t values */
            uint32_t *pc,            /* in: seed1, out: hash1 */
            uint32_t *pb);           /* in: seed2, out: hash2 */

/* handles arbitrarily aligned arrays of bytes */
void hashlittle2(const void *key,   /* array of bytes */
            size_t length,          /* number of bytes */
            uint32_t *pc,           /* in: seed1, out: hash1 */
            uint32_t *pb);          /* in: seed2, out: hash2 */

#endif /* _lookup3_h */
```

A *salt* is a value that perturbs the hash value that the function computes. If we hash the same value with two different salts, we will get two different hashes. Since these functions compute two hashes, they accept two salts.

Here are our Haskell bindings to these functions:

```
-- file: BloomFilter/Hash.hs
{-# LANGUAGE BangPatterns, ForeignFunctionInterface #-}
module BloomFilter.Hash
    (
      Hashable(..)
    , hash
    , doubleHash
    ) where

import Data.Bits ((.&.), shiftR)
import Foreign.Marshal.Array (withArrayLen)
import Control.Monad (foldM)
import Data.Word (Word32, Word64)
import Foreign.C.Types (CSize)
import Foreign.Marshal.Utils (with)
import Foreign.Ptr (Ptr, castPtr, plusPtr)
import Foreign.Storable (Storable, peek, sizeOf)
import qualified Data.ByteString as Strict
import qualified Data.ByteString.Lazy as Lazy
import System.IO.Unsafe (unsafePerformIO)

foreign import ccall unsafe "lookup3.h hashword2" hashWord2
```

```
        :: Ptr Word32 -> CSize -> Ptr Word32 -> Ptr Word32 -> IO ()

    foreign import ccall unsafe "lookup3.h hashlittle2" hashLittle2
        :: Ptr a -> CSize -> Ptr Word32 -> Ptr Word32 -> IO ()
```

We have specified that the definitions of the functions can be found in the *lookup3.h*
header file that we just created.

For convenience and efficiency, we will combine the 32-bit salts consumed, and the
hash values computed, by the Jenkins hash functions into a single 64-bit value:

```
-- file: BloomFilter/Hash.hs
hashIO :: Ptr a     -- value to hash
       -> CSize     -- number of bytes
       -> Word64    -- salt
       -> IO Word64
hashIO ptr bytes salt =
    with (fromIntegral salt) $ \sp -> do
      let p1 = castPtr sp
          p2 = castPtr sp `plusPtr` 4
      go p1 p2
      peek sp
  where go p1 p2
          | bytes .&. 3 == 0 = hashWord2 (castPtr ptr) words p1 p2
          | otherwise        = hashLittle2 ptr bytes p1 p2
        words = bytes `div` 4
```

Without explicit types around to describe what is happening, this code is not completely obvious. The with function allocates room for the salt on the C stack and stores
the current salt value in there, so sp is a Ptr Word64. The pointers p1 and p2 are
Ptr Word32; p1 points at the low word of sp, and p2 at the high word. This is how we
chop the single Word64 salt into two Ptr Word32 parameters.

Because all of our data pointers are coming from the Haskell heap, we know that they
will be aligned on an address that is safe to pass to either hashWord2 (which accepts only
32-bit-aligned addresses) or hashLittle2. Since hashWord32 is the faster of the two hashing functions, we call it if our data is a multiple of 4 bytes in size; otherwise, we call
hashLittle2.

Since the C hash function will write the computed hashes into p1 and p2, we need only
to peek the pointer sp to retrieve the computed hash.

We don't want clients of this module to be stuck fiddling with low-level details, so we
use a typeclass to provide a clean, high-level interface:

```
-- file: BloomFilter/Hash.hs
class Hashable a where
    hashSalt :: Word64       -- ^ salt
             -> a            -- ^ value to hash
             -> Word64

hash :: Hashable a => a -> Word64
hash = hashSalt 0x106fc397cf62f64d3
```

We also provide a number of useful implementations of this typeclass. To hash basic types, we must write a little boilerplate code:

```
-- file: BloomFilter/Hash.hs
hashStorable :: Storable a => Word64 -> a -> Word64
hashStorable salt k = unsafePerformIO . with k $ \ptr ->
                      hashIO ptr (fromIntegral (sizeOf k)) salt

instance Hashable Char   where hashSalt = hashStorable
instance Hashable Int    where hashSalt = hashStorable
instance Hashable Double where hashSalt = hashStorable
```

We might prefer to use the `Storable` typeclass to write just one declaration, as follows:

```
-- file: BloomFilter/Hash.hs
instance Storable a => Hashable a where
    hashSalt = hashStorable
```

Unfortunately, Haskell does not permit us to write instances of this form, as allowing them would make the type system *undecidable*: they can cause the compiler's type checker to loop infinitely. This restriction on undecidable types forces us to write out individual declarations. It does not, however, pose a problem for a definition such as this one:

```
-- file: BloomFilter/Hash.hs
hashList :: (Storable a) => Word64 -> [a] -> IO Word64
hashList salt xs =
    withArrayLen xs $ \len ptr ->
      hashIO ptr (fromIntegral (len * sizeOf x)) salt
  where x = head xs

instance (Storable a) => Hashable [a] where
    hashSalt salt xs = unsafePerformIO $ hashList salt xs
```

The compiler will accept this instance, so we gain the ability to hash values of many list types.[‡] Most importantly, since `Char` is an instance of `Storable`, we can now hash `String` values.

For tuple types, we take advantage of function composition. We take a salt in at one end of the composition pipeline and use the result of hashing each tuple element as the salt for the next element:

```
-- file: BloomFilter/Hash.hs
hash2 :: (Hashable a) => a -> Word64 -> Word64
hash2 k salt = hashSalt salt k

instance (Hashable a, Hashable b) => Hashable (a,b) where
    hashSalt salt (a,b) = hash2 b . hash2 a $ salt

instance (Hashable a, Hashable b, Hashable c) => Hashable (a,b,c) where
    hashSalt salt (a,b,c) = hash2 c . hash2 b . hash2 a $ salt
```

[‡] Unfortunately, we do not have room to explain why one of these instances is decidable, but the other is not.

To hash ByteString types, we write special instances that plug straight into the internals of the ByteString types (this gives us excellent hashing performance):

```
-- file: BloomFilter/Hash.hs
hashByteString :: Word64 -> Strict.ByteString -> IO Word64
hashByteString salt bs = Strict.useAsCStringLen bs $ \(ptr, len) ->
                           hashIO ptr (fromIntegral len) salt

instance Hashable Strict.ByteString where
    hashSalt salt bs = unsafePerformIO $ hashByteString salt bs

rechunk :: Lazy.ByteString -> [Strict.ByteString]
rechunk s
    | Lazy.null s = []
    | otherwise   = let (pre,suf) = Lazy.splitAt chunkSize s
                    in  repack pre : rechunk suf
    where repack    = Strict.concat . Lazy.toChunks
          chunkSize = 64 * 1024

instance Hashable Lazy.ByteString where
    hashSalt salt bs = unsafePerformIO $
                         foldM hashByteString salt (rechunk bs)
```

Since a lazy ByteString is represented as a series of chunks, we must be careful with the boundaries between those chunks. The string "foobar" can be represented in five different ways—for example, ["fo","obar"] or ["foob","ar"]. This is invisible to most users of the type, but not to us, as we use the underlying chunks directly. Our rechunk function ensures that the chunks we pass to the C hashing code are a uniform 64 KB in size so that we will give consistent hash values no matter where the original chunk boundaries lie.

Turning Two Hashes into Many

As we mentioned earlier, we need many more than two hashes to make effective use of a Bloom filter. We can use a technique called *double hashing* to combine the two values computed by the Jenkins hash functions, yielding many more hashes. The resulting hashes are of good enough quality for our needs and far cheaper than computing many distinct hashes:

```
-- file: BloomFilter/Hash.hs
doubleHash :: Hashable a => Int -> a -> [Word32]
doubleHash numHashes value = [h1 + h2 * i | i <- [0..num]]
    where h    = hashSalt 0x9150a946c4a8966e value
          h1   = fromIntegral (h `shiftR` 32) .&. maxBound
          h2   = fromIntegral h
          num  = fromIntegral numHashes
```

Implementing the Easy Creation Function

In the BloomFilter.Easy module, we use our new doubleHash function to define the easyList function whose type we defined earlier:

```
-- file: BloomFilter/Easy.hs
module BloomFilter.Easy
    (
      suggestSizing
    , sizings
    , easyList

    -- re-export useful names from BloomFilter
    , B.Bloom
    , B.length
    , B.elem
    , B.notElem
    ) where

import BloomFilter.Hash (Hashable, doubleHash)
import Data.List (genericLength)
import Data.Maybe (catMaybes)
import Data.Word (Word32)
import qualified BloomFilter as B

easyList errRate values =
    case suggestSizing (genericLength values) errRate of
      Left err            -> Left err
      Right (bits,hashes) -> Right filt
        where filt = B.fromList (doubleHash hashes) bits values
```

This depends on a **suggestSizing** function that estimates the best combination of filter size and number of hashes to compute, based on our desired false positive rate and the maximum number of elements that we expect the filter to contain:

```
-- file: BloomFilter/Easy.hs
suggestSizing
    :: Integer          -- expected maximum capacity
    -> Double           -- desired false positive rate
    -> Either String (Word32,Int) -- (filter size, number of hashes)
suggestSizing capacity errRate
    | capacity <= 0                       = Left "capacity too small"
    | errRate <= 0 || errRate >= 1 = Left "invalid error rate"
    | null saneSizes                      = Left "capacity too large"
    | otherwise                           = Right (minimum saneSizes)
  where saneSizes = catMaybes . map sanitize $ sizings capacity errRate
        sanitize (bits,hashes)
            | bits > maxWord32 - 1 = Nothing
            | otherwise            = Just (ceiling bits, truncate hashes)
          where maxWord32 = fromIntegral (maxBound :: Word32)

sizings :: Integer -> Double -> [(Double, Double)]
sizings capacity errRate =
    [(((-k) * cap / log (1 - (errRate ** (1 / k)))), k) | k <- [1..50]]
  where cap = fromIntegral capacity
```

We perform some rather paranoid checking. For instance, the sizings function suggests pairs of array size and hash count, but it does not validate its suggestions. Since we use 32-bit hashes, we must filter out suggested array sizes that are too large.

In our suggestSizing function, we attempt to minimize only the size of the bit array, without regard for the number of hashes. To see why, let us interactively explore the relationship between array size and number of hashes.

Suppose we want to insert 10 million elements into a Bloom filter, with a false positive rate of 0.1%:

```
ghci> let kbytes (bits,hashes) = (ceiling bits `div` 8192, hashes)
ghci> :m +BloomFilter.Easy Data.List
ghci> mapM_ (print . kbytes) . take 10 . sort $ sizings 10000000 0.001
Loading package array-0.1.0.0 ... linking ... done.
Loading package bytestring-0.9.0.1.1 ... linking ... done.
Loading package rwh-bloomfilter-0.1 ... linking ... done.
(17550,10.0)
(17601,11.0)
(17608,9.0)
(17727,12.0)
(17831,8.0)
(17905,13.0)
(18122,14.0)
(18320,7.0)
(18368,15.0)
(18635,16.0)
```

We achieve the most compact table (just over 17 KB) by computing 10 hashes. If we really were hashing the data repeatedly, we could reduce the number of hashes to 7 at a cost of 5% in space. Since we are using Jenkins's hash functions—which compute two hashes in a single pass—and double hashing the results to produce additional hashes, the cost of computing those extra hashes is tiny, so we will choose the smallest table size.

If we increase our tolerance for false positives tenfold, to 1%, the amount of space and the number of hashes we need go down, though not by easily predictable amounts:

```
ghci> mapM_ (print . kbytes) . take 10 . sort $ sizings 10000000 0.01
(11710,7.0)
(11739,6.0)
(11818,8.0)
(12006,9.0)
(12022,5.0)
(12245,10.0)
(12517,11.0)
(12810,12.0)
(12845,4.0)
(13118,13.0)
```

Creating a Cabal Package

We have created a moderately complicated library, with four public modules and one internal module. To turn this into a package that we can easily redistribute, we create a *rwh-bloomfilter.cabal* file.

Cabal allows us to describe several libraries in a single package. A *.cabal* file begins with information that is common to all of the libraries, which is followed by a distinct section for each library:

```
Name:           rwh-bloomfilter
Version:        0.1
License:        BSD3
License-File:   License.txt
Category:       Data
Stability:      experimental
Build-Type:     Simple
```

As we are bundling some C code with our library, we tell Cabal about our C source files:

```
Extra-Source-Files: cbits/lookup3.c cbits/lookup3.h
```

The `extra-source-files` directive has no effect on a build: it directs Cabal to bundle some extra files if we run `runhaskell Setup sdist` to create a source tarball for redistribution.

Property names are case-insensitive

When reading a property (the text before a ":" character), Cabal ignores case, so it treats `extra-source-files` and `Extra-Source-Files` the same.

Dealing with Different Build Setups

Prior to 2007, the standard Haskell libraries were organized in a handful of large packages, of which the biggest was named `base`. This organization tied many unrelated libraries together, so the Haskell community split the `base` package up into a number of more modular libraries. For instance, the array types migrated from `base` into a package named `array`.

A Cabal package needs to specify the other packages that it needs to have present in order to build. This makes it possible for Cabal's command-line interface to automatically download and build a package's dependencies, if necessary. We would like our code to work with as many versions of GHC as possible, regardless of whether they have the modern layout of `base` and numerous other packages. We thus need to be able to specify that we depend on the `array` package if it is present, and `base` alone otherwise.

Cabal provides a generic *configurations* feature, which we can use to selectively enable parts of a *.cabal* file. A build configuration is controlled by a Boolean-valued *flag*. If it is `True`, the text following an `if flag` directive is used; otherwise, the text following the associated `else` is used:

```
Cabal-Version:    >= 1.2

Flag split-base
  Description: Has the base package been split up?
  Default: True
```

```
Flag bytestring-in-base
  Description: Is ByteString in the base or bytestring package?
  Default: False
```

- The configurations feature was introduced in version 1.2 of Cabal, so we specify that our package cannot be built with an older version.

- The meaning of the `split-base` flag should be self-explanatory.

- The `bytestring-in-base` flag deals with a more torturous history. When the `bytestring` package was first created, it was bundled with GHC 6.4 and kept separate from the `base` package. In GHC 6.6, it was incorporated into the `base` package, but it became independent again when the `base` package was split before the release of GHC 6.8.1.

These flags are usually invisible to people building a package, because Cabal handles them automatically. Before we explain what happens, it will help to see the beginning of the `Library` section of our *.cabal* file:

```
Library
  if flag(bytestring-in-base)
    -- bytestring was in base-2.0 and 2.1.1
    Build-Depends: base >= 2.0 && < 2.2
  else
    -- in base 1.0 and 3.0, bytestring is a separate package
    Build-Depends: base < 2.0 || >= 3, bytestring >= 0.9

  if flag(split-base)
    Build-Depends: base >= 3.0, array
  else
    Build-Depends: base < 3.0
```

Cabal creates a package description with the default values of the flags (a missing default is assumed to be `True`). If that configuration can be built (e.g., because all of the needed package versions are available), it will be used. Otherwise, Cabal tries different combinations of flags until it either finds a configuration that it can build or exhausts the alternatives.

For example, if we were to begin with both `split-base` and `bytestring-in-base` set to `True`, Cabal would select the following package dependencies:

```
Build-Depends: base >= 2.0 && < 2.2
Build-Depends: base >= 3.0, array
```

The `base` package cannot simultaneously be newer than `3.0` and older than `2.2`, so Cabal would reject this configuration as inconsistent. For a modern version of GHC, after a few attempts, it would discover this configuration that will indeed build:

```
-- in base 1.0 and 3.0, bytestring is a separate package
Build-Depends: base < 2.0 || >= 3, bytestring >= 0.9
Build-Depends: base >= 3.0, array
```

When we run `runhaskell Setup configure`, we can manually specify the values of flags via the `--flag` option, though we will rarely need to do so in practice.

Compilation Options and Interfacing to C

Continuing with our *.cabal* file, we fill out the remaining details of the Haskell side of our library. If we enable profiling when we build, we want all of our top-level functions to show up in any profiling output:

```
GHC-Prof-Options: -auto-all
```

The `Other-Modules` property lists Haskell modules that are private to the library. Such modules will be invisible to code that uses this package.

When we build this package with GHC, Cabal will pass the options from the `GHC-Options` property to the compiler.

The `-O2` option makes GHC optimize our code aggressively. Code compiled without optimization is very slow, so we should always use `-O2` for production code.

To help ourselves write cleaner code, we usually add the `-Wall` option, which enables all of GHC's warnings. This will cause GHC to issue complaints if it encounters potential problems, such as overlapping patterns; function parameters that are not used; and a myriad of other potential stumbling blocks. While it is often safe to ignore these warnings, we generally prefer to fix up our code to eliminate them. The small added effort usually yields code that is easier to read and maintain.

When we compile with `-fvia-C`, GHC will generate C code and use the system's C compiler to compile it, instead of going straight to assembly language as it usually does. This slows compilation down, but sometimes the C compiler can further improve GHC's optimized code, so it can be worthwhile.

We include `-fvia-C` here mainly to show how to compile using this option:

```
C-Sources:        cbits/lookup3.c
CC-Options:       -O3
Include-Dirs:     cbits
Includes:         lookup3.h
Install-Includes: lookup3.h
```

For the `C-Sources` property, we need only to list files that must be compiled into our library. The `CC-Options` property contains options for the C compiler (`-O3` specifies a high level of optimization). Because our FFI bindings for the Jenkins hash functions refer to the *lookup3.h* header file, we need to tell Cabal where to find the header file. We must also tell it to *install* the header file (`Install-Includes`); otherwise, client code will fail to find the header file when we try to build it.

The value of -fvia-C with the FFI

Compiling with -fvia-C has a useful safety benefit when we write FFI bindings. If we mention a header file in an FFI declaration (e.g., `foreign import "string.h memcpy"`), the C compiler will typecheck the generated Haskell code and ensure that its invocation of the C function is consistent with the C function's prototype in the header file.

If we do not use -fvia-C, we lose that additional layer of safety, making it easy to let simple C type errors slip into our Haskell code. As an example, on most 64-bit machines, a `CInt` is 32 bits wide, and a `CSize` is 64 bits wide. If we accidentally use one type to describe a parameter for an FFI binding when we should use the other, we are likely to cause data corruption or a crash.

Testing with QuickCheck

Before we pay any attention to performance, we want to establish that our Bloom filter behaves correctly. We can easily use QuickCheck to test some basic properties:

```
-- file: examples/BloomCheck.hs
{-# LANGUAGE GeneralizedNewtypeDeriving #-}
module Main where

import BloomFilter.Hash (Hashable)
import Data.Word (Word8, Word32)
import System.Random (Random(..), RandomGen)
import Test.QuickCheck
import qualified BloomFilter.Easy as B
import qualified Data.ByteString as Strict
import qualified Data.ByteString.Lazy as Lazy
```

We will not use the normal `quickCheck` function to test our properties, as the 100 test inputs that it generates do not provide much coverage:

```
-- file: examples/BloomCheck.hs
handyCheck :: Testable a => Int -> a -> IO ()
handyCheck limit = check defaultConfig {
                        configMaxTest = limit
                      , configEvery    = \_ _ -> ""
                      }
```

Our first task is to ensure that if we add a value to a Bloom filter, a subsequent membership test will always report it as present, regardless of the chosen false positive rate or input value.

We will use the `easyList` function to create a Bloom filter. The `Random` instance for `Double` generates numbers in the range zero to one, so QuickCheck can *nearly* supply us with arbitrary false positive rates.

However, we need to ensure that both zero and one are excluded from the false positives we test with. QuickCheck gives us two ways to do this:

Construction

> We specify the range of valid values to generate. QuickCheck provides a `forAll` combinator for this purpose.

Elimination

> When QuickCheck generates an arbitrary value for us, we filter out those that do not fit our criteria, using the (==>) operator. If we reject a value in this way, a test will appear to succeed.

If we can choose either method, it is always preferable to take the constructive approach. To see why, suppose that QuickCheck generates 1,000 arbitrary values for us, and we filter out 800 as unsuitable for some reason. We will *appear* to run 1,000 tests, but only 200 will actually do anything useful.

Following this idea, when we generate desired false positive rates, we could eliminate zeroes and ones from whatever QuickCheck gives us, but instead we construct values in an interval that will always be valid:

```
-- file: examples/BloomCheck.hs
falsePositive :: Gen Double
falsePositive = choose (epsilon, 1 - epsilon)
    where epsilon = 1e-6

(=~>) :: Either a b -> (b -> Bool) -> Bool
k =~> f = either (const True) f k

prop_one_present _ elt =
    forAll falsePositive $ \errRate ->
      B.easyList errRate [elt] =~> \filt ->
        elt `B.elem` filt
```

Our small combinator, (=~>), lets us filter out failures of `easyList`. If it fails, the test automatically passes.

Polymorphic Testing

QuickCheck requires properties to be *monomorphic*. Since we have many different hashable types that we would like to test, we want to avoid having to write the same test in many different ways.

Notice that although our `prop_one_present` function is polymorphic, it ignores its first argument. We use this to simulate monomorphic properties, as follows:

```
ghci> :load BloomCheck
[1 of 1] Compiling Main             ( BloomCheck.hs, interpreted )
Ok, modules loaded: Main.
ghci> :t prop_one_present
prop_one_present :: (Hashable a) => t -> a -> Property
ghci> :t prop_one_present (undefined :: Int)
prop_one_present (undefined :: Int) :: (Hashable a) => a -> Property
```

We can supply any value as the first argument to prop_one_present—all that matters is its *type*, as the same type will be used for the first element of the second argument:

```
ghci> handyCheck 5000 $ prop_one_present (undefined :: Int)
Loading package array-0.1.0.0 ... linking ... done.
Loading package bytestring-0.9.0.1.1 ... linking ... done.
Loading package old-locale-1.0.0.0 ... linking ... done.
Loading package old-time-1.0.0.0 ... linking ... done.
Loading package random-1.0.0.0 ... linking ... done.
Loading package QuickCheck-1.1.0.0 ... linking ... done.
Loading package rwh-bloomfilter-0.1 ... linking ... done.
OK, passed 5000 tests.
ghci> handyCheck 5000 $ prop_one_present (undefined :: Double)
OK, passed 5000 tests.
```

If we populate a Bloom filter with many elements, they should all be present afterwards:

```
-- file: examples/BloomCheck.hs
prop_all_present _ xs =
    forAll falsePositive $ \errRate ->
      B.easyList errRate xs =~> \filt ->
        all (`B.elem` filt) xs
```

This test also succeeds:

```
ghci> handyCheck 2000 $ prop_all_present (undefined :: Int)
OK, passed 2000 tests.
```

Writing Arbitrary Instances for ByteStrings

The QuickCheck library does not provide `Arbitrary` instances for `ByteString` types, so we must write our own. Rather than create a `ByteString` directly, we will use a `pack` function to create one from a `[Word8]`:

```
-- file: examples/BloomCheck.hs
instance Arbitrary Lazy.ByteString where
    arbitrary = Lazy.pack `fmap` arbitrary
    coarbitrary = coarbitrary . Lazy.unpack

instance Arbitrary Strict.ByteString where
    arbitrary = Strict.pack `fmap` arbitrary
    coarbitrary = coarbitrary . Strict.unpack
```

Also missing from QuickCheck are `Arbitrary` instances for the fixed-width types defined in `Data.Word` and `Data.Int`. We need to at least create an `Arbitrary` instance for `Word8`:

```
-- file: examples/BloomCheck.hs
instance Random Word8 where
  randomR = integralRandomR
  random = randomR (minBound, maxBound)

instance Arbitrary Word8 where
    arbitrary = choose (minBound, maxBound)
    coarbitrary = integralCoarbitrary
```

We support these instances with a few common functions so that we can reuse them when writing instances for other integral types:

```
-- file: examples/BloomCheck.hs
integralCoarbitrary n =
    variant $ if m >= 0 then 2*m else 2*(-m) + 1
  where m = fromIntegral n

integralRandomR (a,b) g = case randomR (c,d) g of
                            (x,h) -> (fromIntegral x, h)
    where (c,d) = (fromIntegral a :: Integer,
                   fromIntegral b :: Integer)

instance Random Word32 where
  randomR = integralRandomR
  random = randomR (minBound, maxBound)

instance Arbitrary Word32 where
    arbitrary = choose (minBound, maxBound)
    coarbitrary = integralCoarbitrary
```

With these `Arbitrary` instances created, we can try our existing properties on the ByteString types:

```
ghci> handyCheck 1000 $ prop_one_present (undefined :: Lazy.ByteString)
OK, passed 1000 tests.
ghci> handyCheck 1000 $ prop_all_present (undefined :: Strict.ByteString)
OK, passed 1000 tests.
```

Are Suggested Sizes Correct?

The cost of testing properties of `easyList` increases rapidly as we increase the number of tests to run. We would still like to have some assurance that `easyList` will behave well on huge inputs. Since it is not practical to test this directly, we can use a proxy: will `suggestSizing` give a sensible array size and number of hashes even with extreme inputs?

This is a slightly tricky property to check. We need to vary both the desired false positive rate and the expected capacity. When we looked at some results from the `sizings` function, we saw that the relationship between these values is not easy to predict.

We can try to ignore the complexity:

```
-- file: examples/BloomCheck.hs
prop_suggest_try1 =
  forAll falsePositive $ \errRate ->
    forAll (choose (1,maxBound :: Word32)) $ \cap ->
      case B.suggestSizing (fromIntegral cap) errRate of
        Left err -> False
        Right (bits,hashes) -> bits > 0 && bits < maxBound && hashes > 0
```

Not surprisingly, this gives us a test that is not actually useful:

```
ghci> handyCheck 1000 $ prop_suggest_try1
Falsifiable, after 1 tests:
0.2723862775515961
2484762599
ghci> handyCheck 1000 $ prop_suggest_try1
Falsifiable, after 3 tests:
2.390547635799778e-2
2315209155
```

When we plug the counterexamples that QuickCheck prints into suggestSizings, we
can see that these inputs are rejected because they result in a bit array that would be
too large:

```
ghci> B.suggestSizing 1678125842 8.501133057303545e-3
Left "capacity too large"
```

Since we can't easily predict which combinations will cause this problem, we must
resort to eliminating sizes and false positive rates before they bite us:

```
-- file: examples/BloomCheck.hs
prop_suggest_try2 =
    forAll falsePositive $ \errRate ->
      forAll (choose (1,fromIntegral maxWord32)) $ \cap ->
        let bestSize = fst . minimum $ B.sizings cap errRate
        in bestSize < fromIntegral maxWord32 ==>
            either (const False) sane $ B.suggestSizing cap errRate
  where sane (bits,hashes) = bits > 0 && bits < maxBound && hashes > 0
        maxWord32 = maxBound :: Word32
```

If we try this with a small number of tests, it seems to work well:

```
ghci> handyCheck 1000 $ prop_suggest_try2
OK, passed 1000 tests.
```

On a larger body of tests, we filter out too many combinations:

```
ghci> handyCheck 10000 $ prop_suggest_try2
Arguments exhausted after 2074 tests.
```

To deal with this, we try to reduce the likelihood of generating inputs that we will
subsequently reject:

```
-- file: examples/BloomCheck.hs
prop_suggestions_sane =
    forAll falsePositive $ \errRate ->
      forAll (choose (1,fromIntegral maxWord32 `div` 8)) $ \cap ->
        let size = fst . minimum $ B.sizings cap errRate
        in size < fromIntegral maxWord32 ==>
            either (const False) sane $ B.suggestSizing cap errRate
  where sane (bits,hashes) = bits > 0 && bits < maxBound && hashes > 0
        maxWord32 = maxBound :: Word32
```

Finally, we have a robust looking property:

```
ghci> handyCheck 40000 $ prop_suggestions_sane
OK, passed 40000 tests.
```

Performance Analysis and Tuning

We now have a correctness base line: our QuickCheck tests pass. When we start tweaking performance, we can rerun the tests at any time to ensure that we haven't inadvertently broken anything.

Our first step is to write a small test application that we can use for timing:

```
-- file: examples/WordTest.hs
module Main where

import Control.Parallel.Strategies (NFData(..))
import Control.Monad (forM_, mapM_)
import qualified BloomFilter.Easy as B
import qualified Data.ByteString.Char8 as BS
import Data.Time.Clock (diffUTCTime, getCurrentTime)
import System.Environment (getArgs)
import System.Exit (exitFailure)

timed :: (NFData a) => String -> IO a -> IO a
timed desc act = do
    start <- getCurrentTime
    ret <- act
    end <- rnf ret `seq` getCurrentTime
    putStrLn $ show (diffUTCTime end start) ++ " to " ++ desc
    return ret

instance NFData BS.ByteString where
    rnf _ = ()

instance NFData (B.Bloom a) where
    rnf filt = B.length filt `seq` ()
```

We borrow the `rnf` function that we introduced in "Separating Algorithm from Evaluation" on page 552 to develop a simple timing harness. Out `timed` action ensures that a value is evaluated to normal form in order to accurately capture the cost of evaluating it.

The application creates a Bloom filter from the contents of a file, treating each line as an element to add to the filter:

```
-- file: examples/WordTest.hs
main = do
  args <- getArgs
  let files | null args = ["/usr/share/dict/words"]
            | otherwise = args
  forM_ files $ \file -> do

    words <- timed "read words" $
      BS.lines `fmap` BS.readFile file

    let len = length words
        errRate = 0.01
```

```
    putStrLn $ show len ++ " words"
    putStrLn $ "suggested sizings: " ++
               show (B.suggestSizing (fromIntegral len) errRate)

    filt <- timed "construct filter" $
      case B.easyList errRate words of
        Left errmsg -> do
          putStrLn $ "Error: " ++ errmsg
          exitFailure
        Right filt -> return filt

    timed "query every element" $
      mapM_ print $ filter (not . (`B.elem` filt)) words
```

We use timed to account for the costs of three distinct phases: reading and splitting the data into lines; populating the Bloom filter; and querying every element in it.

If we compile this and run it a few times, we can see that the execution time is just long enough to be interesting, while the timing variation from run to run is small. We have created a plausible-looking microbenchmark:

```
$ ghc -O2  --make WordTest
[1 of 1] Compiling Main            ( WordTest.hs, WordTest.o )
Linking WordTest ...
$ ./WordTest
0.196347s to read words
479829 words
1.063537s to construct filter
4602978 bits
0.766899s to query every element
$ ./WordTest
0.179284s to read words
479829 words
1.069363s to construct filter
4602978 bits
0.780079s to query every element
```

Profile-Driven Performance Tuning

To understand where our program might benefit from some tuning, we rebuild it and run it with profiling enabled.

Since we already built *WordTest* and have not subsequently changed it, if we rerun ghc to enable profiling support, it will quite reasonably decide to do nothing. We must force it to rebuild, which we accomplish by updating the filesystem's idea of when we last edited the source file:

```
$ touch WordTest.hs
$ ghc -O2 -prof -auto-all --make WordTest
[1 of 1] Compiling Main            ( WordTest.hs, WordTest.o )
Linking WordTest ...

$ ./WordTest +RTS -p
0.322675s to read words
```

```
479829 words
suggested sizings: Right (4602978,7)
2.475339s to construct filter
1.964404s to query every element

$ head -20 WordTest.prof
total time  =          4.10 secs  (205 ticks @ 20 ms)
total alloc = 2,752,287,168 bytes  (excludes profiling overheads)

COST CENTRE                  MODULE                %time %alloc

doubleHash                   BloomFilter.Hash       48.8  66.4
indices                      BloomFilter.Mutable    13.7  15.8
elem                         BloomFilter             9.8   1.3
hashByteString               BloomFilter.Hash        6.8   3.8
easyList                     BloomFilter.Easy        5.9   0.3
hashIO                       BloomFilter.Hash        4.4   5.3
main                         Main                    4.4   3.8
insert                       BloomFilter.Mutable     2.9   0.0
len                          BloomFilter             2.0   2.4
length                       BloomFilter.Mutable     1.5   1.0
```

Our `doubleHash` function immediately leaps out as a huge time and memory sink.

Always profile before—and while—you tune!

Before our first profiling run, we did not expect `doubleHash` to even appear in the top 10 of "hot" functions, much less dominate it. Without this knowledge, we would probably have started tuning something entirely irrelevant.

Recall that the body of `doubleHash` is an innocuous list comprehension:

```
-- file: BloomFilter/Hash.hs
doubleHash :: Hashable a => Int -> a -> [Word32]
doubleHash numHashes value = [h1 + h2 * i | i <- [0..num]]
    where h   = hashSalt 0x9150a946c4a8966e value
          h1  = fromIntegral (h `shiftR` 32) .&. maxBound
          h2  = fromIntegral h
          num = fromIntegral numHashes
```

Since the function returns a list, it makes *some* sense that it allocates so much memory, but when code this simple performs so badly, we should be suspicious.

Faced with a performance mystery, the suspicious mind will naturally want to inspect the output of the compiler. We don't need to start scrabbling through assembly language dumps: it's best to start at a higher level.

GHC's `-ddump-simpl` option prints out the code that it produces after performing all of its high-level optimizations:

```
$ ghc -O2 -c -ddump-simpl --make BloomFilter/Hash.hs > dump.txt
[1 of 1] Compiling BloomFilter.Hash ( BloomFilter/Hash.hs )
```

The file thus produced is about 1,000 lines long. Most of the names in it are mangled somewhat from their original Haskell representations. Even so, searching for doubleHash will immediately drop us at the definition of the function. For example, here is how we might start exactly at the right spot from a Unix shell:

```
$ less +/doubleHash dump.txt
```

It can be difficult to start reading the output of GHC's simplifier. There are many automatically generated names, and the code has many obscure annotations. We can make substantial progress by ignoring things that we do not understand, focusing on those that look familiar. The Core language shares some features with regular Haskell, notably type signatures, let for variable binding, and case for pattern matching.

If we skim through the definition of doubleHash, we will arrive at a section that looks something like this:

```
__letrec { ❶
  go_s1YC :: [GHC.Word.Word32] -> [GHC.Word.Word32] ❷
  [Arity 1
   Str: DmdType S]
  go_s1YC =
    \ (ds_a1DR :: [GHC.Word.Word32]) ->
      case ds_a1DR of wild_a1DS {
    [] -> GHC.Base.[] @ GHC.Word.Word32; ❸
    : y_a1DW ys_a1DX -> ❹
      GHC.Base.: @ GHC.Word.Word32 ❺
        (case h1_s1YA of wild1_a1Mk { GHC.Word.W32# x#_a1Mm -> ❻
         case h2_s1Yy of wild2_a1Mu { GHC.Word.W32# x#1_a1Mw ->
         case y_a1DW of wild11_a1My { GHC.Word.W32# y#_a1MA ->
         GHC.Word.W32# ❼
           (GHC.Prim.narrow32Word#
           (GHC.Prim.plusWord# ❽
             x#_a1Mm (GHC.Prim.narrow32Word#
                           (GHC.Prim.timesWord# x#1_a1Mw y#_a1MA))))
         }
         }
         })
        (go_s1YC ys_a1DX) ❾
      };
  } in
    go_s1YC ❿
      (GHC.Word.$w$dmenumFromTo2
        __word 0 (GHC.Prim.narrow32Word# (GHC.Prim.int2Word# ww_s1X3)))
```

This is the body of the list comprehension. It may seem daunting, but we can look through it piece by piece and find that it is not, after all, so complicated:

❶ A __letrec is equivalent to a normal Haskell let.

❷ GHC compiled the body of our list comprehension into a loop named go_s1YC.

❸ If our case expression matches the empty list, we return the empty list. This is re-assuringly familiar.

❹ This pattern would read in Haskell as (y_a1DW:ys_a1DX). The (:) constructor appears before its operands because the Core language uses prefix notation exclusively for simplicity.

❺ This is an application of the (:) constructor. The @ notation indicates that the first operand will have type Word32.

❻ Each of the three case expressions *unboxes* a Word32 value, to get at the primitive value inside. First to be unboxed is h1 (named h1_s1YA here), then h2, then the current list element, y.

The unboxing occurs via pattern matching: W32# is the constructor that boxes a primitive value. By convention, primitive types and values, and functions that use them, always contains a # somewhere in their name.

❼ Here, we apply the W32# constructor to a value of the primitive type Word32#, in order to give a normal value of type Word32.

❽ The plusWord# and timesWord# functions add and multiply primitive unsigned integers.

❾ This is the second argument to the (:) constructor, in which the go_s1YC function applies itself recursively.

❿ Here, we apply our list comprehension loop function. Its argument is the Core translation of the expression [0..n].

From reading the Core for this code, we can see two interesting behaviors:

- We are creating a list, and then immediately deconstructing it in the go_s1YC loop.

  GHC can often spot this pattern of production followed immediately by consumption, and transform it into a loop in which no allocation occurs. This class of transformation is called *fusion*, because the producer and consumer become fused together. Unfortunately, it is not occurring here.

- The repeated unboxing of h1 and h2 in the body of the loop is wasteful.

To address these problems, we make a few tiny changes to our doubleHash function:

```
-- file: BloomFilter/Hash.hs
doubleHash :: Hashable a => Int -> a -> [Word32]
doubleHash numHashes value = go 0
    where go n | n == num  = []
               | otherwise = h1 + h2 * n : go (n + 1)

          !h1 = fromIntegral (h `shiftR` 32) .&. maxBound
          !h2 = fromIntegral h

          h   = hashSalt 0x9150a946c4a8966e value
          num = fromIntegral numHashes
```

We manually fused the [0..num] expression and the code that consumes it into a single loop. We added strictness annotations to h1 and h2. And nothing more. This has turned a six-line function into an eight-line function. What effect does our change have on Core output?

```
__letrec {
  $wgo_s1UH :: GHC.Prim.Word# -> [GHC.Word.Word32]
  [Arity 1
   Str: DmdType L]
  $wgo_s1UH =
    \ (ww2_s1St :: GHC.Prim.Word#) ->
      case GHC.Prim.eqWord# ww2_s1St a_s1T1 of wild1_X2m {
    GHC.Base.False ->
      GHC.Base.: @ GHC.Word.Word32
        (GHC.Word.W32#
         (GHC.Prim.narrow32Word#
          (GHC.Prim.plusWord#
           ipv_s1B2
           (GHC.Prim.narrow32Word#
          (GHC.Prim.timesWord# ipv1_s1AZ ww2_s1St)))))
          ($wgo_s1UH (GHC.Prim.narrow32Word#
                      (GHC.Prim.plusWord# ww2_s1St __word 1)));
    GHC.Base.True -> GHC.Base.[] @ GHC.Word.Word32
      };
} in  $wgo_s1UH __word 0
```

Our new function has compiled down to a simple counting loop. This is very encouraging, but how does it actually perform?

```
$ touch WordTest.hs
$ ghc -O2 -prof -auto-all --make WordTest
[1 of 1] Compiling Main            ( WordTest.hs, WordTest.o )
Linking WordTest ...

$ ./WordTest +RTS -p
0.304352s to read words
479829 words
suggested sizings: Right (4602978,7)
1.516229s to construct filter
1.069305s to query every element
~/src/darcs/book/examples/ch27/examples $ head -20 WordTest.prof
total time  =        3.68 secs   (184 ticks @ 20 ms)
total alloc = 2,644,805,536 bytes (excludes profiling overheads)
```

COST CENTRE	MODULE	%time	%alloc
doubleHash	BloomFilter.Hash	45.1	65.0
indices	BloomFilter.Mutable	19.0	16.4
elem	BloomFilter	12.5	1.3
insert	BloomFilter.Mutable	7.6	0.0
easyList	BloomFilter.Easy	4.3	0.3
len	BloomFilter	3.3	2.5
hashByteString	BloomFilter.Hash	3.3	4.0
main	Main	2.7	4.0
hashIO	BloomFilter.Hash	2.2	5.5
length	BloomFilter.Mutable	0.0	1.0

Our tweak has improved performance by about 11%—a good result for such a small change.

1. Our use of `genericLength` in `easyList` will cause our function to loop infinitely if we supply an infinite list. Fix this.

2. Difficult: write a QuickCheck property that checks whether the observed false positive rate is close to the requested false positive rate.

CHAPTER 27

Sockets and Syslog

Basic Networking

In several earlier chapters of this book, we discussed services that operate over a network. Two examples are client/server databases and web services. When the need arises to devise a new protocol or to communicate with a protocol that doesn't have an existing helper library in Haskell, you'll need to use the lower-level networking tools in the Haskell library.

In this chapter, we will discuss these lower-level tools. Network communication is a broad topic with entire books devoted to it. We will show you how to use Haskell to apply the low-level network knowledge you already have.

Haskell's networking functions almost always correspond directly to familiar C function calls. As most other languages also layer on top of C, you should find this interface familiar.

Communicating with UDP

UDP breaks data down into packets. It does not ensure that the data reaches its destination or it reaches it only once. It does use checksumming to ensure that packets that arrive have not been corrupted. UDP tends to be used in applications that are performance- or latency-sensitive, in which each individual packet of data is less important than the overall performance of the system. It may also be used where the TCP behavior isn't the most efficient, such as ones that send short, discrete messages. Examples of systems that tend to use UDP include audio and video conferencing, time synchronization, network-based filesystems, and logging systems.

UDP Client Example: syslog

The traditional Unix syslog service allows programs to send log messages over a network to a central server that records them. Some programs are quite performance-sensitive and may generate a large volume of messages. In these programs, it could be more important to have the logging impose a minimal performance overhead than to guarantee every message is logged. Moreover, it may be desirable to continue program operation even if the logging server is unreachable. For this reason, UDP is one of the protocols syslog supports for the transmission of log messages. The protocol is simple; we present a Haskell implementation of a client here:

```
-- file: ch27/syslogclient.hs
import Data.Bits
import Network.Socket
import Network.BSD
import Data.List
import SyslogTypes

data SyslogHandle =
    SyslogHandle {slSocket :: Socket,
                  slProgram :: String,
                  slAddress :: SockAddr}

openlog :: HostName           -- ^ Remote hostname, or localhost
        -> String             -- ^ Port number or name; 514 is default
        -> String             -- ^ Name to log under
        -> IO SyslogHandle    -- ^ Handle to use for logging
openlog hostname port progname =
    do -- Look up the hostname and port.  Either raises an exception
       -- or returns a nonempty list.  First element in that list
       -- is supposed to be the best option.
       addrinfos <- getAddrInfo Nothing (Just hostname) (Just port)
       let serveraddr = head addrinfos

       -- Establish a socket for communication
       sock <- socket (addrFamily serveraddr) Datagram defaultProtocol

       -- Save off the socket, program name, and server address in a handle
       return $ SyslogHandle sock progname (addrAddress serveraddr)

syslog :: SyslogHandle -> Facility -> Priority -> String -> IO ()
syslog syslogh fac pri msg =
    sendstr sendmsg
    where code = makeCode fac pri
          sendmsg = "<" ++ show code ++ ">" ++ (slProgram syslogh) ++
                    ": " ++ msg

          -- Send until everything is done
          sendstr :: String -> IO ()
          sendstr [] = return ()
          sendstr omsg = do sent <- sendTo (slSocket syslogh) omsg
                                    (slAddress syslogh)
                            sendstr (genericDrop sent omsg)
```

```
closelog :: SyslogHandle -> IO ()
closelog syslogh = sClose (slSocket syslogh)

{- | Convert a facility and a priority into a syslog code -}
makeCode :: Facility -> Priority -> Int
makeCode fac pri =
    let faccode = codeOfFac fac
        pricode = fromEnum pri
        in
          (faccode `shiftL` 3) .|. pricode
```

This also requires *SyslogTypes.hs*, shown here:

```
-- file: ch27/SyslogTypes.hs
module SyslogTypes where
{- | Priorities define how important a log message is. -}

data Priority =
            DEBUG               -- ^ Debug messages
          | INFO                -- ^ Information
          | NOTICE              -- ^ Normal runtime conditions
          | WARNING             -- ^ General Warnings
          | ERROR               -- ^ General Errors
          | CRITICAL            -- ^ Severe situations
          | ALERT               -- ^ Take immediate action
          | EMERGENCY           -- ^ System is unusable
                    deriving (Eq, Ord, Show, Read, Enum)

{- | Facilities are used by the system to determine where messages
are sent. -}

data Facility =
            KERN                -- ^ Kernel messages
          | USER                -- ^ General userland messages
          | MAIL                -- ^ E-Mail system
          | DAEMON              -- ^ Daemon (server process) messages
          | AUTH                -- ^ Authentication or security messages
          | SYSLOG              -- ^ Internal syslog messages
          | LPR                 -- ^ Printer messages
          | NEWS                -- ^ Usenet news
          | UUCP                -- ^ UUCP messages
          | CRON                -- ^ Cron messages
          | AUTHPRIV            -- ^ Private authentication messages
          | FTP                 -- ^ FTP messages
          | LOCAL0
          | LOCAL1
          | LOCAL2
          | LOCAL3
          | LOCAL4
          | LOCAL5
          | LOCAL6
          | LOCAL7
                    deriving (Eq, Show, Read)

facToCode = [
```

```
                    (KERN, 0),
                    (USER, 1),
                    (MAIL, 2),
                    (DAEMON, 3),
                    (AUTH, 4),
                    (SYSLOG, 5),
                    (LPR, 6),
                    (NEWS, 7),
                    (UUCP, 8),
                    (CRON, 9),
                    (AUTHPRIV, 10),
                    (FTP, 11),
                    (LOCAL0, 16),
                    (LOCAL1, 17),
                    (LOCAL2, 18),
                    (LOCAL3, 19),
                    (LOCAL4, 20),
                    (LOCAL5, 21),
                    (LOCAL6, 22),
                    (LOCAL7, 23)
          ]

codeToFac = map (\(x, y) -> (y, x)) facToCode


{- | We can't use enum here because the numbering is discontiguous -}
codeOfFac :: Facility -> Int
codeOfFac f = case lookup f facToCode of
                Just x -> x
                _ -> error $ "Internal error in codeOfFac"

facOfCode :: Int -> Facility
facOfCode f = case lookup f codeToFac of
                Just x -> x
                _ -> error $ "Invalid code in facOfCode"
```

With ghci, you can send a message to a local syslog server. You can use either the example syslog server presented in this chapter or an existing syslog server like you would typically find on Linux or other POSIX systems. Note that most of these disable the UDP port by default, and you may need to enable UDP before your vendor-supplied syslog daemon will display received messages.

If you were sending a message to a syslog server on the local system, you might use a command such as this:

```
ghci> :load syslogclient.hs
[1 of 2] Compiling SyslogTypes      ( SyslogTypes.hs, interpreted )
[2 of 2] Compiling Main             ( syslogclient.hs, interpreted )
Ok, modules loaded: SyslogTypes, Main.
ghci> h <- openlog "localhost" "514" "testprog"
Loading package parsec-2.1.0.1 ... linking ... done.
Loading package network-2.2.0.0 ... linking ... done.
ghci> syslog h USER INFO "This is my message"
ghci> closelog h
```

UDP Syslog Server

UDP servers will bind to a specific port on the server machine. They will accept packets directed to that port and process them. Since UDP is a stateless, packet-oriented protocol, programmers normally use a call such as `recvFrom` to receive both the data and information about the machine that sent it, which is used for sending back a response:

```
-- file: ch27/syslogserver.hs
import Data.Bits
import Network.Socket
import Network.BSD
import Data.List

type HandlerFunc = SockAddr -> String -> IO ()

serveLog :: String              -- ^ Port number or name; 514 is default
         -> HandlerFunc         -- ^ Function to handle incoming messages
         -> IO ()
serveLog port handlerfunc = withSocketsDo $
    do -- Look up the port.  Either raises an exception or returns
       -- a nonempty list.
       addrinfos <- getAddrInfo
                    (Just (defaultHints {addrFlags = [AI_PASSIVE]}))
                    Nothing (Just port)
       let serveraddr = head addrinfos

       -- Create a socket
       sock <- socket (addrFamily serveraddr) Datagram defaultProtocol

       -- Bind it to the address we're listening to
       bindSocket sock (addrAddress serveraddr)

       -- Loop forever processing incoming data.  Ctrl-C to abort.
       procMessages sock
    where procMessages sock =
              do -- Receive one UDP packet, maximum length 1024 bytes,
                 -- and save its content into msg and its source
                 -- IP and port into addr
                 (msg, _, addr) <- recvFrom sock 1024
                 -- Handle it
                 handlerfunc addr msg
                 -- And process more messages
                 procMessages sock

-- A simple handler that prints incoming packets
plainHandler :: HandlerFunc
plainHandler addr msg =
    putStrLn $ "From " ++ show addr ++ ": " ++ msg
```

You can run this in ghci. A call to `serveLog "1514" plainHandler` will set up a UDP server on port 1514 that will use `plainHandler` to print out every incoming UDP packet on that port. Ctrl-C will terminate the program.

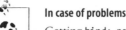

In case of problems

Getting `bind: permission denied` when testing this? Make sure you use a port number greater than 1024. Some operating systems only allow the `root` user to bind to ports less than 1024.

Communicating with TCP

TCP is designed to make data transfer over the Internet as reliable as possible. TCP traffic is a stream of data. While this stream gets broken up into individual packets by the operating system, the packet boundaries are neither known nor relevant to applications. TCP guarantees that, if traffic is delivered to the application at all, it arrives intact, unmodified, exactly once, and in order. Obviously, things such as a broken wire can cause traffic to not be delivered, and no protocol can overcome those limitations.

This brings with it some trade-offs compared with UDP. First of all, there are a few packets that must be sent at the start of the TCP conversation to establish the link. For very short conversations, then, UDP would have a performance advantage. Also, TCP tries very hard to get data through. If one end of a conversation tries to send data to the remote but doesn't receive an acknowledgment back, it will periodically retransmit the data for some time before giving up. This makes TCP robust in the face of dropped packets. However, it also means that TCP is not the best choice for real-time protocols that involve things such as live audio or video.

Handling Multiple TCP Streams

With TCP, connections are stateful. That means that there is a dedicated logical "channel" between a client and server, rather than just one-off packets as with UDP. This makes things easy for client developers. Server applications almost always will want to be able to handle more than one TCP connection at once. How then to do this?

On the server side, you will first create a socket and bind to a port, just like with UDP. Instead of repeatedly listening for data from any location, your main loop will be around the `accept` call. Each time a client connects, the server's operating system allocates a new socket for it. So we have the *master* socket, used only to listen for incoming connections, and never to transmit data. We also have the potential for multiple *child* sockets to be used at once, each corresponding to a logical TCP conversation.

In Haskell, you will usually use `forkIO` to create a separate lightweight thread to handle each conversation with a child. Haskell has an efficient internal implementation of this that performs quite well.

TCP Syslog Server

Suppose we want to reimplement syslog using TCP instead of UDP. We could say that a single message is defined not by being in a single packet, but by a trailing newline character '\n'. Any given client could send zero or more messages to the server using a given TCP connection. Here's how we might write that:

```
-- file: ch27/syslogtcpserver.hs
import Data.Bits
import Network.Socket
import Network.BSD
import Data.List
import Control.Concurrent
import Control.Concurrent.MVar
import System.IO

type HandlerFunc = SockAddr -> String -> IO ()

serveLog :: String              -- ^ Port number or name; 514 is default
         -> HandlerFunc         -- ^ Function to handle incoming messages
         -> IO ()
serveLog port handlerfunc = withSocketsDo $
    do -- Look up the port.  Either raises an exception or returns
       -- a nonempty list.
       addrinfos <- getAddrInfo
                    (Just (defaultHints {addrFlags = [AI_PASSIVE]}))
                    Nothing (Just port)
       let serveraddr = head addrinfos

       -- Create a socket
       sock <- socket (addrFamily serveraddr) Stream defaultProtocol

       -- Bind it to the address we're listening to
       bindSocket sock (addrAddress serveraddr)

       -- Start listening for connection requests.  Maximum queue size
       -- of 5 connection requests waiting to be accepted.
       listen sock 5

       -- Create a lock to use for synchronizing access to the handler
       lock <- newMVar ()

       -- Loop forever waiting for connections.  Ctrl-C to abort.
       procRequests lock sock

    where
          -- | Process incoming connection requests
          procRequests :: MVar () -> Socket -> IO ()
          procRequests lock mastersock =
              do (connsock, clientaddr) <- accept mastersock
                 handle lock clientaddr
                    "syslogtcpserver.hs: client connnected"
                 forkIO $ procMessages lock connsock clientaddr
                 procRequests lock mastersock
```

```
-- | Process incoming messages
procMessages :: MVar () -> Socket -> SockAddr -> IO ()
procMessages lock connsock clientaddr =
    do connhdl <- socketToHandle connsock ReadMode
       hSetBuffering connhdl LineBuffering
       messages <- hGetContents connhdl
       mapM_ (handle lock clientaddr) (lines messages)
       hClose connhdl
       handle lock clientaddr
           "syslogtcpserver.hs: client disconnected"

-- Lock the handler before passing data to it.
handle :: MVar () -> HandlerFunc
-- This type is the same as
-- handle :: MVar () -> SockAddr -> String -> IO ()
handle lock clientaddr msg =
    withMVar lock
        (\a -> handlerfunc clientaddr msg >> return a)

-- A simple handler that prints incoming packets
plainHandler :: HandlerFunc
plainHandler addr msg =
    putStrLn $ "From " ++ show addr ++ ": " ++ msg
```

For our SyslogTypes implementation, see "UDP Client Example: syslog" on page 612.

Let's look at this code. Our main loop is in procRequests, where we loop forever waiting for new connections from clients. The accept call blocks until a client connects. When a client connects, we get a new socket and the client's address. We pass a message to the handler about that, and then use forkIO to create a thread to handle the data from that client. This thread runs procMessages.

When dealing with TCP data, it's often convenient to convert a socket into a Haskell Handle. We do so here, and explicitly set the buffering—an important point for TCP communication. Next, we set up lazy reading from the socket's Handle. For each incoming line, we pass it to handle. After there is no more data—because the remote end has closed the socket—we output a message about that.

Since we may be handling multiple incoming messages at once, we need to ensure that we're not writing out multiple messages at once in the handler. That could result in garbled output. We use a simple lock to serialize access to the handler, and write a simple handle function to handle that.

We can test this with the client we'll present next, or we can even use the telnet program to connect to this server. Each line of text we send to it will be printed on the display by the server. Let's try it out:

```
ghci> :load syslogtcpserver.hs
[1 of 1] Compiling Main              ( syslogtcpserver.hs, interpreted )
Ok, modules loaded: Main.
ghci> serveLog "10514" plainHandler
Loading package parsec-2.1.0.0 ... linking ... done.
Loading package network-2.1.0.0 ... linking ... done.
```

At this point, the server will begin listening for connections at port 10514. It will not appear to be doing anything until a client connects. We could use telnet to connect to the server:

```
~$ telnet localhost 10514
Trying 127.0.0.1...
Connected to localhost.
Escape character is '^]'.
Test message
^]
telnet> quit
Connection closed.
```

Meanwhile, in our other terminal running the TCP server, you'll see something like this:

```
From 127.0.0.1:38790: syslogtcpserver.hs: client connnected
From 127.0.0.1:38790: Test message
From 127.0.0.1:38790: syslogtcpserver.hs: client disconnected
```

This shows that a client connected from port 38790 on the local machine (127.0.0.1). After it connected, it sent one message and disconnected. When you are acting as a TCP client, the operating system assigns an unused port for you. This port number will usually be different each time you run the program.

TCP Syslog Client

Now, let's write a client for our TCP syslog protocol. This client will be similar to the UDP client, but there are some changes. First, since TCP is a streaming protocol, we can send data using a Handle rather than using the lower-level socket operations. Second, we no longer need to store the destination address in the SyslogHandle, since we will be using connect to establish the TCP connection. Finally, we need a way to know where one message ends and the next begins. With UDP, that was easy because each message was a discrete logical packet. With TCP, we'll just use the newline character '\n' as the end-of-message marker, although that means that no individual message may contain the newline. Here's our code:

```
-- file: ch27/syslogtcpclient.hs
import Data.Bits
import Network.Socket
import Network.BSD
import Data.List
import SyslogTypes
import System.IO

data SyslogHandle =
    SyslogHandle {slHandle :: Handle,
                  slProgram :: String}

openlog :: HostName        -- ^ Remote hostname, or localhost
        -> String          -- ^ Port number or name; 514 is default
        -> String          -- ^ Name to log under
        -> IO SyslogHandle  -- ^ Handle to use for logging
```

```
openlog hostname port progname =
    do -- Look up the hostname and port.  Either raises an exception
       -- or returns a nonempty list.  First element in that list
       -- is supposed to be the best option.
       addrinfos <- getAddrInfo Nothing (Just hostname) (Just port)
       let serveraddr = head addrinfos

       -- Establish a socket for communication
       sock <- socket (addrFamily serveraddr) Stream defaultProtocol

       -- Mark the socket for keep-alive handling since it may be idle
       -- for long periods of time
       setSocketOption sock KeepAlive 1

       -- Connect to server
       connect sock (addrAddress serveraddr)

       -- Make a Handle out of it for convenience
       h <- socketToHandle sock WriteMode

       -- We're going to set buffering to BlockBuffering and then
       -- explicitly call hFlush after each message, below, so that
       -- messages get logged immediately
       hSetBuffering h (BlockBuffering Nothing)

       -- Save off the socket, program name, and server address in a handle
       return $ SyslogHandle h progname

syslog :: SyslogHandle -> Facility -> Priority -> String -> IO ()
syslog syslogh fac pri msg =
    do hPutStrLn (slHandle syslogh) sendmsg
       -- Make sure that we send data immediately
       hFlush (slHandle syslogh)
    where code = makeCode fac pri
          sendmsg = "<" ++ show code ++ ">" ++ (slProgram syslogh) ++
                    ": " ++ msg

closelog :: SyslogHandle -> IO ()
closelog syslogh = hClose (slHandle syslogh)

{- | Convert a facility and a priority into a syslog code -}
makeCode :: Facility -> Priority -> Int
makeCode fac pri =
    let faccode = codeOfFac fac
        pricode = fromEnum pri
        in
          (faccode `shiftL` 3) .|. pricode
```

We can try it out under ghci. If you still have the TCP server running from earlier, your session might look something like this:

```
ghci> :load syslogtcpclient.hs
Loading package base ... linking ... done.
[1 of 2] Compiling SyslogTypes      ( SyslogTypes.hs, interpreted )
[2 of 2] Compiling Main             ( syslogtcpclient.hs, interpreted )
Ok, modules loaded: Main, SyslogTypes.
ghci> openlog "localhost" "10514" "tcptest"
Loading package parsec-2.1.0.0 ... linking ... done.
Loading package network-2.1.0.0 ... linking ... done.
ghci> sl <- openlog "localhost" "10514" "tcptest"
ghci> syslog sl USER INFO "This is my TCP message"
ghci> syslog sl USER INFO "This is my TCP message again"
ghci> closelog sl
```

Over on the server, you'll see something like this:

```
From 127.0.0.1:46319: syslogtcpserver.hs: client connnected
From 127.0.0.1:46319: <9>tcptest: This is my TCP message
From 127.0.0.1:46319: <9>tcptest: This is my TCP message again
From 127.0.0.1:46319: syslogtcpserver.hs: client disconnected
```

The <9> is the priority and facility code being sent along, just as it was with UDP.

CHAPTER 28

Software Transactional Memory

In the traditional threaded model of concurrent programming, when we share data among threads, we keep it consistent using locks, and we notify threads of changes using condition variables. Haskell's MVar mechanism improves somewhat upon these tools, but it still suffers from all of the same problems:

- Race conditions due to forgotten locks
- Deadlocks resulting from inconsistent lock ordering
- Corruption caused by uncaught exceptions
- Lost wakeups induced by omitted notifications

These problems frequently affect even the smallest concurrent programs, but the difficulties they pose become far worse in larger code bases or under heavy load.

For instance, a program with a few big locks is somewhat tractable to write and debug, but contention for those locks will clobber us under heavy load. If we react with finer-grained locking, it becomes *far* harder to keep our software working at all. The additional bookkeeping will hurt performance even when loads are light.

The Basics

Software transactional memory (STM) gives us a few simple, but powerful, tools with which we can address most of these problems. We execute a block of actions as a transaction using the atomically combinator. Once we enter the block, other threads cannot see any modifications we make until we exit, nor can our thread see any changes made by other threads. These two properties mean that our execution is *isolated*.

Upon exit from a transaction, exactly one of the following things will occur:

- If no other thread concurrently modifies the same data as us, all of our modifications will simultaneously become visible to other threads.

- Otherwise, our modifications are discarded without being performed, and our block of actions is automatically restarted.

This all-or-nothing nature of an `atomically` block is referred to as *atomic*, hence the name of the combinator. If you have used databases that support transactions, you should find that working with STM feels quite familiar.

Some Simple Examples

In a multiplayer role playing game, a player's character will have some state such as health, possessions, and money. To explore the world of STM, let's start with a few simple functions and types based around working with some character state for a game. We will refine our code as we learn more about the API.

The STM API is provided by the `stm` package, and its modules are in the `Control.Concurrent.STM` hierarchy:

```
-- file: ch28/GameInventory.hs
{-# LANGUAGE GeneralizedNewtypeDeriving #-}

import Control.Concurrent.STM
import Control.Monad

data Item = Scroll
          | Wand
          | Banjo
            deriving (Eq, Ord, Show)

newtype Gold = Gold Int
    deriving (Eq, Ord, Show, Num)

newtype HitPoint = HitPoint Int
    deriving (Eq, Ord, Show, Num)

type Inventory = TVar [Item]
type Health = TVar HitPoint
type Balance = TVar Gold

data Player = Player {
      balance :: Balance,
      health :: Health,
      inventory :: Inventory
    }
```

The `TVar` parameterized type is a mutable variable that we can read or write inside an `atomically` block. For simplicity, we represent a player's inventory as a list of items.

Notice, too, that we use `newtype` declarations so that we cannot accidentally confuse wealth with health.

To perform a basic transfer of money from one `Balance` to another, all we have to do is adjust the values in each `TVar`:

```
-- file: ch28/GameInventory.hs
basicTransfer qty fromBal toBal = do
  fromQty <- readTVar fromBal
  toQty   <- readTVar toBal
  writeTVar fromBal (fromQty - qty)
  writeTVar toBal   (toQty + qty)
```

Let's write a small function to try this out:

```
-- file: ch28/GameInventory.hs
transferTest = do
  alice <- newTVar (12 :: Gold)
  bob   <- newTVar 4
  basicTransfer 3 alice bob
  liftM2 (,) (readTVar alice) (readTVar bob)
```

If we run this in `ghci`, it behaves as we should expect:

```
ghci> :load GameInventory
[1 of 1] Compiling Main             ( GameInventory.hs, interpreted )
Ok, modules loaded: Main.
ghci> atomically transferTest
Loading package array-0.1.0.0 ... linking ... done.
Loading package stm-2.1.1.1 ... linking ... done.
(Gold 9,Gold 7)
```

The properties of atomicity and isolation guarantee that if another thread sees a change in `bob`'s balance, they will also be able to see the modification of `alice`'s balance.

Even in a concurrent program, we strive to keep as much of our code as possible purely functional. This makes our code easier to reason about and to test. It also gives the underlying STM engine less work to do, since the data involved is not transactional. Here's a pure function that removes an item from the list we use to represent a player's inventory:

```
-- file: ch28/GameInventory.hs
removeInv :: Eq a => a -> [a] -> Maybe [a]
removeInv x xs =
    case takeWhile (/= x) xs of
      (_:ys) -> Just ys
      []     -> Nothing
```

The result uses `Maybe` so that we can tell whether the item was actually present in the player's inventory.

Here is a transactional function to give an item to another player, slightly complicated by the need to determine whether the donor actually *has* the item in question:

```
-- file: ch28/GameInventory.hs
maybeGiveItem item fromInv toInv = do
  fromList <- readTVar fromInv
  case removeInv item fromList of
    Nothing      -> return False
    Just newList -> do
      writeTVar fromInv newList
      destItems <- readTVar toInv
      writeTVar toInv (item : destItems)
      return True
```

STM and Safety

If we are to provide atomic, isolated transactions, it is critical that we cannot either deliberately or accidentally escape from an `atomically` block. Haskell's type system enforces this on our behalf, via the STM monad:

```
ghci> :type atomically
atomically :: STM a -> IO a
```

The `atomically` block takes an action in the STM monad, executes it, and makes its result available to us in the IO monad. This is the monad in which all transactional code executes. For instance, the functions that we have seen for manipulating TVar values operate in the STM monad:

```
ghci> :type newTVar
newTVar :: a -> STM (TVar a)
ghci> :type readTVar
readTVar :: TVar a -> STM a
ghci> :type writeTVar
writeTVar :: TVar a -> a -> STM ()
```

This is also true of the transactional functions we defined earlier:

```
-- file: ch28/GameInventory.hs
basicTransfer :: Gold -> Balance -> Balance -> STM ()
maybeGiveItem :: Item -> Inventory -> Inventory -> STM Bool
```

The STM monad does not let us perform I/O or manipulate nontransactional mutable state, such as MVar values. This lets us avoid operations that might violate the transactional guarantees.

Retrying a Transaction

The API of our `maybeGiveItem` function is somewhat awkward. It gives an item only if the character actually possesses it, which is reasonable, but by returning a Bool, it complicates the code of its callers. Here is an item sale function that has to look at the result of `maybeGiveItem` to decide what to do next:

```
-- file: ch28/GameInventory.hs
maybeSellItem :: Item -> Gold -> Player -> Player -> STM Bool
maybeSellItem item price buyer seller = do
```

```
    given <- maybeGiveItem item (inventory seller) (inventory buyer)
    if given
      then do
        basicTransfer price (balance buyer) (balance seller)
        return True
      else return False
```

Not only do we have to check whether the item was given, we have to propagate an indication of success back to our caller. The complexity thus cascades outwards.

There is a more elegant way to handle transactions that cannot succeed. The STM API provides a retry action that will immediately terminate an atomically block that cannot proceed. As the name suggests, when this occurs, execution of the block is restarted from scratch, with any previous modifications unperformed. Here is a rewrite of maybeGiveItem to use retry:

```
-- file: ch28/GameInventory.hs
giveItem :: Item -> Inventory -> Inventory -> STM ()

giveItem item fromInv toInv = do
  fromList <- readTVar fromInv
  case removeInv item fromList of
    Nothing -> retry
    Just newList -> do
      writeTVar fromInv newList
      readTVar toInv >>= writeTVar toInv . (item :)
```

Our basicTransfer from earlier had a different kind of flaw: it did not check the sender's balance to see if she had sufficient money to transfer. We can use retry to correct this, while keeping the function's type the same:

```
-- file: ch28/GameInventory.hs
transfer :: Gold -> Balance -> Balance -> STM ()

transfer qty fromBal toBal = do
  fromQty <- readTVar fromBal
  when (qty > fromQty) $
    retry
  writeTVar fromBal (fromQty - qty)
  readTVar toBal >>= writeTVar toBal . (qty +)
```

Now that we are using retry, our item sale function becomes dramatically simpler:

```
-- file: ch28/GameInventory.hs
sellItem :: Item -> Gold -> Player -> Player -> STM ()
sellItem item price buyer seller = do
  giveItem item (inventory seller) (inventory buyer)
  transfer price (balance buyer) (balance seller)
```

Its behavior is slightly different from our earlier function. Instead of immediately returning False if the seller doesn't have the item, it will block (if necessary) until both the seller has the item and the buyer has enough money to pay for it.

The beauty of STM lies in the cleanliness of the code it lets us write. We can take two functions that work correctly, and use them to create a third that will also behave itself, all with minimal effort.

What Happens When We Retry?

The `retry` function doesn't just make our code cleaner—its underlying behavior seems nearly magical. When we call it, it doesn't restart our transaction immediately. Instead, it blocks our thread until one or more of the variables that we touched before calling `retry` is changed by another thread.

For instance, if we invoke `transfer` with insufficient funds, `retry` will *automatically wait* until our balance changes before it starts the `atomically` block again. The same happens with our new `giveItem` function: if the sender doesn't currently have the item in his inventory, the thread will block until he does.

Choosing Between Alternatives

We don't always want to restart an `atomically` action if it calls `retry` or fails due to concurrent modification by another thread. For instance, our new `sellItem` function will retry indefinitely as long as we are missing either the item or enough money, but we might prefer to just try the sale once.

The `orElse` combinator lets us perform a "backup" action if the main one fails:

```
ghci> :type orElse
orElse :: STM a -> STM a -> STM a
```

If `sellItem` fails, `orElse` will invoke the `return False` action, causing our sale function to return immediately.

Using Higher Order Code with Transactions

Imagine that we'd like to be a little more ambitious and buy the first item from a list that is both in the possession of the seller and affordable to us, but it does nothing if we cannot afford something right now. We could, of course, write code to do this in a direct manner:

```
-- file: ch28/GameInventory.hs
crummyList :: [(Item, Gold)] -> Player -> Player
           -> STM (Maybe (Item, Gold))
crummyList list buyer seller = go list
    where go []                       = return Nothing
          go (this@(item,price) : rest) = do
              sellItem item price buyer seller
              return (Just this)
           `orElse`
             go rest
```

This function suffers from the familiar problem of muddling together what we want to do with how we ought to do it. A little inspection suggests that there are two reusable patterns buried in this code.

The first of these is to make a transaction fail immediately instead of retrying:

```
-- file: ch28/GameInventory.hs
maybeSTM :: STM a -> STM (Maybe a)
maybeSTM m = (Just `liftM` m) `orElse` return Nothing
```

Second, we want to try an action over successive elements of a list, stopping at the first that succeeds or performing a retry if every one fails. Conveniently for us, STM is an instance of the MonadPlus typeclass:

```
-- file: ch28/STMPlus.hs
instance MonadPlus STM where
  mzero = retry
  mplus = orElse
```

The Control.Monad module defines the msum function as follows, which is exactly what we need:

```
-- file: ch28/STMPlus.hs
msum :: MonadPlus m => [m a] -> m a
msum =  foldr mplus mzero
```

We now have a few key pieces of machinery that will help us write a much clearer version of our function:

```
-- file: ch28/GameInventory.hs
shoppingList :: [(Item, Gold)] -> Player -> Player
             -> STM (Maybe (Item, Gold))
shoppingList list buyer seller = maybeSTM . msum $ map sellOne list
    where sellOne this@(item,price) = do
            sellItem item price buyer seller
            return this
```

Since STM is an instance of the MonadPlus typeclass, we can generalize maybeSTM to work over any MonadPlus:

```
-- file: ch28/GameInventory.hs
maybeM :: MonadPlus m => m a -> m (Maybe a)
maybeM m = (Just `liftM` m) `mplus` return Nothing
```

This gives us a function that is useful in a greater variety of situations.

I/O and STM

The STM monad forbids us from performing arbitrary I/O actions, because they can break the guarantees of atomicity and isolation that the monad provides. Of course, the need to perform I/O still arises—we just have to treat it very carefully.

Most often, we will need to perform some I/O action as a result of a decision we made inside an atomically block. In these cases, the right thing to do is usually to return a piece of data from `atomically`, which will tell the caller in the IO monad what to do next. We can even return the action to perform, since actions are first-class values:

```
-- file: ch28/STMIO.hs
someAction :: IO a

stmTransaction :: STM (IO a)
stmTransaction = return someAction

doSomething :: IO a
doSomething = join (atomically stmTransaction)
```

We occasionally need to perform an I/O operation from within STM. For instance, reading immutable data from a file that must exist does not violate the STM guarantees of isolation or atomicity. In these cases, we can use `unsafeIOToSTM` to execute an IO action. This function is exported by the low-level `GHC.Conc` module, so we must go out of our way to use it:

```
ghci> :m +GHC.Conc
ghci> :type unsafeIOToSTM
unsafeIOToSTM :: IO a -> STM a
```

The IO action that we execute must not start another `atomically` transaction. If a thread tries to nest transactions, the runtime system will throw an exception.

Since the type system can't help us to ensure that our IO code is doing something sensible, we will be safest if we limit our use of `unsafeIOToSTM` as much as possible. Here is a typical error that can arise with IO in an `atomically` block:

```
-- file: ch28/STMIO.hs
launchTorpedoes :: IO ()

notActuallyAtomic = do
  doStuff
  unsafeIOToSTM launchTorpedoes
  mightRetry
```

If the `mightRetry` block causes our transaction to restart, we will call `launchTorpedoes` more than once. Indeed, we can't predict how many times it will be called, since the runtime system handles retries for us. The solution is not to perform these kinds of nonidempotent[*] I/O operations inside a transaction.

Communication Between Threads

As well as the basic `TVar` type, the `stm` package provides two types that are more useful for communicating between threads. A `TMVar` is the STM equivalent of an `MVar`: it can hold either `Just` a value or `Nothing`. The `TChan` type is the STM counterpart of `Chan`, and it implements a typed FIFO channel.

---

[*] An idempotent action gives the same result every time it is invoked, no matter how many times this occurs.

A Concurrent Web Link Checker

As a practical example of using STM, we will develop a program that checks an HTML file for broken links—that is, URLs that either point to bad web pages or dead servers. This is a good problem to address via concurrency: if we try to talk to a dead server, it will take up to two minutes before our connection attempt times out. If we use multiple threads, we can still get useful work done while one or two are stuck talking to slow or dead servers.

We can't simply create one thread per URL, because that may overburden either our CPU or our network connection if (as we expect) most of the links are live and responsive. Instead, we use a fixed number of worker threads, which fetch URLs to download from a queue:

```
-- file: ch28/Check.hs
{-# LANGUAGE FlexibleContexts, GeneralizedNewtypeDeriving,
             PatternGuards #-}

import Control.Concurrent (forkIO)
import Control.Concurrent.STM
import Control.Exception (catch, finally)
import Control.Monad.Error
import Control.Monad.State
import Data.Char (isControl)
import Data.List (nub)
import Network.URI
import Prelude hiding (catch)
import System.Console.GetOpt
import System.Environment (getArgs)
import System.Exit (ExitCode(..), exitWith)
import System.IO (hFlush, hPutStrLn, stderr, stdout)
import Text.Printf (printf)
import qualified Data.ByteString.Lazy.Char8 as B
import qualified Data.Set as S

-- This requires the HTTP package, which is not bundled with GHC
import Network.HTTP

type URL = B.ByteString

data Task = Check URL | Done
```

Our main function provides the top-level scaffolding for our program:

```
-- file: ch28/Check.hs
main :: IO ()
main = do
    (files,k) <- parseArgs
    let n = length files

    -- count of broken links
    badCount <- newTVarIO (0 :: Int)

    -- for reporting broken links
```

```
badLinks <- newTChanIO

-- for sending jobs to workers
jobs <- newTChanIO

-- the number of workers currently running
workers <- newTVarIO k

-- one thread reports bad links to stdout
forkIO $ writeBadLinks badLinks

-- start worker threads
forkTimes k workers (worker badLinks jobs badCount)

-- read links from files, and enqueue them as jobs
stats <- execJob (mapM_ checkURLs files)
                 (JobState S.empty 0 jobs)

-- enqueue "please finish" messages
atomically $ replicateM_ k (writeTChan jobs Done)

waitFor workers

broken <- atomically $ readTVar badCount

printf fmt broken
           (linksFound stats)
           (S.size (linksSeen stats))
           n
    where
      fmt    = "Found %d broken links. " ++
               "Checked %d links (%d unique) in %d files.\n"
```

When we are in the IO monad, we can create new TVar values using the newTVarIO function. There are also counterparts for creating TMVar and TChan values.

Notice that we use the printf function to print a report at the end. Unlike its counterpart in C, the Haskell printf function can check its argument types and their numbers at runtime:

```
ghci> :m +Text.Printf
ghci> printf "%d and %d\n" (3::Int)
3 and *** Exception: Printf.printf: argument list ended prematurely
ghci> printf "%s and %d\n" "foo" (3::Int)
foo and 3
```

Try evaluating printf "%d" True at the ghci prompt, and see what happens.

Several short functions support main:

```
-- file: ch28/Check.hs
modifyTVar_ :: TVar a -> (a -> a) -> STM ()
modifyTVar_ tv f = readTVar tv >>= writeTVar tv . f

forkTimes :: Int -> TVar Int -> IO () -> IO ()
forkTimes k alive act =
```

```
replicateM_ k . forkIO $
  act
  `finally`
  (atomically $ modifyTVar_ alive (subtract 1))
```

The forkTimes function starts a number of identical worker threads and decreases the "alive" count each time a thread exits. We use a finally combinator to ensure that the count is always decremented, no matter how the thread terminates.

Next, the writeBadLinks function prints each broken or dead link to stdout:

```
-- file: ch28/Check.hs
writeBadLinks :: TChan String -> IO ()
writeBadLinks c =
  forever $
    atomically (readTChan c) >>= putStrLn >> hFlush stdout
```

We use the forever combinator in the preceding code, which repeats an action endlessly:

```
ghci> :m +Control.Monad
ghci> :type forever
forever :: (Monad m) => m a -> m ()
```

Our waitFor function uses check, which calls retry if its argument evaluates to False:

```
-- file: ch28/Check.hs
waitFor :: TVar Int -> IO ()
waitFor alive = atomically $ do
  count <- readTVar alive
  check (count == 0)
```

Checking a Link

Here is a naive function to check the state of a link. This code is similar to the podcatcher that we developed in Chapter 22, with a few small differences:

```
-- file: ch28/Check.hs
getStatus :: URI -> IO (Either String Int)
getStatus = chase (5 :: Int)
  where
    chase 0 _ = bail "too many redirects"
    chase n u = do
      resp <- getHead u
      case resp of
        Left err -> bail (show err)
        Right r ->
          case rspCode r of
            (3,_,_) ->
              case findHeader HdrLocation r of
                Nothing -> bail (show r)
                Just u' ->
                  case parseURI u' of
                    Nothing -> bail "bad URL"
                    Just url -> chase (n-1) url
            (a,b,c) -> return . Right $ a * 100 + b * 10 + c
```

```
    bail = return . Left

getHead :: URI -> IO (Result Response)
getHead uri = simpleHTTP Request { rqURI = uri,
                                    rqMethod = HEAD,
                                    rqHeaders = [],
                                    rqBody = "" }
```

We follow an HTTP redirect response just a few times, in order to avoid endless redirect loops. To determine whether a URL is valid, we use the HTTP standard's HEAD verb, which uses less bandwidth than a full GET.

This code has the classic "marching off the right of the screen" style that we have learned to be wary of. Here is a rewrite that offers greater clarity via the ErrorT monad transformer and a few generally useful functions:

```
-- file: ch28/Check.hs
getStatusE = runErrorT . chase (5 :: Int)
  where
    chase :: Int -> URI -> ErrorT String IO Int
    chase 0 _ = throwError "too many redirects"
    chase n u = do
      r <- embedEither show =<< liftIO (getHead u)
      case rspCode r of
        (3,_,_) -> do
            u' <- embedMaybe (show r) $ findHeader HdrLocation r
            url <- embedMaybe "bad URL" $ parseURI u'
            chase (n-1) url
        (a,b,c) -> return $ a*100 + b*10 + c

-- This function is defined in Control.Arrow.
left :: (a -> c) -> Either a b -> Either c b
left f (Left x)  = Left (f x)
left _ (Right x) = Right x

-- Some handy embedding functions.
embedEither :: (MonadError e m) => (s -> e) -> Either s a -> m a
embedEither f = either (throwError . f) return

embedMaybe :: (MonadError e m) => e -> Maybe a -> m a
embedMaybe err = maybe (throwError err) return
```

Worker Threads

Each worker thread reads a task off the shared queue. It either checks the given URL or exits:

```
-- file: ch28/Check.hs
worker :: TChan String -> TChan Task -> TVar Int -> IO ()
worker badLinks jobQueue badCount = loop
  where
    -- Consume jobs until we are told to exit.
    loop = do
        job <- atomically $ readTChan jobQueue
```

```
            case job of
                Done  -> return ()
                Check x -> checkOne (B.unpack x) >> loop

        -- Check a single link.
        checkOne url = case parseURI url of
            Just uri -> do
                code <- getStatus uri `catch` (return . Left . show)
                case code of
                    Right 200 -> return ()
                    Right n   -> report (show n)
                    Left err  -> report err
            _ -> report "invalid URL"

          where report s = atomically $ do
                              modifyTVar_ badCount (+1)
                              writeTChan badLinks (url ++ " " ++ s)
```

Finding Links

We structure our link finding around a state monad transformer stacked on the IO
monad. Our state tracks links that we have already seen (so we don't check a repeated
link more than once), the total number of links we have encountered, and the queue
to which we should add the links that we will be checking:

```
-- file: ch28/Check.hs
data JobState = JobState { linksSeen  :: S.Set URL,
                           linksFound :: Int,
                           linkQueue  :: TChan Task }

newtype Job a = Job { runJob :: StateT JobState IO a }
    deriving (Monad, MonadState JobState, MonadIO)

execJob :: Job a -> JobState -> IO JobState
execJob = execStateT . runJob
```

Strictly speaking, for a small standalone program, we don't need the newtype wrapper,
but we include it here as an example of good practice (it costs only a few lines of code,
anyway).

The main function maps checkURLs over each input file, so checkURLs needs only to read
a single file:

```
-- file: ch28/Check.hs
checkURLs :: FilePath -> Job ()
checkURLs f = do
    src <- liftIO $ B.readFile f
    let urls = extractLinks src
    filterM seenURI urls >>= sendJobs
    updateStats (length urls)

updateStats :: Int -> Job ()
updateStats a = modify $ \s ->
    s { linksFound = linksFound s + a }
```

```
-- | Add a link to the set we have seen.
insertURI :: URL -> Job ()
insertURI c = modify $ \s ->
    s { linksSeen = S.insert c (linksSeen s) }

-- | If we have seen a link, return False.  Otherwise, record that we
-- have seen it, and return True.
seenURI :: URL -> Job Bool
seenURI url = do
    seen <- (not . S.member url) `liftM` gets linksSeen
    insertURI url
    return seen

sendJobs :: [URL] -> Job ()
sendJobs js = do
    c <- gets linkQueue
    liftIO . atomically $ mapM_ (writeTChan c . Check) js
```

Our `extractLinks` function doesn't attempt to properly parse an HTML or text file.
Instead, it looks for strings that appear to be URLs and treats them as "good enough":

```
-- file: ch28/Check.hs
extractLinks :: B.ByteString -> [URL]
extractLinks = concatMap uris . B.lines
  where uris s       = filter looksOkay (B.splitWith isDelim s)
        isDelim c    = isControl c || c `elem` " <>\"{}|\\^[]`"
        looksOkay s  = http `B.isPrefixOf` s
        http         = B.pack "http:"
```

Command-Line Parsing

To parse our command-line arguments, we use the `System.Console.GetOpt` module. It
provides useful code for parsing arguments, but it is slightly involved to use:

```
-- file: ch28/Check.hs
data Flag = Help | N Int
            deriving Eq

parseArgs :: IO ([String], Int)
parseArgs = do
    argv <- getArgs
    case parse argv of
        ([], files, [])                     -> return (nub files, 16)
        (opts, files, [])
            | Help `elem` opts              -> help
            | [N n] <- filter (/=Help) opts -> return (nub files, n)
        (_,_,errs)                          -> die errs
  where
    parse argv = getOpt Permute options argv
    header     = "Usage: urlcheck [-h] [-n n] [file ...]"
    info       = usageInfo header options
    dump       = hPutStrLn stderr
    die errs   = dump (concat errs ++ info) >> exitWith (ExitFailure 1)
    help       = dump info                  >> exitWith ExitSuccess
```

The getOpt function takes three arguments:

- An argument ordering, which specifies whether options can be mixed with other arguments (Permute, which we used earlier) or must appear before them.
- A list of option definitions. Each consists of a list of short names for the option, a list of long names for the option, a description of the option (e.g., whether it accepts an argument), and an explanation for users.
- A list of the arguments and options, as returned by getArgs.

The function returns a triple that consists of the parsed options, the remaining arguments, and any error messages that arose.

We use the Flag algebraic data type to represent the options that our program can accept:

```
-- file: ch28/Check.hs
options :: [OptDescr Flag]
options = [ Option ['h'] ["help"] (NoArg Help)
                   "Show this help message",
            Option ['n'] []       (ReqArg (\s -> N (read s)) "N")
                   "Number of concurrent connections (default 16)" ]
```

Our options list describes each option that we accept. Each description must be able to create a Flag value. Take a look at our uses of NoArg and ReqArg in the preceding code. These are constructors for the GetOpt module's ArgDescr type:

```
-- file: ch28/GetOpt.hs
data ArgDescr a = NoArg a
                | ReqArg (String -> a) String
                | OptArg (Maybe String -> a) String
```

The constructors have the following meanings:

NoArg

Accepts a parameter that will represent this option. In our case, if a user invokes our program with -h or --help, we will use the value Help.

ReqArg

Accepts a function that maps a required argument to a value. Its second argument is used when printing help. Here, we convert a string into an integer, and pass it to our Flag type's N constructor.

OptArg

Similar to the ReqArg constructor, but it permits the use of options that can be used without arguments.

Pattern Guards

We sneaked one last language extension into our definition of parseArgs. Pattern guards let us write more concise guard expressions. They are enabled via the PatternGuards language extension.

A pattern guard has three components: a pattern, a <- symbol, and an expression. The expression is evaluated and matched against the pattern. If it matches, any variables present in the pattern are bound. We can mix pattern guards and normal `Bool` guard expressions in a single guard by separating them with commas:

```
-- file: ch28/PatternGuard.hs
{-# LANGUAGE PatternGuards #-}

testme x xs | Just y <- lookup x xs, y > 3 = y
            | otherwise                    = 0
```

In this example, we return a value from the alist `xs` if its associated key `x` is present, provided the value is greater than 3. This definition is equivalent to the following:

```
-- file: ch28/PatternGuard.hs
testme_noguards x xs = case lookup x xs of
                         Just y | y > 3 -> y
                         _              -> 0
```

Pattern guards let us "collapse" a collection of guards and `case` expressions into a single guard, allowing us to write more succinct and descriptive guards.

Practical Aspects of STM

We have so far been quiet about the specific benefits that STM gives us. Most obvious is how well it *composes*—to add code to a transaction, we just use our usual monadic building blocks, (>>=) and (>>).

The notion of composability is critical to building modular software. If we take two pieces of code that work correctly individually, the composition of the two should also be correct. While normal threaded programming makes composability impossible, STM restores it as a key assumption that we can rely upon.

The STM monad prevents us from accidentally performing nontransactional I/O actions. We don't need to worry about lock ordering, since our code contains no locks. We can forget about lost wakeups, since we don't have condition variables. If an exception is thrown, we can either catch it using `catchSTM` or be bounced out of our transaction, leaving our state untouched. Finally, the `retry` and `orElse` functions give us some beautiful ways to structure our code.

Code that uses STM will not deadlock, but it is possible for threads to starve each other to some degree. A long-running transaction can cause another transaction to `retry` often enough that it will make comparatively little progress. To address a problem such as this, make your transactions as short as you can, while keeping your data consistent.

Getting Comfortable with Giving Up Control

Whether with concurrency or memory management, there will be times when we must retain control: some software must make solid guarantees about latency or memory footprint, so we will be forced to spend the extra time and effort managing and debugging explicit code. For many interesting, practical uses of software, garbage collection and STM will do more than well enough.

STM is not a complete panacea. It is useful to compare it with the use of garbage collection for memory management. When we abandon explicit memory management in favor of garbage collection, we give up control in return for safer code. Likewise, with STM, we abandon the low-level details in exchange for code that we can better hope to understand.

Using Invariants

STM cannot eliminate certain classes of bugs. For instance, if we withdraw money from an account in one `atomically` block, return to the IO monad, and then deposit it to another account in a different `atomically` block, our code will have an inconsistency. There will be a window of time in which the money is present in neither account.

```
-- file: ch28/GameInventory.hs
bogusTransfer qty fromBal toBal = do
  fromQty <- atomically $ readTVar fromBal
  -- window of inconsistency
  toQty   <- atomically $ readTVar toBal
  atomically $ writeTVar fromBal (fromQty - qty)
  -- window of inconsistency
  atomically $ writeTVar toBal    (toQty + qty)

bogusSale :: Item -> Gold -> Player -> Player -> IO ()
bogusSale item price buyer seller = do
  atomically $ giveItem item (inventory seller) (inventory buyer)
  bogusTransfer price (balance buyer) (balance seller)
```

In concurrent programs, these kinds of problems are notoriously difficult to find and reproduce. For instance, the inconsistency that we describe here will usually only occur for a brief period of time. Problems such as this often refuse to show up during development, instead occurring only in the field under heavy load.

The `alwaysSucceeds` function lets us define an *invariant*, a property of our data that must always be true:

```
ghci> :type alwaysSucceeds
alwaysSucceeds :: STM a -> STM ()
```

When we create an invariant, it will immediately be checked. To fail, the invariant must raise an exception. More interestingly, the invariant will subsequently be checked automatically at the end of *every* transaction. If it fails at any point, the transaction will be aborted, and the exception raised by the invariant will be propagated. This means that we will get immediate feedback as soon as one of our invariants is violated.

For instance, here are a few functions to populate our game world from the beginning of this chapter with players:

```
-- file: ch28/GameInventory.hs
newPlayer :: Gold -> HitPoint -> [Item] -> STM Player
newPlayer balance health inventory =
    Player `liftM` newTVar balance
              `ap` newTVar health
              `ap` newTVar inventory

populateWorld :: STM [Player]
populateWorld = sequence [ newPlayer 20 20 [Wand, Banjo],
                           newPlayer 10 12 [Scroll] ]
```

This function returns an invariant that we can use to ensure that the world's money balance is always consistent—the balance at any point in time should be the same as at the creation of the world:

```
-- file: ch28/GameInventory.hs
consistentBalance :: [Player] -> STM (STM ())
consistentBalance players = do
    initialTotal <- totalBalance
    return $ do
      curTotal <- totalBalance
      when (curTotal /= initialTotal) $
        error "inconsistent global balance"
  where totalBalance   = foldM addBalance 0 players
        addBalance a b = (a+) `liftM` readTVar (balance b)
```

Let's write a small function that exercises this:

```
-- file: ch28/GameInventory.hs
tryBogusSale = do
  players@(alice:bob:_) <- atomically populateWorld
  atomically $ alwaysSucceeds =<< consistentBalance players
  bogusSale Wand 5 alice bob
```

If we run it in ghci, it should detect the inconsistency caused by our incorrect use of atomically in the bogusTransfer function we wrote:

```
ghci> tryBogusSale
*** Exception: inconsistent global balance
```

Installing GHC and Haskell Libraries

The instructions in this appendix are based on our experience installing GHC and other software in late 2008. Installation instructions inevitably become dated quickly; please bear this in mind as you read.

Installing GHC

Because GHC runs on a large number of platforms, we focus on a handful of the most popular.

Windows

The prebuilt binary packages of GHC should work on Windows Vista and XP (even Windows 2000). We have installed GHC 6.8.3 under Windows XP Service Pack 2; the following paragraphs detail the steps we followed.

How much room does GHC need?

On Windows, GHC requires about 400 MB of disk space. The exact amount will vary from release to release.

Our first step is to visit the GHC at *http://www.haskell.org/ghcdownload.html* (see Figure A-1) and follow the link to the current stable release. Scroll down to the section entitled "Binary packages," and then again to the subsection for Windows. Download the installer; in our case, it's named *ghc-6.8.3-i386-windows.exe*.

After the installer has downloaded, double-click it to start the installation process. This involves stepping through a normal Windows installer wizard (see Figure A-2).

Once the installer has finished, the Start Menu's "All Programs" submenu (see Figure A-3) should have a GHC folder, inside which you'll find an icon that you can use to run ghci.

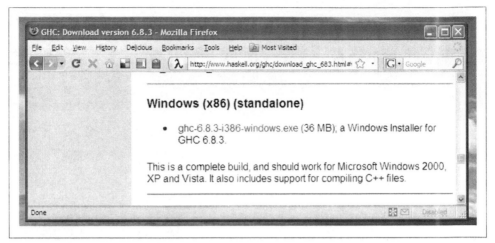

Figure A-1. Screenshot of Firefox, displaying the GHC download page

Clicking the `ghci` icon brings up a normal Windows console window that is running `ghci` (see Figure A-4).

Updating your search path

The GHC installer automatically modifies your user account's `PATH` environment variable so that commands such as `ghc` will be present in the command shell's search path (i.e., you can type a GHC command name without typing its complete path). This change will take effect the next time you open a command shell.

Mac OS X

We have installed GHC 6.8.3 under Mac OS X 10.5 (Leopard), on an Intel-based Mac-Book. Before installing GHC, the Xcode development system must already be installed.

The Xcode software installer may have come bundled on a DVD with your Mac. If not (or you can't find it), you should be able to download it from Apple. Once you've finished installing Xcode, continue on to download GHC itself.

Visit the GHC download page (*http://www.haskell.org/ghc/download.html*) and follow the link to the current stable release. Scroll down to the section entitled "Binary packages," and then again to the subsection for Mac OS X. There is a single installer package available. Download and run it.

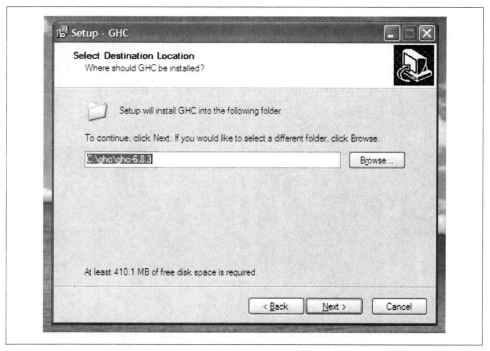

Figure A-2. Screenshot of the GHC installation wizard on Windows

Terminal at your fingertips yet?

Since most of your interactions with GHC will be through a Terminal window, this might be a good time to add the Terminal application to your dock (if you haven't already done so). You can find it in the system's */Applications/Utilities* folder.

The installation process should take a minute or two. Finally, you should be able to successfully run the ghci command from your shell prompt (see Figure A-5).

Alternatives

Both the MacPorts and Fink projects provide builds of GHC.

Ubuntu and Debian Linux

Under both Ubuntu and Debian, you can install a minimal working version of GHC by running sudo aptitude install ghc6 from a shell prompt.

These distros maintain a small core GHC package, which is insufficient for much practical development. However, they make a number of additional prebuilt packages

Figure A-3. Screenshot of the Windows XP Start menu, showing the GHC submenu

```
GHCi                                                    _ □ ✕
returnA :: (Arrow a) => a b b
Prelude> :browse Data.Sequence
(<|) :: a -> Seq a -> Seq a
(><) :: Seq a -> Seq a -> Seq a
newtype Seq a
    = Data.Sequence.Seq (Data.Sequence.FingerTree
                         (Data.Sequence.Elem a))
data ViewL a = EmptyL | a :< (Seq a)
data ViewR a = EmptyR | (Seq a) :> a
adjust :: (a -> a) -> Int -> Seq a -> Seq a
Data.Sequence.drop :: Int -> Seq a -> Seq a
empty :: Seq a
fromList :: [a] -> Seq a
index :: Seq a -> Int -> a
Data.Sequence.length :: Seq a -> Int
Data.Sequence.null :: Seq a -> Bool
Data.Sequence.reverse :: Seq a -> Seq a
singleton :: a -> Seq a
Data.Sequence.splitAt :: Int -> Seq a -> (Seq a, Seq a)
Data.Sequence.take :: Int -> Seq a -> Seq a
update :: Int -> a -> Seq a -> Seq a
viewl :: Seq a -> ViewL a
viewr :: Seq a -> ViewR a
(|>) :: Seq a -> a -> Seq a
Prelude>
```

Figure A-4. Screenshot of the ghci interpreter running on Windows

available; run `apt-cache search libghc6` to find a complete list of these prebuilt packages. We recommend that you install at least the `mtl` package, using `sudo aptitude install libghc6-mtl-dev`.

Since you will probably want to profile the performance of your Haskell programs at some point, you should also install the `ghc6-prof` package.

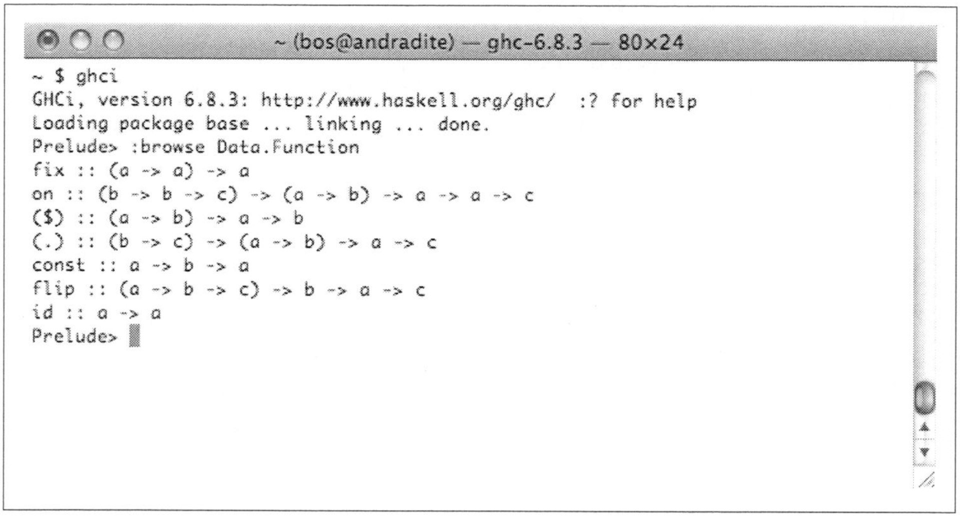

```
~ $ ghci
GHCi, version 6.8.3: http://www.haskell.org/ghc/   :? for help
Loading package base ... linking ... done.
Prelude> :browse Data.Function
fix :: (a -> a) -> a
on :: (b -> b -> c) -> (a -> b) -> a -> a -> c
($) :: (a -> b) -> a -> b
(.) :: (b -> c) -> (a -> b) -> a -> c
const :: a -> b -> a
flip :: (a -> b -> c) -> b -> a -> c
id :: a -> a
Prelude>
```

Figure A-5. Screenshot of the ghci interpreter running in a Terminal window on Mac OS X

Fedora Linux

GHC is available as a standard Fedora binary package. From a shell, all you need to do is run the following command:

```
sudo yum -y install ghc ghc-doc ghc683-prof
```

The base package, containing the ghc and ghci commands and libraries, is *ghc*. The ghc-doc package contains the GHC user guide, and command and library documentation. The ghc683-prof package contains profiling-capable versions of the standard libraries (its version number may have changed by the time you read this).

Once installation has finished, you should be able to run ghci from the shell immediately. You won't need to change your shell's search path or set any environment variables.

FreeBSD

Under FreeBSD, run the following commands:

```
$ cd /usr/ports/lang/ghc
$ sudo make install clean
```

This will download and build GHC from source. You should expect the process to take several hours.

Installing Haskell Software

Almost all Haskell libraries are distributed using a standard packaging system named Cabal. You can find hundreds of Haskell open source libraries and programs, all of which use Cabal, at *http://hackage.haskell.org/*, the home of the Hackage code repository.

Automated Download and Installation with cabal

A command named `cabal` automates the job of downloading, building, and installing a Haskell package. It also figures out what dependencies a particular library needs and either makes sure that they are installed already or downloads and builds them first. You can install any Haskell package with a single `cabal install` *mypackage* command.

The `cabal` command is not bundled with GHC, so at least as of GHC version 6.8.3, you will have to download and build it yourself.

Installing cabal

To build the `cabal` command, download the sources for the following four packages from *http://hackage.haskell.org/*:

- Cabal
- HTTP
- zlib
- cabal-install

Follow the instructions in "Building Packages by Hand" on page 647 to manually build each of these four packages, making sure that you leave `cabal-install` until last.

After you install the `cabal-install` package, the *$HOME/.cabal/bin* directory will contain the `cabal` command. You can either move it somewhere more convenient or add that directory to your shell's search path.

Updating cabal's package list

After installing `cabal`, and periodically thereafter, you should download a fresh list of packages from Hackage. You can do so as follows:

```
$ cabal update
```

Installing a library or program

To install some executable or library, just run the following command:

```
$ cabal install -p mypackage
```

Building Packages by Hand

If you download a tarball from Hackage, it will arrive in source form. Unpack the tarball and go into the newly created directory in a command shell. The process to build and install it is simple, consisting of three commands:

1. Configure for system-wide installation (i.e., available to all users):

   ```
   $ runghc Setup configure -p
   ```

   Alternatively, configure to install only for yourself:

   ```
   $ runghc Setup configure --user --prefix=$HOME -p
   ```

2. Build (this will build each source file twice, with and without profiling support):

   ```
   $ runghc Setup build
   ```

3. Install if you chose system-wide configuration:

   ```
   $ sudo runghc Setup install
   ```

   Alternatively, if you chose configuration for yourself only:

   ```
   $ runghc Setup install
   ```

If you build by hand, you will frequently find that the configuration step fails because some other library must be installed first. You may find yourself needing to download and build several packages before you can make progress on the one you really want. This is why we recommend using the `cabal` command instead.

Characters, Strings, and Escaping Rules

This appendix covers the escaping rules used to represent non-ASCII characters in Haskell character and string literals. Haskell's escaping rules follow the pattern established by the C programming language, but they expand considerably upon them.

Writing Character and String Literals

A single character is surrounded by ASCII single quotes, ', and has type Char:

```
ghci> 'c'
'c'
ghci> :type 'c'
'c' :: Char
```

A string literal is surrounded by double quotes, ", and has type [Char] (more often written as String):

```
ghci> "a string literal"
"a string literal"
ghci> :type "a string literal"
"a string literal" :: [Char]
```

The double-quoted form of a string literal is just syntactic sugar for list notation:

```
ghci> ['a', ' ', 's', 't', 'r', 'i', 'n', 'g'] == "a string"
True
```

International Language Support

Haskell uses Unicode internally for its Char data type. Since String is just an alias for [Char] (which is a list of Chars), Unicode is also used to represent strings.

Different Haskell implementations place limitations on the character sets they can accept in source files. GHC allows source files to be written in the UTF-8 encoding of Unicode, so in a source file, you can use UTF-8 literals inside a character or string constant. Do be aware that if you use UTF-8, other Haskell implementations may not be able to parse your source files.

When you run the ghci interpreter interactively, it may not be able to deal with international characters in character or string literals that you enter at the keyboard.

 Although Haskell represents characters and strings internally using Unicode, there is no standardized way to do I/O on files that contain Unicode data. Haskell's standard text I/O functions treat text as a sequence of 8-bit characters, and do not perform any character set conversion.

There are third-party libraries that will convert between the many different encodings used in files and Haskell's internal Unicode representation.

Escaping Text

Some characters must be escaped to be represented inside a character or string literal. For example, a double-quote character inside a string literal must be escaped, or else it will be treated as the end of the string.

Single-Character Escape Codes

Haskell uses essentially the same single-character escapes as the C language and many other popular languages. The escape codes are shown in Table B-1.

Table B-1. Single-character escape codes

Escape	Unicode	Character
\0	U+0000	Null character
\a	U+0007	Alert
\b	U+0008	Backspace
\f	U+000C	Form feed
\n	U+000A	Newline (linefeed)
\r	U+000D	Carriage return
\t	U+0009	Horizontal tab
\v	U+000B	Vertical tab
\"	U+0022	Double-quote
\&	*n/a*	Empty string
\'	U+0027	Single quote
\\	U+005C	Backslash

Multiline String Literals

To write a string literal that spans multiple lines, terminate one line with a backslash and resume the string with another backslash. An arbitrary amount of whitespace (of any kind) can fill the gap between the two backslashes:

```
"this is a \
    \long string,\
    \ spanning multiple lines"
```

ASCII Control Codes

Haskell recognizes the escaped use of the standard two- and three-letter abbreviations of ASCII control codes, shown in Table B-2.

Table B-2. ASCII control code abbreviations

Escape	Unicode	Meaning
\NUL	U+0000	Null character
\SOH	U+0001	Start of heading
\STX	U+0002	Start of text
\ETX	U+0003	End of text
\EOT	U+0004	End of transmission
\ENQ	U+0005	Enquiry
\ACK	U+0006	Acknowledge
\BEL	U+0007	Bell
\BS	U+0008	Backspace
\HT	U+0009	Horizontal tab
\LF	U+000A	Newline (linefeed)
\VT	U+000B	Vertical tab
\FF	U+000C	Form feed
\CR	U+000D	Carriage return
\SO	U+000E	Shift out
\SI	U+000F	Shift in
\DLE	U+0010	Data link escape
\DC1	U+0011	Device control 1
\DC2	U+0012	Device control 2
\DC3	U+0013	Device control 3
\DC4	U+0014	Device control 4
\NAK	U+0015	Negative acknowledge
\SYN	U+0016	Synchronous idle

Escape	Unicode	Meaning
\ETB	U+0017	End of transmission block
\CAN	U+0018	Cancel
\EM	U+0019	End of medium
\SUB	U+001A	Substitute
\ESC	U+001B	Escape
\FS	U+001C	File separator
\GS	U+001D	Group separator
\RS	U+001E	Record separator
\US	U+001F	Unit separator
\SP	U+0020	Space
\DEL	U+007F	Delete

Control-with-Character Escapes

Haskell recognizes an alternate notation for control characters, which represents the archaic effect of pressing the Ctrl key on a keyboard and chording it with another key. These sequences begin with the characters \^, followed by a symbol or uppercase letter and are listed in Table B-3.

Table B-3. Control-with-character escapes

Escape	Unicode	Meaning
\^@	U+0000	Null character
\^A through \^Z	U+0001 through U+001A	Control codes
\^[	U+001B	Escape
\^\	U+001C	File separator
\^]	U+001D	Group separator
\^^	U+001E	Record separator
\^_	U+001F	Unit separator

Numeric Escapes

Haskell allows Unicode characters to be written using numeric escapes. A decimal character begins with a digit, e.g., \1234. A hexadecimal character begins with an x, e.g. \xbeef. An octal character begins with an o, e.g., \o1234.

The maximum value of a numeric literal is \1114111, which may also be written \x10ffff or \o4177777.

The Zero-Width Escape Sequence

String literals can contain a zero-width escape sequence, written \&. This is not a real character, as it represents the empty string:

```
ghci> "\&"
""
ghci> "foo\&bar"
"foobar"
```

The purpose of this escape sequence is to make it possible to write a numeric escape followed immediately by a regular ASCII digit:

```
ghci> "\130\&11"
"\130\&11"
```

Because the empty escape sequence represents an empty string, it is not legal in a character literal.

Index

Symbols

!= (C comparison operator), 6
" (double quotes), writing strings, 11, 649
&& (logical and), 5
' (single quotes), 649
( ) (parentheses)
  arithmetic expressions, writing, 4
  foldl and foldr function, 94
  operator precedence and, 7
  tuples, writing, 25
(!!) operator, 196
(!) operator, 272, 291
($) operator, 248
(%) operator, 14, 146
(&&) operator, 80
(*) multiplication function, 145
(**) (exponentiation) operator, 8, 145
(*>) operator, 397
(+) (accumulator) option, 93, 145
(++) append function, 80, 120, 317
  fold functions and, 96
  mplus function, 364
(++) append option, 11, 166
  lazy functions, writing, 205
(-) subtraction function, 145
(-) unary operator, 4
(.&.) (bitwise and), 91, 146
(.) operator, 105, 318
(.|.) bitwise or, 91, 146
(/) fractional division function, 145
(/=) operator, 6, 148
(:) list constructor
  pattern matching, using, 51
  recursive types and, 58

splitting lines of text, 74
(:) operator, 202
(::) operator, using type signatures and, 22
(<$>) operator, 248, 397
(<*) operator, 399
(<-) operator, 72, 167, 344
(<>) operator, 120, 125
(<?>) operator, 390
(<|) operator, 323
(<|>) operator, 388
  lookaheads and, 389
(=<<) function, 212
(=<<) operator, 346
(==) operator, 46, 136, 148, 223
(==>) operator, 242, 258, 600
(=~) operator, 198
(>) operator, 223
(><) operator, 323
(>=) operator, 148
(>>) operator, 186, 330, 333, 397
  return calls and, 329
(>>=) operator, 186, 332, 346, 354
  coding style and, 356
  list Monads and, 340
  Monad typeclasses and, 329
  return call and, 335, 367
    reading/modifying state, 348
  state monads and, 347
(>>?) operator, 238, 326
(\\) operator, 258
(^) operator, 145
(^^) operator, 146
(|>) operator, 323
(||) operator, 31, 33, 80
  recursion and, 35

We'd like to hear your suggestions for improving our indexes. Send email to *index@oreilly.com*.

mod function, 146
mode based testing, 259
modifyMVar function, 536
    starvation and, 541
:module command, 3
module declarations, 113
module headers, 122
    writing, 123
modules, 113
Moggi, Eugenio, 443
MonadIO typeclass, 377
MonadPlus typeclass
    Parsec and, 393
MonadReader typeclass, 431
monads, 183–188, 325–357
    common patterns, 431
    error handling, 462–464
    functions, 354–355
    lists and, 340–344
    programming with, 359–381
    state, 346–354
        random values, generating, 349
        running, 352
    transformer stacking and, 441
    transformers, 429–445
        creating, 439
        stacking multiple, 433–436
        understanding, 438–441
    typeclasses, 329
MonadState typeclass, 437
MonadTrans class, 439
Monoid instance, 266
monoids, 320
monomorphic properties, 600
monomorphism restriction, 162–163
mplus function, 364
mtl library, 429, 444
    common patterns in monads, 431
mulitcore programming, 542–560
multiline string literals, 651
multiplication (*) option, 145
mutable arrays, 288
mutable references, 584
MVar type, 533, 536, 539
MySQL, 493

N

\n (newline) character, 11, 73
    CSV files, parsing, 387

-N RTS option, 543
negative numbers, writing, 4
netpbm file format, 235, 275
    color images, parsing, 278
networking, 611–621
newEmptyMVar function, 534
newline (\n) character, 11, 73
    CSV files, parsing, 387
newtype keyword, 155–159
    JSON typclasses and, 159
NF (normal form), 545
Nil, 58
NoBuffering mode (BufferMode), 189
NoMonomorphismRestriction language
        extension, 163
non-strict evaluation, 32
non-threaded runtime, 542
normal form (NF), 545
normal form data, 553
notElem function, 82
null function, 31, 78
null values, 59
nullPtr constant, 415
number systems of barcodes, 269
numeric escapes, 652
Numeric library, 121
numeric types, 144–148, 307–317

O

-o option (ghc), 115
object files, 114
objects, 111, 122
ODBC drivers, 496
offside rule, 64–66
onClicked event handler, 523
onDestroy function, 523
open world assumption, 152–155
openBinaryTempFile function, 174
openFile function, 169, 171
openTempFile function, 174
operators, 5
    defining and using new, 225
    precedence and associativity, 7
-optc-02 option, 579
OPTIONS_GHC clause, 482
or function, 80
Oracle, 493
Other-Modules field, 132
Other-Modules property, 598

About the Authors

Bryan O'Sullivan is an Irish hacker and writer who likes distributed systems, open source software, and programming languages. He was a member of the initial design team for the Jini network service architecture (subsequently open sourced as Apache River). He has made significant contributions to, and written a book about, the popular Mercurial revision control system. He lives in San Francisco with his wife and sons. Whenever he can, he runs off to climb rocks.

John Goerzen is an American hacker and author. He has written a number of real-world Haskell libraries and applications, including the HDBC database interface, the ConfigFile configuration file interface, a podcast downloader, and various other libraries relating to networks, parsing, logging, and POSIX code. John has been a developer for the Debian GNU/Linux operating system project for over 10 years and maintains numerous Haskell libraries and code for Debian. He also served as president of Software in the Public Interest, Inc., the legal parent organization of Debian. John lives in rural Kansas with his wife and son, where he enjoys photography and geocaching.

Don Stewart is an Australian hacker based in Portland, Oregon. Don has been involved in a diverse range of Haskell projects, including practical libraries, such as Data.ByteString and Data.Binary, as well as applying the Haskell philosophy to real-world applications, including compilers, linkers, text editors, network servers, and systems software. His recent work has focused on optimizing Haskell for high-performance scenarios, using techniques from term rewriting.

Colophon

The animal on the cover of *Real World Haskell* is a rhinoceros beetle, a species of scarab beetle. Relative to their size, rhinoceros beetles are among the strongest animals on the planet. They can lift up to 850 times their own weight. The average rhino beetle found in the U.S. is about an inch long, but they can grow as long as seven inches.

Rhino beetles have horns on their heads, resembling that of the rhinoceros, hence the name. The size of their horns is related to how much nutrition they had in larva. In some species, the horns are longer than the bodies, and they can grow as many as four or five horns. They use the horns for digging, as well as for fighting for territory and mates.

Rhino beetles thrive on sap and rotting fruit, specifically bananas, apples, and oranges. Their larvae, which takes between 3–5 years to mature, eat decaying wood, compost, and dead leaves—a kind of recycling for the environment.

The cover image is from an unknown source. The cover font is Adobe ITC Garamond. The text font is Linotype Birka; the heading font is Adobe Myriad Condensed; and the code font is LucasFont's TheSans Mono Condensed.

The O'Reilly Advantage

Stay Current and Save Money

Try the online edition free for 45 days

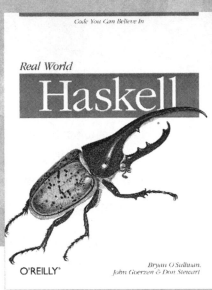

Get the information you need when you need it, with Safari Books Online. Safari Books Online contains the complete version of the print book in your hands plus thousands of titles from the best technical publishers, with sample code ready to cut and paste into your applications.

Safari is designed for people in a hurry to get the answers they need so they can get the job done. You can find what you need in the morning, and put it to work in the afternoon. As simple as cut, paste, and program.

To try out Safari and the online edition of the **above title** FREE for 45 days, go to www.oreilly.com/go/safarienabled and enter the coupon code OKMSLZG.

To see the complete Safari Library visit:
safari.oreilly.com

CPSIA information can be obtained at www.ICGtesting.com
Printed in the USA
BVOW081159061211

277708BV00008B/9/P